THE HIGHLAND PIPE AND

10th Dec, 2014

w.g.y.

John Bàn MacKenzie, 1796–1864. From a calotype by D. O. Hill
and Robert Adamson; courtesy of the Scottish National Portrait Gallery.

William Donaldson

THE HIGHLAND PIPE

AND SCOTTISH SOCIETY 1750–1950

Transmission, Change and the Concept of Tradition

JOHN DONALD

First published in 2000 by Tuckwell Press Ltd

This paperback edition first published in Great Britain in 2008 by
John Donald, an imprint of Birlinn Ltd

Reprinted 2013

West Newington House
10 Newington Road
Edinburgh
EH9 1QS

www.birlinn.co.uk

ISBN 10: 1 904607 76 4

ISBN 13: 978 1 904607 76 2

British Library Cataloguing-in-Publication Data
A catalogue record for this book is available on request from the British Library

Typeset by Hewer Text Ltd, Edinburgh
Printed and bound in Britain by Bell & Bain Ltd, Glasgow

Contents

Acknowledgements

I am greatly indebted to all those who made possible access to the music and research sources upon which this book is based. Firstly, I wish to return most grateful thanks to the Carnegie Trust for the Universities of Scotland, the Scottish Arts Council, and the Harold Hyam Wingate Foundation for generous assistance with research and writing costs. I am obliged also to many individuals, companies and institutions: I wish to record particular thanks for the kindness of Mr. H. G. Bennett, Mr. A. Gillies and Mrs. E. McKillop for access to master copies of the *Oban Times* which has proved an exceptionally rich and useful source, and to the staff of the following libraries and archives: Aberdeen Central Library, especially the staff of the Local Collection; Aberdeen University Library and Dr. Ian Beavan and the staff of Special Collections; the British Library and the British Library Newspaper Library at Colindale; Dundee Central Library; Edinburgh Central Library, and in particular Mr. Ian Nelson and the staff of the Edinburgh Room; Edinburgh University Library and the School of Scottish Studies, who gave permission to consult their tape archives and reproduce material from them; Falkirk Museums and Library Service, in particular Carol A. Sneddon and Marion Scott for information on the Falkirk Mason Lodge; Glasgow City Archives, in particular Dr. Irene O'Brien, for information on the Glasgow Gaelic Club; Glasgow University Library; The Mitchell Library, whose extensive pipe-music holdings greatly furthered the research for this book; Inverness Public Library, in particular Mr. Norman Newton, for references to Alexander MacDonald and Alexander Mackenzie; the former Highland Region Library Service whose flexibility was much appreciated; and the National Library of Scotland.

I am grateful also to the following people who have gone out of their way to provide information: Major (Retd) C. Brown, Records & Welfare Officer, Scots Guards, for information on piper Archibald MacPherson; Col. A. W. Scott Elliot of the Argyll and Sutherland Highlanders for information on John Campbell of Kilberry; Col. A. A. Fairrie, Queen's Own Highlanders Museum, Fort George, for information on John MacDonald; Mr. Stephen J. Fox for information from U.S. sources; Mrs. C. G. W. Roads, MVO, Lyon Clerk and Keeper of the Records, for information on the MacCrimmon Arms; Major Gavin Stoddart and Pipe-Major Bruce Hitchings of the Army School of Bagpipe Music and Drumming for information on Willie Ross; and Mrs. Morag Williams, Archivist, Crichton Royal Hospital, for information on Angus MacKay.

The Carnegie Trust for the Universities of Scotland made possible the microfilming of manuscripts of pipe music and related material which are now deposited, with availability of loan to libraries in the North of Scotland, in Special Collections at Aberdeen University Library. For permission to microfilm and use this deposit, my thanks are due to: Mrs P. M. C. Horrocks for the manuscript of Colin Campbell; The Royal Scottish Pipers' Society for the manuscript of C. S. Thomason's 'Ceol Mor Legends'; The Trustees of the National Library of Scotland for the manuscripts of David Glen, Angus MacKay, Peter Reid and Donald MacDonald; The Piobaireachd Society, for the manuscripts of Angus MacArthur, William Ross and Colin Cameron, and for granting access to the Society's own papers which are also lodged in the National Library.

Assistance with photographs has been generously given by Mrs Lesley Ross Alexander (who also provided much valuable information concerning her grandfather, Pipe-Major Willie Ross); the Managing Director and staff of the *Oban Times:* Dugald B. MacNeill of the College of Piping, Glasgow; and Dr. Deborah Hunter of the Scottish National Portrait Gallery. I am particularly grateful in this respect to Neal Murray of Aberdeen for advice and support. It had been hoped to reproduce much material from the *Oban Times's* rich photographic record, but the original plates were destoyed by previous owners of the paper in the 1970s, and it has not been possible to reproduce photographs from the paper's hard copy to a sufficient technical standard.

It has been my privilege to play with and learn from many piping contemporaries and I am grateful above all to R. B. Nicol of Balmoral who was my main teacher. Two generations of players, of whom I was lucky enough to be one, found his vast knowledge tirelessly at their disposal, and dispensed with a characteristic humanity, humour and generosity that must be for all of us an enduring memory.

Professor Peter L. Payne has given greatly valued support for many years, and I owe a particular debt to Professor Colm O'Boyle, Professor Derek B. Scott, and Dr. W. C. Wotherspoon who read and made detailed comments on the text. The conclusions are, of course, my own and responsibility for any errors the book may contain is mine.

Note on the text

It is difficult to find out about piping. There are a number of books on the subject, but they vary widely in quality and are mostly out of print. There is an extensive periodical literature but it is inaccessible and little-known outside the performer community. Many of the most important musical sources remain in manuscript, and even great libraries cannot be relied upon to possess an adequate spread of printed material. The standard guides to Gaelic culture tend to concentrate on language and literature and say relatively little about music, although by the later twentieth century there were probably more pipers than there were native Gaelic speakers.

The *Oban Times* is a key source for the present book. Although its richness would be difficult to overstate, no Scottish library holds more than about a dozen years of hard copy. The only complete run of the title in Scotland is held by the publisher. Much of the present research was based on a microfilm copy of the years 1875–1929, courtesy of the former Highland Region Library Service, and also at the paper's offices in Oban.

The music text was created using 'Music Publisher 32' by Braeburn Software of Selkirk. Settings from the Highland Society of London MS have been transposed, except in Chapter 7. Otherwise scores are reproduced as they appear in the original sources; no attempt has been made to regularise notational usage.

The verbal text follows the standard conventions. Omissions from quotations are indicated by ellipses in the normal manner and authorial comments enclosed within square brackets. Gaelic terms of art are italicised on their first citation in the text, but not thereafter.

Since the present book can present only a relatively modest sample of the available evidence, it is hoped that the full footnote references will provide a useful guide for further enquiry.

Two scholarly editions of important texts, Frans Buisman and Andrew Wright, eds., *The MacArthur-MacGregor Manuscript of Piobaireachd* (Glasgow and Aberdeen, 2001), and Roderick Cannon and Keith Sanger, eds., *Donald MacDonald's Collection of Piobaireachd vols. 1–2* (Piobaireachd Society, 2006, 2011) have appeared since this book was first published in 2000. They are not referred to in the main body of this work, which draws all primary sources from original manuscript and early printed texts, but I have examined them thoroughly and have taken them into account and they are included here in the bibliography.

Since electronic recordings, other than those discussed in Chapter 20, have not been a source for this book, I have not provided a discography. The catalogues of the piping colleges and leading commercial retailers are the best source of information on the substantial recorded repertoire currently available. For reasons which will quickly become evident to readers of this book, I think there are powerful grounds for concluding that the performance tradition in piobaireachd has been severely compromised by the insensitive and doctrinaire 'official' scores of the Piobaireachd Society. For an idea of how the older idiomatic scores may have been interpreted the reader may consult the sound recordings in my online variorum edition of ceol mor in the 'Set Tunes' series from 2001 onwards in:

http://pipesdrums.com/setTunes.aspx?M=music

The following abbreviations for frequently cited sources have been adopted:

AUL	Aberdeen University Library
EUL	Edinburgh University Library
GUL	Glasgow University Library
HSL	Highland Society of London
HSS	Highland Society of Scotland
NLS	National Library of Scotland
OT	*Oban Times*
PS	Piobaireachd Society
PT	*Piping Times*

Introduction

In January 1880 the distinguished folklorist, John Francis Campbell of Islay, discovered that a small collection of Highland melodies first published in 1828 had been reprinted by the firm of J. & R. Glen of Edinburgh, and hurried to acquire a copy. Its title page stated that it was *A collection of pibaireachd or pipe tunes, as verbally taught by the McCrummen pipers in the Isle of Skye, to their apprentices. Now published, as taken from John McCrummen, piper to the old Laird of MacLeod and his grandson, the late General MacLeod of MacLeod, in the hope that these ancient relics may be thus pre-served for future generations, and tend to keep up and foster that spirit which they have in former times, and are still so well calculated to excite.*[1]

Campbell's interest in the little pamphlet was at once professional and highly personal. He was the foremost living authority on Gaelic folktale, a founder of modern fieldwork methods and a scholar of international reputation thanks to his *Popular Tales of the West Highlands* (4 vols., 1860–2).[2] He was a most unusual man: a cousin of the Duke of Argyll, educated at Eton and called to the English bar, he was also one of the dwindling band of Highland gentlemen who continued to be Gaelic speakers. He had spent his early childhood in the care of a piper, his 'nurse', John Campbell of Lorne, son of Colin Campbell, a member of a famous piping dynasty, and the fascination of the little book of pipe tunes lay in the fact that it was not written in staff notation, but in *canntaireachd*, the syllabic notation system of the Highlands, which J. F. Campbell had last seen as a child, in an old manuscript, leafed through by his nurse as he fingered tunes on the chanter; tunes made out of words – like these:

COGADH NA SITH. Battle or Peace

The True Gathering of the Clans.

I Hodroho, hodroho, haninin, hiechin,
Hodroho, hodroho, hodroho, hachin,

---

1 *Canntaireachd: Articulate Music*, Dedicated to the Islay Association by J. F. Campbell, Iain Ileach. 14th August 1880 (Glasgow, 1880).
2 For biographical information on J. F. Campbell, see Richard M. Dorson, *The British Folklorists: a History* (Lond., 1968), pp. 393–402; see also Frank G. Thompson, 'John Francis Campbell', *Transactions of the Gaelic Society of Inverness*, vol LIV, 1984–1986, pp. 1–57.

Hiodroho, hodroho, haninin, hiechin,
Hodroha, hodroha, hodroha, hodroha,
Hodroha, hodroho, hodroho, hachin,
Hiodroho, hodroho, haninin, hiechin,
Hodroha, hodroho, hodroho, hodroha,
Haninun, haninun, haninun, haninun.[3]

The curious syllables seemed to the child to be filled with mystery and power –
he later wrote that his tutor had given him a glimpse of 'how to rouse men with
strange words out in the isles' – and he had long sought further insight into the
subject, in vain.

The little book seemed to present the perfect opportunity to establish once
and for all what it meant. How did the system work? By what mysterious
alchemy did the piper turn this verbal score which, although it had obvious links
with the sound-system of Gaelic did not make any obvious linguistic sense, into a
tune? The challenge was irresistible: and in the spring of 1880 the famous
folklorist set out to crack it.

Within a few weeks he had roughed out some possibilities and circulated them
amongst his gentlemen acquaintances in the Highland societies of Glasgow and
London, but none could help him. So he turned to the pipers: Ronald MacKenzie,
Pipe-Major of the 78th Highlanders, a leading teacher and competitor; the Queen's
piper, William – 'Uilleam' – Ross, editor of *Ross's Collection*, a standard compilation
of nineteenth century pipe music,[4] and Duncan Ross, piper to the Duke of Argyll,
who eventually turned out to be his most useful source. Duncan could read the
vocables, and play from them at will. But the problems of communication that
Campbell knew to expect from long experience of traditional communities took on
a wholly new dimension when he turned to the pipe and its culture:

We chose a word in a tune, and asked, What is '*hiririn*'?

'That's *hiririn*', said the piper, and played three notes deftly with his little
finger by striking a note on the chanter once. Two were open notes; one
closed. 'Do you know the names of the fingers?' said the teacher.

'Yes', said I, 'that's "ludag," the little finger.'

'Well', said the artist, 'that's "*hiririn*,"' and he played the passage several
times, to show how it was done . . .

'Is *hiririn* the name of the little finger of the right hand; or the name of
the hole in the chanter; or the name of the note; or what else is it?'

'No,' said the master, 'that's "*hiririn*,"' and he played that word over again
cleverly, with the same little finger.[5]

3 Campbell, *Canntaireachd*, title page.
4 This man is usually given the Gaelic form of his name by pipers, and will be
   uniformly thus designated in this book.
5 Campbell, *Canntaireachd, op.cit.*, pp.11–12.

What J. F. Campbell wanted was an explanation, a theoretical statement of some sort, perhaps along the following lines: '*Hiririn* is an onomatopoeic compound 'word' in the vocalic system of musical notation known as canntaireachd, indicating three notes on low A played in succession with varying degrees of rapidity and emphasis; the movement generally signals the beginning or end of a phrase, and is composed of quavers and demi-semi-quavers, and is frequently encountered in those initial musical statements in piobaireachd known as *ùrlars* or 'grounds'; it may be timed in at least three different ways, depending on the musical context, sir . . .'

What he got was a demonstration, a lightning-fast movement of the little finger of the right hand on the chanter, which, with a single stroke, apparently, produced in rapid succession a series of three notes at the same pitch. Very clever. But what was *hiririn*? *Hiririn* was precisely what he had been shown.[6]

Campbell's puzzlement is typical of the cultural barriers which have sprung up around the pipe and its culture since the disintegration of the original audience for this music, namely the Gaelic-speaking Highland middle and upper classes, during the early decades of the nineteenth century, and its replacement by one more populist, but also more technically specialist and arcane thereafter.

Nowadays piping is a worldwide culture with many thousands of performers, composers, teachers and learners, not only in Scotland but in Canada and the U.S.A., Australia, New Zealand and Ireland; there are devotees of the Highland pipe in continental Europe as well, particularly in Brittany. It supports an extensive manufacturing and retail base, involving bagpipe and reed makers, drum manufacturers, makers of kilts and uniforms for bands; a complex web of teaching and regulatory institutions such as the Piobaireachd Society, the Army School of Bagpipe Music, and the Royal Scottish Pipe Band Association; systems of grading and certification for performers, networks of local, national and international competitions for solo players and for bands, and a specialist media, including magazines, radio broadcasts and commercial recordings.

The Highland pipe has become a potent icon, instantly evoking Scotland and the Scots both to themselves and to the wider world, but there is little real knowledge of the instrument and its music beyond the boundaries of the performer community. It exists in a closed world, difficult for outsiders to penetrate. Although the light music of the pipes – marches, strathspeys, hornpipes, jigs and reels – is widely appreciated when played on other instruments (and rightly so, perhaps, because pipe composers have been the most prolific and original contributors to the popular instrumental tradition of

6 Traditional musical cultures vary widely in this respect. Some are 'doing' cultures, with little room for analysis or theory, others are more 'rationalising', where music exists within a context of explicit evaluation and criticism. See Alan P. Merriam, *The Anthropology of Music* (Northwestern University Press, 1964), p.112.

Scotland during the twentieth century), pipers still tend to talk to and amongst themselves, leading to the unusual situation of a performer community which not only generates but to a considerable extent also consumes its cultural product – at any rate in its more sophisticated forms.

The present book aims to widen this understanding a little, because pipers matter. Quite apart from the cultural value of their music, their activities have assumed great institutional and symbolic importance during the past three centuries and, as a result of this, there is more evidence about them than for any other traditional performer group.

They attract our attention above all, perhaps, because they are the creators and custodians of piobaireachd. (Pronounced '*peep*eruchk', of which the English spelling 'pibroch' is a loose imitation. The word itself simply means 'pipering' or 'what pipers do'.) This is an epic mode, involving a series of highly formal variations upon a ground or theme, and in its spaciousness, complexity, and intellectual demand is the highest of the traditional per-forming arts in Britain.[7] It was the first to achieve ideological importance outside the communities which produced it, [8] the first to be affected by modern-style cultural institutions,[9] and the first to develop a literate performer class, which created large quantities of written evidence not replicated in other fields.[10] It provides a rich context for studying the influence of print over long periods of time on an originally oral art form.[11] Best of all, perhaps, it sheds new light on a whole complex of concepts centring on the creation and transmission of culture. By considering what pipers do and why, we can see how it fell to them to wage a great ideological battle in the opening years of the twentieth century about the content, processes, and ownership of 'Tradition'.

---

7 For brief typical accounts of the form, see Roderick D. Cannon, *The Highland Bagpipe and its Music* (Edinr., 1988), pp. 51–104; John Purser, *Scotland's Music* (Edinr., 1992), pp.135–43; and Francis Collinson, *The Traditional and National Music of Scotland* (Lond., 1966), pp. 174–96.

8 Its only possible rival, the high ballad, did not reach a wider public in its full form as a song – tune as well as words – until commercial recordings became available during the 1950s.

9 Such as the Highland Societies of London and Scotland, and the Piobaireachd Society: see below, Chapters 4, 5, and *passim*.

10 The present study is based on a new survey of piping material in the *Oban Times* from 1861 onwards, an incomparably rich and little-known source, containing, in its correspondence columns, features and reviews, millions of words devoted to the pipe and its culture from the late Victorian period onwards.

11 See Peter Cooke, 'The Pibroch Tradition and Staff Notation', in Tokumaru Yosihiko and Yamaguti Osamu (eds.), *The Oral and the Literate in Music* (Tokyo, 1986), pp. 400–13. See also Christine Knox Chambers, 'Non-Lexical Vocables in Scottish Traditional Music', Ph.D Dissertation, Edinburgh University 1980.

I

'Their songs are of other worlds':
Ossian and the Macpherson Paradigm

As the 1750s drew to a close, two young Highlanders were working to present major Celtic art forms to a wider British, and ultimately world, audience. James Macpherson's *Works of Ossian* and Joseph MacDonald's *Compleat Theory of the Scots Highland Bagpipe* were the two great projects of the post-Culloden generation. The first took Europe by storm, was translated into many different languages and brought its author wealth and fame. The second was brought to an abrupt halt by the death in Calcutta at the age of 24 of its brilliant young creator. It was not published until 1803, and then in an edition so limited and corrupt that it was effectively lost for nearly a century thereafter. A reliable text only became available in 1994, nearly two hundred and fifty years after its first composition. Since all Highland art was subsequently, and wrongly, assumed by those outside the Gaidhealtachd to have sprung from the same cultural matrix as the poems of Ossian, the work of James Macpherson is fundamental to an understanding of how the pipe and its music were to be received outside the performer community from the 1760s onwards.

Towards the end of September 1759 on the bowling green of Moffat, a small spa town in the Scottish Borders, a young man presented himself with a letter of introduction to John Home, a distinguished Scottish man of letters whose tragedy, *Douglas*, had lately been the toast of Edinburgh. Home was affable and well-connected, secretary and confidant to the great Earl of Bute and a channel, therefore, to impressive quantities of patronage. Home had served as a volunteer with the government forces during the '45 and made a daring escape from the castle of Doune after his capture at the battle of Falkirk. He was fascinated by the differences between Highland and Lowland culture and was working, rather fitfully, on an ambitious long-term project – a history of the Rising which would relate politics to deeper social and cultural forces.[1] On his research forays into the Highlands he had listened enthralled to translations of epic oral verses recited by the common people, so that the tall, red-headed, highly-educated Highlandman who stood before him was a real discovery. His name was James Macpherson, and he was 22 years old.

Home's questions met with a swift response. Yes indeed, Macpherson knew of

---

1 After many delays this was eventually published as *The History of the Rebellion in the year 1745* (Lond., 1802); see especially pp. v-vi, 1-3. For its contemporary reception, see [James Browne], *A Critical Examination of Dr. Macculloch's Work on the Highlands and Western Isles of Scotland* (Edinr., 1825), pp. 11-14.

such poetry. Better still, he could read Gaelic (by no means a common accomplishment in the English-dominated educational milieu of the time) and had transcripts of Ossianic material actually in his possession:

> When Mr Home desired to see them, Mr Macpherson asked if he understood
> the Gaelic? 'Not one word'. 'Then, how can I show you them?' 'Very easily',
> said Mr Home; 'translate one of the poems which you think a good one, and
> I imagine that I shall be able to form some opinion of the genius and
> character of the Gaelic poetry.' Mr Macpherson declined the task, saying, that
> his translation would give a very imperfect idea of the original. Mr Home,
> with some difficulty, persuaded him to try, and in a day or two he brought
> him the poem on the death of Oscar . . .[2]

Macpherson's caution was understandable. He was probably aware of what had happened to the last volume of Gaelic poems to be published in Scotland, Alasdair MacMhaighstir Alasdair's *Ais-eiridh na Sean Chánoin Albannaich (The Resurrection of the Ancient Scottish Tongue)*, burned by the common hangman at the cross of Edinburgh in 1752 on account of its fiercely Jacobite sentiments.[3] His own were more carefully guarded. Although too young to have taken part in the Rising, he had been well placed to witness its consequences.

He was a gentleman of the clan Macpherson, a first cousin of the chief, born into the 'tacksman' or middle class of Highland society at Invertromie near Kingussie on 27 October 1736. Brought up within sight of Ruthven barracks, under a punitive military regime, he had gained first-hand experience of those parts of the British constitution which were not consecrated to liberty and human rights. For years after the '45, parties of soldiers scoured the country hunting for the chief, Cluny Macpherson, who had rendered himself particularly odious by defecting to the Jacobite side after promising to support the government. As late as 1755 the former local commander, James Wolfe (later to become a major general, and victor of Quebec) was advising that there should be 'a couple of hundred men in the neighbourhood with orders to massacre the whole clan if they show the least symptom of rebellion'.[4]

For those living beyond the Highland Line the '45 was the most momentous event of a momentous century, a desperate affair, described by Alasdair MacMhaighstir Alasdair, who had forsaken his little school in Ardnamurchan to fight as a captain in the Jacobite Clanranald regiment, as 'ane enterprise the

---

2 Henry Mackenzie, *Report of the Committee of the Highland Society of Scotland,
  appointed to inquire into the nature and authenticity of the poems of Ossian* (Edinr.,
  1805), Appendix IV, pp.68–9.
3 For an outline of Alasdair MacMhaighstir Alasdair's life and work, see John Lorne
  Campbell, ed., *Highland Songs of the Forty-Five* (Edinr., 1984, first published 1933),
  pp.33–41.
4 Fiona J. Stafford, *The Sublime Savage: A Study of James Macpherson and the Poems of
  Ossian* (Edinr., 1988), pp.19, 23 *n* 54.

most hazardous and resolute that the history of any person or country can aford'.[5] It had seen Charles Edward Stuart land in Scotland with a handful of companions, seize Edinburgh at the head of a largely Highland army, rout government forces at Prestonpans and Falkirk, and encounter shattering defeat in turn at the battle of Culloden. It is one of the best-known episodes in Scottish history, the subject of countless books and paintings, and of the epic Jacobite song-cycle which celebrated the triumphs and disasters of the campaign and the 'flight through the heather' when the Prince, with a price of £30,000 on his head, was pursued through the western Highlands and the Isles in the summer of 1746.[6]

It was one of the most remarkable events in recent European history, and there were various attempts during the following two centuries to establish a perspective from which it might properly be viewed. Some saw it in dynastic, some in ethnic terms; some as a clash between opposing constitutional theories, some as a struggle between rival systems of social organisation – the triumph of a 'modern' over a 'traditional' type of society.

But Highland historians spoke with a single voice: to them the '45 was an unparalleled calamity, not just for the Jacobite clans who had supported the Prince in '*Bliadhna Theàrlaich*' (the Year of Chairlie) – for the '45 was a civil war, with people from the same district, island, family even, involved on opposite sides – but for the whole of the Gaidhealtachd. 'All this country,' wrote the victorious government commander, William Augustus, Duke of Cumberland, 'are almost to a man Jacobites; and mild measures will not do', and he launched a vigorous campaign of reprisals to determine what a smack of officially sanctioned terrorism might do to adjust the political inclinations of the natives. The distinctive legal framework which underpinned the social organisation of the Highlands, linking commons, tacksmen and lairds in bonds of mutual obligation through a land-tenure system involving liability for military service, was systematically dismantled.[7] Execution and exile weakened the leadership élite, preparing the way for a new generation of Highland lairds more ready to accommodate itself to 'British' norms. Disarming Acts of unprecedented severity were passed.[8] These were aimed at reducing the military potential of the Gaidhealtachd not only by disarming certain sections of the population, but also by prohibiting a

---

5 'Journall and Memoirs of P . . . C . . . Expedition into Scotland Etc. 1745–6. By a Highland Officer in his Army', in George Lockhart of Carnwath, *The Lockhart Papers: containing Memoirs and Commentaries upon the Affairs of Scotland from 1702 to 1715* (2 vols., Lond., 1817), ii, 479–510, (479).

6 See William Donaldson, *The Jacobite Song: Political Myth and National Identity* (Aberd., 1988), *passim*.

7 Bruce Lenman, *The Jacobite Risings in Britain 1689–1746* (Lond., 1980), pp. 277–280; for an account from a less unionist perspective, see Frank McLynn, *The Jacobites* (Lond., 1985); see also A. J. Youngson, *After the Forty-Five The Economic Impact on the Scottish Highlands* (Edinr, 1973), pp.12–13.

8 19. Geo 2. c.39; 20.Geo.2.c.51 and 21 Geo.2.c.34.

distinctive article of clothing, the plaid, which was understood to permit that mobility and endurance which made Highland armies so formidable. Any member of the common people, man or boy, found wearing plaid, philibeg, trews, shoulder-belts, or any item of clothing whatsoever composed of tartan, could expect in theory to face six months' imprisonment for a first offence, and transportation for a second. But the first Act was so badly drawn that Government had to have two further attempts at it, pushing back the date of eventual implementation to 25 December 1748. There seem to have been relatively few prosecutions under its terms.[9]

It is frequently claimed that the pipes, too, were proscribed, but there is no mention of bagpipes in the Disarming Acts, nor contemporary evidence that they were forbidden or discouraged.[10]

The dismantling of the traditional hierarchy of social control within the Highlands was completed by the forfeiture of 41 estates. Most were sold to pay creditors, but 13 were annexed to the Crown, and their rents administered by commissioners 'for the Purposes of civilizing the Inhabitants upon the said Estates, and other Parts of the Highlands and Islands of Scotland, and promoting amongst them the Protestant Religion, good Government, Industry and Manufactures, and the Principles of Duty and Loyalty to his Majesty, his Heirs and Successors . . .'[11] The Gaelic language came under sustained attack. It was viewed as a prime source of disaffection, because it encouraged the people to regard themselves as a race apart and restricted interaction with their neighbours. Steps were taken, therefore, to increase provision of schools in which English alone would be the medium of instruction.

All the misfortunes which overtook the Gaidhealtachd during the following two centuries – the great diaspora known as 'The Clearances'; the inexorable shrinking of the language-base; the alienation of the leadership élite; land agitation and social strife; the threatened extinction of a distinctively Celtic culture beyond the Highland line even – were ultimately traced to the '45.[12]

But the '45 did not just change the Highlands; it transformed the popular culture of Lowland Scotland as well. The adoption as national icons of various elements of Highland costume, music and poetry led to a progressive

---

9 John Telfer Dunbar, *The Costume of Scotland* (Lond., 1981), pp.50–54. The writer Mrs. Ann Grant attended a service in the Rev.Patrick MacDonald's church at Kilmore near Oban in 1773. It is clear from her description that the kirk was ablaze with tartan: *Letters from the Mountains; being the real Correspondence of a Lady, between the years 1773 and 1803* (3 vols., Lond., 1806), i, 56–58. For a detailed recent discussion of these points, see John G. Gibson, *Traditional Gaelic Bagpiping 1745–1945* (Edinr., 1998), pp.25–8, 36–63.

10 See Gibson, pp.28–35, 51–6.

11 Youngson, p.27.

12 By the same token a Stuart restoration was explicitly linked with a revival in Gaelic culture: see William Matheson, ed., *The Songs of John MacCodrum* (Edinr., 1938), 'Introduction' p.xxix.

Celticisation of the public symbolism of Scotland which transformed the
national identity in the generation following the Rising. Robert Burns remarked,
'When political combustion ceases to be the object of Princes & Patriots, it
then . . . becomes the lawful prey of Historians & Poets',[13] and the latter were
given exciting scope by the extraordinary nature of what had just taken place.
John Home captured something of this in his *History of the Rebellion:*

> In the year one thousand seven hundred and forty-five, *Charles Edward Stuart,*
> the Pretender's eldest son, calling himself the Prince of Wales, landed with
> seven persons in a remote part of the Highlands of Scotland. A few days after
> his arrival, some Highlanders (not a very considerable number) joined him,
> and descending from their mountains, undisciplined, and ill-armed, without
> cavalry, without artillery, without one place of strength in their possession,
> attempted to dethrone the king, and subvert the government of Britain. The
> conclusion of this enterprise was such as most people both at home and
> abroad expected; but the progress of the rebels was what nobody expected; for
> they defeated more than once the king's troops; they over-ran one of the
> united kingdoms, and marched so far into the other, that the capital trembled
> at their approach, and during the tide of fortune, which had its ebbs and
> flows, there were moments when nothing seemed impossible; and, to say the
> truth, it was not easy to forecast, or imagine, anything more unlikely than
> what had already happened.[14]

The fame of Charles Edward and his Highland clans made them at once
'*l'admiration et la curiosité de l'Europe*'.[15] He had emerged from the mists
accompanied by a living museum of ancient manners, dress and arts, the last
remnants (or so it was thought) of the once mighty Celtic civilisation which had
dominated Europe, and given instruction through its bardic and druidical
schools to Gaul and all the West. This was no footnote in a dusty classical
text by Livy or Tacitus, but an actual survival from high antiquity, and as such
immediately assimilable to the fashionable theories of primitive culture which
shaped contemporary thinking about man and society. The European intelligentsia was fascinated. How could such people, such a society, be? There was a
clever young Highlander called James Macpherson very ready to tell them.

Macpherson had studied at both of Aberdeen's university colleges, King's and
Marischal, which attracted many students from the Highlands because of the
shortness of the academic year and the city's easy accessibility by sea. In the 1750s
the Aberdeen colleges were at the height of their fame, with a teaching staff of
international reputation in philosophy, aesthetics, classical studies and rhetoric:

13 J. De Lancey Ferguson and G. Ross Roy, eds., *The Letters of Robert Burns* (2 vols.,
　　Oxford, 1985), ii, 82.
14 Home, pp.1–2.
15 Andrew Lang, *Pickle the Spy: or The Incognito of Prince Charles* (Lond., 1897), p.7.

figures like Thomas Reid, founder of the Scottish 'Common Sense' school of philosophy, who was Macpherson's tutor; George Campbell, whose *Philosophy of Rhetoric* dominated its field for upwards of a century; the writer James Beattie (although he came a little after Macpherson's time) whose poem 'The Minstrel' was to become one of the founding documents of the Romantic revival in Britain; above all, perhaps, Thomas Blackwell, the most distinguished Scottish classicist of his period, principal of Marischal College, teacher of Macpherson's teachers, and a man of immense influence.

Blackwell was not a classicist in the narrow linguistic sense, or a writer in the dusty academic mode. His major works, *An Enquiry into the Life and Writings of Homer* (Lond. 1735) and *Letters on Mythology* (Lond. 1748) show him to have been at once a folklorist, a student of myth and a pioneering cultural anthropologist.[16] He offered deep explanations of the nature of mythology, revealing the theories about the world that lay behind the screen of metaphor, and he was author of the definitive Scottish statement on the links between epic poetry and the social organisation of early societies.

His approach was marked by a sophisticated cultural determinism, which suggested that a combination of the right kind of society, geography and climate would produce epic poetry. An additional spark of genius would bring forth a Homer. Blackwell pictured early classical Greece as a turbulent military society marked by a heroic simplicity of manners, and a proliferation of small aristocratic courts. It was uneven in its cultural development because centres of high civilisation were mixed with surrounding pools of relative barbarism. It was mountainous in its geography and divided by rivers and straths, fostering a variety of local cultures, each with its own identity, and it sustained a powerful bardic class drawing inspiration from the traditions of the common people.[17] The whole bore an uncanny resemblance to the Scottish Highlands of James Macpherson's youth.

One idea would have struck Macpherson with particular force: the insistence on a kind of noble barbarism as the essential precondition of great epic poetry. Blackwell wrote:

> I am in the case of a noble Historian [Herodotus], who having related the constant Superiority his *Greeks* had over the Inhabitants of the *Assyrian* Vales, concludes 'That it has not been given by the Gods, to one and the same Country, to produce rich Crops and warlike Men:' Neither indeed does it seem to be given to one and the same Kingdom, to be thoroughly civilized, and afford proper Subjects for Poetry . . . It is thus that a People's Felicity clips the Wings of their Verse . . .'[18]

16 The latter text was begun by another hand; Blackwell completed letters 7 and 8, and
    wrote the remainder of the sequence through to no.19.
17 Blackwell, *Enquiry*, pp. 5, 11–12, 15–25, 104–5, 119–28.
18 Blackwell, pp.26, 28.

Blackwell's insistence upon the creative importance of the audience for the Homeric poems – 'He had not the Inhabitants of a *great luxurious City* to entertain . . . but the martial Race of a wide and free Country, who listen willingly to the Prowess of their Ancestors, and Atchievements of their Kings' – would have increased Macpherson's growing realisation that he was a privileged witness to a living heroic culture.[19] Macpherson went back to Ruthven as a schoolmaster and began to collect traditional Gaelic poetry. But he was restless and hungry for recognition, and soon his own original verse, in English, was finding an outlet in the magazines of the day. His first extended work, a poem in six cantos entitled *The Highlander* published in 1758, showed epic Celtic warriors repelling a Scandinavian invasion, a foretaste, perhaps, of what was to come.

The young man who stood before John Home that autumn day in Moffat represented several strands of cultural possibility: he had personal contact with a heroic 'primitive' culture; potential access to an international literary market hungry for information about the Jacobite clans and the society from which they had sprung; and a powerful theory of culture capable of linking ancient and modern, the oral and the literate, and Celtic with Classical antiquity in a common epic mould.

A few days later Macpherson produced examples, in a startlingly unconventional English prose, of what he claimed was the work of a mighty Caledonian bard called Ossian who had flourished in the third century A.D. Home was stunned. Of Ossian himself he had probably heard, but nothing in his experience could have prepared him for the fresh, original and delicate fragments of prose poetry he held in his hand. This was a discovery of major proportions, a line of noble ancient poetry preserved for centuries within the fastnesses of the Scottish Highlands unknown to the larger world, which, if it were genuine, might have incalculable implications for the balance of cultural power within the United Kingdom. Anxiously he consulted his friend Adam Ferguson, professor of Natural Philosophy at the University of Edinburgh, a Gaelic-speaking Highlander from Perthshire, to whom Home owed most of his knowledge of the language and culture of the Gael. Ferguson confirmed. Yes, he remembered hearing such verses as a child, and there was, he thought, a lot of material like this probably still in existence. Copies of Macpherson's fragments circulated amongst Home's friends in Edinburgh's prestigious Select Society and 'were . . . received with the utmost enthusiasm and delight. Every one read them, and every one admired them; and, altogether, a sensation was created in the world of letters, which it had known but on few occasions before'.[20] In an atmosphere of feverish excitement and expectancy Macpherson was summoned to the capital to meet

---

19 Blackwell, p.119. See also James Macpherson, *An Introduction to the History of Great Britain and Ireland* (Lond., 1771), pp. 188–192.

20 Robert Chambers, ed., *Biographical Dictionary of Eminent Scotsmen* (9 vols., Glasg., 1853–55), vi, 542.

the great arbiter of contemporary taste, Dr. Hugh Blair, minister of the High Kirk of St. Giles and 'literary accoucheur of Scotland'.[21]

Blair was in his early forties and at the height of an outstandingly successful ecclesiastical career. He was as close as one could get in Presbyterian Scotland to being a 'society' preacher, numbering amongst his hearers the Lords of Session, and the other great officers of law and state, the magistrates of Edinburgh, and most of the rank and fashion of the city. It was the most elegant congregation in Scotland, and he regaled it with sermons of unimpeachably chaste composition, containing, as one rather hostile later commentator remarked, 'one grain of the gospel dissolved into a large cooling-draught of moral disquisition'.[22]

Blair was dignified and sedate, a fastidious, dressy, decent man, whose brains were powerful enough to be respectable but not enough to cause alarm. His fashionable lectures on literature and criticism were gratifyingly well attended, and he was soon to be appointed to the chair of Rhetoric and Belles Lettres at Edinburgh University, the first of its kind in Britain. He was the touchstone of good taste in everything from tragedies to teapots and his instinct was held to be infallible; a classically safe pair of hands, guaranteed to ruffle no feathers and leave no hostages to fortune.

Indeed Blair was later assumed to have been the controlling intelligence behind the whole venture, but the reality was rather different. Since he had no Gaelic and little personal knowledge of Highland culture, he was almost entirely dependent on Macpherson for access to the text, and he was to prove little match for Macpherson's powerful and devious intellect.[23] Nevertheless he unhesitatingly assumed the role of literary co-ordinator-in-chief, and wrote a preface for *Fragments of Ancient Poetry, collected in the Highlands of Scotland, and translated from the Galic or Erse Language* which was published in June 1760 and was greeted with high excitement in the capital.[24] As well it might be, for it was

21 Henry Grey Graham, *Scottish Men of Letters in the Eighteenth Century* (Lond., 1901), p.126.

22 Chambers, *Eminent Scotsmen*, i, 255.

23 Mackenzie, *Report*, pp.60–61. That Macpherson was responsible for the intellectual approach is evident from his later prefaces and essays; Blair was forced to rely upon a network of Highland correspondents, chiefly ministers and lairds, such as John Macpherson of Sleat and Donald Macqueen of Kilmuir, who simply tended to confirm in a general kind of way what James Macpherson was saying: see Hugh Blair, *A Critical Dissertation on the Poems of Ossian, the Son of Fingal* (2nd edn., Lond., 1765), pp.140–8. Blair's Whiggish and unionist circle must also have been uncomfortable with the explicitly nationalist thrust of Macpherson's work. For example, see Adam Ferguson's letter to Sir John Sinclair of Ulbster when the latter was compiling the *Statistical Account of Scotland*, urging him to avoid using the word 'Scotland' and substitute instead 'certain northern counties or parishes of Great Britain', quoted in Rev. John Sinclair, *Memoirs of the Life and Works of the Late Right Honourable Sir John Sinclair, Bart* (2 vols., Edinr., 1837), ii, 34–5.

24 Fiona Stafford, 'Introduction: The Ossianic Poems of James Macpherson', in Howard Gaskill, ed., *The Poems of Ossian and Related Works* (Edinr., 1996), pp.v–xxi, (xii).

revealed that the *Fragments* were merely part of a much larger work. A lost epic poem, nearly two thousand years old, existed somewhere in the Highlands, and it might be possible to recover it.[25]

Macpherson was furnished with money and letters of introduction and in August 1760 despatched to the Highlands on the greatest literary big-game hunt of modern times. Several months later he returned laden with transcripts and proceeded to assemble the text of *Fingal, An Ancient Epic Poem. In Six Books: together with Several Other Poems composed by Ossian, the Son of Fingal.* This was published in London in December 1761, to be followed in March 1763 by *Temora, an Ancient Epic Poem in Eight Books: together with Several Other Poems composed by Ossian, the Son of Fingal.* Both were issued together in 1765 as *The Works of Ossian.*[26]

These presented heroic episodes from the wars of the ancient Caledonians, a legendary race of giant warriors led by Fingal, King of Morven, whose deeds were commemorated by his son the blind minstrel Ossian, last of his race. Contemporaries were excited by the boldness and novelty of the diction, which deliberately avoided conventional verse forms in favour of an elevated, loosely-structured poetic prose which emphasised the utter remoteness of the subject matter from a present widely perceived as decadent, whilst at the same time subtly reinforcing a characteristic ambience of cloudy melancholy and loss:

> Whence is the stream of years? Whither do they roll along? Where have they
> hid, in mist, their many-coloured sides? I look into the times of old, but they
> seem dim to Ossian's eyes, like reflected moon-beams on a distant lake . . . As
> flies the unconstant sun, over Larmon's grassy hill; so pass the tales of old,
> along my soul, by night. When bards are removed to their place; when harps
> are hung in Selma's hall; then comes a voice to Ossian, and awakes his soul.
> It is the voice of years that are gone: they roll before me, with all their deeds.
> I seize the tales, as they pass, and pour them forth in song. Nor a troubled
> stream is the song of the king, it is like the rising of music from Lutha of the
> strings. – Lutha of many strings, not silent are thy streamy rocks, when the
> white hands of Malvina move upon the harp. – Light of the shadowy
> thoughts, that fly across my soul, daughter of Toscar of helmets, wilt thou not
> hear the song! We call back, maid of Lutha, the years that have rolled away.[27]

The publication of *Ossian* was a major event. It was translated into most of the European languages and hailed with delight by figures such as Herder (who

---

25 The introduction to *Fragments*, is reproduced in Gaskill, *Poems of Ossian*, pp. 5–6.
26 Gaskill, *Poems of Ossian*, p. xxiii.
27 Ossian represented an extraordinary stylistic coup: looked at merely in terms of
    English language sources, there are obvious traces of the Authorised Version and
    Milton, and James Thomson's great nature poem, 'The Seasons', with perhaps a little
    smack of gentle parody directed against John Home himself, whose epic blank verse
    had been extravagantly admired. The passages quoted are from *Temora*, pp.203, 211.

calmly read 'Fingal' in the middle of a shipwreck),[28] Goethe, Schubert, Hölderlin, Schiller, Madame de Staël, Chateaubriand, and Lamartine; Napoleon carried it with him on his campaigns in an Italian translation, and it became the inspiration for countless other poems and novels, operas, paintings and plays.[29]

But in Britain, the response was sharply divided. There was bitter controversy about the poems' authenticity. Scottish critics, led by Hugh Blair, asserted that they were genuine, while English critics, led by Dr. Samuel Johnson, denounced them as forgeries. Johnson denied that non-literate communities could transmit cultural products coherently over anything like the timespan required and rejected with scorn the notion that a people such as the Scotch Highlanders could at any period have created works of such refinement and moral cultivation. Macpherson's apparent reluctance to produce the 'originals' for inspection led the hostile critics – though few of them were acquainted with the Gaelic language or the habits of oral communities – to conclude that he had made it all up himself.[30]

But the fury of the English intelligentsia was largely directed against a position that was not, in fact, being defended. It appears that Macpherson's work really was based on manuscript and traditional oral sources, however distantly.[31] He had altered names and locations, interpolated huge passages of his own, expressed himself in an English whose sumptuous literary patina and unflaggingly elegiac tone departed significantly from the texts he was ostensibly translating; but such practices were not enormously at variance with the casual editorial standards of the time. He indicated explicitly that he was responsible for weaving together into a coherent whole the fragmentary evidence he had found, justifying his publication of a second version of 'Temora' with reference to fresh materials which had recently come into his possession, adding: 'The story of the poem, with which I had been long acquainted, enabled me to reduce the broken members of the piece into the order in which they now appear'.[32]

His approach was entirely in keeping with contemporary Scottish theories of

28 Uwe Böker, 'The Marketing of Macpherson: The International Book Trade and the first Phase of German Ossian Reception', in Howard Gaskill, ed., *Ossian Revisited* (Edinr., 1991), pp.73–93, (85).

29 See Andrew Hook, 'Scotland and Romanticism: The International Scene', in Andrew Hook, ed., *The History of Scottish Literature Volume 2, 1660–1800* (Aberd., 1987), pp. 307–322, (313–6). See also Kirsti Simonsuuri, *Homer's Original Genius: Eighteenth-century Notions of the Early Greek Epic* (1688–1798) (Cambridge, 1979), p.111. See also Roger Fiske, *Scotland in Music: A European Enthusiasm* (Cambridge, 1983), pp. 31–54. There is a town called Ossian, in Indiana, USA.

30 See R. W. Chapman, ed., *Johnson's Journey to the Western Islands of Scotland and Boswell's Journal of a Tour to the Hebrides with Samuel Johnson, LL.D.* (Oxford, 1930), pp.104–108.

31 Derek S. Thomson, *The Gaelic Sources of Macpherson's 'Ossian'* (Edinr., 1951), *passim*, but esp. pp. 1–12, 79–84; see also *Ossian Revisited, op.cit.*, pp.5–6, 19.

32 *Temora*, p.xviii; see also p.3, *n*, 4,*n*; *Fingal, op.cit*, p.104, *n*. See also *Stafford, op.cit.*, pp.82–85, 124–126.

epic poetry, which envisaged the evolution of unitary, written Homeric texts as a late development resulting from deliberate editorial intervention in a previously oral process. Blackwell insisted that Homer had been a strolling oral poet, whose ballads had been committed to writing as coherent developed epics centuries after his death. Macpherson could easily claim that what the Greek redactors had done might very properly be done again by a modern collector/editor working with the essentially non-literate oral products of the Scottish Highlands.[33]

Had the point of the controversy been merely literary, his position might have been accepted as a reasonable one. But in the domain of cultural politics, the implications of *Ossian* were explosive: if it were 'genuine', then the Scots, like the ancient Greeks and Romans (whom Macpherson also included in the roll of Celtic nations), but pointedly unlike the contemporary English, possessed the ultimate national status-marker: a great foundation epic.[34] Hence the frequent references to Homer and Virgil. *Ossian* was a calculated stroke in the struggle for cultural supremacy within the United Kingdom which had been rumbling on for centuries. Macpherson's demonstration of the seniority of Scottish poetry, and his insouciant tracing of 'British Liberties' to Celtic rather than to Anglo-Saxon roots, were utterly galling to the English intelligentsia and intended to be so.[35] This is why the counter-attack was so ferocious.

But Macpherson's political instincts were highly developed, and his text was furnished with an elaborate apparatus of dissertations and notes intended to meet the arguments likely to be brought against it. It was important to establish very clearly the cultural community to which these poems referred, and this entailed an important sequence of arguments about the origin and identity of the Scottish nation. Some writers had described the Scots as an ethnically loose confederation of peoples – Germanic Picts and northern Angles, and Celtic Scots out of Ireland – brought together by the vagaries of dynastic circumstance. Not so, said Macpherson, appealing to an impressive array of antiquarian lore. With the exception of a later, debilitating, admixture of Saxon stock following the acquisition of the Lothians, the ancient Caledonians were a wholly Celtic

---

33 Blackwell, *Enquiry*, 104–5, 119ff; see also *Temora, op.cit.,*4,*n*. The poems' reception in the Highlands seems upon the whole to have been balanced and realistic. Duncan Robertson of Struan wrote in 1767: 'I have read Fingal, but not with the pleasure that I have heard many of his Exploits repeated in the original Language. It is more than 40 years since I knew the characters of Fingal and his principal Heroes. The Translation seems really surprisingly good, but let any body that understands the Language compare the 7th Book of Temara in the Original (which M'Pherson has given as a specimen), with the Translation, and he'll find a great deall of strength & beauty of expression lost; which is perhaps not so much the fault of the Translator as the deficiency of our modern Language'. Quoted in T. L. Kington Oliphant, *The Jacobite Lairds of Gask* (Lond. 1870), p.354.

34 See Macpherson, *History of Great Britain and Ireland,* pp.6–9.

35 *Ibid.,* pp.223–4; see also L, P, Curtis, jr., *Anglo-Saxons and Celts: A Study of Anti-Irish Prejudice in Victorian England* (Bridgeport: Conn., 1968), pp.8–9.

people, having originated in Gaul and subsequently migrated into the north.[36] Popular mythology might link them with marauding Irish war-bands during the Dark Ages, but Macpherson insisted that the colonisation had taken place in exactly the opposite direction, Ireland being settled subsequently to Britain, the southern parts by Belgic Celts, and the north by Celts from Scotland and the Isles.[37]

Although climate, geography, and political history had subsequently divided the Highland from the Lowland Caledonians in language and social mores, they were essentially a single people.[38] So that the discovery of Gaelic epic poems possessed significance not merely for Highland, but for Scottish culture as a whole. And Macpherson insisted that Ossian was not an isolated phenomenon. He was by far the best and oldest of the bards, it was true, but only one of a succession of brilliant poetic talents preserved in the treasure-house of the Gaelic language, whose recovery bade fair to transform Scotland's standing in the world of learning and culture.[39]

Macpherson was at pains to stress the unique richness of the Scottish Highlands as a receptacle of tradition. He pointed to the deep conservatism of the people, and their social isolation which had restricted external influences whilst strongly fostering indigenous forms. Their military organisation and the spartan austerity of their way of life provided the ideal ambience for a cult of epic nobility to flourish:

> If tradition could be depended upon, it is only among a people, from all time,
> free of intermixture with foreigners. We are to look for these among the
> mountains and inaccessible parts of a country: places, on account of their
> barrenness, uninviting to an enemy, or whose natural strength enabled the
> natives to repel invasions. Such are the inhabitants of the mountains of
> Scotland. We, accordingly, find, that they differ materially from those who
> possess the low and more fertile part of the kingdom. Their language is pure

36 *Fingal*, pp. ii-iii; *Temora*, pp.ii-iv, xiii-xiv.

37 *Temora*, p.vii. For the historical background to Macpherson's thinking see William
    Ferguson, *The Identity of the Scottish Nation* (Edinr., 1998), esp. Chs. 10–11, which
    came to the writer's attention as this book was in the press.

38 *Temora*, pp.v-vi.

39 Macpherson was powerful on the links between language and identity: 'Nations are
    not so tenacious of their customs and manners as they are of their aboriginal tongues.
    The first may gradually vanish in the growing improvements of civil life; the latter
    can only be buried in the same grave with the people themselves. Conquest may
    confine the bounds of a language; commerce may corrupt it; new inventions, by
    introducing new words, may throw the old into disuse; a change in the mode of
    thinking may alter the idiom: but the extirpation of those who speak any original
    tongue is the only means, by which it can be entirely destroyed, even where letters
    have been altogether unknown. It retires from successful invasion into rocks and
    desarts; it subsists with the remains of a people; even mountains and rivers in part
    retain it when the people are no more'. *History of Great Britain and Ireland*, p.241.

and original, and their manners are those of an antient and unmixed race of men. Conscious of their own antiquity, they long despised others, as a new and mixed people. As they lived in a country only fit for pasture, they were free of that toil and business, which engross the attention of a commercial people. Their amusement consisted in hearing or repeating their songs and traditions, and these intirely turned on the antiquity of their nation, and the exploits of their forefathers. It is no wonder, therefore, that there are more remains of antiquity among them, than among any other people in Europe.[40]

The antiquity of Ossian was essential to Macpherson's argument and the point was expounded at length in the 'Dissertations' which accompanied the poems. He pointed to the deep conviction amongst the communities which had preserved them that the pieces were antique. The ideas, manners and linguistic idiom also seemed to indicate great age. In structure they were nobly wild and irregular, which was thought to be the hallmark of 'primitive' poetry. There was no reference to long-established social forms like clanship, and such allusions to Christianity as the poems contained treated it as an intrusive and novel creed.[41]

Macpherson appealed to the fashionable theories of 'conjectural history' currently being developed by Enlightenment thinkers in Scotland and elsewhere. Human societies were thought to pass through a series of clearly-defined stages arranged in a fixed sequence: an age of hunter-gatherers followed by a pastoral age of flocks and herds, then an era of more settled agriculture with tending of crops, and finally the modern mercantile era with its cash nexus and contractual relations.[42] In terms of material prosperity, each stage represented an advance on the previous one, but contemporaries did not regard the process wholly in terms of gain. Blackwell had already noted that it did not 'seem to be given to one and the same Kingdom, to be thoroughly civilized, and afford proper Subjects for Poetry', and the idea of a lost golden age distinguished by high artistic achievement could be traced back to classical antiquity and beyond.[43] The heroic past possessed a potentially strong appeal if it could be shown not to be barbaric in a squalid savage sense, but nobly primaeval; and this Macpherson set himself to do. He radically rearranged the graph of culture, replacing the smooth upward curve with a high initial peak followed by a downward subsequent trajectory, implying that the creative impulse had become so compromised by

---

40 *Ibid.*, pp.ii-iii; see also *Fingal*, 'Preface'.

41 *Fingal*, pp. iv, vii; 'Preface' to *Fragments*, in Gaskill, *Poems of Ossian*, p.5.

42 Macpherson's thinking here seems to have influenced both Adam Ferguson and Lord Kames: see William C. Lehmann, *Henry Home, Lord Kames, and the Scottish Enlightenment: a Study in National Character and in the History of Ideas* (The Hague, 1971), p.190; and George W. Stocking, Jr., 'Scotland as the Model of Mankind: Lord Kames' Philosophical View of Civilisation', in Timothy H. H. Thoresen, ed., *Towards a Science of Man: Essays in the History of Anthropology* (The Hague, 1975), pp.65–89.

43 Blackwell, *Enquiry*, p.26.

commercial values that the present could not hope to equal the past in the production of an enduring poetry.

The lofty, chivalric code of the Ossianic heroes had been framed by the bards and conveyed in language of such power and eloquence as to give it the force of a moral imperative. Art, which had begun by reflecting life, ensured that life in turn attempted to emulate art. In this way heroic values were diffused through Highland society. Every chief believed himself to be descended from a Fingalian hero, and every chief had a bard who could recite the old epics, and in time the office became hereditary. And so bardic succession ensured that the poems were handed down intact from generation to generation.[44]

Macpherson was committed to defending oral tradition as a medium capable of transmitting large-scale cultural forms accurately over considerable periods of time, and he appealed to a spread of similar practices amongst other ancient peoples in support of his ideas.[45] He was prepared to specify the mechanisms of transmission in considerable detail. These involved techniques of disciplined memorisation instilled in the bardic class; their practice of frequent allusion to the established classics which kept knowledge of them current; the public nature of poetry which provided a social brake upon innovation; and the prosodic structures of Gaelic poetry itself which, he thought, inhibited casual mutation.[46]

The oral element was of crucial importance because it was the sole means of access to the 'lost' original fixed authoritative text. Various references in the Dissertations and Prefaces suggest that Macpherson actually believed that such a thing had once existed, and that he was acting as a 'restorer' rather than as an independent creator in his own right.[47] Although he was willing, indeed compelled, to acknowledge the ultimate coherence of 'tradition', he was never entirely comfortable in its presence, regarding variations between the oral versions as probable signs of corruption and loss.[48] Blackwell had been happy to contemplate the 'original' Homeric text as episodic and oral and as having undergone significant change over time, but Macpherson hankered after something a good deal more stable and unitary. He regarded invariance and fixity as the hallmarks of tradition and considered that it was the role of educated mediators such as himself to rescue the products of these forces from disintegrating contemporary oral cultures. This was a task of some urgency. Highland society, he thought, had experienced more rapid change during the last thirty years than in the last thousand. As a result of this its traditional culture stood in serious jeopardy:

---

44 *Fingal,* pp.x-xi.
45 *Ibid.,* p.xiii.
46 *Ibid.,* pp.xi-xiii.
47 Stafford, pp.82–3.
48 Indeed he remarked in *Temora* that 'Probability is all that can be established on the authority of tradition, ever dubious and uncertain', p.xi.

The genius of the highlanders has suffered a great change within these few years. The communication with the rest of the island is open, and the introduction of trade and manufactures has destroyed that leisure which was formerly dedicated to hearing and repeating the poems of ancient times . . . Bards have been long disused, and the spirit of genealogy has greatly subsided. Men begin to be less devoted to their chiefs, and consanguinity is not so much regarded. When property is established, the human mind confines its views to the pleasure it procures. It does not go back to antiquity, or look forward to succeeding ages. The cares of life increase, and the actions of other times no longer amuse. Hence it is, that the taste for their ancient poetry is at a low ebb among the highlanders.[49]

Many generations of readers were to return to *Fingal* and *Temora* and find themselves touched by unearthly beauty and power. Many generations of historians and critics were to acknowledge their outstanding importance in the history of European thought. For this study, however, the significance of Macpherson's work lies in the series of theoretical statements to which it gave rise about the nature of Celtic art. These were caught up and amplified by later writers and established the conventions to which all Highland art forms – and especially the music of the pipe – were subsequently expected to conform outside the Gaidhealtachd. They were as follows:

1. That as Ossian was shrouded in controversy, then all Celtic cultural products might be considered potentially bogus.
2. That antiquity was the distinguishing feature of Highland art and the great period of achievement lay in the past.
3. That its true expression was linked with noble barbarism and rugged natural settings.
4. That wildness and irregularity were its leading formal characteristics.
5. That cloudy melancholy was its most typical emotion.
6. That 'tradition' ought to be, like the societies which sustained it, essentially unchanging.
7. That the fluidity inherent in oral 'variants' must therefore represent corruption and loss.
8. That since the mechanisms of transmission were failing, modern 'tradition' must be inherently degenerative and unable to sustain itself without the intervention of external mediators.

This, then, was the Macpherson paradigm which was to dominate the interpretation of Highland culture outside the Gaidhealtachd during the following two centuries.

49 *Fingal*, p.xv.

2

'Abounding in works of taste and genius': Joseph MacDonald and the Compleat Theory of the Scots Highland Bagpipe

As Macpherson was promoting the claims of Highland poetry, a pioneering collection of piobaireachd, song and dance tunes from oral tradition was beginning to take shape in Sutherland in the hands of a young musician called Joseph MacDonald. This, too, was intended to transform Scottish culture by means of fresh perspectives from Highland sources.

Joseph MacDonald was born on Monday 26th February 1739, the third son of the eleven children of the Rev. Murdo MacDonald, A.M., minister of Durness. The parish lay in the north-west corner of one of the great northern clan territories on the mainland, the Reay country, *dùthaich MhicAoidh*, which stretched from Cape Wrath in the west to Strath Halladale in the east, and from the shores of the Pentland Firth to the mountainous wastes of Foinaven and Arkle in the south. The kirk was in the Clachan of Balnakil, a little to the west of the modern village of Durness, in the crook of the bay formed by the low sandy headland of Fair Aird, where also were situated Balnakil House, the seat of the chief of the MacKay name, Donald, fourth Lord Reay, and the Rev. Murdo's new manse, erected in 1727, when Durness became a separate parish of the recently-established Presbytery of Tongue.

Maighstir Murchadh was a graduate of the University of St. Andrews, and a remarkable man. He was a passionate lover of poetry both in Gaelic and English, who would traverse his scattered and mountainous parish with a volume of Pope or Young in his pocket, and a gifted musician with a powerful and melodious singing voice.[1] This talent was transmitted to his children, most especially to Patrick, the eldest, later to become minister of Kilmore in Argyllshire, and father of the Church of Scotland; Joseph, the subject of this chapter, who entered the service of the East India Company and died in Bengal at a tragically early age; and Flora, who married into the ministry and settled in Edinburgh.[2] To them we owe some of the most important publications in the field of Highland music in eighteenth and early nineteenth century Scotland.

Joseph had a precocious gift. He was given a thorough musical grounding by his father, and was able by the age of eight to lead the psalmody in the kirk of

---

1 Ian Grimble, *The World of Rob Donn* (Edinr., 1979), pp.32–7, and *passim*. See also entry for Murdoch McDonald in Hew Scott, ed., *Fasti Ecclesiae Scoticanae: The Succession of Ministers in the Parish Churches of Scotland from the Reformation, A.D. 1560, to the Present Time* (3 vols., Edinr., 1866–71), iii, 347–8.

2 See entry for Dr. Tough, St. Cuthbert's Chapel of Ease, *Fasti*, i, 127–8.

Durness.[3] The children were encouraged to compose as well as play, and it is said that some of Joseph and Flora's tunes were used for songs by their father's most celebrated parishioner, the poet Rob Donn MacKay.[4] Joseph also made rapid progress on the violin under the tuition of Kenneth Sutherland of Keoldale, factor of the barony of Durness, and on the pipes, probably under Rob Donn's friend George MacLeod, piper to Lord Reay.[5] He also played the flute and the oboe.

He was very able academically. By his early teens, he had made good progress in French and Latin, English and Gaelic (literacy in the latter being by no means common at this time), and his father began to consider a suitable career. Patrick, the eldest son, had already attended the University of Aberdeen, and was currently teaching while he waited for a kirk. But launching another son into the professions would stretch the Rev. Murdo's means. His stipend was a mere £44.00 per annum, and with his large family he was often forced to confide to his diary about 'straitened circumstances', and 'worldly affairs much in disorder'.[6]

But the minister of Durness was a resourceful man and rather good at what the eighteenth century called 'making interest', the art of using well-connected friends and relations to promote oneself or one's dependants in a society where sponsored mobility was very much the order of the day. We find him accordingly, in the spring of 1753, writing on Joseph's behalf to the scholar and physician Dr. John Clephane (probably a connection from his St. Andrews days). Clephane sprang from an ancient Fife family, the Clephanes of Carslogie, near Cupar. He was a Fellow of the Royal Society, and currently practising as a fashionable physician in London. A cultured and witty man, he was a friend of the philosopher David Hume, and had a highly developed interest in art and music – as Murdo was doubtless aware:[7]

> I have not whereupon to launch him out into the Study of Physic or any other Business of Consequence. At present he is with his Brother who teaches a Grammar School in Ross; and the Boy is so caress'd for his Music by the Gentry of best Taste there; that his Head is almost set agog with an opinion instill'd by them, that he may by that very Talent make his Fortune, as many allege of the males and Females of this House, as they all have a singular Turn that way. But what can they make of it in this remote Corner? There have been

---

3 John Glen, ed., *The Glen Collection of Scottish Dance Music, Strathspeys, Reels, and Jigs, Selected from the Earliest Printed Sources or from the Composer's Works* (Edinr., 1891), 'Introduction', entry on Patrick MacDonald, pp.xi-xii.

4 *Ibid.*

5 Roderick D. Cannon, ed., *Joseph MacDonald's Compleat Theory of the Scots Highland Bagpipe* (Glasg., 1994), p. 1.

6 *Fasti*, iii, 348.

7 William Anderson, *The Scottish Nation; or the Surnames, Families, Literature, Honours, and Biographical History of the People of Scotland* (3 vols., Edinr., 1866), i, p.651. See also Ernest Campbell Mossner, *The Life of David Hume* (Edinr., 1954), pp.203, 391.

some here of late from the South of Scotland and from England who alledg'd
that not only the Boys but the Girls also would make Room for themselves in
the Beau Monde, if they were introduc'd to it by Friends of Discretion and
Influence. The younger Boy's Admirers are fond to have him made acquaint
with Geddes the Chief musician, perhaps, of our nation, whom I'm told, is
generously ready to take notice of such a young Creature. Dr. Clephane . . .
could give the most effectual Recommendation to this Purpose . . . by
mentioning his old acquaintance to the good Family, the best Introduction I or
mine could have to their Favour of which I must be ambitious, without
Flattery . . .[8]

'Geddes' was Hugh Rose of Geddes, near Nairn, an accomplished amateur
musician and sheriff-depute of Ross and Cromarty, and, as such, a force to be
reckoned with in the North. He was John Clephane's brother-in-law, having
married the latter's sister Elizabeth.[9] In the shadowy world of political management which lay behind nearly every event of consequence in eighteenth-century
Scotland, this apparently slight fact might have important implications. His
home, Kilravock (pron: 'Kilrake'), was an imposing old country house standing
amongst beautiful policies on the banks of the river Nairn, some seven miles
south-west of the county town. It was a hospitable place, Kilravock, usually
crowded with company; it had been visited by Queen Mary in 1572, and Robert
Burns was to be a guest in September 1787. On one famous musical evening
there, Hugh Rose had entertained Charles Edward Stuart, the Young Chevalier,
just two days before the battle of Culloden.[10]

   Of course, a career as a professional musician would have been the last thing
Murdo had in mind for his son. The cult of the gentleman amateur prevailed in
Scotland at this time, as witnessed by the musical careers of people like Sir John
Clerk of Penicuik, a pupil of Corelli and an accomplished violinist and composer;[11] the Earl of Kelly, a still more talented composer and violinist, who studied
with Stamitz at Mannheim, and was director of the Edinburgh Musical Society;[12]
or the Earl of Eglinton, who published his collection of original strathspeys and

   8 Cannon, *Compleat Theory.*, pp.109–110. In eighteenth-century Scotland one did not
     call on people unknown to one personally without a letter of recommendation from
     an acceptable mutual acquaintance, especially if there was disparity in social rank.
   9 It was a love-match – she was virtually penniless, and had been living at Dunrobin as
     companion to the Countess of Sutherland, who may represent another link with the
     MacDonalds of Durness. See Hew Rose, and Lachlan Shaw, *A Genealogical Deduction
     of the Family of Rose of Kilravock*, Cosmo Innes, ed. (Edinr., 1848), pp.405–457. See
     also, *Scottish Nation*, iii, 362.
  10 David Johnson, *Music and Society in Lowland Scotland in the Eighteenth Century*
     (Lond., 1972), p.28.
  11 Purser, *Scotland's Music*, pp.164–172.
  12 Purser, pp.189–194; see also Johnson, *Music and Society*, pp. 68–84.
  13 Henry George Farmer, *A History of Music in Scotland* (Lond., 1947), p.339.

reels anonymously, as simply 'by a gentleman'.[13] In business and professional circles much the same was true, as we can see in figures like Baillie William Forbes of Rubislaw, Aberdeen, the grandfather of Anna Gordon of ballad fame, a performer and composer who, just like Joseph, was equally at home in classical music and in the Scots instrumental tradition, but whose status came from civic office and the possession of landed property.[14] Of course there were drawbacks to this kind of approach as John Purser notes, surveying eighteenth century Scotland's achievement in 'serious' music: 'Why this lack of major works from a country capable of producing so many great writers and thinkers such as Thomson, Smollett, Ramsay and Hume, and great painters such as Ramsay the younger and Raeburn? The answer is simple enough. To be a painter or a writer was respectable. To be a musician was to be a servant'.[15]

Music was part of his father's larger strategy to enlist the support of powerful people to place Joseph MacDonald in a station of life appropriate to his birth and education. It is not known what the Roses did for him, perhaps a further set of recommendations to still more well-connected people, perhaps something more direct and substantial. It is certain that they were powerful. The family exercised political control of the burghs of Fortrose and Nairn and could also deliver a significant portion of the electorate of Inverness. What made the Kilravock connection so formidable was not only its ability to manipulate feudal super-iorities, which under the old Scots electoral system permitted the manufacture of 'faggot' or fictitious votes, but the family's tenure through several generations of hereditary and other sheriffships. This effectively gave them control of the electoral process in their area of jurisdiction, since only the sheriff could say ultimately who could vote and who could not. To manage such a political machine required a judicious distribution of jobs and favours and Hugh Rose was one of the leading figures in the government interest in the North through which East India patronage was channelled.[16] The reasons for Joseph's later appoint-ment to the Company may well be traced to Kilravock.

At about the age of fifteen, he was sent to study at the grammar school of Haddington, where the master, David Young, was another friend of the Rev. Murdo's, probably also from St. Andrews days. Schools of national reputation capable of attracting pupils from all over Scotland already existed in the eighteenth century and Haddington may have represented the best preparation for eventual entry to Edinburgh University.[17] The town and county of Had-dington (now East Lothian) were politically 'managed' by the powerful

---

14 David Johnson, 'Musical Traditions in the Forbes Family of Disblair, Aberdeenshire', in *Scottish Studies*, vol.22, 1978, pp.91–93.

15 Purser, p.194.

16 G[eorge]. K[irk]. McGilvary, 'East India Patronage and the Political Management of Scotland 1720–1774', PhD thesis, Open University, 1989, pp.64–5; for further details about how the system worked in ways that might have affected Joseph, see pp. 12, 15, 20–21, 34, 74, 80, 162, 173–4, 187–8, 202, 413–4.

17 I am indebted for this point to Donald J. Withrington.

Dalrymple family, who were connected by marriage with the MacKays of Reay in whose confidence Murdo MacDonald evidently stood high, as he boarded and tutored the laird's lively and musical younger son, Hugh (later 6th Lord Reay), a near-contemporary of Joseph.[18]

The Lothians were home to Scotland's legal and administrative élite, dotted with the pleasant seats of powerful people willing to be impressed by a personable young man and possessed of the means to do something for him, especially if he had his still more attractive sister, Flora, with him, as he seems to have done. We know that she was living in the Edinburgh area at this time, and made a considerable impression. Indeed, her father thought that it was Flora's winning ways with the Argyllshire gentry that got her brother Patrick the kirk of Kilmore, then one of the best livings in Scotland.[19]

Joseph seems to have moved comfortably in Edinburgh society, studying painting, and keeping himself abreast of the latest developments in classical music as a pupil and friend of the violinist and composer Nicolo Pasquali, the resident Italian maestro, and other leading musicians of the city.[20] He would have encountered a typically easygoing mixture of the classical and vernacular traditions. In the Musical Societies of Edinburgh and Aberdeen at this time, Scots songs and tunes were regularly included in the programme alongside items from the classical repertoire, so that his interest in the instrumental music of the Highlands is unlikely to have been dampened by his stay in the south.[21] The great movement to collect and publish traditional Scots songs and tunes, which was to culminate in Robert Burns and James Johnson's *Scots Musical Museum* (Edinr., 1787–1803), was already gathering momentum. The final volume of William McGibbon's *Collection of Scots Tunes* (Edinr., 1742, 1746, 1755) appeared while Joseph was in the south, and he may actually have heard MacGibbon play. Collections like Robert Bremner's *Scots Reels or Country Dances* (Edinr. c. 1757), Neil Stewart's *Collection of the best Reels or Country Dances* (Edinr., 1761–4), and David Herd's *Ancient and Modern Scots Songs* (Edinr., 1769) would also have been in active preparation and no doubt the subject of interested discussion in musical circles in the city.[22] These may have fired Joseph's ambitions to do something similar for the Highlands because as soon as he returned from Edinburgh, in about 1758, he threw himself into collecting the song tunes and instrumental airs of his native North-West.

His brother Patrick stated that:

18 Angus Mackay, M.A., *The Book of Mackay* (Privately Printed, Edinr., 1906), p.216.
19 *Fasti*, i, 128.
20 Patrick MacDonald, *A Collection of Highland Vocal Airs, never hitherto published. To which are added a few of the most lively country dances or reels, of the North Highlands, & Western Isles: and some specimens of bagpipe music* (Edinr., n.d., but 1784), 'Preface', p. 1; for further information on Pasquali, see Johnson, *Music and Society*, pp.54–5.
21 Thomas Crawford, 'Lowland Song and Popular Tradition in the Eighteenth Century', in Andrew Hook, ed., *History of Scottish Literature*, pp.123–139, (131).
22 Collinson, *Traditional and National Music*, pp. 206–7; see also Farmer, pp.293, 332.

Although few men felt the charms of the Italian music more sensibly than he did, [four volumes of Corelli were found amongst his effects after he died][23] and although he frequently practised it, his passion for that of his native mountains never abandoned him . . . Upon his return to Strathnaver, he had abundant opportunities of indulging that passion. He then applied himself seriously to make a collection of that music, and to write down the pieces that he knew, or had occasion to hear; and which probably had never before appeared in musical characters. During upwards of two years, which he spent in that country [i.e. *c.* 1758–60], he continued to enlarge his collection, by the addition of such pieces as he heard in different parts of it. He also wrote out some of the best poems that were sung to them, and made a collection of the different kinds of bagpipe-music. From these engaging objects, his attention was for some time diverted, by a proposal that was made him of going to the East Indies, of which he accepted. Before his departure to that country, which was in the year 1760, he wrote out a copy of a number of the vocal airs, which he had collected, and left it with a sister, as a token of affection. All his other collections and papers, relating to Highland music and poetry, he carried along with him[24]

A job with the East India Company was a tremendous stroke for the manse of Durness and the political skills of Murdo MacDonald. The Company offered some of the most sought-after careers in eighteenth-century Britain and the head office at East India House in London was showered with applications on behalf of the younger sons of the English aristocracy. Many of the directors and administrative personnel were Scots, however, and the extensive use of East India patronage in the political management of Scotland meant that candidates from the North might be very advantageously placed.[25]

The Company was well into the second century of its existence and its operations stretched far – into the Indian hinterland, and China, and down into Java and the spice islands of the south-west Pacific rim. It was a fabulously wealthy and powerful organisation, regularly lending money to the British government and in good years paying a dividend of 50%, but it had a relatively compact adminis-tration. In Joseph's time, the business wing in Calcutta probably numbered no more than about fifty or sixty people, plus about five hundred soldiers, although this was changing rapidly as long-established rivalries with the Dutch and French East India Companies broke into actual warfare. The Nawab of Bengal, Suraj ud-Daulah, captured the British settlement at Calcutta on 20 June 1756, leading to the famous Black Hole incident. Robert Clive retook the city in January 1757, and his subsequent defeat of the Nawab at Plassey left the Company as the effective ruler of

23 Cannon, *Compleat Theory*, p.110, *n*, 28.
24 MacDonald, *Highland Vocal Airs*, 'Preface', p.1.
25 P. J. Marshall, *East India Fortunes – The British in Bengal in the Eighteenth Century* (Oxford, 1976), p.12–13.

Bengal. Meanwhile the French and their allies laid siege to Madras. Scots were in the thick of the fighting on both sides, because of the many Jacobite exiles serving with the Dutch and French East India Companies.[26] Hostilities were still going on while Joseph was en route for the Bay, and he must have arrived some time before the final surrender of the French at Pondicherry in 1761.[27]

Although the direct emoluments of the job were relatively modest, the potential for serious wealth came in the Company's expectation that its employees would indulge in private trade. Spectacular success lay within the reach of people from quite modest backgrounds as can be seen in the career of Sir John Macpherson, who succeeded Warren Hastings as Governor-General of India in 1784 and ended up with a baronetcy and a seat in Parliament. He came from the same kind of background as Joseph, a son of the manse from a Highland parish, his father being the noted Celtic scholar Dr. John Macpherson, minister of Sleat.[28] Not everybody could be a Clive, to be sure, but £10,000 or so was a not uncommon outcome of a moderately successful East Indies career.[29] A tidy sum in Durness.

And the tendrils of this sprawling empire reached practically to the manse door. Early in 1757, the Rev. Murdo was reading to a gentleman in the neighbourhood, Donald MacKay of Claiseneach, whose son, Captain George MacKay, had Company connections. They were interrupted by a letter from Hugh MacKay of Bighouse, Lord Reay's brother (and effective head of the MacKay name), soliciting the Captain's support in a matter of local patronage. Murdo noted:

> This incident made me suggest to the parents that, considering their son's ability and benevolent disposition, I greatly wondered how he never called for any of his young countrymen, to whom as I understood by the hint above that he might easily lend a (?hand) by lift, and mentioned my Joseph as a proper person to be offered him as a young adventurer.[30]

He followed this up with a personal letter to George MacKay, who indicated that a place would be found for Joseph in the Company's service and undertook to defray the young man's travelling expenses. This was not a small favour. Candidates required to be nominated by one of the Company's directors, and then find securities for substantial sums of money, perhaps as much as £500 sterling. It cost £40 – the equivalent of almost a year's stipend for Murdo – simply to outfit Joseph for the passage to India.

And of course there were dangers. Mortality amongst Europeans in India was high – about one in three in the civilian wing, and nearly one in two among the

26 McGilvray, pp.20–21
27 See Philip Lawson, *The East India Company: A History* (Lond., 1993), esp. pp. 66–7, 71–5, 89–91.
28 *Scottish Nation*, iii, 63.
29 For the range of potential earnings, see Marshall, pp.214–9.
30 Quoted in Grimble, pp.157–8.

military.[31] But life was an uncertain business in eighteenth century Scotland as well and the Rev. Murdo pushed his anxieties about Joseph's delicate constitution to the back of his mind. Thus one of the brightest young talents in Scotland was dispatched into the middle of an imperial war in a pestilent climate carrying with him a unique, irreplaceable collection of Highland instrumental music.

During the voyage, and at moments of leisure thereafter, Joseph 'arranged and digested' his materials with a view to publication, and compiled an instructional manual entitled *A Compleat Theory of the Scots Highland Bagpipe* which as well as being the earliest is one of the most intelligent and wide-ranging introductions to the music of the pipe ever written. He meant to achieve distinction, not years hence loaded with nabob gold, but in a very much shorter period of time thanks to a major publication on Highland music which he intended to dedicate to his brilliant young contemporary, Sir James MacDonald of Sleat.[32] Macpherson's *Fragments* were now upon the stage, *Ossian* was in gestation, and Edinburgh abuzz with Highland antiquities. The East India appointment presented an irresistible opportunity to raise his family to opulence and consequence; but it removed him abruptly from his community and forced him to work on the scores and the supporting apparatus half a world away from his traditional sources. 'O!' he declared,

> that I had been at more pains, to gather those admirable remains of our ancient Highland music, before I left my native country. It would have augmented my collection of Highland music and poetry, which I have formed a system of [i.e. an editorial scheme with a view to publication] in my voyage to India, and propose to send soon home, dedicated to Sir James McDonald, or some such chieftain of rank and figure in the Highlands, in order that those sweet, noble, and expressive sentiments of nature, may not be allowed to sink and die away: and to shew, that our poor remote corner, even without the advantages of learning and cultivation, abounded in works of taste and genius . . . If Sir James McDonald is not prejudiced, and rendered cold to the Highlands, by his corrupt English education, I hope he will duly prize it. If he is, there is no help for it. I shall next think of addressing it to Mr. McDonald of Glengary, Sir Alexander McKenzie of Coull, or to a society of our Highland gentlemen of best figure and taste, to preserve as a monument of antiquity, or publish, as

31 Holden Furber, *John Company at Work: A Study of European Expansion in India in the Late Eighteenth Century* (New York, 1970; first published Cambridge Mass., 1948), p.27.

32 He was a couple of years younger than Joseph, and was never to see his compatriot's work: he had recently finished his schooling at Eton (which Joseph regarded with deep disapproval) and was currently on the Grand Tour. He died in Rome on 26 July 1766, aged 25. He was the subject of a piobaireachd, 'Sir James MacDonald of the Isles's Salute', composed by Ewen MacDonald of Vallay following a hunting accident in the Uists in 1764 in which he was shot in the leg by MacLeod of Talisker: see Alexander Mackenzie, *History of the MacDonalds and Lords of the Isles* (Inverness, 1881), pp.239–43.

they see proper. But if our Highland gentry degenerate, who knows, but a spirit
for encouraging such a work may arise in the low country? If it meets with no
other encouragement, it will be a first rate entertainment to myself . . . My
good friend Mr. M. [acKay?] at London, has been so kind as to send me a fine
Highland bagpipe, and a suit of Highland cloaths . . . with which I expect yet
to make a conquest of an Indian princess.[33]

But none of this was to be. Joseph MacDonald died in Calcutta in May 1763 'of a
malignant fever' at the age of twenty four.[34]

That there was, once, an actual collection for the *Compleat Theory* to prefix, is
shown by the inventory of Joseph's effects compiled after his death, which lists
three manuscript volumes of 'Highland Musick' bought by a James Ashburner
and now lost.[35] The manuscript of the *Theory* was acquired by General Sir John
MacGregor Murray, chief of Clan MacGregor and Auditor General of Bengal,
who arranged for its return to Scotland. It was eventually published in 1803 by
Patrick MacDonald, the compiler's brother.[36]

The manuscript of the *Compleat Theory* contains 56 pages of detailed
descriptive and analytical prose, accompanied by finger-charts and music
examples in staff notation. The title page is laid out in accordance with the
conventions for printed books of the period, and gives a full indication of the
document's contents and general purpose:

> A Compleat Theory. of the *Scots* Highland Bagpipe. *Containing* All the Shakes,
> Introductions, Graces, & Cuttings *which are peculiar to this Instrument. Reduc'd to
> Order & Method: fully explain'd & noted at Large in 58 Tables & Examples. With
> all the* Terms of Art *in which this Instrument was originally taught by its first
> Masters & Composers in the Islands of* Sky & Mull. *also a full account of the Time,
> Style, Taste, & Composition of true Pipe Musick with Examples of each in the genuine
> & native Style of this Instrument, & an Account of the Rules & method by which the
> Pipe Composition & Time were regulated. To which is added Directions & Examples
> for the proper Execution and Cutting of the Pipe reells Composed by the Same Masters
> in the Isles & Highlands & the First Præludes they Taught, with an Example of a
> March Reel & Jig with their Introductions Cuttings, drawn out at Length, & a
> Description of the Original Intent of Pipe Musick & a Short account of the Nature
> and Compass of the Bellow's Pipes The Whole Carefully collected & preservd in its
> Antient Style & Form without Alteration or Amendment by J. Macdonald*

The conventionality of the literary style – Joseph's courtly Scots English is audibly
a second language and at least a generation out of date – should not dull our
appreciation of just how innovative and difficult was the task which he had set

33 MacDonald, *Highland Vocal Airs*, 'Preface', pp. 1–2.
34 *Ibid.*, p.2; see also Cannon, *Compleat Theory*, p.110, *n.* 25.
35 Cannon, *Compleat Theory*, p.110, *n*, 28.
36 (Edinr., 1803).

himself. Nobody had done anything like this before. He had to take a fluid, oral art form, isolate its underlying structural principles and then demonstrate these to a largely new audience unfamiliar in any detail with the instrument or its music. In addition, he had to find some means of representing that music adequately in staff notation, a process which, likewise, does not seem to have been attempted before and had therefore to be developed from scratch. So the *Compleat Theory* had to perform a number of difficult tasks rather well if it was going to succeed.

The text comprised a series of systematic examples in staff notation showing the basis of piobaireachd technique and illustrating the music's characteristic tonality and expressive vocabulary, accompanied by a detailed verbal commentary. Following the plain scale, there was an example to show 'A Disposition of the Notes in the Taste of this Musick'. Joseph explained: 'By this the Scale is Exercisd, & a nice Ear may easily distinguish the peculiarity of the Style already appearing in this order of the Notes, as Shall be Soon more plain':

He continued:

> The blowing of them [the pipes] must be Strong, Steady & Equal (which at first is a little hard upon evry beginner) as it exercises their breasts & Lungs a Little; but Practise will give them additional Strength of breath & make this familiar & Easy. The Movement of each Finger must be as high as Possible, that they may return with greater Force, For true Pipe Musick, depending Chiefly on the Disposition & Execution of the Fingers, must be so performd, with all the Strength as well as agility of the Fingers, to make it well playd.[37]

An account of the echo beats followed, with one line indicating the melody notes, accented to show the pulse, and a second adding the gracenotes required to execute the movement with an accompanying explanation of how these should be timed:

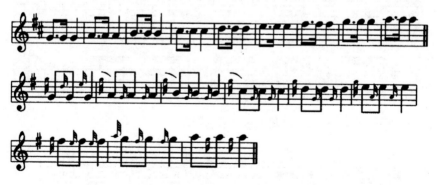

37 Cannon, *Compleat Theory*, p.26.

He then showed how grace notes and melody notes were combined to produce the conventional variations, or 'runnings' as he called them, starting with the *Ludh Sleamhuin* (pron: 'loo slɛvinn' and implying a smooth or sliding movement), which normally occurs immediately after the ground of the tune, remarking: 'This Specimen is enough for evry running of the Kind which will be frequently mett with':

Everything was subsumed under these two basic concepts, the 'cutting' – or gracenote type – and the 'running' – or variation type – the intention being to give a precise but economical impression of the music and how it was produced.

There followed a systematic account of the main types of variation, with remarks on execution, and examples designed to introduce the learner to basic melodic structures. To the modern reader Joseph's notation may well appear antique, with his placement of note stems according to their position on the stave – a practice later abandoned in pipe music – and his technical terms in north-country Gaelic phonetically spelt, but apart from this there is little (with the exception of a handful of murderous-looking later cuttings which even then were apparently seldom played) that would be wholly unfamiliar to a modern piper. Here, for example, is his '11th Cutting' or 'Tuludh', which is much as it would be today, with the exception that it is based on a G/D/A configuration of gracenotes rather than the G/D/G nowadays favoured, giving Joseph's movement a characteristic light and airy feel:

In modern notation, it would look like this:

A fundamental point of Joseph's exposition was that the various cuttings were built out of smaller standard components in a beautifully regular, logical and systematic fashion, such that the light music and piobaireachd formed part of a single progressively more complex system of ornamentation. He showed how closely related the taorluath and crunluath cuttings were, for example, being constructed by simple addition or subtraction of shorter conventional units. The crunluath, 'calld in its Proper Language Creanludh:

is no more than a distinct dividing of the three Notes. This joind with Tuludh . . .

makes up the following running calld Creanludh & Tuludh

as youll See at Large in the Table below'.[38]

The process can be seen more clearly if we examine how one of the longer, more complex – and now obsolete – movements such as the '16th Cutting' –

38 Cannon, *Compleat Theory*, p.48.

– is typically built of overlapping and interlocking units, as follows:

The elegance and precision of such structures is one of his recurring themes.

Joseph MacDonald is the only one of the early commentators to give in any way precise directions about tempo, and his remarks in his section on 'Time' are of great interest.[39] He drew attention to the differences in pace implied by different time signatures, and tried to 'place' the tempi commonly used in piobaireachd relative to familiar types of classical music. Developments in notational practice in the period immediately preceding his own had led to a breakdown in precise directions about the speed at which a piece of music should be played. In the old days, time-signatures such as **C**, **¢** and **$** had indicated fairly exactly the relative proportion of note values, and hence timings, in relation to a more or less agreed standard. But by the early eighteenth century the traditional signatures had come, in general British practice, to indicate simply three broad bands of time: slow, **C**; faster, **¢**; and faster still **$**. Thus Alexander Malcolm in *A Treatise of Musick*, published in Edinburgh in 1721:

> Common Time is of two Species, the *1st* where every *Measure* is equal to a Semibreve . . . the *2d,* where every Measure is equal to a Minim . . . The *Movements* of this Kind of *Measure* are very various; but there are Three common Distinctions, the first is *slow,* signified at the Beginning by this Mark **C**, the *2d* is *brisk,* signified by this **¢**, the *3d* is very *quick,* signified by this **$**; but what that *slow, brisk,* and *quick* is, is very uncertain, and . . . must be learned by Practice.[40]

Various additional terms were therefore used, such as *adagio, allegro,* and *allegretto,* which, although strictly referring simply to the mood of the music, had come by the mid-eighteenth century to possess distinct implications for tempo as well, and these provided a degree of further definition. Malcolm listed them in ascending order:

> *Grave, adagio, largo, vivace, allegro, presto,* and sometimes *prestissimo.* The first

39 *Ibid.,* pp.61–65.

40 Quoted in Robert Donington, *The Interpretation of Early Music* (Lond., new revised edn., 1989, first publ. 1963), p.413; see pp. 410–11 for further British examples.

expresses the slowest Movement, and the rest gradually quicker; but indeed they leave it altogether to Practice to determine the precise Quantity.[41]

There was widespread dissatisfaction with this state of affairs, and although some generations were to pass before the metronome appeared, there were various attempts to establish a reliable objective standard for regulating musical time, sometimes involving clocks or, in the case of Johann Joachim Quantz – a leading theorist of the mid-eighteenth century, teacher of Frederick the Great and a flautist of international reputation – by the rate of the human pulse. Taking eighty beats per minute as standard (and giving directions for adjusting calculations according to individual differences in this particular), Quantz divided each of the two main branches of duple time – namely Common Time **c** and Alla Breve **¢** – into four broad bands of tempo. In his influential *Essai d'une Méthode pour apprendre à jouer de la Flûte Traversière* (Berlin, 1752) he stated:

> how each of the types of metre cited can be put into its proper tempo by using the pulse beat, it must be noted that it is most important to consider both the word indicating the tempo at the beginning of the piece and the fastest notes used in the passage work. Since no more than eight very fast notes can be executed in the time of a pulse beat . . . it follows that there is

> In common time:

> In an Allegro assai, the time of a pulse beat for each minim;
> In an Allegretto, a pulse beat for each crotchet;
> In an Adagio cantabile, a pulse beat for each quaver;
> And in an Adagio assai, two pulse beats for each quaver.

> In alla breve time there is:

> In an Allegro, a pulse beat for each semibreve;
> In an Allegretto, a pulse beat for each minim;
> In an Adagio cantabile, a pulse beat for each crotchet;
> And in an Adagio assai, two pulse beats for each crotchet.

The *Allegro assai* is thus the fastest of these four main categories of tempo. The *Allegretto* is twice as slow. The *Adagio cantabile* is twice as slow as the Allegretto, and the *Adagio assai* twice as slow as the Adagio cantabile. In the Allegro assai the passage-work consists of semiquavers or quaver triplets, and in the Allegretto, of demisemiquavers or semiquaver triplets. Since, however, the passage-work just cited must usually be played at the same speed whether

41 *Ibid.*, p.389.

it is in semiquavers or demisemiquavers, it follows that notes of the same value in the one are twice as fast in the other. In alla breve time . . . which, whether the tempo is slow or fast, is always indicated with a large C with a line through it, the situation is the same, except that all the notes in it are taken twice as fast as in common time.[42]

Some later commentators have regarded this as over-prescriptive, and Quantz himself insisted that musical taste should be paramount, adding: 'No less must good execution be *varied*. Light and shadow must be constantly maintained . . .'[43] However, this is one major strand of the traditions that Joseph was trained in, and since he used its conventions to discuss the music of the pipe, we must consider its basic principles.

Joseph began by pointing out that the relatively limited compass of the Highland pipe did not permit the standard way of 'dividing' a ground, the contemporary system under which melody notes were sustained and elaborated by strings of improvised semi-quaver figures as follows:

He indicated that although, technically speaking, the pipe could sustain a note more or less indefinitely, it did not actually do so in practice. Its limited compass meant that the approach to ornamentation and musical idiom was more laconic than in the most languorous and highly ornamented types of classical music:

> Common & Triple Time (So well known by other Instruments) is here
> diversified, by various Movements of Adagio & Allegro, yet not So numerous
> as in Instruments of Compass, the reason of which is plain. In Common
> Time here, the slowest Movement of Adagio is ¢, this instrument not
> admitting of any slower, For as the Pipe is one Continued, uniform sound a
> semibreve or any Such long Note cannot be swelld, but by an additional
> Strength of Wind, which must occasion a very screaming & rude noise,

42 Johann Joachim Quantz, *On Playing the Flute*, ed. Edward R. Reilly (Lond., 1966): Reilly cites C. P.E. Bach's view that at Berlin 'adagio is far slower and allegro far faster than is customary elsewhere', pp.285–6, and *n*; 284–285.

43 Quantz, p.124. For various caveats about his tempi, see Donington, pp,.391, 408–13.

44 Arnold Dolmetsch, *The Interpretation of the Music of the XVII and XVIII Centuries* (Lond., new edn., 1946), p.327.

besides its being Contrary to the Nature of the Instrument; as when the Pipe
is well blown, it is with the greatest uniformity, & the Reeds have as much
as they are well able to bear. When such a slow Note cannot be swelld
[there is] no other recourse but to the Execution of the Fingers, which by
any shake or Cutting must be awckardly performed; & the small Compass of
a bag Pipe will not admitt of any Flourish of Compass to suply the place of
a Swell. Therefore as all must be diversified by artful & Curious Cuttings,
which constitute the Principall beauty & singularity of true bag Pipe Musick
all long Notes are excluded [such] as Semibreves Breves &c there being no
such notes to be found in Marches which is the slowest species of Pipe
Musick, tho the Pipe is Capable of Sounding as long a Note as an Organ . . .
In Triple time the slowest movement in the Adagio is 3/4 or the Medium of
3/4 & 3/2, as Minuet Time is by far too Quick for the Adagio, & 3/2 Grave
is rather too slow.

As in Common Time there is no movement of Pipe Musick So Slow as
Adagio (c) So in Triple Time there is non so slow as Grave 3/2. [45]

He illustrated these points with a series of graded examples, beginning with 'Pipe
Adagio – Common Time Slowest', quoting the opening bars of the tune
nowadays known as 'The Lament for Castle Dunyveg':

This was followed by a tune in 'Triple Time Slowest':

and then by examples of quicker tempi in duple and triple time:

45 Cannon, *Compleat Theory,* p. 61.

Triple Time Allegro

In the eighteenth century, then, piobaireachd grounds were not all played at the same speed, a stylistic feature uncomfortably apparent in late twentieth-century competitive playing, where timings tended to flatten out into a single tempo, monotonously slow. Joseph's most recent editor, Dr. Roderick Cannon, in an intriguing discussion of tempi, illustrates this point rather tellingly. One of Joseph's examples of 'Triple Time Slowest' is the tune now known as the 'Lament for Duncan MacRae of Kintail'. He set it as follows:

Slow: Siciliana

According to Cannon, the Siciliana '. . . was a slowish, rolling 6/8 or 12/8 rhythm, not unlike the modern 6/8 [bagpipe] slow march', and nowadays 'such movements are often played at a tempo of around 24 6/8 bars to the minute, though some authorities on early music consider that to be too slow'.[47] This would imply a fairly brisk pace, certainly a good deal more lively than the nine bars per minute which Cannon estimates as typical for a modern performance of the tune.

According to Quantz, 'An alla Siciliana in twelve-eight time would be too slow if you were to count a pulse beat for each quaver. But if two pulse beats are divided into three parts, there is a pulse beat on both the first and third quaver'.[48] This would entail the ground of 'Duncan MacRae' being played at about fourteen bars to the minute.

Curt Sachs, the distinguished musicologist and authority on wind instruments, attempted to establish a defining mean tempo for baroque music, a *tempo giusto*, relative to which fast would be fast and slow would be slow. His conclusions were based on contemporary theoretical works and an assumption that our sense of musical time must derive ultimately from physiological rhythms, such as an easy striding walk, or the heartbeat at rest, which would imply a band range of M.M. 60–80. Following detailed examination of eighteenth-century attempts to express time scientifically, he concluded that

46 The extra quaver beat in bar two may be included to indicate more precisely the prolongation of the E.

47 Cannon, *Compleat Theory*, pp.16–17.

48 Quantz, p.287.

the end result would have been noticeably quick and airy to a twentieth-century ear.[49]

Joseph MacDonald acknowledged that piobaireachd had developed independently of the classical tradition, and was essentially an oral form such that 'The first Composers of Pipe Musick having never heard of any other Instrument or known any of the Rules ever invented of Music, except what was suggested to them by Nature & Genius . . . having neither of Common or Triple Time, Crotchet or Quaver but only their Ear to which they must only trust'.[50] Notwithstanding this, it was a highly organised, systematic and rule-bound music, and his constant aim was to demonstrate the elegance and coherence of its underlying structures. He selected for discussion the even four-lined tune, which now makes up about a third of the repertoire, probably because it was closer to the formal expectations of a non-specialist audience than the more common asymmetrical three-lined types discussed elsewhere in this book.[51] He stated:

> it was by the four Fingers of the Left hand that all their Time was measurd & regulated. E.G. An Adagio in Common Time of Such a Style must not exceed or fall short [of] Such a number of Fingers, otherwise it was not regular. If the March was to be but a short Composition, the Ground must be of So many Fingers; for Bars they had no notion of; if a Gathering, commonly of Such a Number; if a Lament, If a March, &c. according to the Occasion it must Consist of Such a Number.
>
> They were sure to have no odd Number in any piece they designd to be regular. Their Adagios when regular, commonly consisted of 4 Quarters. In each Quarter there were Such a number of Fingers (which we Count as Bars) 2, 4, or 8 as the Quarter was Long or short; or as the Bar was Subdivided into more Fingers, according to their Length; & thus they Counted upon their 4 Fingers & measured by their Ear, & when the Finger & Ear Corresponded all was well.
>
> The Ordinar Length of a Pipe Adagio being 16 Fingers, computed about 16 Bars, 4 in each Quarter, The regularity preservd (only by the Help of this Rule) in all their Compositions, being truly Surprising.[52]

He demonstrated the application of these terms in a tune called 'March for a begginner':

49 Curt Sachs, *Rhythm and Tempo: A Study in Music History* (Lond., 1953), pp.202–3, 312–20.
50 Cannon, *Compleat Theory*, p.64.
51 See 'Readers' Guide to Piobaireachd and the Great Highland Pipe', pp.473–4.
52 Cannon, *Compleat Theory*, p.64.

He then offered an illuminating account of tonality:

One woud think the Small Compass of the Bag Pipe woud admitt of no Key but one & that same in a very Confind manner; but in this little Compass they have Contrivd lively Imitations of several Keys, which tho they cannot be calld distinct ones, yet bear a great deal of the Taste; [and] which appear very different the one from the other. As there are no flat Notes in a Pipe so there can be no flat Keys, yet its surprising what a Grave Taste they have contrivd for Laments, which is a quite distinct Taste from the rest, & in several Passages of these, there are to be found some very expressive sentiments of Lamentation or melancholy; & indeed it is hard to say if more cultivated Geniuses could render the Composition of So Small a Compass more expresive. In Keys where one cant have the Liberty of nine Notes, the most fertile Invention & nicest Judgment must be distress'd, & yet the surprising variety & Vicissitude that appears in one Key, by their Disposition of the Notes and art of their Cuttings & Shakes, diversifys the whole & makes it play agreeable to the Ear. The Key for Laments excludes C altogether because it is sharp, & dwells upon the Lower Notes. It takes the Freedom of all the Notes but this. There are other Keys that exclude this Note also . . .[53]

53 Cannon, *Compleat Theory*, p.67. For further information on this point, see Annie G. Gilchrist, 'Note on the Modal System of Gaelic Tunes', prefixed to Frances Tolmie's collection of 'Songs of Occupation from the Western Isles of Scotland', *Journal of the Folk-Song Society*, no.16, vol. IV (London, 1911), pp.150–156. For a thoughtful application of these ideas to piobaireachd tonality, see 'The Bagpipe Scale', from J. P. M.[acLeod of Tain], *OT*, 9/10/1915, p.3, cited in 'Readers' Guide'.

Although he talked of 'Keys', it is clear that Joseph meant what we would now call modes, the 'gapped' scales 'where one cant have the Liberty of nine Notes', claiming that different keys or modes (the terms had not yet quite disentangled themselves in contemporary usage) could be used to express different kinds of emotion. He began with 'A sharp, being also the Key for most of the Martial Marches', quoting the opening bars of the tune nowadays known as 'Donald Gruamach's March':

adding: 'The taste of this Key being

is plainly A Sharp. G being natural makes the style somewhat singular, but not disagreeable . . . There are other Keys for martial Pieces, but this is the most appropriated [i.e. most frequently used] one'.[54]

He then turned to the neighbouring tonal centre, G, and quoted a number of tunes with gapped scales based on low G, low A, B, D and E, which he identified as a 'species of G sharp', quoting as a typical example:

and pointing out that many laments were in this key.

Then followed an example in the mode which 'Inclines by the Taste towards D Sharp', and finally to a tune – -nowadays called 'Lament for Viscount Dundee' – which combined elements of all three, in 'A species of A sharp where C & G are singularly applied':

Rather unusually, the development of this tune was indicated in a selection of later variations:

54 Cannon, *Compleat Theory*, p.68. When Joseph speaks of A sharp and D sharp as keys he uses 'sharp' in the way we would now use 'major'.

Beginning of the first running: 4 fingers; 2 to each Barr

Beginning of the third running [:] 2 fingers eq[ual] to 2 Barrs

Begginning of the 5th & Last Running [:] 4 Fingers, eq[ual] to 4 Barrs

This led into a brief but clear discussion of the 'Method of Composition' showing various ways in which the 'runnings' related to the ùrlar or theme:

> Their Allegro[s] are for the most Part . . . regularly built upon the Ground, to which it Commonly Keeps very Closs, taking in the Heads of the Ground, at Such and such Particular Notes where the Taste of the Adagio Seems to lay: Sometimes at the end of each Second Note, or each Barr, &c according to the Nature & Style of the Ground; & thus by taking in the Heads or Emphatick Notes of the Ground the whole Scope is perceived in the runnings, for Example

Adagio or Ground

First Running

Second Running

In the eighteenth century piobaireachd had not yet assumed the form of a fixed printed text, and did not possess the absolute predictability it was later to acquire. In an oral setting, the well-trained performer had to be able to construct the variations for himself. He had to understand the principles upon which this was done, and be able to make intelligent choices from a fairly wide menu of possibilities. Performance practice in contemporary classical music followed similar lines, at least with regard to ornament, and since piobaireachd variations are basically divisions on a ground (involving the selection of themal notes from the *ùrlar*, between which passages of bridging-work are then constructed of steadily increasing complexity), their construction would have been regarded as lying substantially within the province of the performer even in the written music of the period. The Italian style in which Joseph was trained gave great freedom in this respect.[55] Variations on the theme were positively expected to change between different performances of the same composition, and it is clear from what he says that there was considerable art in this:

> Thus they proceed diversifying the Adagio with all their Various Cuttings, which from [one] to another plays upon the Ear with an agreeable surprise. Then they return & End with the Ground [i.e. they played the adagio again at the end, as is done nowadays.
>
> He continues]: In Marches which Contain a variety of runnings, they return to the Adagio once or twice. It is usual at the running before the Last to return to the Adagio, after which you proceed to the last which is that of greatest Execution.[56]

This rule for repetitions of Ground within the tune, at intervals after variation doublings in tunes of appropriate character, but at all events between the taorluath and crunluath variations, represented standard contemporary practice. Its use was proscribed in the Highland Society of London-sponsored piping competitions during the 1820s as a means of saving time, and by the middle of the following century it was seldom, if ever, to be heard in competitive playing.[57]

Joseph concluded with brief sections on 'Introductions, Graces, Cadencies & Transitions', 'Blowing and Gesture', 'The Cutting of Pipe Reels & Jigs', and a table of 'The original Terms of Art belonging to the Bag Pipe'.

The *Compleat Theory* emphasises the large degree of artistic freedom not only permitted to but positively required of the performer. At several points in the text, the necessity is asserted for performer choice and creative input by the player. Discussing the 'Ludh Sleamhuinn', Joseph declares, 'This Exercise must be all introducd in the manner you See the little Notes Sett down, & the Learner must be always usd with these Introductions untill he can introduce them

55 See 'Of Extempore Variations on Simple Intervals', Quantz, pp.136–161; see also p.113; Dolmetsch, pp. 91, 98, 120–1, 323–39; and Donington, pp. 91, 152–60, 174, 190–1.
56 Cannon, *Compleat Theory*, p.75.
57 See below, p.87.

properly of his own accord, if he has any Taste or Genius, without which no kind of Musick can be well taught him'.[58] In the section 'Introductions, Graces, Cadencies & Transitions', it was stated that 'whenever the Learner arrivd at a Perfect degree of Proficience he was Judge where to dispose these Cuttings properly'.[59] The available cuttings and their manner of execution was predetermined, so that it was *table d' hôte* rather than *carte blanche*, but what to use, and where to put it, was largely up to the player. He was also encouraged to vary the melody line where appropriate in repeats and doublings. The 'Exercise of Lu Sleamhuin . . . Variation or Improvement on the 2nd.' gave an explicit example of this, Joseph remarking: 'Here follows a specimen . . . which is no more than a Doubling of this, or rather a little Variation of it the Second time its playd'. In bars 6, 12, and 15, he departed artfully from the tone row of the singling to vary the beaten track. This was one of the features of piobaireachd playing that was to be seriously undermined by the later introduction of fixed printed scores:

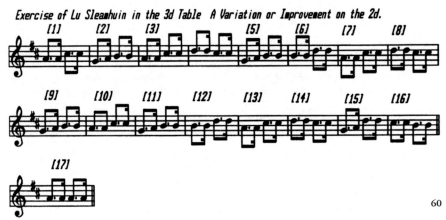

Exercise of Lu Sleamhuin in the 3d Table A Variation or Improvement on the 2d.

60

In Joseph's time, then, 'authority' was located in performance and not in the written score or its institutional sponsors.

Finally, one cannot help being struck by the vocabulary of wonder and delight that Joseph used when contemplating this music and the ingenuity with which it was constructed. He extolled its 'Noble Variety', its 'fertile invention & nicest Judgement . . . sweetness of Taste & richness of Genius . . . Vivacity, glorious Effect, full of Life & Fury'. He spoke about 'nature' and 'genius' but the emphasis was very much upon the 'genius', i.e. upon the sophistication of this music, despite its oral roots. And while he spoke glowingly of its martial capabilities, he stressed that this was only one amongst its several functions, talking of 'the Original Design of the bag Pipe; which was to animate a Sett of Men approaching an Enemy, & to solemnise rural Diversions in Fields, & before

58 Cannon, *Compleat Theory*, p.36.
59 Cannon, *Compleat Theory*, p.78.
60 Cannon, *Compleat Theory*, pp. 36–7.

walking Companys, To play amidst Rocks, Hills, Valleys, & Coves where Ecchoes rebounded . . .'[61] with abundance of compositions in all the different 'Tastes' which amply reflected this variety. Any talk of piobaireachd 'dying away' sprang from fears about its place in the affection of an increasingly alienated Highland gentry rather than from anxiety about its long-term vitality as a form. He spoke from within a living culture, and from an overwhelming sense of its beautiful artifice, organisation and symmetry.

Joseph MacDonald's terms of reference are far removed from the qualities of wildness, rudeness and incipient disintegration which so rapidly came to be accepted as the touchstones of Highland culture in the Lowlands and the South. Indeed it is difficult to imagine an art-form which less met the requirements of the Macpherson paradigm than ceòl mór as described by Joseph MacDonald. But this was precisely the cultural matrix to which the music was expected to comply during the following two centuries.

Joseph MacDonald, his brother Patrick and sister Flora, were amongst the leading tradition-bearers in Highland music during the second half of the eighteenth century. They were of the same generation as James Macpherson and from a similar educational and social background. Yet their lives and work do not at all confirm his picture of cultural production in a Highland context. Although they grew up in the far North-West, in one of the most geographically isolated communities in mainland Britain, they were in contact with the latest thinking in their field. Multi-cultured and multi-lingual, with a wide range of personal and institutional ties on both sides of the Highland Line, they were busily engaged in what they clearly believed to be a vigorously ongoing cultural enterprise.

Macpherson published in 1760 and met with great and immediate success, but it was to be many years before the *Compleat Theory* entered the public domain, and then in a mutilated and defective form. And to understand how this came about, we must now turn to Joseph's brother Patrick MacDonald, the minister of Kilmore.

---

61 Cannon, *Compleat Theory*, pp.64–5.

3

'This warlike and national music':
Patrick MacDonald and the Highland Vocal Airs

So far, we have considered the work of a literary entrepreneur dealing with the epic poetry of the Highlands and a musicologist dealing with the repertoire of the pipe. The work of Joseph MacDonald's elder brother, Patrick, shows how these fields combined, and how perspectives derived from Ossian began to affect the interpretation of pipe music.

Patrick MacDonald was born in the manse of Durness on 22nd April 1729. Like Joseph he had an exceptional musical gift, and like him studied the violin under Kenneth Sutherland of Keoldale. As a child he stayed for some years with his grandfather, Patrick Coupar, the minister of Pittenweem, after whom he was named, and returned to Sutherland to be prepared by his father for the university, entering upon his studies at Aberdeen in 1747. He was licensed as a preacher and, after a spell in teaching, was presented to the Argyllshire parish of Kilmore, amongst the pleasant glens of Lorn. The writer Ann Grant heard him preach in the spring of 1773 and wrote:

> This was an odd old church, almost ruinous. – But when the preacher came in, he roused all my attention – I never beheld a countenance so keenly expressive, nor such dark piercing eyes: he is very like his sister F.[lora] M.[acDonald], and resembles her in a superior musical genius, being a distinguished composer, as well as performer, on the violin.[1]

Although his position as a minister in the Church of Scotland restricted him as a performing musician, Patrick MacDonald enjoyed a considerable reputation as a player throughout his long life, and was able on one occasion when in Edinburgh for the General Assembly (and somewhat to the scandal of his clerical brethren) to stand in at a concert for the maestro Stabilini, when the latter was indisposed.[2]

Patrick was well qualified, therefore, to be his brother's executor, and was involved in two publications designed to bring Joseph's work before a wider public. The first was A Collection of Highland Vocal Airs, Never hitherto published. To which are added a few of the most lively Country Dances or Reels of the North

---

1 Grant, Letters from the Mountains, i, 56–7.
2 Patrick MacDonald died at Kilmore on 25 September 1824 at the age of 95. For a brief account of his life and works, with a portrait, see K. N. MacDonald, 'Rev. Patrick MacDonald of Kilmore. The First Collector of Gaelic Music', in Celtic Monthly, vol. 6, 1898, pp.135–6; see also John Glen, Glen Collection, i, pp.xi-xii.

Highlands, Western Isles; and some Specimens of Bagpipe Music, published in Edinburgh in 1784; the second, a version of the *Compleat Theory* (Edinr., 1803), the manuscript of which had returned to Patrick by devious routes from Bengal. Together they represent the first serious attempt, using the medium of print, to make Highland music more widely known throughout Scotland as a whole.

At the heart of *Vocal Airs* lay the collection of song and dance tunes which Joseph had compiled in the MacKay country in the later 1750s. The original manuscript went to India with him and is presumed lost; but he had made a copy as a keepsake for one of his sisters, probably Flora, and this remained in Scotland. Eighty-six items from it were included in *Highland Vocal Airs,* along with thirty-two piping jigs and reels. There were additional sections of tunes from Perthshire, Argyllshire and the Isles, collected by Patrick himself.

In the eighteenth century, book production was often a collective enterprise. The author would issue a printed prospectus, and order-forms for the proposed work would circulate amongst the booksellers until enough subscriptions came in to – at the very least – guarantee the printer against loss.[3] Potential purchasers could enter into dialogue with the author at this stage and might exercise so much influence upon the finished work that some books were effectively commissioned by their readers. The patronage of important people was as natural a step in publishing as it was in politics and the pursuit of professional careers. It was considered highly desirable to have a big name at the head of the subscription list as an encouragement to the others, hence Joseph's anxiety to have his work taken up by Sir James MacDonald or some of the greater Highland gentry. If the dedicatee took an active interest, he could do much to boost the subscription list and hence a book's chance of making a decent financial return. We can see this process in some detail in the arrangements of Robert Burns, the Earl of Glencairn, and the publisher William Creech to bring out the poet's Edinburgh edition of 1787.[4]

Since it was usual to publish the list of subscribers, we can tell how many copies were printed. At more than 1100, *Highland Vocal Airs* comfortably outsold the first volume of Niel Gow's *Collection of Strathspey Reels,* published the same year in Edinburgh, which has been described as setting 'an out-and-out record for any Scottish music book up to that time'.[5] We can also see what kind of people actually bought it. At 7/6, *Vocal Airs* was quite modestly priced, and the subscription list shows a wide social spread, ranging from the Duchess of Argyll

3 For production costs in publications of this type, see Roderick D. Cannon, *A Bibliography of Bagpipe Music* (Edinr., 1980), pp.61–2, *n* 53.

4 For a brief account of publication by subscription, see D. C. Greetham, *Textual Scholarship: An Introduction* (New York, 1994, first published 1992), pp. 111, 136. On the contemporary blending of politics, patronage and publication, see William Donaldson, 'The Glencairn Connection: Robert Burns and Scottish Politics, 1786–1796', *Studies in Scottish Literature,* XVI, 1981, pp. 61–79.

5 David Johnson, *Scottish Fiddle Music in the Eighteenth Century* (2nd edn., Edinr., 1997), p.220.

(3 copies) to an iron-monger in Oban (1), the bulk being solidly professional – soldiers, and shipmasters, lawyers and surgeons, schoolteachers, merchants and ministers, a visiting French *savant* called Barthélemy Faujas de Saint Fond,[6] and a substantial number of gentlefolk with addresses in Chichester and Bath. The Highland Society of London (to which the first edition was dedicated) was by far the largest subscriber, taking 60 copies, whilst its Secretary, John MacKenzie, took a further 20 in his own name. *Highland Vocal Airs* rapidly established itself as one of the musical landmarks of late eighteenth and early nineteenth-century Scotland, and a further five editions were published during Patrick's lifetime.[7]

The music text was engraved by James Johnson, Burns's collaborator on the *Scots Musical Museum*, who did most of such work in Edinburgh at this time, and there were two substantial introductory articles. Neither was signed. The first of these, the 'Preface', was almost certainly by Patrick and it expertly set forth the work's methodological principles and general scope. Although it was easily the best theoretical statement about traditional music of its period, it had little subsequent influence. The second article, an essay 'Of the Influence of Poetry and Music upon the Highlanders', was a very different piece of work. Pretentious, ill-informed and taking the fashionably gloomy view of Highland culture, it was to loom large in the later literature on the assumption that it, too, was by Patrick MacDonald and carried the stamp of his authority.[8]

But it was not by Patrick. The diarist John Ramsay of Ochtertyre later stated that it was he who had written the 'Essay', and since the two large volumes entitled *Scotland and Scotsmen during the Eighteenth Century* which were posthumously edited from his papers contain a section which closely resembles the text, it seems likely that this was true.[9] Ramsay went on to add that *Vocal Airs* had been seen through the press by the Rev. Walter Young of Haddington, and that Young had written the 'Preface'. Since the contents of the 'Preface' could only have come from an experienced and subtle Highland musician – which Young was not – it seems probable that the latter may have been responsible, at most, for imparting a final gloss to Patrick's prose.[10] Walter Young was a son of

---

6 Archibald Geikie, ed., *A Journey through England and Scotland to the Hebrides in 1784* by B. Faujas de Saint Fond (2 vols., Glasg, 1907), ii, 66, *n*.

7 Cannon, *Bibliography*, pp.110–114.

8 See, for example, John Graham Dalyell, *Musical Memoirs of Scotland* (Edinr., 1849), pp.13, 20, 25, 94, *n*; Lucy Broadwood, 'Introduction' to Tolmie, p. xiii; and Archibald Campbell, 'The Highland Bagpipe, *PT*, vol.14, no.10, July 1962, pp.6–10, (8–10).

9 Born Edinburgh 1736; succeeded to the estate of Ochtertyre near Stirling in 1760; educated at Dalkeith Grammar School and Edinburgh University; later used as a model for Jonathan Oldbuck by Sir Walter Scott in his novel *The Antiquary*. See Alexander Allardyce, ed., *Scotland and Scotsmen in the Eighteenth Century from the MSS. of John Ramsay, Esq. of Ochtertyre* (2 vols., Edinr., 1888), ii, 409–414, and ii, pp.390–1. See also Barbara L. H. Horn, ed., *Letters of John Ramsay of Ochtertyre 1799–1812* (Edinr., 1966), pp. xi–xxviii.

10 *Fasti*, ii, pp.246–7. The obvious person to see the work through the press, if he had

David Young, rector of the grammar school of Haddington, and a near-contemporary of Joseph. He had a considerable reputation 'as the most splendid private [i.e. amateur] musician of his day; he performed with equal grace and effect on the piano, the violin, and the flute'. He was an accomplished arranger of psalm tunes and author of a scholarly treatise on metre.[11]

But Ramsay knew little more than his well-stocked classical library could tell him, and his attitude towards Highland life and culture owed more to *Ossian* than to personal experience. Nevertheless his work helped to initiate a tradition of mediation in which important Highland texts (including those of Donald MacDonald and Angus MacKay) were viewed through highly-coloured Lowland spectacles, to the frequent detriment of their meaning and purpose.[12]

Patrick's transcript of Joseph's song and instrumental airs represented – as he was keenly aware – only one strand of a rich tradition, and a larger scheme began to form in his mind: a more ambitious general work which should reflect Highland popular song as a whole, with particular regard to its strongly marked regional varieties. As he explained in the 'Preface':

> His residence for a considerable number of years in the county of Argyle, gave him frequent opportunities of hearing the airs, that are most common in that part of the country. These he attempted to write down in musical notes. He made several journeys into Perthshire, and other parts of the Highlands, for the purpose of collecting the airs, that are sung in those districts, and that are not so generally known in Argyleshire: and from the singing, and the friendly communications of some respectable gentlemen and ladies, natives of the western isles, he has been enabled to enrich the collection, with a number of beautiful airs, that are, in some degree, peculiar to those countries.[13]

He knew that many of his readers might find the material unfamiliar, and took steps to cope with this, including regularising Joseph's rather free notation, and

cont'd been available, would have been the writer and musician Alexander Campbell, a Perthshire Highlander who later edited an important collection of Highland music entitled *Albyn's Anthology* (2 vols., Edinr., 1816–18). He was related to the MacDonalds, having married MacDonald of Keppoch's widow, making him stepfather to Patrick's wife, Barbara. Campbell had sufficient regard for Patrick to dedicate to him a fine slow strathspey entitled 'Rev. Mr Macdonald of Kilmore' which was set to words by Robert Tannahill and later became one of the classic Scots songs: 'Gloomy Winter's Noo Awa'', see Glen, *op.cit.*, i, iv; for further information on Campbell, see Dalyell, pp.51–3.

11 *Fasti, op.cit.*

12 See Chapters 6 and 8 below.

13 'Preface', p.2. The existence of distinct regional traditions in Gaelic song is echoed by the Nether Lorn Canntaireachd, a contemporary piping manuscript from Argyll which contains more than sixty tunes not recorded elsewhere: see A. G. Kenneth, 'The Campbell Canntaireachd', *PT*, vol.17, no.8, May 1965, pp.18–20 (19).

providing graded examples to help people approaching the Highland idiom for the first time to familiarise their ear. His approach to the problem of multiple variants was equally sensible:

> Musicians well know, that a few variations in the melody of particular passages, do by no means destroy the identity of a piece of music. Hence better or worse editions or sets of the same air will be obtained from different persons, or in different parts of the country. When the publisher had frequent opportunities of hearing an air, he chose that set of it, which appeared to him the best, and the most genuine . . . He did not conceive, that he was authorised to alter, or improve the pieces, according to his own ideas. He leaves that to others. A few appoggiaturas, or grace notes, are occasionally added, in order to give some idea of the style and manner in which the airs are performed. Of these, however, the publisher has been sparing . . .[14]

His restraint seems commendable in a period whose more typical products included George Thomson's *Select Collection of Original Scottish Airs* (Edinr., 1793–1841) complete with sumptuous opening and concluding 'symphonies' (often hilariously unidiomatic) by Haydn, Beethoven, Weber and Hummel.

But Patrick was well aware of the difficulties of harmonising such material according to standard classical procedures:

> As their fundamental harmonies are often ambiguous, and even the keys are sometimes but obscurely marked, or imperfectly established, the proper accompaniment is not so clearly indicated, as it commonly is, in the regular music of the moderns . . . It seemed, therefore, the safest course, to publish the simple melody, and leave it to masters, or others, who might wish to perform particular airs, to frame an accompaniment, agreeably to their own taste and fancy.[15]

Since, however, people were not always adept at constructing harmonies for themselves, and friends urged him to give some indication of what he thought a suitable keyboard accompaniment might look like, he arrived at a typically sensible decision: to arrange basses for the pianoforte to those tunes least liable to harmonic distortion, and to leave the remainder unadorned. Acknowledging the typically modal nature of this music with its 'gapped' scales, he advised the simplest of accompaniments:

> Some of those airs, will probably produce their happiest effect, when sung or played, in a simple expressive manner, without accompaniment, or at most, with a few octaves sounded to the emphatical notes, such as we may suppose were struck upon the harp, in former times. Any regular accompaniment, that

14 'Preface', p.4.
15 'Preface', p.5.

can be set to them, will perhaps weaken, in some degree, their native expression, by giving them a modern, artificial appearance . . . To others of them, the best accompaniment is, perhaps, the bagpipe bass, or the continual repetition of the key note.[16]

Patrick acknowledged the role of collective composition, and his view of tradition as a positively creative medium was strikingly in advance of most of his contemporaries. He denied that tradition was a reflex mechanism by means of which a cultural stock was unchangingly preserved, insisting that it was a living thing. A lot of the old harp repertoire had perished not because tradition was an inherently fragile and wasteful medium, but because it had ceased – unlike the music of the pipe – to be enriched by the creative attention of successive generations. For the same reason, while he was attracted by the idea of a chronological arrangement for the tunes in *Vocal Airs*, and shared his informants' belief that some of them might be very old, he acknowledged that such an order could not be established in a cultural stock sustained by the creative potential of living people. The material was therefore arranged synchronically, by region.

It was typical of Patrick that if he did not know something, he would go and find out at first hand from somebody who did, and he was prepared to travel considerable distances to do this. Thus, when he decided that he needed a section on piobaireachd, he used his family connections with Ronald MacDonald, the laird of Keppoch, to gain access to a notable piper:

> Many respectable subscribers . . . having expressed a wish, that some of the pieces, that are played upon the large or true Highland bagpipe, should be inserted: the publisher was desirous of gratifying them, as far as was consistent with his plan. With this view, he made a journey into the country of Lochaber, where he knew that there was an eminent performer upon that instrument, retained in the family of a gentleman, with whom he was nearly connected: and from his playing, he wrote out four favourite pieces, which he has annexed to the work. Whoever has attempted to execute such a task, and has had experience of the difficulty of it, will readily excuse any imperfections that may be found in the notation of those pieces. The publisher flatters himself, that if such imperfections be discovered, they will not be thought very material, unless perhaps in the quick variations. In performing these upon the bagpipe, it is usual to introduce certain graces and flourishes, which are peculiar to that instrument, and to that species of music; and which can hardly be expressed in notes, or executed, at least, with the same effect, upon another instrument. The publisher, however, has made as near an approach, as he could, to the notes, that were expressed by the performer . . . A compleat collection of that music, would make a large work. Perhaps, such a collection, which may be received with confidence as genuine, is not to be hoped for, till

16 'Preface', p.6.

a performer of genius and ability shall appear, who, being well instructed in the notation of music, may be able to write from his own performance, to explain the graces and modes of execution, that are peculiar to that instrument and music, and to invent and apply proper characters to express them. If such a person shall ever be found, it is not doubted, that the Highland society of London, who have discovered such a laudable zeal for the preservation of that music, will give him suitable encouragement.[17]

Patrick's work was not wholly unprecedented. There had existed since the earliest years of the eighteenth century a genre of fiddle music loosely based on piobaireachd, of which Dr. David Johnson prints several examples in *Scottish Fiddle Music in the Eighteenth Century*.[18] But this was a specifically fiddle form, an impressionistic attempt to capture the 'Highland humours' and making little attempt to reflect the formal characteristics of ceòl mór. So that although Patrick MacDonald's examples of piobaireachd were notated in such a way as to permit realisation on keyboard or string instruments, he produced perhaps the earliest attempt in print to represent the form as a piper would conceive of it.

Opposite is his setting of 'Cha till mi tuille'.[19]

Four piobaireachds were published in *Highland Vocal Airs*: 'Cumha Mhic a h Arasaig – McIntosh's Lament'; 'The same Air contracted, and set with variations for the Violin. Communicated by Mr. Campbell of Ardchattan';[20] 'Cha till mi tuille Never more shall I return. A Bagpipe Lament'; 'A' ghlas mheur A bagpipe Lament'; and 'Coma leam, coma leam cogadh no sith – Alike to me peace or war. The gathering of the clans. A bagpipe March'.[21]

It is an intriguing record, showing, as it does, a fiddle player expert in various branches of Highland music but not piobaireachd – which was evidently a more specialised calling – and as a result sometimes struggling a little with it as a form. For example in 'MacIntosh's Lament', Patrick seems to have mislaid four bars in the ground and then squared up the rest of the tune to make it fit a 28 rather than a 32-bar pattern. In the 'Finger Lock' ('A' ghlas mheur'), his occasional harmonies suggest a hesitant sense of the tune's tonality; whilst there are missing bits in 'War or Peace' ('Coma leam, coma leam cogadh no sith') 'patched' with a couple of rests. But even so, Patrick's settings are of the first interest, in that they are musically aware, and done by someone who was close to the tradition. His notation shows frequent confident directions as to tempi, and a tendency to repeat sections of the

---

17 'Preface', p.7.

18 Pp 119–142.

19 As set, the tune ends with a taorluath fosgailte, but since it lacks Patrick's usual ending signs, the engraver may have excised the crunluath variation to get the piece on to one plate.

20 The subscription list shows this to be Patrick Campbell, esq. of Ardchattan, on the shores of Loch Etive.

21 *Vocal Airs*, pp.38–39, 40, 41, 42, 43.

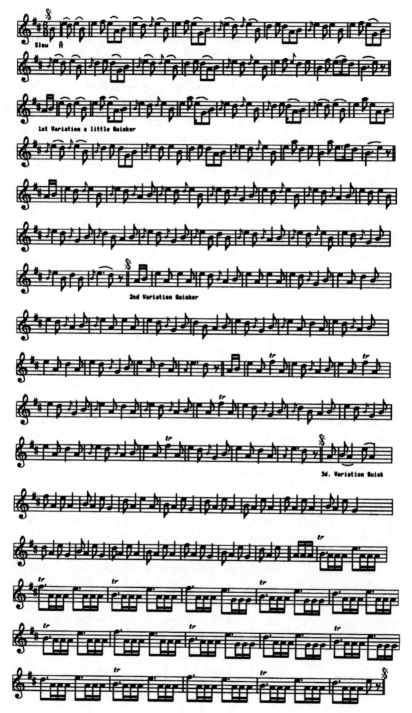

22

tune, including his grounds; indeed, his double barring and frequent use of *Dal Segno* marks may indicate an intention that variations be repeated in a way that has not come down to us elsewhere in performance tradition.

Even within the larger context of its time, *Highland Vocal Airs* was a significant work. A new era was dawning in Europe, and scholars like J. G. Herder and the Brothers Grimm, excited by James Macpherson's discoveries, were beginning to explore the wider implications of popular culture. They shared Thomas Blackwell's sense that the common people were the source of all true creativity and bore ultimate responsibility, therefore, for communal identity. Indeed Scottish thinkers had been working towards such conclusions for at least two generations.[22] It was thought that popular culture, and music and song in particular, possessed immense significance. It was not merely a sign of national distinctiveness – it was its very substance, and interpreted aright, therefore, historical evidence of the highest importance. One of the earliest explicit statements of this position in a Scottish source occurs in the anonymous 'Prospectus' for *Highland Vocal Airs*, undated, but issued probably in 1781.[23] It reads as follows:

> Of the many characters that distinguish one nation from another, their music is not the least considerable. From those airs which are the natural expressions of the feelings that pass within the soul, the genius of a people may be known with more certainty than from the annals of the historian. For this reason the philosopher considers the music of any people as an object not least worthy of his attention, than the man of taste . . . In either of these views it is hoped that the Collection of Highland Airs, now offered to the public, will give satisfaction. The plain and simple spirit that runs through them evinces them to be the music of nature, and the melody of a people uncorrupted in their taste, and simple in their manners. Many of them have another peculiar property, which cannot fail of recommending them to the curious. There is reason to believe that they are of a very remote antiquity. Some of them are handed down as the genuine airs of those ancient Galic poems, translations of which are in the hands of the public [a reference to Ossian]. These were probably adapted to the harp. They have a venerable and antique cast, a tender and elegiac air, in which they differ greatly from the later musical compositions of the Highlands
>
> The Editor has been at pains to obtain the most genuine sets of the different airs, and in writing them out, to follow as closely as he could the manner in which they are sung by the natives . . .
>
> He would not wish to anticipate the judgement of the public concerning

---

22 See William Donaldson, 'Change and Invariance in the Traditional Performing Arts', in *Northern Scotland*, vol.17 (1997), pp.33–54, (34–5).

23 A minute of the Glasgow Gaelic Club, dated 2 October 1781, records the placing of a subscription for 20 copies: Glasgow City Archives.

his work; but hopes, if the Highland poetry is allowed to have merit, that the Highland music will be found congenial to it.[24]

Joseph's *Compleat Theory* had dealt with the courtly, aristocratic music of the Gael; his brother Patrick concerned himself with another side of tradition, demotic popular music and song. His approach was as radical in method as it was in concept; it was based on fieldwork, unlike that of other, typically deskbound, early Romantic theorists, and his sense of the primacy of oral tradition and respect for the things it contained was the most sophisticated of his generation.

Above all one feels a sense of confidence in the future, that it was time for the Gaels to inscribe their own substantial chapters in the book of Scottish song; that the national consciousness must be redefined, and that popular music was the way to do it. When Patrick spoke of rescuing Highland song from oblivion, what he had in mind was the introduction of a living form to a much wider contemporary audience, a very different thing from the antiquarian rearguard action that Walter Scott was to undertake a little later with the Border ballads, moved by the conviction (much influenced by Macpherson) that traditional culture was moribund and could not sustain itself without external intervention.

There was little sense in Patrick that the tradition might be dying, or even at risk; but a very different picture emerges when we turn to John Ramsay's essay 'Of the Influence of Poetry and Music upon the Highlanders'.[25] It was the work of somebody who had little direct personal knowledge of the Highlands and who may not even have seen the collection to which his words were prefixed. He began with a lengthy disquisition on the poems of Ossian, which he saw as the definitive Highland text, in terms of which all others should be viewed. This was scarcely surprising since most of his information came directly from Macpherson, eked out with standard literary sources such as Johnson's *Journey to the Western Islands of Scotland,* Martin's *Description of the Western Isles* and Pennant's *Tour in Scotland.*[26] There was frequent reference, therefore, to the archaic and un-changing character of Highland society, Celtic melancholy and affinity with nature, and the wildness and artlessness of Highland music.

Within a generation, the Macpherson paradigm had assumed such a hold on the Lowland mind that a regiment of Highland musicians might have struggled, in vain, to dislodge it. At its heart lay the notion that the past was intrinsically

---

24 *Proposals for Publishing, by Subscription, a Collection of Highland Vocal Airs, never hitherto published. To which will be added a few of the most lively country Dances, or Reels of the North Highlands and Western Isles.* By Patrick McDonald, Minister of Kilmore in Argyleshire.

25 *Vocal Airs,* pp.8–15.

26 Dr. Samuel Johnson, *A Journey to the Western Islands of Scotland* (Lond., 1775); Donald McNicol, *Remarks on Dr. Samuel Johnson's Journey to the Hebrides* (Lond., 1779); Martin Martin, *A Description of the Western Isles* (Lond., 1703 and later edns.); Thomas Pennant, *A Tour in Scotland and Voyage to the Hebrides, MDCCLXXII* (Chester, 1774).

superior to the present in terms of creative potential. Ramsay declared: 'In giving some account of this remnant of primeval manners, we shall confine ourselves to compositions that are confessedly modern . . . A number of these poems, are accounted beautiful, though inferior, in general, to the specimens published of the works of Ossian'.[27] When we look for information about these 'modern compositions', however, we find precise reference to only one, a fowl-catching song from St. Kilda translated into English prose by a correspondent in Skye. Ramsay made vague general allusion to work songs, 'luinigs' and 'iorrums', but he did not quote a single example either in Gaelic or in translation. Conspicuously little Gaelic appeared at any point, and it is not apparent that he was familiar with the language. Indeed, when he discusses the celebrated harper Rory Dall Morrison in terms which suggest that he considered the sobriquet 'Dall' (meaning 'blind) as an alternative surname, we may wonder about his grasp even of the basic conventions of Highland life.

Ramsay was a dilettante, a collector of 'curious anecdotes relative to Highland poesy', who was quite capable of citing Edmund Spenser and Hugh Blair as authorities respectively on the Bards and Druids. He made much of the music of the harp, tracing its origin to 'the Druidical bards', but he did not quote any of it, refer to any composition by name, or indicate a printed or manuscript source where such music might be found. Since most authorities agree that harping had largely died out in Scotland by the middle years of the eighteenth century,[28] it is unlikely that the author would personally have heard a note of it; yet he did not hesitate to extol it as the inspiration of Ossian and the source of what (little) was of merit in subsequent Highland song.

He regarded Highland poetry and music as existing in a cultural timewarp, opening a uniquely privileged window upon high near-Homeric antiquity. For this to work, it was necessary, as Macpherson had suggested, that the mechanisms of transmission ensure near-immutability over long periods of time, which seemed to require, in turn, that the host society should itself be uniquely conservative and resistant to change. Accordingly we find the author insisting that:

> ancient manners and customs were carefully cherished . . . Neither is it surprising, that this music should have lurked for so many ages in the

27 Ramsay, 'Essay', p.8.
28 But see Alexander Campbell, 'Slight Sketch of a Journey made through parts of the Highlands & Hebrides in Autumn 1815'. EUL, La III: 577: ' "The voice of Harps may yet be heard in the Highlands and Western Islands. As a proof, it is well known that the accomplished ladies of Torloisk are admirably skilled handling the harp', f.11. Presumably, this refers to Marianne MacLean, the lady of Torloisk, in Mull, later Mrs General Douglas Clephane, a great expert on Highland music and an accomplished executant of it also on the harpsichord. See also, Wílliam Matheson, ed., *The Blind Harper: the Songs of Roderick Morison and his Music* (Edinr., 1970), pp.lxxii-lxxiii; and Colm O'Boyle, 'Some Irish Harpers in Scotland', in *Transactions of the Gaelic Society of Inverness*, vol.47, 1971-2, pp.143-71.

mountainous parts of Scotland and Ireland, when we consider the attachment
of every unmixed branch of the Celtae to their original institutions. The
Highlanders have, perhaps, undergone more changes, in the course of the
present century, than for a thousand years preceding.[29]

We see some of the implications of this idea when we turn to his section on the
pipes. He wrote:

> . . . beyond all memory or tradition, the bagpipe has been the favourite
> instrument of that people . . . it is of very high antiquity. It is uncertain at
> what period it was introduced among the Highlanders; but it is neither
> mentioned nor alluded to in the poems of Ossian . . . There is no doubt a
> tradition in the Hebrides, that it was brought in by the northern nations,
> whose viceroys governed those islands for two centuries at least. The Highland
> chieftains, that rose upon their removal, appear indeed to have copied them in
> some other particulars.
>
> The large bagpipe is their instrument for war, for marriage, or funeral
> processions, and for other great occasions. They have also a smaller kind, on
> which dancing tunes are played. In their hours of merriment and relaxation,
> young people of both sexes danced with great alacrity to a species of wild airy
> tunes, the nature of which is universally known. Every morning too, in
> peaceable times, the piper played under the chieftain's windows, strutting,
> with stately steps, backwards and forwards. And, at meal-times, he regaled him
> and his guests with favourite tunes.
>
> These, however, were the least considerable parts of the piper's duty. In
> former times, his presence at funerals was deemed essential. There he played
> certain melancholy tunes, which, in all probability, were connected with the
> *corronach*, or dirge, performed in the days of paganism by the bards over the
> grave . . .
>
> In the days of Ossian, the dirge appears to have been accompanied by the
> harp, an instrument well suited to tender, passionate emotions. But, after it
> had lost its credit, the pipers would, doubtless, attempt to catch the spirit of
> the dirge, as far as it could be accommodated to the bagpipe.
>
> But a very peculiar species of martial music was in the highest request with
> the Highlanders. It was sometimes sung, accompanied with words, but more
> frequently performed on the bagpipe. And, in spite of every change, a *pibrach*,
> or *cruineachadh* [gathering], though it may sound harsh to the ear of a
> stranger, still rouzes the native Highlander, in the same way that the sound of
> the trumpet does the war-horse. Nay, it sometimes produced effects, little less
> marvellous than those recorded of ancient music. At the battle of Quebec, in
> April 1760, whilst the British troops were retreating in great confusion, the
> general complained to a field-officer of Fraser's regiment, of the bad behaviour

29 Ramsay, 'Essay', p.12.

of his corps; 'Sir', (answered he, with some warmth) 'you did very wrong in forbidding the pipes to play this morning: nothing encourages Highlanders so much in a day of action. Nay, even now, they would be of use'. – 'Let them blow, like the devil, then', (replied the general) 'if it will bring back the men'. And, the pipes being ordered to play a favourite *cruineachadh*, the Highlanders, who were broken, returned the moment they heard the music, and formed, with great alacrity, in the rear.[30]

Ramsay stated: 'The contrast between the pipe and the harp tunes is so striking, that one could hardly imagine them to be the music of the same people'. But he did not quote any bagpipe music, or identify any tune by name, or inform the reader where such information might be found. He did, however, have a theory which explained the origin of the music (in remote antiquity, of course) and at the same time deprecated the Gaidhealtachd as a community capable, at least in historically recent times, of serious creative endeavour. Drawing upon the contemporary enthusiasm for Norse antiquities, also visible in Hugh Blair, he confidently ascribed ceòl mór to the Vikings:

> If, then, the martial music, in question, be of Scandinavian origin, it accorded excellently with the bold, impetuous, abrupt, strains of the Scalds. The sound and the sentiment were in perfect unison, and well suited to the feelings of a rugged people, whose trade was war, and whose fury was long considered as irresistible . . .
>
> Neither is it surprising, that the islanders of the middle ages should take an attachment to the music of their conquerors, it being excellently calculated to brace the nerves, and rouze the soul: and it accorded better with their state of society than the harp, which aimed principally at awakening the finer feelings.[31]

When Patrick MacDonald needed to know more about some aspect of Highland music, he consulted a living expert. John Ramsay's response was to burrow ever deeper into his library of classical and Norse antiquities. The fact that nobody, including Ramsay, had the slightest idea what ancient Scandinavian music actually sounded like presented little obstacle. It still existed. Not, indeed, amongst the Scandinavians, but in the form of ceòl mór in the living museum beyond the Highland line where, as was well known, 'manners have been stationary, ever since the northern nations quitted their coasts'.[32]

But here arose a little difficulty. If the Highlanders were as fiercely conservative as the author claimed, how could they have been so deeply influenced by Norse music over so short a period of time? The theory required them to be strongly

30 Ramsay, 'Essay', pp.12–13.
31 Ramsay, 'Essay', p.14.
32 *Ibid.*

susceptible to change and strongly resistant to it at the same time. If the author was aware of this inconsistency, however, he gave little sign of it, going on to offer a number of confident predictions about the current health and future state of Highland music:

> Though the pipers have survived their brethren, the harpers, almost a century, they themselves will, ere long, share the same fate. The present ones are already inferior to their predecessors in knowledge and execution. Nor are they to expect encouragement from their chieftains and gentry, whose manners are formed on a new model: and the spirit of the commons is broken, and directed to objects very different from those of former times.
>
> In less than twenty years, it would be in vain to attempt a collection of Highland music. Perhaps, it is rather late at present; but enough may be got to point out its genius and spirit. The remains of the harp tunes are in most immediate hazard, as all ranks of people are changing their modes of life, with wonderful rapidity. The pipe music is, no doubt, most entire; yet, from its being seldom noted down, a considerable part of it has already perished; and, ere long, the remainder will either be lost, or performed in a slovenly manner.[33]

Having thus dismissed Highland music as a living art, Ramsay reached his concluding remarks. The fact that his approach was almost entirely conjectural and that most of his predictions were contradicted by events shortly after his making them counted for little with subsequent readers whose attitudes towards Highland culture drew upon substantially the same sources as his had done:

> To have allowed such venerable monuments of antiquity to vanish away, would have been a reflection on the taste and liberality of the present age . . . It would be no difficult matter to make the airs more beautiful, and more agreeable to an improved ear; but, if this were done, there would be gross deceit in giving them as originals. Let them, therefore, appear in their native simplicity and nakedness; and, if improvements and variations shall be found necessary, these can be added afterwards.
>
> Though the intrinsic merit of such a publication may not appear considerable to the regular musician, it is, nevertheless, valuable, as a specimen of what was once the delight of a great people. Its very simplicity is a pledge of originality and antiquity . . .
>
> . . . poetry and music had a mighty influence on the minds of the Highlanders. Their poetical tales were (if we may be allowed the expression) pastorals for warriors, and well calculated to inspire the men with an ardent desire of imitating, on some future occasion, their ancient worthies.
>
> . . . Those precepts and examples, which are set before them in the

33 Ramsay, 'Essay', pp. 14–15.

engaging dress of poetry, aided by congenial music, teach them that generous contempt of danger, and even of death, to which the common people of commercial countries seldom attain, till they have been thoroughly disciplined, and familiarized to war.[34]

This militaristic note, which was to resound through much of the later literature, had its roots in the theories of Progress currently being developed by leading thinkers of the Scottish Enlightenment. Assuming that human nature was always and everywhere the same, writers like Adam Ferguson and Henry Home, Lord Kames, had posited a theoretical sequence through which all societies must pass from communities of hunter-gatherers to modern industrial states, each stage involving a corresponding gain in sophistication and wealth. But wealth bred avarice, and avarice corruption, and history contained numerous examples of societies such as ancient Rome which had been founded in spartan warrior virtue, only to fall victim eventually to luxury and moral decay. Kames wrote in *Sketches of the History of Man* in 1774 that 'a military and an industrious spirit are of equal importance to Britain; and that if either of them be lost, we are undone'. Britain possessed a unique advantage over its rivals in sustaining communities at significantly different levels of development, and a number of commentators were coming to see the Highlands as a vital reservoir of the military spirit whose maintenance was essential to the well-being of the United Kingdom as a whole.[35]

In such a scheme of things the great war-pipe of the Gael had an obvious role. Hence Ramsay's willingness to present it as a primitive curiosity valuable chiefly for its animating effects upon Highland soldiers.

Its inclusion in *Highland Vocal Airs* obtained for Ramsay's 'Essay' a significance to which its intrinsic merits in no way entitled it and it went on to shape the ideological agenda until well into the twentieth century. As late as 1962 an influential writer on piping still felt obliged to rebut the theory that ceòl mór was of Norse origin, under the impression that this had been the opinion of Patrick MacDonald.[36]

Why somebody of Patrick's intelligence, and by no means negligible social standing, submitted to such mediation is not clear. Perhaps it was the result of a misguided commission to an old acquaintance whom he could not bring himself to disappoint; but it may also reflect the involvement of the Highland Society of London whose support usually involved surrendering some degree of control over one's project and the way it was presented to the public. The 'Essay' – which set itself to accommodate the new evidence to the comfortable certainties of received wisdom, and bade fair in the process to undo what Patrick MacDonald was actually trying to achieve – may have been a price he was obliged to pay.[37] At

---

34 Ramsay, 'Essay', p.15.
35 Stocking, pp. 65–89.
36 Archibald Campbell, 'Highland Bagpipe', *op.cit.*, pp. 6–10.
37 See below, p.101.

any rate, in the second edition of *Highland Vocal Airs* the dedication to the Highland Society was cancelled, and the collection inscribed to Sir John MacGregor Murray who had arranged the return of the manuscript of Joseph's 'Compleat Theory' to the manse of Kilmore. The 'Preface' and the 'Essay' were removed and the volume contained the music text alone.[38]

But a person of ordinary means might find it difficult to dispense with the Highland Society if he wished to launch new texts into an uncertain market, and the problem of publishing the 'Compleat Theory' arose almost at once. Indeed the proposal came just as the Society was taking delivery of its copies of *Highland Vocal Airs*, when the manuscript was presumably still the property of Sir John MacGregor Murray who had bought it when Joseph died. At any rate we find on 28 April 1785 the following minute in the Highland Society of London's papers: 'Proposed The plan of publication of the Treatise on the Highland-Pipe-Music now under consideration, to Mr. George McKenzie and Mr James Morison, to report their opinion to the Committee'.[39] The response was to remit the proposal to the newly formed Highland Society of Scotland, a sister organisation based in Edinburgh. Membership of the two societies was reciprocal, and they frequently referred awkward proposals to one another in this way, with the implication that all assistance ought to be given short of actual help. The Highland Society of Scotland's Sederunt Book records that on 21 November 1785,

> The Secretary read a Letter which he had received from Mr. Mackenzie Secretary of the Highland Society of London accompanying an Essay by Joseph Macdonald on the Highland Bagpipe Music transmitted to them from the East Indies where the author died, and now sent to this Society for their Opinion how far it merits publication and the Letter Informs that on the favourable Report of this Society the Society of London will print it at their own expense.[40]

The Highland Society of Scotland referred the matter in turn to a sub-committee comprising Sir John Clerk of Penicuik, John Clark of Eldin, James Grant of Corrymony, Dr. Gregory Grant, Dr. Alexander Macdougal, and the Secretary of the Society, William MacDonald of St. Martins, with Grant of Corrymony as convener. Thereafter nothing further concerning it appears in the minutes of either society for nearly twenty years.

The proposal to publish the *Compleat Theory* at the Highland Society of London's own expense put it on a rather different footing from *Highland Vocal Airs* which was published by general subscription, enabling the Society to sell its

---

38 See Cannon, *Bibliography*, pp.110–14.

39 Highland Society of London Papers, NLS, Dep. 268 no 21, Committee Book Gaelic Society 1783: 28/4/1785.

40 Highland Society of Scotland Papers, Ingliston House Library, Sederunt Book One, 21/11/1785.

copies on to its members so that it could support the project while incurring relatively little financial outlay or risk. The internal documents of the Highland Societies during the first several decades of their existence demonstrate a number of recurring tendencies. One was that although specifically dedicated to the promotion of Highland musical culture, they kept up an ethos of rigid 'economy' in this area and would go to considerable lengths to avoid parting with actual money. We will see a little later a number of projects founder because of this.

At some stage, the manuscript must have returned to Patrick MacDonald, because we find in the minutes of the Highland Society of Scotland in July 1804 that he had in the meantime published it himself:

> Sir John Sinclair laid before the Committee a Treatise lately published 'On the Theory Principle and Practice of the Great Highland Bag Pipe Music' composed about 46 years ago by Mr Joseph Macdonald an officer in the service of The East India Company, the manuscript of which was discovered in Bengal by Sir J. M. Murray, and sent by Sir John to the Rev. Mr. Macdonald minister of Kilmore Argyllshire, brother to the deceased who had now published it, the Proceeds to be applied for the benefit of a relation. Sir John stated that this work was likely to conduce much to the Improvement of performers in this warlike and national music and the Committee on the suggestion of Sir John resolved to purchase 20 copies of the Treatise to be delivered to such of the Competitors as had made the greatest progress . . . The Committee beg leave to farther recommend to the Directors of the Highland Society of Scotland to purchase a certain number of copies of said work and to send a dozen copies as a present to the Highland Society of London.[41]

The Directors, however, taking the view that the support of piping was an exclusive responsibility of the Highland Society of London (although this was in breach of their own charter of incorporation), declined to commit funds to the project.[42]

There was another important difference between the *Compleat Theory* and *Highland Vocal Airs*. The title page of the latter indicated that it was 'By Patrick McDonald Minister of Kilmore in Argyleshire'. But the former merely stated that it was 'Printed for Patrick McDonald', with no implication of editorial responsibility. The published text of the *Compleat Theory* was extensively edited by somebody, however, because it differs in many respects from the original MS.[43] Who was responsible for this is not clear, but Joseph's most recent editor,

41 HSS Sederunt Book no 4, pt. 1, June 1803 – December 1808; 14/7/1804.

42 Same, 23/11/1804.

43 For a detailed account of editorially-induced changes between the manuscript and printed version, see C. H. Woodward, 'An Analysis of "A Compleat Theory of the Scots Highland Bagpipe" by Joseph MacDonald. Compiled 1760–63. First published 1803', in *Piping Times*, vol.27, nos.6–10, March-July 1975, pp.21–4, 14–17, 15–17, 14–17, 25–27; vol.28, nos.4–5, 7–8, January-May 1976, pp.28–32, 28–33, 16–19, 29–32.

Dr. Roderick Cannon, cites a grim catalogue of errors of omission and commission including 'wrong notes, notes wrongly timed, holes shown open which should be closed and vice versa . . . columns of holes not properly aligned with the notes. One of the music examples . . . mistakenly repeated . . . a group of six examples printed in the wrong order . . .' and scribal confusion leading to the important technical term 'Tuludh' being rendered as 'Riludh', or 'Iuludh', which does not make sense, and led to much subsequent confusion.[44]

Of the letterpress preliminaries, internal evidence would suggest that none of it, perhaps not even the dedication (once again to Sir John MacGregor Murray), was actually written by Patrick, who was in any case now approaching seventy-five years of age. It may be doubted whether he even saw the proofs. The 'Preface' to the published version of the *Compleat Theory* was a re-hash of Ramsay's 'Essay on the Influence of Poetry and Music on the Highlanders', cobbled together by an anonymous hand in the middle of the Napoleonic wars and taking a line which was even more militaristic and jingo-patriotic than the original. The pipe was presented as the badge of a modern xenophobic nationalism, and as a metaphor for a vanishing world of antique heroism, which formulation was to lie at the heart of the dominant ideology in Lowland Scotland throughout the following century. According to the writer, Joseph MacDonald was

> Enthusiastically attached to his country, and an impassioned admirer of the Heroes of old; he was induced, by feelings of national pride, to attain to an excellence in the theory and practice of their warlike music, from an earnest desire to preserve the remains of it, by introducing a system of notation; because, if any did ever exist, it had been totally lost . . .
>
> Whether or not this instrument, with its chord of drones, is the chorus alluded to by Giraldus Cambrensis, is submitted to the Musical Antiquary. It is said to be mentioned, under the name of Soek Pipe (Penant's Tour to the Hebrids, page 302), in some of the best songs of northern nations, and others conjecture it to be of eastern origin: But, whether of native or foreign invention, it has been, immemorially considered as our national instrument of music; used in war, at tournaments, marriages, funerals, and public exhibitions. In battle it animated the combatants to the most daring exertions. In seasons of peace the Pipers struck up the enlivening morning Cuairts, under the windows of their Chieftains: and, at meal-time, their guests were regaled with favourite marches, or gatherings, complimentary to their several clans. At funerals they played a variety of laments, composed in the elegiac strain, analogous to the corranach, or dirge, performed over the dead, in the days of paganism . . . [which] have now taken the place of the elegant and nervous verses of the Bards, which were admirably calculated to elevate the minds of the rising generations to virtue and military glory. – 'Raise high ye Bards; – raise high the praise of HEROES, that my soul may settle on their

44 Cannon, *Compleat Theory* , pp.3–4.

fame!' [In the original at this point, there follow extensive footnotes, fully half a page in length of heroic quotations from Ossian] . . .

In the Highlands not only has the Harp ceased, but, with the decay of military ardour, the result of a new policy, as narrow as unsound, our martial music has been, for more than half a century, on the decline. It is hoped, however, the annexed treatise will conduce to the preservation of the remains of it; and we earnestly pray that enough of the spirit and virtue of our Ancestors may be kept in such vigour as shall, for ever, preserve the independence of our country, and the Blessings of our invaluable Constitution.[45]

What was going on here was the promotion of their own agenda by third parties of dubious standing under the name of an authority on Highland music, whose control appears to have been minimal, and whose own work was significantly compromised in the process.

It is a pattern which will recur.

The corrupt text of 1803 was twice reprinted, in 1927 and again in 1971. A reliable edition which faithfully reproduced the original manuscript – and therefore for the first time enabled a proper judgement to be made about Joseph MacDonald and his work – did not become available until 1994, nearly two hundred and fifty years after the death of its author. The first serious attempt to bring the pipe and its music before a wider audience in an informed and rational way thus ended in defeat – at the hands of those very forces of ignorance and prejudice which it had been Joseph MacDonald's intention to educate and reform.

---

45 *Compleat Theory* (1803), 'Preface'. This misrepresents the source: Pennant had actually denied that the pipe was of Scandinavian origin.

4

'Clapping of hands and cries of bravo': the Competitions of the Highland Societies of London and Scotland, 1781–1800

The awarding of prizes in competition to promote selected cultural and economic ends appears to have started in Scotland with The Edinburgh Society for encouraging the Arts, Sciences, Manufacturers, and Agriculture. It was founded in 1755 as an offshoot of the Select Society, the city's leading philo- sophical association, which included David Hume and Adam Smith amongst its members. The two societies represented a characteristically Scottish blend of the elegant and the practical, awarding 'premiums' (which consisted as a rule of a piece of plate if one were a gentleman, and a sum of money if one were not) for essays on subjects ranging from biology and aesthetics, to Scotch ale and porter, and the improvement of manure.[1] They were a kind of national academy in embryo, and similar institutions (although generally speaking on a rather grander scale) – such as Cosimo de Medici's *Accademia Platonica*, the *Kongelige danske videnskabernes selskab* at Copenhagen, the *Académie Impériale des sciences* at St. Petersburg, and the *Real Academia Española* at Madrid – had existed for centuries throughout western Europe. These were self-regulating bodies of learned people, sometimes under royal patronage and enjoying state support, and frequently setting themselves to cultivate their national languages by studying the best writers, identifying obsolete or vulgar idioms, and compiling official dictionaries to promote the best contemporary usage. The Select Society of Edinburgh also saw language as its principal focus, except that owing to Scotland's subordination within the Union and the removal to London of the court and government, the language it sought to refine and promote was not Scots or Gaelic, but English.

Although relatively short-lived, the Select Society provided a working model for a number of later institutions including the powerful Highland Societies of London and Scotland, founded in 1778 and 1784 respectively. These latter enjoyed reciprocal membership and though their aims and general corporate style were not identical, can be treated for most purposes as two branches of a single organisation. They were dedicated (1) to establish by statistical and other means of enquiry a full and accurate account of the present condition of the Highlands and western islands of Scotland;[2] (2) to modernise the Highland economy,

---

1 See James D. G. Davidson, *The Royal Highland and Agricultural Society of Scotland A Short History* 1784–1984, (Privately Printed, Edinr., 1984), pp.1–2; Mossner, p. 283.

2 This may have been inspired by the pioneering surveys of the St. Petersburg Academy, then such leaders in the field that Sir John Sinclair of Ulbster (a founding member of the Highland Society of Scotland) personally visited St. Petersburg and

through the establishment of towns and villages, upgrading the communications infrastructure by means of road and bridge building to promote integration into the rest of the U.K., increasing productivity by agricultural improvement, the extension of fisheries, and the introduction of trades and manufactures, developing a co-ordinated approach by landowners, and petitioning for Government support for these activities; (3) they were also to take appropriate steps to preserve the poetry, music and language of the Highlands.[3]

The Highland Societies were hybrid organisations, half board of agriculture, half *Académie écossaise*, and their membership was overwhelmingly landed and titled. They enjoyed close ties with the political establishment and with the Court. In 1793, for example, prompted by the events of the French Revolution, the Highland Society of Scotland unanimously approved a motion expressing, 'Our Loyalty to Our most gracious Sovereign, Our inviolable attachment to Our free and happy Constitution, on the true principles of the Revolution Settlement in 1688, Our firm determination to protect it at the risque of Our Lives and fortunes from every attack from Republicans and Levellers'.[4] This was subsequently translated into Gaelic, printed, and circulated throughout the Highlands. Royal births, marriages, deaths and foiled assassination attempts routinely called forth loyal addresses. There was no President of the Highland Society of Scotland from its foundation to 1850 who was not also a Duke, and – although the Society from the outset took a keen interest in agriculture – no working farmer on its Court of Directors during the first fifty years of its existence.[5] The membership of the Scottish society increased rapidly, rising from 123 in 1784 to more than a thousand by the end of the Napoleonic Wars, and to nearly three thousand by 1850.[6] Although originally dominated by Highland landlords, it eventually contained just about everybody who was anybody in Scotland.[7] It had lady members too, including Sara Drummond, Lady Gwydir, employer of the youthful Angus MacKay.

The Highland Society of London began as a kind of friendly society with cultural leanings: it subscribed to things, it relieved the distressed, it educated the children of deserving London Scots, and it assisted the passages of needy fellow countrymen back to Scotland. It was distinctly keener on the pipes than its counterpart in Edinburgh, however, two of its objects being 'The preservation of the Ancient Music of the Highlands' and 'The keeping up of the Martial Spirit;

cont'd   Moscow when he was planning his *Statistical Account of Scotland*: see Rosalind Mitchison, *Agricultural Sir John The Life of Sir John Sinclair of Ulbster 1754–1835* (Lond., 1962), pp.53–7.

3 Alexander Ramsay, *History of the Highland and Agricultural Society of Scotland with notices of Anterior Societies for the Promotion of Agriculture in Scotland* (Edinr., 1879), pp.47–8.

4 Davidson, p.11.

5 Ramsay, *Highland and Agricultural Society*, p.459–61.

6 Davidson, pp.51–3.

7 Ramsay, *Highland and Agricultural Society*, pp.539–51.

and rewarding the Gallant achievements of the Highland Corps,'[8] activities which it regarded as closely linked. In the opening decades of the nineteenth century it grew rapidly and became very splendid socially. The royal Dukes of Kent and York were members, as was the Prince of Wales – later George IV. In 1815 the Napoleonic Marshal MacDonald, Duke of Taranto, born in France of Scots Jacobite parents, wrote from Paris regretting his inability to attend the annual dinner because of press of other business. By 1810, it was a global organisation with branches in Nova Scotia, New Brunswick and Prince Edward Island, Calcutta, Bombay and Madras.

Both Societies enjoyed the privileges of incorporation, which gave them considerable powers. The scope of their activities was in theory unlimited, whatever it said in their original charter, and their individual members were exempted from liability for any debts which the Societies might incur so that their activities were largely free from financial risk. From an early stage, the Highland Society of Scotland was supporting agricultural schemes with its own money, £100 being voted for this purpose in 1785.[9] Since the majority of its members were landed proprietors, of course, anything tending to promote greater agricultural productivity directly served their own interests: successful initiatives were almost bound, in due course, to result in greater productivity, higher rents, and rising land values. And they were given public money to help them do this, the Scottish Society receiving a grant of £3,000 in 1789 by act of Parliament, out of money paid on restitution of the Forfeited Estates.[10] Premiums were awarded for essays on agricultural improvement (the writer James Hogg got one for a treatise on the ailments of sheep)[11], and published in a series of *Transactions*.[12] The importance that the Scottish Society attached to the agricultural side of its activities may be gathered from the fact that it disbursed some £12,000 on district cattle competitions alone in the period up to 1820, enough to run the annual piping competitions for more than five hundred years. Wealthy individual members were also willing to put up considerable sums in support of objects they favoured. The Duke of Argyll gave £1000 out of his own pocket to encourage the recruitment of Highland officers into the Navy.[13] The Society's income from invested capital, government grants, membership subscriptions and receipts from shows was to become very substantial, enabling it in the period up to 1880 to lay out more than £100,000 in premiums.[14]

Amongst its office bearers the Scottish society numbered a piper, John MacArthur, 'grocer of Edinburgh', who was a member of the celebrated piping

8 Iain MacInnes, 'The Highland Bagpipe: the Impact of the Highland Societies of London and Scotland', M.Litt. Thesis, Edinburgh University, 1989, p.18.

9 Ramsay, *Highland and Agricultural Society*, p.102.

10 *Ibid.*, p. 50.

11 *Ibid.*, p.110.

12 *Ibid.*, pp.416–7.

13 *Ibid.*, p.475.

14 *Ibid.*, pp.494–5.

family from Skye, and one of the finest players then resident in the Lowlands. It also had a bard, the famous Duncan Bàn MacIntyre, and a Professor of Gaelic called Robert MacFarlane. In 1803 these last two offices were abolished as 'totally unnecessary and a misapplication of the funds'.[15] The piper was to follow in about 1817.[16] Four people altogether held the post: John MacArthur, who was succeeded on his death in 1791 by Ronald MacDonald, who died in 1793 and was followed by William Henderson; the latter not giving satisfaction, he was replaced by Donald MacLean in 1799. Judging by the practice of the Highland Society of London which also had a piper, the post was largely honorary and involved little more than turning up in the Society's livery and playing on high days and holidays. It was worth about £10 a year.[17]

In the arena of culture, the Society's interests were mainly linguistic, centring on an enquiry into the authenticity of Ossian and the compilation of a Gaelic dictionary. A committee chaired by the novelist Henry Mackenzie laboured for several years on the questions: 'What poetry, of what kind, and of what degree of excellence, existed anciently in the Highlands, and which was generally known by the denomination of Ossianic, from its universal belief that its author was Ossian, the son of Fingal; and secondly, how far the collection of such poetry, published by Macpherson was genuine?' Its published report running to some three hundred pages was published in 1805 with a copious appendix of supporting documents, and a tentative endorsement of Macpherson's bona fides.[18] It cost the Societies jointly several thousands of pounds to produce. There was a similar scale of layout on the dictionary. Serious work on it began in 1814 under the direction of Dr. John Macleod, minister of Dundonald, Ewen MacLachlan, librarian of King's College, Aberdeen, and the Rev. Mackintosh Mackay, minister of Laggan. It was eventually published in 1828 as the *Dictionarium Scoto-Celticum*, and cost nearly £4,000 raised by subscription and from the Society's own funds.[19]

But these efforts did not mean that the Highland Society of Scotland regarded

---

15 Highland Society of Scotland Sederunt Book no 3, May 1795–June 1803, f.319.

16 Ramsay, *Highland and Agricultural Society*, pp.48–9.

17 NLS. HSL. Dep. 268 no 21: Committee Book Gaelic Society 1783: 19/3/1784: 'Resolved That Mr Secretary Mackenzie be requested to write to Mr [James] Finlay of Glasgow to ask his assistance in procuring an active young man who can play well on the pipe, and who will hire himself as a Waiter, or Servant to Mr Campbell of the Shakespeare, [the Society met in the Shakespeare Head Tavern in Covent Garden] Mr Campbell to maintain him, and the Society to make him an Annual Allowance in proportion to his merit & Good Conduct.' 2/3/1785 – 'Resolved that Twelve Guineas be given to the Piper for this years wages, exclusive of the Highland Dress Complete.' At first the post of piper to the Highland Society of Scotland was more than decorative, however: the early Edinburgh piping competitions were administered by John MacArthur, assisted by the Society's 'Officer', Donald MacDonald. See below, p.75.

18 Mackenzie, *Report of the Committee of the Highland Society of Scotland, appointed to inquire into the nature and authenticity of the poems of Ossian, op.cit.*

19 *Dictionarium Scoto-Celticum. A Dictionary of the Gaelic Language* (2 vols. Edinr., 1828).

the Gaelic language as being in a flourishing condition. Indeed it was quite certain that Gaelic had 'found a refuge in the Highlands of Scotland as a sanctuary in which it might expire', and congratulated itself on having 'seized the happy moment for treasuring up in its archives the words which, though spoken, may soon cease to be heard, and preserving the seal of a decaying record'.[20] Having identified the language as a species of Celtic antiquity – and as such obviously therefore doomed – the Society was content to compile a record while it still existed, and considered its obligations as thereby discharged. There was no further activity by the Highland Society of Scotland in support of Gaelic language or literature for nearly half a century thereafter.[21]

Here, then, we see interest in the Highlands and Gaelic culture channelled through two quasi-governmental agencies dedicated to making more effective the exploitation of the Highlands as an economic and military resource. The full weight of the Scottish landed interest lay behind the Highland Societies of London and Scotland, which enjoyed a complex web of ties with parliament and the crown. The whole undertaking was underpinned by Adam Smith's declaration that the interests of the landlord and the general interest of society were one and the same.

The spirit of capitalistic enterprise which informed the Societies' activities ensured that the mechanism of competition would be central to their approach. Since competition was held to affect the distribution of knowledge as well as of economic resources, it was seen as the ultimate engine of growth and the key, therefore, to cultural as well as to material production.[22] This is an aspect of 'the rage for improvement' frequently overlooked, the idea that the traditional performing arts, language, even, could be taken in hand and governed by the principles of rational management and modern efficiency. Highland bulls and heifers, draught horses, ploughmen, sheep-shearers, poets and pipers – all might be made to compete and be subject to the disciplines of the market.

It was natural, therefore, that the Highland Society of London, casting about for a means to promote the pipe and its music, should seize upon competition as the most effective way of achieving its goal. The minutes record that 'it was determined to institute a Competition of Highland Pipers annually, as the only means within the reach of the Society of preserving and cultivating antient Pipe Music . . . The Black Cattle Fairs held annually at Falkirk, & which led many Highlanders thither, pointed out that place as then the most suitable for such a Competition'.[23]

The Falkirk Tryst, 'that great gathering of men and bestial',[24] was one of the

20 Ramsay, *Highland and Agricultural Society*, pp.135–7; see also Derick S. Thomson, ed., *Companion to Gaelic Scotland* (Oxford, 1983), p.61.
21 Ramsay, *Highland and Agricultural Society*, pp.137–8.
22 D. P. O'Brien, *The Classical Economists* (Oxford, 1975), pp.30–31.
23 HSL, NLS, Dep 268 no 21: Committee Book Gaelic Society 1783, 9/2/1811.
24 John Strang, *Glasgow and its Clubs* (Glasg., 1856), pp.129–30.

leading events of the Scottish year. Thousands of Highland cattle were driven to Falkirk each autumn from the furthest ends of the mainland and the Isles before being sold on into the southern market. It meant long miles on the hoof down the old drove roads through Rannoch and Lochaber and perilous passages in little boats across the Minch; the cattle from Skye were roped together nose to tail and swum across the Kyle to Glenelg.[25] It was half commercial odyssey, half social jaunt, and the poet Rob Donn MacKay lovingly records its pleasures in his journeys thither with Iain MacEachainn and Hugh MacKay of Bighouse.[26] As its names – Capella Varia, Eaglais Bhreac, Fawkirk – imply, the town had once lain within the Gaidhealtachd;[27] even now it was scarcely a day's walk from the Highland Line and little further from either Edinburgh or Glasgow. It was a place to meet friends and do business, the cross-roads of Scotland, and the first of the new piping competitions was held in the town's Masonic Lodge on 12 October 1781, to be repeated, annually at first, and later triennially, for nearly seventy years, although not in its original location, as we shall see.

The Highland Society of London did not at any time directly run these competitions; it relied instead upon local organisations, the first three events coming under the aegis of the Glasgow Gaelic Club (which was an affiliated branch of the London Society), the remainder under that of the Highland Society of Scotland. It was a committee of the Glasgow Club which actually devised the format in consultation with various Highland gentlemen shortly before the first event was held.[28] The London Society maintained overall control by putting up the prize money, some £20.00 per annum throughout the period. Administrative and other costs were met by admission charges, so that the events were, at the very least, self-financing. The competition was advertised as follows:

A handsome Highland Pipe of the best construction is appointed to be given annually by the Highland Society of London to the best Player on that instrument and also forty merks in money – likewise thirty merks to be given to each of the two next best players – The competition to be annually at Falkirk Tryste in October.[29]

Thirteen pipers attended in 1781 at the Masonic Lodge in the Back Row of Falkirk, a small two-story building on a sloping site, situated just north of the High Street. It contained a dwelling house and a Lodge Room, with stables and other offices grouped round a small courtyard in which the pipers actually performed. They wore their everyday clothing and played four tunes of their own

25 A. R. B. Haldane, *The Drove Roads of Scotland* (Lond., 1952), p.75, and *passim*.
26 Grimble, pp.82–3.
27 W. F. H. Nicolaisen, *Scottish Place-Names their Study and Significance* (Lond., 1986; first published 1976), pp. 7–16.
28 Minutes of the Glasgow Gaelic Club, vol 1. Glasgow City Archives.
29 Glasgow Gaelic Club Minutes, 2 October, 1781, Glasgow City Archives.

choice, having drawn lots amongst themselves for the order of play. The judges were ensconced in the lodge-room above where, in order to ensure impartiality, they could not actually see who was playing. The whole event took three days.[30] The winner was Patrick MacGregor (called Patrick *na Corraig*, or 'Patrick of the Finger' because he had lost the ring-finger of his left hand and used the little finger instead), a member of a famous family of players and teachers from Fortingall in Perthshire, known collectively as *clann an sgeulaiche*. He was awarded a prize pipe made by Hugh Robertson of Edinburgh and forty merks in money (about £2.7s. sterling).[31]

This was the first, and the last, of the Highland Society of London's competitions to rely purely and simply upon an informed appreciation of the pipe and its music. The emphasis on spectacle and nationalistic fervour which was to dominate the later events began at an early stage. In 1782, for example, we find that

On the morning of the 16th the Committee preceded by the two victorious Competitors playing on their Bag Pipes which were highly ornamented with Ribbons repaired to the Church Yard of Falkirk, where the two happy victors went in procession, playing the Lament of the Clans in concert thrice round the Monuments of Sir John the Graham, Sir John Stuart & Sir Robert Munro, in presence of the Committee & of many other Gentlemen who attended to do honour to the memory of those illustrious Worthies.[32]

The urge to link the music of the pipes with antique heroism, and a highly-charged all-Scottish patriotism – even to get this quintessentially solo instrument to play ensemble – was already visible.

The reports on the early competitions in the beautifully-turned minutes of the Highland Society of Scotland and in the stately columns of the contemporary press, make the proceedings sound most formal and imposing:

October 1783 – At the annual competition for prizes, given by the Highland Society of London, which was held at Falkirk; the first prize was adjudged to

30 Macinnes, pp.32–3. See also *Falkirk Herald*, 20/04/1935, p.7; James Love, ed., *Antiquarian Notes and Queries reprinted from the Falkirk Herald* (Falkirk, 1908–1928), i,130–2; later on the building became a pub, the Masonic Arms, at the junction of what had become Silver Row and Manor Street, and was demolished in the 1960s to make way for a shopping-centre development.

31 Angus Mackay, *A Collection of Ancient Piobaireachd or Highland Pipe Music* (Wakefield 1972, reprinted from 3rd edn., Aberd., 1899; first published Edinr., 1838), 'Circumstantial Account of the Competitions for the Prizes given by the Highland Society in London, to the best performers on the Great Highland Bag-Pipe, from the year 1781', p.15.

32 NLS Dep. 268, No 15. Highland Society of London Miscellaneous Pamphlets Prospectuses etc., 1781–1895, '15th October 1782. Minute of the Proceedings at the Competition for the prizes of Piping at Falkirk'.

Neil Mac-Lean, Piper to Major Campbell of Airds; the second prize to
Archibald MacGregor, fourth son of John MacGregor, piper to Colonel
Campbell of Glenlyon; and the third to John MacGregor, Piper to the city
guard of Edinburgh. The bard *Ma can T'sior* was introduced, and pronounced
his annual Gaelic poem, in praise of the martial music and prowess of the
Caledonians: and the whole was concluded with a grand procession to the
church-yard . . . On the return of the Pipers from Falkirk, by Edinburgh, it
was conceived by many gentlemen, that an exhibition of their abilities would
be a very agreeable entertainment to the public; it was accordingly arranged,
that it should take place on the following Wednesday, in Dunn's Assembly
Rooms . . .[33]

For the competition of 1783, however, we possess a rare contemporary document:
a detailed eye-witness account of what actually went on, from a privileged insider
who was present throughout the extraordinary events which took place in Falkirk
and Edinburgh in the autumn of that year. It shows a reality – drunken, anarchic,
seething with social antagonism and institutional rivalry – which is very much at
variance with the smooth facade which the Directors of the Highland Society
were accustomed to present to the public. It takes the form of a lengthy
confidential report to John Mackenzie, Secretary of the Highland Society of
London, from a certain Mr. Trigge, man of business to the youthful laird of
Clanranald,[34] who was closely involved in the controversy at Falkirk and the
subsequent decision by the Edinburgh party to commandeer the event and re-
run it in the capital, all of which Trigge observed with high, malicious glee. 'Dear
Sir', he wrote:

> By this time You will think the Pipers have Blowen me below ground when I
> have neither answered Your friendly letter which I recd. at Falkirk the Morng.
> before the Competition nor given You as usewall any history of the particulars
> of that Competition which I am sorry to say will not Add Lusture to those
> concerned but Before I finish this I hope I shall be eable to make not only
> some Attonement for my Sylance and affoord You Some entertainment to the
> Bargain.
>   As I wrote You Clanranald was to Attend in person at Falkirk Competition
> he ordered me accordingly to run an Express Upon the Sunday preceeding to
> secure lodging for himself and friends whow all Sett out that day and came to
> Falkirk Monday Forenoon expecting the Competition would have been held
> upon the Tryst day tuesday – I left Edinr. monday & took my rout by
> Boness where I lodged there that night in company wt. me in the Carriage

33 MacKay, *Ancient Piobaireachd*, 'Circumstantial Account', p.15.
34 John MacDonald, 17th laird of Clanranald, who died in 1794 at the age of 29. At the
    time of the affair at Falkirk he can scarcely have been twenty years old. Mackenzie,
    History of the MacDonalds, pp.435–6.

Mr. Menzies of the Customhouse an excellent Judge of our favourite Ancient Musick . . . and wt. us upon Horseback Professor [John] McArthur and afoot old [Donald] McIntyre from Rannoch [who won the prize pipe in 1785 in his seventy-fifth year] [Donald] Gun late of the 77th. & [John] McGrigor of the City Gaurd getting his lesson upon the Road from McIntyre 3rd Prize at Falkirk he was so vary bade a performer that I thought the poor Fellow would not have been permitted to performe. –

Arriving early on Tuesday morning, he found Clanranald in a state of umbrage because there had been a mix up about the date of the competition and the representatives of the Glasgow Gaelic Club had not yet appeared. Clanranald was unable to convene an ad-hoc bench and, when the Glasgow party turned up that evening, their social overtures were rebuffed:

In the Morng. of tuesday we arrived at Falkirk before Brekfast when I found my Friend Clan[ranald] Just sitting down to Brekfast wt. whom I took parte. he was much displeased (I ommitted [Hugh] Robertson the Pipe maker wt. the Prize Pipes to be among my Army of Pipers) that that mighty Dons of the Committee from Glasgow had not arrived and proceeded upon the stated day and indeed the Competitors were in as bade Blood for detaining them.

   The Clan ordered me to conveen the whole Competitors & that he and Some other Gentlemen there would Sitt as Judges and finish the business, but I advised him agt. that measure however he was determined to returne to Edinr. that [?]Evng . . . But a little before he went about 6 that mighty Webster [i.e. 'wabster' = weaver] as McNabb calls him [James] Findlay wt' Mr. Shoemaker McIntosh[35] cam in greate State to waite on the Clan he went out and I [?] him to the next Room where after some Glasgow Bows Scrapes and will You do us the Honour to Sup with us Mr Blacksmith [William] Robertson & an Old Buttler [Malcolm] McGillivray[36] and so on which being rejected & some appoligeys for not being there Monday so the Clan made them a Bow & was about to Step into his Company when the Gigantick weaver beged he would Honour them wt. nameing any Gentlemen of his Acquanitance to be of the number of Judges he named my friend Mr. Menzies who they accepted of most redily and desired he would be sent to Supp wt. them and he went but finding himself deserted he returned Back to this company not being accustomed to such impolite treatment nor indeed to associate wt. arogant Tradesmen –

35 The Finlay family were important in the textile trade in cotton and linen-weaving and the import and export of yarn: see Anthony Slaven, *The Development of the West of Scotland: 1750–1960* (Lond., 1975), pp.89–90. George McIntosh of Dunchattan, a leading member of the Glasgow business community with interests in glass-making, the manufacture of dye-stuffs, shoe-making and the West India trade, President of the Glasgow Gaelic Club 1780–81. William Robertson was elected President in 1781. Dr. Hugh McLeod was Secretary. See also Strang, pp.147–9, *n*.
36 Malcolm McGilvra, the father of the Glasgow Gaelic Club, Strang, p.146.

There was conflict between the predominantly landed/legal Edinburgh party and the business people from Glasgow about practically every detail of the competition: when it should be held, the delivery of the prize pipe, the appointment of old John MacGregor as the Highland Society's piper, the choice of judges, and, of course, the results. There was an immediate dispute concerning a commission for John MacGregor as piper to the Highland Society of London, the Glasgow people rejecting belated instructions issued to the Edinburgh party to this effect. This resulted in the old man being forced to appear as a competitor, which the Edinburgh people regarded as a deliberate slight. According to Trigge, the results were cooked up in advance by the Glasgow bench, who brought in a leet of beardless boys headed by Neil MacLean, (later appointed piper to the Glasgow Gaelic Club). He stated that the senior pipers were indignant and signed a declaration to the effect that John MacArthur ought to have won, as easily the most able amongst them, and that they would not compete under the auspices of the Glasgow Gaelic Club again. Trigge suggested that the judgement of the Glasgow party had in any case been significantly impaired by drink:

Wedy. Morng. in Mr Menzies & my way to the so much Celebrated Competition called at the Post Office where I found Your letter which I directly produced to the Committee but they said as they did before that they would not pay the least respect to Your letter and that You had used them no as well as the first Year . . . by Sending Agents & Pepole from Edinr & other Places among them I took greate care to behave wt the outmost moderation never saying a Single Word they could possibly find fault wt. by this time the Competition was pretty farr Advanced – McIntosh the only decent person among them brought me Your letter to them & the Minuet which I had Scarce red when the Blacksmith and the Old Buttler was in upon us seemingly in a great rage. I took no notice went to the Large room took my Seat by the Fyre from where I rose not till the Competition was over. But finding old McGregor Compeating I was not pleased then and told Mr McIntosh that I supposed they had done that to Cutt the poor man out of his hundred Merks [presumably the fee due to him as piper designate of the Society] and I was [?] soone going to Stop him however to avoid a Bustle I lett him go on –

I discovered the preceding evening that [John] McAllister Findlay's Goad had been brought in purppose to Act as there Piper & that they determined that McGrigor Should not receive employment and that the Prize Pipes was to be given to Neil M'Lean all of which came out to be true.

The Prizes were now adudged 1st to Neil Macklean 2d to Archd. McGrigor 3d to John McGrigor – McLean the 1st Year of the Competition was Sett down as one of the four Bade Pipers 2nd. the Same and this Year in the Spring he went Six weeks to Young John McGrigor to receive further instruction and in that period he has made Such rapid Progress as to Beat all the Pipers in Scotland – Archd. McGrigor being asked if he thought himself a Boy of 16 Years better than his ffather he said in answer if he was that what for needed he be getting lessons from him . . . the Young Lads were so much dashed that the Prizes were bestowed upon them when so many able performers were there that they were out of all Countenance the oldest of the three not 19 Years – and every Piper there called out when they heard [Professor John] M'Arthur Play that it was needless for them to lift a Pipe where he was and they have signed a declaration to that effect . . . the whole exclaiming aloud they never would come where there were a Glasgow Committee.

This Committee made Choice the preceeding Evng. of McGillavrey to be President to fill the Chair intended to have been the seat of one of the First & greatest Chiftains in Scotland the Clan who says the Chair is now defyled Findlay & Stewart of Balahulish perpetuall Judges wt. the others I believe as Mr. McIntosh told me were not an hour in bed during the Competition the Mug went round ffreely wt. drink to Quench the druith occasioned by the overnights Cups.

At this juncture, two lowland gentlemen, Capt. Clerk of Loanhead and John Clerk of Eldin, who happen to be present, proposed (apparently at the suggestion of Clanranald) that the competition be re-run in Edinburgh promising the pipers ample reward. Most of the latter complied and, despite it being between law terms and also the week of Kelso races, an elegant and appreciative audience was assembled:

Capt. Clark of Lonhead son of Sir Geo. Clark of Penniecook one of the Commissioners of the Customs here and his Uncle John Clark of Eldin Attended at Falkirk and were mostly wt. me dureing tuesday and a parte of Wednd. but seeing things go in the partial manner they did wt a most Noble Spirit as the Clan had before told me that they as lowlanders would redress the Grievances of the Pipers and not only give their aid to encourge these Musicians but to promote the good intentions of the London Highland Society & ordered me to invite the Competitors to Edinr. where they should be treated in the most friendly manner and amply rewarded but nothing would do unless I would assure them that the Glasgow People were not to be there & that the Seat of Competition would in future be removed At length I prevailed upon them all except the four McGrigors . . . McLean came to me too willing to go wt. me but he was Poisioned and went home but [John] McAlister did keep his Word and came in afterwards but out of 28 Tunes wrote down by the Professor and old [Donald] McIntyre for the Performers he could not play one for the History of our Splendid Exhibition I referr You to the enclosed two Printed Copies as published in the Edinr. Evg. Courrant Monday Oct 27th –

The Company was most brileant Honoured wt. the first Ladys in Town the Earle of Buchan his Bror. Lord Advocate Lord Swinton Sir Thos. Dundass &c . . .in short it was astonishing how so Elegant a company could be brought out on so short a notice. The Town this vacancy time and the

Week of the Kelso Races – They were so highly pleased that they called out
for another days Exhibition in Shorte the ?Spirite of Joy and the outmost
Satisfaction was to be seen in every Countenance some of the Ladies &
Gentlemen went to the Tea Room and danced Strathspeys as I had Pipers
that played Reals for the purpose of inspireing the Ladys – The Old Bard I
taught to Clap below his leg which affoorded high fune But this Youll say was
rather harde duty for my poor Corpus and now was obliged to take the whole
Active parte upon my Self & indeed I was wore out by the time I gott home
– In shorte for this four weeks past my habitation has never been free of
Pipeing from morng. to night the Walls may be rent – [37]

What seems to be going on here is a calculated attempt to destroy the Glasgow
Gaelic Club as a credible body in the eyes of the Highland Society of London. We
find Trigge, with easy affability building support amongst the pipers; the opening
of a privileged channel of communication with the London Society, the ostentatious presence of prominent Highland gentry like Clanranald and MacNab to
outface the Glasgow Dons with their purchased acres; the pipers' declaration
repudiating the Glasgow Club (framed by whom?), the seemingly fortuitous
presence of the two Clerks (each a little later to become a Director of the
Edinburgh-based Highland Society of Scotland); the ostensibly spontaneous
suggestion of rerunning the competition in a different place immediately acted
upon, and with a smooth efficiency that suggests prior planning; the rather select
audience which appears out of nowhere at the deadest time in the Edinburgh social
calendar (is this why Clanranald returned so quickly to town?). The more closely
one considers the affair, the more it begins to look like a carefully planned coup.

The Glasgow Gaelic Club went on during the following century to become an
important social and philanthropic institution. But in the eyes of Clanranald and
his ilk, the Glasgow people were social upstarts usurping the privileges of the
ancien régime, and they had to be put firmly in their place. Their president,
George McIntosh, for example, was a self-made man, who had begun life as a
clerk in a tannery, and membership of the Club was effectively limited to Gaelic
speakers, since the society conducted its meetings in that language. And so
control was wrested from a Celtic institution with genuine populist roots by an
agency based in the eastern Lowlands which was aristocratic in social composition and highly ambiguous in cultural outlook.[38] From the ad-hoc committee set
up to oversee the Edinburgh competition in the autumn of 1783, the Highland
Society at Edinburgh, later 'of Scotland' directly sprang. The new Society was
made responsible for the Falkirk competition the following year and upon

---

37 HSL, NLS Dep. 268, Correspondence 1. 1 October 1781 – 30 Sept 1820. Dunn's
    Assembly Rooms lay in West Register Street. In 1787 the competition was held in the
    George Street Assembly Rooms, then in the Adelphi Theatre, and from 1796 in the
    Theatre Royal: see Dalyell, pp.96–7.

38 Strang, p.130.

various pretexts its commissioners, led by John Clerk of Eldin, removed it permanently to the capital, where it took its place amongst the diversions of Leith races week when the town was crowded with people of quality.[39]

The new dispensation at once brought with it a more formal and elaborate structure, seemingly intended to introduce as much variety as possible for the sake of a new and more miscellaneous audience. Competitors played two tunes rather than four as formerly, with no more than about half a dozen being heard at a time without an intermission. The event opened with a salute played by Professor MacArthur, now Piper to the Highland Society of Scotland, and under whose immediate supervision (assisted by the Society's 'officer' Donald Mac-Donald) the event took place.[40] The competition was divided into two parts. In the first, the contestants played a tune of their own choice in order determined beforehand by ballot. During an interval, Duncan Bàn MacIntyre declaimed a poem in praise of Gaelic and the music of the pipes. Then came the second part of the contest in which all the competitors played a set tune, this year *A' Ghlas Mheur* – 'The Finger Lock'.[41] The 'Acts' were further interspersed with 'Several Highland Reels and Strathspeys danced by the Candidates with much Spirit, and the approbation of a numerous and intelligent company of Ladies and Gentlemen who appeared much pleased with the whole performance' and was concluded with a song by the bard Campbell and another piece from Professor MacArthur. A further innovation led to all the competitors and the bards wearing 'Highland dress'. This was to become mandatory a little afterwards.

At the same time, the chilling condescension and social distance which was to mark relations between competitors and sponsors after the Napoleonic Wars, had clearly yet to develop. Not only was the 1784 competition actually run by a piper, but the contestants (sixteen of them who were all apparently able players) were consulted about who they thought should be in the prize list:

On Wednesday the 20th the Judges again met and took the opinion of the Revd. Mr. Robertson McGrigor Chaplain to the Highland Society of Edinr. and of others skilled in Gaelic Music as well as of the different Candidates themselves with regard to the Merits of the different Competitors and determined as follows, viz.

The first Prize of an Elegant pipe and 40 Merks Scots to John McGrigor

39 Highland Society of Scotland, Sederunt Book 1, ff.47–51.
40 *Scots Magazine*, vol.46, Oct. 1784, p.553.
41 In modern conditions this would be unendurably tedious, because each piper would play the same setting (either *Piobaireachd Society*, 2nd ser., i, 8–9, or *Kilberry Book of Ceol Mor*, p.52, see Chs. 18 and 20); and the fact that a single tune could be set as a test piece in this way is an indication, even if no other evidence survived on this point, that the old pipers had their individual settings; and that a gifted individual's interpretation of a tune was an important part of the aesthetic satisfaction that the pipe and its music had to offer. This was lost as soon as fixed printed settings became the norm.

from Fortingall Perthshire who with the additional merit of having already taught above 50 Military Pipers himself is the oldest of six sons taught by their father John McGregor with above 90 other Pipers.

The Second prize of 30 Merks to Donald Fisher from Breadalbane in Perthshire who also possess a great deal of merit for though only a day labourer did by his own study and application arrive at great proficiency and Skill in playing, and the 3rd Prize of 30 Merks was given to Dougal McDougal from Lorne Argyleshire and the prizes were accordingly delivered. At the same time the merits of the other performers were properly acknowledged by the Preses in presence of the Judges, and the whole Candidates were each of them presented with some money in consideration of their Different Merits and for indemnifying their expenses, travelling Charges &c. And a Silver plate was ordered to be engraved and fixed upon the Prize Pipe expressing the preference of John Macgregor in whose favours the first prize was adjudged.[42]

It was at this stage that the idea of the 'rehearsal' was introduced, a mechanism which was to become a useful source of power in later years because it enabled the sponsors to determine who was allowed to play and who was not. But the competition had not yet surrendered to the demands of showbiz; indeed the 1784 formula probably made for a stimulating and worthwhile event. Nor had the balance of cultural power shifted so decisively in favour of the patrons; in 1784 the 'rehearsal' was a means of listening to the players in a more relaxed, non-competitive atmosphere in a serious attempt to establish who was the best:

> That no pains might be Spared in acquiring a knowledge of the Merits of the different performers, the Committee attended at three different rehearsals of the whole of the Candidates besides Several private Meetings previous to the bringing them to the tryal in public.

This was to be the pattern for the next several years.

A number of things can be inferred about conditions of performance from the kinds of tunes the pipers offered. They were mostly quite big and would nowadays be regarded as a fair test of performer and instrument, – tunes like 'Craigellachie', 'The Blue Ribbon', 'Donald Gruamach', 'Mary's Praise', 'Lament for the Only Son', 'The End of the Great Bridge' and 'The Vaunting'. The order of performance for the first stage of the competition on Tuesday 19th October 1784 was as follows:

1. Molladh Mari, or, in praise of Mary, – by Donald Fisher, from Breadalbane, Perthshire.

42 HSS Sederunt Book 1, ff.47-51.

2. Cumhadh an aon Mhic, or, Lamentation for an only son – by Arch. Macgregor, from Fortingall, Perthshire.
3. Piobrachd mhic Dhomail Dhuibh, or Cameron's March, – by John Macgregor, from Glenlyon.
4. Glasmhear, a principal piece, – by John Cumming, piper to Sir James Grant of Grant, Bart.
5. Sliamh an t'Shirreadh, or, Sheriff-Muir, – by Robert Mackay, from Lord Rae's country.
6. Cean drochaid morre, – by John Macgregor sen. from Fortingall, Perthshire.
7. Marshall mhic Allain, or, Clanranald's March, – by John Macgregor jun. from ditto, a boy of eleven years old.
8. [Unknown] by Donald Gunn, piper to Sir John Clerk of Pennycuik, Bart.
9. Failte a Phrainse, the Prince's Welcome, – by Angus Ross, from the estate of Macintosh.
10. Cumhadh an aon Mhic, or, Lamentation for an only son – by James Monro, piper to the Canongate.
11. Failte Mhaircais, the Marquis's Welcome – by Donald Buchanan, from Paisley.
12. Cean drochaid bige – by David Ross, piper to his Grace the Duke of Athol.
13. Colladh a ruin – by Dugald McDugald, from Lorne, Argyleshire.
14. Suan agus Lagan, Stewart's March – by Alexander Lamont, piper to the Laird of Lamont.
15. Failte Shir Sheumais, Sir James's Welcome – by Colin McNab, piper to McNab of McNab.
16. Marshall mhic Allain, or, Clanranald's March – by Duncan Sinclair, from Monteath.[43]

It suggests that the performers were allowed to tune up properly beforehand, thus settling their instruments, and also, perhaps, that they were not penalised for pausing briefly to re-tune during performance. Indeed we know this must have happened, because both of these practices were expressly forbidden in later years. We then see players of stature like John Bàn MacKenzie winning major prizes with slight pieces like 'The Gordon's Salute', which, at the probably crisp tempo of contemporary performances, would not have required the pipe to stay in tune for more than four or five minutes.[44]

We know something about the audience, too, in 1784. One of those present was the celebrated economist, Adam Smith, another his friend, Barthélemy Faujas de Saint Fond, a distinguished visiting French geologist who described the

43 *Scots Magazine*, *op.cit.*
44 MacInnes, p.38; see also Dalyell MSS, Gen 355D f.13.

experience in his book *Voyage en Angleterre, en Écosse et aux Îles Hébrides* published in Paris in 1797. Faujas wrote:

He asked me one day, whether I was fond of music? I answered, that it formed one of my chief delights, whenever I was so fortunate as to hear it well executed. 'So much the better', said he; 'I shall put you to a proof which will be very interesting for me; for I shall take you to hear a kind of music of which it is impossible you can have formed any idea, and it will afford me great pleasure to know the impression it makes upon you'.

Next morning at nine o' clock, Smith came to my lodgings. At ten he conducted me to a spacious concert-room, plainly but neatly decorated, and full of people. I saw, however, neither orchestra, musicians, nor instruments. We sat waiting for more than half an hour. A large empty space in the middle of the room was surrounded with benches which were occupied by gentlemen only; the ladies were dispersed among the other seats. 'These there,' said he, alluding to the gentlemen who sat in the middle, 'are the judges of the competition which is about to take place among the musicians. Almost all of them are landlords living in the Isles or Highlands of Scotland; they are thus the natural judges of the contest; they will award a prize to him who shall best perform a piece of music which is a favourite with the Scots. The same air will be played by all the competitors, no matter how many of them there may be.'

A few moments later, a folding door opened at the bottom of the room, and to my great surprise I saw a Scottish Highlander enter, in his costume of Roman soldier, playing upon the bagpipe, and walking up and down the empty space with rapid steps and a military air, blowing the noisiest and most discordant sounds from an instrument which lacerates the ear.[45] The air he played was a kind of sonata, divided into three parts. Smith begged me to give it my whole attention, and to tell him afterwards the impression it made upon me.

But I confess that at first I could distinguish neither air nor design in the music. I only saw with the piper marching always with rapidity; and with the same warlike countenance. He made incredible efforts both with his body and his fingers to bring into play at once the different pipes of his instrument, [this will have been Fisher tuning up] which made an insupportable uproar.

He received nevertheless great applause from all sides. A second musician followed alone into the arena, wearing the same martial look and walking to

---

45 Faujas elsewhere likened Highland dress to the ancient Roman tunic and toga, a fairly commonplace observation, *vide* the contemporary song which refers to the kilt as 'the garb of old Gaul'. Presumably the apparition thus beheld was Donald Fisher of Breadalbane, playing – there is a little confusion here between morning and afternoon sessions – either 'Mary's Praise' or 'The Finger Lock'.

and fro with the same haughty air. [presumably this was Archibald MacGregor, playing 'The Lament for the Only Son'] He seemed to excel the first competitor; as I judged from the clapping of hands and cries of *bravo* that resounded on every side; grave men and high-bred women shed tears at the third part of the air.

After having listened to eight pipers in succession, I began to suspect that the first part was connected with a warlike march and military evolutions: the second with a sanguinary battle, which the musician sought to depict by the noise and rapidity of his playing and by his loud cries. [presumably as expressed through his instrument: an earlier translation renders this passage as 'he endeavoured by a rapid succession of loud and discordant sounds to represent the clashing of arms, shrieks of the wounded, and all the horrors of a field of battle'.[46]] He seemed then to be convulsed; his pantomimical gestures resembled those of a man engaged in combat; his arms, his hands, his head, his legs, were all in motion; the sounds of his instrument were all called forth and confounded together at the same moment. This fine disorder seemed keenly to interest every one.

The piper then passed, without transition, to a kind of andante; his convulsions suddenly ceased: he became sad and overwhelmed in sorrow; the sounds of his instrument were plaintive, languishing, as if lamenting the slain who were being carried off from the field of battle. This was the part which drew tears from the eyes of the beautiful Scotch ladies.[47]

This passage shows the response of a disciplined and cultivated mind to an overwhelming initial experience and, within its obvious limitations, it is as vivid and detailed a picture of Highland pipers in actual performance as exists in an eighteenth century source. It is not uncluttered by preconceptions, however. Faujas saw and heard what he expected to see and hear, based upon his earlier musical experiences. He was acute enough, for example, to infer the presence of form – the tune was a kind of 'sonata', the ground was an 'andante', and he intuitively sought for a referential intention, i.e. he tried to 'read' it as narrative, talking about the clash of arms, the shrieks of the wounded, lamentations for the slain and so forth. This was, perhaps, inspired by fiddle versions of piobaireachd with which he may have been acquainted, such as 'A Highland Battle', which appears in James Oswald's *Caledonian Pocket Companion*, (15 vols., London, c.1747–69, a major and readily-accessible source) where the different sections of

---

46 Quoted in 'The Pipes', *OT*, 27/9/1884, p.3, which was presumably taken from the London edition of 1799, or from the abridgement in Mavor's *British Tourists* (vol.5, 1814).

47 Faujas, ii, 246–9. What Smith may not have known was that Faujas had encountered the pipes before, at Oban, on his way to Staffa, and absolutely hated them: *ibid.*,i, 319–21; in Edinburgh, however, he was obliged to give the music his considered attention for the first time.

the tune have descriptive labels like 'The battle begins', 'The preparation for a retreat', and 'The lamentation for the chief'.[48]

On the other hand, he records things we might feel inclined to question, such as the pipers' furious pace, bodily agitation, and facial contortions.[49] And he describes other things, like changes in dynamic, the piper's ability to increase or decrease the volume, that he cannot have experienced in actuality. Although he was listening to the cream of the profession in the central belt and southern Highlands,[50] whose playing must have been persuasive to a degree, we gain the impression that Faujas was disturbed by the experience. It may be that he was earnestly trying to respond to it in the approved manner as an example of the nobly barbaric, but had to give up the attempt: 'I confess that it was impossible for me to admire any of them. I thought them all of equal proficiency; that is to say the one was as bad as the other . . .' He shrank before what he perceived as the music's intimidating volume, harsh timbre, and discordant harmonies. But contact with this musical expression of the living epic prompted in this cultivated European a by now familiar pattern of associations: antique glamour, Celtic melancholy, heroism and doom. He concluded:

> I do not know to what period, probably a very ancient one, the institution of these prizes goes back. It is not known if the competition has always taken place in the town of Edinburgh, on account of the distance of the Highlands, or if it was Queen Mary [i.e. Mary Queen of Scots] who transferred it to her capital.[51]

His assumption that the competition was at least two centuries old is a telling one. It was, of course, a brand new event. This was the first time that it had been formally held in Edinburgh.

---

48   For a text of this tune and a commentary, see Johnson, *Scottish Fiddle Music*, pp. 119, 122, 126, 138–42.

49   The earliest instruction manuals prescribe a dignified and stately carriage, and gravity, or at least sedateness, of facial expression. See, for example, Cannon, *Compleat Theory*, pp.79–80; see also Donald MacDonald, *A Collection of the Ancient Martial Music of Caledonia, called Piobaireachd* (Wakefield 1974, facsimile reprint of 3rd edn., Edinr., 1822), 'Instructions for the Great Highland Bagpipe', p.2. That 'facial contortions' were notwithstanding this frequently indulged in may be inferred from popular references to 'the girning piper race'.

50   See MacInnes, pp. 6, 97, 99.

51   Faujas, ii, 253.

5

'A brilliant assemblage of beauty and elegance, rank and fashion': The Competitions of the Highland Societies of London and Scotland, 1800–1844

As the competitions entered the nineteenth century, the programmes became more elaborate and theatrical: new dances, cudgel playing and Gaelic songs were introduced.[1] When the Highland Society of London, anxious as ever about the state of its funds, proposed to make the event biennial, this was strongly resisted by the Scottish society on the grounds that 'such an alteration would be very prejudicial in tending in a Great Degree to Retard the Cultivation of the Antient Martial Bag Pipe music.' In any case, the event was making money; the receipts were in 'considerable surplus'.[2]

The ambience became increasingly militaristic. As the war with France drew to its close, Sir John Sinclair of Ulbster, a prominent lowland 'improver' whose personal acquaintance with the pipe and its music was slight, could be found delivering heady speeches from the Preses chair, full of lofty rhetoric about Highland Gallantry and Waterloo, and the splendid efforts of the Highland Societies on the home front. The latter were especially important because, as he remarked,

> Had it not been for the encouragement granted by the Highland Society of London, and attention given by the Highland Society of Scotland, to the practice of the Highland Pipe, and the liberal countenance bestowed by the patriotic Inhabitants of Edinburgh to these annual competitions, there would not perhaps have been a single piper now living, qualified to rouse by his martial strains, the enthusiastic spirit of his Countrymen.[3]

The evolution of the event from music competition into 'national display', reached its apogee in the early 1820s. There were troops of garishly accoutred dancers, cute little boy pipers (including, on one occasion, Angus MacKay), grizzled war veterans with chestfuls of medals, all in spectacular 'Highland Dress'. They appeared against a painted backdrop depicting romantic Highland scenery arranged in cunning ways so that when the pipers marched on to the

---

1 Highland Society of Scotland, Sederunt Book no 4, pt. 1 June 1803 – December 1808, 14/7/1804.
2 HSS, Sederunt Book no 4, pt. 1, 4/3/1804; 23/11/1804; 6/6/1814.
3 Highland Society of London Papers, NLS, Dep. 268, Minutes, 1814–1816, 26/8/1815.

stage in a body as the curtain went up, it looked as if the Campbells were coming.[4]

The 1822 competition took place in an atmosphere of feverish excitement ahead of the impending visit of George IV, and it provided an ideal opportunity to work up a proper enthusiasm for Celtic chic. The report published in the *Edinburgh Advertiser* was gushingly full, and quite typical of the contemporary press in its tendency to view the proceedings wholly as spectacle:

> On Tuesday last the Annual competition for the Prizes given by the Highland Society of London to the Five best performers on the Great Highland Bagpipe, was held in the Theatre Royal here. The number of pipers who came up to attend the competition was unusually great – no fewer than thirty qualified to compete, besides several who had formerly gained Prize Pipes . . .
>
> From the necessity of limiting the number of Performers at the public Competition, and their general merit as players, the Judges had considerable difficulty, at the previous rehearsal, in selecting those who were to play in public . . . Seventeen pipers were ultimately fixed to compete for the prizes . . .
>
> The performance began by a tune on the prize pipe, precisely at 12 o' clock, so as to interfere as little as possible with the race, which the Stewards had obligingly postponed an hour later than usual. The house was crowded in every part. In the boxes particularly there was a most brilliant assembly of our fair countrywomen; many of whom wore tartan scarfs or other ornaments appropriate to the occasion. Some indeed were remarked in the full Highland costume of tartan robes and bonnets. When the curtain was raised the whole competitors, Pipers and Dancers, were seen arranged round the stage, and the various cheques of the lively tartans worn by above sixty fine Highlanders, in their full native dress, had a very pleasing effect . . .
>
> The decision of the several prizes was announced by their Preses, Sir John Sinclair, as follows: –
>
> The first, an elegant Pipe, handsomely mounted, and adorned with a flag bearing the national emblem of the thistle, and with a silver plate, on which there has since been engraved the proper inscription, with forty merks in money, [*c.* £2.20] to Donald Mackay, piper to Ranald George Macdonald, Esq. of Clanranald, M.P.
>
> The second prize, 60 merks, [*c.* £3.30] to John [Bàn] McKenzie, piper to Duncan Davidson, Esq., of Tulloch . . .

---

4 A contemporary noted that 'two thirds of the audience . . . comes merely to see the dancers . . .' and there can be little doubt about the basis of this appeal: a writer in 1809 says 'in the course of their springs and caperings [the dancers] would doubtless have alarmed the sensitive feelings of a member of the Society for the suppression of vice . . . for the wounded delicacy of the ladies of the pit' and, 1817, 'the exposed limbs of the dancers are sometimes exhibited to the view in a manner altogether superfluous . . .' quoted in MacInnes, pp. 65–6.

Previous to delivering the Prizes, Sir John Sinclair addressed the audience . . . 'It is with much pleasure that I have this day witnessed another competition of Highland Pipers. It is a species of public entertainment to which I have always been partial. It tends to preserve that martial spirit for which the Scottish nation has so long been celebrated; for there is no real Scotsman who would not march to battle with more alacrity to the animating sound of the bagpipe, than to that of any other warlike instrument . . .'

The audience, as usual, was highly delighted with the Highland reels and strathspeys . . . in which the dancers greatly exerted themselves. The peculiar music of the Piobrach . . . perhaps may have something monotonous to an ear unaccustomed to it. The dancing, however, is at once relished by strangers, as well as by natives; and, as Sir John observed, 'if there is not much elegance in Highland dancing, – strength, agility, and spirit, are abundantly displayed'.

After the prizes had been delivered, the preses, in name of the Judges expressed how much the Committee were gratified by so brilliant an assemblage of beauty and elegance, of rank and fashion.[5]

The cost of this elaborate spectacle, and the administrative effort required to mount it, both rose steadily. Against the annual grant from the Highland Society of London, the takings at the door, and cash carried forward from previous years, had to be set the costs of advertising, printing tickets, programmes and posters, theatre hire, paying a band of music, engaging rooms for two days of rehearsals before the show itself, a team of police constables to act as stewards, general clerical support, payments to theatre staff and bill-posters, refreshments for the judges, the prize pipe itself with its ribbons and engraved plate, and the travelling expenses of the competitors, which were normally reimbursed at a rate of about 2d per mile. This amounted annually to a substantial sum. When the races were moved to Musselburgh, however, audience attendance began to decline. On May 5th 1827, the Highland Society of London voted to suspend its subsidy for a year, and as the Scottish society steadily refused to treat piping as a suitable object of expenditure, the contest could not go on. A triennial pattern was adopted, which prevailed until the events were stopped altogether after 1844.[6]

5 *Edinburgh Advertiser,* 2 August, 1822, in HSL Miscellaneous Pamphlets Prospectuses etc., 1781–1895, NLS Dep. 268, No. 19. See also *Kelso Chronicle,* 3 August, 1832, p.3: 'cold indeed must be the Scottish heart that does not warm to the tartan. The form of the mountaineer may be rugged, and his features weather-worn and grave, and the music which he loves so well may seem wild and incomprehensible to ears unused to it; but his heart is kind, and it will not readily be forgotten how his place was ever in the front of battle, and how often the Pibroch, to which he charged, swelled gradually into the proud notes of victory . . .'

6 HSS, Sederunt Book no.9, June 1826 – Dec. 1827, 23/6/1826, 18/6/1827; Sederunt Book no 10, Jan. 1828 – Dec.1829, 24/3/1828; HSL Minute Book, Feb. 1822 – March 1829, 5/5/1827.

Throughout these years, the judges' benches were recruited from the upper echelons of the Highland Societies and it was here, and more especially in the committees which served them, that ultimate power lay. Qualifications for judging were modest: one simply had to be a 'gentleman', an 'enthusiast' and 'in Town' during the competition. A quorum was five, but there was in practice no upper limit on numbers, and the opportunity to see and be seen, and to exercise a little authority in public, seems to have exerted a strong appeal. There were no fewer than 26 judges at the competition in 1800. Often they outnumbered the pipers.[7] In the early years, one might see Highland chieftains such as Clanranald and MacNab and the lairds of Lamont and Coll. But time gradually thinned the numbers of potential judges who may have had informed personal experience of the pipe and its music, and by the mid 1820s the committee was forced to draw up a list of some half-dozen people who actually knew what they were doing (presumably so that one of them at least should always be present). There was even a suggestion that two experienced professional pipers should act as assessors, but this was not adopted.[8]

One of the most important Highland Society judges was Sir John Graham Dalyell, who was responsible for a period of nearly thirty years (1815–1844) for the regulations governing the competitions and their presentation as theatrical events. He left a detailed account of this in his book *Musical Memoirs of Scotland* (Edinr., 1849) and in his extensive unpublished papers now in Edinburgh University Library. Dalyell was an antiquary and naturalist, and scion of an old West Lothian family, born at the house of Binns in August 1775. He had studied at the Universities of St. Andrews and Edinburgh, becoming a member of the Faculty of Advocates in 1796 and of the Society of the Antiquaries of Scotland in 1797, of which he later became vice-president. A prolific author in the fields of literature and history, antiquities and the natural sciences, he was knighted in 1836, and in 1841 succeeded his brother as the sixth baronet of Binns. Freed in considerable measure from the necessity of having to make a living, Dalyell haunted the General Register House, central depository of the Scottish records, and the great Advocates' Library filling voluminous notebooks in a crabbed minuscule hand on subjects like punishment, superstition, and human sacrifice.

Musical Memoirs was an influential work, an account of the musical antiquities of Scotland, beginning with three chapters on the bagpipes and bagpipe music, followed by sections on the organ, and other wind instruments, strings, percussion and keyboards. It is clear that the author did not like the pipe, and regarded its music with distaste. He began in characteristically negative fashion:

7   In 1826 it required 18 judges, headed by the Duke of Gordon, to assess 15 pipers: see
    Ruairidh Halford-MacLeod, 'The Top Twenty Piobaireachds 1824 to 1844 – and the
    influence of Donald MacDonald and Angus MacKay', in *PT*, vol.47, no.8, May 1995,
    pp.50–4 (53).
8   MacInnes, pp.50–2.

Two musical instruments were anciently cultivated by our progenitors – the Harp and the Bagpipe. Their knowledge of the former is transmitted to us only through the relics of history, for national practice has been long abandoned. But encouragement of the latter, as pertaining to the apparatus of war, being still an object of public interest, it claims precedence here on that account, though, from intrinsic quality, perhaps, it would merit none.[9]

The instrument was described as primitive and uncouth, unmelodious in tone and unpleasant to listen to.[10] Bagpipe making was 'but a sorry trade,'[11] and piobaireachds themselves 'airless airs', destitute of refinement or melody.[12] Since Dalyell assumed that ceòl mór was 'ancient', it followed that it must be artistically crude, and since he considered it also to be a plebeian form, it must therefore be inferior from an artistic point of view:

> The frequent deficiency of air, which can admit of no dispute, may be sought in the antiquity of the theme, or in that ignorance and obtuseness restraining the composer from making the most of it; nor are the condition and quality of the performer to be thrown entirely out of account . . .
>
> The Highland piobrachs are very singular compositions in all their varieties and irregularities. They are to be considered no less singular from the rudeness of the instrument for which their expression is designed, and the humble class of composers whom we may presume to be their authors.[13]

He dismissed talk of piping colleges in Mull and Skye on the grounds that Highland society was too primitive to have maintained such establishments in any proper sense and declared that canntaireachd, should it ever be recovered in written form, ought to be deposited in some public library 'as a curiosity'.[14] Nor, said Dalyell, was the repertoire anything like as extensive as some had supposed:

> I doubt whether the number of piobrachs truly amounts to 300. As little worth preserving of this kind is lost, and sufficient encouragement having been given for the last sixty years for such compositions, the sterility of invention, or the imperfections of the instrument, may have repressed that peculiar genius, promising to flourish for time to come. An extraordinary disparity must appear on comparing the national product of centuries, or

9 Dalyell, *Musical Memoirs*, p.3.
10 Dalyell, p.31; see also pp.17, 22, 85, 88, 92.
11 Dalyell, p.8.
12 Dalyell, p.14.
13 Dalyell, pp. 86, 92. In his notebooks, he added that 'the ground, theme or *urlar* scarcely merits the name of a melody.' Edinburgh University Library, Sir John Graham Dalyell MSS, Gen 425D, f.111.
14 Dalyell, *Musical Memoirs*, pp.13, 15.

contrasting the entire store with sometime above an *hundred* operas from the prolific brain of a single modern composer . . .[15]

One would be unlikely to infer from the above passage that about twenty per cent of the entries submitted in the Edinburgh competitions over which he himself had presided were new tunes.[16]

A temperament of Dalyell's rigidly evangelical cast was naturally susceptible to evidence linking the pipes with disorder, profligacy and vice, and he noted with relish how 'gambling, ebriety, nocturnal revels, and gross immoralities accompanied this subordinate species of music'.[17] He recounted anecdotes of its use by murderers, witch covens, and so forth, concluding:

> As the Highlands have been always the grand focus of insurrection here, from
> peculiarity of manners, idleness, and inaccessibility to the arm of the law, a
> language unintelligible to the more civilized districts, and other causes, so has
> the bagpipe been the concomitant of rebellion, as in Ireland.[18]

He repeatedly declared that the music was wild and irregular, despite having access to Joseph MacDonald's *Compleat Theory* and to the published collections of Donald MacDonald and Angus MacKay.[19] Since he referred to few tunes by name, however, and did not venture upon a single musical quotation, it is not evident that he had studied them.[20] He found the piping part of the competitions an ordeal, and welcomed the intervals of dancing, although even that did not escape his censure.[21] By 1822, Dalyell had managed to slim the whole event down to about 4 hours, although this created its own problems, since the rapid succession of performers gave little time for reflection and made it difficult to distinguish between them when it came to drawing up the prize-list. 'It would be vain to deny,' he wrote:

> that the music is of such a peculiar character, – executed on so strange an
> instrument; – containing a series of passages, also, at utter variance with the

---

15   Dalyell, p.17.
16   MacInnes, pp.162: Appendix V(a) details 31 new compositions entered in the
      Highland Societies' competitions between 1781–1844.
17   Dalyell, p.33.
18   Dalyell pp.23–4.
19   For a detailed account of these, see below, Chapters Six and Eight.
20   Dalyell, pp.4, *n* i, 89, 90. His attitude towards the Gaelic language was equally
      contemptuous: 'Among the objects originally designed to be under the special
      patronage of the Highland Societies of London and of Scotland was preservation of
      the Gaelic language. The utility of this will not be readily comprehended, for the
      liberal well know that the cultivation of what is neither the depository of literature
      nor generally understood must be the most unfit medium for extending civilization,
      or promoting the arts'. *Ibid.*, p.115, see also p.16.
21   Dalyell, p.103.

established rules of composition – sometimes offensive alike in melody and in harmony – so wild and warlike – and, above all, produced in hurried succession by a number of performers, several of them on the narrowest parity – is it wonderful that the auditor is bewildered – that the whole combination leaves a very indistinct impression of the qualification of individuals, such as to render the determination of preference seldom an easy matter!![22]

Restricting the number of competitors was one way of keeping the proceedings within bounds. In some years less than half the number who attended were actually allowed to perform.[23] Of the one hundred persons occupying the stage in 1835, only thirteen were pipers.[24]

The problem lay in piobaireachd as a form. It took too long to play to be compatible with the notions of fashionable entertainment which now shaped the Edinburgh competitions. Looking back through the records, Dalyell calculated that there must have been at least fifty-two tunes played at Falkirk in 1781. 'It is no wonder', he added:

> that the competition is said to have lasted three days, for it must be recollected that the *duration* of piobrachs, which seem in their nature to be strictly trammelled by rule, was by no means abridged as at present – an improvement due to later years.[25]

Dalyell was being too modest. It was he himself who had devised the various clever ways of reducing the amount of time that the audience was exposed to the disagreeable necessity of actually listening to ceòl mór. Each competitor was now restricted to a single tune, which had to be played as a kind of summary or paraphrase, omitting the normal recurrences of the ground.[26] Donald MacDonald declared that 'as the chorus of a Song is to the verses, so is the ground of a Piobaireachd to its Variations, and ought to be played after the doubling and where it happens tripling of each measure. It is also the conclusion of each piece, as well as its beginning'.[27] But this counted for little with Dalyell, watch in hand, who cheerfully converted a traditional rondo form into a theme with variations to suit the crowded social calendar of his audience. The pipers were forbidden to tune up on the platform. They were forbidden to re-tune during performance – Dalyell noting in 1825 that 'it was quite common to tune in the middle of any part, and resume where the perfr. [performer] left off.'[28] They were also

22 Dalyell, p.99.
23 Dalyell, p.98.
24 Dalyell, p.100.
25 Dalyell, p.101.
26 MacInnes, p.38, 195–7; see also Dalyell MSS, Gen. 350D f.36.
27 MacDonald, *Ancient Martial Music*, 'Instructions for the Great Highland Bagpipe', p.3.
28 Dalyell MSS, Gen.355D, f.13.

forbidden to end with the usual cascade of tuning flourishes. This allowed the organisers to sprint through a card of eighteen or so players in the space of an afternoon, and still get to the races in time for the off.

The defining moment came in 1818, when John Campbell, the folklorist J. F. Campbell's 'nurse', and son of Colin Mór Campbell of Nether Lorn, brought one of his father's volumes of canntaireachd to the Edinburgh competition. Dalyell recounts what happened next:

> One of the objects of the Highland Society comprehended the preservation of the music of the Highlands – much of it believed to belong to remote antiquity. In consequence, John Campbell, a competitor in performance on the bagpipe, repaired to Edinburgh in the year 1818, at the season of competition, with a folio volume in manuscript, said to contain numerous compositions; but the contents merely resembling a written narrative, in an unknown language, nor bearing any resemblance to Gaelic, they proved utterly unintelligible. Amidst many conjectures relative both to the subject and the language, nobody adventured so far as to guess at either *airs* or *piobrachs*.

The bench of judges actually declined an offer from one of the pipers to translate the notation:

> Murdoch Maclean, a pipe-maker from Glasgow, then also a candidate at the competition, offered to decipher the mysterious manuscript, so as to interpret the true meaning; but from those contracted views, sometimes opposing the most reasonable projects, his proposal received no encouragement, and the owner refused to part with the volume which gave me much regret.[29]

But Dalyell was mistaken. John Campbell did part with the volume. He sold it to Sir John MacGregor Murray who promptly lost it.[30] The episode is significant in showing how power relations had changed during the previous generation, how the status of pipers vis-a-vis the Highland Societies had fallen dramatically since the mid 1780s, and indicating probably also that by this stage the bench had as little Gaelic as the performers had English.

The Societies' approach became increasingly intrusive and authoritarian. In 1822 the two-droned version of the pipe was banned, on the grounds that it gave its players an advantage.[31] In 1828, the Highland Society of London issued fresh regulations governing eligibility to compete: in future, candidates must either be former prizewinners at a 'provincial' Highland gathering; or, failing this, possess a certificate of competence from their commanding officers if they were soldiers, or

---

29 Dalyell, *Musical Memoirs*, pp.9–10.
30 Archibald Campbell, 'The Campbell Canntaireachd MS', in *Piobaireachd Society Collection*, 2nd ser., vol.10, v-vi.
31 MacInnes, p.90.

a testimonial to the same effect signed by three gentlemen if they were civilians.[32] Such a regime inevitably bred an atmosphere of conflict and mistrust, and the increasing subordination of the performer community led to petty vindictiveness, tale-bearing and toadyism. In 1821, Donald MacKay insinuated to the committee that a rival, John Cameron, was

> always cursing and damming the members of the Society and he said there is no justice amongst you and he is going this only once for to hell with the whole of the body for their misconduct and not dealing with justice to him he says that he should have got the Pipes long ago.[33]

If players disputed the results or refused prizes, they faced financial sanctions and disqualification from future competitions. In 1824, Kenneth MacRae, then piper to the Earl of Caithness and one of Donald Cameron's teachers, refused to accept an additional prize, on the grounds that he should have been first in the main competition. The committee offered to turn a blind eye to this offence, and pay his travelling expenses,

> provided he would express contrition for his improper conduct. MacRae being called in and the question put to him he declined to express regret for his conduct, and moreover stated that he considered he had been shamefully used, and was not sorry that he should be refused to be allowed to compete hereafter. In consequence the committee were unanimously of the opinion that no allowance should be made to him.[34]

In 1841, Donald Cameron himself tried to decline a consolation prize for dress, and had to apologise abjectly to the committee before they would let him compete again.[35]

---

32 HSL, NLS, Dep. 268, Minute Book, Feb. 1822 – March 1829, 3/5/1828. For the active support by the Highland Society of London for a network of 'district' Highland games including St. Fillans, Dunkeld, Stirling & Bannockburn, and Strathearn, see NLS, Dep. 268, Correspondence Box 2, 12/4/ 1824; Box 3, 24/6/1828; 15/4/1829, 27/4/ 1829; Box 14, Draft Minutes, 1829–1840, Meeting of Directors of the Highland Society of London, 3/5/1828.

33 Quoted in MacInnes, p.58.

34 Quoted in 'A Page of Old Time Piping. By Archibald Campbell [of Kilberry], Part 2', *OT*, 8/5/1948, p.3.

35 *Ibid.*, part 1, *OT*, 1/5/1948, p.3. For an interesting comment on the decline of 'kindly relations' see Donald Campbell, *A Treatise on Language, Poetry and Music of the Highland Clans: with Illustrative Traditions and Anecdotes, and Numerous Ancient Highland Airs* (Edinr., 1862): 'I have not had an opportunity for some years of hearing the music of the war-pipe under circumstances which entitle me to speak with confidence on this subject, as the meetings of Highlanders are now held under patronage, and I cannot be a party to such repudiation of the feelings which characterised our ancestors as that implies. They clung endearingly and tenaciously to

In striking contrast to their economic undertakings, which usually proceeded on a basis of sound empirical knowledge, the Societies knew little about the actual state of piping, and did not consider it necessary to enquire. Dalyell explained that they wanted to 'revive' the music of the pipe because they thought it was dying; and they thought that it was dying because Patrick MacDonald had said it was in the 'Essay' prefixed to his *Highland Vocal Airs*.[36] They did not know that the 'Essay' had been written by a third party with little personal knowledge of the subject and whose opinions about the wellbeing of Celtic culture were not only, therefore, virtually worthless, but also differed diametrically from those of Patrick MacDonald as set forth in the latter's own 'Preface'. The Societies' approach was entirely utilitarian: they considered that the pipe had a single purpose – to keep up the military spirit of the Gael and, by so doing, to sustain the gallantry of the Highland regiments. A steady flow of pipers into the army was the ultimate goal. But it soon became apparent that the mechanism of competition alone was insufficient to ensure this. Although it might help commanding officers identify good players, it was useless unless the pipers themselves were willing to serve, and it seems that a good many of them were not.[37] Dalyell remarks 'When General the Hon. Sir Alexander Duff proposed enlisting one in 1825 under an assurance that he should not be sent beyond seas, the piper shrewdly demanded "whether the General would give him that in writing?"'[38] The army was not an attractive option when jobs could be had as personal pipers in the civilian sector without coming under military discipline. Only about 20% of the competitors at the Highland Societies' events had any kind of military connection, usually with the militia.[39] As a result, standards in the regular army were low. The Highland regiments could muster only a handful of players of reputation, such as Ronald MacKenzie of the Seaforth, for much of the 19th century.

It was important that a more certain source of supply be secured and accordingly we find the Highland Society of London proposing that pipers should be trained specifically for military service in a new kind of institution, an army school of piping, under the direction of Donald Roy MacCrimmon, the most prestigious player and teacher of his generation.

---

cont'd   the patriarchal chleachda [custom], which fostered and secured the manly
   independence of spirit that could recognise no superiors excepting in the officials
   elected by themselves. But I greatly suspect, since the piper has become a domestic
   musician, that he finds it his interest to cultivate the tastes of strangers; and hence
   that this warlike music has been so toned down as to be a totally different thing from
   what it has been'. pp. 128–9.

36 Dalyell, p.94.
37 For a note on the difficulty Highland Regiments experienced in securing pipers, see
    Diana M. Henderson, *Highland Soldier A Social Study of the Highland Regiments*,
    1820–1920 (Edinr., 1989), p.214.
38 Dalyell, p.114.
39 MacInnes, p.116.

Donald Roy was also a soldier, and a very gallant one, who had served with distinction in the American wars. The younger son of Malcolm MacCrimmon, he was MacLeod's principal piper and occupied Boreraig in 1769 under the usual arrangements which meant that his salary, £5. 11s., equalled his rent, allowing him to retain the rents of his dozen or so sub-tenants. However, the laird was in financial difficulty, the estate was put under trust, and the tacksmen and larger tenants began to find their position threatened. In Donald Roy's case MacLeod proposed to resume half of Boreraig, granting perpetual right to sit rent-free on the remainder.[40] But there was a succession of poor seasons, including the notorious 'Black Spring' of 1771, and plague amongst the cattle. The future looked so forbidding that a number of substantial Skye families, including Flora MacDonald of Kingsburgh and her husband Allan, were reluctantly preparing to emigrate to America. The most common destination was North Carolina which was actively recruiting Highland Scots who, in return for an oath of allegiance to the crown, received substantial grants of land.[41] There was even a song "Dol a dh'iarraidh an fhortain do North Carolina' (I'm going to seek my fortune in North Carolina).[42] And so in 1773 Donald Roy MacCrimmon exchanged the shores of Loch Dunvegan for the American colonial frontier and a plantation of 200 acres in Anson County, on the Cape Fear River, for which he paid one hundred and fifty pounds sterling.[43]

The story of his adventures there is preserved in a Highland Society of London document dated 8 August 1808, entitled 'Lt. MacCruimmen's Case' It begins:

Mr MacCruimmen is one of those unfortunate Loyalists who, on the Breaking out of the American Rebellion in 1775, sacrificed his Domestic Comforts, and his Property which consisted [of] an ample Independence, to his Duty as a British Subject. Animated by Caledonian Spirit, he collected and provided with Arms & Ammunition 40 followers. With these he quitted his peaceful Abode, and, after traversing for 30 days the Blue Mountains & Indian

40 I. F. Grant, *The MacLeods The History of a Clan* 1200–1956 (Lond., 1959), pp. 491, 559–61. For the laird General Norman MacLeod's own account of these transactions, the rage for emigration, and changing habits of chieftainship in the generation following the '45, see the transcript of his fragmentary autobiography 'Memoirs of His Own Life' in Alexander Mackenzie, *History of the MacLeods with Genealogies of the Principal Families of the Name* (Inverness, 1889), pp.149–52.

41 Robert McCluer Calhoon, *The Loyalists in Revolutionary America* 1760–1781 (New York, 1965), p.443.

42 Quoted in Elizabeth Gray Vining, *Flora MacDonald Her Life in the Highlands and America* (Lond., 1967), p.89. On the reasons for the MacDonalds emigrating, see pp.89–91, and for their fate in Carolina, p.101 ff.; for a lively account of the general background to Highland emigration to North Carolina at this time, see James Hunter, *A Dance Called America: The Scottish Highlands the United States and Canada* (Edinr., 1994), pp.11–48.

43 Ruairidh Halford-MacLeod, 'Donald Ruadh MacCrimmon in North Carolina', pts. 1–2, *PT*, vol.49, nos.2/4, November/January 1996/7, pp.33–8, 46–7.

Settlements[44], joined the Army of his Legitimate Sovereign, when he received the mortifying Intelligence that immediately on his departure his house had been plundered, & both his Buildings & Plantations destroyed by Fire, which compelled his Family to fly for refuge to the Hut of a Negro in the woods, where they were concealed for two years. Mr MacCruimmen at the head of his faithful Followers were received by the 84th Regt. of Royal Emigrants in which he attained the Rank of Lieutenant. In 1778 he received Orders to recruit for a Company, which he completed; but, owing to the Casualties of War, he never succeeded to the Rank promised [i.e. Captain]. At this time he served in the British Legion commanded by Lord Cathcart, & participated in the various engagements fought by his Lordship, by Lord Moira, by Generals Small & Tarleton, by the Honble Major Cochrane, Major Sutherland &c whose Military Achievements are well known.

Notwithstanding the many desperate Conflicts in which he was engaged, & in which his Comrades were overpowered by numbers, retaining the spirit of his Caledonian Ancestors, he never once yielded or surrendered himself a Prisoner of War, but preferred a Life of Deprivation & Difficulty. He cut his way through Parties of the Rebels, & eluded their pursuit when 500 Dollars were offered for his Head. In the course of his Service he personally wrested in single Combat their Swords from three Commanding officers of the Enemy, laying their owners prostrate on the Earth, & seized three Stand of Colours. He also at the head of six men compelled the Surrender of a Privateer fully armed.

With the strongest Testimonials of distinguished Valour from his Commanding Officers, he on his return to this Country after the Conclusion of the War applied to the Government for Remuneration and Promotion, & for his loss of Property, his Military Services, & undeniable Rights to the rank of Captain, he only received the half pay of a Lieutenant on 2/4 per day; on which he has since, with much difficulty, supported & educated a large Family.[45]

The new republic was not a welcoming place for ex-Loyalists and like many others he returned to Scotland, settling at first in Skye and later in Glenelg. The enterprise had cost him an eye and a considerable part of his capital. Despite official promises about restitution of losses, he was able to reclaim only a fraction of his outlay.[46] He was therefore in no position to decline a proposal to head an

---

44 This would seem to imply that he had to cross the Appalachians. In those days the territory of North Carolina stretched notionally all the way to the Mississippi, so that Donald Roy's plantation may have lain in what is now east Kentucky or Tennessee, which were subject to intensive settlement at this time.

45 HSL, NLS, Dep.268, Correspondence Box 1, 1 October 1781 – 30 Sept 1820.

46 See Robert O. DeMond, *The Loyalists in North Carolina during the Revolution* (Hamden, Conn., 1964), Appendix C, p.253. Donald Roy apparently re-settled in Canada for a number of years, returning to Scotland about 1790: see Gibson, pp.192–3.

officially sponsored piping college if the Highland Society of London could manage to bring one about.

The General Committee of that body, meeting at the Freemasons Tavern in London, on Saturday 27 February 1808, had before it a lengthy report outlining an ambitious future strategy for the Society. Amongst other things it proposed:

> the establishment of an Academy for the cultivation of the National Pipe Music . . . The cultivation of Pipe Music being necessary for the Highland Regiments, it is natural to expect that, on proper applications being made, Government itself will be induced to lend its aid in realizing what the Society have had for many years in contemplation; that is, the establishment of a College of Highland Pipe Music, of which Lieutenant MacCruimmen was to have been the principal Professor. It is in the power of His Royal Highness the Commander in Chief to comply with the wishes of the Society by promoting Lieut. MacCruimmen from the Half Pay to a higher and permanent rank in the Garrison of Fort Augustus, or of Fort William, which to him would be equivalent to a salary, and being made Professor of the Establishment. Mr MacCruimmen is the last of the celebrated race of Pipers of that name; he is skilled in the theory and practice of the ancient Pipe Music, and is now in the vale of Years.[47]

It was resolved, therefore:

> That the Secretary be authorized to write a Letter in the name of the Society to His Royal Highness the Duke of York stating the anxious wish of the Society for the establishing of an Academy, where the National Pipe Music may be properly taught, and requesting that His Royal Highness will be pleased to recommend Lieutenant MacCruimmen for Permanent Rank in the Garrison of Fort Augustus, or Fort William, where he may act as Professor of the Academy to be established.[48]

The idea was an attractive one from a number of points of view. Donald MacCrimmon would get his cherished captaincy; the new institution would have as its principal the most famous teacher in Scotland, and a building to house it located centrally; there would be much official patronage and prestige and it would not cost the Society a penny. But they needed to introduce their man to the people who mattered, so it was resolved 'That a Ticket for the [annual] Dinner be presented to Lieutenant MacCrumman, to afford an opportunity for judging of his performance on the Highland Pipe'.[49] Also present, with a little artful management, would be Frederick Augustus, Duke of York and Albany,

47 HSL, NLS, Dep. 268, Minute Book, 1802–1808.
48 *Ibid.*, 19/3/1808.
49 *Ibid.*, 1802–1808, f.185.

Commander-in-Chief of the British Army. A high-powered deputation, including the Marquis of Huntly, Sir John Sinclair, Sir John Macpherson, and Sir John MacGregor Murray, was appointed to:

> represent to His Royal Highness that notwithstanding the success with which the efforts of the Society have been attended for the preservation & cultivation of Pipe Music for the Highland Corps in the Army, their endeavours may ultimately prove ineffectual without the establishment of a National Academy in the Highlands of Scotland, whose students shall be instructed in every branch of Pipe Music . . . Lieutenant MacCrummen being, in the opinion of the Society, well qualified for the Appointment of Professor of an Academy of Pipe-Music is far advanced in Years and the last of the celebrated Race of Pipers and Composers of that name, who successively for five centuries presided over a similar Institution in the Highlands, but which has been dormant for 17 Years, from want of pecuniary support. The Society apprehend that, in the event of his death previous to the Establishment of the Academy now proposed, much of the Ancient Music of Caledonia, known to Lieut. MacCrummen alone will be for ever lost . . .[50]

The deputation duly presented the Duke with a written 'disposition' stating the merits of the case. Meantime Donald Roy was in trouble. He had been hanging about in London in expectation of his long-awaited promotion for more than a year, and was now in serious financial difficulty. The Minutes record that:

> About 18 months ago he arrived in London from the Isle of Sky with sanguine hopes of Promotion, & in that period he remitted to his Family £30 in Cash & £10 in Necessaries for their maintenance and Clothing. Between the expences of his Journey, providing apparel for himself, & living so long on Expectations in London he unavoidably got into Debt – To add to his Misfortunes, with the unsuspecting Mind of a Caledonian Soldier he was induced by the earnest Intreaty of a Countryman, on whose honour he placed great dependence, to endorse a Bill of £20. His Countryman departed for the East Indies & the Bill, when due, was not honoured. Upwards of two months ago he was arrested for the amount, & in a few days thereafter a [?retainer] was lodged in the Sheriff's Office for £25 more on his own account. Ashamed to make his case publicly known, he endeavoured for six weeks by his own Individual Efforts to procure his Release; but finding these unavailing, & only sinking him deeper in Debt, he is at length under the necessity, with poignant feelings, to appeal to his Countrymen for their Benevolent Aid to rescue him from Captivity, & to enable him once more to wield his sword against the Enemies of his Country.
> The above Circumstances having been lately communicated to the

50 *Ibid.*, 7/5/1808.

Highland Society, they were pleased to recommend a Subscription among such of the Members as may be still in town for Lieutenant MacCriummen's Relief, & further, the Society have made Application to His Royal Highness the Commander in Chief to grant him Promotion in the Army, which he daily expects. Independent of his Sufferings in Confinement, mortifying most to his feelings & disastrous [?to] his Salvation, should he be unable to extricate himself from Prison when his Promotion shall take place. He therefore prays to the Benevolent to communicate the Distress of a Veteran Soldier, who has been harassed by Poverty for many years past.[51]

And so a man who was the living epitome of the cultural ideals of the Highland Society of London was languishing in gaol on their very doorstep. This was not something that could be referred to a sub-committee. It was August and the town was deserted, but a subscription of about £40 was hurriedly raised and Donald Roy eventually found his way back to Scotland.

In the spring of 1809, the Duke of York fell from power in a high society scandal, accused of trafficking in offices for personal gain. His estranged mistress, Mary Anne Clarke, an actress, shocked the fashionable world by revealing that she had used her lover's authority to peddle positions and influence for money.[52] The Duke was tried before his peers, acquitted, and in 1811 restored to office – but the moment of opportunity had passed for Donald Roy.

In 1815, the Highland Society of London offered the Duke their Presidency. He accepted, agreed to see a deputation about the proposed piping college, then cancelled the appointment, saying that he had put the matter in the hands of the Prince Regent his brother, and not to trouble him about it again. In the spring of 1816 a vacancy occurred for a Barracks Master at Fort William. Might not Donald Roy be appointed to this and still act as 'Preceptor of Pipe Music to such Pupils as might offer'?[53] Evidently not, it would seem, as the issue disappeared thereafter from the minutes.

In view of the immense social power of the Highland Society of London, both as an institution, and in terms of its individual members (which included half the royal family), this repeated failure to persuade the British establishment to support a college of piping is rather puzzling. After all they were not asking for very much: a fairly junior regular commission for a single brilliant old man, and a corner of a barracks somewhere in Scotland. The Duke of York could lose a hundred times the amount at the tables and hardly notice the difference. Indeed, to a good many individual members of the Highland Society the sums involved would have been

---

51 *Ibid.*, Correspondence Box 1, 1 October 1781 – 30 Sept 1820, 8/8/1808.
52 He was not the least raffish of George III's raffish sons, the Dukes of Kent and Cumberland, and, of course, the Prince of Wales, later George IV. A contemporary described him thus: 'His conduct is as bad as possible. He plays [gambles] very deep and loses; and his company is thought *mauvais ton.*'
53 HSL, NLS, Dep.268, Minutes, 1814–1816, 5/4/1816.

little more than small change. Yet in the nearly thirty years that the piping college scheme lay on the table, the possibility that the Society itself might fund the project was never even discussed. One can read one's way through the Highland Society's papers for year after year without finding a single expression of appreciation – or even interest – in piobaireachd as a musical form. It was valued solely for its role in keeping up the military efficiency of the Highland Corps. And this, as all students of Adam Smith well knew, was, ultimately, the business of the state.[54] And if the state declined to act in its own best interests, there, presumably, was an end of the matter. Indeed, more than a century was to pass before the British Army began to accept a responsibility for the training of military pipers in the higher branches of the music, and then only because a civilian body, the Piobaireachd Society, was willing to pay the instructor.[55]

It is not easy to arrive at a positive assessment of the activities of the Highland Societies of London and Scotland in this field. They established the mechanism of the public competition as the central focus of the piping world during the following two centuries. This led directly to an ethos in which piping was seen first and foremost as spectacle, with music coming a distant second to theatrical razzmatazz. Piobaireachd as a form was casually re-modelled to suit the convenience of institutional sponsors whose real interests lay elsewhere. Performance became closely linked to appraisal, and those aspects of the piper's art which most readily lent themselves to comparison, such as brilliance of tone and machine-like accuracy of technique, came to be prized at the expense of subtler qualities like interpretation and expression. The repertoire that could be heard in public became progressively narrower, as judges tended to award prizes to competitors offering one of half a dozen or so favourite tunes.[56] Finally, a traditional, fluid and creatively flexible art form was locked into an institutional nexus in a way that tended to drain autonomy from the performer community and transfer it to external mediators and sponsors.

The Highland Societies were the first institutions to dedicate at least a part of their endeavour to the traditional performing arts and to popular culture. But their approach was founded on the proposition that the inherited ways of doing things were wrong and must be changed, and they found the concepts of 'Improvement' and 'tradition' difficult to reconcile.[57] Indeed, the urge to transform the economic organisation and social mores of the Highlands proved incompatible with the urge to promote its traditional culture, and the latter objective was first modified and then abandoned.

54 Skinner, pp.8–9.
55 See below, p. 306. A further consideration might be that the presence of pipers in Scottish regiments at this period was entirely unofficial since they were paid for by the officers and were not on the establishment: see David Murray, *Music of the Scottish Regiments* (Edinr., 1994), p.109.
56 Halford-MacLeod, 'Top Twenty piobaireachds', p.54.
57 Edward Shils, *Tradition* (Lond., 1981), pp. 100–101.

6

'The only national instrument in Europe': Donald MacDonald and The Ancient Martial Music of Caledonia

The Highland Societies sought from the outset to undermine the oral basis of piobaireachd by reducing it to a fixed written form. They had a number of motives for doing this. One was an antiquarian desire to collect the fragments before they perished, the response of a literate élite who had little personal knowledge of the culture for which they sought to legislate, and whose education encouraged them to regard traditional culture as by definition incapable of sustaining itself without external intervention. But there were also more narrowly institutional forces at work. The mechanism of competition inevitably tended to favour standardisation. If pipers could be induced to play from a fixed written text instead of their own versions of a given tune, they could be more easily compared, and the task of judging made more straightforward. It seemed likely, too, that music thus 'simplified' and 'fixed' would lend itself to teaching in a shorter time, accelerating – and therefore cheapening – the training of pipers for the army.[1]

The extension of the competition system thus became a priority. During the 1820s the Highland Society of London began to promote a network of provincial games, such as St. Fillans, Atholl, and Strathearn, which it aimed to combine into an integrated national system, further deepening the structure of regulation and control. Pipers had first to succeed in this arena, or bear some other kind of formal attestation before they could compete at a national level, thus further weakening their position in relation to the institutional sponsors.[2]

The growth of a public competition circuit marked the passing of the social and economic patterns which had formerly supported a class of professional pipers rooted in the communities which sustained them. The successful High-

---

1 See Ruairidh H. MacLeod, 'The Highland Society of London and the publishing of Piobaireachd' Pts.1–2, *PT*, vol.34, nos.9/11, 1982, pp.25–31, 28–32. For the urge towards standardisation in military music at this time throughout Western Europe, see Murray, *Scottish Regiments*, pp.85–6. There was a similar urge to 'standardise' fiddle music also by the Gows and Simon Fraser: see Samuel P. Bayard, 'Prolegomena to a Study of the Principal Melodic Families of Folk Song' in MacEdward Leach and Tristram P. Coffin, *The Critics & the Ballad* (Carbondale, 1961), pp.103–150, *n.*1, pp.265–6.

2 Highland Society of London Papers, NLS Dep. 268, Correspondence, Box 2, letters concerning Highland Society of London subsidy of Highland Games at St Fillans, Dunkeld, Stirling, and Strathearn, 12/4/1824, 24/6/1824, 15/4/1829, 27/7/1829. Minute Book, Feb. 1822 – March 1829, 7/2/1824.

land musician was moving into a fragmented, economically individualistic, entrepreneurial ethos in which market forces held increasing sway. The piper was beginning to become highly mobile as success in competition led to top jobs with important people, and the published collection began to be seen as the acme of a good career.[3] At the same time, Gaelic-speaking piobaireachd players, trained by oral methods in a fluid traditional form, increasingly performed before benches of narrowly literate English-speaking judges who had the power to make or break them. Creative control over the music, performer choice, the power to realise a tune according to personal aesthetic judgement based upon innate cultural authority – fundamental principles in a traditional art form – all came under attack.

Print as a medium was not inherently deadly to tradition. Indeed its influence on the development of major forms of ceòl beag, such as the competition march, appears to have been largely positive.[4] The effect of translating pipe music into staff notation for descriptive purposes, as in the work of Joseph and Patrick MacDonald, seems likewise to have been neutral. But in the hands of the Highland Societies and their successors the printed text was to become a means of prescriptive control, enabling an authoritative 'standard' version to be established and constituting such bodies as its guardian. In November 1825, Charles Gordon, Secretary of the Highland Society of Scotland, wrote to John Wedderburn his counterpart in the Highland Society of London:

> It is but very recently that any other than *Military* Pipers could write music; –
> those in the country learned their tunes by the ear from some old piper who
> knew as little of music, scientifically, as themselves. A different practice now
> begins to prevail, and I anticipate, very confidently, that the publication you
> are so judiciously about to make will serve essentially to promote it. Under
> the revision which you are personally so well qualified to give to it, it will also
> do much to secure and fix the proper standard for each tune – for at present
> scarcely two pipers play exactly the same *set* of any piobrachd.[5]

In the Societies' view, staff notation was the modern 'scientific' method, in every way preferable to canntaireachd whether written or oral, and it possessed in their eyes one further advantage: namely, that by using it, the piping learner could dispense with a human teacher. Thus the role of the master pipers in instruction and the authority that flowed from it could be substantially weakened.

But there were a number of formidable obstacles in the way of such a programme. It is striking, for example, that at no time was the playing of specific written texts made compulsory at any of the Highland Societies' competitions. It

3 See below, Chapter 9.
4 Donaldson, 'Change and Invariance' p.43; and also below, pp. 216–9.
5 HSL, NLS Dep.268, Correspondence, Box 2, 10/11/1825, Charles Gordon to John
   Wedderburn.

would have been a futile gesture in any case. Not only did the cost of printing and paper make music books a luxury item beyond the reach of ordinary pockets, but many – probably the great majority – of pipers could not read staff notation at all, and this continued to be the case for at least another century.[6] Pipers like Donald MacDonald, Angus MacKay, and Colin Cameron who possessed sufficient command of the medium to commit large numbers of tunes to paper more or less accurately were members of a fairly small élite. Some who could read staff notation, such as Malcolm Macpherson, were reluctant to use it as a teaching medium. Indeed there was a culture of positive orality in the performer community which tended to regard the written symbols of staff notation not just with suspicion, but often with active hostility.[7] This notwithstanding, the Highland Societies and their successors, assisted at first by 'literate' pipers and later by gentlemen amateurs drawn from amongst their own ranks, began the long process of converting piobaireachd, highest and most subtle of the oral arts in Britain, into a literate form with a fixed printed canon possessing prescriptive force.

The committee of the Highland Society of Scotland meeting after the competition of 1806, noted 'how desirable it would be to have the Highland music adapted to the harpsichord, violin and other Instruments', and appointed a sub-committee under Sir John Sinclair of Ulbster to explore how this might be done.[8] Sinclair already knew where to find the necessary expertise: in the person of Donald MacDonald, Pipe-Major of his old regiment, the Caithness Highlanders, now working as a pipe-maker and teacher of the Highland, Northumbrian and Union pipes in the city of Edinburgh. Donald MacDonald is a major figure in piping history, a Skyeman, born in Kingsburgh in 1767, and thought to have been taught by Angus MacArthur, last of the MacArthur line, famous as teachers and composers, whose college had been at Peingown, in Hungladder at the northern end of Trotternish.[9] At the 1806 competition he had been awarded a special prize for 'producing the greatest number of ancient pipe tunes set to music'.[10]

The project must have moved ahead fairly rapidly, because on 3rd November 1808, MacDonald was already able to advertise as a separate publication the tutor which was ultimately to accompany this collection, perhaps to test the market ahead of the larger work:

6 See, for example, 'Grand Bagpipe Competition at Partick', *OT*, 20/10/1900, p.3; 'Bagpipe Competition. Pipers & Pipe Music', 21/3/1903, p.2; 'Eight Pipers Wanted', 24/4/1915, p.1; see also [Seumas MacNeill], 'Ardvasar Seminar', *PT*, vol.41, no.2, November 1988, pp.32–40, (35–6), and Murray, *Scottish Regiments*, pp.301–2.

7 See section on orality in Appendix.

8 Highland Society of Scotland Papers, Minutes of Directors, 28/11/1806, p. 233.

9 Keith Sanger, 'Donald MacDonald', *PT*, Vol. 49, no. 1, October 1996, pp. 24–31; see also Angus MacKay, *Ancient Piobaireachd*, 'Account of the Hereditary Pipers', pp.11–12; and Cannon, *Bibliography*, pp.24–7.

10 Quoted in Sanger, 'Donald MacDonald', p.24.

D. McDonald Musical Instrument Maker and Teacher of Pipe Music, head of
Lawnmarket, Edinburgh, at the request of a number of young gentileman his
pupils has just published a complete set of INSTRUCTIONS for the
HIGHLAND, LOWLAND AND NORTHUMBERLAND BAGPIPES consisting
of three pages price 1sh and 6d and containing all the Cuttings, Shakes and other
Graces with an account of the different times of the music adapted on the above
instrument to which are added various specimens of Bagpipe Music, the whole
being intended as an introduction to a collection of piobrach or the ancient
warlike music of Caledonia and Highland reels which will also soon be published
as soon as sufficient number of subscribers come forward.[11]

Perhaps the subscription lists did not come up to expectations, or there may
have been some other impediment, but there the project rested for a number of
years.

　　Meantime, Donald MacDonald, now pipe-major to the Argyllshire Militia,
continued to do well at the annual competitions, being placed second in 1811 and
winning the prize pipe in July 1817. Later that summer he issued a further edition
of his 'Tutor':

This day is published priced 3sh 6d A New Complete Guide or Tutor for The
Great Highland Bagpipe containing every necessary instruction for enabling any
person even of ordinary capacity to play with Ease and Taste on that celebrated
national instrument. By Donald MacDonald late Piper-Major to the Argyllshire
Regiment of Militia. Published and sold by the Author at his house, Carrubbers
Close, High Street, Edinburgh. D. McDonald carries on the business of Pipe-
making in all its branches and gives lessons on the Highland and Union Pipes &c.
N.B. The Nobility and Gentry who may be desirous of training up Pipers either
for military service or other wise are respectfully informed that every attention will
be paid to the Instruction of such persons on scientific Principles that so they may
acquire the Proficiency which is requisite to qualify them for the discharge of their
duty.
　　Letters (post paid) will be duly attended to.[12]

One reason for his caution may have been that in contemplating a collection
specifically devoted to music for the Highland pipe, MacDonald was venturing
into uncharted territory. As a teacher and maker of the Union pipes, however, he
must have been familiar with recent publications of Irish music, such as
O'Farrell's Collection of National Irish Music for the Union Pipes (Lond.,
1804)[13] and Fitzmaurice's *New Collection of Irish Tunes. Adapted for the Piano*

11　*Edinburgh Evening Courant,* 3/11/1808, quoted in Sanger, 'Donald MacDonald',
　　　p. 25.
12　*Ibid.*, p.25.
13　Cannon, *Bibliography*, pp.81–82.

Forte, Union Pipe, Flute & Violin (Edinr., *c.*1805), more especially since Richard Fitzmaurice actually lived in Edinburgh and had given a demonstration on the Union pipes at the Highland Societies' competition in August 1807 'which was received with great applause'.[14] MacDonald will almost certainly have known him, and may therefore have been quite well informed about the market for certain kinds of pipe music. The goodwill of the Highland Society of Scotland probably seemed assured, and there were a number of recent trends which may have encouraged him to conclude that the time might be ripe for a substantial collection of music for the Highland pipe.

Following the publication of Sir Walter Scott's *Lady of the Lake* (1810), and even more so of *Waverley* (1814), the market for Highland or pseudo-Highland texts was beginning to boom.[15] As the Napoleonic wars reached their climax the exploits of the kilted regiments fuelled this growing enthusiasm. In the spring of 1816, for example, the Black Watch returned to Edinburgh amid scenes of delirious excitement and immense crowds waving tartan scarves and banners.[16] Patrick MacDonald had already demonstrated a considerable appetite in the Lowlands for Gaelic song tunes and piping jigs and reels, and the collections of Alexander Campbell and Simon Fraser of Knockie were about to break new ground. Campbell's collection was published in two volumes in Edinburgh, 1816–1818, and entitled *Albyn's Anthology Or A Select Collection of the Melodies & Vocal Poetry Peculiar to Scotland and the Isles*. It was based on field-work specifically undertaken for the purpose and subsidised by the Highland Society of Scotland. Campbell worked to a detailed programme given to him by Sir John MacGregor Murray, and was answerable to a sub-committee of the Society containing both Sir Walter Scott (a former pupil of his own to whom Campbell had – vainly – attempted to teach music) and the novelist Henry Mackenzie. In the course of his travels he met Donald Roy MacCrimmon and Capt. Niel MacLeod of Gesto from whose collection of written canntaireachd he set a number of tunes in staff notation.[17] *Albyn's Anthology* was eventually to include three songs on Highland subjects with words by Scott and set to piobaireachd melodies – 'The MacGregors' Gathering', 'Pibroch of Donuil Dubh', and 'Lament – (Cha till suinn tuille).[18] Captain Simon Fraser's *Airs and Melodies peculiar to the Highlands of Scotland and the Isles* (Edinr., 1816), was an even more important source. It contained more than two hundred fiddle tunes, including a large number linked with the Jacobite movement, and rapidly became a

14 MacKay, *Ancient Piobaireachd*, 'Account of the Competition of Pipers', p.17.

15 See Donaldson, *Jacobite Song.*, pp.92–3; see also Arthur Mitchell, 'A List of Travels, Tours, Journeys, Voyages, Cruises, Excursions, Wanderings, Rambles, Visits, etc., Relating to Scotland' in *Proceedings of the Society of Antiquaries of Scotland*, 3rd. Ser., vol. 35, 1900–1, pp.431–638; vol. 36, 1905, pp.500–27; vol. 44, 1910, pp.390–405.

16 See James Anton, *Retrospect of a Military Life, during the most Eventful Periods of the Last War* (Edinr., 1841), pp.247–50.

17 Campbell, 'Slight Sketch', ff.47–8.

18 *Albyn's Anthology*, i, 90–7, 82–9; ii, 54–7.

standard work. It also appears to have received the Highland Societies' support.[19]

In October 1818, however, a rival to Donald MacDonald's bagpipe tutor suddenly appeared in the market. It was entitled *The Bagpipe Preceptor; or, the art of playing the great Highland bagpipe rendered perfectly easy to every capacity; by which any one who has a taste for music may soon acquire a knowledge of that grand and warlike instrument, without the aid of a master. To which are added, a few favourite simple airs, calculated to catch the ear and attention of the pupil, and lead him on in the science of music.* It was compiled by 'an amateur' (thought to have been a Capt. Daniel Menzies), and sold by Nathaniel Gow and a number of other music and booksellers.[20] The *Preceptor* used a numerical system to indicate gracenotes derived from the conventions of keyboard thorough bass – and although its compiler declared a wish that 'some abler hand will start up to improve on this original attempt at reducing the study of the Bagpipe to science', he indicated an intention to publish a collection of piobaireachd as a follow-up to the tutor.[21] Although in reality the book was little more than a recruiting pamphlet, painting in glowing terms the attractions of life as a military piper, in a market so relatively small and undeveloped, it represented a threat to MacDonald's position as a teacher, his championship of a truly 'scientific' notation for pipe music, and his long-terms plans for a published collection of his own. If he were forestalled by the compiler of the *Preceptor*, he stood to lose decades of work.[22]

He reacted quickly. Before many months had passed the first edition of his *Collection of the Ancient Martial Music of Caledonia, called Piobaireachd as performed on the great Highland bagpipe* had issued from the press, dedicated to the Highland Society of Scotland. It contained an unsigned 'Preface' describing the pipe and its music, a section of 'Instructions for the Great Highland Bagpipe' aimed at the learner, twenty three piobaireachds in full staff notation, and some two dozen jigs, reels, strathspeys and song airs from Uist and Skye.[23] Presumably he thought that there was insufficient time to issue another

19 HSS Sederunt Book No.5., July 1814–July 1818, ff. 56–7, 102–3. For details of the
    ensuing controversy between Campbell and Fraser, see Mary Anne Alburger, *Scottish
    Fiddlers and their Music* (Lond., 1983), pp.155–8.

20 Cannon, *Bibliography*, pp.23–4, 117–8.

21 *Ibid.*, p.24.

22 It may be that transcripts of his work were circulating and he felt compelled to
    publish them himself before somebody else did, a thing not unknown in traditional
    music circles in Scotland: see Alburger, p.155.

23 The tunes selected for publication were heavily weighted in favour of the popular and
    the known, as we can see from contemporary competitors' lists. See Ruairidh Halford-
    MacLeod, 'Top Twenty Piobaireachds', pp.50–54. For a perceptive note on
    MacDonald's probable reliance on earlier written sources, see Frans Buisman,
    'Dungallon's Lament/Salute Playing Styles and the Exchange of Tunes in Ceol Mor',
    Part 1, *PT*, vol 45, no.6, March 1993, pp.25–9.

prospectus, and he does not appear to have had an explicit promise of support from the Highland Societies. Since the work could be viewed as a response to a Highland Society of Scotland commission, he may have felt that this step was unnecessary. But the Highland Society of Scotland, with two similar titles still in the market, does not appear to have taken his volume up.[24] A little later, therefore, a second impression appeared, with an additional dedication to the Highland Society of London. It read as follows:

To

The Noblemen and Gentlemen

of

The Highland Societies

of

London and Scotland.

The Publisher of the following Work being little known to the World, and making an experiment, too, with regard to our Ancient Pipe Music, hitherto unattempted, or, at least, unaccomplished, felt the danger of ushering it to the Public without sanction or patronage; and, his labours having been devoted to a strictly National Object, he knew no where to turn, with so much propriety, or so much hope, as to those Distinguished Bodies, which boast, not only of almost all the rank, and all the talent, and all the worth, of the Country, but whose exertions have been so assiduously and so successfully employed for the interest and prosperity of Scotland.

He therefore respectfully begs leave to Dedicate this Volume to THE HIGHLAND SOCIETIES OF LONDON AND SCOTLAND, conscious, that if, under their auspices, it fails, it can be worthy of success under no other.

To those, and it is hoped they will be few, who may consider the Music as unworthy of preservation, or adaptation to other instruments, for its own sake, it will at least be curious, as acquainting them with the Strains that delighted and animated our Warlike Ancestors, and of which many had their origin in the most interesting circumstances of dangerous adventure, and romantic attachment; and to those who quarrel with the execution of the undertaking, it may occur, in mitigation, that it was a patriotic feeling that prompted the attempt to redeem, in some degree, from neglect and oblivion what was so dear to our Fathers, and perhaps not unwelcome to many of us, not only from such associations, but from natural taste.

In conclusion, the publisher has only to add to the general voice, his

---

24 For probable dates of publication, and changes between successive editions, see Frans Buisman, 'The Earliest Editions of Donald MacDonald's Collection of the Ancient Martial Music of Caledonia, called Piobaireachd' Parts 1/2, in *PT*, vol.50, no.1–2, October-November 1997, pp. 51–5, 32–4.

heartfelt wish, that both Societies may continue to be cheered in the progress of their unwearied labours, by the increasing prosperity of their Country, and the consciousness of their having already done so much to promote it; and to say how proud he is, at once to grace his undertaking with such names, and to subscribe himself,

    Gentlemen,

        Your humble and grateful Servant,

        Donald MacDonald.[25]

In response, the Highland Society of Scotland subscribed for five copies.[26]

The printer's bill for *Albyn's Anthology* shows costs for a similar volume of about £100 for 100 copies, a substantial sum of money for a person of ordinary means in the second decade of the nineteenth century.[27] Priced at a guinea, Donald MacDonald's collection was unlikely to do much more than cover his outlay at best, so that if he published at his own risk, as he appears to have done, he was likely to be in trouble if the Societies did not take a substantial number of copies off his hands, and their failure to do so involved him in serious loss. His projected second volume of 48 tunes which also contained historical and traditional notes remained in manuscript.[28] General C. S. Thomason, the editor of *Ceol Mor*, records what happened next:

> I am not sure, but I think that Macdonald taught the pipes to my grandfather, the late Mr. J. W. Grant of Elchies in Strathspey . . . Many a time and oft did my grandfather, – as he used to tell me, – write from India to MacDonald beseeching him to send him his copy of the 2nd volume, so long promised to the public; but all in vain as no answer came. He had quite given up all hopes of hearing anything more on the subject when, to his great joy, one day there came to hand the much longed for 2nd volume in manuscript. With the book was a plaintive letter from MacDonald begging my grandfather's acceptance of the book, as no one had shown so much interest in it as he had, and the publication of the first volume had almost ruined the donor.[29]

25 MacDonald, *Ancient Martial Music*, pp.1–2.

26 This impression appears to have been published in the autumn of 1819, MacInnes, p.227.

27 Cannon, *Bibliography*, pp.61–2.

28 The 'second volume' survives in manuscript form, but with the notes set up in type, which suggests that MacDonald risked publishing in 1818/19 only a part – less than a third in total – of what was perhaps already a much larger collection. A specimen title-page for volume two bears the date 1826. NLS. MS. 1680, f.1.

29 C. S. Thomason, ed., *A Collection of piobaireachd, as played on the great Highland bagpipes. Ceol Mor* (facsimile reprint, Wakefield, 1975, first published 1900), p.ii. MacDonald perhaps hoped that Grant might be able to publish the volume. In the event that privilege fell to C. S. Thomason who included its contents in *Ceol Mor*.

A third impression of *The Ancient Martial Music of Caledonia* appeared in July 1822 in response to the wave of Celtic enthusiasm inspired by the visit of King George IV. It was published by Alexander Robertson the music-seller, to whom MacDonald had in the meantime obviously disposed of his interest, and advertised as follows:

> *This day is published, A Collection of Ancient Martial Music of Caledonia as performed on the Great Highland Bagpipe. Now also adapted to the pianoforte, violin &c with a few old Highland lilts. To which is prefixed a complete Bagpipe Tutor by Donald MacDonald. 3rd Edition 21sh.*
> *This work includes the Pibroch of Donald Dhu as well as the Pibrochs of the different Clans.*
> *'Just Published, Heard ye the bagpipe' by R. A. Smith and the 2nd edition of Scottish Melodies by Marshall. Printed by Alex Robertson at his music saloon 47 Princes Street.*[30]

There were two further reprints during the nineteenth century.[31]

Donald MacDonald's main problem was that a market for such a book did not yet exist. When pipers used staff notation at all they tended to work from manuscript, so that from the outset he was forced to aim for the piano-stool rather than the pipe-case, as O'Farrell and Fitzmaurice had done, presenting their work not merely for the Union pipe, but also for the piano-forte, flute and violin. At the same time there must have been some demand for such material, because of the already fairly widespread custom of playing piobaireachd melodies on keyboard instruments. Sir Walter Scott's friend, Dr. John Leyden, recorded on his Highland tour in 1800, that

> At Taynish [in south Argyllshire] we had an opportunity of hearing various species of Highland music performed with grace and execution on the harpsichord. The most characteristic airs which I have heard are Lochiel's and Duntroon's March. With respect to the latter, we heard various anecdotes while we remained in the vicinity of Loch Crinan, particularly a kind of unintelligible story about a piper of one of the hostile clans who was hanged by his friends for betraying them to the Campbells by playing this march. We wished to hear the Mach Lormondh March, but were disappointed.[32]

30 *Edinburgh Courant*, 29 July 1822, quoted in Sanger, 'Donald MacDonald', p.27. R. A. Smith was the leading church musician in Scotland at this time, and arranged the songs of Lady Nairne for publication.
31 Cannon, *Bibliography*, pp.122–3.
32 John Leyden, *Journal of a Tour in the Highlands and Western Islands of Scotland in 1800* (Edinr., 1903), pp.66–7.

Dr. K. N. MacDonald, the authority on *puirt-a-beul,* records his grandfather, Niel MacLeod of Gesto, giving formal instruction in this art to his family:

> . . . he taught his own daughter Jessie to play pibrochs, marches, and laments on the piano . . . Miss Jessie McLeod – my aunt – was a splendid player of pipe music, far and away the best in Skye. She could play 'A Ghlas Mheur', and many other pibrochs, taught by her father. Miss Mary McEwen, a great-granddaughter of Gesto's, who lived with this Miss Jessie McLeod for some years up to the time of her death in 1882, writes . . . 'she told me about her father having taught her to play these lovely pibrochs, she mentioned how cross he used to get if she struck a wrong note on the piano, and how patiently he would play it over on the chanter or pipes'.[33]

In a similar manner, Eliza Ross, niece of James MacLeod of Raasay, made keyboard transcriptions of a number of tunes from the playing of Angus MacKay's father, John MacKay.[34]

But Donald MacDonald was unwilling to compromise by producing an impressionistic score which would lend itself to keyboard or violin as Patrick MacDonald had done. Sitting on top of a keyboard accompaniment in the left-hand staff, potential purchasers would encounter settings of the melodies in full pipe notation, bristling with ornament, and arranged in accordance with a new principle, with which few, if any, of them are likely to have been familiar. The treatment of the opening bars of 'The Finger Lock' (*A' Ghlass Mheur*), are typical of his style:[35]

Not only were Donald MacDonald's settings more detailed and prescriptive than anything which had hitherto appeared, but he substantially revised the inherited notational conventions in a way that was to be adopted by nearly all later writers. It was a bold and simple idea. All gracenote stems pointed up and all melody-note stems pointed down, regardless of their position on the staff. This meant that the melody line was separated typographically from the ornamentation, with a huge

33 'Capt. MacLeod of Gesto as a Piping Authority', K. N. MacDonald, *OT,* 13/7/1912, p.3.
34 Peter Cooke, 'Elizabeth Ross and the Piping of John MacKay of Raasay', *Proceedings of the Piobaireachd Society Conference* (Glasg., 1985), pp.1–14.
35 MacDonald, *Ancient Martial Music,* p.7.

gain in ease of reading.[36] It has sometimes been assumed that with Donald MacDonald and his followers, bagpipe music was adapted to suit the needs of 'scientific' staff notation; it may be truer to say that 'scientific' staff notation was adapted to the needs of the pipe.

Indeed the pipe took precedence over most other considerations in MacDonald's book. With the exception of the Taorluath movement which he re-set to indicate its timing, there were few concession to keyboard players who were instructed to realise the melody simply by leaving out the grace-notes. The arrangements did not sit well under the fingers, and were frequently austere to the point of severity, the production of someone clearly accustomed to thinking harmonically in terms of pipe drones, as we see in the characteristic rocking ostinato figures commonly used to accompany the later movements:[37]

Two features of MacDonald's scores were to create problems in later years. The first involved his treatment of the Taorluath, which he published in a kind of composite form, introducing an A semi-quaver probably to indicate its characteristic timing for performance on keyboard, violin or flute, but which does not actually appear to have been played by pipers before this time. We have seen on p.30 how Joseph MacDonald expressed this movement, and the earliest other surviving staff notation source, the Hannay-MacAuslan manuscript dating from the second decade of the nineteenth century, timed it in a similar fashion:

36 The Hannay-MacAuslan MS, NLS. Dep.201, dating from post 1811, which seems to have been used by Donald MacDonald as a source for several tunes, shows an interim development of this convention, having all gracenote stems pointing up whilst melody notes still have their 'normal' position on the staff: see Frans Buisman, 'An Anonymous Manuscript and its position in the History of Piobaireachd Playing', Part 1, *PT*, vol. 38, no.3, December 1985, pp.23–7 (23–4).

37 MacDonald, *Ancient Martial Music*, p.33.

But there was a notational difference between Hannay-MacAuslan and Joseph MacDonald, and it related to the middle low A in each of these figures. Joseph treated this as a grace-note and timed it as a demi-semi-quaver. Hannay-MacAuslan implied that it was a melody note, and timed it as a semi-quaver. In playing there is not likely to have been an audible difference, but the latter probably provided a visual cue for Donald MacDonald in framing his own multi-purpose version of the taorluath movement as follows:

As it stands, it seems to contain an unrhythmical 'extra' pulse; but MacDonald's version of the movement was probably intended to convey two different sets of instructions. One to non-pipers saying, 'play this':

And one to pipers saying 'play that':

'That' gaining some of its force from the fact that the 'strong' form of the GDG grip used by Donald MacDonald:

instead of the 'weaker' form, GDA:

was the very latest thing in modern piping technique.[38]

And so this compound form established itself as the standard method of notating the taorluath movement for many years, creating the so-called

38 Frans Buisman, 'The Early History of Leumludh', Parts 1–2, *PT*, vol.43, no.9–10, June-July 1991, pp.27–38, 36–51.

'redundant low A'.[39] The spread of ability to read staff-notation, coupled with the growing authority of written or printed texts during the later nineteenth century, seems to have led certain pipers to attempt actually to play it in this form, which led, in turn, to a good deal of controversy when it was pointed out by Lieut. John McLennan and others that it did not actually square with the mainstream of performance tradition.[40]

The clarity with which Donald MacDonald's system distinguished between ornament and melody notes was also achieved at a price, however, in that it required whoever used it to be very sure about what was a grace-note and what was not. He called all his ornamental figures 'appoggiaturas', and gave a typical selection in his section of 'Instructions', called 'Example 5th. Shewing the Appogiaturas':

In contemporary notational practice, then in a period of rapid change, 'appoggiatura' was a highly ambiguous term.[41] Presumably MacDonald used it because he thought that his ornamental notes resembled appoggiaturas in taking time from the following melody note. The problem for the later interpreter is, how much? During the Baroque and early Classical period, the appoggiatura took

  (i) half of an undotted main note
  (ii) two-thirds of a dotted main note;
  (iii) all of the first of two tied notes in compound metre;
  (iv) all of a note before a rest.[42]

But appoggiaturas could be 'long' or 'short' – in which latter case they might have very little value – and only the musical context offered any guide as to which was which.[43] In classical music the appoggiatura was typically a single note, usually a quaver or semi-quaver, set in reduced type, and might be (but was by no means

39 See Buisman, 'Anonymous Manuscript', part 2, *PT*, vol 38, no.4, January 1986, pp.30–4.

40 See below, Ch 16. It would have to be pointed out, however, that this was Donald MacDonald's uniform practice in setting taorluath movements even in his unpublished manuscript which did not have keyboard accompaniments.

41 MacDonald, *Ancient Martial Music*, 'Instructions' p.4. Peter Cooke has pointed out that most of MacDonald's ornaments cannot strictly be called appoggiaturas because these were devices with a precise harmonic role which, he suggested, many of them do not fulfil in piping: 'Letter from Peter Cooke', in *International Piper*, vol.2, no.7, November 1979, pp.20–1.

42 Richard Rastall, *The Notation of Western Music An Introduction*, (Lond., 1983) p. 225.

43 Donington, pp. 203, 206, 208.

always) tied to the following note with a slur. It was played on the beat and took the accent – unless it were a 'passing appoggiatura' in which case it was played before the beat, as many of Donald MacDonald's seem obviously intended to be. Then there was the double appoggiatura form, which bore a rather closer resemblance to the compound ornaments found in piping. Like the single appoggiatura this tended to occupy the scale degrees just above and below the principal note (differing from many pipe ornaments once again) and had the effect of delaying the accent on the following note.[44]

In MacDonald's notation single gracenotes were used to distribute accent and to divide melody notes at the same pitch. To these, the fixed value of a demi-semi-quaver was assigned. But the compound appoggiaturas were different. It seems clear that some of them must have possessed considerable time value, whilst others had virtually none, but which ones, and how much, was left to be determined by the rhythmical context.[45] Ultimately, perhaps, only performance tradition could tell the player how to treat these symbols, and MacDonald's system seems built upon an assumption of ready access to this. For example in a strongly rhythmical tune like *Bodaich na'm Brigis* ('The Carles with the Breeks'),[46] it is possible that the introductory notes on the A and B echo beats were intended to be played as timed, with the exception of the opening one, which is probably a 'cadence E':

But in *Ceann na Drochaid Mhoridh* ('The End of the Great Bridge')[47], the opening figure cannot be treated in this way, because the melody would then start on an awkward off-beat and be a pulse short in the bar. What is set as this:

was presumably intended to be timed somewhat along the lines of:

44 Rastall, p.225.
45 See Cannon, *Compleat Theory*, pp.14–16, for a useful recent overview of this subject.
46 MacDonald, *Ancient Martial Music*, pp.102–5.
47 *Ibid*, pp. III–5.

The result was a system in which the same symbol could mean different things in different contexts, and a conventional expression could be notated in several different ways, even in the same tune. Here, for example, is the opening sequence of *Failte Chlaun Raonuill* ('Clanranald's Salute') from the manuscript of Peter Reid, an important early user of MacDonald's system. Reid was born in Campbeltown probably in 1801, and worked as a clerk in Leith, and later in Glasgow. He was one of the pipers who welcomed George IV to Edinburgh during the royal visit of 1822:[48]

In Reid's setting, the conventional figure:

is also represented like this:

and this:

48 Peter Reid's MS, (dated Glasgow 1826), NLS Acc. 22118, f.19. For further information about Reid, see John MacLellan, 'The Literature of the Highland Bagpipe Peter Reid's Manuscript' in *International Piper*, vol. 3 no. 8, December 1980, pp.14–15.

So that while the G and D notes remain constant in value, the E can apparently range from a demi-semi-quaver to a crotchet.

This potential for ambiguity is of more than theoretical interest. Various later changes in playing styles were to spring directly from the notational conventions established by Donald MacDonald and his contemporaries. As piobaireachd entered the 20th century, written or printed texts were assigned an overriding priority by those who relied upon them as the basis of their authority. A common introductory gesture like:

which was probably timed as follows:

could be transformed into something like this:

for which there was no sanction in performance tradition.[49] Yet the latter, played as written, became mandatory at the leading competitions, effectively displacing more traditional and musically coherent styles, as we shall see.[50]

Learning stories about the tunes seems to have formed an integral part of the piper's training, so that Donald MacDonald's wish to publish what he referred to as 'historical accounts' of his tunes was a logical as well as a commercially attractive step.[51]

Sir John Graham Dalyell noted on 26 March 1839,

> This day the printer of MacDonald's work having called for me I had an
> opportunity of ascertaining some facts from him. The second volume of the

49 Peter Cooke, 'Changing Styles in Pibroch Playing', Part II, *International Piper*, vol.1, no.3, July 1978, pp.11–13.

50 See below, Chapter 18.

51 James Hogg, the Ettrick Shepherd, who knew the book-market as well as anybody during the early nineteenth century, viewed as a key factor in the success of his own song collection *The Jacobite Relics of Scotland*, that it formed 'such a fine text for Highland anecdote.' Donaldson, *Jacobite Song*, p.106.

work was never published. The anecdotes which were promised for it Macdonald was to have received from some gentlemen of the Highlands but he never got them – [52]

Yet MacDonald's unpublished manuscript collection contains notes on some 48 tunes, already set up in type, and forms the earliest known record of its kind. Their stylistic consistency suggests a single author, and it seems possible that this may have been MacDonald himself. Although originally a Gaelic speaker, the author must have been resident in the Lowlands for at least twenty years before he came to compile these notes, and employed in a business capacity which would have required command of an at least adequate written English. The notes are written in a direct and simple style, showing a distinct underlying Gaelic influence, and from a broadly plebeian social perspective in which people of quality are always 'gentlemen' and 'ladies'.[53] There are fairly frequent comments on the musical flavour or technical demands of the tunes which – although tantalisingly brief as a rule – indicate that the author was probably a piper. For example, '*Cruineachadh Chlann a Lain*, or the MacLean's Gathering' is a 'lively and rattling composition.' '*Cumhadh Dhomnuill Bhainn Mhic Chruimmain*, Or a Lament, for the Death of Fair Donald MacCrimmen', 'is the most plaintive Piobaireachd perhaps, now on record'. '*An Bhoalaich*, Or an Intended Lament', 'is a fine air, and very ill [i.e. tricky] to play.'[54]

One very likely source of information will have been the writer's own father, John MacDonald, who was an important tradition-bearer in his own right. He was born probably in the 1720s in Glenhinnisdal in Skye and was for long a servant to Flora MacDonald of Kingsburgh, coming to live with his son Donald in Edinburgh following her death in 1790.[55] As a young man he had been given a shilling by Charles Edward Stuart for helping find fresh drinking water whilst the latter was wandering in Skye disguised as the Irish maid servant Betty Burke. He had caught trout in Loch Leathann for Dr. Johnson's breakfast, and seeing the bulky Englishman walking before Kingsburgh house had asked the minister who he was:

52 Sir John Graham Dalyell MSS, EUL, Gen.353D: f.12. This may possibly have been Capt. Niel MacLeod of Gesto, who was a friend of the MacDonalds and seems to have visited them frequently when in Edinburgh. See Chapter 7.

53 See, for example, the notes to '*Moladh Moraig*, or the Praise of Marion', '*Cumhadh Mhic a' h Arasaig*, or MacIntosh's Lament', and especially '*Cumhadh na Cloinnidh*, Or the Children's Lament', in the section entitled 'History of the Airs in this Volume', NLS, MS. 1680, pp.2, 8.

54 *Ibid*, pp.1, 2, 5.

55 John MacDonald died on 1 August 1827, and was stated in the Canongate Kirk burial records to have been 107 years old. Sanger, 'Donald MacDonald', p.27. However, another source states him to have been a 'raw-boned youth' in 1746: Alex. MacGregor, 'John MacDonald – an Adherent of Prince Charles', *Celtic Magazine*, vol.3, 1878, pp.462–6 (462).

'Sin agad, Iain, an Sasunnach Mór a rinn a' Bheurla'. Thubhairt mi fein, 'ma ta, a' Mhinisteir, bha glé bheag aige ri dheanamh'. 'That, John, is the Big Sasunnach who made the English'. I replied and said, 'Well, minister, he had precious little to do.'[56]

He must have been a striking man, judging by the way he was vividly remembered more than half a century later by the Highland writer Alex MacGregor, who frequently visited the MacDonalds during his student days in Edinburgh:

Old John spoke the Gaelic language with much fluency and idiomatic correctness. Not a word was out of joint, and it was delightful to listen to the grammatical purity of his conversation. His tales and stories about ancient times were endless. It seemed a pleasure to him to speak of the various feuds that existed between the different hostile clans, particularly about the bloody skirmishes in which the Macdonalds of the Isles were engaged with the Macleods of Dunvegan and the Mackenzies of Kintail and Gairloch. He was gifted with a memory extraordinary for its retentiveness, and could repeat ancient poetry for hours on end, which he called 'Bàrdachd na Feinne', or the 'Fingalian Poetry.' John was, however, considerably tainted with various superstitious ideas, for he firmly believed in fairy influences, second sight, and supernatural powers being granted to some, to affect their neighbours' cattle, and deprive cows of their milk. Of second sight in particular, he told a great variety of striking instances, and confidently believed in them all. It was a favourite theme of his to dilate upon the musical proficiency of the MacCrimmons, the family pipers of the Macleods of Dunvegan, and likewise of the MacArthurs, the hereditary pipers of the Macdonalds of the Isles. He acknowledged that the MacCrimmons were more famed for their musical talent, but still that they could not surpass the beautiful and systematic performances of the MacArthurs. He possessed a great relish for pipe-music, when skilfully executed. I am not aware whether he had ever attempted to perform on the bagpipe himself, but I know that he had a correct knowledge of 'Piobaireachd', and could repeat the notes of any lament, salute, or gathering, by the syllabic mode of notation, which was practised by the already mentioned family pipers, in order to preserve their pieces of music from being lost. It was interesting to listen to the old man repeating the various measures of a long 'Piobaireachd' expressed by significant vocables, such as these pipers used to represent the notes and bars of their several tunes. The following will give an idea of that notation: –
    Hi ho dro hi, hi ho dro hi, ha, han an an ha;
    Hi ho dro hachin, hachin, hiuchin,
    Hi dro ti hi, hi an an, an hi ri,
    Ho dro huchin, hi ri o huchin . . .

56 MacGregor, 'John MacDonald', p.465.

I remember calling on worthy John one evening, if I recollect well, in December 1831, when we had a long discussion about pipe-music.[57] John remarked that 'The gathering of the Clans', was a splendid piobaireachd, which was composed at the battle of Inverlochy. He repeated it in the syllabic manner just described. When he had finished it he said, 'Let us go down stairs to hear the same fine piobaireachd from Donald on his large bagpipe'. We did so, and worthy Donald, who was a short, thick-set, very stout man, who weighed about twenty stones, did all justice to the piece of music in question. The aged father, however, who had listened very attentively, addressed his son, and said, 'Donald, my boy you played such a part of the Crànnludh by far too slow, for it ought to be-

   Hiodratatiti, hiodratutiti, hiodratititi, hiodratatiti'.

'Ah! very good, father', said Donald, 'very good, it is easy for these volatile, quivering lips of yours to articulate these notes rapidly, but not at all so easy for my stiff fingers, to extract them from this black, hard, hole-bored stick of mine!' (meaning his chanter).[58]

The legendary and supernatural quality of a number of the stories in Donald MacDonald's manuscript would certainly seem to indicate a writer at home with traditional folk narrative. Discussing '*Cumhadh MhicGilli Chalum Rasay,* or Macleod of Rasay's Lament', for example, he says:

Sir Donald Macdonald of the Isles having got Macleod's sister with child, refused to marry her. Macleod was going to the Lewis Islands, and called upon Macdonald, at his castle, viz. Duntuilm; and, having heard that Macdonald had refused to marry his sister, he (Macleod,) told him, that when he would return from Stornoway, he would take off his head. About a month or two afterwards, Macleod's boat was seen sailing towards the Isle of Skye; Macdonald hearing of this, sent for his dairy-maid, who was said to be a witch: she made use of her art. Macleod and his crew were all drowned; and so near were they to the land, that Macleod's pack of hounds swam on shore. Their bodies were never found. The boat, when found in Ross-shire, had Macleod's sword, struck a plank and a half deep, into the gunnel of it.[59]

Donald MacDonald's version of the famous tale of the betrayal and death of the laird of Duart, attached to the tune '*Cumhadh Iain Ghairbh Mhic a Lean,* Or a

---

57 This date cannot be correct. John MacDonald had been dead for more than four years at this point.

58 MacGregor, 'John MacDonald', pp.464–5.

59 Donald MacDonald MS, f.1; see also the notes to '*Cumhadh Fhionnlaidh,* Or a Lament, for the Death of Finlay', '*Ionnsuidh Aneas Bhig MhicDhomhnuill,* Or Angus MacDonald's attack upon the MacDougalls', '*Cumhadh Chraobh na'n Cheud,* Or a Lament for the Tree of Hundreds', and '*Cumhadh Chleibhair,* Or a Lament for the Death of General Cleaver', ff. 2, 4, 5, 9.

Lament for the Death of Great John MacLean' is not only long and rich, but would also seem to be the earliest recorded text:[60]

Chief of the Macleans, and father to a most mischievous man, but not on account of his evil deeds, previous to what will be said concerning him in this tale. This gentleman got so far as to be styled Sir John Maclean; and it is said that he was the most comely man then in Scotland. He had a pleasure-boat, in which he took great delight; and, almost every day he sailed up and down the Sound of Mull. We shall leave him here, and turn to the king of Spain's daughter, who, one night had a dream, and fancied she saw the most beautiful man that ever lived, taking her by the hand; and when she awoke, she vowed she would never rest, till she should see this man. Accordingly, a frigate was got ready for the purpose; and, almost loaded with silver and gold, she went to sea, and sailed round every part of the navigable globe, – landing every where – going to balls, and making great parties, looking for the person she saw in her dream, but to no purpose. She left no place unsearched; and, having almost lost hope, she determined to try Britain, before she would return to Spain. She came to London, and attended a number of balls, masquerades, and other entertainments, but to as little purpose as before. At last, she sailed round to the West Highlands, and never halted till she came to the Sound of Mull, where she cast anchor, intending to return home in a day or two. However, one morning, as she was looking through her glass, she beheld a fine barge, sailing down the Sound; she waited patiently till it would draw nigh. The sun then rising, was throwing his rays on the water, it being a fine morning in the month of May. The barge was now within a mile of the vessel: and the queen, (being then heir to the throne of Spain), exclaimed 'Here is my man, here is my man coming' . . .

Turning to the 'Preface' of the *Ancient Martial Music of Caledonia*, we find a very different kind of story. Sir John Graham Dalyell thought that 'No editor was employed in publishing the work' but later revised this view concluding that the letterpress portion 'has been obviously written by a person of some intelligence accustomed to literary composition', and this was clearly the case.[61]

It began as follows:

The object of this Publication is, not only to supply a desideratum in our PIPE MUSIC, which has hitherto had no *written* Record, but, at once to facilitate the attempts of Students upon the GREAT HIGHLAND BAG-PIPE, and to accommodate its Music to almost all other instruments, such as the Organ, Piano-Forte, Violin, and Flute. In the progress of this undertaking,

60 Donald MacDonald MS, ff.6–8. I am indebted for this point to Professor Colm O'Boyle.
61 Sir John Graham Dalyell MSS, EUL, Gen.353D, f.12v.

the Publisher has been encouraged by a Prize from the Highland Society of Scotland, as being the first who had succeeded in setting the *Piobaireachd* to Music.

   To accomplish this Work, the Publisher has sacrificed the leisure moments of the last fifteen years, and now, thus encouraged, as well as by the countenance of many enlightened individuals, he presumes to submit to the Public a portion of the result of his labours; and he entertains a humble confidence, that, whatever the learned and the critical may say in other respects, every lover of the wild Melodies of his wilder Country will thank him, for preserving and making familiar to the more fashionable instruments of the day, those strains hitherto confined to the Bag-Pipe, and many of them so worthy of being made universal.[62]

We do not know who wrote this, but it cannot have been Donald MacDonald. Not only is the style impossibly elaborate, but as we shall see the 'Preface' shows ignorance of things which he must have known, and makes statements which he must, likewise, have been aware were untrue. Quite in accordance with standard Scottish publishing practice during the early nineteenth century a plebeian tradition-bearer is being mediated by an anonymous writer of considerably greater 'formal' education and social power, and being reduced to a stereotype, a 'humble individual' soliciting the support of his betters for his 'simple objects' with an apparently cringing sycophancy which is a little ironical when one considers the paltry assistance he was actually given.

   Those acquainted with similar material appended to Patrick and Joseph MacDonald's works would find little to surprise them in the 'Preface' to *Ancient Martial Music*. There was the same antiquarian tone and tendency to sweeping generalisation based on no, or little, or wrong evidence; the same stress upon the antiquity of the pipe and its music; the same appeal to a supposedly age-old heroic tradition; the same sense of the music as characteristically wild and artless, and of the culture which sustained it as enfeebled and approaching its final dissolution unless artificially sustained.

   Since *The Ancient Martial Music of Caledonia* was an important collection – second only to Angus MacKay's amongst 19th century sources – the opinions contained in its 'Preface' were widely disseminated and made an influential contribution to the tissue of ideologically-driven supposition accumulating around the pipe under the names of genuine experts on Highland music who had written not a word of it.

   Donald MacDonald's mediator exploited the current fashion for Jacobite *Kitsch*, intensifying the romantic appeal of his subject by linking it with the gallant doomed clans, heedless, or ignorant, of the fact that the pipes were played all over the Highlands and used by both sides in the '45. Of course the idea that piping was a distinctively Jacobite pastime provided a useful prop for his

62 MacDonald, *Ancient Martial Music*, 'Preface', p.3.

assumption that it was in terminal decline because it provided some sort of 'explanation' for its being in this condition, whilst allowing him at the same time to classify Donald MacDonald's activities as a kind of cultural archaeology with little direct relevance to contemporary creative enterprise:

> After the Battle of Culloden, a powerful check was given to the spirit of the Highlanders; and, with their arms and garb, the Bag-Pipe was, for a long time, almost completely laid aside. In this interval much of the Music was neglected and lost. [a near-quotation from the 1784 Ramsay 'Essay']
> Afterwards, when the internal commotions of the country had completely subsided, and the slumbering spirit and prejudices of our countrymen awakened under the new order of things, the principal, nay only, records of our ancient Piobaireachd, were the memories of those Patriarchs who had proudly sounded them at the unfortunate 'Rising'.[63]

No evidence was offered to support this conclusion. Indeed Donald MacDonald was its living refutation, as were most of the people who had been playing at the Highland Society of London's competitions annually since 1781.[64]

But the notion of proscription once introduced rapidly assumed a life of its own, being taken up and expanded by later writers to such an extent that the author of the 'Foreword' to the 1974 edition of The Ancient Martial Music of Caledonia, Seumas MacNeill, could declare that:

> With the break-down of the clan system following the failure of the 1745 Rising . . . the situation for piping changed drastically. From 1746 to 1782, to play the bagpipe was a criminal offence punishable by death. The various colleges of piping throughout the Highlands were disbanded, but piping continued, albeit on a much reduced scale, carried on by enthusiasts whose contempt for the law was encouraged by their realisation that enforcement of laws in the Highlands has always been difficult, when it has not been impossible.[65]

The intention of much of such writing was to intensify rather than dispel the mystery of the pipe and its music whose secrets were presented as lying behind a screen of impenetrable verbal notation and rude instructional practices. Music, indeed, was scarcely considered to be a quality inherent in piobaireachd at all, but rather as a medium into which it must first be 'translated' before it could begin to be appreciated by people of culture:

63 Ibid.
64 Only one of them, indeed, old John MacGregor of Fortingall, would actually seem to fit this prescription: see Alex. MacGregor, 'The Aged Piper and his Bagpipe', in Celtic Magazine, vol.5, 1879, pp.404–405.
65 MacDonald, Ancient Martial Music, 'Foreword', p.v.

Many who attempted to take down the Tunes from the directions of these Minstrels being ignorant of music, could only describe the sounds by words, which, though rewarded by the Highland Society, as evincing a laudable ambition for the preservation of these relics of our ancestors, it need not be said, would afford little satisfaction to those who wished to know the true character of these Airs. Indeed, so little idea seemed formerly to exist of the mystery of noting down the Pipe Music, that in a sort of College or Academy for instruction on the Great Highland Bag-Pipe, existing not many years ago in the Island of Skye, 'the teachers made use of pins stuck into the ground instead of musical notes'.[66]

And so an obscurely-worded literary source was preferred to the evidence of a living expert, Donald MacDonald – with whom the mediator was presumably acquainted – who could bear personal testimony to these matters, as no doubt could several dozens of contemporary Highland musicians similarly trained. But amongst the 'educated' classes, the present was ceasing to be a context in which it was deemed fruitful to consider the music of the pipe, and so enquiry was directed elsewhere.

To people like the mediator, antiquity was the defining characteristic of piobaireachd as a form, and much emphasis was laid upon this in *Ancient Martial Music* which contained tunes ostensibly dating back to the early fifteenth century. When he declared that a piece like 'The End of the Great Bridge' (a famous tune, still in every serious piper's repertoire) was 'Composed in the Midst of the Battle at Inverlochy 1427. Wherein Donald Balloch of the Isles, was Victorious over the Royal Forces', it seems to have been in the belief that it was a genuine specimen of antiquity, transmitted unchanged over a period of nearly four hundred years, and that the ability of the genre to preserve 'original' texts in this way was one of its most valuable characteristics.[67] The fact that nearly a quarter of the tunes in MacDonald's book had been created within the previous hundred years, or little more, and that all of them were transcriptions of what was currently being played (and in the very latest style), the mediator was not anxious to discuss.[68] To have acknowledged this, and what it meant, namely that piobaireachd was not a relic of antiquity but an ongoing artistic enterprise (to which Donald MacDonald himself was even then making an active contribution),[69] and subject therefore to forces of creative renewal and change inseparable from a living art-form, would have been to call into question the deeply-held assumptions about the unchanging nature of

---

66 MacDonald, *Ancient Martial Music*, 'Preface', p.3.
67 MacDonald, *Ancient Martial Music*, pp.106, 111.
68 For probable eighteenth-century tunes, see pp.1, 23, 34, 68, 92.
69 See, for example, the attractive 'Elchies Salute', in Thomason, *Ceol Mor*, pp.51–3. For the ascription of this tune to Donald MacDonald, see C. S. Thomason, 'Ceol Mor Legends', NLS, MS 3749, f.83.

tradition and its roots in historically remote periods upon which the whole 'Preface' was based.

The problem was, that there was no mention of the pipes in Ossian; indeed there was little reference to them at all in Scotland before the period of the Renaissance. There was also the awkward fact of their known use in Classical times. Some other token of distinction must therefore be found to convey the writer's sense of their unique significance. 'Strangers' he declared:

> may sneer at the pains taken to preserve this wild instrument, because their ears have only been accustomed to the gay measures of the violin, and 'lascivious pleasing of the lute;' but it has claims and recommendations that may silence even *their* prejudices. The Bag-Pipe is, perhaps, the only national instrument in Europe. Every other is peculiar to many countries, but the Bag-Pipe to Scotland alone. There, in the banquet-hall and in the house of mourning it has alike prevailed. It has animated her warriors in battle, and welcomed them back, after their toils, to the homes of their love, and the hills of their nativity. Its strains were the first sounded on the ears of infancy, and they are the last to be forgotten in the wanderings of age. Even Highlanders will allow that it is not the gentlest of instruments; but, when far from their mountain homes, what sounds, however melodious, could thrill round their heart like one burst of their own wild native Pipe? The feelings which other instruments awaken are general and undefined, because they talk alike to Frenchmen, Spaniards, Germans, and Highlanders, for they are common to all. But the Bag-Pipe is sacred to Scotland, and speaks a language which Scotsmen only feel. It talks to them of home, and of all the past; and brings before them, on the burning shores of India, the 'heath-covered hills' and oft frequented streams of Caledonia, the friends that are thinking of them, and the sweethearts and wives that are weeping for them there! And need it be told here, to how many fields of danger and victory its proud strains have led! There is not a battle that is honourable to Britain in which its war-blast has not sounded. When every other instrument has been hushed in the confusion and carnage of the scene, it has been borne into the thick of battle, and, far in the advance, its bleeding, but devoted bearer, sinking on the earth, has sounded at once encouragement to his countrymen, and his own *coronach*.[70]

Here, then, was the argument about music as the substance of national distinctiveness, the mode in which the spirit of the people found truest expression, in its most emphatic early nineteenth century form. The cultural transformation which had been gathering force since the '45, which tended to view all Scots as Highlanders and all Highlanders as Jacobites and the bagpipe and its music as their symbol and summation, here reached its climax.[71]

70 MacDonald, *Ancient Martial Music*, 'Preface', pp.4–5.
71 See Donaldson, *Jacobite Song*, pp. 69–71, 90–4; see also John Prebble, *The King's Jaunt: George IV in Scotland, August 1822 'One and twenty daft days'* (Lond., 1988), *passim*.

The 'Preface', to be sure, contained a number of errors. The bagpipe was not unique to Scotland. It was distributed widely throughout contemporary Europe. Likewise British battles had, from time to time, been won without its aid.[72] And when the mediator gave as his opinion that:

> it must surely enhance the value of the present Publisher's exertions, in recovering so many valuable *Piobaireachd,* when he mentions, that, for nearly twenty years, there has not been above a dozen of different Tunes played at the Annual Competitions of Pipers in Edinburgh.[73]

this was also a mistake. The real number was about 150.[74]

But the roots of the whole argument lay in ideology rather than observation, as is evident from the series of carefully developed contrasts between the civilised and the barbarian, domesticity and wild nature, cultivated taste and primitive passion, which lie at its heart. The fluency of the writing should not be allowed to obscure its deep irrationalism. If, as the mediator claimed, Scots people automatically possessed an intuitive understanding of this music, then concepts such as practice and study, thought and reflection, criticism and theory, the cultivation of taste, indeed the whole gamut of intellectual and aesthetic procedures connected with music as a sophisticated social practice, became irrelevant. Between the music of the pipe and other kinds of music a deep divide was set. If only Scots people could understand it, then it followed that pipe music must adhere to a different aesthetic from 'normal' music. The nationalistic urge to create a distinctive space for piobaireachd was accompanied, therefore, by a seriously weakened expectation that it should conform to recognisable aesthetic principles. And qualities like melodic richness, rhythmical subtlety, structural regularity, beauty even, gradually ceased to be looked for, outside the performer community. Indeed if this argument were pushed to its conclusion, then the less piobaireachd resembled 'proper' music, the more it succeeded in becoming itself. A century later, the Secretary of the Music Committee of the Piobaireachd Society, Archibald Campbell of Kilberry, could be found criticising certain pieces on the grounds that they were 'tuny' – i.e. they were forced to rely mainly on melody for their appeal.[75]

Donald MacDonald was appointed pipe-maker to the Highland Society of

---

72 It was probably in reaction to such hyperbole that the pleasant little anecdote circulated in 19th century Britain to the effect that when military pipers struck up the foe had only two choices: to flee at once, or remain and lose all further desire for life: see W. L. Manson, *The Highland Bagpipe Its History, Literature, and Music with some account of the Traditions, Superstitions, and Anecdotes Relating to The Instrument and Its Tunes* (Paisley, 1901), pp.192–3.

73 MacDonald, *Ancient Martial Music,* 'Preface' p.5.

74 See MacInnes, p.169.

75 Seumas MacNeill and Frank Richardson, *Piobaireachd and its Interpretation: Classical Music of the Highland Bagpipe* (Edinr., 1987), pp.112–5.

London in 1823 and his instruments, with their characteristically robust tone, were much sought after until changing fashions later in the century began to make them obsolete. In 1828 he published *A collection of quicksteps, strathspeys, reels, & jigs. Arranged for the Highland bagpipe* containing 119 tunes. This latter seems to have been a modest success, running to at least three editions during his lifetime, and three subsequent ones after the plates were acquired by the Glen family so that it remained in print for most of the nineteenth century.[76] Donald MacDonald continued to work as an instrument maker and teacher at a variety of addresses in Edinburgh, latterly at 529 Castlehill. He died on the 11th October 1840 of 'ossification of the heart', and was buried next to his father in the Canongate Kirkyard 10 feet west of the east walk and 10 feet south-east of Dumbreck's stone.[77]

When Donald MacDonald said that he had nearly ruined himself by publishing the *Ancient Martial Music of Caledonia* he was probably speaking the simple truth. Within weeks of his death the Highland Society of London received a

> Petition from Mrs. Ann Park, 529 Castle Hill: daughter of the late Donald MacDonald, Pipe Maker to the Said Society . . . Humbly Sheweth that the petitioner's father died on the 11th October last leaving four grand children orphans and two widows of whom he was the sole support.
>
> That the Petitioner makes the present application to the Honorable Society in the hope that they may be pleased to take her case into their consideration . . . the Petitioner and her widowed sister with their young orphans are left in very destitute circumstances.[78]

It is not known what response the Highland Society made.

76 Cannon, *Bibliography*, pp.126–8.
77 Sanger, 'Donald MacDonald', p.29.
78 HSL, NLS Dep.268, Correspondence Box 5, 2 November 1840.

7

'Legible to every musician': the Collections of Angus MacArthur and Niel MacLeod of Gesto

In the spring of 1820, Angus MacArthur, Donald MacDonald's teacher, and former piper to the MacDonalds of the Isles, lay on his deathbed playing the practice chanter. By him sat John MacGregor III, of *clann an sgeulaiche*, piper to the Highland Society of London, pen in hand, copying down what he heard. Also present was musician and society painter Andrew Robertson from Aberdeen, one of the Society's treasurers.[1] MacArthur and MacGregor were being paid. Half a guinea a tune. Eventually there would be thirty of them. And so the 'Highland Society of London's MS' came into being.[2]

By this means, the Highland Society came to possess, as its property – since by paying MacArthur for his work it must be presumed that under common law they thereby acquired his copyright – the central core of a traditional art-form: the cultural equivalent of enclosure and the appropriation of commons. Writing made possible the ownership of tradition. Once it became property, it could be treated in the same way as other sorts of property: it could be more intensively exploited on 'scientific' principles, there could be 'improvements', there could be evictions. The Society planned to promote their collection as a means of fixing 'the proper standard for each tune – for at present scarcely two pipers play exactly the same *set* of any piobrachd', and they proceeded on the assumption that staff notation was best adapted to the process of 'simplifying the process of learning and teaching Bagpipe Music', so that 'these valuable pieces of ancient Music should be forthwith put down so as to be rendered legible to every musician'.[3] Once a fixed written text had been established, it could then be promulgated as the sole acceptable version, confirming the sponsoring institution rather than the performer community as the ultimate source of power, and conferring on one piper's work the cachet of 'authority' at the cost of disfranchising all the rest.

By the middle 1820s, therefore, perhaps a fifth of the repertoire had been translated into written or printed form (for the Highland Society of London was careful to avoid tunes which had already been published by Donald MacDonald)

---

1 See N. T. McKay, 'Andrew Robertson (1777–1845) and his Role in Recording Ceol Mor in Written Form', in *PT*, vol.51, no.4, January 1999, pp.19–24.

2 Now in the National Library of Scotland, NLS MS. 1679. For a brief account of the MacArthur family, see Keith Sanger, 'The MacArthurs Evidence from the MacDonald Papers', in *PT*, vol.35, no.8, 1983, pp.13–17.

3 Highland Society of London Papers, NLS, Dep.268, Correspondence, Box 2, 10/11/1825, Charles Gordon to John Wedderburn. See also Ruairidh Halford-MacLeod, 'Highland Society', pp. 25–31, 28–32.

giving a pretty fair account of the MacArthur style. And the MacArthur inheritance was worth acquiring.

The family was widely diffused, with branches in Islay and Mull, but the first of the MacArthur pipers to the MacDonalds of the Isles appearing in the record was Angus MacArthur, tenant of Hungladder in Trotternish on the north-west tip of Skye near the old MacDonald stronghold of Duntulm. A 'Judicial Rental of the Lands of Sleat and Trotternish' dated 1733 states:

> Charles McCarter in Haunyclater being sworn and interrogate in the Irish [i.e. Gaelic] Language depones that he and Angus McCarter his father possess between them the one penny [land: a pennyland was about 8 or 9 acres] of Hunklater whereof the ordinary rent is eighty four merks of silver duty and Kings meall four pounds sixteen shillings of Cess, twelve merk for tiend, two bolls of meal, two stone of butter and two stone of cheese, no wedders, four hens, ten pecks of horse corn and eight loads of straw and porters mealls conform to use and wont but the deponent being the Laird's piper for his pains he is allowed to retain three fourths of the penny and this is the truth as he shall answer to God. Cannot write.[4]

A later account-book notes payment in September 1735 'To Angus McCarter piper and his son Charles as their wages for 1 year to Whit last £59:6:8'. and 'To Neil McCarter piper as 1 years wages to Whit last £9:5:4'.[5] Angus MacArthur had three sons, Charles, Neil and Iain Bàn. Of these the most important was Charles, who had a considerable contemporary reputation. Angus MacKay's mediator, James Logan, gives the following tale about him, possibly from MacKay himself. It shows a similar tinge of folk narrative that we noted in Donald MacDonald, which in itself may imply something about the standing of the family:

> The most celebrated of this race was Charles, whose musical education was perfected by Patrick òg MacCrummen; and respecting him the following anecdote is handed down: – Sir Alexander MacDonald being at Dunvegan, on a visit to the laird of MacLeod, he heard the performance of Patrick òg with great delight; and desirous if possible to have a Piper of equal merit, he said to MacCrummen one day, that there was a young man whom he was anxious to place under his tuition, on condition that he should not be allowed to return, until such time as he could play equal to his master. 'When this is the case,' said MacDonald, 'you will bring him home, and I will give you ample satisfaction for your trouble'. 'Sir Alexander', says Patrick, 'if you will be pleased to send him to me, I will do all that I am able to do for him'. Charles was accordingly sent to Borreraig, where he remained for eleven years, when MacCrummen, considering him as perfect as he could be made, proceeded to Mugstad, to deliver his charge to Sir Alexander who was then residing there, and where *Eain Dall* Mackay,

---

4 Sanger, 'The MacArthurs', pp.13–14.
5 *Ibid*, p.14.

Gairloch's blind Piper, happened also to be. MacDonald hearing of their arrival, thought it a good opportunity to determine the merit of his own Piper, by the judgement of the blind man, whose knowledge of Pipe-music was unexceptionable. He therefore enjoined Patrick *òg* and MacArthur not to speak a word to betray who they were, and addressing Mackay, he told him he had a young man learning the Pipe for some years, and was glad that he was present to say whether he thought him worth the money which his instructions had cost? Mackay said, if he heard him play, he would give his opinion freely; but requested to be informed previously with whom the piper had been studying. Sir Alexander told him he had been with young Patrick MacCrummen. 'Then,' exclaimed Mackay, 'he could never have found a better master'. The young man was ordered to play, and when he had finished, Sir Alexander asked the other for his opinion. 'I think a great deal of him', replied *Eain*, 'he is a good Piper; he gives the notes correctly, and if he takes care, he will excel in his profession'. Sir Alexander was pleased with so flattering an opinion, and observed that he had been at the trouble of sending two persons to the college, that he might retain the best, so he said the second one should also play, that an opinion on his merits might also be given. Mackay observed that he must be a very excellent performer that could surpass the first, or even compare with him. When Patrick *òg*, who acted as the second pupil, had finished playing, Sir Alexander asked the umpire, what he thought of his performance. 'Indeed, sir, no one need try me in that manner', returned the blind man', 'for though I have lost the eyes of my human body, I have not lost the eyes of my understanding; and if all the Pipers in Scotland were present, I would not find it a difficult task to distinguish the last player from them all'. 'You surprise me, Mackay! and who is he?' 'Who but Patrick *òg* MacCrummen', promptly rejoined Mackay; and turning to where Patrick was sitting, he observed, 'it was quite needless, my good sir, to think you could deceive me in that way, for you could not but know that I should have recognised your performance among a thousand'. Sir Alexander then asked Mackay himself to play, and afterwards he called for a bottle of whisky – drank to their healths, and remarked that he had that night under his roof the three best Pipers in Britain.[6]

Charles MacArthur was also a composer, being credited with 'Sir James MacDonald's Lament', and 'Murray of Abercairnies Salute'[7]. He was successively piper to the young Sir James MacDonald and to his brother and successor, Alexander, later 1st Lord MacDonald, and is thought to have died about 1780, being buried at Peingown. His son Donald ordered a handsome stone for his grave, the only such monument as yet known for an eighteenth-century piper, and a further indication of the family's worldly standing. It bears the words:

6 MacKay, *Ancient Piobaireachd*, 'Account of the Hereditary Pipers', pp.11–12; see also
   'Historical and Traditional Notes on the Piobaireachds', No.XXXI, p.9.
7 Highland Society of London's MS, NLS MS. 1679, tunes no. 23 and 12.

Here ly the remains of Charles MacKarter whose fame as an honest man and
remarkable piper will survive this generation for his manners were easy &
regular as his music & the melody of his fingers will

And there it ends, at the point it had reached when Donald MacArthur was
drowned in the Minch ferrying cattle from Uist to Skye.[8]

Of Charles MacArthur's brothers, Neil became a piper in the 77th and died in
the West Indies in 1762. His son, John, later known as 'professor MacArthur',
was taught by his uncle Charles, and settled in Edinburgh. He composed a salute
for the Highland Society of Scotland.[9] Iain Bàn was one of Sir Alexander
MacDonald of Sleat's pipers in 1745. He died in 1779, leaving a widow, Marian
MacLean (who received a pension from the MacDonald estate), and two sons,
Charles, who became piper to the Earl of Eglinton, and Angus who succeeded his
uncle as piper to Lord MacDonald and moved with him to London in 1796, later
becoming one of the pipers to the Highland Society of London.[10] Angus was also
a composer, and his laments for Lord and Lady MacDonald are preserved in the
Highland Society of London's MS, along with classic tunes such as 'The Big
Spree', 'The Bells of Perth', 'Beloved Scotland, I leave thee gloomy', 'The
Brother's Lament', 'Donald Duaghal MacKay', 'The Lament for the Laird of
Anapool', 'The MacDougall's Gathering' and the lovely nameless tune which
General Thomason called 'Ben Cruachan'.[11]

Angus MacArthur's settings are conspicuously rich and musical, and are
recorded by John MacGregor in a neat and stylish hand.[12] The notation is in an
interestingly transitional style, with gracenote and melody note stems both
written 'up', and, perhaps in order to achieve a visually uncluttered effect,
transposed down a fifth, thus in tune No.13 'Albain Bheadarach' ('Beloved
Scotland'):[13]

8 Matheson, *John MacCodrum*, p.253.
9 NLS MS. 1679, tune no.10 'The Highland Club by J. MacArthur.' For
   published scores see MacKay, *Ancient Piobaireachd*, pp.146–8 and Thomason, *Ceol
   Mor*, p.177.
10 Seumas MacNeill, 'John MacFadyen Remembered', *PT*, vol.42, no.10–11, July-August,
   1990, pp.26–38, 24–8.
11 NLS MS. 1679, tune no.16, 'The Late Lord Mcdonald's Lament – By Angus
   McArthur year 96' and tune no.24, 'Lady MacDonald's Lament, Composed in the
   Year 1790 by Angus McArthur'. For published versions of the nameless tune see
   Thomason, *Ceol Mor*, p.216; and *Piobaireachd Society Collection* (second series), with
   the title 'Gun ainm – Cumha' (Nameless – a Lament), xiii, 420–4.
12 For the transmission of this manuscript and its treatment by later editors see the
   Appendix to the present chapter.
13 From tune No.14 'The MacLean's March' onwards, however, John MacGregor begins
   to tackle the problem created by his bigger grace-note clusters having their stems
   pointing up amongst thickly-crowded melody note stems and beams which often
   makes the effect rather crabbed, by inverting them.

Francis Collinson in his book *The Bagpipe: the History of a Musical Instrument* (Lond., 1975), suggests that 'This was the method used by the classical composers for the notation of the "transposing instruments" of the orchestra, clarinets, trumpets and horns. [i.e. instruments which it was simpler to notate at one pitch, though they actually played at another] It may perhaps be taken as an indication that the Highland pipers were not ignorant of other forms of music'.[14]

MacGregor uses tempo and expression marks in a mixture of Italian and French, indicating that the ground of the 'The Big Spree' should be played *andante con espressione*, that of 'King James VI's Salute' *Legerment*, 'The Highland Club' by J. MacArthur *Animato*, and 'The Bells of Perth', *Vite*. There is also frequent change of time signature for different variations within tunes to signal changes in rhythm and tempo. For example N.28 'The Laird of Anapool's Lament' begins in 3/4 time, changing to 6/8 in first variation, and to 2/4 in variation two which is also marked (in Andrew Robertson's hand) *Andante con express:* with a *ritardando* to emphasise the end of the line.

At first the ground is directed to be repeated after each pair of variations, very much in accordance with Donald MacDonald's rule that 'as the chorus of a Song is to the verses, so is the ground of a Piobaireachd to its Variations, and ought to be played after the doubling, and where it happens tripling of each measure. It is also the conclusion of each piece, as well as its beginning', although this instruction disappears after the first couple of tunes, perhaps reflecting its current interdiction at the Highland Societies' competitions.[15]

In accordance with normal practice up to this point, the first note of echo-beat groups tends to receive the accent, thus:

---

14 Francis Collinson, *The Bagpipe: the History of a Musical Instrument* (Lond., 1975), p.192, *n*. Professor Derek B. Scott points out that this was achieved at the cost of a certain inconsistency: the C gracenotes in 'Albain Bheadarach' above, for example should be natural, but the key signature means they are sharp. Letter to the writer, March 1999. Sensing this difficulty, perhaps, MacGregor abandoned key signatures altogether later in the MS, and this was gradually to become the standard modern practice.

15 MacDonald, *Ancient Martial Music*, 'Instructions for the Great Highland Bagpipe', p.3.

This happens almost invariably on A, usually on B and with decreasing frequency as one goes up the scale, so that even quavers are the most common way of notating this movement on E, F and high G:

There are circumstances where the accent falls on the second note of the group, which is characteristic of Angus MacKay's style, but it seems clear that at this stage these movements were sensitive to their musical context and could be, and were, varied to suit it.

We meet in the MacArthur/MacGregor manuscript for the first time those space-saving devices used by a number of later notators which meant that conventional variations like taorluath and crunluath were not written out in full. These seem to have influenced Angus MacKay in particular who followed them rather closely in his own manuscript collection. A typical taorluath movement would appear as follows:

and a typical crunluath thus:

James Logan said that Donald Roy MacCrimmon had been sent to Charles MacArthur to study the former's 'particular graces' implying that there were significant differences between the MacCrimmon and MacArthur styles on which later commentators have laid some stress.[16] But there is relatively little in general terms in the Highland Society of London manuscript that would seriously trouble a modern piper, except occasionally in the later variations, where we encounter a couple of rather unusual crunluath movements, one typically played off a succession of E melody notes, and with an interestingly different distribution of accent within the movement:[17]

---

16 MacKay, *Ancient Piobaireachd*, 'Hereditary Pipers', p.12.
17 No.12, 'Murray of Abercairnie's Salute'; see also No.23, 'Sir James MacDonald's Lament'.

the other, a fosgailte movement played 'up' with the accent falling on the second rather than the first note of the group, giving a rather attractive rocking effect:[18]

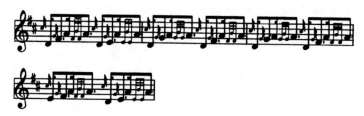

John MacGregor's notation shows a move away from the typical MacDonald 'appoggiatura' style in favour of a less context-bound, more rhythmically explicit style. We can see this in a number of places, such as, for example, the ground of N.14 'The MacLean's March':

where the introductory Es are written nearly always as expressed E quavers, so that when a MacDonald-type semi-demi-quaver GED run appears at the beginning of bar five, in an exactly equivalent rhythmical position, it would suggest that the E should also be given a duration of a quaver, and that the movement be timed like this:

On the other hand, it would seem clear from the context of the first variation of N.24 'Lady MacDonald's Lament', one of Angus MacArthur's own compositions, that the GDE runs must be allotted rather little time value if an obviously flowing melody is not to be seriously impeded:[19]

18 No.7 'Spaidsearachd Bharroch, or the pride of Barroch'.
19 In this example, I have substituted an equivalent movement in bar 24 for its counterpart in bar 8 to illustrate the point without having to reproduce the whole variation.

The fact that MacGregor felt able to omit the GED run at the beginning of the final bar might suggest that in such a context (especially bearing in mind that the passage is marked *moderato*) these things might take very little off the time value of the succeeding melody note.

The pipers seem to have been in good hands with Andrew Robertson, whose occasional notes on the scores suggest that he was more than just the paymaster. He also seems to have been frequently present at the recording sessions so that he was able to talk in general terms about how they had gone. Speaking of N.21, 'Cumha a Chleraich, or the Bard's Lament' he says

> The variation does not perfectly agree with the air in a few bars. This is the only Pibroch in which there appeared the *least* uncertainty in Mr. McArthur's recollection – in all the others there was not the change of a single note in repeatedly whistling them [i.e. playing them on the practice chanter] & *very* seldom even in the time of the dotted crotchets. As it is the foundation of a good Pibroch John McGregor was desirous of recording it which he has done as well as circumstances would admit of. A Robertson.

The next step was to publish the collection. The Highland Society of London Minutes for 1 May 1824 record a quote 'from Mr.[John] Gow for publishing the Piobaireachds written by John M'Gregor from the recitation of Angus MacArthur' at £43.18.0. for 100 copies, and the Society's secretary John Wedderburn was deputed to go ahead with the edition.[20] In August, Charles Gordon, Secretary of the Highland Society of Scotland, wrote suggesting a competition for essays on the history of pipe music, no doubt intended to supply the letter-press portions of the forthcoming edition:

> . . . I beg to mention that a suggestion has been made, – that if the Highland Society of London were to offer a Premium for the best Essay or historical account of the greatest number of ancient Pipe Tunes – showing the occasions on which they were composed or played – giving the original words where extant – ?relative [?relevant] historical sources – very interesting papers might be obtained. I allude to this more particularly at present, as there are several instances of the same Tune being *claimed* by different clans or chiefs – remonstrances are made accordingly; – for instance a Stewart of Atholl has

20 HSL, NLS, Dep.268, Correspondence, Box 2, 3/3/1824.

just been in to say that 'Bodaich nam Brogais' is not a tune of Lord Breadalbane's – and that it belongs to the Stewarts, altho' usually called Lord Breadalbane's March.[21]

In November 1825 Gordon was forced to return a rather negative reply to a request for the various tune MSS for which prizes had been awarded at the Edinburgh competitions over the years which the London Society clearly thought its Scottish counterpart still held:

> In return of your favr of the 6th I am very sorry that it is not in my power to communicate to you any material aid for the Publication of Pipe Music which the Highland Society of London are about to make. The very few Pipers who were qualified to write the piobrachd had generally but *one copy* of the Tunes committed to writing, & which copy they declined to leave with the Committee: altho' they promised to produce a transcript at some time after [the] Competition, and were promised a reward upon their doing so, in nearly every instance the promises of the Pipers were made only to be forgotten. Such tunes as the Judges from time to time got, I now forward to you, that you may make such use of them as they may deserve – if any. There is no occasion to return the manuscript – It is the property of your Society not that of the Judges.
>
> P.S. I recollect the young boy Angus Mackay produced at [the] *last Competition* the best collection I had seen in M.S. of Pipe Tunes. He is the son of Lord Gwydir's piper, & probably it would be well if you had access to the collection.[22]

MacArthur and MacGregor had in the meantime both died. John Wedderburn fell ill, and ceased attending meetings throughout most of 1825 and 1826.[23] On 22 January 1827 he resigned. Whereupon the project disappeared from the minutes, and the edition came to a halt.

At its next meeting, 5 May 1827, the Highland Society of London suspended the subsidy to the Edinburgh piping competition for that year, which meant that it could not go ahead.[24]

Donald MacDonald had lost money on a book of piobaireachd in staff notation, and the Highland Society of London was now showing reluctance, perhaps also on financial grounds, to go ahead. But staff notation was not the

21 *Ibid.*, Charles Gordon to John MacDonald , 9/8/1824; see also John Wedderburn to Rev. D. McCallum, 26/11/1824.
22 *Ibid.*, Charles Gordon to John Wedderburn, 10/11/1825.
23 *Ibid.*, John Wedderburn to the Chairman of the HSL Court of Directors, 31/1/1826.
24 This was at the suggestion of the Highland Society of Scotland in response to a decline in the audience following the removal of Edinburgh races to Musselburgh: *ibid.*, 27/10/1826, C. Gordon to John Wedderburn; see also Charles Gordon to John Macdonald, Box 3, 20/5/1829.

only way of publishing this music. If it were reproduced in canntaireachd vocables, costs could be greatly reduced, because this eliminated the need for engraved plates. Written canntaireachd was, in addition, so economical a medium in terms of space that a couple of dozen tunes could easily be contained in a slender pamphlet. Indeed the sheer bulk of piobaireachd settings written out in full in staff notation was to be an enduring problem and there were experiments with a number of ways of abbreviating settings, from John MacGregor onwards.

In January 1828, the Highland Society of Scotland received a communication from one of its members, a Captain Niel MacLeod of Gesto, in Skye. The Minutes record that

> A letter from Captain Macleod of Gesto regarding the publication of the Tunes noted by him in the syllabic form, as played by the M'Crummins of Skye, was read. The Directors recommended to Mr. Gordon [Secretary of the HSS] to transmit the letter to the Highland Society of London.[25]

The content of this letter is not stated, but related correspondence shows it to have been a request for financial support. The London people did not know what to make of it, and asked the Scottish Society 'how far this work may be considered as a means of cultivating the knowledge of Pipe Music, or of enabling a Piper without previous acquaintance with the Tunes to play the Piobaireachds'.[26] but they did grant a subsidy of ten guineas, and the booklet was 'Very Respectfully Dedicated to The Highland Society of London, by their Grateful and Obedient Servant, Niel MacLeod, Gesto, Captain H. P. Independents, Member of the Highland Society of Scotland.'[27]

MacLeod seems to have published first and asked for support second, avoiding the Societies' mediation and having Prefaces thrust upon him.[28] He also presented them with a rather awkward dilemma. Canntaireachd did not at all

25 HSS, Sederunt Book 10, 6/1/1828, ff.28–9. MacLeod had also written to the Highland Society of London on 24/12/1827 about old pipe tunes, as a checklist of Highland Society papers compiled early in the 20th century reveals; but the letter is now missing from the file, as are a number of other documents relating to this matter.

26 HSL, NLS, Dep.268/27, Rough Minute Book, 3/5/1828, 7/2/1829. See also HSL Correspondence Box 3, 26/7/1828, 28/4/1829, 15/6/1829.

27 There may have been a certain irony in these remarks since the Highland Society of Scotland refused to support the venture: 'Our Society have not voted any thing for it, – they have always abstained from any *direct* patronage of the Bag-pipe or its music, which have been so long and so successfully patronised by the Highland Society of London.' Charles Gordon to John Macdonald, *ibid.*, 28/4/1829.

28 Presumably what the Societies saw in January 1828 was a proof copy. Once subsidy was granted it was easy to add a dedicatory page before the booklet was printed. Charles Gordon noted 'he [Gesto] rates his publication very high and sells each copy at a Guinea. It is certainly a great Curiosity in its way'. HSL, Correspondence Box 3, 26/7/1828.

lend itself to appropriation. The implications in terms of control and power were quite different. If piobaireachd were set in staff notation, then one could quickly acquire a superficial acquaintance with it, whatever one's instrumental background. But to grapple with the music in canntaireachd, one had to be a piper, or have an extensive prior acquaintance with piobaireachd as a form. Here, for example, is the ground of Gesto's tune No.VI 'The Union of Scotland with England, composed by a Scotch piper, commonly called Molluch na Piperin':

I hindro dieliu hiechin, hindro hindrie hiachin,
biedrio dravi hiechin,
hiendo, hindo, hien hin,
betrievi, hievi, hiavi, hiova,
hindro, dieliu, hiechin,
hindro, hi hie, drie haichin,
bietrieo, dravi, hiechin,
hindo, hindo, hien hin,
beetrieviu hie vieo, havieu hovao,
hindro, dieliu, hiechin,
hientro, hiutrie, hiaotro,
bietriea, hierierine.

We have noted the difficulties this was to cause the folklorist J. F. Campbell and his circle some fifty years later.[29] Staff notation could be used to disrupt the monopoly of the master pipers over teaching and transmission, but the verbal notation could not – indeed it had quite the opposite effect, in that one had to place oneself under the tuition of a traditional teacher in order to acquire sufficient knowledge to use it – a course which relatively few amongst the upper echelons of Highland society during the nineteenth century felt able to take.

Pibereach or pipe tunes, as taught verbally by the McCrimmen pipers in Skye to their apprentices. The following as taken from John McCrimmon, piper to the old Laird of MacLeod, and his grandson the late General McLeod of McLeod, at Dunvegan. By Captain Niel MacLeod, Gesto, Skye, was the last such work for more than two generations to be attempted by somebody who was not first and foremost a piper.[30] It contained twenty tunes, including the first published versions of famous pieces such as 'The Lament for the Union', 'MacLeod's Rowing Tune', 'Lament for the Laird of Anapool', 'War or Peace', 'In Praise of Morag' and 'Isabel MacKay', and it was received by the Highland Societies with polite incomprehension. Indeed it is one of the curiosities of piping history that the only source stemming directly from the MacCrimmons was to be system-

---

29 See above, pp.1–3.
30 Cannon, *Bibliography*, pp.123–5 and Cannon, *Highland Bagpipe*, pp.67–9. The edition cited here is that of J. & R. Glen, Edinburgh 1880.

atically ignored by the institutions which set themselves to administer the art for a period of nearly 150 years.[31]

To some extent, the text itself was to blame for this. It must have been difficult to set in type and there are frequent typographical errors which for some reason were not corrected at the proof stage. These problems are compounded by a number of shortcomings in the notation used by Niel MacLeod. Its general consistency would suggest that it was already a developed system, and not simply a phonetic transcript improvised as he went along, but it is by no means as precise as Colin Campbell's 'Nether Lorn' canntaireachd.[32] It may be that diacritical marks were used to differentiate between similar-looking vocables but if so, this feature was not reproduced, and as it stands the printed text does not distinguish between low G and low A, B and C, and E and F except by context. And the context does not always provide a certain guide. If one did not know from other sources, for example, that 'Glengarry's March' ought to sound roughly like this:

one might struggle to arrive at such a conclusion from the following table of vocables even if one were otherwise well acquainted with the form:

> I hin do, ho dro, hin do, ho dro,
> hin do, ho dro, hin do, ho dra,
> hin do, ho dro, hin da, chin drine,[33]

So that while Gesto's collection offers valuable information on how specific tunes were developed in the family tradition represented by Iain Dubh MacCrimmon, some of the finer detail is difficult to interpret, and tunes not recorded in other sources can be difficult to reconstruct.[34] There seems an obvious intention on Niel MacLeod's part to build on the foundation laid by Donald MacDonald, in that only three of the tunes published in *Ancient Martial Music* re-appear in his collection, although in different – and in the case of 'Kiaunma Drochid a Beig, alias the Head of the little Bridge' perhaps superior – settings. Gesto will certainly have known what MacDonald was doing, since the two were well acquainted.

Niel MacLeod of Gesto (*c*.1754–1836) was the representative of an old Highland family, a cadet branch of the house of MacLeod, with lands in

---

31 In the *Piobaireachd Society Collection* (second series), there was a single passing allusion to Gesto in volumes 1–9 [1925–1958] in the course of nearly three hundred pages of music text and notes (p.191).

32 See Appendix.

33 Gesto, p.41.

34 See Frans Buisman, 'Canntaireachd and Colin Campbell's Verbal Notation – An Outline' in *PT*, vol.50, no.3, December 1997, pp.24–30, (29).

Glenelg and Skye, Gesto itself lying on the shores of Loch Harport between Struan and Drynoch. He was the fifteenth and last of the name, a soldier, who had served as a lieutenant in the 116th Regiment of Foot, and as a Captain of Independents. He was also a Justice of the Peace. Niel held Gesto on a lease from MacLeod of MacLeod, with whom he fought a lawsuit about its boundaries of such length and acrimony that when the tack expired in 1825, MacLeod refused to renew it, and the Captain had to flit to Waternish which the Dunvegan family had sold in order to pay off gambling and political debts. Niel's son Kenneth made a fortune in India and later tried to buy back the family's lands, but MacLeod would not part with them. So Kenneth had to content himself with Orbost, Edinbane, Skirinish, Greshornish, Tote, Skaebost and a goodly part of Portree instead. But he was only one of a large and talented family, six sons and seven daughters in all, a number of whose children went on in turn to make names for themselves in Scottish public life during the later Victorian period, especially those of Ann MacLeod, Gesto's eldest daughter, who married Charles MacDonald of Ord in Skye, and was the mother of Dr. K. N. MacDonald, editor of *The Gesto Collection of Highland Music* (1895) and *Puirt-a-Beul* (Glasgow 1901), and Neil MacDonald of Dunach in Argyllshire, who had the brilliant John MacColl for a time as his piper and whose wife, Madeline Brown, was celebrated by the latter in a strathspey, 'Mrs MacDonald of Dunach', one of his earliest compositions. Their sister Flora was married to the poet and essayist Alexander Smith, author of *Dreamthorp* (1863) and *A Summer in Skye* (1865). In the following generation, there was Somerled MacDonald, the portrait and landscape painter, amateur piper and prominent early member of the Piobaireachd Society, who was a son of Lachlan MacDonald of Skaebost, another of the Ord MacDonalds.[35]

Niel MacLeod of Gesto was one of the old school, a gentlemen *aficionado*, himself a player, whose house was a centre of Highland musical culture. His grandson Dr. K. N. MacDonald reported that 'I have heard my mother say that she had frequently been wakened at four in the morning by John MacCrimmon's pipes'.[36] It is not known when he began to form his collection, but the work must have begun some time before 1815, the year in which Alexander Campbell visited him whilst collecting in the Western Isles for *Albyn's Anthology*. Gesto's reputation as an expert must already have been sufficient for the Highland Society of Scotland to direct Campbell to go and see him, especially when we consider that the only other piping source he consulted was Donald Roy MacCrimmon. A manuscript setting by Campbell of 'The Cameron [sic] Gathering in Syllables' preserved in Edinburgh University Library notes that

35 Donald MacKinnon, and Alick Morrison, eds., *The MacLeods – the Genealogy of a Clan. Section Three. MacLeod Cadet Families* (Edinr., 1970), pp.262–294. See also Mackenzie, *History of the MacLeods*, pp.187–200.

36 K. N. MacDonald, 'The Bagpipes and how the MacCrimmons played them', *OT*, 4/7/1896, p.3.

On the following ten pages, is a genuine sett of the Cameron's Gathering in sylables as taught by the MacCrimmons of Sky to their Pupils, as nearly as I can posibly write it from MacCrumin's repeating it, & first noted (without the sylables) to the Pianoforte by Miss Jean Campbell at Gesto & now Copied & noted down more scientifically in my presence by Alex. Campbell, Editor of Albyn's Anthologie. Niel MacLeod, J.P. (Capt. 1/2 pay Independents).[37]

Alexander Campbell had made his own record of this encounter in his 'Slight Sketch of a Journey made through parts of the Highlands & Hebrides in Autumn 1815' in which he states that he worked directly with the original canntaireachd sources, and makes no mention of keyboard transcripts:

23d. Sept. Having made the necessary arrangements regarding the route I was to follow in Skye . . . I set out for Gesto, in order to gain some knowledge of an instrument of which I was hitherto entirely ignorant, – the one I allude to, is, the Bag-pipe.

Captain Niel MacLeod of Gesto is one of those characters, that are distinguished by the phraze, *sui generis*, and he seems to think so. Although dogmatical to excess, and fastidious in extreme, yet, he is neither difficient in the Understanding, nor the better qualities of the heart; proof of which I have personally experienced; and his active zeal will be found eminently subservient to our present undertaking. [i.e. the Highland Society of Scotland's rapidly waning interest in Highland music] To his amiable Lady, and Daughters I owe infinite offices of good will to a Stranger . . . the Captain, with incredible patience, & scrupulous exactness, communicated to me his knowledge of the theory & practice of The Great Highland Bag-pipe, as it is called, in the manner he had acquired his knowledge of it from the famous MacCrummons of Skye.

In order to have it fixed in my mind, the mode by which illiterate men communicate their musical ideas, (being entirely ignorant of notation), to one another, Captain M'Leod permitted me to transcribe from his MS. two popular pipe-pieces or Gatherings, in those sort of Syllables by which Pipers fix in their memory the *themes*, & *variations* of the various compositions performed on the Bag-pipe. After transcribing those syllables, I pricked down opposite to each its appropriate tone, & duration, agreeably to the rules of *rhythmus*, & *melody*, by means of which, the music of this martial instrument may be played by any one the least conversant in the ordinary signs of notation. To these pipe-pieces, I added to my gleanings, seven melodies, (with a stanza of the words to each), from the singing of Mrs. McLeod and her two eldest Daughters . . .[38]

37 EUL, La.ii. 51. ff.172–6.
38 Campbell, 'Slight Sketch', ff.46–8. The 'Slight Sketch' runs to 69 folio pages and although it remains in manuscript seems to have been intended by its author at some stage for publication.

Another shrewd observer encountered Niel MacLeod of Gesto and left a written account of his impressions. Gesto had engaged a young divinity student called Alexander MacGregor, a Gaelic-speaking native of Glengairn in upper Deeside (born 1806), to copy law papers for him in Edinburgh. MacGregor went on in due course to enter the ministry, as assistant and successor to his father at Kilmuir in Skye, (for which he wrote the extensive entry in the *New Statistical Account*), then at the Gaelic chapel in Edinburgh, and finally, from 1853 till his death on 19 October 1881, as the highly-regarded minister of the West Church of Inverness. More importantly, MacGregor was a writer. He translated the Apocrypha into Gaelic,[39] wrote on *Highland Superstitions* (Inverness, 1891), *The Prophecies of the Brahan Seer* (Inverness, 1882), and under his pen-names 'Sgiathanach' and 'Alasdair Ruadh' became a prolific contributor to Celtic periodicals on subjects of Highland history, language and culture. His *Life of Flora MacDonald and her Adventures with Prince Charles* (Inverness, 1882), which ran to several editions, used oral testimony he had collected as a young man in Trotternish within a generation of her death, to reconstruct her role in the '45 with remarkable vividness and detail. One of his chief informants had been Donald MacDonald's father, John.[40]

It was natural enough that Alexander MacGregor should cultivate the MacDonalds when he was studying in Edinburgh, since they were natives of his father's parish. Since he was also a piper (and later a long-serving judge at the Northern Meeting), it seems likely that he also studied with Donald MacDonald, and it was through this connection that he met Gesto. MacGregor appears to have been the earliest writer to offer a descriptive account of canntaireachd, in a published 'Lecture by the Rev. Alexander MacGregor', in *Transactions of the Gaelic Society of Inverness* in 1873.[41] His remarks on 'Piobaireachd agus Ceol nan Gaidheal' identified the main types of ceòl mór, quoted from song texts linked with 'Cha till MacCruimean', 'Seaforth's Salute', and 'The Piper's Warning to his Master', touched upon the MacCrimmons and MacArthurs as pipers to the Macleods of Dunvegan, and the MacDonalds of the Isles, before offering a brief account of canntaireachd as a system, mentioning its use of vocables imitating the notes of the pipe, and quoting from 'Failte a' Phrionnsa':

'An t-urlar
hi o dro hi ri, hi an an in ha rà,
hi o dro hà chin, hà chin hi à chin,
hi o dro hi rì, hi an an in ha rà,
hi o dro hà chin, hà chin hi ì chin . . .

39 *Apocripha air eadar-theangachadh air son a' cheud uair, o 'n Bhéurla ghnàthaichte chum na Gaelic Albannaich* (Lond., 1860).

40 MacGregor, *Flora MacDonald*, p.96, *n*. Biographical details about Alexander MacGregor are taken from 'Memoir of the Author' by his friend Alexander Mackenzie, prefixed to this edition, pp.ix-xx.

41 Vol.2, 1872–3, pp. 6–25.

Siubhal.
hi o dro hi chin, hà chin hà chin,
hi o dro hà chin, hì chin ha chin,
hi o dro hì chin, hà chin hà chin,
hi o dro hà chin, hà chin hì chin . . .

Taobhdudh.
hio dro to, hì dro to, hà dro to, hà dro to,
ho dro to, ha dro to, hi dro to hi à chin.
&c., &c., &c.'[42]

He also wrote knowledgeably about the MacGregor pipers of *clann an sgeu-laiche*.[43]

Gesto presented him with a copy of *Pibereach or pipe tunes, as taught verbally by the McCrimmen pipers in Skye to their apprentices*, which MacGregor later lodged in the library of the Gaelic Society of Inverness.[44]

It is important to consider Alexander MacGregor's credentials as a witness who had some idea about what he was looking at and what it meant, because he says certain things that might significantly alter our view of piobaireachd as an essentially oral process in one at least of the great teaching families.

In the summer of 1880, a portrait of Donald MacDonald's father, John, came into the possession of the journalist and historian Alexander MacKenzie, editor of the Inverness-based *Celtic Magazine*, to which MacGregor was a frequent contributor. He had last seen the picture hanging above the mantelpiece in Donald MacDonald's parlour in Edinburgh some fifty years before, and it occasioned the following reminiscence:

I was in Edinburgh during the winters of 1831, 1832, 1834, and 1835, and in almost all these years old Captain Neil Macleod of Gesto, in Skye, resided in

42 *Ibid*, p.21.
43 MacGregor, 'The Aged Piper', *op.cit.*
44 'Canntaireachd, or Articulate Music', review of J. F. Campbell's pamphlet by 'A.M'. [Alexander Mackenzie] in *Celtic Magazine*, vol 5, 1880, pp.483–89. Archibald Campbell of Kilberry recorded that MacGregor's father had been a guarantor of one of the competitors for the Highland Societies' competitions: 'Kenneth Stewart "from the Isle of Skye" entered for the HS. 1838 competition. His list of tunes, in copperplate handwriting, was endorsed with the following certificate in another hand: "The Bearer can play several new piobrachs and also the Shiosalach or The Chisholm [Chisholm's Salute] composed on the occasion of his being elected member of Parliament for the County of Inverness in the Year 1836 – by R. M'G. Minr. Kilmuir. Skye'. This was the Rev. Robert MacGregor, a native of Perthshire who became minister of Kilmuir in 1822 . . . Both father & son were pipers and the latter is said to have judged piping at the Northern Meeting . . . A[rchibald] C[ampbell] 22/8/55', in Piobaireachd Research Papers of Archibald Campbell (ca. 1903–1963, n.d.), NLS, MS22106, f.8.

Edinburgh . . . He was a tall, gaunt, thin-faced man, with long nose, grey hair, white hat, tartan trousers, and plaid. He was known as the 'Parliament House Ghost', and at times the 'Advocates' Library Ghost', as he frequented these places day and night . . .

He was crazy about 'Piobaireachd', but did not play himself. He knew, I believe, almost every piobaireachd in existence – the names, the composers, their origin, and the causes for composing them. When strolling to and from the Advocates' Library, he very frequently called on, and sat for hours with old John Macdonald, the father of Donald Macdonald, pipe-major to the Highland Society . . . He would make Donald (then about 80 years old, while the father, then also alive, was upwards of 100) play 'piobaireachds' to him, all of which he himself could articulate with his pliant lips in the MacCrimmon noting style. He had a large manuscript collection of the MacCrimmons' 'piobaireachds', as noted by themselves, and part of it was apparently very old and yellow in the paper from age, with some of the writing getting dim. Other parts were evidently more modern, and on different paper. Donald Ban MacCrimmon, who was killed at the rout of Moy, the day before the battle of Culloden, was (Gesto said) one of the best of the MacCrimmon performers; but the best of them all was Padruig Mor MacCruimean. For many ages these pipers noted down their piobaireachds, and Padruig Mor had a daughter who was very expert at noting, and could also play herself when asked as a favour to do so. I should think that the manuscript I saw with him would contain upwards of two hundred 'piobaireachds' from the bulk of it, and out of that manuscript he selected twenty or so, which he published as a specimen. The Macarthurs, pipers to the Clan Macdonald of the Isles, noted their piobaireachds also, but with different vocables. Gesto had one very old-looking leaf of their noting, on which the vocables appeared very faint, but I did not look much at it.

Gesto told me that the vowels a e i o u were the roots of the syllabic notes. The vowel i (pronounced as in Gaelic and Latin – ee) was the root or index of the highest note on the chanter, and u the lowest, and o the next lowest, and then a and e represented the middle notes in the chanter. It was thus the case that such vocables as hi, tri ti, represented the high notes, and ho, hu, the lowest. These they combined by rules of their own, as hio, hiao, hiuo, hi dro to hachin, hidrototatiti, hidrototutati, hidrototutati, hiodrotohachin. I could easily fancy that it would be a very simple matter to fix on syllables, or vocables to represent every bar in pipe music, as it is such regular music in its construction. Any piper of any knowledge who can play the 'urlar' or the tune, and also the first 'siubhal', can easily play the 'taobhluth' and the 'crunnluth'. If you give myself the noting of the first 'siubhal' of any 'piobaireachd', I could easily note down all the other variations, should I have never heard nor seen the 'piobaireachd' before. This regularity in pipe music renders it an easy matter to frame syllables for the 'urlar' and for the first 'siubhal', or variation; and if you have that on some fixed principle, it is easy to add the rest . . .[45]

Parts of this are obviously doubtful. If MacGregor means to imply that Gesto was visiting the MacDonalds during the years stipulated this cannot be right because John MacDonald died in 1825; his son Donald was, likewise, a good deal younger than stated. It appears that Gesto was able to play the pipes although he had given up doing so for some years owing to a lung condition; but MacGregor obviously did not know this. These are the kinds of details which might be expected to fade a little during the passage of fifty years. But when we turn to the main subject of the letter, the nature of canntaireachd as a system, and the existence of a large manuscript collection of it in Gesto's possession, these are facts of a different order, to which the young MacGregor had evidently given considered attention – as we see by the precise details about the number of tunes it contained, its physical condition, the evident age of some of it, the implication that it was the work of several different hands and the reference to an alternative tradition in Skye represented by the MacArthurs who also used canntaireachd vocables as a system of written notation. If his evidence about the papers he saw in Gesto's possession in the early 1830s is reliable, then it means that the MacCrimmon and MacArthur families possessed a form of written notation, and had done so for several generations, and that our ideas about non-literacy and oral transmission may have to be revised.

But Gesto nowhere claimed to have had access to such a source, and no trace of this large manuscript collection has subsequently been found.[46] He invariably described the tunes as having been taken down by himself personally from Iain Dubh MacCrimmon, who appears also as the only named source in the notes headed 'Remarks by Captain MacLeod, as far as he has been informed by the late John Maccrimmon, piper, Dunvegan, Isle of Skye' preserved amongst the papers of his grandson Lachlan MacDonald of Skaebost. For example:

> 1. *Luinagich, alias Auiltich.* – Was played by one of Maccrimmon's predecessors off-hand [i.e. impromptu], at some time when several Highland proprietors were assembled at Dunvegan Castle, and having their pipers attending them.

> 14. *Caugh Vic Righ Aro, alias the son of King Aro.* – Who this son of King Aro was I could not understand from John Maccrimmon, further than that he considered the tune was played in consequence of the death of one of the first chiefs of Mackintosh, killed in battle (perhaps the battle of Largs) with King Alexander against Haco, when a brave chief of Mackintosh fell.[47]

45 *Celtic Magazine*, vol.5, 1880, pp.483–4
46 See Chapter 19 below.
47 *Celtic Magazine*, vol. 8, 1883, pp. 434–5.

Although it later became the focus of a good deal of controversy, the immediate influence of Gesto's *Pibereach* is harder to assess. The size of the print-run is not known but in view of the luke-warm response of the Highland Societies it is not likely to have been large, an impression which its later scarceness would tend to confirm – as well, of course, as the outrageous price that Gesto seems to have charged for it. In any case, the immediate future was to lie with the promoters of staff notation, and canntaireachd was not again to become an issue until the beginning of the twentieth century.[48]

In the meantime, in the autumn of 1829, the finishing touches were put to the final version of one of the most influential theoretical statements about the nature of tradition to appear in the 19th century – the introductory essay to Sir Walter Scott's *Minstrelsy of the Scottish Border*. Scott's pioneering collection of Border ballads had first appeared in 1802, and was an extremely popular work, running to many editions and selling many thousands of copies. It was shortly to be re-issued as part of the Magnum Opus, the revised edition of Scott's collected works designed to pay off his creditors following the failure of his publisher Constable & Co in the financial crash of 1826.[49] Next to *Ossian*, the *Minstrelsy* was the single oral text almost certain to be familiar to the educated classes of Scotland, and its influence on the way they thought about tradition was great. It was also extremely negative. In Scott's pages the ballad appeared as the authentic

48 For some of the wide ranging discussion of the Gesto canntaireachd during the early 1900s, see 'Puirt-a-Beul – Concluding Remarks', from K. N. MacDonald, *OT*, 23/3/ 1901, p.3; 'Highland Music and Canntaireachd', Charles Bannatyne, 30/1/1904, p.3; 13/ 2/1904, p.3; 20/2/1904, p.3; 27/2/1904, p.3; 5/3/1904, p.3; 'Canntaireachd' from 'Eileanach', 9/4/1904, p.3; 'same', from Charles Bannatyne, 30/4/1904, p.3; 'The Secrets of Cainntearachd. Australian Piper's Theory', from Simon Fraser, 11/9/1909, p.2; 'Canntaireachd', from John Grant, 7/10/1911, p.3; 'same', from Charles Bannatyne, 14/10/1911, p.3; 'The Secrets of Canntaireachd', from John Grant, 16/12/1911, p.3; 'same', from Simon Fraser, 20/4/1912, p.3; 'same' from Charles Bannatyne, 4/5/1912, p3; 'same, from John Grant, 11/5/1912, p.3; 'same', from K. N. MacDonald, 18/5/1912, p.3; 'same', from John Grant, 25/5/1912. p.3; 'same', from Charles Bannatyne, 1/6/1912, p.3; 'same', from K. N. MacDonald, 1/6/1912, p.3; 'same', from Charles Bannatyne, 15/ 6/1912, p.3; 'same' from Lieut. John McLennan, 15/6/1912, p.3; 'same' from K. N. MacDonald, 15/6/1912 p.3; 29/6/1912, p.3; 13/7/1912, p.3; 'Sheantaireachd', from Simon Fraser, 23/11/1912, p.3; 'Canntaireachd' from K. N. MacDonald, 30/11/1912, p.3; 'Capt. MacLeod's Collection of Piobaireachd', from K.N. MacDonald, 7/12/1912, p.3; 'same', from Lieut. John McLennan, 7/12/1912, p.3; 'Gesto as a Piper', from Lachlan Bruce [nephew of Sandy Bruce], 28/12/1912, p.3; 'Some Famous Pipers. The Bruces of Glenelg Contemporaries of John MacCrimmon', from K. N. MacDonald, 11/1/1913, p.3; 18/1/1913, p.3; 'The Early History of the M'Crimmons. Related by Themselves to Captain MacLeod of Gesto', from K. N. MacDonald, 5/4/1913, p.3; 17/5/1913, p.3; 'Gesto and the Bagpipe', from Simon Fraser, 3/10/1914, p.3; 'Gesto and the MacCrimmon notation', from Simon Fraser, 9/10/1915, p.3; 'same' from W. C. F, 23/ 10/1915, p.3.

49 Edgar Johnson, *Sir Walter Scott: The Great Unknown* (2 vols., Lond., 1970), pp.172– 207, 1116.

voice of antiquity echoing dimly down the centuries, the creation of a courtly minstrel class whose once heroic art had gradually sunk down the social scale until it had fallen into the hands of the common people, who would corrupt it beyond recovery through a combination of forgetfulness, stupidity, and clumsy interference, if the enlightened collector did not rescue it before it was too late.

Viewed from the study at Abbotsford, the graph of tradition showed an early peak, in the form of a brief period of creativity, followed by an inexorable downward trajectory, representing the subsequent, inherently degenerative process of transmission. It was as if these pieces had been confected in some remote kitchen by a master chef, long dead, then ferried down the corridors of time by a succession of idiot waiters who spilled things and got the plates mixed up. Scott regarded the mechanisms of oral tradition as a 'degraded species of alchymy, by which the ore of antiquity is deteriorated and adulterated'[50] and he declared

> the flatness and insipidity, which is the great imperfection of ballad poetry, is to be ascribed less to the compositions in their original state, when rehearsed by their *authors*, than to the ignorance and errors of the reciters or transcribers, by whom they have been transmitted to us. The more popular the composition of an ancient poet, or *Maker*, became, the greater the chance there was of its being corrupted; for a poem transmitted through a number of reciters, like a book reprinted in a multitude of editions, incurs the risk of impertinent interpolations from the conceit of one rehearser, unintelligible blunders from the stupidity of another, and omissions equally to be regretted, from the want of memory of a third . . . Thus, undergoing from age to age a gradual process of alteration and recomposition, our popular and oral minstrelsy has lost, in a great measure, its original appearance; and the strong touches by which it had been formerly characterised, have been generally smoothed down and destroyed by a process similar to that by which a coin, passing from hand to hand, loses in circulation all the finer marks of the impress.[51]

The fact that ballads had been 'handed from one ignorant reciter to another' led inevitably to the 'deterioration of ancient poetry', although the 'ingenuity of a skilful critic could often . . . revive and restore the original meaning . . .'[52] Scott's approach thus powerfully reinforced Macpherson's anxieties about the reliability of oral transmission in contemporary 'tradition', and it thrust the editor and collector still more emphatically into the equation as the educated mediator without whose intervention it could not sustain itself. Much of the

50 T. F. Henderson, ed., *Sir Walter Scott's Minstrelsy of the Scottish Border* (4 vols., Edinr., 1902), i, 2.

51 *Minstrelsy*, i, 9–10, 12.

52 *Minstrelsy*, i, p.11. See also Thomas Crawford, *Walter Scott* (Edinr., 1982), pp.21–33.

suspicion which came to attach to the performer community in piping as effective custodians of tradition, and the belief that a formal 'education' was all that was required to mediate its products successfully had their roots in this source.

Appendix

The Highland Society of London's manuscript was preserved amongst Angus MacKay's MSS, identified as 'Volume Third 30 Piobaireachds' in sequence with volumes one and two which form his own manuscript collection. It was bought by his pupil Michael MacCarfrae (or MacCaffee) from MacKay's widow with other papers in 1860, then again from MacCarfrae's widow by Dr. Charles Bannatyne in 1904, (see 'Piobaireachd', by Chas. Bannatyne, *Oban Times*, 31/1/ 1920, p.3, and 7/2/1920, p.3, which gives a brief history of routes by which Angus MacKay's papers came down to the twentieth century), and finally by the Piobaireachd Society from Bannatyne's estate following the latter's death on 5 March 1924.

The manuscript is in sequential form with the tunes numbered through from 1 to 30, in an apparently uniform hand not MacKay's, with several bearing written comments by Andrew Robertson or initialled by him. These are nos. 1, 4, 10, 19, 20, 21, 22, 23, 24, 25, 26, 27, 28, and 30. There may originally have been more: the sheets have been cropped for binding and one of the existing signatures has partly disappeared as a result. There is no obvious sign of disturbance in the original sequence of the tunes, which would seem to discount the later idea that only pieces signed by Andrew Robertson were 'authentic'. True, the neat and precise penmanship of the first half of the manuscript deteriorates, but this would be consistent with increasing haste on MacGregor's part – after all his informant was dying – and with larger numbers of tunes being done at a sitting, which would also be consistent with the heavy concentration of Robertson initials in the later stages, implying that he signed these things when he was present but did not feel it necessary subsequently to do so if he had not been, or perhaps more simply that he initialled them to confirm payment, sometimes singly sometimes in batches.

Angus MacKay re-set most of the contents of the MacArthur manuscript in his own style and transposed into the key of A, for his own collection, NLS MS. 3753. He not only had access to the Highland Society of London's MS, but had it actually in his possession, and did not return it when he was finished with it, which may be fortunate when one bears in mind that many of the London Society's papers for this period were later lost in a fire.

The Piobaireachd Society is curiously reticent about the MacArthur manuscript after it came into their possession. Although the manuscript is docketed by Archibald Campbell of Kilberry, 19/7/36, it is seldom alluded to in the volumes of the Society's collection which he edited, and omitted from his account of the MacKay papers in volume 10 of the Piobaireachd Society's Collection, pp.iii-iv. In addition, tunes composed by Charles and John MacArthur such as

'Abercairny's Salute' and 'The Highland Society of Scotland's Salute' edited by
A. G. Kenneth for the Society and published in vol.11, pp.357–9, and vol.12,
pp.374–5, are based on Angus MacKay's transcripts rather than the MacArthur
MS, for reasons which are not obvious. A comment on the manuscript by A. G.
Kenneth in the editorial notes to 'Lament for Donald Duaghal MacKay', vol.13,
p.436, may, however, give a clue. It states that

> Angus MacArthur's version of the tune is much shorter than any of the
> others; he only gives the Urlar and Var.1, which is followed by the instruction
> "D.C." and the initials A.R. These initials represent Andrew Robertson who is
> stated to have examined the 12 tunes which are definitely recorded as having
> been 'written by John MacGregor, dictated by Angus MacArthur and
> examined by Andrew Robertson'. There are in fact only 12 out of the total of
> 30 tunes in this manuscript which bear either his initials or his name, and it
> may be presumed that this was one of the tunes actually dictated by
> MacArthur.

The source for this statement is not given, but can be traced to a note signed by J.
P. Grant in the 'Preface' of vol.1 of the *Piobaireachd Society Collection* (second
series) in 1925, as follows:

> Angus MacArthur's MS., End of 18th Century. Angus MacArthur's MS., or
> the Highland Society of London's MS., contains '12 tunes, written by John
> McGregor, dictated by Angus MacArthur, examined by Andrew Robertson'.
> Eighteen other tunes have been added, perhaps at a later date, possibly by
> John MacKay or his brother Angus. The original volume subsequently formed
> Vol.III of a collection (perhaps John MacKay's). It is written on the clef'.[53]

But the MacArthur manuscript itself would seem to place a question mark over a
good many of these statements.

The compiler of the MS, John MacGregor (1780–1822) won the prize pipe in
1806. He was a pipe-maker and multi-instrumentalist, adept also on the union
pipe, flageolet and German flute, and had been piper to the royal Duke of Kent.
He collapsed and died while playing at the Highland Society's annual dinner later
in the year 1822.[54]

---

53 *Op.cit.*, p.ii.
54 'The Literature of the Highland Bagpipe The Highland Society of London's
    Manuscript', in *International Piper*, vol.1, no.12, 1979, pp.8–11.

8

'A fixed standard for future performers': The Collections of Angus MacKay and Uilleam Ross

Towards the middle of the 1830s a printed prospectus for a proposed new work circulated amongst the booksellers. It declared that:

On or about the 1st of February, 1836, will be published by subscription a Collection of the Ancient Piobaireachds or Pipe Tunes as played by the MacCrimmons and others, with historical notes to the Piobaireachds and a short account of the principle ancient pipers, viz. the MacCrimmons, MacArthurs and MacKays. The Volume will contain 60 Piobaireachds with complete instructions for those desirous of acquiring a minute knowledge of the instrument, and it will be altogether the largest and cheapest work of this kind ever offered to the public.

The first attempt at a work of this nature was made about 30 years ago by Mr. Donald MacDonald of Edinburgh, the celebrated pipe maker. Mr. MacDonald published 23 Piobaireachds, arranged for both pianoforte and the pipe. Circumstances however interfered with the continuation of this interesting collection and, as in the present work, the Piobaireachds will be arranged solely for the Pipe – but at the same time in such a manner as to be easily adapted to the pianoforte, the space thus gained will enable the present editor to give his subscribers a much greater number of Piobaireachds at an expense very little greater than that of Mr. MacDonald's work.

The leading object of the Editor is to preserve in its native simplicity and purity the ancient music of the country, by furnishing a fixed standard for future performers. The Piobaireachds have been collected and compiled with the greatest care and have in the state in which they are now offered to the public obtained the approbation of the best judges of performances on the Scottish Bagpipes and also of the most practised and skilful performers. Trusting that this object will meet with the approbation and the substantial support of all lovers of our national music, the Editor takes this method of making known the work in which he has been for a great length of time anxiously and devotedly employed.

Edinburgh, 8th August, 1835. Angus MacKay, Drummond Castle, the successful competitor for the prize pipe of the Highland Society of London at the general competition held in Edinburgh in July, 1835.

Price of the Work – To subscribers . . . £1–7s.-6d.

To non-subscribers £1–11s.-6d.[1]

1 Quoted in John A. MacLellan, 'Angus MacKay of Raasay', *PT*, vol.18, no.6, March 1966, 10–14, (11).

Although there seems no reason to doubt that the editor had indeed spent 'a great length of time anxiously and devotedly employed' on the project, he was, at the time of writing, a month short of his 22nd birthday. Yet his book *A Collection of Ancient Piobaireachd or Highland Pipe Music* (Edinr. 1838) was to be, by some distance, the most important collection of bagpipe music published during the 19th century.

Angus MacKay was born on 10 September 1813, the third of four piping sons of John MacKay (1767–1848), piper to the laird of Raasay, and himself one of the leading composers and teachers of his generation. Angus's development was precocious. In 1826 he took 4th prize at the Highland Societies of London and Scotland's Edinburgh competition, having already in 1825 won a prize for setting a collection of pipe tunes in the modern 'scientific' staff notation which the Highland Societies were so keen to promote. He lived at a time of rapid change in piping. His father had worked in a traditional setting until late in his career, but Angus moved in a more individualistic, mobile and competitive milieu.

This wider world began to beckon in 1823 when John MacKay, becoming dissatisfied with the atmosphere of retrenchment at Raasay House, accepted an appointment as piper to Lord Gwydir at Drummond Castle near Crieff, exchanging the rugged knowes of Raasay for the spreading pastoral uplands of Strathearn. This move into the southern Highlands by a culturally important family – in itself a new perception: it was scarcely a generation since Donald Roy MacCrimmon and Iain Roy MacKay of Gairloch had been suffered to depart in silence – was probably not the result of chance. News of John MacKay's difficulties had travelled. In July 1821, William MacKenzie, secretary to the Celtic Society, had written agitatedly to Reginald MacDonald of Staffa, Sheriff of Stirling, and secretary to the Highland Society of Scotland:

> I met Mackay, Raasay's piper. The fame of this man is too well known to
> require any praise from me. He is not satisfied with the treatment he is
> receiving, and as his abilities are unnoticed and his allowance so reduced that he
> cannot exist, he talks as a last resource of going to America. To let this man
> leave the Highlands will bring deserved obloquy on these institutions who have
> it in their power to relieve one so capable of preserving in purity the strains of
> our beloved ancestors, and, in the event of his quitting his native land we lose a
> treasure, as he will leave none behind him worthy of being his successor. I asked
> him if he would become a teacher of his instrument if he got a situation by
> which he could live; his reply was that he would do anything rather than leave
> his country. He thought from £40–£50 per annum would be an ample
> provision, and will the London, the Edinburgh, the Fort William, the Tain, and
> the Celtic Societies allow this man to emigrate for such a trifle – for the honour
> of our country, I hope not.[2]

2 Quoted in Archibald Campbell, 'The History and Art of Angus MacKay', *PT*, vol 2.
  no.5, February 1950, pp.8–9 (9).

At Drummond Castle John MacKay went on to teach a number of important players, including John Bàn Mackenzie, Angus Macpherson and Archibald Munro. He left the service of Lord Gwydir (by now Lord Willoughby of Eresby) in 1837, and retired to Kyleakin in Skye, the home of his children Roderick and Kitty, having been granted a pension of £10 a year by the Highland Society of London.[3]

The Gwydirs were part of the new order in the southern Highlands, as extravagance and incompetence thinned the ranks of native landowners and the area began to develop as a sporting and tourist playground. They took a prominent part in the movement to gild contemporary Highland life with a patina of antique Celtic pageantry. Their contingent of Perthshire Highlanders, armed and plaided in what was considered the ancient manner, made quite a splash during the visit of George IV to Edinburgh in 1822.[4] They were enthusiastic pioneers of the Highland games movement and members of both Highland Societies. In 1822 Lord Gwydir was canvassed as a possible president of the London Society. Lady Gwydir was elected an honorary member that same year, and of the Highland Society of Scotland in 1824.[5]

Peter Burrell, Lord Gwydir, was one of the Burrells of Beckenham in Kent and rather well connected. He was related through his mother, Lady Priscilla Bertie, to the Dukes of Ancaster and was heir to Grimsthorpe Castle in Lincolnshire, the family estates in that county, and Gwydir, Caernarvon, hence the title. He was one of George IV's inner circle, hereditary Lord Great Chamberlain, an important office in the royal household, having charge of the palace of Westminster and ceremonial within it, and officiated in that role at the coronations of George IV and Queen Victoria. His wife, the Right Honourable Sara Clementina Drummond-Burrell, Lady Gwydir, was scion of an old Jacobite family, and great-niece of the Duke of Perth. In 1785 the forfeited estates had been restored to her father, James Drummond, 1st Lord Perth, and she was sole heiress of Drummond, and chief of the name.[6] She seems to have taken young Angus MacKay under her wing, making him her personal piper while still a boy, and his ability to read and write staff notation, which was to prove so important to the later history of pipe music was probably acquired at Drummond Castle. Angus's later appointment as royal piper, achieved – according to piping folklore – through the personal recommendation of John Bàn MacKenzie, may have

3 Peter Cooke, 'Elizabeth Ross', p.4.

4 Prebble, *King's Jaunt*, pp.208–9, 288, 294–6. See also their extravagantly Celtic reception of Queen Victoria at Drummond Castle in 1842, in *Crieff: Its Traditions and Characters with Anecdotes of Strathearn* (Edinr., 1881), pp.175–177.

5 Highland Society of London Papers, NLS, Dep.268, Minute Book, Feb. 1822 – March 1829, 2 February 1822, 18/5/1822; see also Ramsay, *Highland and Agricultural Society of Scotland, op.cit.*, p.547, and James Irvine Robertson, *The First Highlander: Major-General David Stewart of Garth* CB. 1768–1829 (East Linton, 1998), p.152.

6 *Complete Peerage*, vi, 680–1. On the death of his mother in 1829, Lord Gwydir succeeded to her title as Lord Willoughby of Eresby.

owed rather more to the continuing interest and support of the powerful people in whose employment he had grown up.[7]

In 1837 he became piper to Walter Campbell of Islay, then in 1840 to Baron Ward of Birmingham (later Earl of Dudley), an English peer who had bought the deeply encumbered Glengarry estates, and finally, on 25th July 1843, he was appointed as first piper to Queen Victoria. Members of the royal family, by virtue of their Scottish titles, had been employing personal pipers for a good many years, so that, in a sense, it was not remarkable for the Queen to have one as well. Happening as it did, however, at a time when the monarchy was consciously realigning itself in terms of cultural affiliation and ceremonial, creating the summer palace of Balmoral, and adopting many of the outward trappings of a 'traditional' Highland landed family, this was to create a unique opportunity for Angus MacKay which, combined with his abilities as a player and editor were to gave him a position of commanding influence in the piping world.

His book, *A Collection of Ancient Piobaireachd*, was innovative in ways which belied its title, and it set out to achieve objects unstated, or only partially so, in the Prospectus. The expressed wish 'to preserve in its native simplicity and purity the ancient music of the country' overlooked the fact that the music was neither simple nor particularly ancient, whilst in such a context the concept of 'purity' was meaningless. Nor was it easy to see exactly how the book could furnish 'a fixed standard for future performers' given its expense and the generally low incidence of literacy in the performer community, although – and this was a sign of things to come perhaps – there were at least twenty pipers amongst the 245 predominantly landed and titled subscribers headed by the Dukes of Sussex and Argyll.

The title-page was set in a typical contemporary pot-pourri of fonts accompanied by an engraving of a piper playing for elaborately accoutred dancers before an idealised Highland castle. Indicating an unprecedented range of content for such a book, it read:

A Collection of Ancient Piobaireachd or Highland Pipe Music, Many of the Pieces Being Adapted to the Piano Forte with full instructions for those desirous of qualifying themselves in performing on this National Instrument. To which are prefixed some sketches of the principal Hereditary Pipers and their Establishments with historical & traditional notes respective of the various pieces.

There was a dedication 'To the Noblemen and Gentlemen of the Highland Society of London, the patronisers of all efforts to preserve the national Manners & Music', and a Preface which declared:

7 Bridget Mackenzie, *Piping Traditions of the North of Scotland*, (Edinr., 1998), p.100.

In preparing the following Collection, the Editor has been diligently occupied for many years; and when it is taken into consideration that Highland Pipe-Music has in a few cases only been committed to regular notation, the difficulty of his undertaking will be appreciated . . .

He hopes the Public will treat with leniency any defects that may be perceived. He avails himself of the opportunity of returning his deep acknowledgements to those noblemen and gentlemen who have so freely encouraged the undertaking, and he has to offer deserved thanks to some literary friends who assisted him in researches for the historical portion of the work.

Finally, he will rejoice if this volume is esteemed a suitable though humble contribution to the yet scanty stock of Highland literature; – if it will preserve, in its native simplicity, the ancient music of Caledonia, and record some particulars, not uninteresting, respecting the origin of the different pieces, and the individuals who commemorated transactions in strains so peculiar and so full of spirit-stirring reminiscences.

Edinburgh, *July* 1838   Aonghas MacAoidh.

The florid prose-style and extravagant social deference resemble similar material in Joseph, Patrick and Donald MacDonald. Like the latter, Angus MacKay was a plebeian intellectual, a native Gaelic speaker whose education in no way equipped him to produce the high-sounding English prose which occupies the letterpress portions of his book. His natural style was a workaday affair, strongly marked by Gaelic phraseology and rhythms, as we see in the following passage from his manuscript collection of light music for the pipe:

This is a brief account of my fathers family John MacKay comonly called Iain MacRuari of Eyre in Rarsair Isle of Skye he was I believe left an orphan with one sister he was reared up by Malcolm Macleod, commonly called fir aire he was there employed as a herd boy &c. and in the house Fir ayre played the pipes & was teaching a young lad my father use to over hear them and pick up his lesson and play the same on the moors while herding . . . he was overheard by Fear aire who taught him and afterwards sent him to the College of Mac Crummine and to the MacKays of Gearloch & he Maried Margaret Maclean or Marearad nion Aonghas – issue Katherine Mhor, a Child who died in infancy Donald Mary, Margaret Cursty, Katherine ogg Roderick, Angus (self) and John . . . [8]

It seems that whoever wrote the letterpress portions of Angus MacKay's book, comprising 'An Account of the Hereditary Pipers', 'A Circumstantial Account of the Competitions for the Prizes given by the Highland Society in London, to the best Performers on the Great Highland Bag-pipe, from the year 1781', 'The

8 NLS, MS.3756.

Bagpipe – History – Effects – Former and Present State of its professors, &c', and the substantial 'Historical and Traditional Notes on the Piobaireachds', it was not Angus MacKay. In all, some thirty-five pages of closely-printed typeset matter, often in double columns, and approaching 30,000 words in length, forming one of the earliest extended accounts of the pipe and its music, appeared under his name. In later years it was widely assumed to be his and, thanks to his immense personal standing as a player, teacher and composer, was very influential in determining how piobaireachd was interpreted, even inside the performer community. But it was actually written by somebody else, and we now know who that somebody was.

On 18 October 1856, a gentleman called James Logan gifted a copy of MacKay's *Ancient Piobaireachd* to the British Library (of which he was a long-time user and ex-employee) with a note that he had written most of the letterpress portions of the text, a claim accepted by the Library and by subsequent scholars.[9] The similarities of language, tone, and subject-matter with Logan's other published writings would seem to place the question beyond doubt.

Logan was an Aberdonian, born in the early 1790s, the son of a merchant, and was educated at the city's Grammar School.[10] He claimed also to have studied at Marischal College, although there is no record of him in the rolls of alumni. He had been intended for medicine or the law, but a severe head injury during his teens induced a temperamental instability, which unsuited him for a regular career. One story says he was hit by a quoit in the quadrangle of Marischal College, another has him struck down by a misdirected heavy hammer at a Highland games on the city's links. At any rate he seems to have gone through the rest of his life with a metal plate in his head and a rooted suspicion of the modern world. A career in painting was his next choice, and in 1821 he settled in London to study at the Royal Academy schools but soon gave this up and took to freelance journalism, by which he lived for many years. This may have involved irregular hours and heavy drinking, but it did give him time to satisfy his insatiable appetite for antiquarian lore and he spent long hours in the library of the British Museum. It may also have been in London that he learned Gaelic, possibly at the classes of the Club of True Highlanders where he quickly became a leading light.

Alasdair MacDonell of Glengarry had founded the True Highlanders in

9 Cannon, *Bibliography*, p.28.

10 This account of James Logan is based on a number of sources, including James Cruickshank, ed., *Logan's Collections* (Aberd., 3rd Spalding Club, 1941); *The Scottish Gael* (2nd edn., Inverness, 1876) edited by Rev. Alex Stewart, 'Nether Lochaber'; and C. N. McIntyre North, *Leabhar Comunn nam Fior Ghaël The Book of the Club of True Highlanders. A record of the Dress, arms, customs, arts and science of the Highlanders. Compiled from printed and manuscript records and traditions and illustrated with etchings of Highland Relics, and the Keltic Vestiges of Great Britain and Ireland* (2 vols., privately printed, Lond., 1881), 'Introduction', i, i-xi; there is an engraved portrait of Logan facing i, v.

1815–16 as a rival to the older Highland Societies, and this was its London branch. The Club had a number of objects. The first was social, to provide a place where Highlanders could relax together, form a network of contacts, and direct a little quiet philanthropy towards distressed fellow Scots. But it also had a cultural role and was dedicated to 'the preservation of the ancient language, music, amusements, and garb of the Gaidheal.'[11] The Club of True Highlanders met monthly in the British Coffee House, and it reflected the pleasantly un-aristocratic side of the Highland community in London. It held a dinner on St. Andrew's Night, a ball at Auld 'Eel, a camanachd at Beltane, and a 'quarterly celebration of eminent Caledonians' (Ossian was in April, Burns in July). There one might meet people like James Logan, William Menzies the Perthshire fiddle player and dancing-master, John Imlah the poet, Robert Ranald McIan the actor and painter, and, when he was in London, the piper, Angus MacKay.[12] The Club was keen on pipers. John MacKenzie of the Caledonian Schools was a member and so was General Thomason's teacher, Donald MacKay, Angus's nephew, and piper to the Prince of Wales.[13] The Club had a 'chieftain', who sat in a ceremonial chair with a drawn claymore before him, a piper 'who is always in attendance, and who, after each of the principal toasts, strikes up some suitable and soul-stirring strain of the mountain music, meanwhile moving majestically round the room' and a henchman with a huge Lochaber axe. There were speeches, and stories, and songs, and many many toasts, some drunk with Highland Honours – which involved standing on one's chair and placing one's foot on the table with fervent Celtic exclamations. The True Highlanders performed this ceremony after the ancient mode, which did not involve hurling the empty glass over the left shoulder as was done, on dubious authority, by the Highland Society of London.[14] At the annual dinner in 1818, Glengarry himself had attended and there was music by Nathaniel Gow and his band and by Glengarry's 'distinguished piper', probably either John MacDonald or Archibald Munro. The Club of True Highlanders was a very Highland affair. Its business was transacted in

---

11 North, i,iv

12 North, ii, 33.

13 North, plate 58 has attractively engraved photographs of John Mackenzie and Donald MacKay, adjoining ii, 34–5.

14 North, i, 30–1; but see also James Logan, *The Scottish Gael; or, Celtic Manners, as Preserved among the Highlanders: being an Historical and Descriptive Account of the Inhabitants, Antiquities, and National Peculiarities of Scotland; more particularly of the northern, or Gaelic parts of the country, where the singular habits of the aboriginal Celts are most tenaciously retained* (2 vols., Lond., 1831), ii, 159, which implies that the custom of standing on the table, as opposed to standing at it, was a later development in the Club of True Highlanders. The custom appears to have been devised by Walter Scott and his circle in the Celtic Society during the second decade of the 19th century. For further details see 'Highland Honours' from 'M', *OT*, 1/7/1911, p.3; 'same' from 'Fionn', 22/7/1911, p.3; for later correspondence on the subject see 19/11/1949, p.3, and 31/12/1949 p.3.

Gaelic, the kilt was *de rigueur*, and tartans were collected from an early date.

Logan was the Club historian and there is an engraved portrait of him captioned 'Jamais Logan Seanachaidh Comunn nam Fior Ghael', showing a long nose (still bearing the marks of the hammer, or quoit,) cold eyes, mutton-chop whiskers, and a plaid secured by a brooch the size of a small soup plate. In addition to his research in the British Museum he undertook a walking tour in the Highlands in 1826 to gather Celtic antiquities for his book, *The Scottish Gael*, a cultural history of ambitious scope published in two volumes in London in 1831, and followed by *The Clans of the Scottish Highlands* (2 vols., Lond., 1845–7) with illustrations by R. R. McIan. On the strength of his growing reputation as a Highland antiquary and, it must be added, his own vigorous canvassing, he was appointed under-secretary of the Highland Society of London in 1839.[15] He lasted less than a year. In 1840 he was sacked again, this time from a post as attendant in the British Museum, the report to the trustees stating 'He is neither punctual nor attentive to his duty, and . . . he was so intoxicated as to be scarcely conscious of what he was doing.'[16] Logan was an abrasive man and a difficult colleague, given to brooding silences and sudden angry outbursts. Later in life he lost his privileges as a gentleman pensioner of the Charterhouse for insulting the management and coming in drunk and obstreperous at unseemly hours of night.

As a scholar he was laborious rather than original, although his tendency to work from cribs supplied by correspondents, and frequent failure to identify his sources, make it sometimes difficult to assess the real extent of his knowledge.[17] He entertained an extravagant regard for Ossian, and unquestioningly accepted the paradigmatic view of Highland culture framed by James Macpherson more than seventy years before. Highland society was interesting because its institutions made it uniquely resistant to change. Its unmixed racial characteristics and geographical isolation made it a storehouse of antique social and cultural practices, and military prowess was its defining characteristic. Logan could go from the days of the Legions to Charles Edward Stuart in a sentence, and with little sense that anything had changed in between. The Celtic world was antique, quaint, and rapidly approaching its demise; yet it could still be sampled by the curious before it entirely disappeared:

> Most of the European nations are now so highly civilized and refined, that it is quite refreshing to meet with those who are yet simple and unsophisticated.

15 HSL, NLS, Dep.268, Correspondence Box 5: Application from James Logan for a clerkship with the HSL, 26/2/1839; Cluny Macpherson writes recommending Logan for the post, 19/3/1839; Logan pleads to keep his job, talking about 'nervous prostration' four inches out of his skull, terrible wound, etc.etc., March 1840.

16 Ruairidh Halford-MacLeod, 'James Logan, Part III', *PT*, vol. 42, no. 5, February 1990, pp. 24–27, (27).

17 For his use of circulars to elicit information, see below. For unacknowledged use of Martin Martin's *Description of the Western Islands of Scotland*, for example, see his anecdote about the piper of St. Kilda imitating birdsong, *Scottish Gael*, ii, 289.

The Gael have preserved a peculiar language, a singular garb, and a mode of
life alike to the nomadic, pastoral state of the most ancient people; and rapid
as the march of innovation has been, they still retain much of their primitive
features . . .[18]

As a playground for the aristocratic tourist, it possessed an obvious attraction:

the Highlands can be traversed in most parts by the best of roads, and its
coasts explored by means of numerous steam-boats . . . Not only have natives
crowded to these romantic scenes and hospitable tribes, but foreigners of
highest distinction have been attracted to this portion of the northern world.
Her Gracious Majesty and Illustrious Consort unbend the bow of Royal
etiquette amid the quietness of a mountain retreat, breaking the monotony of
seclusion by the healthful and exhilarating pursuits peculiar to a Highland life,
deriving entertainment from the athletic and convivial performances of their
loyal Gaelic subjects.[19]

The subscription list of Logan's *The Scottish Gael* was headed by Louis Philippe,
King of the French, and the royal dukes of Sussex and Gloucester, the Prince of
Saxe-Coburg, and the Archduke Maximilian. There were a further three dukes, a
marquis, five earls, several lords, crowds of clan chiefs and landed gentry, and the
whole breathed an atmosphere of opulence and rank. As its cheap re-publication
in serial form during the 1870s indicates, it had originally been too expensive for
ordinary people to buy.[20]

Logan's enthusiasm for costume was typical of his opportunistic approach to
Highland culture, and the idea of a standardised uniform tartan as the outward
badge of clanship was his *idée fixe*.[21] The fact that the so-called 'clan' tartans
often bore but slender resemblance to more traditional patterns and that they had
little traceable existence before the second decade of the nineteenth century did

---

18 *Gaelic Gatherings; or The Highlanders at Home, on the Heath, the River, and the Loch
    . . . From Original Paintings made expressly for this work, by R. R. McIan, Esq. With
    Descriptive Letter-Press by James Logan, Esq, FSA, &c.* (Lond., 1848; reduced facsimile,
    Glasg., 1900), pp.14–18, and also pp.19, 108–9; see also *Scottish Gael*, i,ix, xxiii, ii,
    220–2, 232–3.

19 *Gaelic Gatherings*, pp.15–18.

20 The reviewer in the *Celtic Magazine*, noted it was 'a book now getting very scarce and
    which was never, in consequence of its high price, within the reach of a wide circle of
    readers', vol 1, 1876, p.27.

21 *Scottish Gael*, i, xxii-xxiv, 234, ii, 400–408. His work drew together a number of
    initiatives on Highland history and clan tartans which had been ongoing for years, in
    a desultory kind of way, inside the Highland Society of London. See, for example,
    NLS, Dep.268, Correspondence Box 2, 3 February 1826. The Society's collection of
    tartans seems to have been begun by David Stewart of Garth, see Robertson, *First
    Highlander*, pp.73–81.

not constitute a problem. Historical perspectives could quietly be adjusted to make them appear as a natural and spontaneous outgrowth of Highland culture, as indeed, in a sense, they were.

The generation of 1800 had fought one of Britain's longest wars, at first against the new French republic and then against Napoleon. Scottish society, in particular, had become deeply militarised. The cartoons of John Kay which give such a vivid picture of Edinburgh life at this time, show something of the extent to which militaria penetrated every nook and cranny of civil society, particularly with regard to costume. It had become quite instinctive for people to think in terms of uniform as a means of social differentiation, as we see in Sir Walter Scott's committee planning the ceremonial for George IV's visit to Edinburgh in 1822, which invited even the ordinary citizens to appear in a standardised form of dress.[22] Tartan was the rage of the moment. But which was the 'correct' one? The tartan manufacturers were deluged with anxious enquiries on this score and, business being business, were very willing to provide precise answers. According to Logan

> the stimulus given by the visit of our Gracious Monarch to Scotland, where the great chiefs brought their followers to attend him, and where the Celtic Society, dressed in proper costume, formed his Majesty's body guard, with other circumstances which rendered it necessary for individuals to appear in their peculiar uniforms, have combined to excite much curiosity among all classes, to ascertain the particular tartans and badges they were entitled to wear.[23]

Logan sent his prospectus to various landed and titled persons with a questionnaire about family tartans, relics, history, armorial bearings, slogans, badges, and so on, and was able to include as an appendix to *The Scottish Gael* the first descriptive list of 'clan' tartans.[24] He posed as a champion of genuine tradition, cautioning his readers against 'fanciful' and 'spurious' patterns, but it would appear that he was himself actively involved in the design and promotion of 'clan' tartans. His 'ancient setts' were often mere verbal rationalisations of patterns sent him by the Wilsons of Bannockburn, the leading concern in the contemporary tartan trade, whose normal – and perfectly sensible – approach was to improvise freely with design until they got something that 'took'.[25] But since Celtic culture had been routinely consigned to the past tense by generations of external interpreters, the 'fake antique' was now perhaps the only guise in which the forces of creative renewal could present themselves. At the same time, he had

22 Prebble, pp.97, 100–101, 150–51, 329–30.
23 *Scottish Gael*, i, 237–238.
24 *Scottish Gael*, ii, 400–408.
25 Dunbar, *Highland Dress*, pp. 152–4; see also the same writer's *The Costume of Scotland* (Lond., 1981), pp.88–9.

little more in the way of evidence than a stray reference by Martin Martin to the existence of regional variations in design, and a batch of fabric samples of varying provenance and antiquity. From this slight quarry James Logan raised much of the edifice of 'clan' tartan and its associated paraphernalia.[26]

Similar intellectual methods were applied to the pipe and its music. Here too, Logan's show of specialist knowledge turns out to be superficial, suggesting that his experience of the instrument was very much at second hand, derived from his antiquarian delvings in the British Museum, and interviews with pipers like Donald MacKay (Angus's brother) and George Clark of the Highland Society, to whom he had access in London.[27] For example, the picture of a piper which prefixes the second volume of *The Scottish Gael*, engraved by Logan himself, showed one of the hands wrongly placed; he described the drones being tuned to the E of the chanter, and the presence of a moveable joint in the blow-pipe. His discussion of enharmonic scales seems seriously confused, and the version of 'War or Peace', given in Menzies's figured notation, the only piobaireachd from which he actually quotes, is garbled.[28] Whilst he was familiar with some of the vocabulary of pipe music, therefore, he used it with limited understanding.[29]

But piping was only part of a wider cultural agenda, based on the assumption of the 'clan' as a basic unit of cultural as well as sartorial affiliation. Logan approached piobaireachd in the same way as he did setts of tartan: each 'belonged' to a specific clan, and the suggestion was that nobody else could properly claim it. He was unable to offer any evidence for this, because:

> The suppression of the Colleges for pipers, of which the Mac Cruimins, Mac Artairs, and others, were hereditary masters, has tended much to the misappropriation of Clan music.[30]

Which did tend to draw a veil over the fact that if Angus MacArthur and Donald MacCrimmon were dead, it was but recently so, and their pupils were alive and available for interview. This re-appropriation of the music on a 'clan' basis was one of Logan's goals in the letterpress portions of *Ancient Piobaireachd*, and later, more thoroughly, in his sumptuous *Clans of the Scottish Highlands* (1845–7), published in collaboration with the artist R.R. McIan. Dealing with a distant,

26 Martin, pp.246–7.

27 *Scottish Gael*, ii, 276–7.

28 *Scottish Gael*, ii, 256–7, 294–5; the drone reed drawn on ii, 294 also lacks a bridle.

29 *Scottish Gael*, ii, 269–298.

30 *The Clans of the Scottish Highlands, Illustrated by Appropriate Figures, Displaying their Dress, Arms, Tartans, Armorial Insignia, and Social Occupations. From original sketches by R. R. McIan, Esq. With Accompanying Description and Historical Memoranda of Character, Mode of Life, &c. &c. By James Logan, Esq. F.S.A. Sc., Cor. Mem. Soc. Ant. Normandy, Etc. Author of 'The Scottish Gael,' Introduction to the 'Sar Obair Nam Bard Gaelech.' Etc.* (2 vols., Lond., 1845–7), entry for 'Cameron', vol.i.

substantially oral culture, of which few of his intended readers had personal knowledge, Logan could write things like:

> The Highlanders did not pay a great deal of attention to the armorial marks of distinction – their own peculiar coat armour was the clothing of the clan Tartan. The crest of the Mac Cruimins is a hand holding a pipe chanter, with the motto 'Cogadh no Sith' – Peace or war, a composition of their own. The bearings are on a field argent, a chevron azure, charged with a lion passant, or, between three cross croslets fitchee, gules . . .[31]

with little fear of contradiction. So that we find a version of the past which was at best speculative and sometimes entirely fanciful being invoked to give the sanction of ancient usage to a set of cultural relations which were essentially new.

Logan's 'Account of the Hereditary Pipers' formed the opening section of MacKay's *Ancient Piobaireachd*, and described the line of succession in the MacCrimmon, MacArthur, MacKay, Rankin, Campbell and MacIntyre families. Enormous stress was laid upon the hereditary principle, emphasising the importance of hierarchical social relationships in an aristocratic and deferential society where people were defined by their relationship to social superiors. Logan pictured an idealised regime of semi-feudal dependence in which a stream of 'liberal patronage' was answered by a corresponding stream of artistic tribute and humble regard. But these sketches offered by no means a balanced or objective account of their subject, as we may see in the section on what Logan had been in the habit of calling the 'Mac Rimmons'.

According to Logan, the family was famous all over the Highlands, and widely resorted to for instruction in piobaireachd 'which cannot be acquired except by several years of assiduous study and practice; for the simple reels and strathspeys are far inferior in the estimation of a Piobaireachd player', and such was the extent of their practice that their 'establishment' at Boreraig was regarded as an *Oil-thigh* or college.[32] The township of Boreraig was held rent free, and contained in 1838 a dozen sub-tenants with a rental of £100 p.a., thus identifying the family as members of the 'tacksman' or greater tenant class.[33] Much of the building still survived, a substantial affair, built on an L-shaped plan, with one

---

31 *Clans of the Scottish Highlands*, entry for 'Siol Chruimeinn – The Mac Cruimins', vol.II. I am indebted to the Office of the Lyon Clerk for the advice that 'whatever the origin of these Arms, they were clearly without authority'.

32 For later expressions of the motif that 'there never was a reel in Boreraig', implying that the MacCrimmons played only piobaireachd and disdained lesser forms of music, see 'The Bagpipes and how the MacCrimmons played them', from K. N. MacDonald, *OT*, 4/7/1896, p.3, and 'Pipes, Pipers, and Piobaireachd', by Dr Charles Bannatyne, Part III, 16/5/1903, p.6.

33 For a brief account of the tacksmen in Highland society, see T. C. Smout, *A History of the Scottish People 1560–1830*, (London, 1969), pp.337–8.

wing for accommodation and another for teaching. Due attention was given to picturesque topographical detail, including *Uamh na'm Piobairean*, or the Pipers' Cave, where pupils practised, and *Uamh na'n Calmain*, or the Pigeons' Cave, where MacCrimmon's daughters would play, because they, too, were highly skilled 'being able in his absence to superintend the instruction of the students'.[34] Mention was also made of *Leum an Doill*, or the blind man's leap, a bluff at Dun Bhoreraig from which the famous Iain Dall MacKay was said to have flung himself to escape the ire of jealous fellow pupils.

The narrative continued with a tale about Donald Mór MacCrimmon, the first member of the family about whom anything very definite seemed to be known. Donald had been sent to study with a famous piper in Antrim whose practice was to instruct pupils singly, but he managed to eavesdrop on the lessons of the others and soon learned all that could be taught, so that 'ever since that time the MacCrummens have been allowed to be the best Pipers in Scotland; so much so that no one was esteemed a perfect player, unless he had been instructed or finished by them'.[35]

Donald's brother, Patrick *Caogach* – blinking or squint-eyed Peter – was treacherously slain by a MacKenzie in Kintail, and when MacLeod failed to take vengeance, Donald Mór pursued his brother's killer. Upon his relatives refusing to give him up, he set fire to their houses and several people were killed, the incident becoming known as *Lasan Phadruig Chaogach*, or, 'A Flame of Wrath for Squinting Peter'.[36] Donald fled to the Reay country where he was acquainted with the laird, Donald Duaghal MacKay, who arranged a secret hiding place for him. But Donald Duaghal's wife was a Mackenzie, and soon a party of her kinsfolk arrived commanded by the chief's son and well acquainted where he might be found. MacCrimmon managed to escape, but stole back at night and placed each man's sword and dirk across him as he lay. Recognising that he could have killed them all, the chief's son promised to intercede on his behalf, and Donald Mór, accompanied by Donald Duaghal MacKay, journeyed to Kintail, putting up at the house of Lord Kintail's fiddler. The latter challenged Donald to a drinking bout, thinking to have him overpowered and brought before the laird. But the plot was betrayed and MacCrimmon barricaded himself in his chamber, at which point Donald Duaghal MacKay arrived with the pardon. 'All then dispersed peaceably, and MacKay and MacCrummen proceeded to the castle of his Lordship, where they made merry

---

34 MacKay, *Ancient Piobaireachd*, 'Account of the Hereditary Pipers', p.8. The MacCrimmon women are a recurring motif in the sources, presumably intended to emphasise the family's pre-eminence, since even its females were master players. See, for example, 'Cumha Dhonnachaidh Mhic Iain', from 'Boreraig', *OT*, 27/5/1911, p.3; 'Capt. Neil MacLeod's Book of Canntaireachd', from 'Fionn', 27/7/1912, p.3; for a tale of Elizabeth MacCrimmon, see below pp.211–2; and for Euphemia MacCrimmon, daughter of Iain Dubh, see 'Notices of Pipers', *PT*, vol. 22, no.10, July 1970, p.23.

35 MacKay, *Ancient Piobaireachd*, 'Account of the Hereditary Pipers', p.8.

36 MacKay, *Ancient Piobaireachd.*, p.9.

all night, and next day the Piper returned to Skye, where he remained without much further adventures until his death'.[37]

The later MacCrimmons, including Patrick Mór, Patrick Og, Malcolm, John, Donald Bàn, Farquhar, Iain Dubh and Donald Roy, are disposed of in twenty-two lines. Two centuries of cultural history are summed up by folk tale about blood-feud and vengeance, reflecting the conventional Lowland view of the Highlands as a wild and lawless place shot through by romantic bloodshed and turbulent passions.[38] Within ten years of the death of Donald Roy, the MacCrimmons were already turning into the stuff of legend.

Furthermore, since the 'hereditary' principle continued to apply in the modern Highlands only to the ownership of land, its apparent failure in piping could be used to include the latter amongst the relics of a vanishing civilisation. Logan's identification of the MacCrimmon family as the wellspring of legitimacy – a theme much amplified by later writers – enabled him to imply that the failure of this particular line had been fatal to the art of piping and marked the passing of an age. It also enabled him to ignore its vigorous continuation in the hands of a new generation of master players and teachers whose relationship with the landed élite had significantly altered, and which included as one of its leading lights his colleague, Angus MacKay.

The 'Circumstantial Account of the Competitions for the prizes given by the Highland Society in London, to the Performers on the Great Highland Bag-Pipe, from the year 1781', said a great deal about the ability, generosity, taste and discrimination of the bench, but little about the pipers, except their names, what they won and, sometimes, what they had played. Who their 'masters' were, on the other hand, was recorded very carefully, with full attention to their titles, dignities and territorial possessions. Thrilling speeches from the chair were quoted, extolling the military virtues of the instrument ('there is no sound, which the immortal *Wellington* hears with more delight, or the Marshals of France with more dismay, than the notes of a Highland *Piobaireachd*') and the exciting opportunities for self-sacrifice afforded to the piper in war.[39] The brilliant social credentials of the audience and the bench formed frequent subject of comment, and the proceedings were presented as a gorgeous Highland spectacle, a characteristic passage noting 'between fifty and sixty competitors for the different prizes, ranged on the stage, all equipped in the tartan of their respective clans – a sight most unusual and interesting to strangers.'[40] In a report of some five thousand words dealing with more than fifty years of music-making, there was virtually no critical or evaluative comment on the music itself or how it had been played.

37 MacKay, *Ancient Piobaireachd*, p.10. A royal indemnity to Donald Duaghal Mackay for a raid on Thurso in 1612 shows him to have been accompanied by 'Donald McCruimien ye pyper', see Angus Mackay, M.A., *The Book of Mackay*, pp.126, 414.
38 See Donaldson, *Jacobite Song*, pp.49–53.
39 MacKay, *Ancient Piobaireachd*, 'Account of the Competition', p.18.
40 MacKay, *Ancient Piobaireachd*, 'Account of the Competition', p.20.

Nor were these qualities conspicuously present in the 'Historical and Traditional Notes on the Piobaireachds' which occupied the final section of the text. 'Abercairny's Salute', for example, called forth warm appreciation for the tasteful improvements to the mansion house of Abercairny – to celebrate which 'a grand dinner was given when every one praised the elegance of the new buildings, particularly the dining-room, which was allowed to be in every respect perfect' – but not a syllable about the tune.[41] Likewise 'The Massacre of Glencoe' was made the occasion of a string of fashionably romantic reflections with little trace of musical appreciation:

> . . . A few goats scrambling among the precipices, or eagles soaring high above, may be the only indications of life to meet the traveller's view; and his musings will only be disturbed by the fretful rushing of the rapid Cona, as it dashes over its rugged bed, or the noise of the more impetuous torrents that pour in numerous streams along the mountain side.
>
> Here the contemplative may indulge in a train of sad and serious imagination, not unmixed with less melancholy ideas than the name of this valley is so apt to suggest. On the banks of Cona's echoing stream, it is believed that Ossian first drew breath, and spent his infant years. In this vale, towards the north-west end, the unparalleled atrocity took place, on which the Piper has composed the plaintive and maddening notes of the Piobaireachd which bears its name . . .[42]

It was James Logan who seems to have established the formula, much repeated later, that:

> It is to catch its echoing tones among the blue mountains of its native country; to sit on the heather banks beside the stilly loch and ancient Dun; listening to the notes so sweetly mellowed by distance, as they swell on the evening breeze: to hear the melody wafted wide o'er the silent lake, or breaking through the roaring of the mountain-stream and rushing of the fitful wind, – thus it is to hear the Bag-Pipe as it ought to be heard.[43]

i.e. the music was best appreciated when reduced to a vaguely pleasing hum in the background, as a minor adjunct to a predominantly visual experience.

Logan frequently stressed the antiquity of the instrument and its music. Of 'Tulloch Ard', he declared 'the date of its composition, and its author are unknown', notwithstanding which, however, the tune was 'very old'. 'The MacRae's March' was claimed to celebrate – and presumably, therefore, be

---

41 MacKay, *Ancient Piobaireachd*, 'Historical and Traditional Notes', p.9.
42 MacKay, *Ancient Piobaireachd*, 'Historical and Traditional Notes', p.6.
43 MacKay, *Ancient Piobaireachd*, 'The Bagpipe-History-Effects-Former and Present State of its Professors, &c.' p.22.

contemporary with – the Battle of Park in (probably) 1491. 'The Lament for the Harp Tree' was 'evidently from its style, of very high antiquity'. 'The Young Laird of Dungallon's Salute', although 'the date of its composition has not transpired' was likewise 'very old'.[44] One tune, 'Chisholm's Salute', appeared with a folkish note about ancestral chanters magically bound up with the death of the chief, but no indication that it had first seen the light of day in 1836.[45]

The fact that at least a further nine out of the sixty-one tunes published in *Ancient Piobaireachd* had been composed during the previous half century – five of them by Angus MacKay's own father who was still alive – received correspondingly little emphasis.[46] It was inevitable, given Logan's intellectual debt to James Macpherson, that he should look to the remote past for the period of genuine creativity, and be correspondingly ambiguous about the forces of change and renewal at work during his own period. So that he is quite prepared to tell us that

> . . . although clan gatherings are all more or less old, pipers continued to compose similar music until recently. Several originated in the year 1745, as one by the piper of Cluny, who composed a piobrachd during the battle of Falkirk, which is yet well known; and later instances may not be wanting, but the old gatherings retained their place which they certainly deserve, from the true expression and genuine character of their music. Indeed, the composition of salutes and other piobrachds is now, perhaps, more often attempted than success can warrant; and pipe musicians would acquire greater credit by paying more attention to the inimitable works of their ancestors than to their own rhapsodies. It is alleged, by those who are competent to form a correct opinion, that the present pipers are inferior to their ancestors, and are getting worse. There are certainly many exceptions to this assertion where a musical ear is assisted by knowledge, which the old pipers did not possess. The lists of competitors at Edinburgh shew numerous names of clever pipers; and in London, Mr. MacKay, piper to his Royal Highness the Duke of Sussex, and Mr. Clark, who officiates in the same capacity, to the Highland Society, are excellent; but we must regret that the same cause which led to the decay of oral recitation, impaired our modern list of ancient Gaelic music; for the former celebrated seminaries being no more, a considerable portion of pipe music, from having never been noted down, is already lost. [an unacknowledged

---

44 MacKay, *Ancient Piobaireachd*, 'Historical and Traditional Notes', pp.3, 4, 7, 10, 11, 13.
45 MacKay, *Ancient Piobaireachd*, 'Historical and Traditional Notes', p.7; for the date and occasion of this tune see Chapter 7 *n*. 44.
46 'Glengarry's Lament', by Archibald Munro, 'Lady MacDonald's Lament', by Angus MacArthur, 'The Highland Society of Scotland's Salute', by Professor MacArthur, and 'Lady Doyle's Salute', 'Davidson of Tulloch's Salute', 'The Battle of Waterloo', 'King George III's Lament', and 'MacLeod of Colbeck's Lament' by John MacKay. If one considers compositions originating within the previous century then the number rises to about 16 out of the 61.

quotation from John Ramsay's 'Essay'] 'In less than twenty years', says MacDonald, in his excellent Preface to his Gaelic Melodies, 'it would be in vain to attempt a collection of Highland music'.[47]

We see here a characteristic endorsement of John Ramsay's 'Essay', assumed to be the work of Patrick MacDonald. Although the passage of time had already shown Ramsay's prediction to be wrong, his work confirmed so exactly the expectations created by the Macpherson paradigm that it continued to inform the argument and be cited by the unwary until well into the twentieth century. Logan's work was even more influential in shaping attitudes to the pipe and its music because, just like Ramsay's, it was issued under the name of a genuine expert on Highland music and was assumed to possess an authority to which, in reality, it was in no way entitled.

Although James Logan was responsible for the cultural 'frame' through which the music text was viewed, the construction of that text appears to have been largely the responsibility of Angus MacKay. Obviously, the association with Logan and the Highland Society of London influenced his selection in various ways, causing him to emphasise certain categories of tune, for example, such as those deemed 'ancient', those associated with great aristocratic houses, and with major clans, and also those with links to the Jacobite movement. Since he had access to most of the important contemporary MSS, as well as to his own collection which must already have been substantial, he would have had a wide potential choice.[48] It has sometimes been thought that such constraints alone could explain the inclusion of mediocre pieces like 'The Mackenzies' Gathering', 'The Duke of Argyll's Salute' and 'The Red Hand in the MacDonald's Arms', at the expense of tunes like 'The Lament for the Children', and 'Scarce of Fishing'.[49] The decision to have the text engraved in London seems also to have created problems. MacKay's manuscript copy for *Ancient Piobaireachd* has not survived; but the quality of his other MSS suggests that it will have been clear and technically consistent, so that the numerous errors in the music text of the published book, affecting more than a third of the tunes and ranging from minor note mistakes to serious structural dislocation, would seem to indicate that Angus MacKay had little control over the physical production of the text, and that whoever proofed it, if it was proofed at all, was not a piper.[50] This was doubly

---

47 *Scottish Gael*, ii, 276–7.

48 A.G. Kenneth, 'Some mistakes in Angus MacKay's settings, and where they came from', *PT*, vol. 36, no.6, March 1984, pp.13–14.

49 MacInnes, p.250.

50 The tunes affected are 'Donald Duaghal MacKay's Lament', 'The Mackenzies' Gathering', 'I got a kiss of the king's hand', 'MacRae's March', 'The Massacre of Glencoe', 'Glengarry's Lament', 'The Grant's Gathering', 'Chisholm's Salute', 'Lady Doyle's Salute', 'The Gordons' Salute', 'The MacDonald's Salute', 'Sir Ewin Cameron of Lochiel's Salute', 'Menzies' Salute', 'The MacLeans' March', 'The Red Hand in the MacDonald's Arms', 'The Battle of Sheriffmuir', 'The Viscount of Dundee's Lament', 'Patrick óg Mac Crummen's Lament', 'The Lament for the Harp Tree',

unfortunate as the book became 'the judges bible' – after all, its extensive editorial apparatus gave its possessor a kind of instant expertise, a semblance of genuine knowledge in return for rather modest effort – and a practice grew up amongst competing pipers of playing MacKay, mistakes and all.[51] So that while the goal of a fixed printed text for competitive purposes was achieved, the text was flawed, and there was to be no serious attempt at revision for more than a generation.

Ancient Piobaireachd has sometimes been thought to represent a distinctly MacKay family tradition, in contrast to the MacDonald 'school' which had previously held the field, but it is obvious that Angus MacKay had access to the MSS of Donald MacDonald, Peter Reid, and the Highland Society of London.[52] Thirty eight of his sixty-one tunes also appear in these sources, nine in Donald MacDonald alone (including three from his published book); a further ten appear in both MacDonald and Reid; nine appear in Reid alone; one is given both in MacDonald and the Highland Society of London's MS; and nine tunes appear in the Highland Society's manuscript alone. While MacKay was guided by his sources, however, he did not follow them slavishly, and he introduced a number of significant changes in the prevailing system of notation, apparently designed to standardise and simplify the ornamentation, and to reduce (if not altogether to eliminate) its rhythmical uncertainty:

Donald MacDonald, *Ancient Martial Music,* **p.102**

Angus MacKay, *Ancient Piobaireachd,* **p.5**

cont'd   'Clan-Ranald's Salute', 'The Bells of Perth', 'The Earl of Ross's March', 'The Piper's Warning to his Master', 'War or Peace', 'MacLeod of MacLeod's Lament', and 'Lady MacDonald's Lament'.

51   'As an example of this, let us take "I got a kiss of the king's hand" – Angus MacKay's book. The first part of the ground or *Urlar* has twelve bars, and in the same part in the variations there are only eleven bars. One naturally concludes that there is something wrong in this.

  On comparing the variations with the ground, it is at once apparent that the third bar of the ground is left out in the variations. This little error is known to every leading piper in Scotland, and he plays it wrongly simply because it is in MacKay's book, and if he did play it correctly, most of those who at present act as judges of piobaireachd would say that he was wrong.' See 'The Piobaireachd Society of Scotland', *OT,* 19/9/1903, p.3.

52   But see the manuscript of John MacKay, whose notational conventions are very

The above example shows MacKay's typical procedure, which involved either specifying a time value for one element of the appoggiatura to show its rhythmical value in relation to surrounding melody notes, or reducing it to a single gracenote so that ambiguity was eliminated:

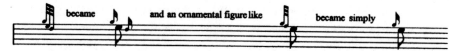

One effect of this conscious drive towards a simpler, plainer approach to decoration – perhaps to ensure that the resulting notation could be more easily interpreted by keyboard players – was to sacrifice a good deal of the rhythmical and harmonic subtlety which had characterised the written tradition up to that point. As we may see, for example, in a typical passage from the ground of the 'Lament for Donald Duaghal MacKay', firstly from the Highland Society of London's manuscript and secondly from MacKay:[53]

Sometimes MacKay preserved an appoggiatura present in an earlier source, but indicated its timing by making small changes of value within it, which was to become a favourite device of later editors:

cont'd   similar to his brother Angus, NLS, Acc.9231. For the view that notational differences between Angus MacKay and Donald MacDonald reflected two divergent traditions in late eighteenth and early nineteenth century piping, see Archibald Campbell, *Kilberry Book of Ceol Mor* (2nd edn., Glasg,, 1953), 'Introduction', p.12.

53 See Frans Buisman, 'The Reflexive Shake: An Ancient Piobaireachd Ornament', Parts 1–4, *PT*, vol.41, no. 8–9/11–12, May-June, August-September 1989, pp.21–31, 47–53, 38–40, 22–7.

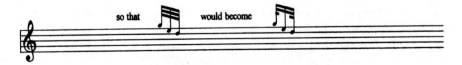

What had in the past been variable, therefore, a matter of taste or judgement, musical context, performer choice, now tended to assume a single fixed form. We can see what this might imply by considering one of the most frequently occurring conventional movements, the so-called 'echo beats'. We have already seen these accented in a number of different ways.[54] MacKay generally notated them as follows:[55]

They fell into two groups, A – D, and E – high G. In the first, the opening E quavers received the accent, in the second, the dotted quaver which formed the second component of the movement. There may have been a pleasing unity from a typographical point of view, but they did not always fit very well into their musical context if played as written, especially in tunes which have the movement on A as their opening gesture and whose rhythmical pattern was disrupted when the preceding E introductory note was incorporated into it, anticipating the accent.[56] Specifying the value of introductory notes was certainly useful in contexts where there might be room for doubt. This was less so, perhaps, in those where their ability to be played 'long' or 'short' might be advantageous, representing the difference between a flowing richly decorated musical line, and one divided into breathlessly short note-groups punctuated by frequently interjected quaver E's, say, each of which had a fixed duration regardless of what was happening around them. Here, for example, is the opening sequence of 'Isabel MacKay', firstly as set by Donald MacDonald and then by Angus MacKay:

54 See above, pp.127–8.

55 For an example of MacKay's occasional use of a differently-timed movement on low A, see *Ancient Piobaireachd*, p.131, and for two different timings of this movement within the same tune in his unpublished papers, see 'The Sutherlands' Gathering' and 'The MacKays' March', NLS, MS 3754, ff.45–7, 50–52.

56 For a suggestion that Angus's father, John MacKay, may have played the introductory E short and the first of the low A's long, and that Angus may have been over-zealous in his standardisation of the appoggiaturas, see Cooke, 'Elizabeth Ross', p.6, 7, 9–10. This latter point was taken up by Dr. Cooke in 'Changing Styles', pp.12–14, 11–13, and also in a letter to *International Piper*, vol. 2, no. 7, November 1979, pp. 20–1.

Donald MacDonald's MS, NLS 1680, f.254, with the title 'The Battle of Maolroy'

Angus MacKay, *Ancient Piobaireachd*, p.26

The later variations were subjected to a similar standardisation. There was more involved than just detail. The crunluath fosgailte, for example, was rendered in a way that seems to violate the underlying point of the movement.[57] The term 'fosgailte' means 'opened', and in piping terms what happened in a fosgailte movement – previous to *Ancient Piobaireachd* – was this:

Pre-MacKay fosgailte: throw on E played off 'open' B, C or D

Angus MacKay's fosgailte: the throw is played off A, and has become 'duinte' or 'closed'

The power of MacKay's sponsors was so great, however, that by the early twentieth century, his 'fosgailte' movement had displaced the older form.

Angus MacKay frequently took an independent line with regard to melodic contour, time signature, and number and type of variations, with results that were not always happy. In 'The MacRae's March', for example, which appears in the Highland Society of London's MS, his changes to the distribution of accent in the ground, reversal of the timing of the taorluath, and removal of the insistent Fs up to which it was played in the original source, considerably weakened the point of the tune.[58]

'John Garbh MacLeod of Rasay's Lament', was translated into 3/4 time rather than the common time in which it was set in Donald MacDonald's manuscript and which more naturally reflected the phrase pattern of the melody.[59] MacDonald's siubhal was removed in favour of a trebling of the taorluath

57 But see Frans Buisman, 'Gleanings from pre-Mackay Piobaireachd: Clialudh', *PT*, vol. 39, nos 3–5, December-February, 1986–87, pp.34–8, 33–6, 36–41.

58 MacKay, *Ancient Piobaireachd*, pp.21–2; NLS, MS 1679, No.22.

59 MacKay, *Ancient Piobaireachd*, pp.23–5; Donald MacDonald's MS, NLS, MS 1680, ff.20–4.

and crunluath movements, so that the balanced and tasteful arrangement of paired variations in the earlier version was replaced by something simpler and, perhaps inevitably, more monotonous. There was a similar approach in 'The Massacre of Glencoe' where MacDonald's attractive thumb variation and siubhal were cut and the tune proceeded rapidly to the later variations, based on a tone row which was distinctly less pleasing than MacDonald's one.[60]

Although there are exceptions to this rule, the general tendency of Angus MacKay's editorial practice was to make tunes plainer, shorter, and structurally more simple.

It is clear that *Ancient Piobaireachd* was only the first instalment of a much more ambitious project. In the later 1830s and early '40s, MacKay went on to complete one of the largest manuscript collections of piobaireachd ever assembled, written out in fair copy using the shorthand conventions pioneered by John MacGregor in the Highland Society of London's MS. There were nearly two hundred tunes in all. The contents included transcripts from existing manuscript sources, and material collected from his father, John MacKay, and other tradition-bearers. In 1841 he took the papers to the Edinburgh competition, and offered them for sale to the Highland Society of Scotland. The Society referred them for an opinion to Sir John Graham Dalyell who advised against purchase, stating, 'It is impossible to judge of them [the tunes] without hearing them on the instrument . . . I have no doubt that Mackay has made a selection of the best music for the collection he published and that much of the content of these volumes may be secondary matter'.[61] And so the sponsoring institutions lost, for a time, the opportunity to acquire virtually the whole tradition. Of course Dalyell was right, in a sense: the decisive step from the Highland Societies' point of view – the transfer of authority from performance to score – had already taken place. At the final Edinburgh competition in 1844 tunes from Angus MacKay's book dominated the competitors' lists.[62]

Ancient Piobaireachd went to a second edition in 1839. Although always scarce, and therefore expensive (copies were changing hands for between £5–£10 by the 1890s), it strongly influenced what was heard in competition during the century following its publication. Most copies were owned by the gentlemen enthusiasts who occupied the judges' bench; its contents circulated amongst pipers in manuscript.[63]

In 1843 MacKay edited a collection of light music entitled *The Piper's Assistant*, which ran to several editions. From 1849 onwards he began to compile a

---

60 MacKay, *Ancient Piobaireachd*, pp.28–30; Donald MacDonald's MS, NLS, MS 1680, ff.119–24.
61 Sir John Graham Dalyell MSS, EUL., Gen 374D ff.19–20
62 Halford-MacLeod, 'Top Twenty piobaireachds', Part 3, pp.23–6.
63 'Pipe-Major Meldrum on Champions Past and Present. A Veteran Piper's Reminiscences'. Part 4, *OT*, 20/7/1940, p.5. For the price of second-hand copies of MacKay see John Grant, *Piobaireachd its Origin and Construction* (Edinr., 1915), p.23.

manuscript collection which eventually contained some five hundred tunes of this type. Presumably he contemplated further publications, but serious illness put a stop to whatever plans he may have had. In 1854 Angus MacKay became violently insane, probably as a result of tertiary syphilis, and was confined first in the London Bedlam and then in the new and prestigious Crichton Royal Asylum near Dumfries.

His Bedlam diary records that:

> many of the things I dreamed about happened at Dunvegan Castle. The following met there, my mother and the queen and the Lords and Dukes of Clan Donald . . . It appeared as if God were moving backward and forward along the passage and around my room. It seemed to me that the world had come to an end.[64]

The historian of the Crichton Royal gives details of the symptoms:

> His case notes from the London Asylum refer to a 'dangerous delusion respecting the Queen and Prince Albert' while those from Crichton Royal record: 'His wild declamations refer to persons of rank and to their transmutations into one or other or into himself – his marriage to Her Majesty and his repudiation of Prince Albert' . . . MacKay . . . 'sings, shrieks, hoots in exact imitation of the owl and howls in every conceivable cadence'. The *Scotsman* newspaper latched on to this detail with the inference that it was little wonder since 'they had taken his pipe away from him'. [65]

On the 21st March 1859, he was drowned in the River Nith attempting to escape.

His papers (including the Highland Society of London's MS) were bought from his widow and preserved by Michael MacCarfrae (or MacCaffee), a former pupil who was piper to the Duke of Hamilton. They are now in the National Library of Scotland.

Although *Ancient Piobaireachd* was mediated as a classic product of Celtic antiquity, it was an innovative and forward-looking text, whose enthusiastic embrace of standardisation was very much of the age of Paxton and Brunel and contemporary movements in engineering, architecture and the applied arts. Conservative thinkers like John Ruskin and William Morris, had they concerned themselves with things like bagpipe music, would have found it disturbing.

While Angus MacKay's career was a success, as the world would have reckoned it, it was carved out in difficult times. Instead of a highland laird, however grand, he worked for a head of state, of whose establishment he necessarily formed a much less important part. Instead of a clearly defined role, and well understood

---

64 Bound in with 'MacKay's Music' Vol IV, NLS, MS 3756.
65 Morag Williams, *History of the Crichton Royal Hospital* 1839–1989 [Dumfries: n.d. but 1989], p.79.

social standing, he had to improvise a place for the pipe and its music in the hierarchy and ceremonial of a royal court at a time of rapid change. Instead of a secure, if moderate, landed income paid directly to himself by a number of dependants, enjoyed by right of succession (which, in normal circumstances, gave considerable personal autonomy to the likes of the MacCrimmons and the MacKays of Gairloch) he had a wage. He was a servant, who could be – and eventually was – dismissed. Under the new dispensation, master pipers may have been better off than their predecessors in terms of disposable income, but this was at the cost of a serious decline in status and security, marked by a descent from the middle ranks of the old Highland society to the servant sub-class of Victorian Britain. When changing circumstances began to make it possible for pipers to make a decent living by their art without entering service, then, like John MacColl and Willliam McLennan they did so, shunning the inherited culture and the social dependency it entailed.

In the educated and genteel parts of the Victorian world where people could afford to buy big books of pipe music as cultural curios, and absorb their opinions about Gaelic Scotland from middle-class newspapers and magazines, the Macpherson paradigm continued to dominate attitudes throughout the second half of the nineteenth century.

We see this in *Ross's Collection of Pipe Music* (Lond., 1869), one of the most important mid-Victorian editions. The music text was compiled by the Queen's piper, Uilleam Ross, but the cultural parameters of the work were set out in an introductory essay, 'The Bagpipe and its Music', written by the Dean of the Chapel Royal, the Rev. Dr. Norman MacLeod, the ebullient, fast-talking, cigar-smoking 'Norman of the Barony' (a high-profile inner-city parish in Glasgow), editor of the popular religious periodical *Good Words*, and a leading figure in the post-Disruption Church of Scotland. Ross almost certainly knew him personally and commemorated his death in 1872 with an interesting little lament entitled 'Cumha Thoirmaid Mhoir Mhic-Leoid'.[66] The Doctor was a frequent visitor at Balmoral, a confidant of the Queen, and one of her favourite preachers. And he was passionately fond of music.

Norman MacLeod came of a long and distinguished line of Highland divines. His father, also named Norman, had been a notable campaigner for the Gaelic language and writer on Highland subjects, famous under his pen-name 'Caraid nan Gaidheal' ('Friend of the Gael'); his brother-in-law was Archibald Clerk, minister of Duirinish, in Skye, whom we will shortly encounter writing about the MacCrimmons in the *New Statistical Account*. MacLeod was born in Campbeltown, and brought up at Campsie in Stirlingshire and later in Glasgow, where his father was minister of St. Columba's; but he did have Gaelic and he was interested in piobaireachd, at least at a verbal level. For example, we find the following note in his 'Journal' in 1841:

---

66 Ross, *Collection*, pp.62–3.

Highland Music. – The pibroch; the music of the past and gone, of lonely lakes, castled promontories, untrodden valleys and extinguished feuds, wild superstitions, and of a feudal glory and an age of romance and song which have fled on their dun wings from Morven. It is fit only for the large bag-pipe in the hall of an old castle, with *thuds* of wind and the dash of billows as its only accompaniment.

It is deep sorrow that is checked by lofty pride from breaking.[67]

Unfortunately he did not actually know very much about bagpipe music. He was more familiar with it as an ideological construct than as a musical form, typically, perhaps, of his day and generation. Norman MacLeod was a formidably clever man, a fluent writer with a genuine expressive gift, but if one were in search of a comprehensive collection of conventional platitudes about the pipe and its music – with the single concession that it was 'carefully composed' – it would be difficult to find a better example than his prefatory essay to *Ross's Collection*.

He invoked the whole gamut of inherited stereotypes – the idea that the music made its characteristic appeal to emotion rather than to reason; that it did not conform to normal aesthetic criteria and was therefore unintelligible except to those of Celtic blood; that it enabled its listener to lay aside maturity and educational sophistication and recover the spontaneity and innocence of child-hood; that it was inextricably linked with wild natural scenery, highland dress, military ardour, and the baronial panoply of a hierarchical landed society; that it was a survival from a lost heroic age and spoke most typically of sorrow and dispossession, and that it was, indeed, the swan-song of a doomed civilisation. The essay looked forward as well as back, however. When it spoke of 'the joy of grief' which loved to brood upon its own loss, it not only invoked the words of Ossian, but carried its readers to the very threshold of the 'Celtic Twilight' movement which was to dominate the cultural agenda in the later decades of the nineteenth century:

The Music of the Highlands is the Pibroch of the Great War Pipe, with its fluttering pennons, fingered by a genuine Celt, in full Highland Dress, as he slowly paces a Baronial Hall, or amidst the wild scenery of his native mountains. The Bagpipe is the instrument best adapted for summoning the Clans from the far off Glens to rally round the standard of their Chiefs, or for leading a Highland Regiment to the attack amidst the roar of battle. The Pibroch is also constructed to express a welcome to the Chief on his return to his clan; and to wail out a lament for him as he is borne by his people to the old burial place in the Glen, or in the sainted Isle of Graves. To those who understand its carefully composed music, there is a pathos and depth of feeling suggested by it which a Highlander alone can fully sympathise with; associated by him, as it always is, with the most touching memories of his home and country; recalling the faces

67 Donald MacLeod, *Memoir of Norman MacLeod, D.D* (Toronto, 1876), p.106.

and forms of the departed; spreading forth before his inward eye panoramas of Mountain, Loch, and Glen, and reviving impressions of his early and happiest years. And thus, if it excites the stranger to laughter, it excites the Highlander to tears, as no other music can do, in spite of the most refined culture of his after life. It is thus, too, that what appears to be only a tedious and unmeaning monotony in the music of the genuine Pibroch, is not so to one under the magic influence of Highland associations. There is, indeed, in every Pibroch a certain monotony of sorrow. It pervades even the 'welcome', as if the young Chief who arrives recalls also the memory of the old Chief who has departed. In the 'Lament' we naturally expect this sadness; but even in the 'Summons to Battle', with all its fire and energy, it cannot conceal what it seems already to anticipate – sorrow for the slain. In the very reduplication of its hurried notes, and in the repetition of its one idea, there are expressions of vehement passion and of grief – the 'joy of grief', as Ossian terms it – which loves to brood upon its own loss, and ever repeats the one desolate thought which fills the heart, and which, in the end, again breaks forth into the long and loud agonising cry with which it began. All this will no doubt seem both meaningless and extravagant to many, but it is nevertheless a deliberately expressed conviction.

The characteristic poetry of the Highlands is Ossian, its music the Pibroch, and these two voices embody the spirit, and sing the praises of '*Tir nam' beann nan' Gleann's nan' Gaisgeach*'.[68]

When we turn to the music text we find ourselves, as often happens, in the presence of a different kind of intelligence, every bit as resourceful as MacLeod's in its own medium, and aesthetically gifted beyond his conjecture.

Uilleam Ross (1823–1891) was a grand-nephew of the famous John Bàn MacKenzie, born in Knockbain by the Beauly Firth, and so came from the Strathconon/Strathglass/Black Isle triangle which produced so many talented performers during the nineteenth century. Indeed, he was one of the few players of quality to be found in the regular army at this time, serving as pipe-major of the Black Watch when he won the prize pipe at Inverness in 1853. From 1854 to 1891 he was first piper to the Queen. In some ways he looks like a rather traditional figure, a master piper rising to eminence by dint of success at competition, a pipe-maker also, publishing a collection depending on his personal fame and authority for its success – Donald MacDonald, perhaps, a couple of generations on. But he lived in a different world. Uilleam Ross was first and foremost a businessman, a musical impresario working the market and using the British establishment to promote himself in the most effective way. His *Collection* was published in 1869, with a second extended edition in 1875/6, and by the time of the third edition in 1885, it included forty piobaireachds and more

---

68 'The Bagpipe and Its Music' by The Rev. Norman MacLeod, quoted from Ross, *Collection*, 3rd edn., 1885. The Gaelic toast means 'The Land of the Bens, the Glens and the Heroes'.

than four hundred pieces of ceòl beag. Up to this point, publications of pipe music had tended to concentrate either on piobaireachd or on light music, but not both.[69] The astute Uilleam Ross, sensing an opportunity for a new kind of mixed anthology, devoted roughly equal space to each. His book eventually ran to six editions, being more or less continuously available until the expanding *Piobaireachd Society Collection* (second series), and various more modern collections of light music, led to its demise in the 1930s.

Like its predecessors, *The Ancient Martial Music of Caledonia* and *Ancient Piobaireachd*, *Ross's Collection* was aimed mainly at the judges' bench and was published by subscription. Seventeen of its 124 subscribers were pipers, including William and Alexander MacDonald of Glentruim, Alexander McLennan of the Inverness-shire Militia, J. F. Farquharson, piper to the Duke of Edinburgh, J. F. Campbell's informant Duncan Ross, piper to the Duke of Argyll, and Aeneas Rose, piper to the Duke of Atholl; but at 30/- it would have been beyond the purses of most of their colleagues.[70] The Highland Society of London subscribed; the Highland Society of Scotland did not.

Every piobaireachd in the collection was published in staff notation for the first time, and these included some of the greatest tunes in the tradition, such as 'The Lament for the Children', 'Scarce of Fishing', 'The Lament for Donald Bàn MacCrimmon', 'In Praise of Morag', 'MacCrimmon's Sweetheart', 'The Lament for Mary MacLeod', 'The Battle of the Pass of Crieff', 'The Lament for the Only Son', 'The Old Woman's Lullaby', and 'The Blue Ribbon'.

The light music section was also innovative. It contained early versions of a good many tunes which were to become standard pieces, including the marches 'The Marchioness of Tullibardine', 'The Edinburgh Volunteers', 'The Balmoral Highlanders', 'The Abercairney Highlanders', 'The Glengarry Gathering', 'The Stirlingshire Militia', 'The Atholl Highlanders March to Loch Katrine', 'The 74th's Farewell to Edinburgh', 'Highland Wedding', 'Leaving Glenurquhart', and 'The 71st Highlanders'; strathspeys like 'The Cameronian Rant', 'Tullochgorm', and 'MacBeth's Strathspey', and the reels 'Duntroon', 'The Rejected Suitor', 'Over the Isles to America', and 'The Smith of Chillichassie'. Ross published some lovely tunes, especially the new competition material which was beginning to absorb the main creative urge in piping; but some were instantly forgettable, the results in many cases of what looks like a trawl through the pipe-cases of his service acquaintances. In an oral setting, indifferent material was discarded, neither remembered nor reproduced. As a result only the good survived. In a context of musical literacy, however, this in-built quality control was removed. The junk was not immediately forgotten. It was printed first. Then forgotten.

---

69 Donald MacDonald had included a section of 'Airs Composed in the Islands of Uist and Skye' at the end of his piobaireachd collection, but it was relatively insignificant in comparison with the space devoted to piobaireachd.

70 Cannon, *Bibliography*, pp.146–50. See 'List of Subscribers' attached to first edition, pp.133–4.

The compiler drew upon his own extensive manuscript collection of piobair-eachd,[71] and although this seems to have been derived in the main from the MSS of Angus MacKay, his published versions were often more fluent and idiomatic than MacKay's and he included several settings of quality from living master players such as Duncan Campbell, Colin Cameron, and Alexander MacDonald. There was a particularly attractive version from the latter of 'The Lament for Duncan MacRae of Kintail' (here called 'Colin MacRae of Invereenat's Lament') and a setting of 'The Desperate Battle of the Birds' from Colin Cameron, which was strikingly better than the sketchy account of the piece to be found in MacKay. Ross also included a number of his own compositions including the slight but graceful 'Rev. Dr. Norman McLeod's Lament':

'Cumha Thoirmaid Mhoir Mhic-Leoid'.   Ground and line 1, 1st variation. *Ross's Collection*, p.62.

He was keen on the virtues of a precise and consistent staff notation and anxious to correct what he saw as the shortcomings of his predecessors.[72] His section of 'Instructions' included at the beginning of the book, although largely cobbled together out of Donald MacDonald and Angus MacKay's books, does contain some very interesting remarks on the timing of various piobaireachd movements. He writes:

> The following bars in Macdonald, Mackay, or Ross's Piobaireachd ought to be played as written here; although often written with Grace notes; as the 2nd. half of the 3 following bars:

71 NLS, MS. 3040.
72 See I. H. MacKay Scobie, *Pipers and Pipe Music in a Highland Regiment* (Dingwall, 1924), p.20, *n.*45.

All the run down Grace notes in Macdonald's Piobaireachds ought to be played with a rest on the E. Grace note . . . [three musical examples follow] If the Rules laid down . . . were adhered to in all the tunes in Macdonald's Book: The objections that most Pipers have had to them would to some extent be corrected: As the great difficulty of Pipe playing is in the Grace notes.'[73]

Despite Angus MacKay's attempt to establish a standard 'gairm' movement, we find Uilleam Ross using several, showing that any one of the low As could be accented, depending on the time-signature and surrounding rhythmical context. To the Victorian masters it was part of a web of delicate expressiveness and not yet the mere rattle it was to become in the pages of later editors:

There is more involved here than mere technical nicety. These movements occur frequently and their timing has an important effect on expression. Many tunes have the 'gairm' as their opening gesture, and quite small apparent differences in timing have expressive consequences which are anything but superficial. For example, one may compare the standard 20th century setting of 'The Battle of the Pass of Crieff' in the *Piobaireachd Society Collection* (second series), which is usually played as written, with the more idiomatic and rhythmically plausible version which appears in Uilleam Ross:

'The Battle of the Pass of Crieff'. Ground, line 1. *Piobaireachd Society Collection* (second series), i, 15

'The Battle of the Pass of Crieff'. Ground, line 1. *Ross's Collection*, p.75

73 Ross, *Collection*, pp.ix-x.

As a rule Ross did not follow MacKay in setting crunluath fosgailte movements in a closed form. In a tune of this character one would usually find something like:

'Melbank's Salute'. Crunluath doubling, line 1. *Ross's Collection*, p.19

Ross also routinely tempered MacKay's partiality for E cadence-notes, which sometimes afflict the latter's settings like a musical stammer, even where it seems likely that MacKay's manuscript was his source for a tune:

'MacDonald of Kinlochmudeart's Salute'. Ground, line 1, Angus MacKay's MS., i, 173

'Kinlochmuidart's Lament'. Ground, line 1, *Ross's Collection*, p.28

In many ways, however, *Ross's Collection* was founded in established practice. It was a mediated text designed to be consumed first and foremost by people outside the performer community and was framed to meet their expectations. It was published by subscription and not on the open market, and bore an unmistakable aura of official sanction. Ross was presented as the Royal Piper – '*Piobair Na Ban-Righ*' – and the book was dedicated, by permission, to the Queen. The music was thus presented within an explicit relationship of clientage and dependency. The engraved title-page showed Ross, dignified, bearded, swathed in the elaborate costume deemed suitable – by his employers – for the Victorian piper, his instrument festooned with heraldic banners and ribbons, providing a pleasing background hum for the figures strolling in the gardens of Balmoral in tasteful Celtic déshabille and to all appearances paying him not the slightest heed. The sponsors pictured on MacKay's title-page were at least obliged to dance when he played, and were as uncomfortably trussed up in cross-belts and scarf plaids as he was.

The music text of *Ross's Collection* leaves three overriding impressions: firstly of the continuing creative vitality of piobaireachd, seen in the unostentatious way in which new compositions mix indiscriminately with the old; secondly, the variety of interpretation which continued to flourish a generation after a major attempt by the sponsoring institutions to restrict it, showing master pipers taking what they wanted from MacKay but declining to be dictated to either in notational practice or musical style; thirdly, and perhaps most markedly, a sense of social and cultural division, of piping partitioned into carefully segregated communities of producers and consumers, differing widely in income, status, language and outlook. In order to consider this more fully, we must now turn to the performer community itself and the ethos which prevailed within it.

9

'Men who made the pipe their business': the Performer Community, 1750–1900

When we turn to the performer community, we find ourselves in a different mental world. The Macpherson paradigm was able to influence directly only those who were literate in English, which, in a Highland context, meant effectively the middle and upper classes. Attempts to introduce the paradigm directly into the performer community, such as the presentation of superbly bound editions of Ossian's poems as prizes in the piping events at St. Fillans Games in the 1820s, appear to have been ineffectual.[1]

Scotland was a predominantly Protestant country whose Reformation had run a vigorous course. In order to sustain an individualistic community of believers relating directly to God through the medium of the holy scriptures, the ability to read had to be widely diffused and the provision of a school in every parish was an important goal. To some extent, therefore, Scottish popular culture was based on print from an early date. The Lowlands were awash with broadsides, song-slips and chap-books from the seventeenth century onwards. But when we turn to the Highlands and to Gaelic culture we find a very different situation. There, written and print media were much less likely to impinge upon popular culture owing to the limitations imposed on formal schooling by the large size of Highland parishes, and the fact that Gaelic was spoken by the overwhelming majority of the people. For much of our period the language was without a fixed orthography, supported a relatively small corpus of printed texts, and was frowned upon as a medium of officially-sanctioned instruction. The introduction in 1872 of the Board School system and mass compulsory education meant, however, that by the end of the 19th century, literacy in English had become a common possession.[2] For pipers this might represent a considerable degree of empowerment as it enabled them to use print media to pursue their own agenda, as we shall see. But it also meant increased vulnerability to certain aspects of the culture that print media sustained, amongst which were the Macpherson paradigm and its related concepts.

In the eighteenth century piping was a profession in which a performer could make all, or part, of his living. There was also a corps of gentlemen amateurs such as Ewen MacDonald of Vallay, or Captain Malcolm MacLeod of Eyre, and a

---

1 See David Webster, *Scottish Highland Games* (Edinr., 1973), pp.9, 13.

2 Laurence J. Saunders, *Scottish Democracy* 1815–1840 (Edinr, 1950), pp.261–4; see also Victor Edward Durkacz, *The Decline of the Celtic Languages* (Edinr., 1983), 27, 45–8, 123.

large – perhaps very large – number of occasional players who made no regular part of their living from piping, and do not normally appear, therefore, in the records.[3] Women played as well, sometimes to a high standard, although it seems not to have been considered appropriate for them to do so publicly. Professional piping covered a wide social spread, ranging from humble town pipers such as the McLennans of Inverness, to the respectable middle ranks of Highland society as represented by the MacCrimmons and the MacKays of Gairloch. Whilst it was always a specialised calling, degrees of professionalism varied. In a rural economy most pipers were of necessity also farmers, but some had other occupations, such as innkeepers or schoolteachers. Although the training was long and exacting, piping need not be the performer's main life-long source of remuneration. It could be taken up and laid down at need, as witnessed by the career of John MacDonald, who gave up his post as a schoolmaster and tutor in the MacKay country in the 1770s, to go as pipe-major with MacLeod's Highlanders (73rd of foot, later 71st, H.L.I.). He served in India and China, and was present at the siege of Gibraltar. When he had his fill of adventure, he came back to teaching – and to *dùthaich MhicAoidh* – as schoolmaster of Tongue.[4]

At the heart of the tradition were the important teaching families, the MacCrimmons and the MacArthurs in Skye, the Rankines in Mull, the Campbells and others in Argyll, the MacIntyres and MacGregors in Perthshire, the Bruces in Glenelg; the MacKays in Gairloch, MacDonalds in Glenurquhart, the Mackenzies in Strathconon, MacRaes in Kintail, McLennans in the Black Isle, Cummings in Strathspey, and MacKays and others in Sutherland.[5] The most important centres were recognised as 'colleges', and to them young men might be sent from considerable distances, and for varying periods of time, to complete

3 There is a vivid account of Malcolm MacLeod in James Boswell's *Journal of a Tour to the Hebrides with Samuel Johnson, LL.D.* (Lond., 1785, and numerous later editions); for a note on Ewen MacDonald, see Alexander Cameron, *History and Traditions of Skye* (Inverness, 1871), pp.141–2. A relatively small number of pipers at any period appear in the written record, or achieve a reputation that outlives their own generation: for an indication of the size of the performer community at the end of the nineteenth century see MacKenzie, *Piping Traditions, passim.* During the past two centuries it appears to have been extensive.

4 MacKay, *Ancient Piobaireachd,* 'Historical and Traditional Notes', p.10, 13–14; Angus Mackay, M.A., *Book of Mackay,* p.217–18. For a stimulating discussion of professionalism and the social rewards of musicianship in traditional societies see Merriam, pp. 125–39, to which the present chapter is much indebted.

5 See 'The Poetry of Piobaireachd. Part 1', by 'Gleannach' [Alexander MacDonald], *OT,* 18/4/1925, p.3; see also, Ruaridh Halford-MacLeod, 'Early MacCrimmon Records', *PT,* vol.29, no.5, Feb. 1977, pp.10–13, 'The MacCrimmons and the '45', vol.29, no.6, March 1977, pp. 11–13, and 'The End of the MacCrimmon College', vol.29, no.8, May 1977, pp.15–18. For a satire on the leading pipers towards the end of the 17th century, by Lachlann MacLean, which refers slightingly to Conduiligh MacRaing, and 'that twister MacCruimein', see Colm O'Boyle, ed., *Eachann Bacach and other MacLean Poets* (Edinr., 1979), pp.54–9, 221–8.

their training. The most well known of these were the MacCrimmon college in Duirinish, the MacArthur college at Hungladder in Trotternish, and the Rankine college at Kilbrennan, Mull, the last important teacher at which may have been Eoghan MacEachain 'ic Chonduiligh who died in 1783.[6] About the year 1700, the Rev. David Kirkwood wrote that 'Pipers are held in great Request, so that they are train'd up at ye Expense of Grandees & have a Portion of Land assignd & are design'd such a man's Piper',[7] and we see in 1698 the Earl of Breadalbane order his chamberlain to 'Give McIntyre ye piper fforty pounds scots as his prentises(hi)p with McCrooman till May nixt as also provyde him in what Cloths he needs and dispatch him immediately to the Isles'.[8] In some cases the resulting contractual relations might be highly formal. There is an indenture from the year 1743, binding David Fraser to serve Lord Lovat as his piper, in return for maintenance, specified payment, and meeting the cost of his tuition in Skye under Malcolm MacCrimmon:

At Beaufort the Nynth day of March One thousand seven hundred and forty three years, It is Contracted and Agreed upon betwixt the Right Honourable Simon Lord Fraser of Lovat, On the One part And David Fraser his Lordships servant Brother german to William Fraser Tacksman in Bewly his Lordships Musician, And the said William Fraser as Cautioner and surety for his said Brother On the other part, In manner following That is to say, Whereas the said Simon Lord Fraser of Lovat has out of his own Generosity Cloathd and mantaind the said David Fraser for these severall Years past, And has also bestowed upon him during that time for his Education as a Pyper with the now deceast Evan McGrigor his Lordships late Pyper, And that his Lordship is now to send him upon his own Charges to the Isle of Skie, in order to have him perfected a Highland Pyper by the famous Malcolm Mcgrimon whom his Lordship is to reward for Educating the said David Fraser, Therefore, And in Consideration of his Lordships great Charity kindness and generosity The said David & William Frasers have become bound And hereby bind and Engage themselves Conjunctly and severally, That the said David Fraser shall honestly & faithfully serve the said Simon Lord Fraser of Lovat or his heir and Successor by Night & by day, For the haill Space of Seven full & compleat years from & after the Term of Whitesunday next to come, And that he shall never do or Committ any thing inconsistent with or contrary to that duty & Obedience which a faithfull

---

6 For the Rankins see Matheson, *John MacCodrum*, pp.251–2, suggesting that the last of the Rankin pipers – Hector – did not leave Mull until 1804. See also 'The Name MacRankine', *OT*, 14/11/1942, p.3. For a recent overview of the various conflicting accounts, see Keith Sanger, 'Mull and the Maclean Pipers', *PT*, vol.42, no.9, June 1990, pp.38–43.

7 Quoted in Collinson, *Bagpipe*, p.151,*n*.

8 Halford-McLeod, 'MacCrimmon College', p.18.

Servant Owes to a bountifull Master, But shall serve them uprightly to the outmost of his Skill and Capacity, For which Cause And on the other part the said Simon Lord Fraser of Lovat binds and obliges himself And his Lordships heirs Executors and Successors whatsomever To Mantain the said David Fraser his servant during the space above mentiond in Bed Board & Washing & to furnish & provide him in Cloaths Shoes & Stockings And likeways to Satisfie and pay to him Yearly and ilk year the sum of Fifty Merks Scots money in name of Wages during the said Space of Seven years Commencing from Whitesunday next, And in the Meantime to Send him with all due convenience to the Isle of Skie to be perfected a Highland Pyper by the above namd McGrimon, The Charge and Expense whereof his Lordship is to defray As said is. Lastly the Said Simon Lord Fraser of Lovat binds and Obliges himself & his foresaids, And the said David & William Frasers bind & Oblige themselves Conjunctly and severally their heirs Executors and Successors To Implement & perform their respective parts of the premisses Ilk One to another Under the penalty of Ten pound Sterling by & attour performance & for the more security both partys Consent to the Registration hereof In the books of Councill & Session Or any other competent Register within this Kingdom That Letters of Horning & all other Execution needful may pass hereon in form as effiers & to that effect Constitute Their Procurators & In Witness whereof (Written upon stamped paper by Hugh Fraser Secretary to the said Lord Lovat); His Lordship & the said William & David Frasers have subscrived thir presents Consisting of this & the preceeding page Place & date above mentiond before witnesses John Forbes Servant to his Lordship & the said Hugh Fraser.[9]

David Fraser was born in 1716, and died on 27th December 1812. He was 'out' in the '45, present at the battles of Falkirk and Culloden, and he fashioned a beautiful lament for Lovat when the latter was executed following the Rising.[10]

Our knowledge of the older teaching dynasties comes largely from oral sources. The first substantial written account of the MacCrimmon family appeared in Angus MacKay's *Ancient Piobaireachd* (1838), viewed through the highly coloured spectacles of James Logan, and the story lost little in its elaboration by later writers.[11] But the real MacCrimmons lived in a prosaic enough world, as tacksmen or larger tenants on the MacLeod estates in Skye, making a living from their various farms, and also from teaching. References to MacCrimmon pipers can be traced in the Dunvegan muniments back to the later

9 Scottish Record Office: E769/12/5/8/11, quoted in *International Piper*, vol.4, no.5, September 1981, pp.12–13.

10 'Cumha Mhic Shimidh. Lord Lovat's Lament', in *Ancient Piobaireachd*, pp.141–143. See also Fred. T. MacLeod, *The MacCrimmons of Skye Hereditary Pipers to the Macleods of Dunvegan* (Edinr., 1933), pp.156–7.

11 See below, Chapter 19.

seventeenth century. In the course of the following hundred years they occupied the farms of Boreraig, Galtrigal, and Borrodale in Duirinish. They were paid a notional salary which normally equalled their rent, so that they sat rent free, the rents and services of their sub-tenants coming to them and not the laird.

The estate papers show that in 1711 thirty merks were paid for '2 pypes bought to MacCrimmon MacLeod's principal pyper', with a further payment in 1714, of 57 merks 9s. to Patrick Morrison, Merchant in Edinburgh 'for livery cloathis to MacCrimmon, MacLeod's pyper.'[12] There were payments made to various other pipers, sometimes MacCrimmons sometimes not, maintained at the same time in different parts of the estate, and this appears to have been a common practice at the time. For example, Donald Bàn MacCrimmon, killed at the Rout of Moy during the Rising of 1745, for whom the famous lament was made, was based in Harris, and would probably have been second piper on the MacLeod establishment.[13]

The MacCrimmon pipers found themselves in a similar situation to other tacksmen in the West Highlands during the second half of the 18th century, as the increasingly absentee lairds pushed their demands for cash rents to unimaginable heights – in many cases, indeed, far beyond what the properties could bear. 'Kindly' tenancies like theirs were transmuted into money payments. Notional salaries went down, while real rents went dramatically up. Donald Roy gave up Boreraig in 1773 and emigrated for a time to America while his brother Iain Dubh seriously contemplated doing the same, but between them they continued to occupy various MacLeod tacks for more than fifty years after their 'college' supposedly closed.[14] The MacCrimmon pipers had always moved around, sometimes on one farm, sometimes on another, and teaching must have taken place wherever they happened to be at the time. The notion of a fixed institutional-style college at Boreraig owes more to James Logan than to reality. Nor is it clear that the leading MacCrimmon pipers ever stopped teaching. There is an eye-witness account of Donald Roy MacCrimmon with his pupil Alexander Bruce dating from the second decade of the nineteenth century.[15]

The nearest contemporary account of the MacCrimmon family in terms of worldly circumstance, comes from the pen of the Rev. Archibald Clerk, minister of the parish of Duirinish, and published in 1845 in the *New Statistical Account of*

---

12 Grant, *MacLeods*, pp.376–7. See also Halford-MacLeod, 'MacCrimmon Records',
    pp.11–13.

13 Grant, *MacLeods*, p.490. For the tune, see 'Cumha Dhonhnuill Ban Mhich
    Cruimmen. Donald Bain Mac-Cruimmon's Lament', in Ross, *Collection*, pp.34–40.
    There was a considerable disparity in income between the principle piper and the
    others on the MacLeod estates: R. C. MacLeod, ed., *The Book of Dunvegan* (2 vols.,
    Aberd., 1938–9), ii, 92, records that 'In the early days of the [18th] century payments
    were made to pipers in each district – £26 6s. 8d. Scots to each – while McCrimmon
    received £166 13s. 4d. Scots'.

14 Grant, *MacLeods.*, pp.490–91, 559–61.

15 See below, pp.183–4.

Scotland, a comprehensive social, economic and physical survey of Scotland, parish by parish, mainly compiled by the local ministers. Clerk was a son-in-law of Norman MacLeod ('*Caraid nan Gaidheal*'), and his account was written in 1841, less than twenty years after the death of Iain Dubh MacCrimmon. Although presented very much from the perspective of the 'big house', giving credit to dubious tales about the Italian origin of the family, and treating their 'college' as a modern-style institution, the piece as a whole seems based on first-hand knowledge, recently acquired:

> It is well known that the great bag-pipe, the instrument on which the national music of Scotland was chiefly played for so long a time, and which has still so striking an effect in rousing the martial spirit of the Highlanders, was cultivated with greater success by the Maccrimmons, the hereditary pipers of the Macleods, than by any others in the Highlands. The name of Maccrimmon, whether on fanciful or on conclusive ground we pretend not to say, has been derived from the fact of the first musician who bore the name having studied his profession at Cremona in Italy. Certain it is that, what rarely happens, high musical talent as well as high moral principle and personal bravery, descended from father to son during many generations in the family of the Maccrimmons. They became so celebrated that pupils were sent to them from all quarters of the Highlands, and one of the best certificates that a piper could possess was his having studied under the Maccrimmons. Finding the number of pupils daily increasing, they at length opened a regular school or college for pipe music on the farm of Boreraig, opposite to Dunvegan Castle, but separated from it by Loch Follart. Here, so many years of study were prescribed, regular lessons were given out, certain periods for receiving the instruction of the master were fixed. The whole tuition was carried on as systematically as in any of our modern academies; and the names of some of the caves and knolls in the vicinity still point out the spots where the scholars used to practice, respectively on the chanter, the small pipe, and the *Piob mhor*, or large bagpipe, before exhibiting in presence of the master. Macleod endowed this school by granting the farm of Boreraig to it, and it is no longer ago than seventy years since the endowment was withdrawn. It was owing to the following cause: The farm had been originally given only during the pleasure of the proprietor. For many ages the grant was undisturbed: but when the value of land had risen to six or seven times what it was when the school was founded, Macleod very reasonably proposed to resume one-half of the farm, offering at the same time to Maccrimmon, a free lease of the other half *in perpetuum*; but Maccrimmon, indignant that his emoluments should be curtailed, resigned the whole farm, and broke up his establishment, which has never been restored.
>
> The Maccrimmons were well educated, intermarried with highly respectable families, and were universally regarded as vastly superior to the common class of the country people. A son of the last family piper holds the rank of captain

in the British army, and is said to inherit the musical talents of his race.
There are a few of them still residing in this parish, but they are born of what
was reckoned a very low marriage for Maccrimmon, and they do not possess
either the talents or respectability of their progenitors. A Maccrimmon still
acts as piper to Macleod, but he is not descended of the Boreraig
Maccrimmons, who appear to have renounced their profession with their
endowment.

We know not whether there were establishments similar to that of Boreraig
in other parts of the Highlands; but it certainly is to be regretted that it was
dissolved, and also that we have not minuter information as to the mode of
training pursued by those who were universally acknowledged to be the first
masters of bagpipe music.[16]

Iain Dubh MacCrimmon is a shadowy figure of whom we catch a glimpse in
extreme old age sitting by the fire fingering his staff, unable any longer to play the
pipes.[17] But we know rather a lot about his brother, Donald Roy: his emigration
to Carolina, his gallantry in the wars of Independence, his half-pay lieutenancy,
and his role in the Highland Society of London's attempts to revive the
MacCrimmon college with state support during the early years of the nineteenth
century. There are a number of written accounts of Donald Roy but only one, it
would appear, from the pen of another musician who had some idea of who –
and what – he was listening to.

This dates from the autumn of 1815 when Alexander Campbell was gathering
material for his forthcoming collection of Highland music and song, *Albyn's
Anthology*, and is recorded in his journal now preserved in the library of the
University of Edinburgh. Campbell explains:

I . . . proceeded to Glenelg, now the property of Mr. Bruce [who had
recently bought it from MacLeod], on a farm belonging to whom, I was to
find Lieut. Donald MacCrimmon, the celebrated performer on the Great
Highland Bagpipe, to whom I had letters of introduction from two of his
principal friends, the Sheriff of Uist and Captain [Niel] McLeod of Guesto.

Lieut. MacCrimmin's present residence is in Kirktoun, near Bernera
barracks, Glenelg. When I called, I found that he was at his farm in Glenbeg,
a *long mile's* distance from his present place of abode. I had little time to spare
and, rather than await his home-coming, I set out to find him. And on my

16 Vol.14, 'Inverness – Ross and Cromarty', (Edinr., 1845), pp.322–60 (339–40). See also
   'The MacCrimmons', from A. R. Macdonald, Waternish, Skye, *OT*, 3/7/1920, p.3,
   stating that in the later 18th century they took to soldiering, and identifying Ensign
   Donald Maccrimmon of the 42nd., killed at the battle of Toulouse in 1814, Lieut.
   John of the 78th and Capt. Patrick of the 79th, a Major Maccrimmon in Glenelg,
   and a Norman Scalpa Maccrimmon, captain in the 74th.
17 'Ceol-mor agus Clann MhicCruimein', le N. Ros, B.D. *Celtic Monthly*, vol.18, no.2–4,
   February-April 1910, pp.26–8, 45–7, 65–7 (65).

coming to the spot, I found him leading in his corn with the assistance of some neighbours of his own name, amongst whom he is a sort of Chieftain. He is upwards of '*three-score and ten*': rather thin, stoops a little – is about the middle size – has all the appearance of having been in his earlier years handsome: his countenance, tho' not very animated, is pleasing: and, when he had the use of an eye, the sight of which he lost in action, his features, one can easily imagine, must have, occasionally, assumed great animation.

We walked home together: – on our way the conversation naturally turned to the subject of my present pursuits. Altho' conversible & polite, I did not find him very zealously inclined to enter, all at once, into my views; for, as I understood, afterwards, he had but lately experienced disappointment and mortification in some projects of a similar nature to that which I have undertaken; consequently, his enthusiasm has suffered a wound; the recovery from which is very doubtful: which is to be much lamented indeed.[18]

His family consists of his wife & daughter, with whom we dined. As I had come such a distance to hear him perform on his favourite instrument, and converse with him concerning the theory & practice of the Great Highland bagpipe, he sent for Alexander Bruce, Piper of Glenelg, a favourite pupil of his own, who played several pieces in a stile of excellence, that while it excited applause, reflected much credit on his able Preceptor, who encouraged him occasionally with approbation.

After a few glasses of his own good toddy, MacCrummin seized the pipe – *put on his hat* (his usual custom)[19] – breathed into the bag – tuned the drones to the chanter – gave a prelude in a stile of brilliancy that flashed like lightning, and commenced FAILTE PHRIONNSAH, in tones that spoke to the ear, and affected the heart. Thro' the whole of this fine *Salute*, he shewed a masterly command of the instrument; – the manner in which he moves his fingers seems peculiar to himself, the effects he produces by this means are admirable – there is not a sound lost – not the quickest appoggiatura, how rapid soever the movement or the variation – and the regular return to the subject or *theme* of the piece, is in fine contrast with the more intricate passages. Are the talents of MacCrimmin doomed to decay in solitude? This

18 Presumably this refers to the collapse of the Highland Society of London's plans to set up an army school of piping with Donald Roy as its 'professor'. See Chapter 5.

19 This gesture has been misunderstood subsequently, since owing to heavy involvement of pipers with the British Army during the 20th century, it is now considered to show a lack of respect on the part of a competitor to appear bonnetless before a bench of judges normally composed of social superiors. But MacCrimmon's bonnet had the opposite implication: it was an assertion of his standing as a gentleman: he would not play uncovered before people he regarded as social equals. Hence his insistence when playing at Dunvegan when the laird had company, that he did so in MacLeod's presence and with his hat on. (A practice noted by Sir Walter Scott, on his visit to Dunvegan just the summer before: see J. G. Lockhart, *The Life of Sir Walter Scott, Bart.*, Lond., 1896, p.283).

veteran, in *a double sense*, is the *seventh in succession* of the MacCrummons of Skye – his brother John is older than he – but is now, by reason of his great age, unable to perform.

After taking leave of MacCrumman and his family, I retired to my quarters in the Public-house at the end of the village. Alexander Bruce, the Piper of Glenelg, came along with me, and over a glass, he communicated to me many interesting particulars regarding the mode of training pipers, by his celebrated Preceptor, which I have taken notes of & may hereafter prove useful. Sandy Bruce and I parted about mid-night, after which I lay down to enjoy a few hour's sleep.[20]

In terms of income and status, Donald Roy was rather a complicated case, perhaps, but we have information on the emoluments of at least one other MacCrimmon, namely

John McGrimon, who was originally piper to the MacRaes of Conchra, the greatest landed branch of the clan, holding estates near Dingwall, with wadsets [mortgaged property] in Lochalsh and Kintail. This John had 80 merks salary yearly from Duncan McRae, the tutor of Conchra . . . out of the lands of Innerskinnaig. Apparently, about 1715, McGrimon became piper to Seaforth, for although up to 1718 his salary had been paid by the tutor of Conchra, after that year he had the lands of Easter Leckachan in lieu of his salary of 80 merks. He also held part of Wester Leckachan conjunctly with another tenant.[21]

Considered simply in cash terms, this looks like a fairly moderate income. Contemporary Highland schoolmasters earned about 100 merks per annum, but they might not have the land and the personal dependants and status that came with it, and money or a money-equivalent would in any case have been only part of the piper's income.[22] During the 1760s, Donald MacLeod, who was piper to George, 5th Lord Reay, had a salary of £21.6s.8d. a year. plus land and a house.[23] This was about the same as the forester earned, the average rental for a tacksman in the Reay country being about £30.00 a year. In the 1780s, Sir James Grant's piper, John Cumming, was paid in money and meal, with a house, garden ground, and the right to cut peats.[24] In some districts, pipers seem to have been supported by a tax levied upon the community as a whole. William MacKay in his account of *Urquhart and Glenmoriston* (Inverness, 1893), a parish situated on

20 Campbell, 'Slight Sketch', ff.62–4.
21 'The MacCrimmon Ancestry', from 'D. R. M', *OT*, 28/5/1910, p.3.
22 See Robert Smith, 'Poem *on the Building of the Schoolhouse of* Glenshee', in *Poems of Controversy Betwixt Episcopacy and Presbytery*, (Edinr, 1869, first published 1714), p.1
23 Angus Mackay, M.A., *Book of Mackay*, p.213.
24 George A. Dixon, 'From the Past', in *PT*, vol.36, no.5, February 1984, pp.35–6.

the west side of Loch Ness, quotes a statement to the effect that until the early years of the 19th century:

> There has always been a Piper in Urquhart belonging to the Family of Grant, whose sallary has constantly been paid by a small portion of oats from each tenant. The tenants want to get free of this Tax, but it is submitted whether or not it is not better to continue it, as the Tax is small, and, being in use to be paid, it is not very sensibly felt. If you let it drop, the Highland Musick is lost . . .[25]

The social standing of the MacCrimmons was not unique. It was echoed by at least one other of the important teaching families, the MacKays of Gairloch, as we see in a remarkable document entitled 'Reminiscences of a Long Life' compiled in Canada by John MacKay, stipendiary magistrate in New Glasgow, Pictou County, Nova Scotia, and published in the *Oban Times* in February 1935. The writer was a son of Iain Roy MacKay and great-grandson of the famous piper and poet Iain Dall MacKay. When he was born, in 1794, his family had been pipers to the Lairds of Gairloch for upwards of a century. In some ways the 'Reminiscences' paint a broadly expected picture: the holding of lands rent-free by virtue of office, the social leadership entailed by the resulting tacksman status, the possession of servants, the easy familiarity with the lairdly family and neighbouring gentry, often permitting, as here, a degree of travel with consequent social polish and cosmopolitan outlook. But some things are not quite what might be casually assumed about a Highland piping family in the eighteenth century: its careful 'respectability' for one thing; its devoutness – to the point of severity – in matters of religion for another; then there is the ability to afford, and the desire to pursue, a Lowland education, giving mastery of English and access to an all-British literate culture, subsequently used to reinforce the family's local standing:

> My forefathers on my father's side were originally (I believe) from Lord Reay's country, the most northerly parts of the mainland of Scotland; and those on the mother's side from Kintail. My mother was a MacRae and traced connection through some second or third cousin with Sir Roderick Murchieson, the eminent geologist and President of the Royal Society of Great Britain. A grand ancestor of that gentleman was at one time Episcopal minister of Kintail, and my mother was also a descendant, by her mother, of the same Episcopal clergyman – his name was Murchieson. My father, grandfather, and great-grandfather, were successively pipers to the Lairds of Gairloch, and as such held free lands under successive Lairds. My great-grandfather was blind, and was known far and near under the name 'Piobaire Dall', that is 'the blind piper.'

25 *Urquhart and Glenmoriston*, p.462, *n.*

He was a poet as well as a piper, and some of his pieces are published in almost all collections of Gaelic songs, especially in MacKenzie's collection published in Glasgow in 1841, in which work there is also a short sketch of 'the blind piper's' life. The celebrated Gaelic poet 'William Ross' was this blind man's grandson by a daughter; and thus William Ross and my father were first cousins. I have no recollection of seeing William Ross, for he died quite a young man; but I remember seeing his father, John Ross, often at our house.

My grandfather, Angus MacKay, was, I believe, a good scholar – a rare thing in the Highlands in those days. When a young man he travelled a good deal with the young Laird, Sir Alexander MacKenzie, and they were on the closest intimacy during the rest of their lives. They both died comparatively young; the Laird first, my grandfather attending him on his death-bed. My grandfather, Angus MacKay, left two children, my father and a sister. Of my grandmother on my father's side I do not know much; only that she was a Fraser, and related to MacKenzie of Baddachro. Baddachro and my father were thus first cousins, and the late Donald and Murdoch Fraser, Robertson's Lake, were relations of my father on the same side.

Both my father and his sister had some education. My father was some time at Thurso, Caithness-shire, and was also at Inverary, Argyllshire, at school. He must have understood the English language well, for he was the best (extempore) translator of English into Gaelic that I ever heard attempt it.

My father, beside being the recognised and paid piper of the Gairloch family, was also gamekeeper, and had charge of the woods and forests on the Estate; and as a matter of course this threw him into the company of the Lairds and of all strangers that might get permission to hunt on the estate; and this introduced him to the best company in the place, strangers or otherwise.

This short sketch of the history of my fore-fathers will show that although not wealthy, they were respectable, and held good positions in the country of their nativity, and enjoyed advantages not attained by many in those days in the Highlands of Scotland. And far better than all this, I have good reason to believe they were all God-fearing people, my grandfather, Angus MacKay, eminently so.

. . . With respect to my own father I can testify that he was verily a painstaking man. There was a large family – ten girls and two boys – besides generally a servant man. We were some ten miles from the nearest church: very few could go and very few did go. I have no recollection of seeing a Minister in our house for the purpose of catechising. There were about ten families in the village, and my father kept worship and reading every Sabbath day for all the villagers. None understood English but himself, and there were no Gaelic books in those days. Even the Bible could not be got in Gaelic. My father translated from the Bible, and from Boston, Baxter and Dyer, and then after the reading was over and the villagers dismissed the family exercises would commence. He was very exacting upon his children in these exercises, and insisted on the strictest compliance with all his requirements in the matter of our tasks and lessons.

. . . The formation of the lands on the south side of the loch differs greatly from that on the north. Here the mountains are thrown back leaving a broad margin of comparatively low ground between them and the loch, with a good deal of arable and cultivated land. Three small rivers fall into the loch from this side, each forming a considerable strath (or dale); and at the time of which I speak there might be ten families residing in each of them. My father farmed one of these straths for many years, and there I was born in 1794, and there I passed my childhood and boyhood until I was eleven years of age.

[follows a glowing evocation of growing up in this wonderful place, concluding] . . . We left the Loch and came to Pictou in the summer of 1805."[26]

Hereditary piping dynasties such as these may have been neither as ancient nor as 'hereditary' as the Victorians liked to suppose. So long as the talent and the will to perform this kind of function remained within a family, succession might continue. But this may have been a matter of two or three generations as a rule, rather than the centuries so often assumed. John MacKay stated that three generations of his family had been pipers to the lairds of Gairloch, but the laird – perhaps with an eye to the power and antiquity of his family – made rather larger claims. In the appendix to Osgood Hanbury Mackenzie's *A Hundred Years in the Highlands,* along with information on local superstitions and wildlife notes, there was a section on 'The Famous Gairloch Pipers' which traced the line of succession back to a Rory MacKay born about 1592.[27] In some ways, the idea was a useful one, in that it gave precise physical shape to lines of teaching and learning and sometimes perhaps to distinctive schools of musical interpretation; but it could also be misleading. Since access to instruction was not based upon consanguinity, a particular 'school' might continue for generations amongst people over a widely scattered geographical area who were not in any way connected by blood. In this sense, the formation of piping dynasties never ceased. Indeed we can see new ones such as the MacKays, the Bruces the MacKenzies, the Camerons and Macphersons come into being during the nineteenth and early twentieth centuries.

The song-collector Alexander Campbell was not the only person to hear Sandy Bruce play and commit his impressions to writing. We have a detailed

---

26 'Reminiscences of a Long Life', by John MacKay, *OT,* 2/2/1935, p.3. For further information on the MacKays of Gairloch, see MacKay, *Ancient Piobaireachd,* 'Account of the Hereditary Pipers', pp.12–13.

27 See 'The Famous Gairloch Pipers' in Osgood Hanbury Mackenzie, *A Hundred Years in the Highlands,* (new edn., London, 1949), pp.190–94. The author was brother of Sir Kenneth Mackenzie, 13th of Gairloch.

account of this from a later date, from the pen of Dr. K. N. MacDonald, editor of *The Gesto Collection of Highland Music* (Leipzig, 1895), and *Puirt-a-Beul* (Glasgow, 1901). He was one of the Ord MacDonalds, a son of Niel MacLeod of Gesto's eldest daughter, Ann, and had frequently heard him play. He wrote

> . . . about 40 years ago an old piper named Sandy Bruce from Glenelg, used to come about my father's place at Ord, in the parish of Sleat, and as he had been a pupil of the last of the MacCrimmons, John MacCrimmon, piper to MacLeod of MacLeod, and under the superintendence of Capt. Niel McLeod of Gesto, who was an adept at the MacCrimmon system of teaching and style of playing, Bruce had every advantage of picking up and becoming proficient in the MacCrimmon style and time, as he had been taught by no others. It is quite clear also that the MacCrimmons were very studious, and practiced a great deal. I have heard my mother say that she had frequently been wakened at four in the morning by John MacCrimmon's pipes, and as Bruce was at Gesto with MacCrimmon he would have had full advantage of being kept upon proper lines both by Capt. McLeod and MacCrimmon.
>
> I have listened to him scores of times, both before rising in the morning, and at other times, and I remember clearly and distinctly that his matchless playing was always especially in the 'urlar' ground or Adagio, *very slow indeed*, a long pause, and a long breath, and altogether different from the style of modern pipers. He was also slow and methodical in the first variation and even in the 'Taorluath' and subsequent variations the pace was not of the 'Deil among the tailors' style, but animated and clear, every note could be heard. His step was also slow and measured, none of your military swagger, and he stood still as a statue over the more rapid passages. He was a short thick-set man, with a rather massive face, not unlike Neil Gow in expression. He wore a tartan short-tailed coat with round silver buttons, and he looked and felt proud of his function as a piper. Though he could play other music, and especially slow marches most beautifully, and reels and strathspeys, yet the pibroch was his forte. He could not, however, play dance music upon the great pipes. He had a smaller pair for this class of music, and played a *good deal slower* than we do at the present day.[28]

Sandy Bruce's sons, John and Peter, were taught mainly by their father, and they taught in turn George and Angus MacDonald of Arisaig, who won considerable fame in competition during the later Victorian period. Both the younger Bruces emigrated to Australia, where John became personal piper to various wealthy Scots expatriates and kept a hotel called 'The Highland Chief' in Melbourne. His brother Peter is thought to have taught Simon Fraser, who later claimed that the

28 'The Bagpipes and how the MacCrimmons played them', *OT*, 4/7/1896, p.3.

true MacCrimmon line of teaching had descended through him, and been preserved in Australia after it had died out in Scotland.[29]

As relations with landed proprietors became more narrowly contractual, pipers became more mobile, and the practice of working in several different settings during the course of a career became the norm. John Bàn MacKenzie, one of the leading 19th century masters, shows the pattern beginning to develop. He was born in Achilty in Strathconon, Easter Ross, in 1796, one of a large and poor family, and was able to study with Donald Mór McLennan of Moy (born c. 1783), and with John MacKay (Angus's father) in Raasay, as a result of his fees being paid by a local benefactor, Alexander MacKenzie of Millbank. He became piper first to George Falconer MacKenzie of Allangrange in the Black Isle, then to Duncan Davidson of Tulloch near Dingwall, and finally for a period of nearly thirty years, until he retired in 1861 at the age of 65, to the Marquis of Breadalbane at Taymouth castle in Perthshire. The latter move was probably enforced. John Bàn had been helping the much-married laird of Tulloch conduct a secret amour with Maria MacKenzie, the heiress of Applecross, and carried a message to her from Tulloch begging her to elope. Which she duly did, not with the laird, but with the piper who was a famously handsome man.

He was a gifted and successful teacher, training both his sons, Donald (1833–1863) and John Ronald, the former an able player who won the prize pipe at Inverness in 1847 and the gold medal, also at Inverness, in 1853, and whose death from smallpox in the spring of 1863, called forth one of the best-known Victorian piobaireachds, 'His Father's Lament for Donald MacKenzie'.[30] He also taught Donald Cameron, and Duncan Ross, who was J. F. Campbell's informant in his canntaireachd enquiries. John Bàn died on 23 April 1864 at the age of 68, and his line of teaching came down mainly through his nephew Ronald (1842–1916), who had lived with John Bàn as a child in Perthshire, later became pipe-major of the 78th, and was himself an influential teacher.[31]

Donald Cameron was born at Contin in Strathconon in 1810 and developed precociously as a player. He received his early instruction from Donald Mór McLennan, and then from John Bàn MacKenzie, Kenneth MacRae, and John MacKay's sons. This tendency to study with several different masters seems a characteristic feature of instructional routines at any period for which we have precise knowledge. He also became a close personal friend of Angus MacKay. He

29 K. N. MacDonald, 'Some Famous Pipers. The Bruces of Glenelg. Contemporaries of John MacCrimmon', in *OT*, 11/1/1913, 18/1/1913, p.3; for further information about Simon Fraser, see below Chapter 19.

30 First published in Thomason, *Ceol Mor*, pp.246–7.

31 For details on John Bàn MacKenzie and his family, see Angus Fairrie, *The Northern Meeting* 1788–1988 (Edinr., 1988), pp. 167–70; see also MacKenzie, *Piping Traditions*, pp.27–33, 57–60, 77–8, 82–5, 88–9, 94–100. For some distinctive points of the MacKenzie style, see Frans Buisman, 'A Note on the MacKenzie Manuscripts', *PT*, vol. 43, no.5, February 1991, pp.47–53.

moved around less than John Bàn, becoming Piper to Sir James MacKenzie of Rosehaugh, near Avoch in the Black Isle, about 1830, and then in 1849 to Col. K. W. S. Mackenzie of Seaforth at Brahan Castle a few miles south-west of Dingwall. He attended the Highland Societies' competitions at Edinburgh from 1830 onwards, being placed second in 1838, and winning the prize pipe in 1844. He won at the Northern Meeting at Inverness in 1843, took the former winner's gold medal there in 1849, and the 'King of Pipers' title at the competition organised by the Club of True Highlanders for winners of the former winners' gold medal in 1867. Donald Cameron's eminence was thus of a new sort, reflecting the rise of the 'competition circuit', which was gradually taking the place of the old annual and triennial events in Edinburgh. It was no longer a case of appearing once or twice and then retiring, as former winners at Edinburgh had been obliged to do. As the Highland games movement gathered force, there sprang up a network of public competitions which did not disqualify former winners, so that they could establish professional ascendancy in a way not possible hitherto, as well as adding quite substantially to their incomes. This development was underpinned by the transport revolution in mid-Victorian Britain, signalled by the screw steamer and the railway system, which made it possible for champion pipers to compete on a regular basis all over Scotland.

Donald Cameron taught his sons, Colin, (1843–1916), Alexander (1848–1923), and Keith (c.1853–99), as well as Alexander (1835–1883) and William MacDonald of Glenurquhart. Colin and Alick Cameron were famous and much-sought-after teachers, the latter training John MacDougall Gillies who was himself to become one of the most important teachers in the early twentieth century. Donald's younger brother Sandy Cameron also won fame as a player and teacher (prize pipe at Inverness, 1846; gold medal, 1862), but after a spell with the Earl of Seafield, did not make his living as a piper. He went into business in Edinburgh and then kept the Museum Inn at 9 William Street, Greenock.[32] His nephew, Alick Cameron (also known as Sandy), moved in and out of professional piping in a similar way. He was piper to the Marquis of Huntly at Aboyne, wining the prize pipe at Inverness in 1867 and the gold medal for former winners in 1870. Then he took a job on the railways and worked for a while with the bagpipe makers Peter Henderson, before ending his career as piper to Lochiel at Achnacarry. For people such as John Bàn MacKenzie, professional piping represented upward mobility and they stayed with it throughout their lives; for others, the opportunities it offered were more equivocal, and they might move in and out in search of economic or social advantage.[33]

The Macpherson pipers can be traced to the later 18th century, beginning with Peter Macpherson, who moved from Badenoch to Skye, and married a sister of

32 'Notices of Bagpipe Makers'. Pt. 12, by Jeannie Campbell, *PT*, vol.51, no.5, February 1999, pp.26–29 (28).
33 For details about Donald Cameron and his family see Fairrie, pp. 170–2; see also Mackenzie, *Piping Traditions*, pp.65–75.

the Bruces. His son, Angus Macpherson, who was born about 1800, is said to have studied with Iain Dubh MacCrimmon, John and Peter Bruce, and John MacKay. Angus's son, Malcolm Macpherson 'Calum Pìobaire' was piper to Cluny Macpherson and lived at Catlodge in Badenoch. He was taught by his father, and by Angus MacKay and Archibald Munro, and taught in turn a cluster of leading players including Angus Macrae, Robert Meldrum, William MacLean and John MacDonald of Inverness. Although he retired from Cluny's service in 1877 (unlike some workers in Victorian Scotland, master pipers could apparently afford to do this), he continued teaching to the end of his life, dying as a result of a fishing accident in 1898. With his long hair and bushy beard, Malcolm Macpherson may have seemed the very image of the old style piper, working in a traditional setting until the dawn of the twentieth century. But he was a roving, raffish sort of figure who had worked in his younger days for the customs and excise, playing the pipes on revenue cutters up and down the west coast and, when based in Greenock as a ships' carpenter, he had played with Sandy Cameron (the elder) in one of the earliest pipe bands.[34] For nearly a generation he plundered the competition circuit and was regarded by many as easily the best piobaireachd player of his generation. He won the prize pipe and gold medal at Inverness, gold medals at Oban and Birnam, first prizes at Portree, Blair Atholl, Aberfeldy, Kingussie, Grantown and Dunkeld. He competed at the Edinburgh Exhibition of 1886 and won two gold medals, one of which carried with it the championship of the world for piobaireachd. Of his sons, perhaps the most interesting was Angus (1887–1976) who became piper to the Scots multi-millionaire Andrew Carnegie at Skibo Castle and in New York and was for many years tenant of the Inveran Hotel on the banks of the river Shin in Sutherland, a favourite resort of anglers and pipers. Angus was also a writer and his autobiography, *A Highlander Looks Back* (Oban, 1970, first edn. 1953), tells us a good deal about his career. He started as a clerk on the Highland Railway but gave this up in favour of piping and dancing, which promised a better return. There was a powerful strain of bookish mysticism in Angus Macpherson. It was in his generation that the Paradigm began seriously to affect the performer community. He was strongly influenced by the 'Celtic Twilight' movement and wrote of the power of inspiration, of the natural world as a source of moral virtue, of druids and bards, and of pipers as their successors in the old Celtic wisdom. Angus's son, Malcolm R. Macpherson, who died in Edinburgh in 1966 was also a champion piper.[35]

The relationship of pipers with the landed élite was subject to continuous

34 Fairrie, p.176.
35 Macpherson, *A Highlander Looks Back* (Oban 1970; first edn., 1953): see especially pp.64–5. For further details on the Macpherson pipers see Fairrie, 176–8; see also W. L. Manson, '"Callum Piobair" The World's Greatest Pibroch Player', in *The People's Friend*, September 26, 1898, pp.709–710; and Mackenzie, *Piping Traditions*, pp.3–4, 70–1, 268–70, 275–86.

revision in the light of social and economic change. One can see this in the papers of the Oliphants of Gask, an old Perthshire family whose best known member was the songwriter Lady Nairne. Her father, Laurence Oliphant, had been Aide de Camp to Charles Edward Stuart during the '45 and his children had been given a thoroughly Jacobite upbringing. Yet even in such conservative settings the traditional performing arts were ceasing to find support as the nineteenth century dawned. Indeed they might encounter active hostility and disapproval thanks to the strain of pietistic evangelicalism which was beginning to affect many of the leading Scottish families. In 1821 the laird's sister wrote:

> A few days ago Robert Arthur asked to speak with me and said he wished to go to the Highlands for a month to get *edication*. I asked if he could get 'edication' no nearer than the Highlands, I found by his reply that the chief object of his studies would be the bagpipes. I dissuaded him from bestowing much time upon an accomplishment which would never be of any real use to him and added that he could attend Mr McFarlane's evening class for reading and writing, and he said that he would go, when the dancing class was over. I asked what the dancing class meant, and found that the school-master had given up his room to an itinerant dancing master, who gave lessons in the evening.

Of course, this was no sooner discovered than it was put a stop to.[36]

The distinguished judge and writer, Henry Cockburn, noted in his journal for 31 August 1841, an encounter with a leading player who now kept the inn at Ballachulish:

> Angus [Cameron] was the best piper in his day, and, when only eighteen, gained the competition prize at Edinburgh [July 1794] . . . Though giving great praise to old rivals, and to young aspirants, he bemoaned the general decline of the art, for he said that there was not now one single '*real* piper – a man who made the pipe his business', in the whole of Appin. I suggested that it was probably owing to the want of county militia regiments, for the Highland colonels used to take their pipers with them. But he eschewed this, saying that we had plenty pipers long before the militia was heard of. I then suggested the want of training. 'Ay! there's a deal in that, for it does tak edication! a deal o' edication'. But then, why were they 'no edicated'? So he hit it on the very head, by saying it was the decline of chieftains, and their castles and gatherings. 'Yes', said I, 'few of them live at home now'. 'At hame! ou, they're a' deed! an' they're a' puir! an' they're a' English!'[37]

36 E. Maxtone Graham (E. Blair Oliphant), *The Oliphants of Gask: Records of a Jacobite Family* (Lond., 1910), p.402.
37 Henry Cockburn, *Circuit Journeys* (Edinr., 1888), pp.107–8.

As landed proprietors sought to maximise the cash return on their properties, the old adage that it was a poor estate that could not keep the laird and the piper without working began to seem increasingly out of touch, and in this sector the demand for 'real pipers', steadily declined.[38] We find in 1821, for example, that

> at the time the Inverness-shire Militia were last assembled for training, Col. Grant asked Lieut. Col. Gordon, when on his way to Inverness, to let him know in case he should happen to hear of a man of good character, who could, when occasion required, play a good tune on the Bag Pipe, and who, if he were disposed to come and settle there, could be rendered useful either as a workman or a tradesman. A person to be his piper and nothing but a piper he did not wish for.
>
> Colonel Gordon, however, mistook Colonel Grant, and sent to Cullen House a professional piper, who, although he pleased his employer could do nothing else, and piping could only occupy a very small part of his time. He was therefore sent back to Inverness, to have his account settled and a sum paid in compensation.[39]

On all but the largest estates it came to be expected that the piper would discharge a range of additional functions such as forester, gamekeeper, fisherman, or chauffeur, which considerably lessened the attractiveness of this sector to the highly skilled personnel who occupied the upper reaches of the profession.[40] One of the defining moments came at Taymouth when John MacDougall Gillies (1854–1925) was first piper. Gillies's family came from Glendaruel in the Cowal district of south-west Argyll, but he had been brought up in Aberdeen, and had studied with Sandy Cameron (the younger) at Aboyne, winning the piobaireachd at Braemar in 1875, and the prize pipe at the Northern Meeting the following year. Taymouth was, or ought to have been, a highly desirable appointment. The vast neo-gothic pile at the head of Loch Tay was centre of the Breadalbane estate, one of the biggest landed properties in Scotland. Amounting to nearly a quarter of a million acres in Perthshire and almost as much again in Argyll, it supplied a princely income – about £55,000 per annum – to successive Earls and Marquesses of Breadalbane, which was as well, perhaps, for they were men with expensive tastes. It was the focus of the early movement to exploit the southern

---

38 The 'poor estate' remark is quoted in C. A. Malcolm, *The Piper in Peace and War* (Lond., 1927), p.96, attributed to John MacDonald, piper to Glengarry.

39 'Miscellaneous Gleanings, 1788–1837', by Duncan Warrand, *OT*, 6/1/1940, p.3.

40 David Ross, writing of the later years of the nineteenth century said, 'their position in the household was that of Piper and Valet and companion to the Gentleman, and they were greatly respected, and all they were required to do was to be in attendance and ready to play the pipes when required. Later their status changed and many of the pipers were expected to act as servants. Therefore their position in the household became less attractive and many of them left to seek other employment', 'Some of the old pipers I have met', *PT*, vol. 26. no. 4, January 1974, pp.9–17 (9)

Highlands for sporting and tourist purposes – hence the Breadalbane clearances –
and of stage-managed Celticism on the grandest scale. The post of first piper at
Taymouth was held for many years by John Bàn MacKenzie, and later by
Duncan MacDougall, who some thought the best all round player in Scotland
during the second half of the nineteenth century. It was probably the biggest
private piping establishment in Scotland, being able, under the direction of the
first piper, to turn out more than two dozen players all told for the lavish
'Highland' entertainments given by its proprietors.[41] In 1819, for example, in an
interesting anticipation of the visit of George IV to Edinburgh some three years
later, Prince Leopold, afterwards King of the Belgians, was entertained at
Taymouth Castle with a Highland games involving some 2,000 tartan-clad
tenants. In the Autumn of 1842, Queen Victoria and Prince Albert were treated
by the old Etonian second Marquess to three days of extravagant spectacle, with
piping and dancing and Gaelic song, the surrounding hills ablaze with illumina-
tion.[42] The Castle was occupied by the family only occasionally, however. Much
time was spent abroad and at their London home in Park Lane. As one source
records,

> Lady Breadalbane arrived from the London residence. Her Ladyship, not in
> the best of moods, had heavy gambling losses in London. On her last night in
> London she had lost £72,000 on the turn of a card.
>
> She sent for the factor and ordered all these pipers doing nothing but
> playing pipes to sweep the drive. MacDougall Gillies felt so insulted he
> fetched his pipes and belongings and left for Glasgow . . .[43]

But Gillies was a man who made the pipe his business and he continued to make
it so, although not on the land or in the employment of the landed élite. For at
least a century pipers had worked in urban settings, and figures such as Hugh
Robertson, Donald MacDonald, Murdoch McLean, William Gunn and Donald

41 'When HRH the Duke of Cambridge visited Taymouth Castle in 1882, the
    Breadalbane Pipe Band of 16 Pipers under the leadership of Pipe-Major McDougall
    entertained H. R. H. and the distinguished company present, every evening during
    diner and after to choice selections of pipe music, and so highly delighted was
    H. R. H. with the performance that he sent for Pipe Major McDougall to the
    drawing room, and in complimenting the band on their playing said he had heard all
    the pipe bands of the British Army, but had never before listened to such grand pipe
    music' Typescript: 'Notes on Duncan MacDougall, Aberfeldy, the Queen's
    Bagpipemaker – 1898' from a reprint of 'An interview with the Queen's Bagpipemaker
    – by a Lady Correspondent' reprinted from the People's Journal, 4/11/1893: Seton
    Gordon Papers, NLS, Acc 7451 Box 19/3: Notes on Pipers and Piping.
42 William Marshall, Historic Scenes of Perthshire (Edinr., 1880), pp.427–9; see also
    William A. Gillies, In Famed Breadalbane (Perth, 1938), pp.212–220.
43 Alexander MacAulay, 'The Art and History of the MacDougalls of Aberfeldy', PT,
    vol.16, no.4–5, January-February, 1964, pp.7–10, 9–14, (4: 10).

MacPhee figure prominently in the record. As industrialisation gathered pace, the cities grew in importance as centres of power and patronage, opportunity and employment. By 1900 one Scot in four was a Glaswegian. Careers based in landed settings became progressively less common and within Gillies's own generation urban pipers came to dominate the profession.[44] In Glasgow he became manager of Peter Henderson's, the bagpipe firm, President of the Scottish Pipers' Association, and teacher of a talented generation of city pipers including James Taylor, George Yardley, Robert Reid and William Gray, as well as a number of gentlemen amateurs including Archibald Campbell of Kilberry.[45] His predecessor at Taymouth, Duncan MacDougall, had negotiated his own terms, which involved work on a part-time basis only, and starting only when MacDougall could conveniently move his pipe-making business to Aberfeldy, which by then had good road and rail links and an appropriate commercial infrastructure.[46]

The MacDougalls came originally from Lorn and had evidently been pipers there for many generations; but Duncan MacDougall had a craft background and came of a family of pipemakers. His grandfather, Allan, had started the business in Perth in the 1790s and Duncan's father had transferred it to Edinburgh in about 1861. His own instruments and those of his son Gavin were regarded as the summit of the pipe-maker's art in Victorian Scotland and are still much sought after. When Duncan MacDougall, who was also an outstanding player, won the prize pipe at Inverness in 1870, he acquired thereby an instrument of his own making.[47]

The entrepreneurial strain we see illustrated here in a piper who was willing to work in a traditional setting, but only if he retained a degree of commercial independence, a kind of hybrid between service and a business career, is echoed by another leading piper of this generation, Uilleam Ross. Robert Meldrum, who knew him well, wrote that:

> When the Prince Consort heard of [Angus MacKay's] death, at a dinner of
> the officers of the Highland Brigade at Chobham . . . he sent word to the
> general officer in command of the Brigade to send up to Windsor the pipe-
> major with the black beard (Hardie of the 79th, a native of Skye) to be piper
> to the Queen. Hardie had not been long at Windsor when the English
> footmen began to mock his Highland accent. After vainly warning them, he at
> last threw off his coat and gave two of them a hammering. Her Majesty held

44 By 1927, indeed, James Campbell, Queen Victoria's last piper, could describe Glasgow
   as 'the centre of the piping world', 'A Royal Piper', *OT*, 17/12/1927, p.2.
45 'The Late Mr. J. McDougall Gillies. A Famous Piper', *OT*, 26/12/1925, p.3.
46 For example MacDougall used a lot of 'sea ivory' for his mounts – walrus and sea
   lion tusks and the blades of swordfish – which he was able to buy in Dundee when
   the whalers came in: Seton Gordon, 'Typescript: "Notes on Duncan MacDougall"',
   NLS, Acc.7451 Box 19/3, 'Notes on Pipers and Piping'.
47 MacAulay, 'Art and History', (5:11).

an enquiry and Hardie was discharged. The luck of the black beard next fell to William Ross, pipe-major of the 42nd, a native of Ross-shire, and he held the post for many years. When he had got settled down in Buckingham Palace, he asked the Queen to make him an allowance for living outside the palace. This was granted, and he immediately began to make pipe reeds and bags, and engaged a turner and began to make pipes. He supplied the five kilted regiments that were in existence at that time, and made a big business.

As Pipe-Major of the 93rd . . . I sometimes handed him sums of £20. The full ivory mounted pipes won by me at the Northern Meeting were made by Ross . . .

It is told that Lord Rollo, getting into conversation with Ross the Queen's piper at a dinner of the Highland Society of London, asked him what the amount of his income was. Ross replied that he had 10d a day Army pension, £200 a year and all found with the Queen, £30 from the Highland Society, £20 from the Gaelic Society, besides his profits on the sale of pipes and pipe equipment. Lord Rollo at once exclaimed 'You d – – – – – fellow! You are better off than I am'.[48]

During the later nineteenth century professional piping covered a fairly wide social range and its financial returns seem to have varied considerably. It was able to attract and retain people whose qualifications would nowadays have led to middle-class careers (or who managed to combing piping with such careers), like William McLennan who was an architect, John Smith, Pipe-Major of the 93rd, who had trained as a teacher, and J. F. Farquharson, piper to the Duke of Edinburgh, who was a physician. William Campbell who won the Inverness medal in 1897 as second piper to Queen Victoria had received quite an elaborate formal musical training, and had studied law.[49] There was Angus MacDonald of Morar, a leading pupil of the Bruces and of Duncan Campbell of Foss, who as well as being a champion piper was estate factor of South Morar and party agent in Arisaig for a succession of Liberal M.P.s.[50] New occupational groups created by urbanisation and industrial growth such as the railways and the police were also a frequent recourse of pipers. Angus Macpherson worked for the railways, as, for a time, did John MacDougall Gillies. John McLennan, (1843–1923), the leading representative in his generation of another of the important piping dynasties, was a superintendent of police in Edinburgh (although he is usually known as Lieutenant John). He was the ninth child of Duncan (1781–1869) and Catherine McLennan, who had moved from Mellon Charles near Aultbea in

48 Robert Meldrum, 'On Champions Past and Present', *OT*, 6/7/1940, p.5, 13/7/1940, p.3. Meldrum is slightly out in his dates: Angus MacKay died in 1859.

49 Mackenzie, *Piping Traditions*, pp. 79–81; 'A Veteran Piper's Reminiscences', from 'Piobair', *OT*, 6/7/1940, p.3; Jeannie Campbell, 'J. F. Farquharson', in *PT*, vol. 50, no.11, August 1998, pp.52–5; 'The Queen's Second Piper', *OT*, 2/10/1897, p.2.

50 'Death of a Well-Known Piper', *OT*, 22/4/1922, p.2.

Gairloch to the Braes of Kilcoy in the Black Isle during the 1830s, and he had walked to Dundee at the age of 19 to join the force. His great-grandfather, Murdo McLennan (born *c.* 1700) had played at Culloden. His grandfather, Duncan McLennan (1759–1837), who was a pupil of Angus MacKay of Gairloch and may have married the latter's daughter Ann, was shot in the legs during the Black Watch mutiny of 1779 and survived to play at Waterloo. His uncle was Donald Mór McLennan of Moy.[51] Although he was a senior police officer, John McLennan made the pipe his business every bit as much as MacDougall Gillies or Angus MacKay. Through his teaching activities – his son, George Stewart McLennan is often considered the most technically accomplished player as well as the best composer of light music in the first half of the 20th century – and his published work as an editor and theorist, John McLennan was a powerful voice in contemporary piping. His books, *The Piobaireachd as MacCrimmon Played it* (Edinr., 1907) and *The Piobaireachd as Performed in the Highlands for Ages, till about the Year* 1808 (Edinr., 1925), and his frequent contributions to the *Oban Times* gave him a greater influence than he could ever have enjoyed as a personal piper. McLennan was an ideologue, the source of whose power lay in the sophisticated popular print media which had sprung into being during the communications revolution in Victorian Scotland. Here was somebody quite unlike the Logans or Ramsays: a piper achieving a powerful individual voice by skilful use of the new technologies in printing, publishing and distribution which only a specifically urban infrastructure could sustain. He had numerous successors.[52]

There were two important changes in the social context of piping during the nineteenth century: the gradual decline of the tie with the land, and the rise of the competition circuit. The two were closely related. The Highland games movement began as an adjunct to aristocratic social gatherings such as the Northern Meeting, founded in 1788 at Inverness, and the Argyllshire Gathering which began at Oban in 1871.[53] The Northern Meeting was 'the culminatory point of the Highland season . . . Half the London world of fashion, all the clever people that could be hunted out from all parts, all the north country, all the neighbourhood from far and near, without regard to wealth and station . . . flocked to this encampment in the wilderness during the fine autumns . . .'[54] There was hunting, and horseracing, balls and dinners, and much seeing and

---

51 For further details of the McLennan family, see Fairrie, pp.172–5.

52 Mackenzie, *Piping Traditions.*, *passim*, but see especially pp.34–5, 46–7, and 164–173. McLennan frequently used the Gaelic form of his Christian name 'Ian', but in this book 'John' is used to avoid confusion.

53 Fairrie gives a detailed history of the Northern Meeting; for a brief account of the Argyllshire, see Jeannie Campbell, 'The Argyllshire Gathering – The Early Years', in *PT*, vol.42–3, no.9–11/2, June-August/November 1990, pp.30–4, 15–19, 40–5, 32–5.

54 Elizabeth Grant of Rothiemurchus, quoted in Iain Colquhoun and Hugh Machell, *Highland Gatherings: being accounts of the Braemar, Northern and Luss Meetings* (Lond., 1927), pp.117–8.

being seen. The fashions were of the highest, and tartan everywhere. The games began in 1837. They quickly gathered a momentum of their own, and were largely attended, making a significant annual contribution to the economy of Inverness.[55] In 1848, there were steamers running from Glasgow, Leith and London, and coaches from Dingwall, Caithness, Perth, Fort William, Aberdeen and Elgin.[56] This ostensible celebration of aristocratic chic was underpinned by hard-headed business acumen which prompted a ceaseless promotion of commercial popular culture in pursuit of ever larger audiences. By 1890 the event was attracting about 10,000 paying spectators. There were boat races and bicycle races, and pigeon shooting and military bands, novelty events, hot air ballooning and lady parachutists. And in the middle of all this one could, in theory, hear some of Scotland's finest professional pipers.[57]

After the end of the Edinburgh competitions in 1844, the Northern Meeting became the premier piping event in the country, with two competitions run on successive days, the first for a prize pipe, the second for previous winners who played for a gold medal awarded by the Highland Society of London. Even in pre-railway days the Northern attracted top players. They did not have to pay entry fees (a common feature at other games), and for a number of years their travel expenses were met. Above all, the prize money was good, £8 for a win in the piobaireachd for much of the later nineteenth century – three or four times what was on offer at the smaller games. A similar pattern developed at the Argyllshire Gathering at Oban and, as the nineteenth century drew to its close, it took its place alongside the Northern as the big event that at some stage of his career a professional piper would expect to win if he were to be acknowledged as a player of the foremost rank. Games tended to specialise – Crieff, for example, was the main venue for heavy athletics – and the major competitions in piping were at Inverary, Lochaber (Fort William), the Breadalbane Highland Gathering at Aberfeldy, and the games at Cowal, Portree, and Braemar.

Braemar shows an interestingly different pattern, having its roots in a plebeian social initiative which was subsequently taken over and re-defined by the gentry. It originated in a craft-guild, the Braemar Wrights, who in 1800 organised an annual 'Walk' to raise funds to assist sick and distressed members. An invitation to Lord Fife to become its patron after Waterloo initiated a series of dramatic changes, however. The committee began to fill up with local lairds, the wearing of the kilt became mandatory, the name was changed to the 'Royal Highland Society', and the main focus of activity became the staging of an annual games:

---

55 Not only in accommodation, catering, and transport, but in the drapery and costumier trade as well, see 'The Northern Meeting Muddle', the *Scottish Highlander*, 24/9/1891, p.4.
56 Colquhoun, p.147.
57 Colquhoun, pp.134–63.

In the year 1832 . . . The Marquis of Caermarthen (afterwards Duke of Leeds) took a nineteen years' lease of Mar Forest, north of the Dee, together with the adjoining forest of the Bachen and Slugan Glen on the Invercauld estate. He at once began to take a keen interest in the affairs of the Society. He presented each of his gamekeepers and retainers with a complete Highland costume of his own Dunblane tartan (Viscount Dunblane being one of his subsidiary titles) and carefully drilled them so that they might present a smart appearance. His example was shortly followed by the Earl of Fife and Mr Farquharson of Invercauld, who presented each of the members residing on the remaining portion of their Braemar estates with a costume of their own clan tartan, Duff and Farquharson respectively.

General Sir Alexander Duff of Delgaty, brother of the fourth Earl of Fife, took a great interest in the Duff Highlanders, and spent many hours in drilling them, so that they might acquit themselves creditably when on parade.[58]

And so a movement which had been started by working people trying to take greater control of their lives and whose objects were charitable, gradually became host to elaborate ceremonial designed to reinforce the social leadership of the landed élite and the pseudo-feudal dependence upon it of the rest of the rural population. Highland games gave visible shape to class-based division between competitors and sponsors, between those who performed and those whose superior social standing entitled them, with varying degrees of competence, to judge. The games represented two opposite, and ultimately irreconcilable, impulses: while at the forefront of the new mass popular entertainment market in a rapidly modernising country, they were dedicated at the same time to proclaiming the values of a characteristically rural and hierarchical order. The apparent object was entertainment. The real agenda was about deference and social control.

The physical scale of the larger Highland games meant that different parts of the ground might be devoted to different events, each attracting a specialist audience. Piping was seldom the central focus. Sometimes it took place in an out of the way corner of the ground, and might impinge rather little upon a casual spectator. As is evident from contemporary newspaper reports, the main reasons for attending Oban and Inverness for a good many of those present were the agreeable rituals of the fashionable world and the niceties of haute couture. An observer of the Argyllshire Gathering in 1895 noted:

All day people were arriving by train and steamer, and soon the little town was gay with smartly-clad ladies in yachting and travelling dresses and well-known county lairds and others in Highland dress, young and old, all greeting

58 *Ibid.*, pp.85–86. The games at Luss show a similar general pattern at a later period: see p. 90.

one another to the week's festivities . . . Most people were in tailor-made gowns; I noticed one girl in a brown and green checked suit, the coat short in front, with very long tails behind, and with this she wore a brown felt hat with white cock's plumes, as did also her sister, and very smart they looked. There were several bright blue coats and skirts, and those with flowery hats looked so pretty. Three sisters, evidently from a yacht, wore blue serge skirts, reefer coats, and men-of-war straw hats; while another girl was in blue serge with white piqué facings. Nearly everyone left early to go to numerous 'At Homes', both onshore and on the yachts . . .

Of course the Balls, held on the evenings of Wednesday and Thursday, were the chief attraction to most of us . . . The first person to be noticed on entering the building was Maclaine of Lochbuie, who was, as usual, all important and indefatigable, and amongst other well-known faces, most of whom were accompanied by parties, were Campbell of Kilberry, Campbell of Dunstaffnage, Campbell of Inverneil, Sir Fitzroy MacLean of Duart, Patten MacDougall of Gallanach, Forsyth of Quinish, Lloyd of Minard, Colonel Cheape of Carsaig, Stewart of Coll, Burnley Campbell of Bailliemore, and the newly-elected county member, Nicol of Ardmarnock. There were not many debutantes this year, but I noticed one of Lochbuie's daughters one night in white, and the second with bunches of pale pink on her gown . . . There were some lovely diamonds worn by chaperones and dancers . . . most beautiful lace . . . amongst other pretty frocks was one of gold and silver brocade with bunches of scarlet, and the wearer of this had lovely diamond stars in her hair; while another lady, carrying a shower bouquet of pink carnations, had a pale-blue satin dress with velvet bodice and a big black sash. A piquant little lady wore a quaint gown of pink and white with a low diamond tiara, while a young married woman was in white satin with black chiffon and old lace, with lovely stars forming a tiara in her hair, and carrying a bouquet of brilliant scarlet . . . The daughter of one of the lords of the county . . . each night wore a tartan sash over her shoulder, and a sprig of bog myrtle in her hair.[59]

The greatest expansion of the games movement came in the 1860s onwards, as the growth of the railway network made it economically attractive for upland and rural communities within reach of large urban centres to host such events. As incomes rose and working hours were reduced the modern leisure industry began to take shape in mid-Victorian Britain, bringing the music-hall and the seaside holiday, and, in Scotland, the Highland games. Ballater started in 1864, Aboyne in 1867, Crieff in 1870. Unlikely places deep in the Lowlands whose links with Gaelic culture had been severed centuries before sprouted Highland games along with the rest. David Webster notes that:

59 'The Argylleshire Gathering: a Lady's Letter', *OT*, 21/9/1895, p.3. For a rich photographic record of this aspect of the Games scene dating from the 1920s and '30s, see Fairrie, pp.60–106.

In the Buchan area alone there were games at Fyvie, Delgaty, Gamrie, Crudie, New Byth, New Pitsligo, Bonnykelly, New Aberdour, Rosehearty, Rathen, Peterhead, Mintlaw, Maud, Ellon, Auchnagatt, Slains, New Deer, Crichie, Longside, Fraserburgh, Hatton, Plaidy, Turriff, Garmond and many others. In these small places, crowds of around 7000 were not by any means uncommon.[60]

What this meant was money for pipers; some were able to make substantial sums from the games circuit, especially if, like John MacColl, they were also dancers and athletes.[61]

John MacColl was born at Kentallen in Appin on the shores of Loch Linnhe on 6 January 1860, youngest of the seven children of Dugald MacColl, the tailor of Kentallen, and his wife Elizabeth MacInnes. In his later teens he worked as a quarryman at Bonawe to save enough money to go and study with Donald MacPhee in Glasgow, under whom, with his brilliant natural ability, he made rapid progress. He won the Oban medal in 1883, the gold medal at Inverness in 1884 and the former winners' medal there in 1888. After a spell as piper to Neil MacDonald of Dunach, he made his living entirely from the games circuit and from teaching, as his son John Carruthers MacColl later recalled:

> He did tell me of finishing a dance, throwing off his kilt (having running shorts underneath), competing in the hundred yards race and then putting his kilt and things on ready for the next dance. This, of course, was just as a professional to augment his prize money for the day. Naturally his major earnings came from playing the pipes, dancing and teaching.
>
> Before the establishment of the Army School of Piping in Edinburgh under the late Pipe-major William Ross there was an arrangement whereby my father taught individuals and groups of pipers attached to various Highland regiments, which meant travelling around Scotland in the winter months visiting Campbeltown, Inverary, and even at times the Outer Hebrides.
>
> In the summer months, from June to the end of September, there were games in all sorts of places – villages and towns throughout Scotland, and even England and Ireland. He was away from home practically all summer travelling round the Games with only short breaks of a day or two back to Oban. My mother often told me of the excitement of these visits and the presents for the family – my sisters, brother and myself. It must have been lucrative in these days as he told me – and it is recorded – that he could earn £40 in an afternoon from piping, dancing and athletics – quite a lot of money in the eighties and nineties of last Century![62]

60 Webster, p.22.
61 The fullest recent account of John MacColl is Seumas MacNeill, 'The Life and Times of John MacColl', *PT*, vol.50, nos.5–8, February-May, 1998, pp.18–22, 46–9, 22–5, 19–23.
62 *Ibid.*, 7: 23.

There was little at which John MacColl did not excel. As well as being an outstanding composer of ceòl beag (he was one of the founding fathers of the modern 'competition march'), he was an expert yachtsman and golfer, a shinty internationalist, and a Gaelic singer, at which he also competed.[63] Little more than half a century lay between the birth of John Bàn MacKenzie and John MacColl, but in terms of professional opportunity piping had been transformed.

Just how relentlessly commercial the competition circuit had become is suggested by a story of Robert Meldrum, a leading military piper in the later Victorian period. He was born in Tomintoul (1851) and joined the Seaforth at the age of 16, serving under Ronald MacKenzie, before going to the 93rd as pipe-major on the recommendation of the Queen's piper Uilleam Ross, who intended Meldrum to be his successor. Being a soldier meant that he could not compete as often as his civilian rivals, so that when he got a chance to play, he did not like to miss it. He records that

> I had gone to this gathering knowing nothing of an unfortunate, although perhaps amusing, difference between the pipers and the management. On my arrival, William McLennan met me and asked me what the devil I was doing there.
>
> I replied that I was not afraid of any of them, and asked why I should not be there.
>
> He explained that they had protested against the smallness of the prizes, and that they were not going to play.
>
> I replied that I had paid for my return ticket to Inverness, and was going to play. Eventually Angus Macrae and [John MacDougall] Gillies played, although they had protested, but MacColl and McLennan did not. They got into some trouble for booing those who played. Gillies got the piobaireachd and I was second. The judges praised my playing but for my reed. Someone had removed my own reed and substituted another.[64]

There was much contemporary unease about the games circuit. It was attacked as a grossly inaccurate reflection of Highland culture, a mere 'carnival of muscle', rootless, vulgar and commercial. Glengarry's daughter, Caroline MacDonnell, wrote in 1885 to the *Oban Times*:

> Various efforts are being made to revive the old Highland games, but it seems to be either unknown, or entirely overlooked, that they were the pastime of the people – whereas now, several persons endeavour to gain a livelihood by them, which materially alters their character, and has introduced a theatrical style of dancing, quite foreign to the real Scotch steps and mode of executing them. Tossing the caber and throwing the hammer are quite different now from what they were between fifty and sixty years ago.

63 Colquhoun, p.100.
64 Meldrum, 'Reminiscences', pt. 5, *OT*, 27/7/1940, p.5.

The Highland fling and Gillie Callum are seldom, if ever, danced to the end, only a few steps of the former, and the first and easiest half of the latter, being now sufficient to elicit great applause and win the highest prizes!! Other feats of strength and agility are wholly unrepresented.

Then, as to the costume itself, that is indeed badly represented; doubtless from many persons considering the 'Military Regulation Kilt' a model for the old Highland kilt, when, in point of fact, they are not even made alike.

You will therefore see that instead of perpetuating these old games and costume, the gatherings (as now conducted) are only producing a very singular burlesque – which is generally received as the old style.

Having given my opinion so freely, it may be as well to state that my father is commonly allowed to have been the last Highland chieftain of the old type who encouraged such sports among his people, and therefore I have seen them in my childhood.[65]

Not only were the games seen as fraudulent from a cultural point of view, they were thought to be reactionary and socially divisive as well. In a climate of bitter land agitation and social unrest, land-raids, rent-strikes and evictions, which eventually led to the formation of the Highland Land Law Reform Association, the Crofters' Party and the Napier Commission, it was difficult for the Highland gentry to rebut the charge that they were a group of ruthlessly exploitative rentiers prepared – as the recent 'Battle of the Braes' in Skye had demonstrated, and the deployment of troops in Lewis, Tiree and elsewhere – to impose their policies of land management by force if necessary.

Urging a boycott of the Argyllshire Gathering in 1884, a correspondent of the *Oban Times* (itself under embargo by the gentry because of its support for the crofters' cause) declared:

this raises a very important question to Highlanders. Are they going to be duped to make exhibitions of themselves to please the vanity of such men, to make them appear important in the eyes of Cockney spectators? Men who care no more for them, in fact a great deal less, than they do for the sheep on the hill-sides. Do they not show by their conduct of these Gatherings that the whole thing is a sham, that they are making a show of the natives to entertain their friends? Are not the balls with which the meetings terminate strictly confined to the gentry, *an cead na cuideachd,* ['with the company's leave'] and strangers, but debarred to the plebeian natives? When will my countrymen be wise and let those pseudo chiefs if they wish to make an exhibition to their friends, muster their cheviot faced and antlered retainers as an example of the prowess of the land? I trust my countrymen will take this matter to heart, every action of this kind is a step in advance for our cause, let them show by

65 'Highland Gatherings', *OT*, 22/8/1885, p.3; for the 'carnival of muscle' quote see Leader Column, 16/9/1899, p.4.

their absence from these *shows* that they have awakened to a sense of their position and will not any more be made puppets for the amusement of Cockney visitors, or to flatter the vanity of Highland lairds.[66]

Protests by one of the judges, local laird John Campbell of Kilberry, that he had not evicted anybody were denounced as hollow on the grounds that all the tenants who could be evicted already had been, and there was hardly anybody left on the estate.[67]

The railing-off of the Northern Meeting park in 1891 to create exclusive new areas for the gentry drew a stinging comment from the editor of the *Scottish Highlander*, Alexander MacKenzie, in which he compared it to 'a fifth rate menagerie' and enquired which was the dangerous side of the fence.[68] But the Northern had by this stage become quite dizzyingly posh. Its historian Angus Fairrie notes that 'The list of those present at the Balls . . . read like an international 'Who's Who'. Princes, Dukes, Ducs, Marquises, Earls, Counts, Comtes, Barons . . . eminent Indian grandees such as the Maharaja Holkar of Indore, Princess Sophia Duleep Singh, the Maharaja Gaekwar of Baronda . . . they made the Northern Meeting as distinguished and cosmopolitan a gathering as anything in the world.'[69]

Moves to widen the appeal, to create a kind of 'Highland Eisteddfod', were set in motion in Argyllshire in 1890 and the first 'Mòd' took place in Oban on 17 September 1892. Even this was regarded as potentially exploitative. A correspondent of the *Scottish Highlander* wrote, echoing the feelings of many ordinary Gaels, that the Mòd, too, would be used to reinforce the ascendancy of the landed élite, and that any implication of inclusiveness and social harmony would be quite illusory:

> . . . although I would advise delaying it just now, I hope soon, if the people get enlarged holdings, they may be able to afford the expense of going to Oban or Inverness for a day or two to take part in or to witness the competitions. At the present time they have been reduced to such poverty by the oppression of the rich that they are mostly quite unable to give any assistance either by competing or paying, and the object instead of being a true Highland gathering would be degraded into a meeting for making sport for the Philistines. An eloquent example may be found in the Northern Meeting and many other Highland games.[70]

66 'The Oban Games', from 'The Old Man of Storr', *OT*, 13/9/1884, p.3.

67 'Evictions on Kilberry Estate', from 'Caolasadaich', *OT*, 3/10/1885, p.3.

68 'The Northern Meeting. A Descent into Snobbery,' *Scottish Highlander*, 24/9/1891, p.2.

69 Fairrie, pp.52–4.

70 'A Highland Eisteddfod', from Ewen MacDonald, *Scottish Highlander*, 25/12/1890, p.3.

During the second half of the nineteenth century there was a dramatic increase in competitive piping, a corresponding enlargement of the cadre of judges, and a substantial increase in the power of the bench. But few Victorian judges had more than an amateur acquaintance with the pipe and its music and many did not possess even that. Landed wealth and formal education were the chief qualifications for the role. As a result, decision-making was arbitrary and conservative and much swayed by reputation, so that the best chance of winning was being known to have won before. This tended to create a small élite of regular prizewinners, and it was difficult – and expensive – for younger players to break into the charmed circle. Archie MacNeill, born in Govan in 1879, gives a vivid picture of what this was like as the century neared its end:

> In the summer of 1897 the Queen Victoria Diamond Jubilee Highland Games were held at Helensburgh, and many of the best known pipers were competing. Many of the pipers wore their medals etc. It was at these Games that I met J.[ames] A. Center from Edinburgh. He told me he was twenty-nine years old, and that the first year that he had gone round the Games it had cost him forty pounds and he had hardly made a penny. At that time it seemed to be a case of serving your apprenticeship, and a young piper, no matter how well he played, never got a chance . . .
>
> I had entered for the piobaireachd competition, and when the judges asked what tune I was going to play I told them 'Seaforth's Salute'. I was then requested to play the groundwork and one of the variations as that would be sufficient – not much encouragement for a beginner. However, I played the tune right through from beginning to end. I had paid my entry money and I could not reason why I should carry out their instructions. However, I was compensated as I won the local competition of the March, Strathspey and Reel. One of the judges criticised my outfit. I wore a heather-coloured tunic instead of the usual silver braid and buttons [in competition at this time, pipers were required to play in costly full Highland evening dress, or full dress uniform if they were soldiers].[71]

Dr. Charles Bannatyne, himself a judge, wrote bitterly to the *Oban Times* in 1904:

> Round and round goes the wheel, and the same old names turn up year after year till some day there appears a judge of strong character and sound judgement, who recognises the merits of some struggling young player, and lo!

---

71 'Early Piping Days', *PT*, vol.12, no.6, March 1960, pp.16–22 (22). John MacDonald of Inverness recollected that on one occasion a judge 'informed me that I would have been placed higher up in the prize-list if I had marched off on the left foot instead of on the right' – see 'The Art of Piobaireachd Playing. Interesting Address by Pipe-Major MacDonald, M.B.E.', *OT*, 13/7/1935 p.3.

another name is added to the judging wheel, and perhaps one of the hitherto
unbeaten old fogies dies of old age or disappointment at the judge's non-
recognition of his illustrious name, and thus a vacancy occurs in the merry-go-
round, and another young player fills the vacancy who played for it years
before. Here are the facts in programme form: – Grand piping competition –
piobaireachds, marches, strathspeys and reels. Big prizes. All the élite of the
piping world have entered. So, to this grand fiasco go Patrick MacCrimmon,
Donald Cameron, Angus MacKay, and a host of smaller fry, who can play
almost as well as they and perhaps on this occasion play better. But the judges
know them not, and they pipe in vain, and here is the prize-list:-Piobaireachd
– 1. Patrick MacCrimmon; 2. Angus MacKay; 3. Don. Cameron. Marches – 1.
Angus MacKay; 2. Patrick MacCrimmon; 3. Donald Cameron. Strathspeys
and Reels – 1 Donald Cameron; 2. Patrick MacCrimmon; 3. Angus MacKay.
You see poor Donald is a little behind the others in prize money, but, never
mind, the North Polar games are to-morrow, and very likely Donald will get
the better of Patrick and Angus, and so the wheel goes round.
. . . this is no fantastic picture, but stern reality . . .[72]

Given such difficulties, some young pipers preferred to concentrate on track and
field events, where arcane considerations of authority and reputation did not pre-
determine the outcome, where they did not have to bear written accreditation
from social superiors before they could even enter (as was the case with piping
events at a number of games, including the Northern Meeting), and where
victory and defeat were normally unequivocal. Robert Meldrum recalled one of
his own pupils, Donald Ewen Macpherson of Skye, 'who was a most promising
piper, playing some splendid piobaireachds, but he preferred the athletics side of
the games and while Pipe Major of the Royal Scots won the wrestling championship of the Services'.[73]
    Competing pipers formed only a small proportion of the performer
community at any time. Well-informed contemporaries of Charles Bannatyne
and Archie MacNeill thought that, in a way, they were living through a great
age of piping, with more people playing than ever before. But this would not
be evident from the competition circuit at the turn of the 19th and 20th
centuries, where the same dozen or so names – John MacColl, William
McLennan, Angus MacRae, George and Angus MacDonald, John MacDougall Gillies, John MacDonald of Inverness, G. S. McLennan, and Willie Ross
– dominated the prize-lists at the big open competitions year after year. In
Victorian Scotland (and the Empire), there were pipers everywhere. We know
about a few of them because they were observed by somebody interested in
piping, like General C. S. Thomason, for example, who received his main
training from notable champions like Sandy Cameron and Donald MacKay

72 'Bagpipe Judging at Competitions' OT, 23/7/1904, p.3.
73 Meldrum, 'Reminiscences', OT, 17/8/1940, p.3.

(the younger), whose 'stock of piobaireachd seemed inexhaustible', but the foundations of whose knowledge were laid by Mackie, the head gardener at Elchies in Speyside, otherwise completely unrecorded.[74] As would have been, but for Thomason, the driver of his train at Nursingpore in Bengal, also a piper, who refused to start for Allahabad until the General had finished playing 'The Big Spree'.[75] Or they rose to eminence in some other field, like Alex. Fettes of Aberdeen, composer of 'The Glendaruel Highlanders', who was several times mayor of Port Elizabeth in South Africa.[76] Or they might enter history by dint of specialist knowledge, like the policeman Robert MacGregor of Muir of Ord, an early member of the Govan Police Pipe Band, whose lifelong interest in canntaireachd led to published pieces in the *Oban Times* and correspondence with Sheriff J. P. Grant of the Piobaireachd Society.[77] Or there may have been some other thing notable in their life, or death, like Alexander Gray from Fort William who played for the passengers on the Comet steamer which plied between Inverness and Glasgow via the Caledonian Canal, and was lost in its wreck on 17 October 1825 along with eighty other souls.[78] Or often, perhaps, like William Sutherland of Airdrie, who was an engine-man at a coal pit, and a very fine player, they might be remembered for the range of their gifts as multi-instrumentalists, poets, singers, raconteurs and composers.[79]

The curious reticence about living pipers we noted in James Logan was a regular feature of mediated texts originating outside the performer community until well into the twentieth century. It was consistent with the pattern of assumptions – that the significant period of creativity had lain in the distant past, that tradition was antique, unchanging and now in process of dissolution – that had reappeared in successive generations of formally 'educated' commentators from the time of James Macpherson onwards. Unlike Macpherson's informants, however, pipers were highly visible practitioners of a contemporary art form in a society which not only tolerated, but to some extent positively encouraged deviant behaviour in its musicians. Pipers made livings (sometimes not very creditably), got drunk, fell into debt, ran off with other people's women, went mad – and did other kinds of untidy all-too-human things. Societies acknowledge musicians in many different ways ranging from direct payment and various other kinds of subsidy and gifts, to less tangible but perhaps not less valuable

74 B.D. MacKenzie, 'General Thomason and Ceol Mor', in *Transactions of the Gaelic Society of Inverness*, vol. 57, 1993, pp. 58–72, (60, 63).

75 *Ibid.*, p.64.

76 J. D. R. Watt, 'Death of a Well-Known South African Piper', *OT*, 18/6/1921, p.3.

77 See Robert MacGregor, 'Clan MacKinnon Salute', *OT*, 28/10/1916, p.3; 'MacKinnon Music', 24/2/1917, p.3; and 'MacIntosh of Borlum's Salute', 13/12/1919, p.3.
Piobaireachd Society Papers, Correspondence 1895–1928, NLS Acc.9103 /8, Robert MacGregor to J. P. Grant, 22/12/1919, 2/1/1920.

78 Mackenzie, *Piping Traditions*, pp.249–50.

79 See H. S. Strafford, 'The Late Dr Charles Bannatyne', *OT*, 22/3/1924, p.5.

things such as recognition, status and tolerance.[80] One of the rewards of the
master player of the Highland pipe, for example, is to enjoy a vigorous afterlife in
the rich and frequently scandalous Valhalla of piping folklore, which is full of
examples of non-standard behaviour particularly with regard to drink. The story
of the fairy chanter, for example, tells how at a great competition at Dunvegan,
MacCrimmon was expected to carry off the honours, but when the time
approached for him to perform . . .

> MacLeod glanced in the direction where he expected to see MacCrimmon
> preparing to acquit himself bravely, but to his annoyance there was no sign of
> him. Calling a boy, a young MacCrimmon, to him, he bad him search for
> and bring back MacCrimmon. In short time the boy returned with the tidings
> that MacCrimmon was hopelessly drunk . . .

The chief in desperation nominated the lad as his picked piper and the fairies
appeared with a magical silver chanter which gave him such mastery that he easily
won the contest.[81] Alexander MacDonald, in *Story and Song from Loch Ness-Side*,
tells of Finlay MacLeod, the piper of Glenmoriston, entered for competition by
his laird, James Grant:

> MacPhàdruig put Finlay forward one year to compete at the Inverness
> Northern Meeting Games. When, however, Finlay's turn to appear came
> round he did not find himself, it would seem, in the best condition to play
> for a prize. Grant was much annoyed. 'Is this your treatment of me, now,
> Finlay?' said he. 'James, my man', replied Finlay, 'get you the pipes on my
> shoulder, and I will do my best for you'. This was done, and he played so
> well as to win the prize.[82]

Robert Meldrum records of more recent times that

> on the night before the Northern Meeting at Inverness Malcolm
> Macpherson and Sandy MacDonald, Glentruim, got so engrossed in their
> own jollification that they forgot that they had to play at the first
> night's ball and did not arrive until the first reel had been danced.
> Their masters were so angry that they took them down to the station
> and sent them home, waiting to see the train had started. But the
> pipers got out at Forres and returned to the Northern Meeting to enjoy
> themselves in the crowd and laugh at the woes of their friends trying to

---

80 Merriam, pp. 125–6, 130, 133–9.
81 MacLeod, *MacCrimmons of Skye*, pp.70–1.
82 Alexander MacDonald, *Story and Song from Loch Ness-Side being principally Sketches of
Olden-Time Life in the Valley of the Great Glen of Scotland with particular reference to
Glenmoriston and Vicinity* (Inverness, 1914), pp.108–110.

tune their pipes and whispering and grumbling in secret about the incompetent judges.[83]

An article in the *Oban Times* relates how Willie Ross's mother, Mary Collie, then aged 14, had played the concertina all night at a Highland ball because the pipers were too drunk to play.[84] In some ways, then, it might be difficult, except in time of war, to present pipers as heroic figures because contemporary notions of the heroic included ancillary concepts like 'gentility' and 'respectability' to which they could not always be accommodated. There were complex motives, therefore, behind the urge to detach pipers from their music in order to preserve its fancied antique and heroic tone, to elevate them on the one hand into icons, and on the other to reduce them to the mere recipients of tradition instead of – what they actually were – its ultimate architects and trustees.

During the nineteenth century, the upper echelons of pipers gradually deserted the land and although the army was beginning to attract people of high ability such as Robert Meldrum and Willie Ross, general standards of playing there were low and the main focus of piping lay, as it had always lain, elsewhere.[85] There was a decreasing likelihood, therefore, that the view from the big house or the officers' mess would be either accurate or well-informed as the 20th century dawned. Statements about decline and fall in piping originating in such quarters should therefore be treated with caution.

With the spread of literacy, however, the idea of a fixed 'original' text, and its corollary that variety and change were signs of corruption and loss, brought power relations between the performer community and the mediating institutions to the point of crisis. The relative primacy of the printed text vis-a-vis oral testimony raised urgent questions about the nature and location of 'authority' in a way that could no longer be avoided and the closing decades of the nineteenth century were to witness much anxious debate.

---

83 'Pipe-Major Meldrum on Champions Past and Present', *OT*, 13/7/1940 p.3.

84 'Three Generations. Pipe-Major Ross's Family', *OT*, 22/8/1942, p.2. Archibald Campbell wrote of his teacher, Alexander Cameron, that 'Poor old Sandy Cameron's life was a long history of losing jobs, through his failing, until Allan Cameron found him practically begging on the streets and brought him into a haven of refuge at Achnacarry', Seton Gordon Papers, NLS, Acc.7451, General Correspondence, 1913–1926, 10/11/1925.

85 Archibald Campbell, 'The Highland Bagpipe'. Part II, *PT*, vol.14, no.11, August 1962, pp.6–9 (8–9): 'In many regiments within my own recollection the general level of individual performance was deplorably low. This was because the number of the bands had to be kept up. Enough ready made pipers could not be enlisted, and men had to be taken from the ranks and taught hurriedly and therefore taught badly. Such is still the situation to some extent . . .' The writer was born in 1877.

10

'Many a lonely hour I copied piobaireachds on the mountain side at Ronald's bidding': Literacy, Orality and the Manuscripts of Colin Cameron, John MacDougall Gillies and David Glen

The second half of the 19th century saw an increase in the importance of written rather than oral procedures, both in recording the repertoire of piping and also in teaching methods.

There has been little study of teaching and learning in piping. But amongst teachers there appears to have been a degree of specialism from a relatively early period. Some concentrated on giving a sound basic instruction, such as Donald Mór McLennan of Moy, with whom a number of important mid-Victorian players began their careers. Others, like Calum Pìobaire, seem to have concentrated on master-class teaching for people who were perhaps already well established as players. It seems to have been common for pipers to study with several different teachers and, while the process of instruction might often begin within the family, it was frequently completed outside it. The Report of the Judges of the Highland Society of Scotland at the Edinburgh competition of 1784 had commended 'John McGrigor from Fortingall Perthshire who with the additional merit of having already taught above 50 Military Pipers himself is the oldest of six sons taught by their father John McGrigor with above 90 other Pipers.'[1] Learning also went on during and after the period of formal instruction by studying the work of peers.

Ability was more important than consanguinity. Calum Pìobaire reportedly said 'I have three sons, and if I rolled them all into one, I still could not make a piper out of him'[2] and his most important pupil was John MacDonald of Inverness, the son of a friend. Almost as important as the individual personnel was the line of teaching, the descent of instruction through a succession of master players and teachers which students of traditional societies call 'genealogies of learning'.[3] These supplied the performer's credentials. They were the guarantee of his privileged access to authoritative teaching, an acknowledgement of the regard in which he usually held his instructors and – by extension – the people

---

1 Highland Society of Scotland Papers, Sederunt Book One, 'Report of the Judges named by a Committee of the Highland Society of Edinr. at request of the Highland Society of London relative to the Competition for Prizes given to the best performers on the Highland great Pipe determined at Edinburgh the 20 October 1784'. We should perhaps remind ourselves that this would be only a part of the total output of just one of the important teaching families in the generation following the '45 when piping was supposedly proscribed.

2 R. B. Nicol in conversation with the writer, Ballater, 27/3/1976.

3 Jack Goody, ed., *Literacy in Traditional Societies* (Cambridge, 1968), p.13.

who had taught them. Piping reached the present through a myriad of such genealogies of learning, great and small, and it is these which are referred to when the names of the MacKays, the MacDonalds, the Bruces, the MacKenzies, the Camerons and the Macphersons are invoked. The idea that such lines of instruction might also entail the existence of clearly-defined stylistic 'schools', however, with the implication that the piping world was divided into rival musical 'clans' – is a late one. It appears to have originated with General C. S. Thomason in *Ceol Mor* in 1900 and, although fairly frequently alluded to by later writers usually outside or on the fringes of the performer community, finds little support in the evidence.[4] Thomason's own papers make it clear that there was not a uniform 'Cameron' style during the second half of the 19th century. On the contrary, there seems to have been a widely diffused common idiom in which all good players were schooled. John MacDonald, who had been taught by his father, Alexander, and had studied with Alexander Cameron as well as the Macphersons and was steeped in the playing of George and Angus MacDonald of Morar, stated that all the old players approached the music in a broadly similar fashion.[5] A good 19th century training provided a broad interpretative trajectory within which the cultivation of an individual style was a valued characteristic. People taught by the same teacher, even members of the same family, would have subtle differences from each other, as we shall see.

There is little direct evidence about the teaching process before the end of the 19th century, but it appears that women were quite frequently involved.[6] John Johnston tells of an Elizabeth MacCrimmon, who had been courted by a pupil of her father's, and had come with him when he became piper to the laird of Coll:

---

4 See below, Chapter 11. The present writer found only four references to the 'Cameron School' or the 'Macpherson School' in the *Oban Times* during the first half of the 20th century, one of them from Thomason: see 'The Piobaireachd Society and the Cameron School of Piping', 29/09/1906, p.3. See also 'Piobaireachd Playing', from Angus Macpherson, 17/1/1920, p.3, and 'Piobaireachd', from Charles Bannatyne, 7/2/1920, p.3. Lieut. John McLennan pointed out at an early stage how dubious the idea was: 'not only do the pupils of the one school argue with the other as to the proper setting of a tune, but the pupils of the same school do not agree': 'Piobaireachd Society's Music', 14/5/1910, p.3.

5 'The Piping Reminiscences of John MacDonald M.B.E.' *OT*, 4/4/1942, p.5. His pupil R. B. Nicol said that MacDonald laid great stress on this point: 'to all intents and purposes, they all played the same way, making allowance, of course, for little individual preferences', R. B. Nicol in conversation with the writer, Ballater, 28/6/1976. The 'Reminiscences' were assembled at Inveran in 1941 in consultation with Angus Macpherson and writer and naturalist Seton Gordon: see Seton Gordon Papers, NLS, Acc.5640/2 (1) 'Some notes of a conversation Seton Gordon had with John MacDonald on Saturday May 3rd 1941'; and correspondence, 20/11/41, f.27.

6 For information on how the instructional sections in Donald MacDonald and Angus MacKay's books may have been used, see Frans Buisman, 'A Stock Tune in Older Piobaireachd Teaching and a device of Practising and Instruction' in *PT*, vol. 40, no. 7, April 1988, pp.44–9.

Duncan Rankin, of the Mull pipers, went to study a while with 'Donald Ruadh McCrimmon'; another pupil from Morar happened to be there also, and both appear to have been smitten by the charms of McCrimmon's daughter, named Bess, or likely Elizabeth. The Morar swain, when well learned, went home to his own country, but suddenly returned with a friend to bring matters to a point. The lady understood their errand at once, and slipped to the other end of the house, took up her father's bagpipes, and played 'Sann a bha 'n t-sheotrich air Bodich na Morthir', [there was naught but sloth amongst the carles of Morar] a tune well known to the young man, and at once understood, with its import on that occasion, and thinking it was MacCrimmon himself who played it as a broad hint, he told his companion that their errand was useless, and immediately departed without saying a word about their business. Rankin married her shortly thereafter, and came to the island of Muck, where he was piper to that family for a long time, and when the family removed to Coll, he came there with them, and was there the remainder of his days – both of them are buried in Killinaig, in that island. She could play the pipes as well as her father's pupils, and on one occasion in Grisipool House, Coll, during her husband's temporary illness, played in the passage during dinner, and none of the gentlemen present distinguished any difference, though her husband was one of the greatest pipers in the Highlands in his time, having come through both the great seminaries in Mull and Skye, with the highest proficiency . . .When her husband, who was rather quick tempered, found fault with his pupils about their playing of particularly difficult portions of tunes, would abruptly retire and leave off his tuition in anger, she would take her distaff, and lift the necessary fingers on it, showing them to perfection where they lacked.[7]

A woman was also responsible for some part at least of John Bàn MacKenzie's tuition, according to his pupil Duncan Ross:

Many a story did old John Mackenzie tell me when I was turning his lathe for him [presumably when making pipes] and learning music with him. He was four score when he died and that is more than twenty years ago. It must be nearly a hundred years since he was in Raasay, learning 'Ceòl mòr', great music, from Mackay . . . they only played Ceòl mòr on the pipes, battle tunes, and laments, and salutes, and such like. They had cattle in one end of their house. Mackay used to turn his back to the pupils, and play the tunes.

7 'Dr. K. N. MacDonald and Bagpipe Playing', from John Johnston, *OT*, 12/9/1896, p.3. See also, 'The MacCrimmon Ancestry', from 'Fionn', 30/4/1910, p.3 and 21/5/1910, p.3, querying the chronology for Elizabeth MacCrimmon and suggesting that she must have been a daughter of an earlier generation than Donald Roy's; and John Johnston's replies, supplying further information and dates, 14/5/1910, p.3, and 28/5/ 1910, p.3.

Mackay's sister used to sit by the fire, and dictate the words of Canntaireachd, and sing them as the piper played.[8]

Pipe-Major William Ross (1878–1966) for many years instructor of the Army Class at Edinburgh Castle, and one of the most famous of 20th century players, was largely taught by his mother, Mary Collie.[9]

The apparently vigorous survival of oral methods of instruction until the very end of the 19th century is attested by John MacDonald of Inverness (1865–1953), whose reminiscences were published in the *Oban Times* in 1942. MacDonald came from a family of professional pipers, his father, Sandy, being piper to the Earl of Fife, and his uncle, William, to the Prince of Wales. In the first three decades of the 20th century he enjoyed an outstandingly successful competitive career, and was for a number of years closely involved with the Piobaireachd Society as adviser and instructor. He made the first commercial recordings of piobaireachd, and the tracks he cut for Columbia in the winter of 1926–7 of 'The Lament for the Children', 'The Lament for Donald Ban MacCrimmon', 'The Lament for Patrick og MacCrimmon', 'The Little Spree', and 'MacCrimmon's Sweetheart' – although the tunes had to be abridged to fit the discs, and suggest that by this date his style had been influenced by the Piobaireachd Society's published settings – make it clear that he was a very fine player.[10] He received his initial teaching from his father, and from

---

8 Campbell, *Canntaireachd*, pp.33–4.
9 I am indebted for this information to William Ross's grand-daughter, Mrs. Lesley Ross Alexander. Mary Collie could still play the chanter at the age of 82 and was noted in 1934 as having attended the Northern Meeting every year since 1892: Seton Gordon Papers, NLS, Acc.5640/2 (1), 12/10/1934. Piping in Rogart is said to owe much to four MacLeod sisters from Mull: see Mackenzie, *Piping Traditions*, p. 258. Bessie Brown, sister of R. U. Brown of Balmoral, was also an active and successful teacher. She was fiercely proud of her ability to build a sound technique from scratch, and used to pour jocular scorn on her brother and his friend R. B. Nicol, who did most of their teaching at advanced level: 'Them? Teach pipin'? They nivver taught a piper in their lives. They're jist finishers o' pipers, french polishers. Sittin' at the fire croonin' piobaireachd. Tchach!' Bessie Brown in conversation with the writer, Banchory, August 1975.
10 See 'Record Performer. Piobaireachd and Gramophone. Pipe-Major John MacDonald', *OT*, 26/3/1927, p.5: since the recording session had been organised by the Piobaireachd Society, MacDonald may have been deliberately playing in their style. The above biographical information is partly from R. B. Nicol and R. U. Brown, pupils of John MacDonald, in conversation with the writer. See also 'Famous Pipe-Major's Death. John MacDonald, M.B.E., Inverness. An Appreciation. By Seton Gordon', *OT*, 13/6/1953, p.3; the written sources for John MacDonald's life are rather scattered, but further information will be found in Macpherson, *Highlander Looks Back*, pp. 71–6; see also the following sources in *Piping Times*: 'The Late Pipe-Major John MacDonald M.B.E. of Inverness An Appreciation By Col. J. P. Grant of Rothiemurchus' vol. 5, no. 10, July 1953, pp.4–6; 'John MacDonald of Inverness M.B.E.' by Seton Gordon, vol.14, no.5, February 1962, pp.6–7; 'Some Memories of John MacDonald' by Pipe Major Donald MacLeod, vol.14, no.6, March 1962, pp.6–7;

Calum Pìobaire's son John. The master approved: 'You have made him good', he said, 'now I will make him great'. John MacDonald considered the time he spent studying with Malcolm Macpherson, and the oral methods the latter employed, as crucial to his development as a player:

> I received most of my tuition in piobaireachd from Calum MacPherson, at Cat Lodge, Badenoch. Calum was easily the best player of piobaireachd I have ever known. He hardly ever played March, Strathspey and Reel; only piobaireachd and Jigs. Each morning, he used to play Jigs on the chanter while breakfast was being got ready – he would sit on a stool near the peat fire as he played. But his heart was in piobaireachd. He excelled in heavy low hand tunes. It was inspiring to hear him play 'My King has Landed in Moidart'; another grand tune of his was 'Cillechriosd'; I never heard anyone play 'Donald Dughal MacKay' in a way that appealed to me so much. Calum had very strong fingers, and I never once heard him missing Crunluath gracenotes. As I have said Calum played a few Jigs on the practice chanter before breakfast, I can see him now, with his old jacket and his leather sporran, sitting on a stool while the porridge was being brought to the boil. After breakfast he would take his barrow to the peat moss, cut a turf, and build up the fire with wet peat for the day. He would then sit down beside me, take away all books and pipe music, then sing in his own canntaireachd the ground and different variations of the particular piobaireachd he wished me to learn.
>
> It was from these early associations of Malcolm Macpherson that I realised that piobaireachd must be transmitted by song from one piper to another in order to get the soul of it; the lights and shades. Most of the piobaireachd players of the present day rely on the score, but you cannot express in musical notation what you would like to. It is really impossible . . . Present – day piping is in danger of losing its soul and expression, its sentiment. The tendency now is to play with the hands, not with the brain, and the transmission by canntaireachd is now almost lost . . .[11]

Of course this is a picture of self-consciously traditional instruction deliberately resisting the encroachment of writing and print, and it seems clear that during

cont'd 'More Memories of John MacDonald', by Donald MacLeod, vol.14, no.8, May 1962, pp.14–15; Frank M. Richardson, 'Memories of John MacDonald of Inverness', in *Proceedings of the Piobaireachd Society Conference*, 1985, pp. 1–15; 'Interpretation', in MacNeill and Richardson, pp. 66–107; and Raymond Eagle, *Seton Gordon The Life and Times of a Highland Gentleman* (Moffat, 1991), pp. 177–8, 229–31. See also Fairrie, pp.179–80. The most recent account is in Mackenzie, *Piping Traditions*, pp.1–13, note, however, that John MacDonald was not unmarried, as stated, but was twice married and widowed; and he died on the 6th, not the 8th of June 1953; also the piper captioned as 'Robert Reid' in the photograph of MacDonald's funeral on p.12, is Robert U. Brown.

11 MacDonald, 'Piping Reminiscences', *op.cit.*

the later Victorian period methods centring on these were steadily gaining ground.[12] Everything depended on the training and outlook of the teacher, and his perception of the pupils' needs. Robert Meldrum, who was also taught by Calum Pìobaire (amongst others), described a teaching regime in which canntaireachd was only one of a number of instructional techniques: 'I was not taught by means of it,' he said, 'nor did I teach by means of it myself. But it was always used in teaching as a help. The fingering was shown, and the teacher sang, each in his own way, the tune he was teaching. It is almost indispensable for correct timing and phrasing'. He went on to add, 'In my young days publications were scarce and dear; and we did much manuscript work'.[13]

John Grant, author of *Piobaireachd: Its Origin and Construction* (Edinr., 1915), and a frequent contributor to the *Oban Times* on piping subjects during the early decades of the twentieth century, had studied in his youth with Ronald MacKenzie for a period of about seven years, and his training reflected the latter's strenuous belief in the virtues of musical literacy. MacKenzie was a thorough and painstaking teacher, starting his pupils on the chanter, then moving them on to a goose (a practice chanter attached to a bag with a blow-pipe, but no drones, sometimes used to ease the transition between the practice chanter and the full pipes). He taught music theory and was keen on writing tunes in manuscript as a means of mastering them. 'To finger the notes', he said, 'was after all a parrot style of memorising; but to write them separately and minutely was to acquire an experience in the art of theory and the creation of pipe music which no other thing in the world of music could supply'. Grant added, a little ruefully perhaps, 'Many a lonely hour I copied piobaireachds on the mountain side at Ronald's bidding'.[14]

Such scenes must have occurred many times during the later 19th and early 20th century, as written and printed sources began increasingly to influence the tradition. The trend is marked by growing numbers of manuscript collections created by pipers like Ewen Henderson, Duncan Campbell, Colin Cameron,

---

12 It is clear that John MacDonald regarded certain publications of light music with affection: 'I had several of these small books and like many others, lent them and never had them returned. There was a small cardboard covered book printed by Alex Glen, Angus MacKay, Gunn and some others of that day, which was not elaborate enough for the later players but would be interesting to many today. It was from Angus MacKay I discovered 'Hope Vere'. I heard the late Willie McLennan play it at Kingussie Games when I was a lad of 19 and it haunted me for years until I came across this small book which I looked upon as a gold piece.' Letter to Dr. W. M. MacPhail, 14/12/1939, in J. H. Shone, ed., *Some Letters of Archibald Campbell of Kilberry 1935–1949* (Cockenzie, 1980), p.56.

13 Meldrum, 'Reminiscences', *OT*, 20/7/1940, p.5, 16/11/1940, p.3.

14 'Famous Piper of the Past', from John Grant, *OT*, 27/6/1936, p.3. See also 'Fifty-Two Years Piping Record. Mr John Grant. Edinburgh', 20/3/1948, p.5. Even wealthy amateurs found key texts like Angus MacKay's book difficult to come by. The only way the youthful C. S. Thomason could get a copy during the 1850s was to borrow one and transcribe it: 'Honouring General Thomason. The Author of "Ceol Mor"', 10/7/1909, p.5.

Donald MacKay (the younger), John MacDougall Gillies, Uilleam Ross, D. S. MacDonald and David Glen.[15] Sometimes, as in Henderson's case, these were fairly modest affairs, informal, private documents, perhaps containing tunes or settings which were new, or outside the normal range of the compiler's repertoire. Henderson served with the 1st Scots Guards, 1853–74, and his manuscript contains 28 piobaireachds and assorted light music.[16] In other cases, such as Uilleam Ross's (85 piobaireachds) and for much of its length Colin Cameron's manuscript (84 piobaireachds), we encounter substantial, highly finished texts either used, or probably intended to be used, as a basis for publication. With David Glen (191 piobaireachds) we see an attempt to give a comprehensive account of the tradition in the half-century following the death of Angus MacKay.

As the games circuit grew, the demand for music suitable for competitive purposes became more diverse. Ceòl beag, the light music of the pipes, comprising marches, strathspeys, reels and jigs began to assume a more important role in the repertoire of the professional piper. Since the medium helped to shape the content of the material transmitted, the spread of musical literacy and the writing technologies which accompanied it began to affect musical structure. This was particularly evident in ceòl beag, where the rise of the written score was accompanied by the emergence of a new form, the 'competition march', which rapidly established itself as an important genre. The traditional quickstep seems to have been in existence in a form suitable for playing on the pipes for at least a century.[17] In order to make it sufficiently formidable as a test in competition, technical demand had to be raised. This meant the introduction of elaborate variations on the basic theme, requiring high levels of dexterity to execute, an increased use of rich and complex ornament, and a considerable enlargement of the form itself, the typical two-part format with eight bars to the part growing to four, or possibly even six or eight parts. It took nearly two generations for these developments to achieve their stable modern form, but the basic formula was already in place by the 1850s.

Eclectic borrowing from other areas of traditional instrumental music may have

15 Ewen Henderson MS, Glasgow University Library, MS Gen. 1458; Duncan Campbell MS, formerly in the possession of the Piobaireachd Society, now lost – see A. G. Kenneth, 'Re-Publishing Piobaireachd', in *PT*, vol.24, no.10, July 1972, pp.8–11; Colin Cameron MS., National Library of Scotland, MS 3745; Donald MacKay MS., GUL, MS Gen. 1455; John MacDougall Gillies MS, GUL, MS Gen. 1457; William Ross, MS., NLS MS 3040; D. S. MacDonald MS., NLS MS 3110; David Glen MS., NLS MS 22120.

16 For a biographical note with portrait, see F. Maurice, *The History of the Scots Guards from the Creation of the Regiment to the Eve of the Great War* (2 vols., Lond., 1932), ii, 53, 120.

17 See 'Competition Marches', from 'Perthshire Highlander', *OT*, 16/3/1940, p.3; same, from Archibald Campbell of Kilberry, 30/3/1940, p.3; and 'Pipe Music in Highland Regiments', from 'Piobair', 13/4/1940, p.3. For a general account of the development of light music for competitive purposes see Cannon, *Highland Bagpipe*, pp.134–43. There is a useful note on Hugh MacKay (1801–1864) one of the pioneers of the competition march in 'Notices of Pipers', *PT*, vol.24, no.5, February 1972, p.18.

been responsible for the speed with which this happened. Pipers were (and are) frequently multi-instrumentalists, and a degree of expertise on the fiddle was fairly common amongst them. Even where this was not so, they still participated in an inherited common popular musical idiom to which fiddlers had made a substantial contribution.[18] The practice of building extended conventional variations on traditional airs was well established in the fiddle repertoire. As soon as the basic intellectual leap had been made – that although it possessed a much narrower compass, the Highland pipe could support broadly similar musical structures – a 'competition march' repertoire could rapidly be achieved since much of the necessary musical vocabulary was already in place.[19] There had long been dialogue between the different branches of the popular instrumental tradition. Pipe music had influenced the 'long variation sets' favoured by fiddlers in the 18th century. Now procedures developed by fiddle players returned to enrich the music of the pipe. Here is the air and two variations of the famous old tune 'The East Neuk of Fife' in an 18th century fiddle setting:

'The East Neuk of Fife', David Johnson, *Scottish Fiddle Music in the 18th Century*, pp.92-3

Variation 10 is an earlier version of what became the final part of one of the classic competition marches, 'Highland Wedding'.[20]

18 Henderson, *Highland Soldier*, records the 42nd. trooping home from Halifax, Nova Scotia in 1852: '. . . the Band played after Mess also the Pipes and old McLean the Pipe-Major danced and played the fiddle like a five year old.' p.226. John MacDonald of Inverness played the contents of a new collection of light music for R. B. Nicol and R. U. Brown on the fiddle because he did not think it would be proper to do so on the pipes, since the book had not yet been published. (R. B. Nicol in conversation with the writer, Ballater, 30 July 1975).

19 See Johnson, *Scottish Fiddle Music*, *passim*, but especially. pp. 4, 6–7, 15, 53–5, 66–7, 119–24.

20 *Pipe-Major W. Ross's Collection of Highland Bagpipe Music* (5 vols., Lond., 1923–1950),

Ewen Henderson's setting of one outstanding early competition tune, Angus MacKay's 'The Balmoral Royal Highlanders March' shows how these procedures were used:[21]

The Balmoral Royal Highlanders March. By Angus MacKay. Copy Mr. Lamont. From Ewen Henderson's MS. f.1

cont'd   i, 22–3. The tune appears to owe its modern form to Donald Cameron: see Piobaireachd Society Papers, NLS, Acc. 9103/21, Music of Colin Cameron 19th-20th century, assembled by A. G. Kenneth, for a setting here called 'Lord Breadalbane's March' docketed 'Donald Cameron Brahan Castle 1862. Noted by C.[olin] Cam.[eron] Coposed [sic] by D[onald] Cam.[eron] B.[rahan] Castle 1856.' This may be compared with the much shorter and cruder version in Angus MacKay's MSS., NLS, MS 3755, f.27, where it appears as the 'Breadalbane Fencibles' Quickstep'.

21 Glasgow University Library MS Gen. 1458, f.1. It is marked 'Copy Mr.

Such methods permitted the simultaneous co-existence, as autonomous entities, of large numbers of sometimes quite narrowly differentiated compositions, which in an oral context might be fleeting realisations of a flowing continuum of related ideas. Only musical literacy and writing technology could make this fixity and definition possible. There was a further effect on compositional technique as visual elements became more important, so that the 'shape' of a tune on the page began to contribute to its aesthetic, tempering the purely acoustic considerations which prevailed previously. Finally the concept of 'mastery' came to include the ability to understand and manipulate the symbols of written music before one could enter fully into possession of the tradition, as we see with Ronald MacKenzie and his pupils. Indeed, this can be seen developing within a generation in a single important family.

'Mr Donald Cameron's Music Book, Brahan Castle. Presented from Alexander Corbit; as a token of respect, May 5th 1859' contains 84 piobaireachds and is one of the most important Victorian manuscripts. It came into the possession of John MacDonald of Inverness along with other papers of the Cameron family in 1949, was bought by the Piobaireachd Society for £5.00, and immediately deposited in the National Library of Scotland.[22] The first three tunes are notated by Donald Cameron in a rather tentative hand, the remainder in a bold and fluent script by his eldest son Colin, piper to the Duke of Fife. The last tune in the book is dated 'Nov.22nd 1869.'

The collection falls into three sections and offers a fascinating record of a distinctive family style drawing eclectically upon earlier notational systems and showing the influence of a number of identifiable written sources. The largest of these, the first 51 pieces in the collection, appears to be drawn largely from Cameron family tradition and includes 'The Groat', 'The Lament for the Union', 'The Sound of the Waves against the Castle of Duntroon', 'Beloved Scotland I leave thee Gloomy', 'The Lament for Donald of Laggan', 'The Unjust Incarceration', 'The End of the Great Bridge', 'Lament for the Only Son', 'Lament for Donald Ban MacCrimmon', 'Scarce of Fishing', 'The Blue Ribbon', 'The Battle

---

cont'd Lamont', presumably William Lamont of Inverey. As this will have been the latest stuff from Deeside where to some extent the form was pioneered, Lamont, a Deeside man, will probably have been its channel. For details of the Lamont Manuscript, now lost, see Roderick D. Cannon, *General Preface to the Piobaireachd Society Collection* (Glasg., 1997), p.14; see also Kenneth, 'Re-Publishing Piobaireachd', pp.8–11.
   Nineteenth century pipers frequently used conventional mordent or trill signs to indicate doublings and throws. Often, with those of more casual hand, it is difficult to tell exactly which was intended, and it was always an approximation in any case. In cases of doubt I have used the standard trill sign throughout in the musical examples which follow in this and subsequent chapters.

22 Piobaireachd Society Papers NLS, Acc. 9103/9 Correspondence 1929–1950, 11/5/1949, 30/5/1949, 11/6/1949. The manuscript was 'Deposited on indefinite loan' on 15 July 1949 by Archibald Campbell and does not appear to have been actively used in the preparation of vols. 9–10 of the Society's second series subsequently edited by him.

of Waternish', 'The Old Woman's Lullaby', 'The Lament for the Children', 'The Big Spree', 'The Battle of the Pass of Crieff', 'MacCrimmon's Sweetheart', 'In Praise of Morag', and 'The Laird of Anapool's Lament'.

Next comes a section transcribed from the 'Seaforth MS' of Angus MacKay, a collection of eleven tunes made in 1854 ostensibly 'for the private use' of Col. Keith Stewart-Mackenzie of Seaforth, but which came into the possession of the Cameron family and was amongst the papers acquired by the Piobaireachd Society in 1949. MacKay had supplied these tunes with full volume and page number references to his own manuscript collection and these are reproduced in the Cameron transcript. Each bears the additional words 'Copyright Colin Cameron', as if perhaps at one stage he had intended these first two sections of the manuscript to form the basis of a published work. The tunes here include 'Weighing from Land', 'The Lament for Colin Roy MacKenzie', 'The Blind Piper's Obstinacy', and 'The Lament for the Departure of King James'.

Finally there is a section of 30 tunes which apparently derive from the manuscripts of Duncan Campbell of Foss. These are written in a less finished style, and contain amongst others 'The King's Taxes', 'The Daughter's Lament', 'The MacDonald's Salute', and 'The Lament for the Castle of Dunyveg'.

As might be expected, the tunes in the Cameron manuscript are steeped in the MacKay tradition. Donald Cameron's teacher, John Bàn MacKenzie had been a pupil of John MacKay and Donald had himself studied with John MacKay's sons, and counted Angus as a friend. Yet it is noticeable that while the last two sections of the manuscript follow Angus MacKay's notational conventions, the opening 'Cameron' section of the manuscript frequently departs from these, as in the following example where expressed values for introductory notes are avoided in favour of gracenote clusters more redolent of the MacDonald style. This seems further confirmation that Angus MacKay's notational practice did not carry all before it in the generation following the publication of *Ancient Piobaireachd*:

Cumha na Mairbh Lament for the Dead. Angus MacKay's MS, i 64

Lament for the Dead. Cumah na Marbh. Composed by Professor MacArthur. Colin Cameron's MS f.13

Colin Cameron also develops the tune differently from Angus MacKay, doubling the thumb variation where MacKay had a singling only, and in general terms his is the musically superior setting. He writes out his later movements in full, as well, avoiding MacKay-type contractions, although his father, Donald, had used them.

The tune nowadays known as 'The Daughter's Lament' (ff.127–8), appears in the Cameron manuscript twice, under different titles. In the section of material from Duncan Campbell, it bears the 'Daughter's Lament' title, as in Angus MacKay's manuscript (i, ff.123–4) to which it is thought Duncan Campbell had access. In the 'family' section of Colin Cameron's manuscript, however, the tune appears as 'General Clavers's Lament', as it does in Donald MacDonald's manuscript ('Lament for the death of Genl. Cleaver. Cumhadh Chleibhar' ff.277–282) which is clearly the source of the Cameron text. The only difference is that MacDonald's second variation (in which the ground receives its final elaboration) is omitted which, as is frequently the case with the deft and tactful Cameron stylings, would make good musical sense. The piece may have been copied from a floating transcript, but it seems more likely that Donald Cameron had access to Donald MacDonald's MSS when he was in Edinburgh for the Highland Society of London's competitions, and had copied the piece there. This would in turn suggest that whilst Colin Cameron's manuscript may have contained transcripts of material hitherto circulating orally, it was certainly in part a synopsis of earlier written sources in the possession of the Cameron family and its circle:

Lament for the death of Genl. Cleaver. Cumhadh Chleibhar. Donald MacDonald's MS. f.277

General Clavers's Lament. Colin Cameron's MS. f.30

It is noticeable that in tunes which are common to both Angus MacKay's and Colin Cameron's manuscripts, the latter is usually more explicit rhythmically. MacKay often elects for long strings of even quavers, but in Cameron most things are dotted and cut, giving a more precise guide to the nuances of expression:

Cumha na Suipeirach Big. Lament for the little Supper. Angus MacKay's MS. ii.16.

An t'shuipear bheag. The Little Supper. Colin Cameron's MS. f.52

Cameron's version of 'The Lament for the Only Son' ('Cumha an aona mhic'. ff.36–8), while practically identical to MacKay in the ground, has a thumb variation unlike either of the settings in MacDonald or MacKay, and an end-note – 'The Taorluadh and Crunluadh can be played into four or five parts. Colin Cameron.' – suggesting that the way a tune was developed still lay within the performer's province in the middle years of the nineteenth century. 'Millbank's Salute', (f.72) a MacKay tune, composed by Angus's father, likewise shows individual differences in timing, as well as being judiciously abbreviated by discarding Angus MacKay's tripling movement. Even so, the ground is probably still developed beyond its potential, a tendency of John MacKay compositions, at least as recorded by Angus. Where there are possible sources in MacDonald and MacKay, therefore, there are numerous subtle differences in the Cameron versions. Their settings are closely related to both these earlier strands of tradition but are ultimately independent of either.[23] Indeed the stylishness of Colin Cameron's settings sometimes makes Angus MacKay seem prolix and heavy-handed by comparison.

The range of expressive nuance in the Cameron manuscript is also fairly striking. For example, Donald Cameron uses two different double echo beats on A in the space of three tunes:

Eallach from Catherine's Lament, f.1   Gairm from The Groat, f.3

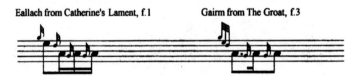

The manuscript also sheds interesting light on the timing of ECA or EBA 'cadences' or concluding movements. Although it was stated by the

---

23 Compare for example 'The End of the Great Bridge', ff.34–5, with MacKay MS. i, 186–8, and MacDonald, *Ancient Martial Music*, pp.111–15.

Piobaireachd Society's editor, Archibald Campbell, claiming the authority of the Cameron family, that these should be played as even quavers or crotchets, this is not supported by the Cameron manuscript, where such movements are expressed in flexible ways to achieve an appropriate rhythmical fit with the surrounding musical context.[24] For example, in the tune entitled 'The British Army' ('An t'arm Dearg'. ff.26–7, nowadays generally known as 'The Red Speckled Bull'), the timing varies from a characteristically semi-quaver/dotted quaver/crotchet pattern to crotchet/quaver/quaver, or quaver/quaver/crotchet pattern as follows:

Concluding movements from The British Army. An t'arm Dearg. f.25

The British Army. An t'arm Dearg. Ground: line 1

The British Army. An t'arm Dearg. Doubg. of var 1st

Master players were expected to have a distinctive style and piobaireachd versions were often identified as 'D. Cameron's' or 'D. Campbell's set' or suchlike. Similarly, Sandy MacDonald, the father of John MacDonald of Inverness, was acknowledged as a source in Uilleam Ross's *Collection*.[25]

To give more permanent expression to that most elusive of things, an

24 See James Campbell, ed., *Sidelights on the Kilberry Book of Ceol Mor Notes on instruction received by Archibald Campbell of Kilberry* (Glasg., 1984), p.11.

25 See, for example, reference to 'Colin Cameron's setting' of a tune in 'Puirt-a-Beul', *OT*, 30/3/1901, p.3; see also *Ross's Collection*, pp.92, 103, 104.

individual 'style', may have been a powerful inducement to master pipers to expend the considerable time and labour necessary to compile a written account of their personal repertoire, bearing in mind that a good player would have at least a hundred piobaireachds, perhaps double that in exceptional cases. Work on recording tunes might take place in intensive bursts, with considerable gaps – perhaps of years – and a big manuscript might be the work of a lifetime. John MacDougall Gillies's piobaireachd manuscript book, which contains more than seventy tunes, was begun in the winter of 1879 and was still being added to well into the 20th century. Like Colin Cameron's manuscript it is highly finished and precise throughout most of its length; the tunes are signed and dated, with the earlier titles in a beautifully executed 'Celtic' script.

Many tunes in this source occur also in Angus MacKay's manuscript. Whether MacDougall Gillies had direct access to it is not clear, but if he had, then the material was comprehensively re-set during transcription. Here, for example, is the first line of the ground of 'Glengarry's March', firstly from MacKay, and then from Gillies:

Cill Chriosda. Glengary's March. Angus MacKay's MS. i, 169

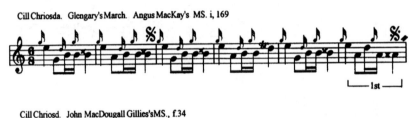

Cill Chriosd. John MacDougall Gillies's MS., f.34

Gillies's implied 2/4 timing gives a more plausible feel to the tune in rhythmical terms. His introductory Es – if they were intended to be played as timed – are considerably shorter than MacKay's, forcing the accent on to the Gs and As at the beginning of bars and giving a more satisfyingly dramatic treatment than MacKay to the alternation of G and A with B and D, which lies at the heart of the melody.

It is believed that MacDougall Gillies did have access to the manuscripts of Duncan Campbell of Foss, Peter Reid and Colin Cameron. He was heavily influenced by the Camerons but was not dependent on them for his expressive vocabulary, having many little stylistic touches of his own, as we can see in his treatment of 'MacCrimmon's Sweetheart'. He had two attempts at this, the second likely to be preferred to the first as being less square and deliberate, and with a better sense of line. Although it resembles Colin Cameron's setting, it is not identical:

MacCrummen's Sweetheart. John MacDougall Gillies's MS., version 1, f.50

MacCrummen's Sweetheart. John MacDougall Gillies's MS., version 2, f.50

MacCrummin's Sweetheart. A Mhuil Duin. Colin Cameron's MS., f.86

Delicacy of pointing and subtly varied expression is characteristic of MacDougall Gillies's style. We note how he varies the accent in 'Mary's Praise', with the introductory Es given different lengths, the little cut down to B at the beginning of bar six in the ground, and again in the interesting syncopation at the start of bar two of the doubling of the thumb variation with its contrasted timing at the beginning of bar six:

Mary's Praise. John MacDougall Gillies MS., f.52

Doubling of Thumb Variation

It is important to note that a whole palette of expressive nuance was available to the Victorian masters in a way that had ceased to be to their successors a century later, as the spread of the fixed printed text undermined the creative autonomy of the performer community.

One indication of the fullness with which the tradition had been translated into written form (and of how relentlessly thorough Angus MacKay had been) is that only a relative handful of tunes – largely new and recent compositions – are recorded in the later Victorian manuscripts which had not already appeared in earlier sources. The amount of shared material in later nineteenth century collections shows that Victorian masters enjoyed access either directly or indirectly to all the major existing sources. Written scores had become important not just for recording the repertoire but for transmitting it as well. Robert Meldrum gives an example of its working:

> I have already mentioned my friendship with Pipe-Major Duncan Campbell. That friendship was responsible for the adding of two good pibrochs to our collection – 'Lament for Captain MacDougall' and 'Hey for the Old Pipes'. Duncan lent me a roll of tunes possessed by his predecessor at Taymouth – John Bain Mackenzie. I copied out these two and sent them to MacDougall Gillies. I returned the roll to Duncan and it went with his son to America'.[26]

Written scores formed a highway of communication for a very real musical community, until their acquisition by wealthy gentlemen amateurs during the twentieth century removed them from circulation and closed what had been an open door.

David Glen's manuscript collection (NLS. MS. 22120) was compiled during the opening decade of the twentieth century and contains some 191 tunes. Glen was a pipe-maker and music publisher, very much in the mould of Donald MacDonald. But he worked in a more favourable commercial environment as technological change made printing and publishing cheaper and the Victorian habit of serial publication increased the availability of otherwise expensive texts. He was born in Edinburgh in 1853, a son of the bagpipe maker Alexander Glen, and was taught by Gilbert Gordon, piper to Lord Panmure and later keeper of the Black Bull Inn at Perth. Although he is not thought to have competed, David Glen was apparently an able player, bracketed by contemporaries along with John MacDougall Gillies, John MacColl, and John MacDonald of Inverness.[27] He was also the most prolific publisher of bagpipe music in nineteenth century Scotland. His titles included *David Glen's Collection of Highland Bagpipe Music* (Edinr., 1876 – 1900) which was the defining collection of ceòl beag of its period, and one of the musical treasures of Victorian Scotland. Its seventeen parts eventually contained more than a thousand tunes. *Highland Bagpipe Music* was attractively produced, well-printed on good-quality paper, and although the

---

26 'More Reminiscences by Pipe-Major Meldrum', *OT*, 16/11/1940, p.3.
27 See 'The Piobaireachd Society's Publication', from Charles Bannatyne, *OT*, 19/3/1910, p.3.

complete cloth-bound edition cost 20/-, or 11/- each if bought in two parts, the separate volumes with their stylish paper jackets could be acquired for a distinctly affordable 1/- each. These sold well over eighty thousand copies and remained in print for nearly a century. Indeed the present writer was able to buy one of the fourth thousand of the fourth part in Fraserburgh in 1956. A tutor was issued in 1881, uniform with this edition, which itself sold more than twenty-five thousand copies during the century-or-so that it remained available and in the face of stiff competition from at least three similar publications. *A Collection of Ancient Piobaireachd or Highland Bagpipe Music. (A number of which are now published for the first time) To which are prefixed tables showing the fingering required for producing the grace notes and cuttings. Carefully arranged and revised by David Glen,* began to issue from the press in 1880. Part One was priced at 10/- and contained a dozen tunes. Amongst those hitherto unpublished were 'The Battle of Waternish', 'The Lament for MacDonald's Tutor', 'King James VI's Salute', 'Campbell of Cawdor's Salute', and 'The Lament for the Old Sword'. Parts Two and Three appeared in 1895 and 1896, respectively, and added 'Captain Donald MacKenzie's Lament', 'MacLean of Coll's Lament', 'The MacIntyres' Salute', 'The Battle of the North Inch of Perth', and 'Clan Chattan's Gathering' to the published repertoire. By 1907 Glen's *Collection of Ancient Piobaireachd* extended to seven parts, containing one hundred tunes altogether and covering the classic heart of the repertoire. These were available either as a single bound volume with historic, biographical and legendary notes to the tunes by 'Fionn' (journalist and Celtic scholar Henry Whyte) at £1.15/-, or in seven separate parts at 4/- a part. The collection was also available in single sheets each containing one tune priced at 1/-. Fionn's notes could be bought separately at 3/-.

In 1900, Glen issued *The Music of the Clan MacLean*, following an approach by the Clan MacLean Association 'as to the possibility of my collecting and publishing the Music of the MacLeans'. He already had in his possession 'a good many of this Clan's pibrochs not hitherto published . . .' and the collection was to contain 'a number of pibrochs very little known, which now appear in print for the first time'. He noted that 'I have also to tender my special thanks to Mr. John Johnston, Isle of Coll, who journeyed specially to Glasgow, in order that I might write down from his playing, several tunes belonging to this Clan which were, so far as I could learn, only known to himself, and which his ancestors had learned from the Rankins, who were the hereditary Pipers of the MacLeans of Coll and Duart.'[28] The volume included versions of 'Hector MacLean's Warning', 'The Lament for John Garve MacLean', 'MacLean of Coll Putting his Foot on the Neck of his Enemy', 'MacLean of Coll's War Galley', 'MacLean of Lochbuie's Lament', 'The MacLeans' Blue Ribbon', 'The Lament for Sir Lachlan MacLean', 'The Lament for Hector Roy MacLean of the Battles', and 'John Garve MacLean of Coll's Broadsword'. The edition was produced with the active support of Colin Cameron and General C. S. Thomason. His final large work

28 Glen, *Music of the Clan MacLean* (Edinr., 1900), 'Preface'.

was *The Edinburgh Collection of Highland Bagpipe Music Pibrochs, marches, quicksteps, strathspeys, reels & jigs, compiled & arranged by David Glen* containing more than five hundred tunes and issued in eleven parts (1903–8).[29]

The Glen manuscript as we now have it – large as it is – must therefore be merely one of a series of such manuscripts compiled by this indefatigable collector and arranger of music for the Highland pipe. David Glen was at the centre of a web of written sources and living informants. He had access directly or indirectly to the MSS of Donald MacDonald, Angus MacArthur and John MacGregor, Angus MacKay, John MacKay jr, Duncan MacDougall's transcript of Duncan Campbell of Foss's manuscript book (then apparently still in the possession of Sir Charles Forbes of Newe). He had personal contact with Dr. Charles Bannatyne (currently working on a key to the Gesto Canntaireachd), Lieut. John McLennan, Colin Cameron, General C. S. Thomason, and John MacDougall Gillies, all of whom supplied him with material. And these were just the big names. We should probably also include, at least potentially, every piper who visited his shop, or dealt with him by post.

The resulting manuscript looks like an attempt to arrive at a complete account of the tradition in piobaireachd, as it was known at the beginning of the twentieth century. Glen conspicuously omitted certain classic tunes found in previously published sources, such as 'MacIntosh's Lament', 'My King has Landed in Moidart', 'The Lament for Patrick Og', 'The Bells of Perth', 'The Earl of Seaforth's Salute', 'The Finger Lock', 'Donald Gruamach's March', 'Mary's Praise', 'The Lament for Donald Ban MacCrimmon', 'The Blue Ribbon', 'Scarce of Fishing' and 'In Praise of Morag', which he obviously regarded as having reached a satisfactorily stable condition following generations of creative attention. But it is clear that in later Victorian Scotland when a tune had been published it was not regarded as having thereby assumed a fixed and final form. It remained open to debate, revision and creative accretion. This is apparent in the large number of previously published tunes included in the Glen MS, such as 'MacLeod's Controversy', 'The Battle of Sheriffmuir', 'The Earl of Ross's March', 'The Half-Finished Piobaireachd', 'MacLeod's Rowing Tune', 'The Vaunting', 'Lament for Viscount Dundee', 'MacDonald's Salute', 'Glengarry's March', and 'Too Long in this Condition', all of which received editorial attention. Even where there was only one source for a tune, Glen would seldom follow it to the letter, as in the typical changes he makes to Angus MacKay's version of 'Grain in Hides and Corn in Sacks', which appears to have been the sole written source:

29 Cannon, *Bibliography*, pp. 37–9, 159–71, 176–84, 202–3, 208–9. See also, 'Notices of Pipers – Glen, David' in *PT*, vol.21, no 5, February 1969, p.15. See also "Puirt-a-Beul – Cille Chriosda'", a letter from David Glen to the *OT*, 30/3/1901, p.3, in which he states 'The notes of this setting were given to me by the greatest living authority on this class of pipe music, namely Colin Cameron, late piper to the Duke of Fife . . .'

Gràn a Seichanan's Sial am Pocanan   Grain in hides and seed in bags. Angus MacKay's MS. i, 249

Var. 1.

Gràn a Seicanan 's Siol an Pocanan. Grain in Hides & Corn in Sacks. David Glen's MS. f. 74

Var 1.

Glen wrote to the *Oban Times* in the spring of 1910 explaining some features of his notational style:

> the best and oldest method of writing all the various movements in
> piobaireachd is the treatise written by Joseph MacDonald in 1760, and
> published in 1803. This method – after many years of study – is the one I now
> use in my own Piobaireachd Book. The method I use in writing the themal
> grace-notes is my own, and, I think, is an advance on any hitherto in use.[30]

Glen is one of the handful of people (Angus MacKay was another) known to have had a copy of the *Compleat Theory*. Since his notational practice was closer to that of Donald MacDonald and Angus MacKay, he is presumably referring here to specific devices of Joseph MacDonald, such as the writing of complex crunluaths as a single integrated figure and to

30 'Piobaireachd Movements', from David Glen, *OT*, 16/4/1910, p.3.

the use of the slur to indicate smooth transition between various movements:[31]

MacNeil of Barra's Pibroch (or Grand March). David Glen's MS. f.348

He had begun in *Ancient Piobaireachd* (1880) by setting his introductory notes in Angus MacKay's style, moving closer to Donald MacDonald in *Music of the Clan MacLean*, (1900):

Notation of introductory notes by David Glen, 1880-1900

Ancient Piobaireachd (1880)   Music of the Clan MacLean (1900)

He described the intended timing in a note to 'Caismeachd Eachainn Mhic Ailein Nan Sop':

> When played on any other Instrument than the Bagpipe, all the Semi-quavers E & D Grace Notes must be played to complete the Melody. The Demi-semiquaver Grace Note G, which precedes these notes being only a Bagpipe 'Accent Note' should be omitted, as also all the other 'Pipe' Grace Notes. The E in Cadence may be at the performer's pleasure – played as if written with a pause over it and held out beyond its proper duration:[32]

Example

Whilst MacKay would have assigned a fixed length to these notes, Glen reasserted the principle of performer choice. By doing so he revived the dilemma which had beset notators of pipe-music for nearly a century, namely, what was a melody note

---

31 The suggestion of James Campbell in 'The Elusive Appoggiatura', *PT*, vol.40, no.9, June 1988, pp.22–5 that Glen's ties indicate the presence of an intended appoggiatura is not supported by the example above which represents his general later practice.

32 *Music of Clan MacLean*, p.12.

and what was not, what had time-value and what had not? And how much time? Dissatisfied with his solutions in *Music of the Clan MacLean*, Glen evolved the style we see in the Manuscript which avoided the awkward appearance of MacKay on the page by setting introductory notes in reduced type with their stems pointing up as Donald MacDonald had done, but preserved the advantages of MacKay's more explicit system by specifying note-values fairly exactly.

The Glen Manuscript is the first 'piper's workshop' we can look into in this way. Earlier written sources had presented their conclusions merely, giving little indication of the process of musical reasoning which lay behind them. Here, however, one can watch an attractive musical intelligence going about its business, weighing one version against another, working out the most appropriate combination of variations for a given theme, trying to reconcile apparent inconsistencies in earlier sources, and throughout striving for the most artistically pleasing effect.

Glen not only maintained a critical independence of his sources but he was careful to indicate what he had done to them. His treatment of the tune 'The MacDonalds are Simple. Tha Clann Domhnuill Socharach' shows his typical method.[33] He notes 'No Doubling is given to Taorluath in MSS. from which this was copied. One will be added by me on next page'. Which was duly done in an appendix marked 'Taorluath-a-mach. by D.G.' The main source here was Angus MacKay's MS, although there were settings also in Colin Cameron and John MacDougall Gillies which he may have seen, and with whose style he would certainly have been familiar.[34] He added a taorluath a-mach to balance up MacKay's crunluath a-mach, and also a taorluath singling (not present in MacKay) from a version in Colin Cameron. He often recorded alternative interpretations of tunes. In 'His Father's Lament for Donald MacKenzie', here called 'John (Bàn) McKenzie's Lament for his son Donald (1863)' (ff.16–19) he had a version ending with standard taorluath and crunluath movements and also one with a taorluath and crunluath breabach:

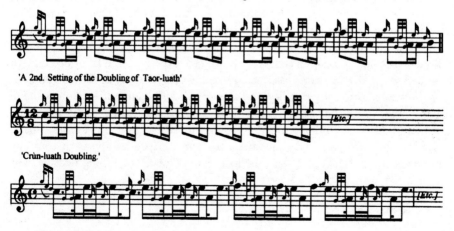

John (Bàn) McKenzie's Lament for his son Donald.   'Doubling of Taor-luath'.   Glen MS. f.18

'A 2nd. Setting of the Doubling of Taor-luath'

'Crùn-luath Doubling.'

33 Glen MS., ff.47–49.
34 Cameron MS, ff.136–137; Gillies MS., ff.13–14.

'A 2nd Setting of Doubling of Crùn-luath'

Glen's approach thus differed from that of C.S. Thomason whose work will be discussed in the next chapter. Thomason sought the theoretically correct 'original' text and was willing to re-construct it if he was dissatisfied with the existing versions. Glen sought the 'best' setting from an aesthetic point of view, so his willingness to synthesise 'traditional' texts had a different justification. It was itself entirely 'traditional', being what pipers had always done. A similar spirit led him to search out alternative titles for tunes. For example the piece now known as 'I am Proud to Play a Pipe', appears as 'The Earl of Cromarty/ Cromartie's Salute; Hey for the Old Pipes; Dastirim gu'n Seinnm Piob; Dancing or Marching to the Music of the Pipes; I would like fine to play the Pipes.' He preserved every title he could find, aware that it was in their nature to vary.[35]

The written score drew its value from the professional standing of its creator, but it was ultimately independent of him. It could survive him. It could pass into the possession of a third party and be bought and sold like any other commodity. In an oral setting the master teacher was a kind of 'living library', giving him an irreplaceable personal importance, as we see in the anxieties about the possible loss of John MacKay in 1821.[36] But the teacher who based his approach upon the mastery of literate skills was working, ultimately, towards his own dissolution. In the 20th century the printed or written text came increasingly to be identified as the ultimate source of authority in preference to the living master.

The move from orality to an institutionally-sponsored print culture could involve a cognitive shift which might alter quite significantly the way the piper related to his art. In an oral context, he was required to master the general content of the repertoire and particular techniques for handling it. He had an active role in the creative organisation of the resulting knowledge. But the transition from orality to print meant replacing an efficient, economical (indeed free) storage system with an external, mechanically produced, expensive and laborious one. In normal use, a written score was treated like any other source, open to acceptance or rejection, creative intervention and change; but in a competitive context where a published score possessing prescriptive force was required to be played as written, a different kind of remembering – more passive, more rote, more visual – was brought into play.[37] By the later 20th century such an approach could be presented as 'normal', and the principal of the College of Piping declare that:

35 Glen MS. ff.52–3.

36 See above, p.146.

37 See Ruth Finnegan, *Oral Traditions and the Verbal Arts: a Guide to Research Practices* (Lond., 1992), pp.114–116; see also Shils, pp.92–3.

although a piper does not apparently play from a score, there is nothing extemporaneous about his performance. The composer has decided which variations he will use and how exactly he will apply them. The piper memorises the piece from the score and plays this exactly, at least so far as the notes and gracenotes are concerned.[38]

But this was the result of imposed change and the transition from an oral to a literate milieu was not swiftly or painlessly achieved. Reporting the Northern Meeting in 1910, where competitors were required to play one of six set tunes in the versions published by the Piobaireachd Society, the *Inverness Courier* noted that:

The cold, gusty wind was not favourable to the piping, but the weather did not account altogether for the somewhat poor performance of the large proportion of the competitors, who failed before the end of the tunes. It appears that the Piobaireachd Society's rule that the competitors must play the music in strict accordance with the score is one that many young pipers find it difficult to comply with. It is to be hoped that in future more time will be given by them to the thorough preparation necessary to enable them to commit the tunes accurately to memory.[39]

In order to prepare the Society's settings of the set tunes, of course, existing settings had to be *un*learned, which many contemporary performers found difficult, especially as they frequently considered the modern arrangements to be incorrect and musically inferior to those already acquired. One competitor complained about being '. . . bored beyond expression by having to relearn and afterwards unlearn certain "wrong" versions, published in high places'.[40]

The rise of the fixed score diminished the role of the player and narrowed the concept of the art. Within a generation of the debacle at Inverness, John Grant – whose own training had involved much manuscript work – could dismiss with scorn the idea that a piper must have 195 piobaireachds before being considered a finished player on the grounds that 'To memorise and play 195 tunes would amount to at least a minimum of 600 pages of music, 7,200 staves, 28,800 bars, and 491,200 notes' and that therefore the real number could not have been more than about forty or fifty at most.[41] The narrowness and rigidity of this approach could make the learning of piobaireachd intolerably arid to a sensitive musical intelligence and placed demands upon precise visual memory to which many

38 MacNeill and Richardson, p.46.
39 'Northern Meeting Fashionable Attendance in the Park. Games Programme. Piping and Dancing', *Inverness Courier*, 23/9/1910, p.5.
40 'The Piobaireachd Society's New Collection', from 'Luceo', *OT*, 10/8/1912, p.3. See also 'Piobaireachd Society of Scotland and "Ceol Mor"', from G. Sharp [Henry Whyte], 31/10/1903 p.3.
41 'The MacCrimmons and a Monument', from John Grant, *OT*, 5/7/1930 p.3.

performers felt themselves unequal. John MacKay of Strath Halladale, a notable collector and composer of ceòl beag, declared:

> Oh I loved the piobaireachd but I never learned piobaireachd. It is a constant marvel to me how a piobaireachd player can memorise pages and pages of piobaireachd.[42]

The imposition of the fixed text, reinforced by the competition circuit and the power of its sponsoring institutions, drove a wedge between those pipers who played piobaireachd and those who did not (another historically recent phenomenon), narrowing repertoires and disfranchising a sizeable proportion of the performer community from active participation in the higher branches of its art.

---

42 In interview with Robbie Shepherd: broadcast in 'Pipeline', B.B.C. Scotland, 5/1/1997 (originally transmitted 1983). For further details of John MacKay, see Mackenzie, *Piping Traditions*, pp.236–41; see also his collection of pipe music, *The Music of MacKay* (n.p., 1984).

II

'Within the reach of poor pipers': the Collections of Donald MacPhee and General C. S. Thomason

With the collections of Donald MacPhee and David Glen, the publication of pipe-music entered a new phase. Hitherto books of piobaireachd music had been luxury items, costing considerably more than the weekly wage of a working man.[1] MacPhee, however, by concentrating simply on music text was able to bring out his *Collection of Piobairachd* in 1879 at 15/-, half the cost of Uilleam Ross's book, which had gone to its second edition less than three years before. But MacPhee was addressing a very different sector of the market from Ross.

Between 1850 and 1875 the wages of ordinary people had risen in real terms by as much as a third. A corresponding increase in leisure time and a boom in popular publishing followed. An interlocking network of technological changes – the automation of paper-making, steam-driven presses, mechanical typesetting – rapidly drove down the price of printed matter. Norman MacLeod of the Barony, speaking as editor of the periodical *Good Words* to the letterpress printers of Glasgow at their annual soirée on 14 January 1860, said that 'it is no exaggeration to say that the men now before me print every single morning in Glasgow more words, produce more matter, in twenty-four hours than was ever written by the hand during twenty-four centuries before the invention of printing.'[2] Access to print culture was transformed.

MacPhee's *Collection* was 'Dedicated to the Noblemen and Gentlemen of the Highlands of Scotland', but it was not a mediated text. There was no high-flown editorial apparatus, elaborate engravings, or Ossianic allusions, and it was published in the open market, without subscription or institutional sponsorship. By the 1890s it was available in two handy volumes priced at just 4/- each, at a time when reprints of Angus MacKay's book still cost a guinea.[3] And while those who bought MacKay got a fair amount of chaff amongst the wheat, the quality of MacPhee's tunes – 37 in all covering much of the central core of the

---

1 When Uilleam Ross published in 1869, working class incomes ranged from about 14/- a week for a general labourer, to about 35/- a week for top skilled trades such as instrument makers and engine drivers. See Geoffrey Best, *Mid-Victorian Britain 1851–75* (Lond., 1979), pp.111–17, 137–8.

2 See William Donaldson, *Popular Literature in Victorian Scotland* (Aberd., 1986), pp.ix, 1–34.

3 Cannon, *Bibliography*, pp.131, 175. For MacPhee's light music collection and tutor, see *ibid.*, pp.171–4.

repertoire (along with two new piobaireachds of his own composition) – was extremely high. It included 'The Piper's Warning to his Master', 'The Sound of the Waves against the Castle of Duntroon', 'The Lament for Patrick Og', 'Mary's Praise', 'The Desperate Battle', 'The Prince's Salute', 'Too Long in this Condition', 'The Piobaireachd of Dhomhnuill Duibh', 'Seaforth's Salute', 'MacGregor's Salute', 'Macintosh's Lament', 'The Bells of Perth', 'Donald Gruamach's March', 'MacCrimmon will never return', 'Lament for the Departure of King James', 'MacLeod of Rassay's Salute', 'The Glen is Mine', 'The Finger Lock', 'The Carles with the Breeks', 'The MacKay's Banner', 'Clan Ranald's Salute', 'My King has landed in Moidart', and the 'Lament for Ronald McDonald of Morar'. Donald MacPhee's book was the first published collection of the classical music of the Highland pipe intended first and foremost for pipers. His *Selection of Music for the Highland Bagpipe* (Glasg., 1876) containing 150 marches, strathspeys and reels, and his *Complete Tutor for the Highland Bagpipe* (Inverness, n.d.), which were selling for 2/- or 3/- each by the nineties, were likewise widely used.

As its title page records, the *Collection* was 'newly arranged and revised . . . by Donald MacPhee', and virtually all of its contents had already appeared in published sources, the majority in Donald MacDonald and Angus MacKay's books. MacPhee edited his sources fairly lightly on the whole, simplifying and up-dating MacDonald's grace-note system, silently correcting MacKay's typographical errors, occasionally re-distributing accent, and making minor adjustments in the variations so that they followed the themal notes of the grounds more closely. Occasionally, though, his interventions were more drastic. In 'Clan Ranald's Gathering to the Battle of Sheriffmuir in 1715' he replaced MacDonald's tasteful tripling movement and crunluath fosgailte with a taorluath and crunluath variation in *dùinte* form, creating thereby a tiresome reiteration of Bs which by no means enhanced the tune. It would seem that this was MacPhee's decision, as the only other source, Angus MacKay's MS, does not show this feature.[4] MacPhee's gairm usually showed the accent on the initial low A and he did not normally vary this for the eallach.[5] His crunluath fosgailte, like Uilleam Ross's, was written in the 'opened' form; and there was a similarly selective approach to other aspects of MacKay's notational practices; for example, the expressed time-values of MacKay's introductory notes were usually converted back into traditional-style gracenote clusters:

---

4 The edition used here is the photographic reproduction of the 2nd edn., issued in two
   volumes by Logan and Co., (Inverness, n.d.), in *The Bagpipe Works of Donald
   MacPhee* (Wakefield, 1978); MacDonald, *Ancient Martial Music*, pp.68–70; MacKay
   MS, i, 171–2.
5 See *A Collection of Piobaireachd*, part 1, p.1.

Donald MacPhee, *A Collection of Piobaireachd*, pp.1, 21, 27

Patrick óg MacCrummen's Lament, Angus MacKay, *Ancient Piobaireachd*, p. 82

Patrick Og Mac Crimmon's Lament, Donald MacPhee, *A Collection of Piobaireachd*, p. 8

Donald MacPhee was born in Coatbridge about 1841 and, although both his parents came from Islay, he may have been one of the earliest major players who was not primarily a Gaelic-speaker. He worked as a miner in his youth before becoming associated with the Forbes Brothers who were Highland dancers and exhibition-fencers. He is thought to have been taught piping by Donald Galbraith in Coatbridge.[6] MacPhee had a fine technical gift and soon emerged as a successful competitive piper and Highland dancer. Robert Meldrum heard him at Aberdeen in 1870 and considered him a fine player both of piobaireachd and of light music.[7] In about 1873 MacPhee set up as a pipe-maker and teacher in Glasgow with premises in West Nile Street and later at 17 Royal Arcade. Apparently he prospered but his career was cut short by premature death on 9th December 1880.[8] The business was taken over by Peter Henderson and under the management of John MacDougall Gillies went on to become became one of the leading bagpipe-making firms in Scotland.[9] MacPhee's most important pupil was John MacColl who composed 'Donald MacPhee's Lament' in his memory and promoted his settings in competition, which was to provoke in the autumn of 1883 the first of many piping controversies in the columns of the *Oban Times.*[10]

The *Oban Times* was an outstanding example of the penny-weekly newspapers

6 Jeannie Campbell, 'Notices of Bagpipe Makers' Part 13, *PT*, vol.51, no.6, March 1999, pp.37–43 (37).

7 Meldrum, 'Reminiscences', Part 1, *OT*, 29/6/1940, p.5.

8 David Baptie, *Musical Scotland Past and Present* (Lond. 1894), pp.113–14.

9 See advertisement by Peter Henderson giving notice that he had just taken over Donald MacPhee's business, *OT*, 1/5/1880, p.4.

10 'A Famous Piper. John MacColl', *OT*, 17/8/1935, p.2.

which formed the basis of the dynamic new popular print-culture of Victorian Scotland, developed after the repeal of the Stamp Act in 1855. It was founded in 1861 and passed into the ownership of the Cameron family in 1882. Under the editorship of Duncan Cameron and his successors it rapidly established itself first as the 'county' newspaper for Argyll, then as the main popular paper for the Highlands as a whole, and latterly as the leading newspaper for the world-wide Gaelic community. It was advanced Liberal in politics and supported the crofters' cause in the land agitation of the 1880s, leading to its boycott by the lairds, who refused either to take the paper or to place advertising with it. The *Oban Times* saw itself first and foremost as a vehicle for popular opinion, giving full coverage to local news via a web of district reporters and devoting extensive column space to correspondence from its largely plebeian readers. Popular culture, the language, literature, folklore and music of the Highland community was its major focus. There was frequent discussion of tales and songs, folkloristic belief and practice, and every aspect of material culture, as well as countless contributions on place names and history, Gaelic idiom, vocabulary and orthography. There were exhaustive accounts of the activities of Highland and Celtic societies in Scotland and further afield, including the Pan-Celtic Congress and the Welsh Eisteddfod, and much political comment both local and national. Above all, from the early 1880s onwards the *Oban Times* gave extensive column-space to every aspect of the Highland pipe and its music, from the minutiae of canntaireachd theory to the aesthetic merits of the latest published collections. The paper developed into the major channel of communication for the world community of pipers. There was discussion on the instrument itself and its leading makers, on reeds and reed-making, tunes and tune-titles, piping history and folklore, biographies of famous players, the structure of piobaireachd, styles of playing and the evolution of technique, notational conventions, composition and publishing, the competition circuit, and relations within and between the various institutions which set themselves to promote the art. Between letters, reviews, features, news items and leaders, the paper devoted millions of words to the subject. If one had access to no other source, it would be possible to construct a detailed history of piping from about 1880 onwards from the *Oban Times* alone.

John MacColl, then at the beginning of his career, had won at the Argyllshire Gathering in the autumn of 1883, playing a setting of 'MacLeod of Raasay's Salute' from the published book of his teacher Donald MacPhee. He was attacked for doing this in the columns of the *Oban Times* by a pseudonymous correspondent, 'Vanduara', who wrote to the paper on piping subjects several times during the closing decades of the 19th century:

> . . . it is frequently noticed, even at some of the best gatherings, that
> competitors mis-place parts of the tune, and again leave some parts out
> altogether . . . such cases are at times overlooked, and the judges as if it were
> to show their own ignorance or carelessness on some of these occasions have

awarded the bunglers first honours, to the infinite disgust of all the other professionals. As a case in point I may just here state that McColl, who was lately awarded the silver cup presented by the Marquis of Lorn, and competed for at Oban, did not lift the variations of his piobaireachda of[f] the ground work of the t[une], an error sufficient of itself to have put him *hors de combat.*[11]

What was at issue was not error in any technical sense, but the right to play a setting which was not Angus MacKay's. MacColl, well aware of his critic's drift, appealed to performance tradition, claiming that the interests of piobaireachd were not well served by reducing it to a single written text, and described the variety of interpretations amongst contemporary masters as confirming his freedom to play what he liked:

I know I did not play it exactly as some of the professionals he refers to would, for I did not wish to do so. I was speaking to some of them about the tune on many occasions, but they could only say – 'That is not the way it is in MacKay's book'. I believe some of them never spent five minutes to look if MacKay took the variations properly of[f] the ground work. If 'Vanduara' or any of his professionals takes the trouble to compare MacKay's book and MacPhee's, on the tune of 'MacLeod of Raasay's Salute' (this being the tune referred to), and carefully look how each bar in the ground work is carried on in the Taorluadh and Crunluath variations, they will, if they properly understand how a Piobaireachd is composed, come to the conclusion that in one of the bars MacKay put the 'cart before the horse', this being the great blunder for which 'Vanduara' thinks I should have been put *hors-de-combat.* Why is this case taken as an exception? I know pupils, and sons of one of our best authorities for Piobaireachd, who all play a different style.[12]

His antagonist was not persuaded. 'Vanduara's' arguments, although not always clearly expressed, reflected the growing tendency during the later years of the 19th century to ascribe absolute authority to a single published source, sanctioned in the case of Angus MacKay's book by its use by the bench during the previous two generations:

Perhaps I am not fairly correct to say MacColl blundered the variations, since he tells us that they were played as found in MacPhee's book. Now, I would be very sorry indeed to say a single unjust thing against MacPhee, especially that he has for some time gone over to the majority. That he was

11 'Bagpipe Competition', from 'Vanduara', *OT*, 10/11/1883, p.5. An annotated master copy of the *Oban Times* identifies 'Vanduara' as M. Gilmour from Johnstone near Paisley.

12 'Bagpipe Competition, from John MacColl, *OT*, 24/11/1883, p.5.

undoubtedly a first-rate reel and strathspey player I never heard disputed, and
his book, so far as these tunes are concerned, is admitted by all a standard
work. It was a pity MacPhee did not rest content with this. His book on
piobaireachd was a failure, and no man in his senses could have hoped for
success when venturing to alter and reset a class of music that has been the
production of Highlanders, whose names as famed composers and performers
on the great Highland bagpipes have been handed down for many generations
by worthy followers of these great men. It was folly; nay, more, it was pure
madness to have undertaken such a task; while such men as John
MacClennon [?lives], known by the sobriquet of 'Big John', not because of his
personal bulk, but in honour of his well-deserved fame as an authority and
proficient performer of piobaireachd. Next comes the well-known Donald
Cameron, who died some years ago, and who was, perhaps, the best authority
since the days of the MacRemmonds. Donald left sons; they are still alive, and
famed as piobaireachd players. All these and many more good men I could
name refuse to accept MacPhee's book. MacPhee was nowhere as a
piobaireachd player, and as a proof of this it needs only to be stated that he
competed over twelve years at Inverness and never succeeded in getting
anything above a third prize in that class. And this is the author of the book
that John MacColl would wish to champion against MacKay's book and the
overwhelming authorities herein named.[13]

What MacColl and 'Vanduara' were ostensibly arguing about was this:

MacLeod of Raasay's Salute, Ground line 2, MacKay/MacPhee

Tone row in taorluath doubling, line 2, Angus MacKay

Tone row in taorluath doubling, line 2, Donald MacPhee

the placing of two notes in the fourth bar of the second line of the variations.
MacKay had the phrase contour ACEC, as against MacPhee's AECC. Ironically,
one of MacPhee's leading characteristics as an arranger was to frame his variations

---

13 'Bagpipe Competition', from 'Vanduara', *OT,* 8/12/1883, p.6; see also 'Bagpipe
   Competition', from John MacColl, 15/12/1883, p.6.

to shadow the themal notes of the ground even more closely than his sources, as he does here.

The controversy wandered on into the spring of 1884, rather like a game of postal chess, attracting intermittent attention from a number of other correspondents, until eventually MacColl succeeded in drawing from 'Vanduara' an admission that MacKay's book 'although the best authority, is not infallible':

> The errors, however, are undoubtedly printers' errors, and nothing is more
> certain than this, when we look at McKay's Banner as put down in the book.
> The ground work of the tune is correct. When a variation does not agree with
> the ground it is faulty. This is what is wrong with McKay's *Banner* in
> McKay's book. But . . . [none] of the living or dead authorities would play
> the variation as found in McKay's book; because they know it to be an error,
> and they know also that it had no foundation with McKay.[14]

But the argument was only superficially about music. What it was really about was power. The transfer of 'authority' to the printed text with its accompanying tendency to confer authenticity on the work of one piper whilst disfranchising all the rest, became explicit here. On the one hand there was a power of autonomy and entitlement, involving the freedom to play as one wished, or at the very least to select without undue restraint from pre-existing sources. On the other, there was the power to discipline and regulate, enabling its possessor to define and to control and to exercise the prerogatives of a privileged interpreter, which included granting esoteric significance to certain texts and refusing it to others. The concept of 'authority' espoused by 'Vanduara' and his like was brutally simple. Only Angus MacKay and those attuned to his purpose were deemed to possess it. Whilst asserting MacKay's quasi-scriptural authority, however, 'Vanduara' was forced to defend the details of a flawed text as nonetheless inspired and when forced to concede the presence of error, to vest final authority in an élite of true interpreters who, by a mystical process not explained, had alone been granted access to MacKay's intentions.

Although the fixed standard text was assuming *de facto* recognition on the competition circuit, the machinery to enforce its use was not yet in place. The basically sound quality of Donald MacPhee's settings, coupled with their attractively cheap price, ensured that they went on being used. The plates were bought by Logan and Co. and then by Patersons, and the *Collection of Piobairachd* remained in print for more than fifty years after the compiler's death.[15] 'Niall Mor a' Chamais' writing to the *Oban Times* in 1905 praised it as 'accessible to every piper from its moderate price,' and described MacPhee as 'a first-rate player, who was also a thoroughly scientific musician', concluding: 'sensible, easily-read, rhythmical, and admirable – Donald MacPhee's and David

14 'Bagpipe Competition', from 'Vanduara', *OT*, 29/12/1883, p.6.
15 Cannon, *Bibliography*, pp.174–6.

Glen's great collections, [form] the only modern standards.'[16] In 1923 the Cowal Committee subsidised classes for young piobaireachd players in Glasgow taught by Robert Reid at a merely nominal charge. Donald MacPhee's were the preferred settings and the tunes were 'Struan Robertson's Salute', 'Too long in this condition', and 'MacLeod of Raasay's Salute.'[17]

As the twentieth century dawned, therefore, the work of Angus MacKay was receiving a largely uncritical endorsement by those whose concern was with 'authority', while being treated with rather greater caution by the musically aware. Although certain of MacKay's ideas, were taken up and adapted by his contemporaries, his desire to establish a standard text found, at best, equivocal support amongst pipers. In the social classes from which the bench was recruited, however, it was a different story. They clung to MacKay's book and considered departure from it, even in the smallest detail, as 'wrong'. Their formal education encouraged them to look for a fixed, original, authoritative score and they consistently failed to grasp that variety and fluidity were inherent qualities in traditional music, signs not of corruption and decay but of well-being and vitality. Indeed this search for a wholly non-existent 'authority' was to mislead even C. S. Thomason, the most formidable musical intelligence of the age in piping.

Charles Simeon Thomason was born in India, at Azangarh in the North West Provinces on 25th May 1833, the son of John Thomason of the Bengal Civil Service and Maynard Grant. His mother was a scion of the Grants of Elchies on Speyside and it was mainly here that her son was brought up following her death in 1839. In an atmosphere rich in Highland music and song, Thomason learned Gaelic and studied the flute and the pipes.[18] His grandfather, J. W. Grant, had been a gentleman pupil of Donald MacDonald, and had been sent the manuscript of the proposed second volume of MacDonald's collection when it became clear that it could not otherwise be published. Thomason noted:

. . . my grandfather, who spent 45 years of his life in the Bengal Civil Service, was [Donald MacDonald's] pupil &, in his younger days, an enthusiastic piper. When MacDonald's first volume was published Mr. Grant was in India. The second volume alluded to so freely in the first as about to contain historical notes pertaining to both volumes was eagerly looked forward to & formed the subject of many a letter from Mr. Grant when postal communication was the sport of long sea voyages in sailing ships via the

16 'The Piobaireachd Society's Collection of Bagpipe Music', *OT*, 13/5/1905, p.3.

17 H. S. Strafford, 'Instructing Boys in Bagpipe Playing', *OT*, 15/12/1923, p.3.

18 He was later a prominent member of the Gaelic Society of London: 'London Highland News', *OT*, 3/10/1903 p.5. See MacKenzie, 'General Thomason and Ceol Mor', pp.58–72, and 'The Life and Work of General Thomason', in *PT*, vol.49, no.5–6, February-March 1997, pp.37–44, 33–41. See also Thomason's obituaries in the *Oban Times*: 'An Seanalar MacThomais', 22/7/1911, p.4; and 'Death of Major General Thomason. The Author of "Ceol Mor"', *same*, p.5, both written by 'Fionn'.

Cape. I have heard my grandfather relate how, after many fruitless attempts to extract a reply, at last, to his great surprise, a letter was received by him from MacDonald together with his second vol. in manuscript. This vol. though containing historical notes on many of the piobaireachdan in it, unfortunately contained no such notes pertaining to those in the first vol. as promised. MacDonald wrote that he had been almost ruined by the publication of the 1st vol., & not being in a position to undertake that of the 2nd. begged to present to my grandfather its manuscript original, in the hopes that he, who of all his patrons had evinced the greatest interest in his work, would some day find himself in a position to perpetuate it.[19]

Grant had the manuscript copied by one of his daughters and this copy was presented to Thomason along with his grandfather's pipes, made by Donald MacDonald, when he gained his commission in the Bengal Engineers in 1852. Before being posted to India he studied with Sandy McLennan, son of Donald of Moy and with Donald Cameron's brother, Alexander Cameron. Thomason wrote:

I was fortunate enough to come to terms with Donald's brother, Sandy, who then had a small place in the High Street, where all pipers of note were accustomed to congregate when in Edinburgh. A full size and a half size stand of pipes lay always at hand on the table for the use of all comers; music was always kept well agoing. I must there have heard the best pipers in Scotland, though they were unknown to me even by name. I was too much a tyro to form any opinion as to the merits of the performers, but I used to listen greedily to their conversation regarding the capabilities of the several pipers of the day. The opinion of the majority was certainly in favour of Donald as the best piper of the day, but he was close run by [John] MacLachlan. As regards execution both were held to be equal but MacLachlan's style was characterised as 'light,' whereas that of Donald was held to be 'the true MacCruimen style'.[20]

Thomason sailed for India in 1854, taking with him the family pipes, a large collection of piobaireachd MSS copied for him by his aunts and a transcript of Angus MacKay's book which he had made himself, an indication of how scarce printed copies had become even at this period. The labour involved in this first interested him in the possibilities of an abbreviated system of

19 C. S. Thomason, 'Ceol Mor Legends', NLS MS. 3749, ff.83–4.
20 'Ceol Mor', from C. S. Thomason, *OT*, 2/1/1904, p.3. John McLachlan was piper to Neil Malcolm of Poltalloch. He edited a collection of light music entitled *The Piper's Assistant* (Edinr., 1854). McLachlan's sister, Agnes, was said to have been influential in forming her husband Donald MacPhedran's distinctive style: see 'MacPhedran's Pipe Tunes' from 'Cean-na-Drochaid', *OT*, 8/9/1906, p.3.

musical notation which was to become the foundation of his later editorial work.[21]

Everything was lost in the fall of Delhi during the Indian Mutiny in May 1857. Thomason barely escaped with his life, making his way by devious routes to rejoin the British forces, using his knowledge of the canal system to lead his small party through hostile territory full of marauding insurgents. He took part in the later siege of Delhi, approaching its walls in disguise to map out possible lines of attack and was one of the group of sappers who blew in the Kashmir gate under murderous fire to launch the British assault upon the city. When he came home on leave in 1860–3, he found his grandfather unwilling to risk the original manuscript returning to India, whilst he himself felt unequal to the task of transcribing its many pages. In the autumn of 1862 he met Donald Cameron at the Northern Meeting, having resumed his lessons with Donald's brother Sandy, and encountering a friend there, Capt. Forbes of the 78th (Ross-shire Buffs), arranged that the pipers of that regiment would copy the work. When the manuscript returned to Elchies in 1863, however, little had been done and when Thomason next met Forbes, by now commanding the 78th (which had in the meantime become the 2nd battalion Seaforth Highlanders) in India in the 1880s, there was no trace of the project in the regimental records.[22] It seemed that not all sections of the performer community (least of all, perhaps, the military wing) could be relied upon to respond to old piping MSS with either enthusiasm or understanding. Nor did any of the institutions available to him seem capable of offering intelligent support. Thomason began to conclude that if he were to accomplish anything there was little option but to do it himself. It took another ten years, another furlough in 1869–71, and the support of a leading civilian piper to make good what had been lost at Delhi.

The piper was Donald MacKay (the younger), nephew of Angus MacKay, then with Sir George Grant at Ballindalloch, just eight miles up the Spey from Thomason's Scottish home, 'Laggan House', which the latter had built near his grandfather's place at Elchies. MacKay was one of the rising generation of important players who were not native Gaelic speakers, being brought up in London and educated, like D. C. Mather, at the Caledonian Schools. He was a pupil of Donald Cameron, and evidently a favourite, being married from Donald's house at Maryburgh. In Donald MacKay Thomason once again had contact with an important player on whose time he had some claim and who was able to provide access to important manuscript sources. He noted that:

> Angus MacKay . . . left at his death a large quantity of M.S. piobaireachdan,
> the most of which were purchased by the Duke of Hamilton. A very large
> portion of this collection evidently found its way (perhaps indirectly) to
> Ballindalloch . . . whilst another portion, including what is known as the
> 'Seaforth Collection' eventually came to his nephew Donald MacKay, H.R.H.
> the Prince of Wales's Piper . . .

21 'Honouring General Thomason. The Author of "Ceol Mor"', *OT*, 10/7/1909, p.5.
22 Thomason, 'Ceol Mor Legends', ff.84–5.

Donald Cameron strongly objected to pupils who even thought in anything but Gaelic, but made an exception in favour of Donald MacKay (the nephew of his former master), who as Piper to Sir George Grant of Ballindalloch, when I first made his acquaintance, did full justice to his teacher by winning the gold medal at the Northern Meeting in 1872.[23]

Not only was MacKay trained in the style of Donald Cameron, but he had copies of Donald MacDonald and Angus MacKay's tunes which had been amended or certified as 'correct' by his teacher, whom Thomason regarded as the greatest master of his generation. In order to make the most effective use of his time he began to work out a system of musical shorthand, using a repertoire of devices in part adapted from standard musical notation but including also a series of special symbols which enabled conventional piobaireachd movements to be represented by a single sign. In these sessions at Laggan House in the early 1870s the first steps were taken towards an explicit acknowledgement of fundamental musical structure in piobaireachd, a subject which – owing to the widespread, but quite mistaken, belief that this music was intrinsically wild and irregular – had lain dormant since the days of Joseph MacDonald.

Most of the effort went into what has since become the core of the modern competition repertoire – tunes like 'The Blue Ribbon', 'The Lament for the Children', 'The Lament for Donald Bàn MacCrimmon', 'The Lament for Donald Duaghal MacKay', 'Donald of Laggan', 'The Earl of Antrim', 'The End of the Great Bridge', 'The Glen is Mine', 'The Lament for the Harp Tree', 'I got a Kiss of the King's Hand', 'The Little Supper', 'MacDonald of Kinlochmoidart's Lament', 'MacCrimmon's Sweetheart', 'Mary's Praise', 'MacIntosh's Lament', 'Scarce of Fishing', 'The Rout of Glenfruin', 'The Big Spree' and 'The Lament for the Union'. Indeed, the contents of the manuscript which Thomason

23 Thomason, 'Ceol Mor Legends', ff.247–8. It would appear that this is a different and much larger set of papers than what is now called the 'Ballindalloch MS' which is the personal manuscript book of Donald MacKay, currently deposited in Glasgow University Library (MS. Gen 1455) which contains 22 tunes as follows; 'The End of the Great Bridge', 'Milbank's Salute', 'The Rout of Glenfruin', 'Lady Margaret MacDonald's Salute', 'The Lament for Donald of Laggan', 'The Sinclair's March', 'The Lament for the Death of Samuel', 'The End of the Little Bridge', 'MacCrimmons Sweetheart', 'The Lament for the Union', 'The Red Ribbon', 'McKenzie of Gairloch's Salute', 'Farewell to the Laird of Islay', 'His Father's Lament for Donald MacKenzie', 'The Battle of Waternish', 'The Earl of Antrim's Lament', 'The Highland Society of London's Salute', 'Colin Macrae of Inverinate's Lament', 'Mary's Praise', 'The Frasers' Salute', 'The Lament for Red Hector of the Battles', and was compiled between 1867 and 1892: see Cannon, *General Preface*, p.16. Thomason's own manuscript collection, now deposited in Glasgow University Library (MS. Gen. 1456) was compiled between 1870 and 1878 and includes a copy of 'Borlum's Salute' taken from what Thomason calls 'The Ballindalloch MS' which is not in Donald MacKay's manuscript book, although it is in Angus MacKay's MS., a further indication that he must have had access to parts at least of this important source from a relatively early stage.

compiled at this time tend to support the later suggestion that he had a personal playing repertoire of about sixty tunes.[24]

As soon as one started to do something even as simple as this:

The End of the Little Bridge, Ground line 1, Donald MacKay, Ballindalloch MS.

2nd Variation

the structural links between the various phrases of the tune began to become apparent.

Thomason's symbols were cleverly improvised from existing notational signs, by devices like attaching to the note indicating a gairm or double-echo beat the sign for a 'mordent' or 'turn' in a way that was both logical and economical of labour and space:[25]

The Lament for the Earl of Antrim, Ground line 1, General Thomason's MS (1870-1878)

The next step was to increase lateral compression by aligning symbols on the axis of the note stem, so that the gairm, for example, could be represented like this (with various minor modifications to indicate differences in timing):

For echo-beats he adopted a minim with a hooked tail, thus replacing five signs with one:

Later on he achieved still greater economy by eliminating the tails, which were difficult to construe in the more complex combinations (and presumably were

24 Somerled MacDonald, 'The Piobaireachd Society's Music', *OT*, 16/7/1910, p.3: 'For the benefit of those not in the know, I may here remark that the General could play upwards of sixty piobaireachd on the pipes'.
25 For a discussion of Thomason's distinction between the 'gairm' and the 'eallach', see Cooke, 'Changing Styles' Pt.2, pp. 11–13.

also rather fussy to engrave), representing such movements by a semi-breve or crotchet note-head with a dot or a star above the stave to indicate accent. This could be assigned an arbitrary value without the aid of hooks and flags because it was not used elsewhere in the system:

There were various kinds of brackets to indicate repeated sections and first and second endings; each division of the tune was numbered, and a system of abbreviations adopted ('L' for Lemluath singling, 'T' for Taorluath and so on) to indicate the number and type of variations to be played. By such means the music could be represented in a precise yet highly compressed manner:[26]

26 'Revised Edition of Notation', *Ceol Mor*, p.16.

The system had been largely worked out by 1893, although it was to go on being developed until at least 1905, and it enabled even lengthy piobaireachds to be written on a single page. Eventually Thomason could represent 'The Carles wi' the Breeks', which had taken Donald MacDonald four folio pages, in a mere four lines:

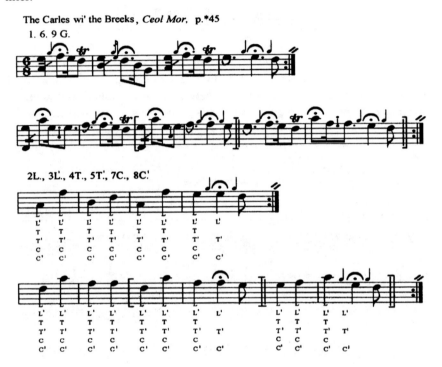

His sessions with Donald MacKay ended in November 1871 and by the following year he was back in India, where he began the final period of his military career, heavily involved in engineering projects on harbours, road and irrigation systems, studying piobaireachd by night on solitary postings, brushing up his Gaelic, turning a set of pipes with his own hands from some ebony he bought in Colombo, and busily occupied with administrative duties as Secretary for Public Works for Central India.[27]

The day after he retired, in 1888, he turned to his piobaireachd collection and the problems of imposing order on a large body of written material assembled during the course of half a lifetime. A series of difficult decisions presented themselves. By now he was determined to publish. But what? The obvious choice was an edition of Donald MacDonald's MS, the original of which he now possessed; but by about 1890 he had decided not to do this, or at least not to do this merely. He noted:

27 Mackenzie, 'General Thomason', pp.64–5.

It is now more than two years since I began to carry out my long cherished project of editing and publishing the collection of piobaireachds which I have succeeded in making on my own account. Retirement from active public service had then given me the necessary leisure for a time & the elaboration of the abbreviated notation (which alone makes the undertaking possible) had then begun to assume practical form, after having engaged my attention in a fitful way, ever since I learned my first piobaireachd from A. Cameron in 1852.

It was whilst thus engaged in the work of compilation that the original of MacDonald's second vol in MS. came to me as an heirloom and its incorporation in 'Ceol Mhor' is the result.

Many would, I daresay, argue in favour of my publishing this 2nd Vol line for line and note for note, but not only would the cost of such a work (appreciated only by a very few) be prohibitive, but I am sure that such a course would only be courting . . . disaster . . .

The fact is, the originals of MacDonald compiled during the end of the last century are full of obvious errors of omission and commission. His trip through the northern Highlands & Islands, undertaken with a view to rescuing this beautiful music from the extinction with which it was threatened after the proscription following the rising of 1745 was, (– & I speak from memory of conversations with my grandfather –) largely subsidised by the Highland Societies of London and Scotland. The notation & even the science of music in those days was very different to what it is now, & it is not at all with a view to laying disparaging stress on them that I allude to these errors. The wonder to me rather is that, MacDonald should have accomplished so much & this wonder will, I am sure, be shared by all those who have succeeded, after much practise, in committing to paper the music of a piobaireachd reaching them only through the ear. To this must be added the serious drawback of the errors in the playing of those whose music MacDonald was noting down. To this day such errors – demonstrable errors – may be detected in the performances of our best pipers & to this failing must be attributed much of the neglect that has been the lot of MacDonald's collection . . . Fortunately the music of the piobaireachd, speaking generally, follows such recognised rules, that corrections, even now, are anything but arbitrary for those who closely study the subject. The application, now for the first time, of rules as to metre has much facilitated this work of correction, & the adherence strictly to practical lines of which the abbreviated system of notation alone admits – places the corresponding phrases of the air in such clear juxtaposition that, as to my work of correction, I have been able with full confidence to submit it to the verdict of the best pipers of the day, a remark which applies especially to corrections in the work of Donald MacDonald, to whom lovers of the piobaireachd owe so much . . .[28]

28 Thomason, 'Ceol Mor Legends', ff.83–8.

Thomason was an educated and cultured man, but he was an engineer not a historian, and was correspondingly unable to appreciate at its actual worth the apparently authoritative testimony to be found in the letterpress portions of the standard published sources under the names of distinguished Highland musicians. As a result, it seemed to him that piobaireachd stood in double jeopardy. He gave a ready credence to Donald MacDonald's mediator and similar writers of that school, believing that a stringent disarming act after the '45 had outlawed the pipes and done very nearly fatal damage to the music:

> it was, in those days, often as much as a man's life was worth, if he were
> convicted of being a piper . . . Naturally, under such circumstances, the
> piobaireachd, which, up to that time had been the natural expression of the
> musical genius of the whole of the Highlands, languished, and threatened
> soon to become as extinct as the dodo.[29]

He shared the conventional view that the Highland Societies had rescued piobaireachd from destruction, believing, incorrectly but tellingly, that MacDonald had undertaken 'fieldwork' with their support. He regarded the published record as hopelessly corrupt, leading to such bad and unmusical playing that it would, unless action were taken, eventually destroy the art.[30] And it seemed to Thomason that oral transmission represented a still more serious threat. He thought that this fluid and volatile medium was inherently incapable of sustaining texts in a stable form and seemed to generate much error and corruption over relatively short periods of time. Thomason, with his highly-developed and unselfconscious literacy was moved by a fundamental assumption – that the real tune was located in the written or printed score which, if 'correct', took priority over any other form. If oral versions differed from it, they were 'wrong':

> As an instance of this I may quote the case of 'MacIntosh's Lament.' I learned
> this from Sandy Cameron in 1852–3, and he had been taught by his brother
> Donald Cameron, the best piper of his time. I have a list of D.[onald]
> MacKay's piobaireachdan with full particulars as [to] the sources from whence
> he derived his versions, and from this list I see that D. MacKay learned
> 'MacIntosh's Lament' direct from Donald Cameron. When I played over the
> tune to D. MacKay in 1870 he pointed out to me that I was playing it
> wrong, as my Ground did not agree with the variation. As it was then 17 or
> 18 years since I had learned the tune from Sandy Cameron, and as in the
> meantime I had heard many pipers playing it – no two alike – I thought it
> more than likely that the going astray was mine, and so I very carefully took
> down D. MacKay's set and have played it ever since. A few months ago I had

29 *Ceol Mor*, 'Introduction', p.i.
30 *Ibid.*

this tune played to me by Keith Cameron, Corporal Piper in the 2nd H.L.I. Keith Cameron is old Donald Cameron's son, was taught by his uncle Sandy and plays it just as I did when D. MacKay corrected me! In 'Ceol Mor' I am giving both sets, which not only differ from each other but from the set given by Angus MacKay, who taught Donald Cameron; and yet in the variations all three versions agree. It is fortunate that they do agree with each other so far, as we thus have some clue as to the really correct setting . . .

From what I have already said regarding the variations that have occurred in the settings of 'MacIntosh's Lament' since it was published by Angus MacKay a telling lesson may be learned. If my critical notes on the 'Massacre of Glencoe' be studied, it will be seen how much greater has been the divergence in the rendering of this piobaireachd in the longer interval since D. MacDonald took it down . . . The divergences go on increasing so markedly with the antiquity that I am, as a rule when correcting, driven to depend on internal evidence rather than on living authorities, and with the experience acquired by long study, I really often feel myself in a position similar to that of the late Professor Owen reconstructing his extinct saurian from the single fossil bone which is all that he sometimes had to guide him.[31]

Reconstruction. That was the master concept. What had been lost could be found again by a proper appreciation of underlying structure. Structure held the key to everything. With his tidy engineer's mind Thomason determined to prevent piobaireachd from any longer being 'the sport of tradition'. By reducing to coherent form and then publishing accurately the entire existing corpus of ceòl mór (with the exception of a handful of pieces in Uilleam Ross's, Donald MacPhee's and David Glen's books in which there might be a commercial interest) he could undo the damage of centuries.

As if to confirm that this was no mere fancy bred of isolation and over-exposure to indifferent military piping, Thomason found his anxieties echoed in the *Oban Times* from an almost uncannily similar point of view. A correspondent calling himself 'Piobaire' wrote to the paper's 'Celtic Notes and Queries' column in November 1883 about the stories attached to the well-known tunes 'The Lament for the Only Son' and 'Too Long in this Condition', claiming that they had been lost because piping folklore was disintegrating, and that piobaireachd itself was dying because it had not been written down properly:

The tunes or piobaireachds, 'The only Son's Lament,' and 'Too long in this Condition' have no story attached to them to identify the particular time or circumstances in which they were composed, though, no doubt, they were of an exceptional kind. I made the same enquiry from the old piper from whom

---

31 *Ceol Mor*, 'Introduction', pp.vi-vii. Sir Richard Owen was a distinguished palaeontologist, and author of numerous works including *History of British Fossil Reptiles*, (4 vols., Lond., 1849–84).

I learned them, but though he practiced under a pupil of the celebrated
MacKay, of Dunvegan, successor to the MacCrimmons, and though he also
made the same enquiry from the great pipers of the day whom he knew, he
could not find any story connected with these piobaireachds farther than what
their names imply. Of course, most of the piobaireachds had a story attached
to relate the circumstances under which they were composed, and these tunes
likely had theirs too; but as far as I could find out from old masters, they are
now lost, and I am afraid the tunes themselves are destined to follow. I am
aware they are both to be found laid down in some pipe music books, but I
could never reconcile the way they are put down there to the way the old
masters played them. In fact, they cannot be taken up properly from books,
hence piobaireachds are almost now lost – and a great loss it is to the
Highlander, among his several losses. This is the result of the suppression of
piping after the disastrous '45 . . .[32]

A correspondent signing himself 'Another Celt' wrote in the summer of 1893
declaring that not only were performance standards falling owing to poor tuition,
but that the quality of the audience was declining as well:

. . . as to piobaireachds, two conditions must exist before they can be
melodious or intelligible; and that is, that the performer must be a thorough
good hand who has acquired that peculiar music from a tutor of
acknowledged ability, and that the listener must be a genuine specimen of the
race for whom that music was composed. When these conditions meet, the
music can be well left to stand on its merits. At the time piobaireachds were
appreciated and understood, they were quite intelligible to those who used
them; but, no doubt, the exceedingly powerful players had a great deal to do
with this. But the suppression of piping after the '45 destroyed the music for
ever, as was intended it should, and what we have now is only the shadow . . .
I really believe there is not one living in Scotland who can now play the
'Massacre of Glencoe' as the great masters played it, and so of others. They
can never be properly taken up from books, and alas! where are now the
tutors? This has the most to do with the meaninglessness of Piobaireachds
heard now-a-days, and to listen to them with English or Englified ears does
the rest.[33]

'Piobaire' and 'Another Celt' were one and the same man, a crofter called John
Johnston from the isle of Coll, who was to continue to issue jeremiads on the
decay of piping in the columns of the *Oban Times* until well into the 20th
century. As a result of these the General entered into private correspondence with
him. Despite his public pronouncements on the decay of the old stories,

32 *OT*, 17/11/1883, p.6.
33 *OT*, 26/8/1893, p.3.

Johnston was still able to contribute a number of items to the growing collection of piping folklore called 'Ceol Mor Legends' which Thomason had been compiling for years and hoped eventually to publish when he had finished *Ceol Mor*.[34] Johnston was to exercise so powerful – and negative – an effect on the General's thinking, that this connection should be considered more closely.

We have seen how it was possible for people outside the performer community to believe that piping was in danger of extinction when the growing sales of bagpipe-music (including books of piobaireachd), the expansion in bagpipe-making and corresponding increase in numbers of players suggest that something very like the opposite must have been the case. Yet in Johnston, we have an apparently authentic voice from inside the performer community echoing the pessimistic view. John Johnston of Coll is one of the few Victorian pipers whose outlook can be considered in detail because of his extensive journalistic work. When he wrote to the *Oban Times* in 1883, he was aged about forty and a noted local man. He had been taught piobaireachd by his uncle, Hector Johnston, a pupil of John MacMaster, which latter had succeeded Neil Rankin as piper to the laird of Coll and been – as Johnston believed – a pupil of John MacKay of Raasay and a friend and colleague of Donald Roy MacCrimmon.[35] Johnston was a leading member of the community, active on the School Board, in the affairs of the Free Kirk, and in advanced Liberal politics where he took a keen interest in the Land Question. He was regarded as the leading tradition-bearer of his generation on Coll, the son of a father similarly gifted, and was well versed in Highland history, both written and oral.[36] He contributed frequently to the paper's correspondence columns on a wide range of subjects under his own name and a number of pseudonyms.[37] He was also 'District Correspondent' for Coll, supplying pieces on island affairs on a weekly basis, so that it is possible to piece together a picture of the man and his community with some precision.

John Johnston was spokesman for the remnants (some 500 souls) of a once flourishing population and the hardships and difficulties of island life were his constant theme.[38] He spoke of a crippling sense of isolation. The anchorage of

34 It quite often happened that letters published in the *Oban Times* might lead to private correspondence between interested parties. This was another way in which the paper acted as an information exchange.

35 'Dr. K. N. MacDonald and Bagpipe playing', from John Johnston, *OT*, 12/9/1896, p.3; 'The MacCrimmon Ancestry', from John Johnston, *OT*, 28/5/1910, p.3. 'Piobaireachd Playing', from John Johnston, *OT*, 22/11/1919, p.3.

36 For a brief history of the Johnston family see Rev. A. MacLean Sinclair, 'The Johnstons of Coll', *OT*, 14/7/1900, p.3.

37 His style is sufficiently distinctive to identify a number of his pseudonymous contributions to the *Oban Times*.

38 *New Statistical Account*, Argyllshire, 'Parish of Tiree and Coll', pp.195–222; *Third Statistical Account*, The County of Argyll, 'The Parish of Coll', pp.132–5. In 1841 there were 1,442 people on Coll, by 1861 almost half the population had been evicted.

Coll was rocky and dangerously exposed to the south and west. There was no pier and passengers had to transfer from the mail steamer via a rowing-boat piled high with goods and chattels, a perilous proceedings at the best of times. In heavy weather during the winter the island was effectively cut off. People watched in frustration as the mail steamer shuddered down the Minch to Tiree past their very doorsteps because it could not put in at Coll. The telegraph cable was uprooted in an Atlantic gale and there was no sign of replacement. There were no proper roads on the island and in winter parents often had to carry their children to school on their backs over the moss. In spring the fishing grounds were stripped by fleets of east coast trawlers whose lights were like a small city on the sea at night, causing Johnston to declare that 'Altogether, it comes to this, that capitalism has driven the poor off the land to the sea; and now it begins to drive them from the sea.'[39] The old Coll fairs which had once brought people to the island from all over the west were a thing of the past. Except for the occasional sporting tenant and returning tribes of *Colaich* during the Glasgow Fair, the island was seldom visited and seemed to be slipping into an irreversible spiral of decline.

There was little piping on the island, and although Johnston competed at the local Tiree games, his only opportunity to hear top-class playing was on the Coll people's annual jaunt to the Argyllshire Gathering.[40] As he wrote to the naturalist and piping enthusiast Seton Gordon, 'Regarding the MacPherson pipers you mention, I never met with any of them. Being on an isolated island I had the chance of meeting people of that kind but seldom'; he was cut off both from the mainstream of Scottish life and from piping culture.[41] Johnston had a style of playing cadences as a tumbling run of even semi-quavers which was noted by David Glen who recorded some of his repertoire for *The Music of the Clan MacLean*, noting of '*Cas air amhaich a Thighearna Cholla* – The Laird of Coll placing his Foot on the Neck of his Enemy', that 'This tune was written down by the Compiler from the playing of Mr. John Johnston of Coll, who played the 'G E D cadence' as given in Example 1st. The usual method of playing this cadence is given in Example 2nd.':[42]

39 'District News: Coll', *OT*, 13/11/1896, 29/4/1899, 3/6/1899, 15/7/1899, 22/7/1899, 19/8/1899, 30/12/1899, 2/6/1900, 18/5/1901, 14/9/12, 18/1/1913; see also 'Improvements on the Island of Coll', 8/7/1899, p.2; 'Meeting in Coll', 13/4/1907, p.2; and 'The MacLean Chiefship', 11/2/1899, p.3, in which Johnston claimed to be the great grandson of one of the Rankin pipers to the lairds of Coll.

40 'District News', *OT*, 10/10/1885, 14/1/1899, 21/7/1900, 10/1/1903, 27/7/1907, 7/9/1907.

41 Eagle, p.75.

42 Glen, *Music of the Clan MacLean*, p.22 *n*. Seton Gordon, who knew Johnston personally, confirmed that this was his usual style in such movements: see Eagle, pp.78–9.

Example 1st.

Example 2nd

Glen did not endorse the style, setting Johnston's tunes in accordance with his own notational conventions. There appears to be no other record of this way of playing, and given the rather unattractive quality of the results if played as timed (and Johnston was later to praise Glen's notation for its accuracy), it raises interesting questions about the source.[43] Johnston's repertoire contained material not recorded elsewhere; but his introductory sequences look like an attempt to play a written source as written, the source in question having obvious links with Donald MacDonald's *Ancient Martial Music of Caledonia.*

There are also questions about his reliability as a guide to piping history. The contention that John MacKay had succeeded the MacCrimmons as piper to MacLeod at Dunvegan is supported by no other reputable source and was challenged by a number of correspondents, including a representative of the MacCrimmon family.[44] The tales and legends associated with pipe-tunes supplied by other readers of the *Oban Times* during these years cast doubt on his sweepingly negative view of the state of piping folklore and the conclusions he drew from it. As to the basis of his knowledge, his numerous pieces on Highland history show that John Johnston was a well-read man, and it seems possible that the source of much of what he said about piping was derived in one way or another from the prefatory essays attached to the collections of Patrick MacDonald, Donald MacDonald, and Angus MacKay. This may explain why his views were so similar to those of General Thomason.[45]

Thomason possessed a unique concentration of sources. He had everything committed to paper by Donald MacDonald, much of Angus MacKay (thanks to the Ballindalloch papers, and the assistance of the barrister and antiquary

43 'Modern Pipe Playing', from John Johnston, *OT*, 13/9/1919, p.3. See also 'Clan MacLean Music', from Lieut. John McLennan, criticising Johnston's tunes on grounds of structural irregularity, *OT*, 15/12/1900, p.3.

44 'Dr. K. N. MacDonald and Bagpipe playing', from John Johnston, *OT*, 12/9/1896, p.3; 'The MacCrimmon Family', from James MacKinnon, 26/9/1896, p.3; 'The Last of the McCrimmon Pipers', from K. N. MacDonald, 10/10/1896, p.3; 'The McCrimmon Family', from John Johnston, 17/10/1896, p.3; 'The McCrimmons', from Norman McCrimmon, 24/10/1896, p.3.

45 For an example of his style as an historian, see 'The Norwegian occupation of Coll', *OT*, 23/10/1920, p.3, 27/11/1920, p.3.

P. E. Dove, who owned a complete transcript of MacKay's piobaireachd MSS, which the General was later able to buy), much material from Colin Cameron, his brother Sandy (the younger), Lieutenant John McLennan, John MacDougall Gillies, Donald MacKay, and, of course, all the important published texts. He had a network of piping correspondents, and the *Oban Times* to keep him up to date and publicise his views. By the same token, he was fifty-seven years old and keenly aware that his time might be short.

During the next five years, sitting at his desk in 'East Laggan', the house he had built for his retirement by the lake in Naini Tal, a pleasant hill-station in the foothills of the Himalayas in northern Uttar Pradesh, the General edited his way through very nearly the entire corpus of piobaireachd as it was then known. He sought to establish a 'correct' text, where necessary reconstructing a hypothetical 'original' by examining the different written versions and applying the insights about structure he had begun to form when studying with Donald MacKay during the early '70s. Although its formal application to piobaireachd was new, the editorial method employed by Thomason had existed for some centuries.[46] It involved evaluation of the documentary evidence by constructing a model of 'correctness' so that 'original' and 'non-original' material could be distinguished by careful collation of sources when differences amongst earlier notators were difficult to reconcile. The object was to arrive at the presumed intentions of the original composer. And insofar as piobaireachd had accumulated a body of written texts and could be supposed to conform to a literate model of composition and transmission, the approach could produce quite interesting results.

The problems confronting such an edition were great but each was met and overcome. The first was sheer scale. A collection of more than 270 tunes on the lines of MacKay or MacDonald would occupy nearly 1,000 pages and weigh more than a stone. But the General's abbreviated notation system could get a tune of any ordinary length onto a single oblong-shaped page, roughly 4 x 8 inches, producing a plump but portable volume. The General engraved the music plates himself, with substantial reduction in time, error and expense. The text was reproduced by photo-zincography courtesy of the Army Surveying Service. The resulting book was published in parts, and there were reduced rates for professional players, the object being, as Thomason explained, of 'reducing the cost of my book to a figure placing it within reach of poor pipers – a matter surely of the first importance'.[47] Thomason was well aware that this was the first

---

46 Greetham, pp.299–300; for a brief account of Karl Lachmann (1793–1851) a textual scholar who, although working at an earlier period and with rather different materials (in this case the various legends of the ring of the Nibelung), used an approach not dissimilar in essence from that of Thomason, see pp.320–23.

47 Piobaireachd Society Papers, NLS, Acc.9103/8: Correspondence 1895–1928, Thomason to William Stewart of Ensay, 13 July 1905. For the complex publication history of *Ceol Mor* see Cannon, *Bibliography*, pp.190–5.

collection of piobaireachd in staff notation by someone who was not a champion player; indeed Donald MacKay told him that he would have half the pipers in Scotland after his blood. But potential resistance was to be disarmed by a full explanation of editorial principles in the prefaces of the various editions, and also in the columns of the *Oban Times* to which the General became a frequent contributor.

Indeed it was a letter to that paper from a correspondent signing himself 'Celt' which spurred Thomason to his first public statement in a pamphlet entitled *Ceol Mor Notation. A New and Abbreviated System of Musical Notation for the Piobaireachd as Played on the Highland Bagpipe, with Examples* (Dehra Dun, 1893), setting out the principles upon which his edition was to be based.[48] 'Celt' had written from Edinburgh on 8 August 1893:

> Sir, – Can you or any of the numerous readers of the *Oban Times* inform me how it is that Piobaireachd is the only species of the music of the Gael that has neither time, tune, melody, nor rhythm in it? Did the composers intend to puzzle and annoy, or is it the performers who vie with each other in prolonging unconnected, meaningless sounds? I have recently listened to a champion playing what he called the 'Massacre of Glencoe', but really no one could make head or tail of it, and [I] am at a loss to understand how an intelligent being could call it a musical performance. I am, &c.[49]

The letter was a typical statement of the 'recitational' position, which enjoyed a good deal of support amongst contemporary *aficionados*. This was a modern version of the idea that piobaireachd was a wild and irregular music which did not adhere to 'normal' aesthetic patterns and could not therefore be represented by normal notational practices. 'Unhappily', one such writer had complained,

> no pipers hitherto appear to have had sufficient musical knowledge to notice that the ground of a piobaireachd has no rhythm known to European music. It has a *prose* rhythm – a recitational rhythm – which *cannot* be expressed by any 'time' mark . . . You might as well attempt to give the scansion of a passage in Demosthenes or Cicero as of the ground of a piobaireachd.[50]

Thomason had once taken this view himself but intensive work with the sources had led him to revise his opinions considerably. He replied to 'Celt':

48 Cannon, *Bibliography.*, pp.44–6.
49 'Piobaireachd', *OT*, 12/8/1893, p.3. 'Celt's style is not unlike that of Dr. Charles Bannatyne (1868–1924), a frequent correspondent on piping subjects. For further correspondence triggered by this letter from General Thomason and others, see 26/8/1893, p.3, 2/9/1893, p.3, 17/3/1894, p.4 (which is a review in a second leader of Thomason's *Ceol Mor Notation*), 8/9/1894, p.3, 29/9/1894, p.3, 8/12/1894, p.3, 9/3/1895, p.3.
50 Thomason, *Ceol Mor.*, 'Introduction', pp.iv–v.

. . . No one denies the faultiness of this music as now existing amongst us. Every piper knows it, and if I myself did not see it I should not have spent so many years of my life in trying to correct its errors – a fact which in itself is proof positive that, to my mind, the errors are corrigible. The 'Ceol Mor' collection when published will be found to be a far more extensive one than is generally supposed to have survived. I think, moreover, I may confidently assert that, as given in 'Ceol Mor', the music differs little from the original compositions. There is no self laudation in this, for I am careful, as far as possible, invariably to give the name of my authority and coadjutor. It is not possible, however, always to quote an authority, and here a peculiarity of piobaireachd music comes to our aid. Almost every piobaireachd gives unmistakable evidence of having been originally composed on definite rule. For instance, let us take 'The Blue Ribbon' (Grant's), one still well known to pipers. The 'urlar' ground or theme consists of sixteen bars, of which six form the first bar [a slip, this should be line], six the second, and four the third. Now, the air in reality is formed of only six bars. Let us call them A, B, C, D, E, and F. The use to which these bars are turned constitutes the air when placed thus:

A--B--A--B--C--D
A--B--C--D--E--F
A--B--C--D

[Example as it would appear in *Ceol Mor* notation]

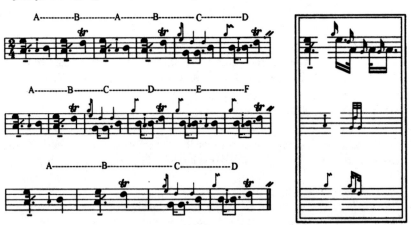

The rule or method herein is obvious; and, if the whole piobaireachd consists simply of so many following variations, comparisons between the urlar and variations, or between variations, render easy corrections of omission – the most common – and of commission. I have taken this as the simplest illustration, of which I can think, of the principle which pervades the corrected renderings of the coming book, 'Ceol Mor'. The rule for each piobaireachd is not easy to detect in this music written hitherto as prose, and in the more modern music, with the end of each line marked. Such marking does not catch the eye, and, moreover, often finds itself in the wrong place, thus completely destroying the sense of the air and much misleading the player. In 'Ceol Mor', the poetic form of writing is adopted throughout, so that it will be easy for anyone to satisfy himself whether the composer's meaning has been rightly interpreted or not . . .[51]

Applying these principles to some 173 piobaireachds from his collection he found that 112 were in the same basic regular three-lined form, containing varying numbers of bars but always arranged in the proportion 3, 3, 2 or (less commonly) 2, 3, 2. In his last preface, dated from Grantown-on-Spey in September 1905, Thomason demonstrated the application of his method in further specific cases:

> . . . with two unimportant exceptions the metres in CEOL MOR prove to be one of the three following, viz.: – Equal barred of two or four lines; three lined of metre 3,3,2, and three lined of 2,3,2 metre . . .
>
> In the case of a three lined air it will be found that the figures representing the metre in bars, if divided by 1, 2, 3, 4 or 5, as the case may be, will give us a result of 3,3,2, or 2,3,2, and this divisor will be the number of bars in each section . . .[52]

He went on to show how the principle could be used even with core material from the competition repertoire:

> The metre of 'I got a kiss of the King's hand', given in bars is 12, 12, 8, and in sections ABC-BDC-BE. The music of the 'Urlar' given by A.[ngus] MacKay is, I believe, quite correct, but when we come to the first variation we find the metre to be 11, 12, 8. There is evidently a bar missing in the first line, but what is the bar? Analysing the first section of the 'Urlar' we can distinctly trace two phrases in it, each phrase consisting of two bars, the first of which bars is identical in both phrases, and it should be the same in the variation, but the third bar is wanting. If, therefore, at this point we insert the first bar, we shall get the metre correct . . .[53]

51 'General Thomason on Piobaireachd', *OT*, 8/12/1894, p.3.
52 *Ceol Mor*, 'Rhythm in Sections', pp.1–2.
53 *Ibid.*, pp.2–3.

In MacKay's book 'I got a Kiss of the King's Hand' was, as Thomason noted, a bar short in line 1 from Variation 1 onwards; but pipers could be penalised for playing 'wrong' by bookish benches if they did not follow it note for note, so Thomason emended it as follows: [54]

Angus MacKay, 'I got a Kiss of the King's Hand', var.1, line 1, *Ancient Piobaireachd*, p.14

C. S. Thomason, 'I got a Kiss of the King's Hand', var.1, line 1, *Ceol Mor*, p.156

Missing sections of text could thus be restored either on internal grounds by comparison with other variations of the same tune, or contextually by analogy from tunes of similar construction:

'Lord Lovat's Lament' . . . I have never heard this played, and my appeals to piper friends for correction met with no success; but a record of D.[onald] Cameron's correction of the first two lines, as given to me by D.[onald] MacKay, saved us. D. MacKay could not remember the correction for the third line and I had given up the air as lost. The corrections, as far as I had them, gave me a metre of 8, 12, 4, which left a deficiency of 4 bars in the last line to bring it into the 2, 3, 2 category. To discover the four missing bars I carefully studied the third lines of all the three line airs in my collection with the following results. Out of 189 pieces thus studied I found in 99 the first section of the third line the same as in the first line, in 38 more this was approximately the case, and in 44 the first and third lines did not conform at all. Under these circumstances I determined to supply my deficiency from the first line, and was not a little surprised when I began dealing with the Taorluath that A. MacKay had supplied half the deficiency,

54 'Whenever a competitor takes on himself – no matter how good his authority – to stray from these books, the judge will say, "You played very well, but I cannot give you the prize. You went wrong in your ground; the book has it an "E", and Alastair Deirg, the best piper since the MacCrimmons, plays it the same way, but you made it an "F"', 'The Bagpipe and how to play it', from 'Celt', *Oban Times.*, 1/8/1896, p.3. James Campbell, ed., *Further Sidelights on the Kilberry Book of Ceol Mor* (Glasg., 1986), quotes Archibald Campbell: 'I have heard (a) John MacColl (b) Angus MacRae (c) [Robert] Meldrum assail fiercely General Thomason's emendation of the first line of the variations of a Kiss of the King's Hand, which is now accepted by everyone . . . That was a conspicuous example of brilliant performers becoming slavishly accustomed to what . . . contemporaries would dub as ridiculously and obviously wrong.' p.25.

and from the same source. So I have every reason to be satisfied with that correction.[55]

Sometimes, though, a phrase or line might be longer than the formula suggested and in this case extraneous material could be located and removed. 'The Cameron's Gathering' (sometimes called 'The Gathering of the Clans') is a case in point. There were settings of the tune in Angus MacKay's, Colin Cameron's, Uilleam Ross's, and John MacDougall Gillies's MSS, and they all had the same little peculiarity – an apparently 'extra' bar in the 'B' phrase of the tune.[56] And this happened not just in the ground, but throughout the variations. Here is the first line of the ground from Colin Cameron's manuscript with the General's emended version below:

'The Camerons Gathering', ground line 1, Colin Cameron's MS, f.75

['Extraneous' bar]

'The Camerons' Gathering', ground line 1, *Ceol Mor*, p.32

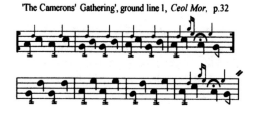

Two things happen in the *Ceol Mor* version, one structural, one stylistic. Firstly, the penultimate bar of the B phrase is excised wherever it or its variants occur; secondly, an E cadence is adopted in the final bar of both A and B phrases to balance out the rhythm and give a less abrupt feel to the phrase endings.

55 *Ceol Mor*, 'Rhythm in Sections', p.3. If one wished to treat 'Lord Lovat's Lament' as a three-line tune, this might be a plausible enough reading, although a little repetitive in line three caused by using only material already present in the tune, emphasising Thomason's need to proceed cautiously if he were to have his settings adopted; even so, his version seems musically superior to Simon Fraser's four-line setting published in the *Piobaireachd Society Collection* second series, viii, 248–9. For a useful overview of the various published texts, see G. F. Ross, *Some Piobaireachd Studies* (Glasg., 1926), p.26.
56 MacKay MS., ii, 93; Uilleam Ross MS., ff.125–7; John MacDougall Gillies MS., ff.3–5.

Yet Thomason had a light editorial touch as a rule. Sometimes what looks like quite drastic emendation entailed little more than supplying a missing portion of the ground and then adjusting the following variations to fit. His version of 'The Gathering of the MacDonalds of Clanranald' was based on a source in Donald MacDonald's manuscript in which there were a number of irregularities – half a bar missing at the end of the repeat of the ground, and in some (but not all) later variations; a couple of bars missing in the tripling movement, and again in the crunluath doubling – which spoiled an otherwise attractive tune.[57] Proceeding by analogy from a setting in Angus MacKay's manuscript which suggested that the form was probably 4: 4, 4 (although MacKay's variations were also irregular), the General was able to produce a symmetrical and idiomatically plausible reading and effectively recover a famous tune which had not been represented adequately by the written or printed record.[58]

Thomason's system of notation could cope with the form in all its complexity. It only *looked* home-made, thanks to the hand-engraved plates. He was keenly aware at the same time that no notational system could ultimately do more than echo the subtleties of actual performance. Discussing one of the crunluath-types, he noted:

> According to the author's experience, the pointing of the Breabach given in
> the various examples hitherto published, and in manuscript, is very seldom
> that adopted by pipers in practice . . . The pointing of these triplets really
> affords greater scope for taste than for dogmatising.[59]

Thomason did not regard his readings as prescriptive. Indeed he was anxious to uphold the autonomy of the performer and foster the higher expressive skills. He hoped these might be strengthened by a clearer grasp of form, particularly in the management of *rubato* which he viewed as exceptionally important in good piobaireachd playing. He urged the younger performer:

> to cultivate his taste with advantage in studying the meanings in the playing of
> masters of the art to whom he may be fortunate enough to get access; and
> eventually it will help him in giving a meaning of his own . . . For expression it is
> chiefly on his pauses that he must rely, and not necessarily on all that he may find
> in [the] Ceol Mor book, as many of these are only impressions of my own
> feelings, which may differ from his. As a rule, we may suppose every section to be
> marked by a pause of greater or less extent; but this rule must not be slavishly
> followed or we may get a sing-song style as painful as that heard in the reading of
> poetry by whose who are not adepts. Such pauses are found essential to Ceol Mor
> – hence the frequent grace note cadences; and it is in the management of his

57 MacDonald MS., ff.73–75.
58 MacKay MS., i, 156–7; *Ceol Mor*, p.46.
59 *Ceol Mor*, 'Ceol Mor Notation', p.6.

pauses (almost entirely) that a piper can show his taste. He should, in fact, treat his Piobaireachd as a song . . . even for this purpose temporarily quickening or slowing his time, but always of set purpose, and reverting to the ordinary as soon as the object of such exceptional departures from rule shall have been attained.[60]

Ceol Mor was the first collection of piobaireachd whose letterpress sections were written by the editor of the music text; but there were significant differences in outlook between the two parts of the book. Thomason moved amongst pipers with an ease and acceptance extended to few gentlemen amateurs.[61] Yet his formal education made him susceptible to the Macpherson paradigm and many of its assumptions appear in his work. He believed that piobaireachd was an ancient music which had once existed in a pure and unitary form, reflecting the creative intentions of its original composers; that its continued existence was endangered by the mechanisms of oral transmission, which were essentially degenerative so that pipers could not be trusted to transmit the music accurately; that the multiplicity of versions must indicate error and confusion; and that by an appeal to compositional first principles he could strip away the detritus of centuries and recover the 'original' text.

He had been taught by Sandy Cameron and by Donald MacKay. *Ceol Mor* had been compiled with the help of Colin and Keith Cameron and it was Thomason's proud hope 'that the book will be fairly representative of the school of Donald Cameron, in which I was educated.'[62] But he was disturbed by the variety of interpretations he found in the Cameron family. They had all received their teaching from a single source, yet they timed things differently and took individual routes through tunes. Thomason was the greatest collector and editor of his age but he had little instinctive sense for oral tradition and how it might work. Confronted with a number of spontaneously occurring variants it did not occur to him that this might be a natural and healthy state of affairs and that therefore his quest to reconstruct an 'original' text might represent a serious misconstruction of the evidence.

---

60 *Ceol Mor*, 'Rhythm in Sections', pp.4–5.
61 See below, pp.298–300.
62 *Ceol Mor*, 'Introduction', p.vii. However he stated elsewhere that 'I first met Donald Cameron more than 30 years ago, and though I was the pupil of his brother Alexander, and met them both again when home on furlough in '61 and '62, strange to say I could not get Donald to play to me. The only explanation that was ever offered me for this was that Donald knew my anxiety, even then, to book all that came within my reach as regards Ceol Mor, and he had a horror of any "chiel takin' notes". Then even more than now very few pipers could write down what they heard – I myself was a beginner at that art – and possibly Donald dreaded the results of inaccurate reporting. He had no real musical education himself, and scoffed at the idea of anyone presuming to write down from ear. Fortunately his followers thought differently . . .', see 'The Piobaireachd Society and the Cameron School of Pipers', *OT*, 29/09/1906, p.3.

For example, of the thirty one tunes he got from Donald MacKay, which had been explicitly approved as 'correct' by Donald Cameron, Thomason accepted final editorial responsibility for no fewer than fifteen, amongst them some of the greatest tunes in the tradition including: 'Patrick Og', 'Donald of Laggan', 'MacCrimmon's Sweetheart', 'The Harp Tree', 'Donald Gruamach's March', 'Craigellachie', 'Viscount Dundee' and 'The Big Spree'.[63] His view that the inherited corpus of written and printed scores was seriously corrupt sprang directly from his wider cultural assumptions. In 1893 he had written:

> The progress of my labours with my manuscript, hitherto unpublished tunes, to which 'Ceol Mor' was originally confined, so encouraged me and seemed to reveal so many unsuspected beauties, that I could not resist the temptation of extending my researches to the published tunes of MacDonald and MacKay. The conclusion at which I could not help arriving was, that both had given to the public a mine of wealth, the value of which had hitherto been entirely concealed by errors as to time and metre. As an instance, I would ask could there be a more beautiful air than the 'Sister's Lament'? And yet I had never heard any piper play it. I had myself tried it over many a time without being able to make anything of it; but suddenly its correct metre and time seemed to flash on me, and through a long illness (typhoid fever), which immediately followed that discovery two years ago, that beautiful piobaireachd never left me . . .
>
> I honestly think that it is only due to the technical errors so obviously permeating most of our published piobaireachd music as to make much of it all but unintelligible, that piobaireachd playing is now in such a languishing condition. [64]

Yet he did very little to Donald MacDonald's setting of 'The Sister's Lament' when he published it in *Ceol Mor*, except to convert the echo beats to the MacKay style and suggest a (sensible) alternative reading in a single bar towards the end of the last variation.[65] Ideology and observation were curiously at odds in C. S. Thomason. His bookish cultural expectations led him to talk about widespread error at the same time as his insight as a musician led him to respect the basic coherence of the tradition, and his settings, on the whole, did not differ very dramatically from those of MacDonald and MacKay. Thomason's musical gift was strongly in evidence in the pages of *Ceol Mor*. His settings were often sweetly playable and as a composer he was capable of real distinction, with a number of his own pieces appearing in the collection. One of them, 'Hail to my Country', is perhaps the loveliest of 19th century piobaireachds and became a

63 *Ceol Mor*, 'Index. Revised in 1905', pp. i-xiv.
64 *Ceol Mor*, 'Introduction', pp.viii, x.
65 *Ceol Mor*, pp.23–4; see also *Ancient Martial Music*, pp.53–55, and MacKay MS., i, 151–2.

great favourite.[66] The technical sections of his book contained the most systematic and extensive account of piping ornament since the days of Joseph MacDonald, and it was long and detailed engagement with the text which led him to declare that 'Ceol Mor is in every respect subject to the ordinary laws of Music', deliberately contradicting received opinion.[67] Indeed if his approach could be criticised, it might well be on grounds of being too narrowly technical. Considered in musical terms there was really no logical reason why pipers should play 'wrong'. It required a grasp of the institutional context, the bench and the competition circuit, to appreciate why this might be happening. The power relations which governed professional piping in Scotland in the closing years of the 19th century were a feature to which the General, long in India, gave little weight. But he was to experience that power, painfully, and at first hand, before many years had passed.

66 *Ceol Mor, op.cit.,* p.369. Pipers played it for love rather than money. It was not admitted – for reasons to be considered later – into the charmed circle of 'competition tunes'.

67 'Celt' wrote to the *Oban Times* declaring 'I believe it is one of the seven deadly sins to say that pibroch can be reduced to the rules of ordinary music – at least it is the sin I hear most railed against. However, it is to the General's credit that he has managed to do what others looked upon as an impossibility', 9/3/1895, p.3.

'Prepare, Sunart, for Ardnamurchan has gone to wreck': The Pipes and the Celtic Revival

The Victorian period saw piping transformed. But in educated, middle and upper class Scotland, it was as if nothing had happened. As the twentieth century dawned the familiar misconceptions about the pipe and its culture continued to be pronounced. Here, for example, is Dr. Norman Hay Forbes of Forbes, writing in 1897 on 'The Highland Bagpipe: Its History, Music and Romance' in *The Celtic Monthly*, a typical source of 'bright' and conventional opinions about the Highlands and Highland life. Behind the charmingly bogus facade of technical expertise (lifted straight out of Donald MacDonald, although the misunderstandings are the writer's own) lies the usual hotchpotch of assumptions intended to increase rather than to diminish the mystery and romance of the subject-matter. It could have been written at any time during the previous three generations:

In a history of the manners and customs of Scotland the bagpipe would fill an important page, its music a weird, wild melody, deeply sentimental in essence, the voice of nature, the expression of deep human emotions in martial, festive, amatory, or mournful strains, stimulating good and true passion, soothing bitter sorrow . . . The old Highlanders loved the simplicity of the music of the chanter with its limited compass, and, like the Spartans, refused all embellishments of arts as innovations, even though they promoted personal convenience . . .

In halls of joy and in scenes of mourning, the Highland pipe prevailed. It has fired the hardy sons of Caledonia in battle, it has welcomed them back again after their toils, to the longed-for homes of their love, and to the hills and valleys of their birth. Its strains were the first sounded in the ears of infancy, and they are the last to be forgotten in the dreamy wanderings of age. Even Highlanders will allow that it is not the gentlest of instruments; but when far away from their heath-clad mountain homes, what sounds, however sweet, however meritorious, could thrill round their warm heart, like one passionate burst of their own wild native pipe? . . .

In playing a piobrachd the 'ùrlar' or ground work theme, generally in common time, is first played, followed by the 'siubhal' or variation, of which there is most usually a doubling and often a trebling, the time quickening, and the last being generally termed 'Taorluidh' or fast movement, the 'ùrlar', like a chorus, is then repeated, and variation second commences . . . the fourth variation, which has only a doubling, and the repetition of the 'ùrlar' leads to the 'crunluath' or round, quick, and yielding movement, which has its doubling, trebling, and quadrupling, the latter part in 9/8 time, being the quickest of all runnings, extending through sixty-four bars, the piece closing with the opening strain additional . . .

Among the most beautiful and pathetic of laments may be mentioned *Cumha Mhic a' Arisaig* or 'The Macintosh's Lament,' 'Lochaber no more,' 'The Flowers of the Forest', [and] 'The Land o' the Leal' . . .[1]

As the list of tunes in the final paragraph shows, Forbes is by no means sure what a 'piobrachd' actually is. The music is presented as wild and irregular, appealing to primitive emotion, as speaking with 'the voice of nature' (and not, therefore, of conscious art), as being quintessentially martial whilst at the same time evoking powerful sentiments of 'hame and infancy'. The tradition from which it springs is represented as essentially static and communicating its full meaning only to Celts. The article was illustrated by a print of 'A Highland Piper' with bag uninflated and fingers wrongly placed.

Here is W. G. Burn Murdoch addressing the Edinburgh Celtic Union in 1895 on the subject of 'The Early Celtic Music'. He is assuring his audience that the distinguishing feature of Highland music is its utter simplicity. Indeed, it is this very quality which makes it so difficult to remember:

> . . . the older and more simple tunes . . . are so wrapped up in our beings – so much part of our souls – so long passed down to us that not only do we have the associations of times and places where we have heard them readily brought to us, but we have as well impressed on us the actual sensations that were felt long ages ago by those who have preserved the tunes for us – the Druids, Culdees, Priests, and Bards . . . Do we not hear more in these tunes than we can read in history. Do they not raise certain vague thoughts, formless pictures of wondrous grandeur . . . so powerfully do they picture to me the days of the past, that I believe it were better to lose our national records, our monuments, our museums, and the collections of dusty relics of antiquity, than to lose more than we have already lost of this music of the past.[2]

Thus Burn Murdoch neatly completes the Macpherson paradigm by adding the elements of huge antiquity, and threatened extinction which Forbes had over-looked. This was not history; still less was it folklore. The paradigm released its educated and sometimes distinguished adherents from all normal considerations of scholarship or even intellect. It was a declaration of ethnic faith, intended to be proclaimed rather than examined, a system of verbal gestures confirming the speaker as an adept of the mystic Celtic lore. As the reports of countless after-dinner speeches in the Victorian press reveal, expert practitioners could go on like this for hours.

1 Vol. 5–6, 1897, pp.216–218, 237–40.
2 *OT*, 14/9/1895, p.3.

The late-Victorian generation of English public schoolboys whose estates lay in Scotland often tried to find their way back to their Celtic roots. This could involve the assumption of Gaelic forms of their names, transforming John Campbell, say, into 'Iain' or 'Seoc' MacDiarmid, and recourse to Gaelic salutations and endearments in correspondence. But the piece on the pipe and its music contributed to *The Galley of Lorn* in 1911 by Stewart MacDougall of Lunga, one of the early doyens of the Piobaireachd Society, contains such dubious Gaelic and basic ignorance of the instrument as to suggest this process of self-conscious Celticism must often have been fairly superficial:

'Thig Crioch air an T'saoghal
Ach mairidh gaol is ceol.'
('The world passes, but love and music live for ever.')

The Bagpipes are among the oldest of musical instruments and have been known in some form or other in many countries, but with no country have they been more intimately associated at any period than that of the Gael of Alabainn . . . Piobaireachd music is an epitome of the history of the Highlands – the Clan gathering: the march to the battlefield: the glad notes of victory: the welcome to the Chief or Prince; and the Lament for the fallen – all have their story to tell . . .
    The Harp, or Chlarsaich, of old was played by the Bards to accompany their songs of warriors' deeds, of love, of mirth and of sorrow, but the Pipes – the Piobh Mhor – gathered the Clansmen for the fray and inspired them with hope and courage . . . The piper of a staunch Jacobite, Macdonald of Aberarder, was wounded in the face at Culloden, but he survived many years, and played when leading the concourse at the funeral of his master. Roads in the neighbourhood were then of a very primitive type, and on the march of 15 miles the piper's foot was deeply cut by a sharp stone. Though suffering much he never took the chanter from his lips until the consecrated ground was reached, but from that day he never played again . . .
    Of late years great efforts have been made by the Piobaireachd Society to raise the standard and improve the general playing of our pipers, and also to rescue and resuscitate old Piobaireachds, many of which had almost passed into oblivion . . .[3]

Even people who were well informed about the pipe and its music could indulge this vein, if they possessed the requisite degree of formal education. Here, for example, is W. L. Manson, whose book, *The Highland Bagpipe Its History, Literature, and Music with some account of the Traditions, Superstitions, and Anecdotes Relating to The Instrument and Its Tunes* (Paisley 1901), was the first extended study of the subject and is still consulted as a work of reference. Manson

3 *Galley of Lorn*, March 1911, pp.43–4.

was heavily influenced by James Logan (probably assuming he was listening to Angus MacKay) and his account is based on the familiar assumptions: that the pipes were proscribed after the '45 and suffered serious decline as a result;[4] that pipe music was the quintessential expression of the mystical Celtic spirit;[5] that the music was ancient;[6] that it was primitive and artless and not bound by normal aesthetic rules;[7] that the pipe was a nobly barbaric, essentially military, instrument best heard at a distance in a natural setting;[8] that the music was the property of specific clans who alone had the right to use their ancestral tunes;[9] that oral tradition was a degenerative medium and that the period of legitimate creativity lay in the past so it was largely futile for contemporary pipers to attempt to compose;[10] that the appeal of the music was ultimately irrational, such that only Celts could understand it.[11] There was in Manson a pervasive sense of nostalgia and loss, a feeling that for Highland society the glory had well and truly departed:

> The only gathering of the clans we have nowadays are the gatherings in the halls of our big cities, where a thousand or two of people bearing a common name meet under the presidency of the next-of-kin of the chief of olden times, and drink, not mountain dew, but tea, and have Highland or Jacobite songs sung to them by people whose profession is singing, and applaud dancers and pipers who dance and pipe because it pays them to do so. This is very far removed from the time when the *Piob Mohr* was in the zenith of its power, though when one gets enthused with the atmosphere of such a meeting, and forgets the slushy streets outside, and the telegraph and the railway, and other nineteenth century things that have made the Highlands impossible, the song of the hundred pipers is quite sufficient to make the blood course quicker, and to translate one for a moment to other scenes and other times. But it is only for a moment. The prosaic present comes back with a reality that will not be denied, and one remembers with a sigh that the song is but a sentiment, and that never more will the gathering cries of the clans re-echo through the glens, the fiery cross pass from hand to hand, or the peal of the pibroch ring from clachan to clachan in a wild cry to arms.[12]

4 Manson, *Highland Bagpipe*, pp.56–7.
5 *Ibid.* pp.74–5.
6 *Ibid.* pp.76–7.
7 *Ibid.* pp.77, 78, 79, 89, 96.
8 *Ibid.* pp.78, 82–3, 84, 85, 288.
9 *Ibid.* pp.99, 301.
10 *Ibid.* pp.295–6.
11 *Ibid.* p.92, although Manson elsewhere remarked that anybody capable of responding to serious music ought to be able to appreciate well played pipe music, p.77.
12 *Ibid.* p.11. A similar complex of ideas informs a contemporary work, A.[lexander] Duncan Fraser's *Some Reminiscences and the Bagpipe* (Edinr., n.d. [but 1907]), although critical of Manson at several points.

The final third of the nineteenth century was a time of uncertainty and foreboding amongst many who concerned themselves with Gaelic culture. Generations of growing religious fervour had culminated in the triumph of the Free Kirk in 1843 throughout much of the Highlands and the stern and puritanical outlook which it often fostered was thought to be doing serious damage to traditional culture.[13] The folklorist, Alexander Carmichael, whose *Carmina Gadelica* (6 vols., Edinr., 1900 ff.) was one of the definitive Victorian studies reported an informant as saying:

> . . . the good ministers and the good elders preached against them and went among the people and besought them to forsake their follies and to return to wisdom. They made the people break and burn their pipes and fiddles. If there was a foolish man here and there who demurred, the good ministers and the good elders themselves broke and burnt their instruments[14]

Norman MacLeod of the Barony, a determined foe of pharisaical humbug wherever it might occur (and especially in the Free Kirk), declared that:

> A minister in a remote island parish, once informed me that 'on religious grounds' he had broken the only fiddle in the island! His notion of religion, I fear, is not rare among his brethren to the far west and north . . . the old songs and tales are also being put under the clerical ban in some districts, as being too secular and profane for the pious inhabitants. What next? Are the singing-birds to be shot by the kirk-sessions?[15]

13 'The Old Legends and Superstitions of the Hebrides', *OT*, 22/6/1867, p.3.

14 Alexander Carmichael, ed., *Carmina Gadelica Charms of the Gaels Hymns and Incantations With Illustrative Notes on Words, Rites and Customs, Dying and Obsolete; orally Collected in the Highlands and Islands of Scotland* (6 vols., Edinr., 1900–71), i, xxvi.

15 Norman MacLeod, 'Reminiscences of a Highland Parish', in *Works by Norman MacLeod. D.D.* (Lond., 1891), p.15, *n* 1. See also Campbell, *Popular Tales*, 1, vii, xx, xxiii. How well founded the resulting pessimism about the survival of traditional culture was may be judged by the mass of material collected in the western Highlands and the Isles by 20th century fieldworkers: see Malcolm Chapman, *The Gaelic Vision in Scottish Culture* (Lond, 1978), pp.123–4. K. N. MacDonald, himself a musician, said 'I remember quite well when music and singing were at a very low ebb in Skye, but they never died out, and when the cause of depression went down music was the first thing that revived . . . now there are fiddlers and pipers in almost every village, and the majority of the women are good singers . . .', 'The Violin and Strathspey Music', *OT*, 20/4/1912, p.3. Fraser, *Reminiscences*, gives numerous examples of Free Church opposition to traditional culture and instrument breaking and burning. The author, A. Duncan Fraser, was a Gaelic-speaking physician, originally from Argyllshire, who had practised for several years during the 1870s in Skye. He supports MacDonald's view of the resilience of the traditional performing arts, pointing out that owing to the interchangeability between instrumental and vocal culture, instrumental traditions could and did survive destruction of the instruments: one could not kill the music unless one were prepared to kill the people. The focus of both studies is on Highland rural districts, but piping had already largely migrated to the towns and cities where it was immune from clerical censure.

Yet there was little comfort either in the secular sphere where the forces of modernisation were thought to be, if anything, still more perilous to the old lore. Steamships and railways, telegraph and penny post brought many benefits to the Highlands. But they were also thought to have exposed once remote communities to unprecedented external influence. This, together with the spread of tourist-related *Kitsch*, intensified anxiety that the language, tunes, songs and tales which formed the distinguishing marks of the Gaidhealtachd might very quickly become a thing of the past.[16] The Gaelic Society of Inverness, a learned body founded in 1871 to compensate for the neglect of Celtic studies by the British Academy and the Royal Society of Edinburgh, was moved to appoint a Folk-Lore Committee under the convenership of the journalist and historian Alexander Mackenzie to co-ordinate efforts to collect such material throughout the Highlands before it was too late.[17]

This sense of external threat was underlined by a rabid anti-Celticism within the British establishment, moved by social Darwinist theories which regarded the races of man as locked in a struggle for supremacy which must eventually be won by the Anglo-Saxons whose psychological maturity, political success, and guardianship of the old Teutonic liberties uniquely qualified them to govern themselves and others.[18] The Celts were seen as inferior in racial endowment, a violent, indolent and feckless crew who, having sprung from an alien cultural tradition and having never experienced (as they were in any case temperamentally unsuited for) 'liberty,' must acquiesce in the leadership of their betters and rule by an iron hand. To a world-view capable of defining the Irish people as sub-human savages and the Welsh language as the curse of Wales, the cultural identity of the Scottish Gaels was the merest bagatelle:

For years, we had thought that the Kelt was dead, and comfortably interred; and willingly, gladly, had we added a stone to his cairn. He had careered

16 'Bag-Pipe Competition', *OT*, 31/12/1881, p.5, The Chairman, Walter Douglas Campbell, stated: 'There was a great danger, in these days of rapid travelling and keen competition, of our nationality being destroyed in the process of general levelling that was so much spoken about. Why should Scotchmen, who had such a glorious past, such a noble present, and such a bright future, allow themselves to be robbed of their nationality? They must see that the landmarks were not destroyed in the great cry for cosmopolitanism. These landmarks were their songs, their music, their language, and their dress, and so long as these were efficiently maintained there was no fear of their nationality being difficult of recognition'.

17 *OT*, 27/3/1875, p.2.

18 This was a later version of the cultural supremacism which James Macpherson had attacked so powerfully a century before. For a comment on Anglo-Saxon supremacism in the mid Victorian period, see Donald Campbell, *Treatise*, pp.130–1. For an illuminating discussion of ethnocentric theories of government at this time which, although concerning itself specifically with Anglo-Irish relations, is applicable, broadly speaking, to the whole of the 'Celtic fringe', see Curtis, pp.8–15, 20, 28, 33–4, 39–44, 50–1, 69–70, 74–89, 109.

through literature for a considerable time, and had done not a little to ruin the English language by mis-spelling the words that are most frequently in use . . . [and] insisted upon interlarding his dialogues with 'whatefer' and 'moreover' to a nauseating degree . . . No longer, we fondly thought, were our notions of decency to be offended by the sight of his scanty kilt, nor our nostrils irritated by the combined efflorescence of his snuff and the intoxicating effluvium of Talisker or Glenlivet. 'Claymore', we believed, was thenceforth to be taboo in polite conversation, and 'Oich! Oich!' was to cease as an interjectional form of speech. He was dead as Queen Anne or Malcolm Ceanmòr, and the world was well rid of him.[19]

To certain English intellectuals, however, the few positive qualities that the Celts were thought to possess, their penchant for dreams and fantasies, their affinity with the sensual and the primitive, their readiness to revolt against the despotism of fact, might form a useful counterpoise to the materialistic pragmatism sweeping through the metropolitan culture. To the image of the Anglo-Saxon – 'masculine', responsible and restrained – could be opposed, or better still, absorbed and transformed, that of the idealised Celt – 'feminine', childlike and passive. Those reared in the English public school system, which by now included most of the Scottish landed élite, were instilled with such notions from a tender age. But the real Gaels were little disposed to accept a role as the fey and feckless denizens of a Celtic Twilight constructed for its own ends by a neighbouring cultural superpower. They had read Matthew Arnold, just like everybody else, and had noted his remarks that '. . . this great primitive race, all, with one insignificant exception, belongs to the English empire; only Brittany is not ours; we have Ireland, the Scotch Highlands, Wales, the Isle of Man, Cornwall . . .'[20] They appreciated the hazard that such a programme might entail to the real products of Highland culture and, aware that the goal was assimilation, were determined to resist it.[21]

Equally worrying, perhaps, was the sense of leadership crisis within the Gaelic world, the conviction that the institutions intended to promote Highland culture were rapidly losing touch with their goals, and that the upper classes were increasingly becoming alien, incompetent and aloof.[22] The Scottish Pipers'

19 'The Rampant Kelt', first published in the *Pall Mall Gazette*, reproduced in *OT*, 13/6/1896, p.3. The article concludes 'shall we confine him, as the Romans did of old, to the north of the wall of Antoninus? Or – happy thought – could we not banish him entirely?' 'His ancestors tried to do so', remarked a later correspondent grimly, 'and the result was that about 30,000 of their carcasses were left at Stirling Bridge . . .', 27/6/1896, p.3.

20 Matthew Arnold, *On the Study of Celtic Literature and other Essays* (Lond., Everyman, n.d.; originally published 1867), pp.133–4. See Chapman, *Gaelic Vision*, pp.81–99.

21 Arnold, pp.8–9, 20–21, 69–70, 82–3, 104ff. For resistance to assimilation see, 'The Gaelic Renaissance', *OT*, 10/11/1906, p.3, and 'The National Language', 16/3/1907, p.3.

22 'Highland Music', leader, *OT*, 21/11/1891, p.4; 'Scottish Music', 27/2/1897, p.4.

Society, formed in Edinburgh in 1882 and rapidly dubbed the 'Stockbridge Highlanders', had a membership restricted to gentlemen amateurs. It became a prominent social institution and its splendidly tartan levee, was, a contemporary noted, nearly as popular as the Boat Club fancy dress ball.[23] The problem, as a correspondent of the *Oban Times* observed in 1887, was 'there are about sixty pipers in number connected with this Society, who profess to play the pipes, and these put together – teacher and all – (spare me the remark), would, as the saying is, "not make a good piper."'[24]

Like all generalisations, of course, this must be treated with caution. We might consider, for example, the contrasting cases of George Douglas Campbell, (1823–1900) the 8th Duke of Argyll, and his son, Lord Archibald Campbell (1846–1913), each a reactionary, perhaps, but in interestingly different ways. Argyll was a former President of the Highland Society of Scotland and of the Royal Society of Edinburgh, Lord-Lieutenant of the county and a classic example of the 19th century 'British Peer'. He was also the *bête noir* of the *Oban Times* who regarded him as the very worst sort of 'improving' landlord. A keen amateur scientist and early opponent of evolutionary theory, he wrote a famous defence of property rights in the Highlands, *Scotland as it Was and as it Is* (Edinr., 2 vols., 1887), linking the landed élite with the forces of Civilisation and Progress and blaming the locals for causing their own problems by their ineradicable backwardness and stupidity. Lord Archibald Campbell was a different kind of man. Although an old Etonian, an alumnus of Cambridge, and a partner in the city banking firm of Coutts and Co., he had been raised by a Highland nurse, like his friend and cousin the folklorist J. F. Campbell, and identified strongly with the traditions of the people. He was the editor of *Waifs and Strays of Celtic Tradition 1. Argyllshire Series* (London, 1889) and a number of similar works. An inveterate wearer of the kilt, he defended the antiquity of tartan and the philabeg, and was active in promoting the re-introduction of the harp. His theories of culture were strongly ethnocentric. The character of the Celt, in his view, was an unstable compound of explosive violence and tender sentiment which required particularly strong and tactful leadership; yet he was considered sufficiently a friend of the Gael for the gifted William Laurie to compose the 'Lament for Lord Archibald Campbell' which was 'considered to be a masterpiece of the day' – a tribute pointedly withheld from his father.[25] His daughter the Hon. Elspeth Campbell was to become prominent in the movement to 'revive' Celtic music, and a leading member of what contemporaries called 'the Mòd Squad'. She played the pipes, and served for many years on the General Committee of the Piobaireachd Society which was founded in 1903 and

23 'Scottish Pipers Society Ball', *OT*, 15/3/1884, p.3. For an account of this society, see N. A. Malcolm Smith, ed., *The First One Hundred Years A History of the Royal Scottish Pipers' Society* (Dunfermline, n.d.).

24 'The Recent Bagpipe Competition', from 'Tullochgorm', *OT*, 31/12/1887, p.3.

25 See 'A Famous Ballachulish Piper. Pipe-Major Wm. Laurie', *OT*, 16/12/1916, p.5.

was, like *An Comunn Gaidhealach*, an attempt to re-organise to meet a perceived threat to the traditional Gaelic arts.

The numerous Highland societies were criticised as mere facades, existing largely for the purpose of an annual dinner and a little genteel self-congratulation while doing little to foster the language and culture of the Gael.[26] In a leader column in August 1887, the *Oban Times* declared: 'Till recently Highlanders were evidently unable to do anything without evoking the aid or presence of some lord or duke, who turned in course of time all patriotic attempts to the benefit of his order rather than to the good of the people and their abused interest', and it neatly summed up the situation in its spoof report on the first annual gathering of the great Clan MacSneeshin:

Sir, – You must know that, during the recent clan fever, the Clan MacSneeshin, in a commendable spirit of emulation, formed themselves into a society on the usual lines. Among the chief objects of our society are the fostering of Highland sentiment, the cultivation of our ancient language, and encouragement of the wearing of the picturesque dress worn by the MacSneeshins on many a hard fought field. With these laudable objects in view we set manfully to work, and it will interest you very much to know that our first attempt towards their furtherance has been made with conspicuous success. The first annual reunion of the Clan MacSneeshin is an accomplished fact! Our chief, Mr Taddeus MacSneeshin-Smythe (of Finsbury Pavement, London), occupied the chair, and his introductory address, of which I present you with a brief résumé, was received with tumultuous applause. 'It gave him much pleshaw, he said, to be present at this, he had no doubt the first, peaceful gathering of the ancient Clan MacSneeshin. It was the first time he had crossed the bordaw – (cheers) – and he was agreeably surprised to see so many decent, well-dressed people present. (Applause). It showed that the Celt had good qualities which Saxon civilisation was calculated to bring to the surface. As for himself, he was not one of those who believed that the Celt was utterly bad. (Cheers). He asserted firmly and with confidence that there were some men of Celtic blood whose qualities would do no discredit to the great Anglo-Saxon race! (Loud cheers). He would not detain them longah. He heard the pipahs tuning up their – aw – pibrocks outside. The pibrock was a most interesting instrument – at a distance. (Laughter). He would merely renew his expression of pleshaw at being present at such a meeting – an event, he might say, which was most significant of the progress of civilisation'. (Loud cheers). A most enjoyable programme was then duly entered upon. The famous Camlachie comic elicited roars of laughter by his clever sketch entitled 'Tonal MacIlwham'. His imitation of the Highland

26 See 'A Proposed "Glasgow Pipers' Society"', *OT*, 10/12/1887, p.3; 'Glasgow Inverness-Shire Association. Sensational Address by President', 14/10/1899, p.3; 'Highland Societies and their Work', 21/10/1899, p.3.

accent was most natural, and his Highland costume excruciatingly funny. As his kilt was the only one in the hall the chief surveyed it with evident interest. Miss Arabella MacSneeshin's rendering of that interesting old Celtic air 'Daisy Bell' evoked an enthusiastic encore,[27] and Mr Browne-MacSneeshin's 'Man that Broke the Bank at Monte Carlo' was much appreciated. The customary Gaelic song followed, and was good-naturedly applauded by a considerable section of the audience. The Camlachie comic, whose reappearance was hailed with tremendous applause, then gave his inimitable rendering of –

> 'My name is Mr Smiler
> My heid's as big's a biler,'

and fairly brought down the house. An assembly followed, at which, owing to the lateness of the hour, it was found necessary to dispense with one item of the programme, viz. the usual Highland reel. The waltz music by Herr Snuffenberg's band was all that could be desired. The foregoing brief report of the proceedings of our first reunion will, I think, convince you that the society is entering upon a successful career, and that the objects for which it was instituted are in no danger of being lost sight of.[28]

There seemed, then, a pressing need to overhaul the voluntary agencies concerned with Gaelic culture, and there was much looking outwards to other parts of the Celtic world for models of how this might be done. Interest in the *Eisteddfod* led to the establishment in 1891/2 of the *Mòd* and *An Comunn Gaidhealach*, dedicated to the promotion and encouragement of Celtic literature, music and home industries and there was active interest in the Irish *Feis-Ceoil* and the Pan-Celtic Society.[29] Alexander Carmichael returned from the first Congress of the Pan-Celtic Society in Dublin in 1901 impressed with the richness of Breton musical antiquities and the progress which had been made in the work of collection there. He was dismayed that perhaps thousands of Scottish Gaelic traditional poems and songs might have been lost during the previous two centuries and prayed 'for an earthquake to shake up the dry bones of Highland apathy'.[30] Indeed it was L. A. Bourgault-Ducoudray's collection of Breton folk songs which prompted Marjorie Kennedy Fraser to search for similar material in

---

27 Better known as 'A Bicycle Built for Two', written by the well-known vaudeville composer Harry Dacre.

28 'Clan MacSneeshin – First Annual Gathering', *OT*, 2/12/1893, p.3.

29 See 'The Irish Feis Ceoil', *OT*, 8/1/1898 p.2; 'A Highland Eisteddfod. Meeting in Oban', 18/10/1890, pp.2, 4, 1/11/90, p.3; 'An Comunn Gaidhealach', Leader, 2/5/1891, p.5; 'The Celtic Wave', Leader, 21/09/1907, 4; 'The Pan Celtic Congress', 5/10/1907, p.2; 'Some Noted Workers in the Celtic Revival. The Founders of the Mod', by A. M., 27/11/1920, p.3.

30 'The Antiquity of Gaelic Music and Song', by K N. MacDonald, *OT*, 26/10/1901, p.3. See also K. N. MacDonald 'Gaelic Music', 11/12/1897, p.3.

the isles.[31] There was an attempt to revive the harp and in 1892 David Glen's cousins, J. & R. Glen of Edinburgh, made the first modern clarsachs.[32]

It is notable how frequently Gaelic culture was placed within a wider non-British context. The journalist and translator Lachlan MacBean, editor of *Songs of the Gael* (Edinr., 1890), writing on 'The Gaelic Revival and the Mission of the Celt', declared:

> It is, broadly speaking, an outburst of race feeling shown in love of country, and people, and language, and music, and traditions – not an unprecedented phenomenon in the . . . world. It may be compared with the Slavonic dreams of a united race that adds a tinge of romance to the politics of Russia and the Turkish principalities, or to the Greek revival, which led to the resurrection of Greece; or even to the old Hebrew patriotism so vividly portrayed in our bibles. In all these instances, the race feeling has been allied with politics or religion – in our case, it is almost entirely literary or social; and yet in the case of Gael, and Greek, and Jew, and Slav, the great object in view is the welfare of the race and the triumph of its genius.[33]

According to a reviewer of *Lyra Celtica: An Anthology of representative Celtic Poetry* (Edinr., 1896), 'The Celtic Renasence is upon us with all its seductive power and witchery of expression. Not only in this country does it effloresce . . . but in France and Germany in particular, Celtic students and savants are working with a fervid interest to unearth beautiful fragments of a dim, mysterious but heroic past'.[34] And the following month the current issue of the *Zeitschrift für Celtische Philologie* was reviewed in the *Oban Times*.[35]

Much energy went into the promotion of the Gaelic language and the 1890s witnessed the publication of several important new grammatical studies, including Alexander MacBain's *Gaelic Etymological Dictionary* (1896). But it was difficult to banish the sense of underlying malaise. The Ossian controversy broke out anew, with K. N. MacDonald forced to defend Macpherson's work against the charge of J. F. Campbell and Hector MacLean that not a line of it could be found in the heroic oral poetry of the Gael.[36] There were gloomy

---

31 Louis Albert Bourgault-Ducoudray (1840–1910), *Melodies populaires de Basse-Bretagne* (Paris, 1885). See also Marjorie Kennedy-Fraser, *A Life of Song* (Lond., 1929), pp.100–101.

32 'The Mod at Oban', by Lord Archibald Campbell, *OT*, 2/9/1893, p.3; 'The Harp or Clarsach', from 'Fionn', 24/3/1894, p.2; 'The Harp Institute', 4/4/1896, p.2. The Mòd was culturally conservative: for the active discouragement of new composition by An Comunn, see 'Gaelic Song and Music', from 'Mac', 26/4/1924, p.3.

33 Pts. 1–3. *OT*, 27/4/1895, p.3; 4/5/1895, p.3; 11/5/1895, p.3.

34 *OT*, 21/3/1896, p.3.

35 *OT*, 4/4/1896, p.3.

36 For the progressive re-construction of the Gaelic text during the 19th century, and a review of the end of century controversy, see 'What Ossian?', *OT*, 22/2/1902, p.4.

accounts of decline in Gaelic psalmody[37] and of the withdrawal of the upper classes from active participation in the native instrumental music.[38] The antiquity of Highland dress was challenged and the authenticity of the Highland Games called into serious question.[39]

The music of the pipe was seen as a key to the problem of self-definition. A people who could produce such an instrument and such music must surely be the antithesis of the 'hysterical degenerates' which the Celtic Twilight thesis seemed to require.[40] Yet in the piping world also there were anxieties about the well being of tradition. There was a worrying lack of precise information, even about quite recent periods, shown, for example, in the debate about the MacCrimmon genealogy which began in the later 1880s and wandered on well into the twentieth century. How and when had their connection with the house of Dunvegan ended? Some said with Iain Dubh, others with Donald Roy, still others that it had continued in a different line, ending with Kenneth MacCrimmon in about 1840. There was even a suggestion, as we have seen, that John MacKay, Angus's father, had been the last great piper to the MacLeods of Dunvegan.[41] 'Fionn' tried to make sense of the succession in 1889 and was still struggling with it twenty years later.[42] There were nagging doubts that the pipe itself might not be particularly ancient, nor, indeed, have originated in Scotland.[43]

37 'Gaelic Psalmody', Leader, *OT*, 14/4/1894, p.4. See also 'Scottish Music', Leader, 27/2/1897, p.4, reporting a lecture recently given in Glasgow by the Scottish composer Hamish MacCunn: 'the pity of it all is, as Mr MacCunn remarked, that . . . [there] has come an attitude which a certain class of people assume towards anything in the vernacular – a "kind of superior attitude, and a conviction that Scottish music is slightly vulgar, that it is hardly the thing for young ladies and gentlemen to sing, and that it had better be dropped."'

38 'Scottish Dance Music and its Composers', Leader, *OT*, 19/10/1895, p.4.

39 'Lord Archibald Campbell and the Tartan Question', *OT*, 14/3/1891, p.3; 'The Tartan Revividus', Leader, 4/4/1891, p.4; 'Highland Dress and Ornament', Leader, 23/9/1899, p.4. For Highland Games, see above pp. 202–3.

40 'Pipes, Pipers, and Piobaireachd. By Dr Charles Bannatyne', *OT*, 2/5/1903, p.2; Part II, 9/5/1903, p.2; Part III, 16/5/1903, p.6.

41 See 'Dr. K. N. MacDonald and Bagpipe playing', from John Johnston, *OT*, 12/9/1896, p.3. See also, 'The MacCrimmon Family', from James MacKinnon, 26/9/1896, p.3; 'The Last of the MacCrimmon Pipers', from K. N. MacDonald, 10/10/1896, p.3; 'The MacCrimmon Family', from John Johnston, 17/10/1896, p.3; 'The MacCrimmons', from Norman MacCrimmon, 24/10/1896, p.3; 'Ceol Mor', from C. S. Thomason, 23/1/1904, p.3; 'The MacCruimein Bagpipe Style', from C. S. Thomason, 6/2/1904 p.3; 'The MacCrimmon Ancestry', from 'Fionn', 30/4/1910, p.3; 'The MacCrimmon Ancestry', from John Johnston, 14/5/1910, p.3; 'The MacCrimmon Ancestry', from 'Fionn', 21/5/1910, p.3; 'The MacCrimmon Ancestry', from John McLennan, 'D.M.R.', John Johnston, and 'Fionn', 28/5/1910, p.3; 'Piobaireachd', from Chas. Bannatyne, 10/1/1920, p.3.

42 See 'The MacCrimmons of Dunvegan', by 'Fionn', *OT*, 21/9/1889, p.5, and 'A MacCrimmon Certificate', from 'Fionn', 16/10/1909, p.3.

43 'Scotland, the Scots, and the Origin of the Highland Bagpipes', *OT*, 1/4/1899, p.3.

The litany that the music of the pipe was 'lost and neglected' and in a 'languishing condition' had been pronounced routinely by the leadership élite in Scotland for more than a century. But there was a new sense that the publicly performed repertoire was becoming dangerously narrow and stereotyped and that a handful of senior professionals were dominating the prize-lists year after year, stifling younger talent. Some appealed to the conventional 'explanation' for this, and saw it as a sign that the music was dying. Others, more realistically, suggested that the cause lay in the environment of competition, which made pipers reluctant to venture beyond the limited range of stock pieces familiar to the bench, that the problem lay therefore with the audience and in particular the landed and titled element from which the cadre of judges was recruited.

In September 1903 a series of influential articles appeared in the *Oban Times* under the title 'The Passing of the Piobaireachd' by a writer signing himself 'A.M.'. It was followed by a second series in 1905. The 1903 articles were re-issued as a pamphlet and became quite a *cause célèbre;* but nobody knew who 'A.M.' was. The initials, certainly, were famous. They had appeared at the foot of many a piece by the Highland journalist and historian Alexander Mackenzie, editor of *The Celtic Magazine* and *The Scottish Highlander,* and a brave and tireless campaigner in the Crofters' cause. But Mackenzie had died in 1897, and the identity of the *Oban Times's* A.M. was never revealed. What could be gauged from the pieces themselves was that the writer was a polished prose stylist with a formal education of which the classics had clearly formed part, and seemed well informed about competitive piping and the conditions under which it took place. The analysis was gloomy: 'One after another the old families are giving place to the English merchant. The old customs are fading, the old language is dying, while year by year the colonies and the Lowland town reap their Highland harvest and leave the empty land emptier still'. Never had there been more pipers, said A.M., or more enthusiastic audiences for the more vulgar kinds of performance. But 'real pipers', the masters of piobaireachd, how many were there in the world – ten perhaps? And were matters in this respect not going from bad to worse?

> The decadence of the piobaireachd is strikingly apparent to anybody who
> attends three or four Highland games in the summer, and listens carefully to
> half a dozen of the leading pipers of the day competing for the piobaireachd
> prize. That he will hear fine playing is unquestionable. For sheer brilliancy
> and accuracy of execution, and (in one or two cases) scholarly interpretation
> of the music, the exhibition will be all that could possibly be desired. What is
> depressing, however, is to hear the same old round of six or seven tunes
> played time after time, day after day. 'The Glen is Mine', 'The Massacre of
> Glencoe', 'I got a kiss of the King's hand', 'Pibroch of Donuil Dubh',
> 'Donald Dugald MacKay', 'Moladh Mhairi', and 'Glengarry's Lament', are
> most frequently heard. There are a few more, which are not played quite so
> often – 'The Blue Ribbon', 'MacKay's Banner', 'Seaforth's Salute', 'Too long

in this condition', 'Clan Chattan's Gathering', 'Lament for the only son', 'The battle of Waternish', 'McCruimen's Sweetheart', and 'Chisholm's Salute'. These are all very beautiful tunes no doubt, but do they represent all the piobaireachd music which has been composed for the pipes? As far as the general public is concerned, and pipers who are not members or pupils of the old piping families, it is a melancholy fact that they do. There can be only one reason for this, namely, the utter lack of interest in and proper appreciation of piobaireachd prevailing among Highlanders of the present day. This is why the judging of piobaireachd playing at many of the games is so scandalously bad as to discourage pipers from making any effort to improve themselves as masters of piobaireachd music. This is why no attempt is being made to preserve and record the many fine old tunes which still exist, but which will be lost ere long . . .[44]

A.M. condemned the Highland lairds for failing to sustain the class of master players and the general run of Highland societies for devoting their energies to the accumulation of funds with which they then did little or nothing. Most writers on piping revealed few signs of genuine knowledge, and altogether there was so little to foster a lively and informed interest in the classical music of the pipe that apart from the effort and enthusiasm of the master pipers there seemed little to prevent it from foundering in general ignorance and apathy:

There is said to exist an association, styled the [Royal] Scottish Pipers' Society founded some twenty years ago, with its headquarters in Edinburgh, and professing as its object the encouragement of piping. The writer has been informed that it has a large membership, composed entirely of officers of the army, and gentlemen of high social position from all over Scotland, and that its financial condition is most satisfactory. That a society like this should sit on the fence, and do nothing is perhaps the most lamentable feature of the whole miserable business . . .

Not that the professional competitor is one to be sneered at or held up to reproach in any way. On the contrary he is a man who should be, and is, appreciated in the abstract, and admired and respected in the concrete. He is hustled by pompous stewards, he is put on a platform to play amid the din of a brass band and the hooting of steam merry-go-rounds. He is frequently the victim of cruel injustice at the hands of ignorant judges. Yet he takes a host of annoyances, which might tempt Job himself to commit a breach of the peace with philosophic cheerfulness, blended with that polished courtesy, which is his invariable characteristic . . . And in this he gets no assistance from the numerous writers on Highland subjects of the present day. Articles do appear, have appeared quite lately, in Highland newspapers and periodicals, but nearly

44 'The Passing of the Piobaireachd. By 'A. M.'' Part 1, *OT*, 29/8/1903, p.3.

every one is a farrago cooked according to the same recipe, and that recipe a simple one. Take Angus MacKay's book, boil down the preface and the notes, and serve hot, with a few quotations from Neil Munro's 'Lost Pibroch' . . . It is not far off the truth to say, that nothing in the shape of descriptive writing has ever been published in Gaelic or English by anyone possessing a technical knowledge of piobaireachd music . . . We want to see fewer letters appear in the papers complaining that one piper plays a tune one way, and one another; letters talking about a committee, forsooth, to decide upon an official setting for every tune, and to provide for the damnation of every player of a non-official style, and the destruction of the individuality of piping, its most characteristic and pleasing feature.[45]

A.M. argued that piobaireachd was not a rude and ancient but a modern sophisticated music, but that there had been an entire failure to appreciate this fact or what it might mean for the study of historically recent Scottish culture. Popular taste was so corrupt that a flimsy affair like 'MacIntosh's Lament' was held up as a standard of excellence while better compositions which did not echo its trite phraseology were condemned out of hand. Standards were being dragged down by the deplorable ignorance of the bench: 'pipers play piobaireachd solely in order to win prizes in competitions, judged frequently by men without the slightest elementary knowledge of the subject':

> . . . there is no time to waste. Men are dying, tunes are perishing, knowledge is waning. There are four pipers alive in Scotland to-day, and should they all, by some evil chance, die to-morrow, piobaireachd playing would receive a blow which might kill it outright . . . all that is hoped for is that some reader of this paper, which circulates among Highlanders in every quarter of the globe, will be induced to think over the matter, and to consider what he personally can to do save Ceol Mor. 'Prepare, Sunart, for Ardnamurchan has gone to wreck!' and if the piobaireachd dies, then dies also the spirit of the Scottish Gael.[46]

It is now possible to identify A. M. Annotated master copies of the *Oban Times* show the source of both series as 'Campbell Kilberry/ Campbell, India/ Campbell, Dehli'. The initials probably stand for 'Aonghas MacDiarmid' a Celticisation of the name of Angus Campbell of Kilberry, a representative of an old Argyllshire family, then practising at the English bar, although the views expressed seem likely to be the joint conclusions of all three of the Kilberry brothers, John, Angus and Archibald. To preserve the authors' incognito, the letters were probably routed via Archibald, the youngest, then with the Indian

45 Same, Part 2, 5/9/1903, p.3.
46 Same, part 4, 19/9/1903, p.3.

Civil Service.[47] Their object was to publicise the Piobaireachd Society which the Campbell brothers had just founded to address the problems described above.

47 Archibald Campbell was identified as 'A.M.' in an unsigned obituary notice in the *Oban Times* in 1963, reprinted with the title 'Highland Bagpipe Music's Finest Authority' *The Piper Press* no.5, March 1998, pp.20–23 (21). Tentative support for this idea was offered by James Campbell in 'History of the Piobaireachd Society', in *Proceedings of the Piobaireachd Society Conference*, 1977, pp.30–48 (30), and accepted by Roderick Cannon in *Highland Bagpipe*, pp.90, 176. But the letters resemble the prose style of Angus rather than of Archibald Campbell who does not appear to have claimed personal authorship at any stage. A Gaelic version of Archibald Campbell's initials would have been 'G.M.', Gilleasbuig being the equivalent form for Archibald. Angus was the most active of the three brothers in the Piobaireachd Society's early affairs and died in 1908 at the age of 35.

13

'Binding the Piper with Chains of Gold': The Piobaireachd Society, 1902–1914

In the autumn of 1902 a carefully selected group of Scottish gentlemen received the following printed invitation:

> Kilberry, Argyllshire, 1902
> Sir,
>   I have the honour to inform you that it is proposed to form a Society, having as its objects the *Preservation of Old Highland Piobaireachd, and the diffusion of knowledge concerning them.*
>   It is, I think, an undoubted fact, that very few Piobaireachd are at present generally known or played even by the best Professional Pipers, and that many of the most beautiful are never heard at all.
>   It is proposed, in the first instance, only to invite those who are believed to have the above-mentioned objects really at heart, and who have themselves some knowledge of Piping, to become Members. Will you kindly let me know by the 1st November, whether you wish to become a Member of the Piobaireachd Society?
>   It is intended to hold a Preliminary Meeting at some central place as soon after that date as possible, to settle the Constitution of the Society, the Subscription, and the best method to adopt for furthering our objects.

It was issued by Capt. John Campbell, yr., of Kilberry, representative of a prominent Argyllshire family whose estate lay in Knapdale at the head of Kintyre. Campbell had been educated at Harrow and Sandhurst and was a serving officer in the Argyll and Sutherland Highlanders. He was a man of scholarly temperament, who had become a soldier in deference to family tradition. He was also an enthusiastic amateur piper – like his lawyer brothers, Angus and Archibald who were co-founders of the Society and his supporters through the difficulties that followed.[1] Their careers made it difficult for the Campbells to attend meetings – even the opening session of the Piobaireachd Society of Scotland which took

---

1 When these remarks were made there was more piobaireachd available in published form than at any time before or since. Ross's, MacPhee's, Thomason's and at least four volumes of Glen's collection were all in print containing between them approaching 300 tunes. For further details about John Campbell see 'Myth of Kintyre', the *Herald*, 8/8/1998, p.19. For a piping house party at Kilberry Castle on the eve of the Great War, see 'The New Year at Kilberry', *OT*, 21/1/1911, p.2.

place in Edinburgh on Monday 19th January, 1903, in Dowell's Rooms, 18 George Street with Capt. Charles A. H. MacLean of Pennycross in the chair. Four others were present – Capt. Malcolm MacNeill, D. B. MacDougall, Somerled MacDonald, and James MacKillop jr. of Polmont. A committee was appointed and qualifications for membership drawn up, stating that 'the Candidate for election must be a player of Piobaireachd on the Highland Bagpipe, or the Committee must be satisfied that the Candidate has the love of Piobaireachd thoroughly at heart'. James MacKillop was appointed Secretary and General Charles Simeon Thomason nominated as President. A prospectus was drawn up specifying the aims of the new Society. These included the acquisition of printed and manuscript sources, but made no reference to field collecting or oral tradition. Professional pipers were excluded from membership.

The fourteen founder members came mainly from landed and military backgrounds, and included Capt. (later Sir) Colin Macrae, and Capt. (later Major) William Stewart of Ensay, the painter Somerled MacDonald (great-grandson of Niel MacLeod of Gesto), and the Hon. Elspeth Campbell, daughter of Lord Archibald Campbell. Many were also members of the Scottish Pipers' Society.[2] The Piobaireachd Society of Scotland was intended to be small and select, little more than a study group at first, which, as its members' knowledge increased, might eventually begin to issue definitive scores and provide a pool of genuinely knowledgeable judges for the bigger competitions.

But events quickly took on a momentum of their own. The entry qualification was relaxed and the original band of enthusiasts, drawn mainly from the lesser and middle gentry, was swamped by the great aristocracy and its clients who had little time for so studious and gradual an approach. By the summer of 1903 the Duke of Hamilton, the Marquesses of Graham, Tullibardine, and Bute, and the Earl of Dunmore were already members. That year, the fourteen were joined by a further 38 and in 1904 by another 28 members, most of them wealthy and well-connected and very few of them players. By 1905 the Society's connections with the upper echelons of the British establishment had become so intimate that its effective headquarters had moved to London and in its minute-book, the sobriquet 'of Scotland' was struck out. It was now under royal patronage and receiving financial support from about a dozen Highland and other regiments. Within three years of its formation the Piobaireachd Society represented a concentration of power so formidable that it could be spoken of in the same breath as the Royal Highland and Agricultural Society of Scotland.[3]

Almost at once it was resolved to sponsor a major professional competition at the Argyllshire Gathering under stringent new rules. Instead of competitors

---

2 See Smith, *Royal Scottish Pipers*, p.13.
3 Piobaireachd Society Papers, NLS, Acc 9103/1 Minute and Cash Book; Acc.9103/5 Printed rules and lists of members, 1905, 1910, 1913, 1932, 1935, 1973; Acc.9103/8: Correspondence 1895–1928, Angus Campbell to William Stewart of Ensay, 3/7/1905. See also 'Bagpipe Music – The Piobaireachd Society's Collection', *OT*, 6/5/1905, p.3.

nominating their own lists, as formerly, the Society was to determine which tunes were to be played and, instead of their own settings, competitors were obliged to use a standard score, to be played as written. A sum of £20 and a Gold Medal was voted as first prize. The set tunes, selected by General Thomason and Colin Cameron, were reproduced from *Ceol Mor* and distributed free to intending entrants.[4]

A.M.'s third letter appeared in the *Oban Times* on 19 September 1903. In the adjoining column was an article, largely written by General Thomason, announcing the new Society:

> The Piobaireachd Society of Scotland was instituted in January last, and in view of the promised revival of the piobaireachd, it will be of interest to publish some particulars of its aims and intentions
>
> The office-bearers are: – President, Major-General C. S. Thomason, R.E.; secretary and treasurer, Mr J. MacKillop, jr.; committee, Captain Colin MacRae, Captain C. A. H. MacLean of Pennycross, Captain Kenneth Cameron, R.A.M.C., Captain Malcolm MacNeill, D.S.O., Somerled MacDonald, and Major S. MacDougall of Lunga.
>
> The objects of the society are: –
>
> (a) The encouragement, study, and playing of piobaireachd music on the Highland bagpipe.
> (b) To collect piobaireachd MSS and Legends, and publish tunes which have never before been published, and to correct, when possible, tunes already in print which are known to be wrong.
> (c) The general advancement and diffusion of knowledge of this ancient Highland music.
> (d) Eventually, by offering adequate money prizes, to hold piobaireachd competitions, to be judged by members of the society. A list of tunes to be played at such competitions to be selected by the society.

The article explained that the proscription of the pipes after the '45 had left the music in 'a languishing and tottering condition'. There were numerous errors in the published versions owing to the difficulty of writing the music down and the limited education of the compilers. This had resulted in different versions of many tunes unfortunately gaining currency. The regularity of the form made it possible to correct many of these errors, however, and this the Society would do. It would judge where necessary between different renderings of conflicting authorities and take steps to preserve and publish the manuscript sources. The Society would also have regard to the verbal lore of the pipe and would collect and publish stories relating to the tunes. Since one of the main objects was to increase the repertoire heard in public the Society would issue set tunes for the

4 NLS, Acc. 9103/1, 16/3/1903, 4/6/1903, 14/8/1903.

competitions it sponsored. This would foster new talent by ensuring that all competitors started on an equal footing. The writer concluded:

> The society believe that the falling off in piobaireachd playing is largely due to two reasons – First, that so many pipers have different settings of the same tune, and they are afraid to play certain settings, in case their setting may be different to that which the judges think the correct thing; second, that many tunes are so long that the pipers are afraid to play them, as a long tune is a much greater strain both on the fingers and on the pipes than a short one. A set of pipes might stand splendidly for 'Glengarry's Lament', but would go all out of tune in playing 'Donald Ban MacCruimein's Lament.' The society shall, as much as possible, select tunes of equal length, so that all the pipers may be put on the same footing, and not one get a very short tune to play and another a very long one, which happens often under existing rules.
>
> With regard to the settings of tunes, the society, after much consideration, has decided to adopt 'Ceol Mor', collected by Major-General Thomason, R.E. The reasons for this are:- First, that 'Ceol Mor' is the only large collection of piobaireachd in existence; second, that the society will be able to distribute six piobaireachd in abbreviated 'Ceol Mor' settings, with key to the notation, amongst the pipers at a very small cost. With no other book of piobaireachd can this be done, as neither the society nor the pipers could afford the expense of buying so many tunes written out in full.
>
> The Society does not guarantee that 'Ceol Mor' is free from mistakes, or that the settings in it are the best, but it is a standard from which all can play the same setting, and this will put all competitors on an equal footing.
>
> If after the competition each year any competitor can point out errors in a tune, or give a better setting on some good authority, the committee of the society will thoroughly consider his suggestions, and should they decide to adopt them, they will be glad to pay those who assist them in trying to correct the tunes as much as possible.
>
> The society hope by this means at some future time to be able to publish the best and most correct book of piobaireachd in existence, and to restore the ancient Highland Piobaireachd to the exalted position it held when the College existed in Skye under the far-famed MacCruimeins.
>
> The society will select only those who are thoroughly acquainted with the tunes to act as judges at these competitions, so that the pipers may have absolute confidence in them.
>
> The tunes for next year's competition will be:-
>
> 'The Desperate Battle Perth'.
> 'The King's Taxes'.
> 'Lament for MacLeod of MacLeod'.
> 'The Earl of Seaforth's Salute'.

'The Groat'.

'Lament for the Earl of Antrim'.

The committee has decided to let pipers have these tunes free of charge this year, and they may be had on application to the secretary of the society.[5]

There were immediate protests from the performer community about the idea of set tunes. The difficulty was not the number, but the labour involved in bringing existing repertoires into conformity with the prescribed scores. If adopted more widely, it would mean pipers having to keep up substantial lists of such pieces to competition standard and since only top professionals had the time to do this, it would effectively prevent the semi-professional or occasional player being heard.[6] David Glen did not think that distributing music free was a good idea at all. Sensing a threat to his position as Scotland's leading publisher of bagpipe music, he offered to supply the Society with the set tunes at a price it could hardly refuse (although it did).[7] Most disturbing of all, perhaps, was a campaign against the adoption of Thomason's system of notation, prompted by a dissident group inside the Society itself, leading to a partial boycott of the first competition at the Argyllshire Gathering in September 1904.[8]

Pipers familiar with conventional notation could read Thomason without much difficulty and acknowledged the system to be 'clever' and 'intelligible'. But those starting from lower levels of musical literacy – as many did – found it a more formidable challenge. More importantly, the new requirement to play fixed standard texts meant laboriously unlearning existing settings, which was harder than getting up a tune from scratch. Some thought that it would be simpler for competitors to submit a written setting of what they meant to play and be judged on it.[9] But the players were knocking on a locked door. While Thomason sought dialogue some of the other founder members regarded the performer community as the main threat to the Society's programme and were resolved above all else to disrupt its control of the repertoire.

In September 1903, Capt. William Stewart of Ensay was elected to the Society's committee. He was a military man – Argyll and Sutherland Highlanders and Lovat Scouts – and a Highland proprietor with a seat at Obbe (later Leverburgh) in South Harris. He claimed to have some knowledge of Gaelic and

5 'The Piobaireachd Society of Scotland', *OT*, 19/9/1903, p.3

6 'The Passing of the Piobaireachd', from 'A Highlander', [John Grant], *OT*, 17/10/1903, p.3.

7 'The Piobaireachd Society of Scotland', from David Glen, *OT*, 26/9/1903, p.3.

8 'John MacColl was the ring leader, and said to me that Ceol Mor was all the General's own invention. I remember Angus MacRae's words to me "What is the use of talking about the thing when the man is daft?"' Seton Gordon Papers, NLS, Acc. 7451, Archibald Campbell to Seton Gordon, 19/9/1942.

9 'Piobaireachd Society of Scotland and "Ceol Mor"'. from 'G. Sharp' [Henry Whyte], *OT*, 31/10/1903, p.3.

a large collection of piping manuscripts. He was appointed at the same time as a judge at the Northern Meeting, sitting with fellow Piobaireachd Society members, the Earl of Dunmore, Somerled MacDonald, and Major E. W. Horne of Stirkoke.[10] In December 1903 he joined Colin MacRae and James MacKillop on the sub-committee to select the tunes and settings for the Piobaireachd Society's 1905 competition, two to form a quorum.[11] From this a number of consequences were to follow.

At the Society's General Meeting in London on Monday 6 June, with C. S. Thomason in the chair, the bench for Oban was appointed. It comprised Capt. Colin MacRae, Col. Duncan Campbell of Inverneill, Capt. William Stewart of Ensay, Somerled MacDonald, Capt. C. A. H. MacLean of Pennycross, Capt. Ian Forbes, yr of Rothiemay, Angus Campbell of Kilberry, Capt. Malcolm MacNeill and James MacKillop jr of Polmont. The General declined to join it.[12]

On Tuesday 13th September 1904 the first Piobaireachd Society competition took place. The *Oban Times* reported that:

Tuesday morning broke rather unpromisingly . . . Towards noon, however, the sun broke through . . . with the prospect of a fine afternoon and with the military attractions on the card, the numbers gradually swelled, and during the remainder of the day the pay-boxes were kept exceedingly busy . . .

The first part of the programme was occupied with the piobaireachd competitions. For the principal event nineteen competitors entered, but the whole of the contestants did not put in an appearance. The Society is, however, gratified by the response made to its initial efforts, and also with the piping results. The competitive tunes . . . were [titles follow] . . . the setting being that of 'Ceol Mor', the distinguished author of which, (Major-General Thomason) was present during the day. The first prize – a gold medal and £20 – fell to Mr. John MacDonald, Inverness, for 'The King's Taxes'. This is rather a hard tune, the proper getting up of which presents some difficulties, but MacDonald gave an excellent rendering of it. Pipe-Corporal Geo. Stewart McLennan, 1st Gordon Highlanders, a young piper, carried off the second prize with the 'Lament for the Earl of Antrim', which he played carefully and well. The third prize winner was Corporal Piper W. Ross, 1st Scots Guards, who played 'The Desperate Battle' with good effect. The fourth prize fell to James A. Center, Edinburgh, who made a very promising appearance.[13]

---

10 Fairrie, pp.57, 204, 225. For Stewart's involvement in the mysterious disappearance of Col. Jock MacDonald's elephant tusk and later mysterious acquisition of a new ivory chanter, see Campbell, 'History of the Piobaireachd Society', p.43.

11 NLS. Acc. 9103/1, 15/12/1903.

12 *Ibid.*, 6/6/1904.

13 'The County Gathering', *OT*, 17/9/1904, p.5.

Most of those who had been present at the General Meeting in June were to meet again after the Gathering for the A.G.M. in the Station Hotel at Oban on the afternoon and evening of Thursday 15th September 1904. But General C. S. Thomason was not amongst them, having received warning of an intended coup in which he was to be deposed as President and many of the Society's original goals overturned.

In his absence, Charles Adolphus Murray, 7th Earl of Dunmore, was called to the chair. He was an old Etonian who had served in the Scots Guards and owned considerable parts of Inverness and Stirlingshire. He was a strapping figure of a man, then in his sixty-fourth year, a Christian Scientist, noted traveller, prominent member of the Northern Meeting, and Commanding Officer of the 4th (Volunteer) Battalion Cameron Highlanders whose Pipe-Major was John MacDonald of Inverness.[14] With Dunmore in the chair, a motion was proposed by Wllliam Stewart seconded by Colin Macrae, 'That in future all Piobaireachd printed for the Society, or issued by it, be in the ordinary system of notation'. An amendment by Angus Campbell 'That the form of notation in which tunes are to be issued be left in the hands of the Committee' was unsuccessful. On Dunmore's formal election as President, James MacKillop declined to continue as Secretary/Treasurer and the post fell to William Stewart of Ensay.[15] During the year that followed most of the Society's playing members resigned.

In the spring of 1905 *The First Part of a Collection of Piobaireachd Selected and Edited by the Piobaireachd Society* was published, containing the next batch of set tunes – 'Craigellachie', 'John Garve Macleod of Rasay's Lament', 'Patrick Og', 'MacCrimmon's Lament', 'The Prince's Salute', 'Isabel MacKay' and 'Saurachan' or 'The March of the Clan Macrae'.[16] It was compiled by William Stewart of Ensay. Thomason had always been treated with respect by his critics but Ensay's work was received with derision. The *Oban Times* reviewer was characteristically blunt:

> It will be observed that with the exception of 'The Prince's Salute' taken from Donald MacDonald's Collection, the other five tunes are from Mackay's Collection. Beyond correcting obvious misprints, the tunes are reproduced very much the same as they are given in these two Collections. Nor does the society seem to have any standard for writing piobaireachd music, for MacDonald's system is accepted when the tune is lifted from his Collection, while MacKay is allowed to write the same musical phrase in his fashion in tunes taken from his work. This want of uniformity is anything but satisfactory, and is not in keeping with the power claimed by the Society 'to

---

14 *Complete Peerage*; Fairrie, p.179. According to Col. Jock MacDonald, Dunmore had difficulty distinguishing one end of a chanter from the other: see Campbell, 'History of the Piobaireachd Society', p.43.

15 NLS. Acc. 9103/1, 15/9/1904.

16 Inverness, 1905.

decide between the diverse renderings of conflicting authorities'. There are some other irregularities in MacKay's and MacDonald's settings of certain tunes which experience, as well as science, has taught pipers to play in a manner different from what is written, and in several cases subsequent editors in reproducing the tunes in which such blemishes occur, have submitted the more excellent way with a precision begotten of scientific knowledge. The Piobaireachd Society has allowed these incongruities to remain, leaving it to the competitor to interpret them to the best of his knowledge, and by so doing has shirked the very work they were expected to perform. One wonders why, with so many unpublished MSS in its possession, the Society should have been content to reproduce six tunes which are already in the hands of every piper.[17]

Ensay's 'Preface' and 'Critical Notes' were typical of the mediated texts which had prefixed the work of Highland musicians for upwards of a century. They spoke about Ossian and the Celtic Renaissance, and trotted out the timeworn clichés about the antiquity of the pipe, its military virtues, and the wild irregularity of its music, declaring that 'Art must not be tied by rule'. Their ostentatious parade of Gaelic lore was dismissed by Henry Whyte under his pen-name 'Fionn' in a crushing review:

> The few Gaelic words and phrases introduced do violence to the grammar of that language. The genitive case seems to be unknown to the compilers. Before issuing the second part, the Society ought to revise carefully the music and letter press of Part 1., and purge it of all its errors.[18]

A little later, the following 'Notice to Pipers' appeared on the front page of the *Oban Times*:

> David Glen has in the Press, and will shortly publish, the Three Test Tunes given out by the Piobaireachd Society for their this year's Competitions,

---

17 'The Piobairachd Society's Collection', *OT*, 25/3/05, p.3 [anonymous, but by Henry Whyte]; see also same, from Niall Mor a' Chamais [Dr. Charles Bannatyne], 1/4/1905, p.3; and John McLennan, 13/5/1905, p.3, 17/6/1905, p.3.

18 'Scottish Piobaireachd Society. The Historic Notes, etc' *OT*, 29/4/1905, p.3. Henry Whyte ('Fionn'), (1852–1913), came from Easdale in Argyllshire. A prolific writer, and Glasgow correspondent of the *Oban Times*. Journalist, historian, musician, editor and translator, and one of the founders of An Comunn Gaidhealach (he wrote the bulk of its Gaelic manifesto), Whyte was a leading figure in the Gaelic movement, and recognised as 'the most widely known Scottish Gael of his day'. Drawing on his very extensive knowledge of the historical background of the repertoire of the pipe, he wrote the historical notes for David Glen's *Collection of Ancient Piobaireachd*, and in 1904 published *The Martial Music of the Clans*: see 'The Late Mr Henry Whyte. A Noted Celtic Figure' *OT*, 3/1/1914, p.5.

together with the other Three Tunes given in the book this Society has just published. The Six Tunes have been carefully revised and arranged, and are written in such a form that they may be read by any Musician . . . Post Free 3/- Single Tunes, 1/- each.

The paper noted 'It is hardly to be expected that the Piobaireachd Society will accept these revised versions at their competitions, but all piobaireachd players will welcome them as distinct improvements on previous settings, and models of careful editing'.[19] Alongside Glen's advertisement another notice appeared and ran for several weeks. It said:

> To Pipers. Caution. The Piobaireachd Society's Revised Setting of Six
> Piobaireachd. This is the only Edition authorised by The Piobaireachd
> Society, and from which the competitors will be judged. Published only by
> Logan & Coy. Inverness. Price 3/2. Post Free.

As the *Times* had inferred only the Society's settings, played as written, would be accepted at competitions under its control.

To allay the ensuing storm of protest the Society's President, the Earl of Dunmore, issued a public statement. In a letter to the *Oban Times*, dated from the Carlton Club, London, he attempted a blanket rebuttal of the charges, claiming that the Society's versions were its own and not 'lifted' from existing sources, that they were consistent in style, unambiguous with regard to interpretation, and that the final text had been arrived at by experienced playing members in consultation with leading professional pipers. He went on to state that the Piobaireachd Society was supported by the great majority of Highland and other Scottish proprietors, by the Highland Society of London, by the officers of many Highland regiments, and was under the gracious patronage of His Royal Highness the Prince of Wales, K.G. etc. Implying that in the circumstances opposition was downright disloyal, if not actually treasonable, he insisted that Stewart of Ensay had done a first rate job and appealed to the paper to drop its apparent hostility to a great national project.[20]

His remarks were received with open contempt. Lieut. John McLennan, in a letter pointedly dated from 'Parliament Square, Edinburgh', went through the collection tune by tune compiling a detailed catalogue of its technical deficiencies and concluding:

> The letter . . . states that the tunes were corrected by members of the Society
> 'possessing a thorough practical as well as a theoretical knowledge of
> Piobaireachd'. No one will doubt the statement, coming, as it does, from so

19 *OT*, 1/4/1905, p.1. See also 6/5/1905, p.1. Glen's versions of the set tunes were reviewed on 29/4/1905, p.3: 'Piobaireachd New Settings of Test Tunes'.
20 'Bagpipe Music – The Piobaireachd Society's Collection', 6/5/1905, *OT*, p.3.

high an authority, but it is only fair to say that they have left no trace of such knowledge in the book.[21]

Dr. Charles Bannatyne, writing under the pseudonym 'Niall Mor a' Chamais' dismissed the settings as 'ridiculous' and showing 'a poverty of musical imagination and judgement' and went on to criticise the Society's tendency to wrap itself in 'tradition' which, when examined, turned out to be bogus: 'Lord Dunmore states that the Society had the MS. authority of two of the most celebrated players of Ceol Mor of a past generation. The present writer happens to know the two celebrated players referred to, and he can testify that one of them strongly objects to the Society's "sett" . . .'[22] 'Fionn' also wrote again, claiming to have detected more than 150 textual errors which he offered to correct in red ink if Dunmore would send him a clean copy, adding that the 'Gaelic in the letterpress is little short of an insult to intelligent Gaels . . .'[23]

The Society held an Extraordinary General Meeting in London on 6 June 1905. At it the Marquis of Tullibardine proposed a vote of thanks to Stewart of Ensay and that he should be invited to prepare the tunes for the following year. John Campbell of Kilberry, seconded by his brother Angus, moved that the music for 1906 should not be proceeded with in the present notation. He was ruled out of order by the chair and Tullibardine, seconded by MacDougall of Lunga, carried an amendment that the edition should continue in its current style. John Campbell then moved that the role of the Secretary be redefined and the duties of the post re-distributed. This was referred to a sub-committee with the Campbells in a minority. Shortly afterwards John and Angus Campbell, James MacKillop and General C. S. Thomason resigned from the Piobaireachd Society.[24]

In his open letter of resignation Angus Campbell described the intentions of the founders and the reasons for their dissatisfaction with the present state of affairs. His assumptions were revealing: including a typically exaggerated view of the shortcomings of the published record based on a simple equation of variety with error, and the conviction that what could be heard in competition gave an

---

21 'The Piobaireachd Society's Collection of Bagpipe Music', *OT*, 13/5/1905, p.3.
22 *Ibid.* Charles Bannatyne (1868–1924), was a graduate of Glasgow University, and practised as a physician in Lanarkshire. Of an old Bute family, he was brought up in Arran, and was taught piping by William Sutherland of Airdrie. A keen all-round musician with a fine tenor voice, he was in considerable demand as a judge of piping, being connected particularly with the burgeoning pipe band movement. A talented composer of pipe music, his reels 'The Blackbird' and 'The Brolum' remain favourites; he was founder of the Pipers' and Dancers' Union, and had one of the largest collections of old piping MSS in private hands. A frequent contributor to the *Oban Times* on piping subjects.
23 'The Reviewer of the Piobaireachd Society's Collection of Bagpipe Music', *OT*, 13/5/1905, p.3.
24 NLS. Acc. 9103/1, 6/6/1905.

accurate picture of the extent of the surviving repertoire. He stated his belief, accordingly, that the leading professional pipers 'were, with few exceptions, men who could play, most brilliantly, a very small number of tunes' who were able with the complicity of ignorant and conservative benches to dominate competitive piping and effectively stifle the art. Since they had a vested interest in ensuring that their pupils knew even less than they did, it was difficult for talented young players to get a proper training or appropriate reward for their efforts. The published scores were virtually unobtainable and full of errors, which made the acquisition of an extensive repertoire all but impossible. The appearance of *Ceol Mor* presented a golden opportunity, therefore, to do something about this. Here was practically the whole repertoire in a single volume, written in a 'scientific' manner so that anybody who knew a little about piobaireachd 'could add any number of tunes he pleased, self-taught, to his stock'. Thomason had distributed copies widely amongst the leading professionals but only about three of them had given him active support. The remainder mostly condemned the book realising that it represented a direct challenge to their monopoly of knowledge. This, Angus Campbell explained, was the real reason why he and his brothers had founded the Piobaireachd Society, regardless of what it said in the published Prospectus:

> . . . I assert without hesitation that but for the publication of 'Ceol Mor', the Society would never have come into existence . . . the urgent necessity of forcing it, if need be, down the unwilling throat of the professional (not in his interests, but in the interests of the cause of Highland music), were the bonds which brought the founders of the Society together.
>
> I want to emphasise the point that they started with a deep distrust of the opinion of the leading professionals on any question of reform; and that this distrust has not, in the founders and their supporters, diminished with experience. The original idea was to confine the membership to those having sufficient knowledge to form their own opinions, for fear that at any time the Society might be governed by a majority who, lacking that knowledge, would not unnaturally be guided each by the opinion of his favourite among the various 'Champion Pipers'. You know how well grounded that fear was; and how the opening of the Society to those who have no personal knowledge of the subject has led the Society, rightly or wrongly, to defer almost slavishly to the opinions of the 'Champions'.

The Society had agreed to subsidise a new and improved edition of *Ceol Mor*, but nothing practical had been done and a year later, without giving it a proper trial, the abbreviated notation had been abandoned, a move, in Campbell's view, fatally prejudicial to the Society's goals: 'I do not believe that the publication by the Society of every known Piobaireachd, in full notation, would do any good: at the present rate it would take nearly 50 years and the results would weigh about a hundredweight. And, after all, the possessor of the collection would have nothing beyond what, in "Ceol Mor" notation, he could carry in his sporran'.[25]

Although Thomason would have supported the view that the tradition was at risk and that ultimate authority should reside in the written or printed score, this frank acknowledgement that the Campbell brothers viewed relations with the performer community in terms of power and conflict would have surprised and saddened him. His own letter of resignation reflected with quiet dignity on the painfully *ad hominem* attacks which had been made upon him and the lengths to which his opponents had been prepared to go to discredit *Ceol Mor* and the man who created it:

Grantown-on-Spey,
July 13th, 1905.

Dear Ensay,
From the few words that I addressed to those present at the Piobaireachd Society's Meeting in London last year, I hoped it would be sufficiently evident that my sole interest in the Society lay in the apparent possibilities of placing at the disposal of those interested in our National Music the valuable records that are in my possession.

. . . For [*Ceol Mor*] I never claimed infallibility. I proclaimed distinctly to all that I looked upon it only as a basis for correction, and how I earnestly sought for such correction from every piper I knew or met is well known to the whole fraternity. Others apparently shared my views, hence the 'original' Piobaireachd Society, who devoted much time and attention to framing the laws which seemed to suit the case. Beyond approving these laws and from anything but the music I purposely refrained from interfering.

. . . From what was brought to my notice privately I had more than suspicion of what would be the drift of the meeting held at Oban last year, and promotion of discord, being my last object, will explain my non-attendance on that occasion. What did actually take place fully justified my action. The policy of the Piobaireachd Society to-day is so entirely opposed to that of its originators that . . . I feel it now my duty to resign membership . . .

It is no secret to me that some have said that my relations to the Piobd. Society are somewhat tainted with a suspicion that I relied on their assistance to exploit my book, 'Ceol Mor', as a pecuniary venture. Anyone who knows me will hold this opinion at its true value, but I think I might have been spared this insinuation . . . Profits I never expected, but I candidly confess that I did look to the Society to help me in reducing the cost of my book to a figure placing it within reach of poor pipers – a matter surely of the first importance:

25 NLS, Acc.9103/8 Correspondence 1895–1928, 3/7/1905. Like his brother, Archibald, Angus Campbell had taken up piping as an adult enthusiast. See Seton Gordon Papers, NLS, Acc.7451, Archibald Campbell to Seton Gordon, 14/1/1929.

and my failure in realising these hopes has been a far greater disappointment to me than the pecuniary loss to which I own . . . Opposition from any educated member I never expected . . . but my experience of the last year strikes me as a very queer example of the good old saying: 'Clann nan Gaidheal gualainn a Cheile'. ['Children of the Gael shoulder to shoulder'] . . .

Yours truly,

C. S. Thomason.[26]

As if to emphasise the disarray within the Society, there followed a debacle at the Argyllshire Gathering involving a serious difference between the bench of judges and the committee. A.M. described the incident in his second series of articles:

At Oban, there was a large entry of competitors, and a good percentage of them actually played. There was also a large bench of judges – no fewer than five . . . but I am inclined to think that once more Mr MacKillop was the only one who was really qualified for the task.

The day was cold, and there were frequent heavy showers, which was no doubt the principal cause of the many breakdowns. Still there were several fine piobaireachd played. Among the best competitors, in the opinion of many outside the ring, was George Allan, of the Scottish Horse, who played the 'Prince's Salute'. When the result was announced, he was found to have been placed third – not any too high most people thought. However, when the prize-list was read out at the end of the second day's games, his name did not appear in it.

Inquiry as to the reason of this elicited the following almost incredible story, which I give only because I was assured of its substantial correctness on unimpeachable authority. There was a disagreement among the judges as to whether Allan should be disqualified for playing a setting different from that published by the Society; but eventually he was awarded . . . the third prize. This showed that the majority of the judges at all events were satisfied that what he had played did not depart in any marked way from the Society's so-called 'standard' setting. The next day, however, a meeting of the committee of the Society reversed the decision of its own judges, and removed Allan's name from the prize-list. In other words, the Society, having appointed five judges – including its President and Secretary – reversed a decision of those judges by the verdict of a committee, some of whom had not been on the ground when the tune was played! . . .

I may add that though they disqualified Allan, they paid him the amount of his prize, thereby once more upsetting the decision of – this time – their committee.[27]

26 NLS, Acc.9103 /8.
27 'The Passing of the Piobaireachd. Two Years Later. By "A. M."', Part 1, *OT*, 7/10/ 1905, p.3.

A.M. went on to offer a damning assessment of the Society's activities during the previous two years, concluding that it had fallen at every hurdle. The outcome to date had been one seriously-flawed publication and seven competitions. The holding of competitions had been declared to be a matter of minor importance, but the Society's effort had so far lain in that direction to the exclusion of virtually everything else. A stated aim had been to raise the calibre of the bench and guarantees had been given that the Society's judges would be 'thoroughly acquainted' with the tunes. This was one of the main reasons given for restricting competitors to set tunes in the first place. Yet A.M. felt inclined to doubt that any of the judges (with one exception) were adequately prepared to the extent that they could personally play even two of the six set tunes. Still, he thought the 1904 event had been a success and while 'true that some of the most famous pipers abstained from it . . . it could not have been expected that everyone would at once fall in with such a novel idea as that the tunes were to be selected by those who gave the prize, instead of by whose who sought it. And, it must be remembered, the winner was John MacDonald, Inverness, who is perhaps the most complete "artist" among present day exponents of piobaireachd'. But even before the competition there was considerable hostility to the *Ceol Mor* notation inside the Piobaireachd Society, said A. M.; a lever was made of the abstentions, and 'normal' notation was adopted in its place. As soon as Thomason had been removed the prize money was slashed (from £20 to £7). Although the number of test tunes was dropped from six to three, at the Lochaber Gathering one of the three, 'The Prince's Salute', was not given to any competitor. At Portree none of the Society's members turned up to judge. At Oban, in 1905, it was questionable whether any of the bench, except MacKillop, could personally play the tunes.

Under Thomason the Piobaireachd Society had been open and reasonable, continued A. M., but this had changed dramatically following his departure. The Society had no shortage of wealthy members and its financial position ought to have enabled it comfortably to afford the most expert professional help. Its failure to do this, and the poor quality of the subsequent publication, had been a major disappointment to lovers of Highland music:

> There was a general hope that the recording of piobaireachd music would be reduced to a method, if not at first to a science, and that published collections would cease to be, as they are at present, sealed books to all except the trained piper, whom long familiarity has accustomed to their peculiarities. This hope has proved a vain one.
>
> The drawbacks to Angus MacKay's notation are too generally admitted to require exhaustive description, but they are nowhere more prominent than in the first volume of the Piobaireachd Society's Collection. The chief of them is undoubtedly the haphazard way in which grace notes are written as full notes and vice versa, an inconsistency probably due to the fact that those who first applied staff notation to piobaireachd music found a difficulty in marshalling the notes into bars, owing to their ignorance of the theory of music. This difficulty

they ultimately surmounted by making notes which they could not fit into the
time of the bar, grace notes, and then, being thus launched into a certain system,
making confusion worse confounded by endeavouring to be consistent to it.[28]

The letterpress parts of the *Collection* had been an even bigger flop. No authority
had been quoted by name and there was no indication of how the tunes should
be played. The carefully cultivated impression of collective responsibility was
entirely misleading: the first volume of the Piobaireachd Society's Collection had
been the work of a single man. A number of the playing members of the Society
had privately assured A.M. that they had not been consulted and he could not
find a professional player who had been either. The situation was aggravated by
the Society's assumption of absolute authority and refusal to enter into dialogue:

> Not only no good, but actual harm, will be done if this course of action be
> continued. It is only by showing readiness to receive and weigh the suggestion
> of everyone competent to give assistance that the Society can command
> respect, and ultimately inspire confidence – otherwise it can gain neither.[29]

Simply contributing a few more prizes to the competition circuit was not an
appropriate way for a body like the Piobaireachd Society to spend its money
while its future publications, if they were like the first one, seemed unlikely to
add to existing knowledge. The Society should not have abandoned Thomason
and the *Ceol Mor* method but having done so, 'it is hopeless to expect that it will
ever be of any real service to the cause of piobaireachd'. A. M. concluded that this
was 'a lamentable ending to a promising undertaking', and ended with the plea:
'If the Piobaireachd Society is to fail, is there no one in the Highlands to take up
the task of saving Ceol Mor?'[30]

It seemed as if all the failings of the old-style Highland associations which had
led to such talk about leadership crisis and the arrogance and incompetence of the
landed élite – were appearing once again in the new Piobaireachd Society. The
atmosphere of recrimination and bad faith which followed the overthrow of
Thomason caused at least one of the leading professionals, John MacDonald of
Inverness, to consider his position. He had been asked to assist in the preparation
of the Society's second volume, but as the winter of 1905/6 progressed he became
increasingly uneasy about his role and wrote to James MacKillop for advice.
MacKillop was frank:

> Dear MacDonald,
> I received your letter with enclosure this morning, for which many thanks. It
> is very difficult for me to know what to advise, as I am no longer a member

28 *OT.*, 14/10/1905 p.3.
29 *Ibid.*
30 *Ibid.*, Part 3, 21/10/1905, p.3.

of the Piobaireachd Society, and anything I say might be considered to be prejudiced . . .

I will tell you how we were treated last year, and you can form your own opinion. Major Stewart asked [John MacDougall] Gillies and me to revise the music, which we did very carefully. After we had done it, Major Stewart would not allow the corrections and alterations, and stuck to his own ideas about the music. When the tunes were published, and people began to criticise and find fault with them, Major Stewart would listen to nothing, and said that we had revised the music, which was absurd, as although we had revised the tunes, our suggestions had been quite ignored. And you know when Allan played our setting of the 'Princes Salute' at Oban, Major Stewart insisted on having him disqualified, although he told Gillies and myself that if any piper played our setting, it would be allowed at the Society's Competitions.

If the Society would guarantee that your corrections and suggestions would be accepted and carried out, it would be all right revising the music, but I am sure they will not do this, as Major Stewart thinks nobody knows anything about Piobaireachd but himself, and if you suggest anything that is not agreeable to him, he will on no account accept it, but after the music is published, and people begin to point out the mistakes, he will say that you revised the music. So you see it is not a very nice job trying to assist the Society. I think your reputation is much too good to run the risk of being treated like this . . .

I am writing to you as a brother piper, and hope you will treat this letter, and what I have written to you as strictly private, as I would not express my opinions to anyone on this subject, except to yourself and Gillies . . .

We certainly intend to start another Society, but it must be gone about very cautiously.

Anytime you are South you might let me know, and I would try to meet you in either Glasgow or Edinburgh, and we can have a talk over matters . . .[31]

Four further volumes of the first series were published (1906–1912) and met with a similar reception. Not only was Ensay's knowledge inadequate, but he had a constitutional inability to work with other people which meant that when advisers like Charles Bannatyne and John MacDonald, were brought in to ensure that his work met an acceptable standard they were simply ignored. In May 1906, he casually informed MacDonald: 'I have had to direct the printers to proceed with printing the music for this year so please do not trouble to correct the proofs, as they would be too late. I trust to have some help from you with the next lot.'[32] Somerled MacDonald found his work treated in a similar manner:

31 NLS, Acc.9103/8, James MacKillop to John MacDonald, 15/1/1906.
32 *Ibid.*, Stewart of Ensay to John MacDonald, 15/5/1907

On one occasion at Inverness, I had gone over the 'Children's Lament' and one or two other piobaireachd with Mr Alexander Cameron, Pipe-Major John MacDonald, and Pipe-Major [Willie] Ross. I had written out the tunes in long hand from General Thomason's book, and these three professionals corrected any mistakes there were to the best of their ability, and passed the settings as correct. I then forwarded them to the secretary [Stewart of Ensay], but after waiting for some time and receiving no acknowledgement, I wrote again about them as I valued the settings. He replied that he considered the tunes absolute rubbish, but that he would return them if they had not already found their way to the waste-paper basket![33]

The sweeping powers of the Secretary/Treasurer under the Piobaireachd Society's original constitution meant that if he had the President's support – which he did – Ensay could do virtually what he liked.

Some of the performer community turned to C S. Thomason to protest against the unscrupulous things that Stewart was doing to his text, and in a letter to the *Oban Times* in September 1906 the General raised a number of issues. The Society, he said, was making silly mistakes, refusing to consult pipers, becoming dogmatic and arbitrary, and worst of all deliberately misrepresenting the traditional authorities cited in support of its settings:

The grievance is this – and Alick Cameron particularly wishes me to mention his name in connection therewith – that Donald Cameron's name should be unjustifiably alluded to as affording a precedent for what most of the professionals regard as 'innovation' in Major Stewart's music, the adoption of which are, by the rules, rendered compulsory on all competitors.

. . . he says that the first variation of 'The Prince's Salute', as given by him, is as the pipers of the old Highland School, and notably Donald Cameron and Malcolm MacPherson, played it. Alick Cameron indignantly denies this, and that he is right as to the facts on which his protest is based I too am in a position to testify. When I was editing this tune for my book . . . Keith Cameron begged of me to [use] his father's sett, which I took down from Keith's playing and gave in 'Ceol Mor'. I think it was in 1903 that Mr J. MacKillop . . . and I made a pilgrimage to Colin Cameron at Maryburgh to correct this and some other setts in my book. Colin corrected only one note in this tune, and as his correction was in accordance with the context I adopted it and circulated it amongst my friends who had copies of my book. I think that this makes it pretty clear that Donald Cameron did not play as Major Stewart states. What Malcolm MacPherson played I cannot say, as I only heard him play once, and then not this tune[34]

33 'Piobaireachd Society's Work', from Somerled MacDonald, *OT*, 9/4/1910, p.3.
34 'The Piobaireachd Society and the Cameron School of Piping', *OT*, 29/09/1906, p.3.

As if to demonstrate how these things should be done, Thomason called a meeting of pipers in Edinburgh in the spring of 1907. He had been anxious for some time about the pipe scale and the widely varying characteristics of contemporary chanters. Just the year before, a leading piobaireachd player had found himself suddenly in charge of a pipe band and finding that his chanter could not be tuned with the others wrote asking if he could borrow one of the General's. This rekindled the latter's interest in a question which had laid sporadic claim to his attention for more than a decade. He consulted the military school of music at Kneller Hall, and the head instrument maker at Messrs. Boosey in London. He read Herman von Helmholtz's *Sensations of Tone* and A. J. Ellis's 'Musical Scales of Nations throughout the World'.[35] Assisted by Colin Cameron and Angus Campbell, he assembled three groups of pipe chanters for comparative testing, the first of which included the Drummond Chanter, the Culloden Chanter and the Dunvegan Chanter, all thought to be of early date; a second historically more recent group by bagpipe makers now dead; and finally a batch of contemporary chanters.[36] The most obvious thing to emerge was the extraordinarily wide range of pitch and tone. It was clear, too, that pitch had been a good deal lower in the past, and that the most variable of all the notes was high G, especially important because of its prominent use in piobaireachd.[37] This was what the General had feared. Modern pipe-makers were too interested in light-music, he thought, as a result of which the note was becoming progressively sharper. Without some fixed standard there seemed nothing to prevent a drift towards a pitch and timbre which might eventually prove quite unsuitable for ceòl mór. He observed that 'We still have with us a good stock of players of the old schools, who are rich at least in the traditions of the MacCruimeins. The Piobaireachd soul is not yet dead in these men, nor is the intuitive perception of what is the true chanter scale. Let us make the most of this valuable asset while it is still with us'. He insisted that everything should be in the hands of the pipers and pipe-makers and published a useful table showing the frequencies of the various chanters he had tested as a basis of discussion.[38]

The meeting was well attended. John MacDonald of Inverness, Lieut. John McLennan, Farquhar MacRae and John MacDougall Gillies were present, and numerous gentlemen amateurs, including Charles Bannatyne, Angus Campbell, Capt. Colin MacRae, James MacKillop, John Bartholomew, and Somerled MacDonald. Thomason said that 'It was for pipers to say what the scale should be, not for amateurs . . . As pipers they got into extraordinary habits . . . The tendency was for a man to take up his own chanter and work at it year after year and say "There is none other like it". It was wonderful what the ear got

35 *On the Sensations of Tone as a physiological basis for the Theory of Music*, trans., Alexander J. Ellis (Lond., 1875).
36 'The Scale of the Highland Bagpipe Chanter. By Major-General C. S Thomason. Part 1', *OT*, 17/11/1906, p.3.
37 *Ibid.*, Part 2, 24/11/1906, p.3.
38 *Ibid.*, Part 3, 5/1/1907, p.3.

accustomed to, bad music and all . . .' He envisaged two pitches being established, one in the older lower style for playing piobaireachd and the other near the modern higher pitch for playing light music. He then went on to reeds: 'They knew how kittle a thing a pipe reed was. They could not get two to agree, and when they got them to agree they put them down for five minutes and they disagreed'. Since the problem with the usual material, arundo donax, was that it absorbed moisture, he suggested various synthetic alternatives and entered a plea for a scientific study of reeds to do away with the present hit-or-miss methods.

When the meeting was thrown open to general discussion John MacDonald expressed anxiety about the high G in contemporary chanters. MacDougall Gillies suggested that until they had perfect reeds they were unlikely to develop a perfect chanter. John Dickson, the reedmaker, said that moisture lay at the root of the problem; he had tried various materials, including whalebone, but had difficulty with the latter in getting the sides of the blades to meet. But reeds and chanters were not the only variable, and the meeting went on to discuss fingering as well. Should the high G be made with the F finger down? Should C be open or closed? At this period, it would appear that fingering was still a highly individual affair and this, too, had a bearing on pitch:

> Lieut. McLennan said . . . he was judge along with a famous player once, and saw him put away a very good pibroch player for lifting the G finger [i.e. for playing an open C]. He was judge with another famous piper on another occasion, and he put away a man for doing the other thing [i.e. for playing a closed C]. He came across a very fine piper, the finest reel and strathspey player ever he heard. Two or three of them thought he did not play according to scale [i.e. he habitually 'false fingered']. Another gentleman in town played D and E up [i.e. without simultaneously covering various holes on the bottom hand of the chanter]. He said that he had been taught to play that way by Roderick MacKay, Angus MacKay's brother, piper to the Queen. This piper said the MacKays held that if they had the note and the finger below it open, that was all right . . .

Angus Campbell said he had asked Sandy Cameron about this point and been told 'Judge by the sound; if the reed is getting flatter, lift more fingers, and sharpen up in that way'. A committee of pipers, reedmakers, bagpipe makers and gentlemen amateurs including John McLennan, Somerled MacDonald, Dr. Bannatyne, John MacDougall Gillies, John MacDonald of Inverness, John Bartholomew, John Dickson, James MacKillop, R. G. Lawrie, James Center and Farquhar MacRae was elected to explore the matter further.[39]

---

39 'The Bagpipe Chanter Scale. Standard Pitch Problem. Meeting of Experts', *OT*, 4/5/ 1907, p.2. This discussion prompted a series of detailed and illuminating letters on reed-making from John H. Shearer of Huntly, see 'The Bagpipe Chanter Scale', 18/5/ 1907, p.3, 'Bagpipe Reeds', 31/8/1907, p.3, and especially 'Bagpipe Chanter Reeds', 5/ 10/1907 p.3.

If the openness and co-operation of Thomason's meeting in Edinburgh in the spring of 1907 had been intended to place a question mark over the Piobaireachd Society's way of doing business, it could hardly have been more effective. That a society of gentlemen enthusiasts containing a handful of amateur players should seek to assume control of the classical music of the pipe and dictate to professionals how the repertoire should be interpreted raised the question of cultural authority in the most pressing fashion. What *was* tradition? How did it work? Above all, to whom did it belong?

To some, the Society's attempts to impose a fixed 'authoritative' text seemed doomed from the start, since the characteristic tendency of the oral mode to work through multiple variants dissolved the subject in a wash of relativity.[40] No authority could logically rest on guardianship of an 'original' text if there was no original text to guard. To others, the Society's bungling had a simpler explanation. It could not offer a coherent account of the music because the music had ceased to be coherent: in an act of collective despair it had been deliberately sabotaged by the master teachers in the generation following the '45. Charles Bannatyne, writing as 'Niall Mor a' Chamais', declared:

> The Piobaireachd Society and their advisers either do not know, or choose to
> ignore, the influence of the '45 on the classical music of the Highland bagpipe.
> The ban of proscription and the crushing grasp of tyrannical revenge led the
> old-time pipers to conceal the melodies of Ceol Mor under the garbage of a false
> and misleading rhythm, and the later pipers, such as Donald MacDonald,
> Angus MacArthur, and Angus MacKay, who really knew the true melodies, were
> just as anxious to conceal them, and succeeded. So they taught rubbish to, and
> wrote it for, their pupils, and all the time laughed up their sleeves; and now the
> descendants of those misled pupils assist a well-meaning but misguided society
> to perpetuate gross errors, which are apparent to any musician.[41]

There was not a shred of evidence to support this idea. But that did not diminish its appeal and it found lodgement in several quite important minds, including that of Lieut. John McLennan.

McLennan was a prolific correspondent of the *Oban Times* during the first two decades of the 20th century, and one of the Piobaireachd Society's most consistent critics. In the summer of 1907, for example, he condemned its awarding prizes 'not, mark you, for the best player of the best versions – but for playing in the unmusical manner in which the editor has been pleased to note down the tune', adding 'any competitor who wades through this rigmarole should certainly get the first prize.'[42] In June of that year he brought out his own collection entitled *The Piobaireachd as MacCrimmon Played it with Instructions*

---

40 'The Passing of the Piobaireachd', from 'J. D. R.', *OT*, 16/9/1905, p.3.
41 'The Piobaireachd Society's Collection', from Niall Mor a' Chamais 17/6/1905, p.3.
42 'The Piobaireachd Society's Publication,' *OT*, 27/6/1907, p.3.

how to Read and Understand Music, containing a mixture of light music and ceòl mór including 'The men went to drink', 'The End of the Little Bridge', 'Clan Chattan's Gathering', 'Clan Ranald's Gathering', 'The Duke of Atholl's Salute', 'The Lament for the Earl of Antrim', 'The Rout of Glenfruin', 'Glengarry's Lament', 'I got a Kiss of the King's Hand', 'Lord Lovat's Lament', 'MacDonald of Boisdale's Salute', 'MacCrimmon's Sweetheart' and 'Mary's Praise'.[43]

McLennan was determined to challenge the Piobaireachd Society's recent statements concerning the metrical irregularity of ceòl mór by demonstrating its fundamental melodic and rhythmical coherence. Endowed with a keen sense of form, he rebelled at the playing of contemporaries affected by recitationalist theories which led them to play without a regular pulse, or who gave too scrupulous adherence to the exact time values of imperfectly notated scores. He believed that Ensay had been misled by the superficial inconsistencies of the written tradition into supposing that piobaireachd was a wild and rude music which possessed no regular rhythmical pulse, and had edited his scores in such a way as to reflect this belief. In his own notational practice – he had apparently studied music at Heriot Watt College – McLennan aimed at new standards of precision. He adopted the minim rather than the crotchet as the basic unit of time in order to achieve a richer and more accurate rhythmical palette and used this to work his way back to what he believed to be the *status quo ante*.[44] He welcomed Thomason's ideas but sought to achieve abbreviation by simpler means. His scores were typeset using the conventions descending from MacDonald and MacKay, but he was able to get a whole tune on to a single folio page by means of a new and ingenious system. Each bar was numbered, and the order of playing specified in a numerical table – such as 'Play 1.2.4–2.3.4–2.4' – so that whole parts could be fitted into a single line, achieving compression without compromising clarity.

Working with Dr. Charles Bannatyne, McLennan had reached the conclusion that terms of art such as 'taorluath' and 'crunluath' were distortions of a once simple descriptive system derived from Gaelic cardinal and ordinal numbers to indicate which fingers were involved in execution. 'Taorluath' was really 'trì-lugh' 'activity of three fingers' and 'crunluath' 'ceithir-lugh', or 'activity of four fingers' and so on.[45] He suggested, further, that these movements had been written inaccurately for almost a century, appearing with an extra, or 'redundant', low A which was not sounded in playing, and that notational practice should be revised to reflect this. There was some stir at the time, but the suggestion was adopted in the more important publications and soon became the normal way of representing the

43 Edinr., privately printed, 1907. For a detailed and hostile commentary by Charles Bannatyne, see *OT*, 10/8/1907 p.3.
44 For a lucid defence of McLennan's reasoning here see 'The Piobaireachd', from 'Loch Duich', [the annotated master copy of the *Oban Times* reveals this to have been a person called Welsh, writing from London] *OT*, 11/6/1910, p.5.
45 See 'Highland Music and Canntaireachd', from Charles Bannatyne, *OT*, 30/1/1904, p.3, 13/2/04, p.3, 20/2/04, p.3, 27/2/04, p.3, 5/3/04, p.3.

movement. It emerged, however, that some pipers actually played the 'redundant low A' and regarded those who did not as 'wrong', and as the implication dawned on the performer community about what this might mean for the transmission of the tradition during the 19th century, it was to trigger a major controversy.[46]

McLennan criticised a number of contemporary stylistic vices including unnecessary prolongation of introductory Es, jerky timing of the siubhal, and exaggerated concluding movements which he traced, once again, to the influence of the printed scores. He called them 'Sitirichean an Eich – Raoichden an Asail agus geumnaich a Mhairt' (the neighing of the horse, the braying of the ass, and the lowing of the cow), which meant this:

instead of this

The Piobaireachd As Performed in the Highlands for Ages, till about the Year 1808, Preface.

They were, he claimed, the result of 'unqualified men writing music they knew little or nothing about, thereby making bagpipe playing a variety of wild and meaningless notes, as if Momus, the god of mockery, was trying his best to show the piper as a full-grown clown'.[47] McLennan's point was a timely one, and it became increasingly applicable as the 20th century progressed. 'When my book appeared', he wrote:

> it was much denounced, notwithstanding which it had a sale far beyond my expectation; but when another man puts out a book which will be more simple, more concise, more intelligent, more musical, easier to learn and retain in the memory, I shall be the first to applaud him, and admit that I have been superseded . . . Other writers as well as myself wrote as we thought proper, and forced no man to play our setting. The Society, on the other hand, put out their tunes as the ancient music of Scotland, and bind pipers with chains of gold to play them.[48]

46 See Chapter 16.
47 John McLennan, *The Piobaireachd As Performed in the Highlands for Ages, till about the Year* 1808 (Edinr., privately printed, n.d. but 1924). For a thoughtful and well-informed review, probably by Alexander MacDonald ('Gleannach'), see *OT*, 16/8/1924, p.3.
48 'Piobaireachd Society's Music', *OT*, 14/5/1910, p.3.

The printed score, however inaccurate and unmusical, was not inherently deadly, therefore. For this to happen its use had to be made compulsory as was increasingly happening in modern competition. McLennan added:

> The practice and regulations promulgated within the last century or so
> regarding pibroch playing compel men of real musical genius to become more
> or less imitators of pipe playing . . . without any enquiry into the facts, we
> calmly conclude that what we now hear are the ancient melodies of our
> ancestors. Contracted views reared on scanty information . . . [lead] us to
> believe that the composers of former times did not insist on the regularity of
> metre but insisted on the maxim that 'Art must not be tied by rules'.[49]

McLennan felt that to tackle these problems it was necessary to get behind the façade of deliberate distortion which obscured the written scores as a result of a group of master players deliberately teaching 'wrong' in the generation after the '45:

> The Pipers who survived the battle of Culloden (16th April 1746) not only
> kept the Pibroch among themselves but were unfortunately enabled to exhibit
> it in so mysterious a form as not only to impose on, but to perplex the
> understanding of their pupils . . . Any person, with the slightest knowledge of
> music listening to the best pibroch players of the present day must feel that
> the performance is exceedingly disconnected and meaningless, all through,
> dwelling too long on the E and low A notes, not keeping time to the
> melody . . .'[50]

Thus two separate and ultimately unconnected ideas – the notion of proscription and the belief that poor notational practice had distorted the

---

49 'The Piobaireachd. By Lieut. John McLennan', *OT*, 22/2/1919, p.5, quoting Stewart of Ensay's remarks in the Preface to the first volume of the Piobaireachd Society's new *Collection*. Further on this point, see 'Piobaireachd Playing', from John McLennan, *OT*, 23/10/1920, p.3: ' The piper may have a far better setting of the tune, but he dare not play it, and his own natural abilities are curbed; he must simply play note for note what is put before him; he is simply a tracer or a copyist, and is not allowed to become an artiste'.

50 *The Piobaireachd as MacCrimmon Played it*, p.8. The idea was held up to ridicule by Charles Bannatyne in a hostile review of McLennan's book, although he had expounded it himself under a pseudonym not two years previously: 'Hoity, toity! What a study these simple minded, aye, often illiterate men of genius must have had to evolve such diabolical ingenuity and dishonesty, and what a fine type of freemasonry and telepathy must have existed among their hundreds to make the so-called "mysterious form" so common to all the hundreds of melodies and their multiplied setts'. McLennan regarded this, reasonably, as an act of treachery. Just a week or two before Bannatyne had written to him privately praising the work and appearing to accept its conclusions: *The Piobaireachd As Performed*, 'Preface'. McLennan responded with a long and reasoned defence of his book in 'The Piobaireachd as MacCrimmon Played it', *OT*, 24/8/1907, p.3.

music – were combined to produce an attractively simple explanation of why the published scores 'disagreed' with one another and sometimes departed from what a generation of largely orally trained players regarded as good idiom. There was a powerful additional sense that the Piobaireachd Society was dangerous and, if it were not checked, would do serious damage. It is significant that a man as able as John McLennan, representative of an old piping family whose grandfather had actually reached maturity during the 1770's, should prove so susceptible to the complex of ideas deriving ultimately from the letterpress portions of Patrick and Donald MacDonald and Angus MacKay. Two sets of skills were required to interpret such documents adequately: insight into the musical text and a historiographical awareness which, given the state of knowledge at the time, few contemporaries could be expected to possess.[51] The result was a limited ability to assess the ideological weighting of key portions of the published evidence. With the spread of literacy, these mediated texts began inevitably to affect the perception of the music inside the performer community, and in the early 20th century the Macpherson paradigm was to leave its characteristic marks of pessimism and uncertainty on a number of important traditionbearers.

At the Piobaireachd Society time was working its changes. Dunmore died in August 1907 and was succeeded by Brigadier-General Simon Fraser, 14th Lord Lovat, a military peer who had raised his own regiment, The Lovat Scouts, for service in the South African War and was to be the Society's President for many years to come. Stewart of Ensay fell ill, but continued as convener of the Music Committee. In February 1908 MacKillop wrote to John MacDonald, 'I fear there is small chance of improvement in the Piobaireachd Society. I have heard nothing as to what they propose to do. In a Society where everyone imagines he knows everything there is to be known, and where no one really knows anything, the whole thing is a huge farce'.[52] When Ensay died in the summer of 1908 there was an immediate problem because few current members of the Society could even begin to attempt to edit the texts.[53]

In 1907, the Society had begun to appoint teachers to conduct courses on the set tunes for aspiring young players. John MacDonald was responsible for Inverness and the Outer Isles, John MacColl and William Laurie for Argyll and the west, Gavin MacDougall for Perthshire and John MacDougall Gillies for Glasgow. It was not considered possible to appoint G. S. McLennan for Aberdeen, because he refused to change his personal style in order to teach

---

51 See, for example, his attempt to trace the descent of the MacCrimmon family into remote Irish pre-history, 'The MacCrimmon Pipers. By Lieut. Ian McLennan. Part 1', *OT*, 3/5/1919, p.3.

52 NLS, Acc. 9103/8 – J. MacKillop to John MacDonald of Inverness, 22/2/1908.

53 NLS, Acc. 9103/1, 10/9/1908.

the Society's settings.[54] As the *Piobaireachd Society Collection* grew, of course, so did the dilemma it presented for the teachers and in July 1910 Somerled MacDonald wrote:

> This means that the Society is now doing a real harm, and it is difficult to understand how the masters can teach settings which they themselves have so often condemned . . . It would also be interesting to know how the masters explain this matter to their pupils.[55]

In 1909 Lovat obtained the agreement of the War Office that candidates for appointment as pipe-major in the regular army should be trained by the Society's chief instructor John MacDonald, and the first course was held in Inverness beginning on 15th October 1910. It ran for three months and consisted 'of a lesson of at least one hour for each pupil, on four days in each week, and 50 lessons in all'. The Board of Examiners was made up of three Piobaireachd Society members and three army officers and at the end of the course 'The Board will examine candidates in Pipe playing, in reading and writing music, and will grant parchment certificates to those who are successful, qualifying them for promotion to the appointment of Sergeant-Piper' [i.e. Pipe-Major]. It was also agreed that henceforth only holders of the certificate would be eligible for this appointment, much as only 'certificated' pipers had been eligible to enter the later Edinburgh competitions of the Highland Societies of London and Scotland. Thus the Piobaireachd Society secured one of the early objectives of the Highland Societies by bringing into existence what was in effect an Army School of Piping.[56]

There had been increasing blurring of the distinction between civilian and military since the army reforms of the early eighties had created the new volunteer reserve and a number of leading pipers such as John MacDonald (4th Camerons), John MacDougall Gillies (5th H.L.I.), and William Laurie (8th Argyll and Sutherland Highlanders) took advantage of part-time soldiering as a useful addition to their incomes. This placed them under a pseudo-military discipline, and also at a disadvantage with regard to the Piobaireachd Society in which their part-time officers often held senior positions. Its President, Lord Dunmore, was C.O. of the 4th Camerons. He had also employed William Laurie as a personal piper.[57] Later on Willie Ross was appointed Pipe-Major of the

---

54 NLS. Acc. 9103/1, 20/7/1907, 6/7/1908, 5/7/1909; see also 'Piobaireachd Classes in South Uist. A Nursery of Pipers', revealing that John MacDonald's teaching there was largely owing to local initiative, *OT*, 26/3/1910, p.2. For the perceived unsuitability of G. S. McLennan as a Piobaireachd Society instructor see Acc. 9103/2: Loose Minutes 1905–6, 1910, 1913–14, 1919–21, 1955–68, 1975–7: Minutes of the AGM of the PS, held in the Station Hotel, Oban, on Thursday 11th September 1913.

55 'The Piobaireachd Society's Music', from Somerled MacDonald, *OT*, 16/7/1910, p.3.

56 NLS Acc. 9103/1, 5/7/1909; printed AGM Minutes, Inverness 1909.

57 'A Famous Ballachulish Piper. Pipe-Major Wm. Laurie', *OT*, 16/12/1916, p.5.

Lovat Scouts, which was to all intents and purposes the Piobaireachd Society's private regiment, raised by Lovat, and commanded by the Secretary of its Music Committee, Col. J. P. Grant of Rothiemurchus. And so the control of the upper echelons of the performer community which had begun to be lost by the landed élite in the drift to the cities, was to some extent regained by indirect but perhaps no less effective means. The Piobaireachd Society was now in a position of considerable strength. It controlled the major piping competitions, what was played at them, and how it was played. Through its network of instructors it was often able to determine who might receive higher instruction in the art and who might not, and ensure that its own scores were actively taught.[58] Without its approval, military pipers could not reach the final rung in the ladder of promotion. Finally, its expanding role as an employer of key pipers restricted opposition to its activities by people like John MacDonald who was its paid instructor and John MacDougall Gillies who held its publishing contract. Only people like John McLennan who were outside its power structure could afford to take an independent line, at least in public.

And yet the Society was vulnerable. Its acute shortage of practical knowledge and skill made it dependent on 'outside' sources for the set texts upon which its power was founded, while its social inflexibility and limited vision meant it was consistently unable to achieve a credible standard in this area. Following the death of Ensay the task of producing the set tunes devolved upon a sub-committee comprising Colin MacRae and John Bartholomew and Stewart MacDougall of Lunga. They immediately enlisted the help of John MacDonald, John MacDougall Gillies and Willie Ross, although with the typical proviso that this was done:

> on the distinct understanding . . . that the Sub-Committee reserve to
> themselves full discretionary power as to the settings to be accepted and
> printed. It was . . . agreed to include . . . any authorised variants of the tunes
> selected . . . It was also agreed that these variants were not to be used for
> competition purposes.[59]

The new committee proved little more receptive to advice than Ensay had been, and its relationship with the professional players was rigidly *de haut en bas*. And so volume IV of the Society's Collection appeared in the Spring of 1910 to the by now almost predictably hostile reception.[60] But there was a growing feeling in the piping world that things could not go on like this, and as Charles

---

58 See, for example, the Society's advertisement informing pipers about the settings for this year's competitions, and reserving the right to admit [and therefore equally to withhold admission] to its classes, *OT*, 26/2/1910, p.1.

59 NLS, Acc. 9103/1, AGM, Oban, 10/9/1908.

60 See, for example, 'The Piobaireachd Society's Publication', from John McLennan, *OT*, 5/3/1910, p.3 and 26/3/1910, p.3; same, from Charles Bannatyne, 12/3/1910, p.3, 19/3/1910, p.3.

Bannatyne proposed a conference in Edinburgh of all interested parties, the Society came under attack from a powerful new source close to the dissident Campbells.

On the 26th March 1910 a long letter headed 'The Piobaireachd Society's Publication' and signed 'Padruig Og' appeared in the *Oban Times*. It strongly supported the stance taken by the Society's critics but it carried the argument well beyond the music text: the Piobaireachd Society was denounced as aristocratic, authoritarian, secretive, London-based, and musically illiterate. It was also very rich. But how did it spend its money?

> . . . A large sum is spent on publishing music shown to be incorrect in quality and in quantity most unnecessarily full – the taor-luath and crun-luath beats being printed in all the volumes 'in extenso', and incidentally wrongly – a sheer waste of paper, time and money.
>
> Again, one of the objects of the Society is to correct those tunes already in print, which are found to be wrong. But we find the mistakes corroborated by this Society which may, I fear, by its name, command among an ignorant posterity an influence greater than that of Donald MacDonald and Angus Mackay.
>
> . . . the society is guided by a number of well-meaning enthusiasts, and it is no secret that they are blind enthusiasts on the subject of piobaireachd music . . . And yet this Society professes to dictate to the piping world what is correct and what is not correct . . . The Society's paid instructors are bound, willy nilly, to perpetuate the blunders . . . [and] the competence of the Society's judges, with one or two honourable exceptions, must be a matter of grave doubt . . .
>
> Why is it that the Society, whose objects are in every way admirable and deserving of the support of all lovers of Ceol Mor, has failed so lamentably?[61]

The letter went on to describe the Society as 'the laughing stock of all piobaireachd players' and to call either for its radical reform or summary dissolution. 'Padruig Og' was John Peter Grant, yr. of Rothiemurchus (1885–1963), who was eventually to become President of the Piobaireachd Society and do much to shape its activities during the middle years of the twentieth century. He was then in his twenty-fourth year and studying law at Edinburgh University having attended Winchester and Magdalen College, Oxford. He was a close

61 'The Piobaireachd Society's Publication', *OT*, 26/3/1910, p.3. James MacKillop had seen 'Padruig Og's letter before its publication and responded enthusiastically: 'I have gone over your letter, and think it is splendid, and very much to the point. I think you should be very particular in keeping your identity absolutely secret, the same as A.M. has done.' NLS, Acc. 9103 /8 – J. MacKillop to 'Dear Grant' 16/3/1910. See also draft letter to the *Oban Times* from 'Padruig Og', 21/3/1910: the handwriting is that of J. P. Grant, and the published text is docketed 'Grant of Rothiemurchus' in the annotated master copy of the *Oban Times*.

associate of the Campbell brothers and an enthusiastic amateur pupil of John MacDonald of Inverness.[62] He had not been a member of the Society, but his views were quickly endorsed by someone who had – Somerled MacDonald, one of its founders and a long-serving judge, who publicly conceded the accuracy of nearly everything the critics had alleged:

> . . . In 'Padruig Og's' letter we have the plain truth, and a good many useful suggestions . . .
>
> At one time I was on the Music Committee of the Society; yet my word was not taken on any single point. Neither was any advice taken from any professional . . . I do not believe that any first-class professional would pass the last number, or indeed any of the numbers, published by the Society as correct . . .
>
> I deny that the committee is composed of the best amateur players. Indeed, I should be surprised to hear that there existed a single passable player in the Society.
>
> With regard to the judging the decisions have been questioned over and over again. I have judged for the Society at Oban, Fort William, and Inverness. And at these three meetings I have only come across one other judge who could play all the tunes. At Fort William one of the judges could neither play the pipes nor had he any knowledge of competitions or pipe music whatsoever. To my amazement this 'judge' asked me, while the piper was still tuning up his pipes if he had begun to play his tune! It used to be a rule in the Society's competitions that the piper should not be allowed to tune his pipes on the platform. It has since struck me that perhaps this rule was made in order to enable the judges to guess with tolerable accuracy when the piper actually did commence. When the second competitor began to play the same judge enquired if it was the same man playing another 'piece'. It was at this meeting that some of the competitors told me they had practised the misprints, as they suspected the judges would go exactly by the book, they presumably having no other knowledge to guide them . . .
>
> I hope the Piobaireachd Society will even at the eleventh hour realise the necessity of putting its house in order, and will not be led further into a pathetic self-deception . . . The first important step is the immediate recall of the publications complained of. Failing the Society following this course, I would suggest that a new Society be formed to counteract its misdeeds, and the members should be very carefully chosen, and also, most important of all, that it should include professional players who would have full control of the publication department, assisted, if they liked, by some of the amateurs. I am, etc.[63]

62 See 'The New Year at Kilberry', *OT,* 21/1/1911, p.2; NLS, Acc. 9103/8 – J.P. Grant to John MacDonald, 11/3/1913.

63 'Piobaireachd Society's Work', from Somerled MacDonald, *OT,* 9/4/1910, p.5.

The inaugural meeting of the Scottish Pipers' and Dancers Union, intended to represent the performer community was held in Glasgow on Saturday 26 November 1910 with Charles Bannatyne in the chair.[64] At the end of it, twenty eight potential members gave in their names, including John MacDougall Gillies and John MacDonald. The basic idea was that competitions should not be judged by gentlemen amateurs of limited knowledge wielding fixed texts, but by distinguished former competitors on agreed principles, with pipers to be judged 'on any recognised setting of a tune they care to play'.[65] At its own meetings, the Union aimed to vary the ceaseless diet of competition by securing papers on music and piping history from visiting speakers with discussions and recitals by leading players. At a lecture-recital in Glasgow the following spring Bannatyne gave a talk on the history of the pipe and there were selections from MacDougall Gillies, John MacColl and William Gray.[66]

Meantime the impasse at the Piobaireachd Society was about to be resolved. There was little talk now amongst the secessionists of forming a new society. The wealth and power of the original organisation was a mighty lever waiting to be used if the requisite intelligence could be applied. J. P. Grant was already at work to acquire the manuscript sources on which an authoritative edition could be based. In June 1910 James MacKillop gave him a letter of introduction to Colin Cameron, then living at his father's house, Seaforth Cottage, in Maryburgh, adding: 'I fear you will find him a very feeble old man, and not very strong mentally, however it will be interesting in after life, just to be able to say that you knew him'.[67] In his reply Cameron said his hands, like his friend General Thomason's had become 'weak & shaky . . . at one time I played *Ceol Mor* rather well, but alas that day is gone'.[68] As a result perhaps of his ceaseless editorial labours, the General had developed scrivener's palsy which was slowing the work of revision on *Ceol Mor*. By now written communication was possible only by typewriter, laboriously, and Grant was giving much-needed secretarial help.[69] Grant was also working in close association with Archibald Campbell, the

---

64 'The Scottish Pipers' Union', from Charles Bannatyne, *OT*, 22/10/1910, p.3: same, from 'Loch Sloy', [Pipe-Major Donald Macfarlane of Oban], 5/11/1910, p.3; same, from 'Ceol Mor' [John Grant], 12/11/1910 p.3 and 26/11/1910, p.3; 'Scottish Pipers' Union. Inaugural Meeting', 10/12/1910, p.3; 'Scottish Pipers' Union', from 'Gilleasbuig' [Archibald Paterson], 24/12/1910 p.3; same, from 'Blue Ribbon', 7/1/1911, p.3.

65 *OT*, 17/12/1910, p.3.

66 *OT*, 'Scottish Pipers' and Dancers' Union. Lecture by Dr. Bannatyne, 22/4/1911, p.2. the Union appears to have fallen into abeyance during the Great War.

67 NLS, Acc. 9103/8, J. MacKillop to J. P. Grant, 13/6/1910.

68 *Ibid.*, Colin Cameron to J. P. Grant, 18/6/1910.

69 *Ibid.*, C. S. Thomason to J. P. Grant, 5/8/1910. He was also being assisted by John Campbell of Kilberry, see 'Letter from John Campbell dated Kilberry, Argyllshire, 15/10/1909, to Lord Lovat, indicating that he was working on 'the 2nd edition of Genl Thomason's "Ceol Mor" which I and many others are so anxious to see produced.' Piobaireachd Research Papers of Archibald Campbell (ca. 1903–1963, n.d.), NLS, MS. 22107, f.8.

youngest of the Kilberry brothers.[70] The latter was born in 1877 and educated at Harrow and Pembroke College, Cambridge, entering the Indian Civil Service in 1900 and eventually rising to be a junior High Court Judge on the Lahore circuit. He was nearly ten years Grant's senior and very much the dominant partner, displacing Grant as editor of the Piobaireachd Society's second series when he returned permanently to the United Kingdom in the later 1920s. In the summer of 1910 he was home on furlough, going the rounds of the games – dismissing Cowal, in a memorable phrase, as 'the wild beast show at Dunoon' – and he visited Thomason at Grantown to arrange for photographic copies to be made of the MSS of Donald MacDonald and Angus MacKay.[71]

Thomason was seen both as an asset and as a liability. While he made a splendid figurehead, he had a mind of his own and was not inclined to rest on his laurels and it was felt that his uncompromising honesty could easily wreck the delicate negotiations going on between the secessionists and the Society. MacKillop wrote to J. P. Grant on 23 August 1910:

> Yes, the General is a problem, his friends really require to try and save him from himself. I have had frightful difficulty in the past, trying to prevent him doing the most stupid things. He is completely out of touch with the present day pipers, and a lot of his ideas, about the scale, and the way notes should be played, etc., are theoretical rot, and as you say, will only put people against him, and hurt the Ceol Mor cause. It is also a tremendous mistake for him to rush into the Oban Times as it will certainly do him more harm than good, but he is very difficult to persuade about anything. If he would leave things alone, and be content with the great work he has already done, I am sure we could get the P.S. into line, but he would expect the P.S. to take up all his fads. I am going to do my best at Oban, to try and bring about a compromise with the P.S. It would be in the interests of piping in Scotland, and the time is now ripe for it . . . I see no difficulties in the way except the General, and I think we might manage to deal with him. Lunga and Colin MacRae are very keen that something should be done . . .[72]

Meantime there had been a major discovery. In 1909 a notice had appeared in the *Oban Times* advertising an old 'Culloden' set of pipes for sale under a box number. It was answered by leading Scottish advocate and legal writer, John Bartholomew. Bartholomew was one of the most prominent society Celticists of his generation, a former Secretary of the Scottish Pipers Society, member of the

70 NLS, Acc.9103/27, 'Memoranda etc concerning the history of piping, mostly undated, but including the agreement, 1911, between Kilberry and Rothiemurchus relating to their joint ownership of their music', which contains a formal 'Memorandum of Agreement' to that effect.
71 NLS, Acc. 9103/8, Archibald Campbell to J.P. Grant, 19/8/1910.
72 *Ibid.*, James MacKillop to J. P. Grant, 23/8/1910.

MacCrimmon Memorial Trust, President of the Celtic Union, Vice-President of the Edinburgh Gaelic Musical Association, member of the Music Committee of the Piobaireachd Society and a prominent piping judge. The advertisement led him to a Miss Ann Campbell in Oban.[73] He examined the pipes, bought them, and was preparing to leave when Miss Campbell mentioned that she had some books which she thought had to do with piping and asked if he would like to see them. She then produced the two volumes of Colin Campbell's 'Nether Lorn' Canntaireachd which were thought to have been lost for nearly three quarters of a century. Bartholomew bought them at once and passed them to J. P. Grant who had a transcript made and, encouraged by John MacDonald, set to work to master the system.[74] He noted:

> After all the controversies about Gesto's Book you can understand that many
> pipers were a bit sceptical about this tremendous discovery. One critic even
> without seeing the manuscript condemned it as a patent forgery, but
> scepticism was pretty general as to the recovery of the system of the notation.
> It fell to me to convince one of these who had been on duty abroad at the
> time of the discovery [probably Archibald Campbell] . . . the test was that he
> would play me a tune which I did not know, I would write it in Canntd. as
> he played, & then play it back on the practice chanter. Well he played & at
> the end confessed to 2 mistakes, which were duly rendered in my play back,
> & that converted him.[75]

Not only was the Campbell canntaireachd a good deal more systematic and coherent than Gesto's but it also – most excitingly – contained some sixty tunes not recorded elsewhere. Grant prepared eight well-known pieces of which the Canntaireachd gave attractive or unusual readings for publication in the original notation.[76]

The secessionists and their allies were the only people of their social class in Scotland who could even begin to cope with the Society's publication programme and the Society knew it. In April 1911, J. Graham Campbell yr. of Shirvan, wrote to J. P. Grant about the growing atmosphere of rapprochement:

73 For biographical details see 'Mr John Bartholomew of Glenorchard. President of the
    Celtic Union', *OT*, 30/5/1914, p.5.
74 NLS, Acc. 9103/8, John MacDonald to J. P. Grant, 28/2/1911. For some of the
    difficulties in construing the text, see letter from John Bartholomew to Archibald
    Campbell, in Piobaireachd Research Papers of Archibald Campbell, NLS., MS 22117,
    ff.66–7.
75 NLS, Acc.9103/26, 'Memoranda Relating to Canntaireachd', 'Canntaireachd or the
    Syllabic Notation', p.6.
76 *Ibid.*, draft essay by J. P. Grant on the Nether Lorn Canntaireachd. The tunes were
    'Lament for the Only Son', 'Clan Chattan's Gathering', 'Massacre of Glencoe',
    'Lament for the Harp Tree', 'The Unjust Incarceration', 'The Groat', 'The Battle of
    Auldearn', and 'The Rout of Glenfruin'.

I fell in with Colin MacRae on the boat & we talked P.S. the whole way to Glasgow . . . He said why will these fellows, (you, Archibald Campbell, etc.) have nothing to do with the P.S. is it personal feeling? I said No they are frightened of being put in the same position as they were before of being outvoted by a crowd of ignorant sassenach deadheads.

He said well on what terms will they come back?

I said guarantee them a capable Music Committee with full charge of all matters relating to music and answerable to nobody for their actions & they'll probably come back (except perhaps Kilberry & Somerled MacDonald who might not).

He said All right we'll put them all on the Music Committee, & be only too glad if they'll run the show their own way.

. . .I took the opportunity to put the dirk into him about the music & said the whole thing ought to be revised & authorities shown for settings & proper notes Etc. He said he didn't know there was anything wrong with the music! but if wrong it shd certainly be revised & he agreed about authorities. He is really absolutely sound on the whole thing & damned keen to see the thing run on proper lines . . .

I hope you will fall into line if offered reasonable terms (which I am sure you will be) as the P.S. properly run wd do a tremendous amount of good, & all this scrapping & squabbling is damned sickening when everyone ought to be working together to keep the music of our country alive.[77]

In June, Colin Cameron wrote excitedly. He had heard rumours about a cache of MacCrimmon MSS at Dunvegan. He thought that all MacCrimmon pupils had to note down their tunes as part of their training and that quantities of such material might still exist, opening up the possibility of another find as big, or even bigger, than the Campbell Canntaireachd.[78] J. P. Grant at once wrote to Norman MacLeod of MacLeod who agreed to a search of the castle although warning that 'a lot of papers were destroyed some years ago'.[79] Indeed the omens were not good. Various people had been through Dunvegan in recent years, including the family's historian, Canon R. C. MacLeod who wrote 'There is a lot of old music in some of the cupboards in the library at Dunvegan and what you want might be there . . . I believe that, when Lord Hill had the Castle, his housemaid used old papers in the Muniment room to light fires with and many

77 NLS, Acc. 9103/8, J. G. Campbell to J. P. Grant, 10/4/1911; see also letter from Archibald Campbell to J.P.Grant, 20/12/1911 'we ought if we rejoin to snaffle the secretaryship . . . Lovat . . . offers to resign in favour of Jock [i.e. Capt. John Campbell] but this would be a mistake and a misfortune as he is the sort of fellow we want to carry with us . . . I am ready to agree to anything provided that the music is declared provisional and we are well represented on a music committee of actual pipers.' quoted in James Campbell, 'History of the Piobaireachd Society', p.41.
78 NLS, Acc.9103/8, Colin Cameron to J. P. Grant, 15/6/1911, 19/6/1911, 22/7/1911.
79 *Ibid.*, Norman M. MacLeod to J. P. Grant, 10/7/1911.

valuable documents which we know were at Dunvegan in the 17th and 18th centuries have disappeared'.[80] In the middle of all this, on 12th July 1911, General Thomason died at his home at 103 Warwick Road, Kensington. Norman MacLeod wrote to Grant: 'Poor old Thomason. He was very enthusiastic and I am afraid was very sensitive.'[81] He was buried in Inverallan Churchyard, Granton-on-Spey. The notice of his death in the London *Times* did not mention piping.[82]

In the end, Grant's search for MacCrimmon papers proved fruitless, but he sent MacLeod a haunch of venison for his trouble and turned his attention to the lost third volume of the Campbell Canntaireachd.[83] This had been brought by John Campbell to the 1818 competition in Edinburgh and purchased by Sir John MacGregor Murray, thereafter disappearing from view. Grant wrote to Miss A. G. Murray MacGregor, the historian of Clan MacGregor, who replied:

> You are quite right that I am an 'enthusiast' in everything highland and many of the family papers of my forbears have come under my ken but none I fear in connection with *pipe* music . . . I am afraid I cannot give you any trace of John Campbell's missing volume of piobaireachd. Most of my Grandfather's papers have passed through my hands (he died in 1822) but not the volume to which you refer.[84]

She regretfully declined Grant's gallant offer of a dance at the Northern Meeting Ball on the grounds that she was now 82 years old.

On 1st April 1912, the Piobaireachd Society moved formally towards détente with the secessionists. Behind the polite rhetoric, it was an unconditional surrender. Archibald Campbell, James MacKillop, and Somerled MacDonald were appointed to the music committee and it was recommended that Captain John Campbell of Kilberry become Vice-President of the Society. The music committee were to have a Convener and Secretary appointed by themselves, all the previously issued music of the Society was to be revised, and an advertisement to that effect was placed in the *Oban Times*. J.P.Grant was elected a member of the Society, and the new-look music committee, now comprising Grant, John Campbell, James MacKillop and R. S. Munro, took in hand the revision of the Society's publications. John Campbell and his brother Archibald formally re-joined the Society. The new rules allowed people to be removed from the roll of members; insisted that members could recommend only persons personally

---

80 *Ibid.*, R. C. MacLeod to J. P. Grant, 22/7/1911.
81 *Ibid*, Norman M. Macleod to J. P. Grant, 28/7/1911.
82 Smith, *Royal Scottish Pipers*, p.65.
83 NLS, Acc.9103/8 , 16/8/11, confirming that Grant had found nothing at Dunvegan. See also A. MacDonald to J. P. Grant, 25/7/1911: 'I feel very funny when I think of that Goth of a maid lighting fires with probably McCrimmon piobaireachds . . .', and same 26/2/1912.
84 *Ibid.*, A. G. Murray MacGregor to J. P. Grant, 20/9/1912.

known to them; decreed that AGM's be henceforth held only in Scotland; removed control from the AGM, at which on previous occasions the small band of piping enthusiasts had found themselves ambushed and outvoted, vesting it in a general Committee of 12 Members and a Music Committee of 7. The Secretary's role was re-defined in a way that meant the holder of this office could no longer control the Society. Real power now lay with the Music Committee and its Secretary, J. P. Grant, yr. of Rothiemurchus.[85]

Signs of change were quickly apparent. The requirement that only the Society's settings be played in their competitions, which had caused so much conflict in the past, was suspended for that year, although the Society continued to nominate the tunes.[86] In the meantime Grant had tracked down Peter Reid's MS. Its owners considered it as a 'family relic' and would not part with it, but he continued to scour the country for manuscript sources.[87] In his report to the AGM in 1913, he listed the Society's holdings as follows:

When the Committee was appointed, the Society's collection of music (besides that which they had published) consisted of two volumes, photographs of Donald Macdonald's unpublished MS., and three of Angus Mackay's unpublished MS., presented by Captain Campbell of Kilberry, in April 1911.

It has now the use of the collection made by Messrs Archibald Campbell (Kilberry), and J. P. Grant, which contains *inter alia* –

Printed
    Donald Macdonald's Collection
    Angus MacKay's Collection
    McPhee's Collection
    D. Glen's Collection
    D. Glen's Edinburgh Collection
    Ceol Mor: General Thomason
    Historical Notes: Henry Whyte
    Gesto's Cainntearachd
    (1) Copy Cainntearachd Collection, 2 vols., Colin Campbell, 1797. 169 tunes
    (2) Copy Angus MacArthur's MS. 30 tunes

85 NLS. Acc. 9013/1, Minutes, 1/4/1912, 21/5/1912, 20/9/1912, 13/12/1912, 15/1/1913.

86 See 'Piobaireachd Society's New Rules' from 'A Lover of Piobaireachd', *OT*, 15/2/1913, p.3. 'Piobaireachd Society's Competitions, 1913', from J. P. Grant, 8/3/1913, p.3. The move was generally welcomed, but see 'The Piobaireachd Society's New Rules' from 'Competitor' [probably John Grant], and same from Lieut. John McLennan declaring the new rule 'a great forward movement', 29/3/1913, p.3.

87 NLS. Acc. 9013/8, James A Reid to J. P. Grant, 14/2/1913; W. M Bliss to ?J. P. Grant, 20/8/1913; Donald Alex Campbell to J. P. Grant, 10/9/1913, 17/10/1913; W. Langrish, to J.P.Grant, 23/10/1913; ? to ?J.P.Grant, 7/11/1913; R. C. Bruce Gardner to J.P.Grant, 14/4/1914.

(3) Photos Donald Macdonald's MS., 2 vols., 49 tunes.
(4) Photos Angus Mackay's MS., 3 vols., 181 tunes,[88]

To this was shortly to be added the Skinner MS, 61 tunes compiled by Duncan Campbell of Foss, and, thanks to the good agency of Lieut. John McLennan, the MS. of Donald MacDonald jr.[89]

J. P. Grant was also anxious to use the Society's resources to promote piobaireachd as a living art, and to this end, the Music Committee proposed to the AGM of 1913 that a competition in piobaireachd composition be held. But the Hon. Elspeth Campbell moved that the proper publishing of the older tradition was more important and the moment passed. The Great War intervened and the proposal lay dormant for fifty years.

88 NLS. Acc. 9013/1, 11/9/1913.
89 *Ibid.*, Draft Report Aug 1913 – 1914, it adds, 'Through the kindness of ex-Lieut. Jno. McLennan, Edinburgh, another MS. was put in the Committee's hands to copy. According to Lt. McLennan it was written by Donald Macdonald, son of Donald Macdonald . . . It contains 41 tunes, and at first sight promises to clear up a good many difficulties in some [of his father's published and manuscript tunes]'.

14

'Merry Christmas Scottie Guardie':
The Great War and its Aftermath

During the 1914–18 war the clubs and societies, games, competitions, virtually the whole civilian institutions of piping were suspended. The war dominated everything. There was an enormous increase in Scottish military capability and therefore in the demand for pipers. The 71st. H.L.I., for example which had begun the war with two regular and two territorial battalions, ended up seventeen battalions strong, two regular, nine 'New Army' and six territorial, all on active service.[1] The Royal Scots had also grown to seventeen battalions by the end of the war. Each battalion had its complement of pipers. More than 254 served with the H.L.I. and more than 249 with the Royal Scots.[2] When the British Expeditionary Force landed in France in 1914, it included seven units with pipers. By the end of hostilities there were more than a hundred. It is thought that over 2,500 pipers were involved on the Western Front alone.[3]

There was an immediate call for men and instruments in the advertising columns of the *Oban Times*. By October the 7th Camerons were appealing for pipes on loan, to be returned after the end of hostilities.[4] The 6th H.L.I. advertised for pipers, proclaiming that 'This Battalion wears the Kilt'.[5] The 11th Gordons wanted a Pipe-Major, the successful candidate to be liable for home service only with additional pay, and also ordinary pipers, inviting them to 'State amount of extra pay required'.[6] The 2/5th Argyll and Sutherland Highlanders, the King's Own Scottish Borderers, the Royal Army Medical Corps, even the Royal Naval Division advertised for players.[7] There were pipers in units from all

1 Malcolm, p.118.
2 Sir Bruce Seton, and John Grant, *The Pipes of War A Record of the Achievements of Pipers of Scottish and Overseas Regiments during the War 1914–1918* (Glasg., 1920) pp. 73–82, 105–114.
3 Seton and Grant, p.46.
4 'Bagpipes Wanted for Lochiel's Highlanders', *OT*, 17/10/1914, p.5.
5 'Pipers and Drummers Wanted', *OT*, 19/12/1914, p.1. Listening to Scottish soldiers fretting about possible abolition of the pipes, kilts, and other signs of visible nationality at this time, one could be forgiven for thinking that they sometimes regarded the British War Office as a greater threat than the Germans: Seton and Grant, pp. 3–8, 67.
6 'Pipe-Major Wanted', *OT*, 16/1/1915, p.1; 'Pipers', 13/2/1915, p.1.
7 'Pipers. Pipe-Sergeant and Pipers. Wanted for Service in the 2/5th Battalion Argyll and Sutherland Highlanders', *OT*, 20/2/1915, p.1; 6/3/1915, p.1; 'Eight Pipers Wanted' 24/4/15, p.1; 'Lord Graham's Appeal for Pipers', 16/1/1915, p.3.

over the U.K., in the London, Tyneside and Liverpool Scottish and in English regiments commanded by Scots. They were particularly well represented in formations from Canada, South Africa, Australia and New Zealand.[8] When American forces entered the war some of them had pipers too.[9]

As the fighting intensified the obituaries began to accumulate in the *Oban Times*. They were laid out in standard typographical boxes, with photographs of young men in ill-fitting uniforms and a paragraph or so saying how they had died, under headings like 'A Brave Son of Skye', 'A Brave Mull Soldier'. During quiet periods there might be three or four a week but in the great battles the little boxes spread across the inside pages:

'A Heroic Uist Piper Killed. Deep regret is felt over the district of Iochdar, South Uist, on official information being received . . . Piper Angus Morrison, 16th Seaforth Highlanders of Canada . . . killed in action . . . recovering the lost guns when the Canadians were gassed by the Germans . . . 32 years of age . . .'

'Piper Ross – Hero. Official notification has been received of the death in France of Lce-Corpl. R. G. Ross, of the 1/5th Seaforth Highlanders . . . bullet wound in the head . . . prior to mobilisation gamekeeper . . . gone out to help a comrade who was shot . . . buried side by side . . .'

'Highland Piper's Bravery . . . Sergeant-Piper Neil MacLeod, 1/8th Scottish Rifles . . . killed in action at the Dardanelles . . .23 years of age . . . took a great interest in the Boys' Brigade movement and taught several Boys' Brigade pipe bands in Glasgow . . . a Turkish gun got their range and dropped three high explosive shells right into the trench . . .'

'A Brave Islay Piper . . . Peter McNiven . . . killed at the Dardanelles in a gallant attack on the Turkish forts . . . as modest, intelligent, kindly and gentle a lad as ever left Islay . . .'

'With the Gordon Highlanders . . . Corporal John Campbell . . . killed in great advance on 25th September . . . wounded for the sixth time . . . piper in the band of the 2nd Gordons . . . noted athlete . . . championship of Egypt and the Soudan for long-distance running . . . 29 years of age . . .'

'Death of a Noted Highland Piper . . . Archibald MacPhie Ramage, Scottish Rifles . . . big engagement at the Dardanelles . . . 23 years of age . . . genial young man and a gifted piper, having won a number of cups and medals in the keenest competitions . . .'

8 Seton and Grant, pp.143–7, 150–60.
9 Seton and Grant, p.37.

'Brave Uist Piper. Alexander MacEachen, Cameron Highlanders . . . died from his wounds . . . took part in the great charge around Loos . . . wounded in the head by a German bullet . . . remains brought to South Uist by way of Kyle of Lochalsh, and though the weather was boisterous and the ground was covered with snow, every man in the district turned out to the funeral . . .'

'Piper Duncan Mackenzie . . . Scottish Rifles . . . member of the 86th Glasgow Boys Brigade and Eglinton Toll Pipe Bands . . . killed in France on 17th November while carrying the wounded from the field.'[10]

And it went on for many months after the Armistice, as some posted missing were discovered to be dead and others died of disease and wounds. Sometimes the cameos were celebratory and one had to read the small print to discover whether the subjects were living or dead. On 5th January 1916 one of these drew the readers' attention to 'A Gallant Uist Family. Five sons with the colours'. The sons were those of Mr and Mrs Ronald MacDonald, Garrahellie, South Uist. Four of them were pipers.

Casualties were heavy. The Scottish regiments lost – at a conservative estimate – more than 1,000 pipers killed and wounded during the course of the War, and many of these losses were sustained during the first year of the fighting as they played their units into action at Mons, and Le Cateau, Ypres, Loos and Neuve Chapelle.

The 1st Gordons took 18 pipers out to France. At the roll call at Cambrai on 26th August 1914, only two remained. The Scots Guards also suffered heavy losses, with 7 pipers killed and 17 wounded by the end of the first year.[11] Such losses could not be sustained and after the autumn of 1915, they were less frequently to be found playing their companies over the top. Even so, during the course of the war the Seaforth lost almost one hundred and fifty pipers dead and wounded and the Royal Scots nearly a hundred.

The military maps show the situation in the autumn of 1914 as the war of movement ground to a halt and trench warfare set in. The line was a great sagging loop of grey/blue held by the French, with a bright red bulge around Ypres, representing the British. Facing them was the massed green of the German VIth Army commanded by Crown Prince Rupprecht of Bavaria. If the British could not hold the Salient and the Germans broke through, they would turn the Allied flank, drive rapidly towards Paris, and the war would be over – like everybody said – by Christmas.

But the British did not lose Ypres. Barring the way down the Menin road was the flower of the old regular army, or what remained of it, and near the tip of the Salient, the 2nd Battalion Scots Guards.

---

10 *OT*, 17/7/1915, p.2; 7/8/1915, p.2; 16/10/1915, p.2; 23/10/15, p.2; 6/11/1915, p.2; 20/11/1915, p.2; 27/11/1915, p.2; 25/12/1915, p.2.

11 Seton and Grant, pp.124, 71–3.

They had not had been having a good war. Landing at Zeebrugge in October to defend Antwerp, they had been forced to cover the retreat of the Belgian army and now found themselves in the line, in the thick of the desperate defence of Ypres. On the night of the 26th October, they were heavily shelled. The primitive trenches collapsed and men were suffocated before they could be dug out. The Germans overran their position. The C.O. was lost and many men taken prisoner. When they counter-attacked they were fired upon by their own artillery and suffered further losses. When eventually they were withdrawn on the night of the 29th-30th October they were reduced to two hundred men commanded by a captain. By the end of November they had lost a further four officers and one hundred and thirty six other ranks.[12]

So it was as a representative of a small and rather shattered band that piper Archibald Macpherson, of Bunessan, Isle of Mull, found himself on Christmas morning, 1914, experiencing one of the most curious events of the War: 'We had a glorious time of it on Christmas Day', he wrote to relatives in Glasgow:

There was a keen frost and snow falling slightly. On Christmas Eve the Germans shouted from their trenches, which are only 100 yards from ours, in these terms – 'A merry Christmas, Scottie Guardie. We are not going to fire to-morrow; we will have a holiday and a game of football'. Our fellows agreed. Next morning, sure enough, the Germans came out of their trenches, and began to saunter over to ours unarmed. At this, our chaps went over half-way to meet them. They greeted one another like the best of friends and shook hands. You would have thought the war was at an end. We exchanged cigarettes for cigars, tobacco, etc. They brought over ever so many things as souvenirs. A German officer gave me a button off his coat for my capstar. We were chatting all day.

I was talking to a German who was four years in London. He could speak fine English. I asked him when did he think the war would be over. He said in six months' time. I remarked that they were getting the worst of it now; and he said that if they were beaten it was taking four countries to do it. They said they were getting tired of it. They seem to be as well off as we are, and have plenty of everything. One German gave our officer a letter to post to a lady he knows in Essex. I had such a funny feeling talking to our enemy, who would seek to shoot us on the morrow; but there was another surprise for us. Next day, they came over and stood up on the trenches. We could walk and go where we liked.

Later the same night we heard that they were going to make an attack, so we prepared for it by getting our artillery to shell them; but not a rifle shot was fired, and they didn't attack. Next morning, being the third morning of peace, they came over half-way to inquire what was the matter with our

12 J. E. Edmonds, *History of the Great War: Military Operations France and Belgium*, 1914 (2 vols., Lond., 1922), ii, see index under 'Foot Guards, Scots, 2nd. Bn.'.

artillery last night, that it had killed a lot of their chaps. They came to the conclusion it was the French. All day they never fired a shot. In the evening we were relieved by the [unit name erased by censor]. The Germans knew we were being relieved, and asked us to tell them not to fire, and if they got the order to fire to fire high, and they would do the same. I don't know how they got on since, but we are going back to-morrow. That would never end the war, would it? I think the Germans are tired of it, and would never shoot if we didn't shoot first. I must say some of them were very nice fellows, and did not show any hatred, which makes me think they are forced to fight. I wrote you a letter telling you we made a bayonet attack. I wonder if you got it. We lost a few men. The Germans helped us to bury them on Christmas Day.[13]

Piper Archibald Macpherson was wounded at the battle of Neuve Chapelle on the 11th of March 1915 but survived the war, serving with the Guards until November 1921.[14]

His Pipe-Major, Willie Ross (1878–1966), competitor, teacher and composer, also survived and went on to become the most famous all-round player in 20th century Scotland. He was born on 14 June 1878 at Camsorie, Glen Strathfarrar, Inverness-shire, the second of the six children of Alexander Ross (1854–?), head forester of Struy and his wife, Mary Collie (1854–1944) of Monar. His main piping teacher was his mother and he also had instruction from his father and his mother's uncle, Aeneas Rose (1832–1905), piper to the Duke of Atholl. Ross joined the Scots Guards in 1896 and became Pipe-Major of the 2nd battalion in 1905. He saw active service in the Boer War and throughout the Great War until invalided out with rheumatism in June 1918. He refused a commission and for nearly forty years thereafter dominated the piping world from his eyrie in Edinburgh Castle where he taught the army class. He personally trained a whole new generation of senior military pipers until eventually there was hardly a Pipe-Major in the British Army who had not been through his hands.

Three master players, Willie Ross (2nd. Scots Guards), G. S. McLennan (1st Gordon Highlanders), and William Laurie (8th Argyll and Sutherland Highlanders) went to the war. Two of them came back. William Laurie, one of the most fresh and original composers of *ceòl beag* of the early twentieth century died, aged thirty five, at a military hospital in Oxford on 28 November 1916.[15] The first two were career soldiers; Laurie was a civilian, a champion piper making a little extra with the volunteer reserve, mobilised with his battalion on the sudden

13 'Mull Piper at the Front. Talking with the Enemy', *OT*, 23/1/1915, p. 3.
14 Archibald Macpherson re-enlisted with the Royal Engineers on 3 January 1940. I am indebted for this information to Major (Retd) C Brown, Records & Welfare Officer, Scots Guards.
15 'A Famous Ballachulish Piper. Pipe-Major Wm. Laurie', *OT*, 16/12/1916, p.5.

outbreak of war in August 1914.[16] John MacDonald of Inverness was called-up for active service with the 4th Camerons at the same time. But MacDonald, already 49 years old, was taken seriously ill and invalided out.

Such opportunities for heroic self-sacrifice had not presented themselves for several generations and the rhetoric linking the pipe with patriotic exertion and military virtue reached levels unknown since the Napoleonic Wars. The British commander Field Marshal Earl Haig wrote:

> Wherever Scottish troops have fought the sound of the pipes has been heard, speaking to us of our beloved native land, bringing back to our memories the proud traditions of our race, and stimulating our spirits to fresh efforts in the cause of freedom. The cry of 'The Lament' over our fallen heroes has reminded us of the undying spirit of the Scottish race, and of the sacredness of our cause.
>
> The Pipers of Scotland may well be proud of the part they have played in this war. In the heat of battle, by the lonely grave, and during the long hours of waiting, they have called to us to show ourselves worthy of the land to which we belong. Many have fallen in the fight for liberty, but their memories remain. Their fame will inspire others to learn the pipes, and keep alive their music in the Land of the Gael.[17]

In November 1915 Sir Bruce Seton of Abercorn, wrote to the *Oban Times* appealing for information for an intended commemorative volume on the role of pipers in the war: 'There must at present be many pipers in hospital in this country who could give me most valuable information about casualties which have occurred near them in the field, and I ask you to publish this letter in order to inform these men that I shall be very glad to hear from them . . . Letters from men at the front referring to pipers will also be of great value . . . The record will be published privately, and the entire sale proceeds will be devoted to the orphans of pipers.'[18] The book appeared in 1920 under the title *The Pipes of War* (Glasg., 1920), and in it Seton wrote, echoing the writer of the preface to Donald MacDonald's book a hundred years before, that:

> The piper, be he Highlander, or Lowlander, or Scot from Overseas, has accomplished the impossible – not rarely and under favourable conditions, but almost as a matter of routine . . . In doing so he has sacrificed himself; and Scotland – and the world – must face the fact that a large proportion of the men who played the instrument and kept alive the old traditions have

---

16 McLennan died in the prime of life in 1929 as a result of a lung complaint picked up in the trenches: see 'Pipe Major George Stewart McLennan' in Peter Graham and Brian MacRae, eds., *The Gordon Highlanders Pipe Music Collection* (2 vols., Lond., 1983–5), ii, viii-xvi.

17 Seton and Grant, foreword.

18 'A Record of Pipers', *OT*, 6/11/1915, p.3.

completed their self-imposed task. With 500 pipers killed and 600 wounded something must be done to raise a new generation of players; it is a matter of national importance that this should be taken in hand at once, and that the sons of those who have gone should follow in the footsteps of their fathers.

This is the best tribute that can be offered to them.

The Piobaireachd Society intend to institute a Memorial School of piping for this purpose, and all profits from the sale of this book will be handed over to their fund.[19]

The problem from the Society's point of view was that with a number of its leading members away at the war, coherent decision-making was difficult. It was discovered, for example, that somebody, nobody seemed able to say who (but actually the Society's President, Lord Lovat), had taken upon himself to appoint John Grant as instructor to the first of the revived army classes. This had not given satisfaction. Grant was a minor civil servant with the Board of Health who taught piping to boys in his spare time. He had published (privately) a rather superficial book about piobaireachd, a collection of rather unoriginal compositions (also privately), and for many years supplied the newspapers with hectoring and muddled letters about piping and related subjects.[20] He called himself 'Pipe-Major' and had once served as a piper in a volunteer battalion of the Seaforth, but he was by no means the premier player or teacher in Scotland. He had been trying to insinuate himself into the Society's good offices for years, however, and this perhaps was his reward.[21] The course did not go well. It is said that he began with the tune 'Drizzle on the Stone', which he illustrated by solemnly emptying the contents of a water jug onto the ground. Each of the students wrote to his commanding officer asking to be returned to his unit, which was apparently the first time this had happened in the annals of the British Army.[22]

When the Music Committee of the Piobaireachd Society reconvened after the war (J. P. Grant in particular having distinguished himself, winning the M.C. and rising to command the Lovat Scouts with the rank of brevet Lieut-Col.), they terminated John Grant's appointment, engaging Willie Ross in his place. John Grant protested furiously and demanded compensation.[23] Nobody knew what

19 Seton and Grant, p.vii.
20 *Piobaireachd its Origin and Construction* (Edinr., privately printed, 1915); *The Royal Collection of Piobaireachd* (Edinr., privately printed n.d. but 1908).
21 Piobaireachd Society Papers, NLS, Acc 9103/1 Minute and Cash Book, Annual General Meeting, Inverness, 20/9/1907; same, 11th September 1913; Acc.9103 /8 Correspondence 1895–1928, John Grant to J. P. Grant, 30/9/1912. See also 'Honour to Piobaireachd Scholar', *OT,* 14/5/1921, p.5.
22 R. B. Nicol, in conversation with the writer, Ballater, 25 January 1977.
23 NLS, Acc.9103 /8 Correspondence 1895–1928, John Grant to Colin MacRae, 15/9/1919; J. P. Grant to Colin MacRae, 20/9/1919. In view of his existing full-time employment, his claims of financial ruin seem a little overstated: for brief biographical details of Grant see 'Edinburgh Letter: Pipe Music Champion Mr John Grant', *OT,* 30/8/1941, p.3.

terms he had been engaged on but it was thought that he had nothing in writing, and eventually a cheque for £25 changed hands. The Society was keen to get its old chief instructor, John MacDonald of Inverness, but the appointment to the Army Class was part-time by fixed annual contract and MacDonald had in the meantime taken up a well-paid full-time job with the drinks firm Youngers as their representative in the north and west of Scotland, and had found them generous employers, willing to give him leave to teach and compete. The only one of the senior pipers whose style was acceptable to the Society, whose military status was acceptable to the army, and who had the financial flexibility to take on the job at all (thanks to his pension, his teaching fees and his appointment as Pipe-Major of the Lovat Scouts) was Willie Ross, who duly began his long and distinguished tenure at the Castle. He did not know that the Society intended to re-instate MacDonald as soon as it could raise enough to pay a full-time salary.[24]

24 NLS, Acc.9103/2, Loose Minutes, 1905–6, 1910, 1913–1924, 1919–21, 1955–63,
     Extraordinary General Meeting, London, 15/7/1919, Annual General Meeting 18/11/
     1920; Report of the Music Committee, 13/1/1920.

15

'This canker growing every year': The Post-War Period, 1919–1925

Since it was too soon after the war to issue its own texts, the Piobaireachd Society allowed competitors to select the tunes for 1919 from a stipulated list of published sources. While leaving open the possibility of playing from something not on the list, the wording of the announcement in the *Oban Times* sent a clear signal to the player anxious not to put at needless risk the cost of his entry-money, transport, accommodation and loss of pay. It stated:

> The tunes will be accepted as correctly played, if played according to the settings in the published collections of Angus Mackay, William Ross, David Glen, Donald MacPhee, The Piobaireachd Society, or in Ceol Mor. Competitors must, if asked, give the judges their authority for the settings to be played. Any setting other than those above-mentioned may be played; but in this case, if the judges do not think that the authority quoted is sufficient, they may take into consideration, in making their award, the merits of the setting adopted.[1]

What might constitute sufficient 'authority' – such as another published text like, say, Donald MacDonald, or a manuscript source, or a taught setting of a master teacher, or personal aesthetic judgement – on this the Society was silent. So that the performer had no practical way of deciding where 'authority' might be deemed to lie except by reference to previous experience, which suggested that the answer was not likely to be an enlightened one.

In September 1919, John Johnston wrote from the isle of Coll claiming that the whole orientation of piping was being wrenched from its traditional bearings. Piobaireachd playing seemed to him to be in a state of irretrievable decline. There was a great variety of styles nowadays whereas in the past the old masters had all played the same way. The published scores were hopelessly wrong. The new prominence of ceòl beag was leading to rushed technique and expression – even the instrument itself was deteriorating in power and tone:

> . . . compared with ancient piobaireachds as played by the great pipers of old, the present mode of playing is immensely wide of the mark, both as to the construction of the tunes and the notes. This is so much the case that one

---

1 'Comunn na Piobaireachd (The Piobaireachd Society). Competitions – 1919', *OT*, 26/7/1919 p.1.

who acquired them at first-hand from the great performers of the old days
would scarcely know them, being in another garb altogether. Present-day
pipers will no doubt demur at this, and refer to the notation in piobaireachd
books, but these are fully as wide of the mark as the present performers, with
the exception, perhaps, of a few by the late David Glen, of Edinburgh, who
could take down the notation very correctly . . . It will perhaps be news to
present-day pipers that the old famous ones did not play anything but 'Ceol
mor'; not one finger of marches or reels, nor would they listen to such but
held them in disdain, and so did the chiefs of the day, though they are almost
the only thing held in esteem now, piobaireachds being shoved aside as if they
are of no value, but their being lost almost altogether in their original charm
and form is the principal cause of this, and even the marches and reels
themselves are rapidly deteriorating into a hotch-potch of fingers and notes
played at lightning speed, as if each one wanted to try who plays faster, thus
murdering the pipes altogether, as the instrument was meant to play
somewhat slow and clear that it might have room to speak, and not to use
fingers and notes upon it as fast as a shower of large hail . . . [The pipe] did
not attain to its great perfection till the time of the famous McDonald, of
Edinburgh, whose make exceeded all others in their loudness and power. A
few of them may be seen in the Highlands yet, and have peculiarities of their
own, the bores in the parts being considerably larger than the present ones,
that of the chanter itself being fully an eighth of an inch larger in diameter
than modern makes, and the other parts in proportion, making their sound to
be heard at a considerable distance. It was far in excess of present makes in
charm and symmetry. It appears present ones are getting gradually smaller in
the bore from year to year, so that their sound is nothing like what it was.
What is the gain in this I cannot see, but think it the other way. I would
impress upon modern players, if they want the piping to continue in its
former charm and preponderance over all other music, at least in the open,
and in any case to Highlanders, let them attempt to revert to the old mode of
playing, or they will soon play out of the power of the pipes to follow them
altogether.[2]

A lengthy correspondence followed about the state of modern piping. Some took
a positive view, like the correspondent signing himself 'Loch Sloy' [Donald

2 'Modern Pipe Playing', from John Johnston, *OT*, 13/9/1919, p.3. These statements
   were expanded in two further letters from Johnston headed 'Piobaireachd Playing', 22/
   11/1919, p.3, and 19/6/1920, p.3. For a comment from another writer on the inferiority
   of modern pipes see 'The Highland Bagpipe', from 'Druim na Cour', 4/7/1925, p.3:
   'The Highland bagpipe owes nothing whatever to the 19th century except a bad top
   G note and an inferior F, which at their best are half imperfect, and at their worst are
   hideous . . . The old pipes were powerful, organ-toned instruments, with a deep,
   mellow, natural volume of sound – a great contrast to much of the thin, sharp,
   strained tones of many pipes to-day'.

Macfarlane of Oban, son of Hugh Macfarlane who had been a pupil of John MacColl and of Archibald Munro's brother-in-law Archibald Steuart] who asserted that all was well, and that present day players were equal, indeed probably superior to, their predecessors. It was quite wrong to suggest that the tradition had been lost: piobaireachd had been handed down intact by a known succession of master teachers guarding their instruction with jealous attention to detail and scrupulously passing it on exactly as they had received it. In any case it was not in the nature of tradition to change, invariance was its defining characteristic: 'the playing of piobaireachd never changes . . . to condemn what we have would be disaster.'[3] Among the defenders of modern piobaireachd playing, the assumption of fixity was strong, the belief that people had always played as at present and that if the written record showed differently then it must be 'wrong'. In effect, then, supporters of this view were upholding the primacy of oral over written tradition in the conviction that the medium guaranteed the essential stability of the message.

Adherents of the fixed original text were forced to less optimistic conclusions. One wrote: 'When the old piobaireachd . . . were created, they were each composed by one man. No tune had two different settings, and only one setting should exist'.[4] The problem was that the 'original settings', if they had ever existed, were irrecoverably lost, and it was difficult to found a unitary concept of 'authority' in a written tradition which was itself so diverse. Indeed if the written tradition bore testimony to anything it was to the fact that change had plainly taken place during the previous hundred years. Writing technologies brought the sheer pastness of the past into strong relief, with a heightened sense of its difference to and distance from the present.[5] It seemed evident that there had been a number of schools and that these had differed from one another in quite noticeable ways. Which was the 'authentic, the 'true MacCrimmon' style? None, claimed Simon Fraser from Warnambool in Australia. He had seen ways of playing alter during his own lifetime. This, he claimed, was because the MacArthurs, the MacKays, the Campbells and their pupils had mistakenly tried to develop a personal style and depart from the sacred MacCrimmon text, 'altering the tunes in many ways and all having different systems of notation, so it is not to be wondered at that the real thing is all but lost'.[6]

---

3 'Playing of Piobaireachd', from 'Loch Sloy', *OT*, 25/10/1919, p.3; 29/11/1919, p.3; 'Piobaireachd in Mull', from 'Loch Sloy', 10/7/1920 p.3.
4 'The Piobaireachd Society's New Rules', from 'Competitor' [probably John Grant], *OT*, 29/3/1913, p.3. See also 'The Passing of the Pibroch' , from 'J. D. R', 16/9/1905, p.3; and 'Piobaireachd Society's Work', from 'Mal Dhonn' [John Grant], 30/4/1910, p.3 which stated: 'The composers unalterably laid down the law, and said what was to be what, and no-one now has the right to tamper with their original compositions in any respect . . . one might as well attempt to alter the Lord's Prayer as to change a piobaireachd in any detail from its originally composed form'.
5 See Eric A. Havelock, *The Literate Revolution in Greece and its Cultural Consequences* (Princeton, 1982), *passim*, but esp. pp.3–38.
6 'The Playing of Piobaireachd', from Simon Fraser, *OT*, 17/7/1920, p.3.

This view was disputed by Dr. Charles Bannatyne. The written tradition could be projected back for a hundred and fifty years, he declared, and a clear and consistent line of development could be traced through it:

> What is the ancient and correct method of playing piobaireachd? It may be postulated that the present day method is that of the Mackays, coming down through Angus Mackay, and the Camerons, but where it originated none can tell. It is easier and not so fine as the methods of MacArthur, Donald MacDonald and Mr. Johnston, whose style closely resembles that of these masters. I am conversant with Mr. Johnston's method through the noting and playing of the late Mr. David Glen, and so I claim to know something of it. Donald MacDonald, a Skyeman, was taught by Angus MacArthur, who was taught by his uncle, Charles MacArthur, who in turn had been taught by Patrick Og MacCrimmon, ergo Angus MacArthur's and Donald MacDonald's method of piobaireachd playing, also Mr. Johnston's, is the true MacCrimmon method, while that of the Mackays is, well, that of the Mackays.[7]

Some of the written record was trustworthy, then, and some was not; but textual scholarship could disentangle which was which, and in a series of letters to the *Oban Times* starting in December 1919, Bannatyne set out to establish the line of transmission on a reliable basis. It was wrong, he said, to look for a single style of interpretation. The thematic range of piobaireachd was wide and tunes could not all be treated in the same way. It was true that the light music of the pipe was being played faster than formerly, but this was not so in piobaireachd. In the latter case, indeed, tempi were actually dropping and many performers played at the same dead slow pace regardless of whether the tune was a lament, salute, or gathering. 'Ceol Mor' he wrote, 'is not a "perpetual funeral", nor is it a necessity to play, even a lament in the dragging rhythm many piobaireachd players seem to consider a sine qua non . . . Even a lament . . . need not be a crawl'.[8] He denied that the old masters had played nothing but piobaireachd, and as the possessor of one of the largest collections of piping manuscripts then extant he felt able to declare 'I can find nothing to teach me that piobaireachd is only a shadow of its former glory . . . each player's method and setting of tunes combined, form the only true method of Ceol Mor, and each traces back to the greatest school'.[9] But this attempt to demonstrate unity in diversity did little to satisfy those who regarded tradition as fixed and considered all change as evidence of decline and

---

7 'Modern Pipe Playing', from Dr. Chas Bannatyne, *OT*, 20/9/1919 p.3.
8 'Piobaireachd Playing', from Charles Bannatyne, *OT*, 10/7/1920, p.3. For a further comment on the growing tendency to play piobaireachd too slowly, see 'Piobaireachd and Piper Saints', from Malcolm MacInnes, 12/2/1921, p.3.
9 'Piobaireachd Teachers and Players', from Charles Bannatyne, *OT*, 20/12/1919, p.3, 3/1/1920, p.3.

fall. The variety of present day styles could not to their minds be adequately explained as having legitimately descended from a lost 'original' if that original had been distinguished, as they assumed it to be, by an unvarying uniformity.

Lieut. John McLennan supported Bannatyne's reservations about Angus MacKay, stating of his book that: 'there is not a single correctly written tune in it, not only are the notes badly timed and grouped together, but in some cases are an insult to intelligence . . . His historical notes are misleading in several cases, and are contrary to reliable contemporary writers in other cases'.[10] This drew a stinging rebuke from Calum Pìobaire's son John (or 'Jockan') Macpherson, who declared that the mistakes in MacKay's book were the printer's fault and that 'Mr. MacLennan's letter . . . must fill all true lovers of piobaireachd with shame and indignation'.[11] He went on to challenge McLennan's right to speak at all, implying that, in contrast to the giants of the past, authority was something which nobody now living could reasonably claim. Pressed to its conclusion, this argument had serious consequence, since it meant asserting continuity with the past at the cost of denying relevance to the present. For people who thought like Macpherson, 'tradition' was over and done with, it was a book whose final chapter had long ago been inscribed. The only legitimate role for the current generation was to transmit it unaltered, a condition fatal to the vitality of a living culture if it were effectively observed.

In the spring of 1920 J. P. Grant brought out the Piobaireachd Society's new batch of set tunes and met with the usual hostile reception. Bannatyne wrote to him privately, drawing attention to numerous editorial shortcomings and urging a more consistent and intelligent approach:

> With a little care, the music would have been beyond all but the most captious criticism. As it stands it lays the compilers open to charges of
>
> (a) Defective knowledge of: (1) Notation
>   (2) Piobaireachd
> (b) Defective ear as to melody & quantity.
>
> As notes possess quantity so do sounds & the appended examples show it: type hieruren. Each is a correct form. The centre one is D Glen's. The Third is MacArthur's & D. MacDonalds. Glen's is the remains of a former groping after truth in which the D grace note, which should only just be heard, is too obtrusive. The following form has nothing to recommend it & I never heard it in Ceol Mor. It is defective in every attribute of good notation & is nearly unplayable in piobaireachd.

---

10 'Piobaireachd', from John McLennan, *OT*, 14/2/1920, p.3.
11 'Piobaireachd', from John Macpherson, *OT*, 6/3/1920, p.3.

Charles Bannatyne to J. P. Grant, 12/4/1920, concerning the Piobaireachd Society's 'Gairm'

	D. Glen	MacArthur/MacDonald	Piobaireachd Society 1920

     Correct   Wrong

> Mr. MacLennan [in *The Piobaireachd as MacCrimmon played it*] wrote . . .
> certain forms as grace notes but his beat was the minim & therefore his small
> notes had greater Comparative value than the Society's where the crotchet is
> the beat. With the latter in use it is wise to look for the 'pitfall & gin' of the
> formula 'When in doubt as to quantity write certain piob notes as grace
> notes'. In company with a celebrated piper I went over the music to find if it
> were playable. It is, but if competitors play it as written it will present the
> most hilarious exhibition ever heard by this or any other generation.[12]

But J. P. Grant refused to accept that he had misunderstood McLennan or that
the latter's authority was dubious, despite Bannatyne's assertion that: 'his
knowledge of Ceol Mor leaves much to be desired. His remarks about superfluous notes in beats &c &c a painful remembrance of hearing the magnificent
technique of his son George [G. S. McLennan] prostituted in playing his father's
fads are sufficient corroboration of this . . .'. 'I do not intend to argue the matter',
Bannatyne continued, 'Many things found eventually wrong can be propped up
by argument. Your Society "pays the piper" & is therefore entitled to "call the
tune". I know of no piobd music ancient or modern presenting a similar
appearance to the Society's . . .'[13]

Nor, it would seem, did anybody else. A correspondent signing himself
'Dunvegan' wrote to the *Oban Times* criticising the 1920 tunes as a 'grossly wrong
method of writing piobaireachd' and went on to speak of 'the untimely death of
ancient piobaireachd caused by the appearance of a foreign method of writing the
ancient classical music of our forefathers'. Another talked about their 'new and
unwarrantable style'.[14]

12 Pibaireachd Society Papers, NLS, Acc.9103/8 Correspondence 1895–1928, Charles
    Bannatyne to J. P. Grant. 12/4/1920.
13 *Ibid.*, 16/4/1920, 29/4/1920.
14 'The Piobaireachd Society's Music', *OT*, 22/5/1920, p.3. I have not so far traced a
    copy of the Society's set tunes for this year, but it seems probable that at least some
    of the complaints were about J. P. Grant's adoption of McLennan's method of
    notating the taorluath and crunluath movements omitting the so-called 'redundant
    low A'. See NLS, Acc.9103/8 Correspondence 1895–1928, John McLennan to J. P.
    Grant, 3/12/1919; and 'Piobaireachd Society Tunes for 1920', from John McLennan,
    OT, 17/4/1920, p.3.

The prevailing uncertainty was well captured in the summer of 1920 by a young competitor who wrote from Glasgow requesting advice. He was in a most awkward position. His tutor (obviously John MacDougall Gillies) had made numerous changes in the writer's books of music. Was he allowed to do this? When they differed, what was he to follow, the living master or the published score?

> I am a young piper of eight years' experience, and am at present learning four of the tunes for the junior competition by a thorough and qualified and competent tutor, who, I believe, is recognised as an authority, and is an adviser to the Piobaireachd Society.
>
> I am being taught four tunes – one from Mackay's, two from Glen's, and one from the Piobaireachd Society's Collections. Now, in every tune my tutor has made some alterations in pencil or ink. I have heard from pupils of other tutors that they are asked and taught to play the tunes as they are written in the books. When I submit my tunes and the names of the collections to the judges, who have these collections before them when judging, they will find I am not playing the tunes as they are written in these books.
>
> I have every faith in my tutor, and I am not qualified to dictate to him as to whether he is right or wrong, because these alterations may have something to do with misprints. Like many other young players, I think it is very hard to go on learning tunes, and then find at the competition that the judges will not listen to me or may disqualify me for not playing the tunes as they are written.
>
> When some pupils hear other players play the tunes as written in the books and taught by competent tutors, they wonder what is the right or the wrong way in playing. This is a matter which requires clearing up a bit, and I earnestly appeal to the Secretary of the Piobaireachd Society to give young pipers a lead in this matter, and state in the columns of the 'Oban Times' what young players should do.[15]

But there was no response from the Society.[16] Some thought that there was more to this than the natural secretiveness of power and the doubtful quality of J. P. Grant's ear: the roots of the problem lay in the competitive context within which pipe music was normally heard and the alarmingly low level of knowledge in the audience, particularly of piobaireachd. The pipe was linked with powerful emotions of patriotism and military zeal. It was one of the great national symbols; but even the Highland public was largely ignorant of its music and

15 'The Piobaireachd Society's Tunes. Junior Competitions', from 'Mal an Righ', *OT*, 5/6/1920, p.3.

16 He had to be content with a cynical little note from McLennan saying in as many words 'play the rubbish, laddie, if you want a prize', 'The Piobaireachd Society's Music', from John McLennan, *OT*, 12/6/1920, p.3.

culture, and especially in the higher social echelons. There was a lot of loose talk, but little real appreciation. In the summer of 1920 this formed the theme of an anxious leader in the *Oban Times*:

> It would be useless to deny that as regards the characteristics of language, dress, dancing and music – especially pipe music – a large section of the Highland public is ignorant. At present, even among musical Highlanders, how many are there who could give the most elementary information on the Highland pipe, its construction and the peculiar features of its music? The result of this ignorance cannot fail to tell upon piping in general. It is only necessary to examine the conditions under which the best pipe music is demanded. Imagine the leading violinists and pianists, if they had to perform at 9.30 a.m. on a September morning in the Highlands, their shelter nothing but a small roof, which in no way prevents rain, snow or a piercing wind reaching them, paralysing their fingers and playing the very mischief with those reeds that for weeks past they have been coaxing into condition. Added to the vagaries of the weather, they are lucky if their music is uninterrupted by the screech of a passing train or the explosion of a pistol within a few yards distance . . . but what of the audience? Perhaps no hall could be found large enough to contain those Highlanders who talk glibly and with so little knowledge of their national instrument. They are not present. The grandstand is empty . . .
>
> It is not upon pipers themselves that the chief blame for ignorance lies. The great need is for an educated public opinion. A much higher standard of knowledge is required, especially among officers of piping regiments and the class from whom judges for the Highland Games are selected. Instead of taking the lead in these matters . . . these people have been content to neglect the language, to learn nothing of their dress but what their tailors could teach them, to dance and to judge piping by the light of nature.[17]

But these were just the kind of people who joined the Piobaireachd Society and tried to impose their ideas about bagpipe music on the performer community using the competition circuit of which their social power gave them control. John McLennan wrote again in the autumn of 1920:

> For many years now the Pibroch has been played more as a comparatively meaningless jargon of notes than anything else, void of form or melody, and much more so since the Piobaireachd Society came into existence . . . The piper may have a far better setting of the tune, but he dare not play it, and his own natural abilities are curbed; he must simply play note for note what is put before him; he is simply a tracer or a copyist, and is not allowed to become an artiste.[18]

17 *OT*, Leader, 'The Highland Bagpipe', 5/6/1920, p.4.
18 'Piobaireachd Playing', from John McLennan, *OT*, 23/10/1920, p.3.

He contrasted the labour and cost involved for the piper in competing with the uncertainty of the system and its paltry material rewards. Players were forced to distort their own often considerable talent to bring it into conformity with the frequently ill-formed musical ideas of gentlemen amateurs who enjoyed the privileges of regulation without responsibility and patronage without expense:

> It would appear that to play a piobaireachd properly one must go (even a Doctor of Music) to some of the Society's teachers, and learn how to time each note . . .
>
> Before a man can compete he must learn six pibrochs annually, and it takes, say, three hours per day, or eighteen hours a week, to learn one tune, or 108 hours in all, besides the time he must practice. He has to pay his return railway fare from, say, the South of Scotland to Inverness, pay hotel fare for two nights and two days, also lose four days' pay, all for a prize of £8, and a gold clasp! Something must be done to make the pibroch popular it is evident, and the first point is to play the tune as it was originally, a melody – not the monotonous jargon we hear at Highland Games . . .[19]

Malcolm MacInnes wrote from Johannesburg agreeing: 'That the opinion is correct requires no further proof than the attitude of every audience, Highland or non-Highland, who find that, with some exceptions the ground is played with such lapses that they wonder what has become of the melody'.[20] He went on that Highland culture had been bedevilled by bungling and deception for centuries, from Macpherson's *Ossian* down to 'the "collection" of chants and songs, going on recently', of which 'the greater . . . quantity is composed and written at the desk and the piano' (a reference to Marjorie Kennedy-Fraser and her associates). Given that intellectual shoddiness had been the hallmark of the mediators of Highland culture, he continued, what reason was there to suppose that the Piobaireachd Society would be any different? But even this did not elicit a response.

The performer community, struggling to reconcile the annual texts with traditionally-transmitted playing styles, could not ultimately escape the dilemma that if what they had been taught was right, then much of what the Society was doing must be wrong. There had been fierce opposition to the official scores from the outset, but the instinctive deference normally paid to social rank and formal education had hitherto imposed a degree of restraint upon this. The Society's critics had, after all, to have the confidence to pit their informal, largely orally-transmitted lore against the vast array of privileged sources to which it was believed to have access. By the early twenties, however, the Society was increasingly identified as the ultimate source of the malaise. In December 1922 a correspondent signing himself 'C.D.' published an extended commentary on 'A.M.'s famous first series. He described the Society's editors as bungling

19 'The Piobaireachd Society's Music', from John McLennan, *OT,* 2/4/1921, p.3.
20 'Piobaireachd and Piper Saints', from Malcolm MacInnes, *OT,* 12/2/1921, p.3.

amateurs, little more than beginners in understanding or technique, who were none the less attempting, with astonishing effrontery, to give instruction to people far their superiors in the art. The problem was not the fancied proscription of the instrument, or the equally fancied revolt of the master players after the '45, the ignorance of the audience, the vagaries of oral tradition, or the deficiencies of the written scores. The greatest danger to the classical music of the pipe was the Piobaireachd Society of Scotland:

> In the old days, before the Piobaireachd Society commandeered Oban and Inverness Gatherings, one could hear Piobaireachd playing at its best; of course, the lazy and unenthusiastic piper who wanted as much money as he could with as little trouble as possible, often played the same old tune year after year (but then he played it well), but with that exception the most of performances were good and the feeling and expression superb. What is it now? Alas! a sad and destructive change. Tunes are selected for competitors by men who cannot play them themselves, nor could they do so with a lifetime to practice a year's selection. Very often tunes without melodious beauty, and with only a month or two to practice, what is the result? Many of the best men have broken down, and no wonder . . .
>
> There is no need to print every year old tunes in new forms. It is all humbug . . . Whoever prepares the tunes at present are void of the faintest idea of piobaireachd, and promoters of a freakish style . . .
>
> . . . the blind leading a man who has the gift of a keen vision is folly . . . Where did they get their knowledge? . . . They are juniors and learners in the eyes of a genius in piobaireachd . . .[21]

The Society's settings were clumsy and unmusical, said 'C. D.', and its editors were doing unheard-of things to the form, such as adding a MacDonald-style fosgailte as final a-mach movements:

This practice seems to have started in 1922 with 'The Groat' and was repeated in 'Glengarry's March' in 1923. Angus Macpherson issued a vigorous protest against it:

21 'The Passing of the Piobaireachd by "A.M."' from 'C.D.' *OT*, 2/12/1922, p.3.

I maintain with all due respect that there is not a piper living to-day (and
certainly never dreamed of among those now dead) who can put a Crunluath
Mach on either of those two tunes nor any such tunes requiring a Crunluath
Fosgailte, and that the invented Crunluath Mach is simply the doubling of a
Crunluath Fosgailte or open Crunluath, and quite out of place after the
singling and doubling already in keeping with the tunes referred to.[22]

Later he described it as

a most mischievous introduction to piobaireachd playing . . . entirely
wrong . . . such a thing was never known in the history of bagpipe playing
until published by the Society . . . Neither the Piobaireachd Society nor any
other body can bring forward any piobaireachd book ever written prior to the
formation of the Piobaireachd Society to contradict my statement.[23]

The fact that he was right did not induce the Society to enter into discussion on
this point. Or to abandon the practice.

A correspondent signing himself 'Hold Fast' said:

With a view to attempting senior competition work, I have from time to time
obtained copies of tunes required to be played by the Piobaireachd Society,
and, on proceeding to try and render the pieces as required by our ancestors,
I find just what Mr Macpherson points out. Old tunes have been so altered as
to become degraded. Those placed as I am, away from tuition for the greater
part of the year, feel therefore rather upset when endeavouring to put the
genuine old interpretation on such tunes as those for this year's competitions.

And he went on to talk about '. . . alteration for the worse . . . all sense of feeling
obliterated . . . self contradiction . . . mutilation . . . departure from 'first
principles' in tune building'.[24]

'Bratach Bhan' agreed. Not only was the fosgailte a mach unknown in
practice, but the Society was also silently removing the traditional instructions
to repeat the ground at various points within the tune which had serious
implications for structure, effectively turning piobaireachd from a rondo-type
form into something more resembling a simple theme with variations:

They are undoubtedly at fault in adding Crunluath Mach to certain tunes
where it was never intended by the composer and in making the playing of
both styles of Crunluath Fosgailte compulsory. The one in general use at the

22 'Piobaireachd Playing', from Angus Macpherson, *OT*, 17/3/1923, p.3.
23 'Piobaireachd Society's Music', from Angus Macpherson, *OT*, 21/4/1923, p.3;
    'Piobaireachd Playing', 17/5/1924, p.3.
24 'Piobaireachd Playing', from 'Hold Fast', *OT*, 7/6/1924, p.3.

present day, and usually known as 'the MacKay Method', is favoured on account of its being heavier and more distinctive, and is quite sufficient in itself without the addition of the lighter and more easily made one. The fact is, most of the tunes are already overburdened with variations, many of which must have been added later. Some people have a mania for this sort of thing. This practice in no way augments the beauty of the tunes. The result is that the main theme or 'Ground' of the piece is lost sight of in a multitude of variations, and in fact is entirely forgotten long ere the finish of the tune.

This was never the intention of the composer, his idea being naturally to focus attention on the principal part and keep the mind concentrated on the theme of the tune instead of the variations; which are after all merely embellishments. This is strikingly apparent in tunes like 'Queen Anne', 'The Union', 'Dun Naomhaig', and 'Dun Dornaig' – where the melody is contained in a few phrases of great beauty of expression and made designedly short for convenient repetition at intervals of the piece. Hence the familiar injunction to 'Repeat the Urlar' placed in the middle and end of the tunes in the older publications which we of a more enlightened age foolishly discarded altogether. It is almost unnecessary to add that all tunes were not made on this basis; it would be absurd, for instance, to repeat or to expect a repetition of the 'Urlar' in 'The Harp Tree', or 'Donald Ban McCrimmon', the 'Ground work' of those being of such dimensions as to make a repetition of them neither necessary nor desirable. There are other and much smaller tunes where the repetition of the 'urlar' does not hold good ('The King's Taxes' for example), for here the beauty of the tune is in the variations. The return to an old Piobaireachd custom like this would do much to enhance the value of the playing and would be a much happier addition to the tunes than superfluous 'Crunluaths', whether 'Mach' or 'Fosgailte'.[25]

'Bratach Bhan's' point was a cogent one, and the evidence entirely in his favour. But the Society did not acknowledge his criticisms or change its practice. Indeed, at the junior competition at Cowal that year, 1923, two competitors were waved off the boards for attempting to repeat the ground between the taorluath and crunluath variations in 'The Little Spree' and 'Glengarry's Lament' although it was clearly indicated that this should happen in MacKay's and Glen's books, which were the set texts. It was not enough to follow instructions. Competitors had to become skilled at sifting what the authorities said in order to discover what it was they actually meant. In such circumstances, competition became a lottery.[26]

'A Lover of Piobaireachd' pointed out that by now this kind of thing had been going on for twenty years and the Society was prevailing. It was not just a case of people playing 'the modern corruptions' for the sake of a prize and then reverting

25 'The Piobaireachd Society's Music', from 'Bratach Bhan', *OT*, 7/4/1923. p.3.
26 'Juvenile Piobaireachd Playing', from 'Musician', *OT*, 15/9/1923, p.3.

to their former style. The inherited performance styles were fading and, unless decisive action were taken, would quickly disappear. Then there would only be one way to play – and that would be the Piobaireachd Society way:

> Mr MacPherson and 'Hold Fast' are not alone in their protests against the massacring of our ancient Piobaireachd as handed down to us by the McCrimmons. The real question is, how is this mutilation to be arrested – so abhorrent to the true ear – if we are to hand down to future generations the cherished melody as it actually should be played.
>
> I fear not so long as the Piobaireachd Society remain indifferent to protests by players with undoubted reputation. There are always to be found players who will comply with the Society's settings for the honour of gaining the valuable prizes they offer and so long as this continues, there will be two schools of thought – the old and the modern – consequently when the old school have gone west to join the McCrimmons there will probably be nothing left but the modern style. How sad to see this canker growing every year while we have eyes to see and ears to hear and a remedy at hand.[27]

In the decade following 1915 a generation of master players and commentators fell silent. Colin Cameron died in 1916 and his brother Sandy in 1923; John McLennan also died in 1923 and in the spring of 1924, suddenly, in his fifty-sixth year, Dr. Charles Bannatyne.[28] And on 17 December 1925 at his home at 409 Great Western Road, Glasgow, the manager of Peter Henderson's, ex-Pipe-Major of the 5th Battalion H.L.I., champion piper and teacher, John MacDougall Gillies. The *Oban Times* obituarist recorded his career: piper to Breadalbane and for nearly thirty years to the Glasgow Highland Club, twenty-two years as manager of Henderson's, five times winner of the Cowal Shield with the H.L.I., all the premier honours in solo piping, at his first big competition at Braemar in 1875,

> taking first place with MacCrimmons Sweetheart, a tune which he finished with a different flourish from that known today. In the following year he won the prize pipes at Inverness with 'Piobaireachd Donald Dhu.' Two nights prior to his death he performed at the Highland Club, Glasgow, and played in masterly style 'The Lament for the Only Son'.
>
> His stock of Piobaireachd seemed inexhaustible, and what a treat it was to hear him render 'Thanaig mo Righ air tir am Muideart,' 'The Earl of Seaforth's Salute', 'War or Peace', 'A Flame of Wrath for Squinting Peter',

---

27 'Piobaireachd Playing', from 'A Lover of Piobaireachd', *OT*, 21/6/1924, p.3. A point echoed by the reviewer of John McLennan's *The Piobaireachd as performed in the Highlands for Ages, till about the Year* 1808 (Edinr., privately printed, n.d., but 1924), 16/8/1924, p.3.
28 'The Late Dr Charles Bannatyne', *OT*, 22/3/1924, p.3.

'Donald Ban MacCrimmon', and many other old masterpieces too numerous to mention. Even to the initiated, he could express piobaireachd in a manner which created astonishment and admiration.

While at Taymouth Castle, he and the late Sandy Cameron used to adjourn to the Tower and there play to their hearts' content. Mr. Gillies used to say he never heard anything finer than Sandy's playing of 'The Ribean Gorm' on a fine summer evening with a gentle breeze carrying it far up the glen. Variation after variation of this most symmetrical and beautiful tune, rolled around singlings, doublings, and treblings, embedding the urlar in the crunluath-a-mach as even as a wheel on a mill-lade.

Mr MacDougall Gillies taught many pipers, and several of his pupils have carried off the highest honours. His pupils included Pipe-Major Gray, Pipe-Major Reid, Pipe-Major Yardley, Pipe-Major Jas. Taylor, H.L.I., and Pipe-Major J. O. Duff, who have all been winners of the medals of the Highland Society of London at Oban and Inverness. He held the position of President of the Scottish Pipers' Association. He was a member of St. Columba Parish Church. He belonged to the old school, and always maintained the dignity of his profession. Of a most kindly nature and unassuming in disposition, his death will be a great loss to the piping world. He leaves a widow and two sons to mourn his loss.[29]

---

29 'The Late Mr J. MacDougall Gillies. A Famous Piper', *OT*, 26/12/1925, p.3. For corrections to some of the dates, see 'Pipers and Piping' from 'Battack Feimein', 9/1/1926, p.3.

16

'Pipers' Challenge':
The 'redundant' low A Controversy, 1925–1930

The great 'redundant' low A controversy which agitated the piping world during the mid 1920s and '30s had its immediate source in the suggestion by Lieut. John McLennan in *The Piobaireachd as MacCrimmon Played it* (1907), that the taorluath and crunluath movements as written in the works of Donald Mac-Donald and Angus MacKay and their followers had an extra, or 'redundant', low A which was not sounded in playing, and that the standard notation should be revised to omit the note as follows:[1]

Angus MacKay, *Ancient Piobaireachd*, p.159 'The Glen is Mine', taorluath singling

'Redundant' low A

John McLennan, *The Piobaireachd as Performed in the Highlands*, p.1, 'ditto', tri-luth singling

Angus MacKay, crunluath singling

'Redundant' low A

John McLennan, ceithir-luth singling

The explosive implications of this idea took some time to emerge. The Great War interrupted normal activities, and McLennan was dead when the crisis broke in

1 See Chapter 13 pp.302–3.

the autumn of 1925. But the adoption of his style in the post-war publications of the Piobaireachd Society and in the first volume of Willie Ross's *Collection* (1923) – whose classic status was at once recognised – brought matters to a head. It became clear that a number of people actually played the 'redundant' A. They thought the written record accurately represented the movements concerned. They held, moreover, that this was the only true and authentic method of execution, that McLennan was a reckless meddler and the 'new' style an act of cultural vandalism.[2]

Even non-playing contemporaries were disturbed (when not merely amused) by the vast expenditure of intellect, emotion and ink that followed. To outsiders it seemed a trifle, and they shook their heads over pipers' apparent willingness to shed blood over a semi-quaver. But the question was of the utmost consequence. The whole of the later variations in piobaireachd were founded on these movements and the question of their 'correct' interpretation was inextricably bound up with the relationship of literacy and orality in traditional culture, the ability of a disciplined cadre of tradition bearers to transmit basic information accurately and, ultimately, the nature of tradition itself and the role – if any – of diversity and change within it. Those who regarded the coherence of the written record as an article of faith, were flatly contradicted by those who gave priority to performance tradition and, therefore, to oral transmission. It seemed that one of these must be wrong. But which?

On 21st November 1925 a letter was published in the *Oban Times* from A. K. Cameron (1882–1956) an expatriate Scottish sheep farmer in Montana, on what had recently been Indian territory on the western fringes of the Great Plains. Cameron came originally from the Beauly area and had emigrated in 1902, visiting Scotland only once thereafter in 1927. He appears to have learned his piobaireachd in the States, being taught by his employer, Thomas MacRae, formerly of Kintail and now a rancher at Wolf Springs about 70 miles north-west of Miles City in Custer County on the Yellowstone River. MacRae had been a pupil of Ronald MacKenzie. But the main influence on Cameron was Simon Fraser with whom he was in regular correspondence and from whom he absorbed a powerful strain of religious mysticism which he applied to piobaireachd, as we shall see.[3] Both regarded the McLennan style as an innovation, and were concerned by its recent adoption in the published sources:

In my view the taor-luath and taor-luath a mach, the crun-luath and crun-luath breabach are wrong. A note is omitted in each movement . . . A note is

---

2 The taorluath exercises prefixed to David Glen's influential *Collection of Ancient Piobaireachd* (p.iv), for example clearly indicated that the 'redundant A' should be played.

3 John V. Pearson, 'A North American "Piping Fanatic": Alexander K. Cameron (1882 – 1956) Montana's Bagpipe Essayist', M.A. Thesis, University of Montana, 1981, pp.10–13, 23, 35, 38, 39, 54–5, 66.

also omitted in Pipe-Major Ross's new book. I advise all bag-pipe players to play these movements as they are written in all the standard works on pipe music . . . All these composite notes can be played and written in perfect time . . . We all know that . . . by omitting a note in the taor-luath it is much easier to play 'big' marches at 112 and 120 beats per minute. But omitting a note in any of these movements is sacrificing music for execution and speed, and therefore a few of us play the taor-luath the old way.[4]

William Gray, whose *Bagpipe and Drum Tutor* was criticised for promoting the McLennan style, retorted that it was in fact the true traditional method. Gray had come from Mull originally, and served with the City of Glasgow Police, rising to the rank of Lieutenant. He was a leading pupil of John MacDougall Gillies and a noted solo competitor, winning the Argyllshire Medal in 1909. He was a prominent figure in the band movement, being Pipe-Major of the Glasgow Police and, during the War, of the 2nd. Argyll and Sutherland Highlanders. He seems to have been one of the first professionals to be admitted as a member of the Piobaireachd Society, and was another disciple of Simon Fraser's – although not at this stage. Gray insisted, as McLennan had done, that the movements in question had been written differently from the way pipers actually played them.[5]

Not so, claimed John Grant: *his* teachers had taught him to play the movements exactly as they were written. Grant was a permanent fixture in the piping controversies of the early 20th century, feeding the *Oban Times* with a letter – sometimes two – a week for the greater part of thirty years. He was often dogmatic, long winded, and rude, and his main value lay in his knack of irritating people more musically aware than himself into correspondence. At any rate, he claimed the older written forms represented the true MacCrimmon style and 'Any man who cannot play Taorluath and Crunluath as Mackay writes them is not a piobaireachd player'.[6]

Gray denied this, suggesting that there must be something strange about the way Grant had been taught. Usage in the written record was merely scribal, said Gray, and had arisen because the earlier scores were mainly intended for playing on instruments other than the pipes, and it was necessary to include the additional A to give some idea of the timing. He appealed to 'the unanimity which exists among the players who have inherited the traditional teaching as to the correct way of fingering these movements in spite of recorded staff notation', adding that he had won all his prizes playing in the manner recommended in his *Tutor* and nobody had ever suggested that it was untraditional or wrong.[7]

4 'I.[s] F.[ada] M.[ar] S.[eo] S.[inn]' ['Too long are we thus', a pseudonym of A. K. Cameron], 'D Note in Pipe Music', *OT*, 21/11/1925, p.3.
5 'Taorluath and Crunluath Notes', from William Gray, *OT*, 5/12/1925, p.3. See also William Gray and John Seton, *Bagpipe and Drum Tutor* (Glasg., 1922), pp.19, 21.
6 'Taorluath and Crunluath Notes', from John Grant, *OT*, 19/12/1925, p.3.
7 'Taorluath and Crunnluath in Piobaireachd', from William Gray, *OT*, 2/1/1926, p.3.

This was immediately contradicted by John Grant. The 'redundant' A was supported not only by written tradition, he claimed, but also by the overwhelming weight of performance practice, although he did not identify anybody other than himself who played in this manner. Gray retorted that amongst the leading performers who played as he did were Sandy Cameron, MacDougall Gillies, Willie Ross, G.S. McLennan, and William MacLean, and he challenged Grant to make a public demonstration of his claims.[8] Seton Gordon followed up the point urging Grant to list the important players who used the 'redundant' A. Neither he – Gordon – nor anybody he knew had heard it played, and if, as claimed, it really was the 'old' style, then it had disappeared within the space of three generations with important implications for the ability of 'tradition' to transmit information accurately over relatively short periods of time.[9]

Grant suggested that at an earlier stage of his career, Lieut John McLennan had himself notated the movements in question using the 'redundant' A and that therefore he must also have played it, but this was rejected by the latter's son G. S. McLennan who had now retired from the Gordons and was running a pipe-making business in Aberdeen:[10]

> He always wrote Taorluath and Crunluath as they are played by all properly taught pipers. Evidently I must remind Mr Grant that it was my father who first introduced this method, now under discussion, of writing these and other grace notes . . .
>
> The subsequent adoption of his method of writing these notes by so many responsible and discriminating writers is, I think, very good proof of the soundness and utility of the same. Previously Taorluath and Crunluath, like so many other notes in pipe music, were written as they were not played. Taught pipers, however, knew what was intended, and the thing passed at that. I know many pipers to-day who, from sheer force of habit, still write the redundant low A, although they never play it. Apart from all this, I am perfectly certain that there is no piper with an ear who will not readily admit that the Taorluath and Crunluath movements played as written by Lieut. John McLennan, Pipe-Major Wm. Gray, The Piobaireachd Society and Pipe-Majors Wm. Ross and James Robertson are more solid and much better piping than when played with the redundant low A. The former is deep and solid, while the latter is shallow and insipid.[11]

Grant was supported by J. F. Farquharson, former piper to the Duke of Edinburgh, who wrote stating that he had been taught the crunluath movement

8 'Taorluath and Crunluath Notes in Piobaireachd', from William Gray, *OT*, 23/1/1926, p.3.

9 Same, from Seton Gordon, *OT*, 30/1/1926, p.3.

10 Same, from John Grant, *OT*, 6/2/26.

11 Same, from Geo. S. McLennan, *OT*, 20/2/1926, p.3.

by John Bàn MacKenzie, Donald Cameron and Duncan Campbell 'the same as in MacKay's book, note for note', and by A. K. Cameron, although the latter conceded that the overwhelming majority of pipers did actually play in the McLennan style.[12] Grant meantime claimed that he had played the redundant low A movement to John McLennan who had not faulted it, and that McLennan had removed the offending A's without authority and as a matter of mere personal taste. Although acknowledging that he had never heard McLennan play, he dismissed the latter's knowledge as 'vague and shallow'.[13]

On 20th March 1926 G. S. McLennan wrote again to defend his father's reputation:

> With regard to the letter of Mr J. F. Farquharson . . . other pupils of the pipers he mentioned played Taorluath and Crunluath without the redundant low A. I am afraid the letter does not carry the weight it might otherwise do. I notice he only mentions Crunluath. Donald Cameron's sons, famous players, did not play these notes as Mr Farquharson does, nor did Murdo McLennan, who was taught for years by John Ban Mackenzie . . .
>
> Considering the fact that Mr Grant had almost twenty years in which to write all he wanted to regarding my father's book, when he could have been answered by the author himself, I think it is unbecoming, to say the least, for him to write now as he does regarding him.[14]

Angus Macpherson also confirmed that though many pipers wrote the 'redundant' note through sheer force of habit, none of the good ones played it – including his own father, who was taught by Angus MacKay, and MacKay played in the 'modern' manner, whatever he may have written.[15]

Meantime Grant had declared his intention to give William Gray a public demonstration of the points at issue and a meeting was fixed for Thursday 25th

12 'Taorluath and Crunluath Movements', *OT*, 6/3/1926, p.3. For further details of J. F. Farquharson, see *PT*, vol.50, no.11, August 1998, pp.52–5. 'Taorluath and Crunluath Movements', from 'Is Fada Mar So Sinn', *OT*, 13/3/1926, p.3. Archibald Campbell visited Farquharson in this connection and wrote to Seton Gordon: 'Farquharson told me that I played the redundant A. He thinks he plays it himself but he does not. He plays Taorluath & Crunluath just like other people. It is true that when preparing to show the note slowly he puts in the redundant A, but it is not there when he plays it fast.' Seton Gordon Papers, NLS, Acc.7451, General Correspondence 1927–9, 5/10/1929.

13 'Taorluath and Crunluath Movements', from John Grant, *OT*, 27/2/1926, p.3; 13/3/26, p.3.

14 Same, from Geo. S. M'Lennan, *OT*, 20/3/1926, p.3; 3/4/1926, p.3.

15 'Taorluath and Crunluath in Piobaireachd, from Angus MacPherson, *OT*, 27/3/1926, p.3, 15/1/1927, p.3, 16/3/1929, p.3. John MacDonald of Inverness also wrote later supporting the 'modernist' position, see 'The Piping Reminiscences of John MacDonald M.B.E.', 4/4/1942, p.5.

March 1926 in the Oddfellows Hall in Forrest Road, Edinburgh, under the auspices of the Tir nam Beann Society.

The *Oban Times* was not given to banner headlines, but on this occasion it came close:

TAORLUATH AND CRUNLUATH.

THE PIPERS' CHALLENGE.

MEETING IN EDINBURGH.

PIPE-MAJOR JOHN GRANT, EDINBURGH

AND

PIPE-MAJOR WILLIAM GRAY, GLASGOW.

UNIQUE PIPING DEMONSTRATION AND DISCUSSION.

SPECIAL REPORTS.[16]

The hall was packed and in an atmosphere of intense excitement John Grant recounted his piping lineage, and demonstrated his contentions on the practice chanter. He talked a lot, but was apparently not much of a player and did not manage to convince the audience. Willie Gray, by contrast, said little except to contradict Grant and indicate by his manner that he thought his opponent was an idiot. Indeed Gray's truculence considerably weakened support for his views, and it is evident that whatever the abilities of each as a piper and authority on tradition there was little to choose between them in terms of public-relations skills.

> . . . Pipe-Major Grant led off the debate. He traced the history of the
> Piobaireachd from the time of the great MacCrimmon masters . . . explained
> their position as hereditary pipers . . . how they devoted their whole lives to
> their art . . . how they invented and developed the system of 'Canntaireachd'
> . . . how they founded the school at the Castle of Dunvegan . . . mentioned
> the famous pipers who originated from Borreraig – the MacArthurs, the
> MacKays, the MacLeans or Rankins, the Campbells, and the MacIntyres.
> He detailed the MacCrimmon system of teaching . . .

As Grant droned on the audience became restless. Given its specialist nature – half the piping establishment was present – a lengthy exposition of basic piping history was not the most arresting fare, especially when it was not easy to see what relevance it had to the case.

> Mr Grant stated he was taught by Pipe-Major Ronald Mackenzie, a pupil of
> John Ban Mackenzie, who was taught by Angus MacKay, and who in turn
> was taught by John 'Dubh' MacCrimmon. Surely that is a direct line, he
> added. Positively he could assert that he received the assurance of Ronald

16 *OT*, 3/4/1926, p.5.

Mackenzie that John Ban Mackenzie always played the Taorluath as written by Mackay. Is there any reason, he demanded, why Angus MacKay should insert the 'A' in all his tunes if he did not intend it to be played? Is there any reason why John Ban Mackenzie should say he played it, and as a matter of fact taught Pipe-Major Ronald Mackenzie to do so, if he did not? Is there any reason at all for these men to tell falsehoods about the matter? To my mind, he continued, there is none.

These great pipers, traditionally taught, played the Taorluath and Crunluath notes giving effect to the 'A'. I play it in the same manner, and I demand to know from Pipe-Major Gray and also from Pipe-Major [Willie] Ross, whose name has been brought into the controversy, what authority they have in altering the compilation of Angus MacKay as they have done in their books. I say emphatically they are wrong, and if they cannot play the Taorluath as written, then they are not proficient in their art, and are not Piobaireachd players. All the standard works on the Piobaireachd include the 'A' in the Taorluath, are all these works wrong?

At this point he offered the floor to Gray who suggested that he get on with the playing, whereupon Grant launched into another rambling discourse on the various kinds of piobaireachds and their histories, until, eventually, accompanied by two of his pupils,

> The Pipe-Major then selected 'The Mackintosh's Lament' from Angus Mackay's book, as being an exceptionally fine example of the Taorluath and played the piece through on the Chanter. Concluding, he asked Pipe-Major Gray if he had rendered the Taorluath giving effect to the 'A', and was greatly taken aback when met with a direct negative. He played the single note again and again, but was unsuccessful in persuading Mr Gray to admit the correctness of his execution.

Gray claimed that Grant played the taorluath movement exactly the same way as he did himself. In practice the 'redundant' A was so short as to be inaudible. Gray then wrote up a McLennan-style movement on the blackboard and stated that this was what Grant had actually played, waving the latter's objections aside:

> Pipe-Major Gray stated emphatically that the redundant 'A' could not be rendered in time and rhythm, and that the Taorluath was not played by the hereditary pipers or their pupils the way it was written by Angus Mackay . . .
> 'I am not here as an orator,' continued Mr Gray, 'my time is limited. I must catch a train for Glasgow, and, so far as I am concerned, Pipe-Major Grant has signally failed to convince me from his playing that he is correct in his assertion. As a further test, I will ask him to play the "Leamluath" in "The Glen is Mine."'

Pipe-Major Grant did so; but beyond a smile and a significant shrug of the shoulders which indicated his opinion Pipe-Major Gray made no remark.

Sir John Lorne MacLeod in a few words thanked both gentlemen for their demonstrations of the niceties of a very fine point, and the proceedings terminated.

The whole affair from the point of view of an impartial spectator was left in a very unsatisfactory state. Neither side is, in any degree, any further forward.

But if anybody thought that that was the end of John Grant, they were mistaken. The following week's *Oban Times* contained two letters on the subject of the 'redundant' A, claiming that he could easily have had three or four top pipers at the meeting to demonstrate his points. Why he had not done this in the first place and spared himself humiliation at the hands of a player of genuine class like Willie Gray was left to conjecture.[17]

At this point Malcolm MacInnes entered the fray pointing out that the Gesto canntaireachd had three syllables for the appropriate movement, not four as Grant's theory would appear to require. The timing of piobaireachd songs and the poetry of the bards set to piobaireachd tunes also supported the 'modern' timing. He added that even if the latter was an innovation, it was a better way of doing the movement. Since nobody now played in the 'old' style, and nobody living seemed actually to have heard it, the balance of the evidence was entirely in favour of the 'modernists'. In his view, the 'traditionalists' were wrongly preferring the book to living tradition. He reminded readers that the old notators had been taking down orally dictated texts from the pipers playing 'slow' and may have been led into error by attempting to record an already distorted performance. He pointed out that in a traditional art form there may well have been more than one way of doing most things anyway and that modern pipers actually demonstrated this, many of them in practice omitting the second low G and giving more air to the following A in consequence.[18]

Much of the impetus behind the 'redundant low A' controversy throughout, although his presence was not apparent until this point, came from Simon Fraser in Australia, who had been in correspondence with a number of the protagonists. In November 1929 he wrote to the *Oban Times* under his own name:

I have been requested by some pipers to answer the question. Did John MacCrimmon use the low A in Taorluath and Crunluath as written by D. MacDonald, Angus MacKay, and other writers of Piobaireachd. Most certainly he did. I know this beyond any doubt. Those pipers who do not play the low

17 'Taorluath and Crunluath Demonstration', from John Grant, *OT*, 10/4/1926, p.3.
18 'Styles of Pipe Tunes', from Malcolm MacInnes, *OT*, 5/6/1926, p.3; see also
   'Movements in Piping', 11/9/1926, p.3, and 'Taorluath and Crunluath', 16/10/1926, p.3;
   25/12/1926, p.3; 15/1/1927, p.3; and 'Noting of Pibroch', 24/8/1929, p.3.

A have not been properly taught, and it is a great pity that they are trying to lead other pipers astray.

I have been criticised myself a good deal over the MacCrimmon notation, but none of my critics have had the courage to come and put me to a practical test in this matter. Had Donald MacDonald written the MacCrimmon notation under the ordinary notes this trouble would not have arisen. My father was present when several persons advised him to do this, but he would not do so. Gesto, his son Norman, Alexander Bruce and his three sons all played the low A: so did Donald Cameron and his sons. As none of my critics ever came to try and upset what I have said and written, it is very strong evidence that what I say is correct, and I would advise those revivals [sic] to play their own way and leave others alone. I am etc., Simon Fraser.[19]

But Simon Fraser's statements must be treated with caution, as we shall see in Chapter 19. In the summer of 1929 Somerled MacDonald (the great grandson of Niel MacLeod of Gesto) argued in a series of long and thoughtful letters on Joseph MacDonald's *Compleat Theory*, the earliest written source on this subject, that those who favoured the 'redundant' A were wrong, and that the pupils of the Bruces did not play it.[20]

MacDonald, MacInnes and others brought arguments of frequently impressive subtlety to bear on the subject, but it is possible that the explanation was rather simple. Ronald MacKenzie alone of later 19th century masters seems unequivocally to have played the 'redundant' A, and it is noticeable that most of the people who wrote in its defence had been taught either by him or by his pupils. It is possible that the technique may have been introduced by MacKenzie, who is known to have placed a high value upon written scores, (and perhaps other teachers of similar mind) in an attempt to render the texts of MacDonald and MacKay *literatim*.[21] So perhaps the 'modernists' were the 'traditionalists' and the 'traditionalists' were the 'modernists' after all. In the hall of mirrors of piping controversy it was sometimes difficult to tell.

An important factor in determining attitudes was whether the writer was familiar with the work of Joseph MacDonald, whose *Compleat Theory of the Scots Highland Bagpipe* had been out of print for more than a century and had become exceedingly rare. When we realise that Lieut. John McLennan had studied MacDonald, then his absolute certainty that the 'redundant' low A

19 'Noting of Pibroch', from Simon Fraser, *OT*, 23/11/1929, p.3.
20 'Joseph MacDonald and Piobaireachd Notation', from Somerled MacDonald, *OT*, 8/6/1929, p.3; 20/7/1929, p.3; 3/8/1929, p.3; 15/3/1930, p.3; 14/6/1930, p.3. For the Bruce pupils, see 5/7/1930, p.3.
21 'Famous Piper of the Past', from John Grant, *OT*, 27/6/1936, p.3. But see Piobaireachd Society Papers, NLS, Acc.9103/10 Correspondence 1951–54, William Gray to J.P.Grant, in which Gray speaks of 'the redundant "A" of which my old friend and tutor John MacDougall Gillies was really the instigator', 14/8/1954.

really was redundant becomes at once intelligible, since the corresponding movement in Joseph, the 'IIth Cutting', was timed exactly as the 'modernists' claimed.[22] Thomason knew the work, as did David Glen, Charles Bannatyne and Henry Whyte ('Fionn'), but its republication in 1927 by Alexander MacDonald ('Gleannach') of the Gaelic Society of Inverness burst upon most of the piping world with the force of revelation.[23] Its authority was immediately challenged: some hailed Joseph as an expert on the instrument and its music and an epitome of taste and judgement; others dismissed him as an ignorant outsider, a mere youth, a fiddle player meddling with things he did not understand. Some went so far as to declare the work a forgery.[24] The editor was unable to allay the storm of controversy. Alexander MacDonald died suddenly of a heart attack shortly after the book was published leaving his daughter, Mairi A. MacDonald, to fight a twenty-year campaign to vindicate his reputation.[25]

Part of the problem lay in the very fact of Alexander MacDonald's scrupulousness. Since the manuscript of the *Compleat Theory* was currently lost, he had taken the difficult decision of reproducing exactly the earliest available text, namely the published version of 1803, although it was known to be corrupt. However, he supplied extensive notes and commentary in order to demonstrate the fundamental coherence of the work. The editor's own interests were primarily linguistic, and related to the derivation and meaning of the Gaelic terms of art; but the attention of many of his readers was directed elsewhere, and there was much anxious conning of the text for proof – or disproof – of the 'redundant' low A.[26] Most people felt that the 'modernists' had the better of the ensuing long and intricately technical argument, and it emerged – much later – that the passage on which the advocates of the 'redundant' A placed greatest reliance did not form part of the original *Compleat Theory* having been interpolated into the 1803 text from an

22 'The Passing of the Piobaireachd', from John McLennan, *OT*, 26/9/1903, p.3.
23 'Ceol Mor', from C. S. Thomason, *OT*, 2/1/1904, p.3; 'Joseph MacDonald's Treatise on Bagpipe Playing', from Charles Bannatyne, 11/8/17, p.3; 'Piobaireachd', from Charles Bannatyne, 10/1/1920, p.3. The volume was published as *A Compleat Theory of the Scots Highland Bagpipe" By Joseph MacDonald Compiled, 1760/63; First Published, 1803 A Reprint Now published by Alexander MacDonald Glencona, Inverness* (Glasg., 1927). For preparatory articles by Alexander MacDonald on the history of the pipe and Gaelic terms of art in piping, see 'The Highland Bagpipe', from 'Gleannach', *OT*, 16/5/1925, p.3; 18/7/1925, p.3; 'Taorluath and Crunluath Movements in Piobaireachd', 6/2/1926, p.3; 12/2/1927 p.3.
24 Review: 'A Complete Theory of the Scots Highland Bagpipe. A Musical Genius of the Eighteenth Century', *OT*, 27/8/1927, p.3; Part 2, 3/9/1927, p.3; 'Noting of Piobaireachd', from Malcolm MacInnes, 11/5/1929, p.3.
25 'Tragic Death of Inverness Town Councillor. Mr Alex. Macdonald, Glencona', *Inverness Courier*, 7/2/1928; 'The Joseph MacDonald "Theory"', by Mairi A. MacDonald, *Scots Magazine*, vol.60, 1953, pp.210–215.
26 MacDonald, *Compleat Theory* (1927), 'Preface to the Present Issue'.

unknown source.[27] To a casual observer the debate could easily appear narrow and pedantic. Considering the range of possibilities for discussion offered by Joseph MacDonald's text this obsessive focus on how many gracenotes there should be in certain movements might have seemed almost wilfully perverse. But what was going on was a searching examination not so much of the art itself, but of the conditions which made it possible: whether the content of what had been received was coherent, whether the mechanisms of transmission were reliable, whether cultural authority was located in written or oral sources, and in the present or in the past; whether invariance or change was the defining characteristic of tradition.

Joseph's work could be interpreted in a number of ways. The optimists found concepts and procedures which seemed to differ little from the present. Contemporary finger technique, for example, seemed to be a continuous development of that of Joseph's day, and if present methods were slightly different, they could convincingly be defended as improvements. To such as these the past was a comforting and familiar place, founded in an acceptance that a 'traditional' culture could change but still be 'traditional', that change and loss were not synonymous. The pessimists, on the other hand, found in Joseph's pages a tale of discontinuity and destruction, proof that during the preceding century and a half, whole movements, whole variation types, perhaps even whole genres of piobaireachd had disappeared without trace. It was well known, they argued, that traditional cultures were inherently stable owing to the ability of the mechanisms of transmission to sustain them without significant variation over lengthy periods of time. But in this case important change seemed demonstrably to have taken place. By that token 'tradition' had been compromised. Perhaps fatally. Proscription of the pipes after the '45 had severed the arteries of transmission. Not even Iain Dubh MacCrimmon had been properly taught. 'Authority' had been lost and during the past century the performer community had failed to protect its inheritance. They had added their own ideas to what they had been taught.

---

27 See for example 'Chanter Notes and Fingering', from A. McDonald, Glencona, *OT*, 24/9/1927, p,.3; 'Noting of Piobaireachd', from Malcolm MacInnes, 11/5/1929, p.3; 'Joseph MacDonald and the Noting of Pibroch', from Somerled MacDonald, 8/6/ 1929, p.3; 'Noting of Pibroch', from Malcolm MacInnes, 29/6/1929, p.3; 'Joseph MacDonald and Piobaireachd Notation', Somerled MacDonald, 20/7/1929, p.3, 27/7/ 1929, p.3, 3/8/1929, p.3; 'Noting of pibroch' from Malcolm MacInnes, 24/8/1929, p.3; 'Pipe Music Terminology' from 'J. C.', 24/8/1929, p.3; 'Problems in Piping', from 'Piper', 14/9/1929, p.3; 'Joseph MacDonald and Pibroch Notation. Part 1' from 'Grip', 26/10/1929, p.3, Part 2, 2/11/1929, p.3, Part 3, 28/12/1929 p.3; 'Piobaireachd Society Publications', from Malcolm MacInnes, 30/1/1937, p.3; 'The Origin of Piobaireachd', from Malcolm MacInnes, 17/6/1939, p.3; 'The Compleat Theory of the Bagpipe by Joseph MacDonald. The Taorluath Beat', from 'A Correspondent', 31/8/1946, p.3; 'Joseph MacDonald's Theory of the Highland Bagpipe Music', from Mairi A. MacDonald, 14/8/1948, p.3. For the interpolated passage see Cannon, *Compleat Theory*, p.95.

They had wantonly departed from the inherited text. The evidence for this was contained in the written scores of Donald MacDonald and Angus MacKay. Their difference from one another was an unmistakable sign that the true original style had been lost. The pessimistic view rested, once again, upon the literate concept of an original fixed text, from which perspective alone, perhaps, could creativity be regarded as destructive.

Yet few even of the gloomiest observers thought the position irrecoverable, although they varied in their prescriptions. If the written tradition was incoherent, then perhaps by detailed study and comparison, the principles of composition could be re-established, and the true original style edited back into the scores.[28] This was the position of G. F. Ross of Calcutta, a frequent contributor to the *Oban Times*, who in the autumn of 1926 brought out a slim volume entitled *Some Piobaireachd Studies*, containing amended versions of some twenty-eight tunes with a lengthy introduction explaining his views.[29] His work was based on two premises: firstly, that since the light music of the pipes was metrically regular this must also once have been true of piobaireachd; and, secondly, that all correct metre must conform either to the 6 6 4 or the 4: 4 4 pattern. Anything else was wrong. Ross studied form by means of moveable wooden blocks, each carrying a single bar written out in staff notation. By manoeuvring these on a grooved board so that each bar of the variations was placed directly under its corresponding bar in the ground he was able to establish whether, according to his criteria, the tune in question possessed internal

28 G. F. Ross, *Some Piobaireachd Studies* (Glasg., privately printed, 1926), p.5. For a long and rather sceptical review, see 'Some Piobaireachd Studies', By G. F. Ross'. Parts 1–3, *OT*, 22/1/1927, p.3; 29/1/1927, p.3; 5/2/1927 p.3. Ross's *A Collection of MacCrimmon and other Piobaireachd* (1929) was reviewed as 'The Pibrochs of MacCrimmon and Others', 19/10/1929, p.3. For a selection of letters of G. F. Ross to the *Oban Times* see '"Canntaireachd" or the Vocal Method of Recording Piobaireachd', 30/6/1923, p.3; 'The Prince's Salute', [under the pseudonym 'Piob Mhor' and dated from Calcutta], 15/11/1924, p.3; 'Piobaireachd. "Campbell of Cawdor's Salute"', from 'Piob Mhor', 26/12/1925, p.3; advertisement for *Some Piobaireachd Studies*, 6/11/1926, p.2; 'The MacCrimmon Genealogy Evidence from Dates and Times', 1/12/1934, p.3; 'The MacCrimmon Genealogy', 12/1/1935, p.3. '"Lament for Rory Mor" and "Lament for the Children"', 7/9/1935, p.3.

29 'Introductory Remarks', pp.4–7; 'Some Notes on MacCrimmon Canntaireachd', pp.8–17; 'The Playing of the Leumluth, Taorluth and Crunluth Beats', pp.18–22. The tunes were 'Lament for Alistair Dearg', 'Lament for the Earl of Antrim', 'The Big Spree', 'The Blind Piper's Obstinacy', 'The Blue Ribbon', 'The Cave of Gold', 'Cawdor's Salute', 'The Lament for the Children', 'Chisholm's Lament', 'The Lament for the Dead', 'Donald Gruamach's March', 'The Lament for Donald of Laggan', 'The Lament for Finlay', 'In Praise of Marion', 'Salute on the Birth of Rory Mor', 'Lament for John Garve MacLeod', 'Lady Elisabeth MacDonald's Lament', 'Lord Lovat's Lament', 'Macintosh's Banner', 'Mackinnon's Lament', 'MacNeil of Barra's Lament', 'Mary's Praise', 'The Massacre of Glencoe', 'The Piper's Warning to his Master', 'The Lament for Samuel', 'The Stuarts' White Banner', 'Flame of Wrath for Squinting Peter', and 'King George III's Salute'.

consistency.[30] Those which failed the test were declared to be 'mutilated' and amended, sometimes drastically.

Ross made much of the virtues of consistent editorial method systematically applied, but a good many of his ideas had their ultimate source in Simon Fraser of Warnambool in Australia with whom he had for some time been in private correspondence. Fraser was a mysterious and charismatic figure who presented himself as the voice of the true way crying in the Outback. He had little personal reputation as a player, but his world-wide network of correspondents gave him considerable influence during the first three decades of the 20th century. He claimed to have been taught by Peter Bruce, and to have inherited the authentic MacCrimmon and MacArthur teaching which had been allowed to die out in Scotland – hence Ross's conviction that the lost 'original' style had in fact survived and could be restored to the text.[31] The results sometimes involved quite radical departure from the mainstream of performance tradition. Here, for example, is 'The Lament for Donald of Laggan' which had come down in a fourteen bar form like this:

Cumha Dhomhnuill a Lagain, Donald MacDonnell of Laggan's Lament, MacKay MS, ii,94

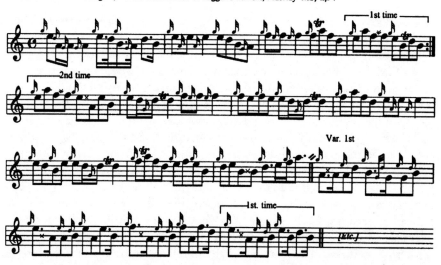

Thomason had left the tune as it stood, but in G. F. Ross's scheme, the ground was two bars short and he made up the number to the required sixteen using phrase materials already present in the tune.[32] Why he also thought it necessary to reverse the order of bars in the opening line – so that what had been bars three and four in other settings became bars one and two in his – was not explained:

30 *Ibid*, p.6.
31 For discussion of Simon Fraser at greater length see Chapter 19, pp. 408–414.
32 *Ceol Mor*, p.231.

Lament for Donald of Laggan. (V11 of Glengarry). (1645).

Bars 1 & 5	2 & 6	3 & 7	4 & 8

It seems likely, however, that this was at the prompting of Simon Fraser who left two settings of the tune, one like Angus MacKay's and one like G. F. Ross's.[33] Why Fraser thought the tune should take this form is not known.

Ross's views were not calculated to endear him to the Music Committee of the Piobaireachd Society. He mounted a sustained attack on its methods, rejecting the playing of the opened fosgailte as an a mach variation, criticising the Society's timing of the gairm and eallach as 'undoubtedly an incorrect method', and spoke slightingly of J. P. Grant's work on canntaireachd.[34] Equally gallingly, perhaps, he supported the 'traditionalists' in the 'redundant' low A controversy, offering a defence of the form which was by some distance the most persuasive of the period.[35] But his settings did not win favour, and since he could not force people to play them, unlike the Piobaireachd Society, they did not succeed in dislodging the earlier versions. G. F. Ross's work shows in a particularly clear form the dilemmas which confronted the world of piping at this time. Transferring 'authority' to the written score raised the immediate problem that the written scores did not agree with one another. For those who believed that 'tradition' should speak with a clear and undivided voice, it followed that something must be wrong, and it fell to the wealthy and educated possessors of those scores to establish by various forms of divination what the 'original' message ought to have been.

33 Ross, *Some Piobaireachd Studies*, p.25; text reproduced from *Collection of MacCrimmon and other Piobaireachd*, pp.34–5. See B. J. Maclachlan Orme, ed., *The Piobaireachd of Simon Fraser with Canntaireachd* (n.p. 1979), pp.258–9.

34 *Some Piobaireachd Studies*, pp. 8, 14, 16, 17.

35 *Ibid.*, pp.18–22.

The cultural importance of piobaireachd saw it become a battleground of contending forces, and the first three decades of the 20th century witnessed the performer community locked in struggle with the forces of institutional control for the right to define tradition. Yet if ceòl mór resembled only too disturbingly the trench warfare in which many of its exponents had recently taken part, ceòl beag, the light music of the Highland pipe, was quite untouched by notions of fixed texts and institutional regulation. The performer community remained in control of the music and a very different order of things prevailed.

17

'Leaving Lochboisdale by Steamer at Midnight':
The Light Music of the Pipe Transformed, 1850–1930

The century following 1850 was a period of immense creative vitality in ceòl beag. A succession of gifted composers, such as Angus and Hugh MacKay, John MacColl, D. C. Mather, John MacLellan of Dunoon, Roderick Campbell, William Laurie, William Fergusson, G. S. McLennan, Willie Ross, John Wilson, and Peter MacLeod, Donald Shaw Ramsay, Donald MacLeod, and a host of others enriched the repertoire to such an extent that the pipe overtook the fiddle as the major source of creative renewal in the popular instrumental tradition. Even James Scott Skinner, the great fiddle virtuoso, wrote for what he called 'the flutterin' blades', and leading accordion players like Jimmy Shand and Bobby MacLeod also composed in the piping style.[1]

The mechanism of competition, so harmful to piobaireachd when combined with institutional regulation and prescriptive scores, was a major creative influence in ceòl beag. We have already noted how the competition march developed. Similar processes were at work in other parts of the light music repertoire. The strathspey and reel, for example, grew from a typically two-parted form intended mainly as an accompaniment to dancing, into something much more formidable technically, involving perhaps as many as six or eight parts. This might be the result either of fresh composition, or, as commonly happened, by development of existing material, as with Donald MacPhee's 'Islay Ball' or 'The Caledonian Society of London' where additional parts were supplied by another composer, in the latter case John MacDonald's sister Nelly MacDonald of Craigellachie.[2] The process was broadly similar in a good many cases: the third part being an elaboration of the first, and the fourth part of the second, with, in the case of the strathspey, frequent use of triplets and heavily-ornamented figures difficult of execution, as we see in the last part of 'The Islay Ball':

---

1 Piobaireachd Society Papers, NLS, Acc. 9103/21, 'Music of Colin Cameron 19th-20th century, assembled by A. G. Kenneth': Pipe quickstep 'The Lovat Scouts', J. Scott Skinner, Monikie, 15 May 1908 inscribed to Colin Cameron. See also 'Dundee City Police Pipe Band', 'Kirkwall Bay' and 'Master David Anderson Shand', by Jimmy Shand, in Donald Shaw Ramsay, ed., *The Edcath Collection of Highland Bagpipe Music and Drum Settings* (3 vols., Edinr., 1953–1968), i, 18, 36, 46; and 'Murdo Mackenzie of Torridon' by Bobby MacLeod in Jas. Robertson and Donald Shaw Ramsay, eds., *Master Method for Highland Bagpipe With a Selection of Modern and Traditional Marches, Strathspeys, Reels and Jigs* (Lond., n.d., but 1953), pp.18–19.

2 George S. McLennan, *Highland Bagpipe Music* (Aberd., 1929), p.27.

There was much elaboration of song airs like 'Bonnie Anne' or 'The Yowie wi' the Crookit Horn' and shuttling of material between different time-signatures and rhythmical patterns, so that 'The Reel of Stumpie', also known as 'Young Rory', could become, with a little attention from Donald Cameron, the classic competition march 'Highland Wedding'.[3] There were purloined fiddle tunes, often with their compass cut down to fit the pipe, classic reels like 'Miss Girdle' and 'Rachael Rae' and strathspeys by Gow, Marshall and others that pipers couldn't bear not to play. One famous 6/8 march 'The Bugle Horn' was, as its title suggests, an affectionate reworking of a bugle call, in this case of B Coy. Seaforth Highlanders:[4]

---

3 See NLS, Acc. 9103/21, 'Music of Colin Cameron' for an early setting of 'Highland Wedding' as a march – here called 'Lord Breadalbane's March' – docketed 'Donald Cameron Brahan Castle 1862. Noted by C.[olin] Cam.[eron] Coposed [sic] by D[onald] Cam.[eron] B.[rahan] Castle 1856.' For typical Victorian adaptation of song airs to the pipes see *Ross's Collection*, pp. 118, 120, 127, 128, 129, 136, 137, 145, 146, 151, 153, 171, 184, 188, 190, 197, 198, 200, 215, 230, 231, 249, 251, 254, featuring tunes such as 'A Man's a man for a' that', 'And sae will we yet', 'Because he was a bonny lad', 'The Bonnie house of Airlie', 'Up and waur them a' Willie', and similar material.

4 For typical bugle calls see Murray, *Music of the Scottish Regiments*, pp.52–4.

There was a common stock of building blocks, formulaic phrases like:

which crop up with minor variations all over the place, but sometimes whole
parts, whole tunes even, might go wandering. A number of the new competition tunes were actually medleys, combining bits and pieces of different airs like
'Donald Cameron's Hotchpotch' – still a leading competition march – or the
reel 'MacAllister's Dirk' whose third and fourth parts as nowadays played were
once a separate tune called 'The Glen where the Deer is'; or 'The Smith of
Chilliehassie' which is a compound of 'The Lads of Mull' and 'The Black
Haired Girl'.[5] 'The King's Gun Reel' provided part of 'The Rejected Suitor',
and 'Sir John Mackae's Reel' most of 'The Sheepwife'. 'Arniston Castle's first
two parts were a separate tune called 'J. D. K. McCallum Esqrs. Strathspey'
whilst its third part was once the first part of 'Glenspean Lodge'.[6] Parts three
and four of 'Struan Robertson' were once the first two parts of 'Mrs Campbell's
Favourite.'[7]

In the published collections we can see many bits of this and that in the
process of evolving into something better. Tunes received attention from every
creative personality through which they passed and so they tended to improve
with the passage of time as good ideas were kept and inferior ones discarded.
This would go on until nobody thought they could reasonably improve on
what they had got, or a change of fashion prompted a re-think about the
inherited repertoire. For example, the jig 'The Maid of Edrachaolis', as
published by Uilleam Ross, was a fairly nondescript affair; but it had potential,
and by the time it found its way into *David Glen's Collection of Highland
Bagpipe Music* around the turn of the century, somebody had given it a good
deal of loving attention:

5 *Ross's Collection.*, pp. 181: also appearing under the title 'Glengarry's Dirk', in
   Donald MacPhee, *A Selection of Music for the Highland Bagpipe* (Inverness, n.d.),
   p.13; for 'The Smith of Chilliehassie', see *Ross's Collection*, 182, 183, and see also
   'Old Willie Duncan', p.163; for Uilleam Ross's own setting of the Chilliehassie
   tune, see p.206.

6 *Ross's Collection*, pp.172–3, 181, 235. For the later parts of 'Mrs MacLeod of Raasay',
   see D. S. MacDonald's 'Mackintosh's Reel', p. 181; for the third part of 'The
   Shepherd's Crook', see 'Seaforth's Strathspey', part one, p.195. For what eventually
   became 'Willie Davie' see 'The Miller's' Fair Daughter' and 'The Waterloo Reel', pp.
   167, 246.

7 MacPhee, *Selection*, p.24.

'The Maid of Edrachaolis, Uilleam Ross's Collection, p.187

The Maid of Edrachaolis. David Glen's *Collection of Highland Bagpipe Music,* iv, 11.

There was even an occasional nod towards the classical music of the pipe, as we see in the march called 'The Conundrum', Peter MacLeod's affectionate parody of 'Glengarry's Lament':[8]

8 MacLeod had a wooden leg, his right, and piping folklore relates that when he marched, the second pulse in the bar received the clump of the wooden leg, shifting the accent, an effect perhaps played with here in the cheekily unresolved pattern of threes held against fours. One of the most original composers of the twentieth century, Peter MacLeod was a Lewisman who came to Glasgow in 1900 to work as a shipwright. Industrial injury led to amputation and halted his competitive career. For a brief biography with a photograph, see *OT,* 8/2/1930, p.7. But see Angus J. MacLellan, 'From the Past', *PT,* vol.50, no.4, January 1998, pp.17–20 (17–18), which queries the wooden leg story. For photographs of MacLeod in later life, see *PT,* vol.51, no.6, March 1999, p.7.

Glengarry's Lament, Angus MacKay   *Ancient Piobaireachd*, p.31

The Conundrum, *Pipe-Major W. Ross's Collection*, iv, 16.

Solo playing provided the impetus for most of the competition material, but during the second half of the nineteenth century the pipe band rose to prominence and much new material, technically less demanding but often of great loveliness, began to be written for it, especially by the military – as one might perhaps guess by some of the titles: 'The 79th's Farewell to Gibraltar' by John MacDonald of Tiree who may also have composed 'Dornoch Links'; 'The 25th's Farewell to Meerut' by John Balloch of the 1st K.O.S.B.; 'The 72nd's (or the 42nd's) Farewell to Aberdeen', also known as 'The Boy's Lament for his Dragon', probably written by William MacKay; 'The Barren Rocks of Aden' by James Mauchline of the 78th, with additional parts by Alexander MacKellar, also of the 78th; 'The Drunken Piper' by Alexander MacLeod, Pipe-Major of the 26th Cameronians; and 'The Badge of Scotland', the classic 4/4 pipe march, by John MacKay Pipe-Major of the Argyll and Sutherland Highlanders.[9]

Until about the middle of the nineteenth century, pipers in the army had been attached to individual companies and had no formal role as a unit playing ensemble. Likewise battalion drum-corps were used for military communication, or accompanying the fifes, which most Highland regiments also had, rather than the pipes. However during the second half of the century that most familiar of modern Scottish icons, the corps of pipes and drums playing ensemble, began to develop in the army and in civilian contexts. Involving as it did perhaps considerable numbers of performers, it was predominantly, although not exclusively, an urban phenomenon.[10] The Govan Burgh Police Pipe Band

9 For brief accounts of a number of these composers see 'Some Well-Known Army Pipers' in Malcolm, pp.247–65.

10 The early history of the pipe band remains obscure, but see Murray, *Music of the Scottish Regiments*, pp.111ff., and *passim*. Many pipers did not welcome these developments. An army pipe-major signing himself 'MacVourich' wrote to the *Oban Times* in 1925, 'Sir, - If you will protect me I will write about drumming and piping . . . But I have fears for my life. Drummers are terrible fellows, and if my name and hiding place were revealed they might come and drum near me, and I would sooner die of old age . . . There have been many bad things that have crept in recent times into Highland art, and the drums drowning pipe music is one of the worst', 'Bagpipe Drumming', 28/2/1925, p.3.

was formed by public subscription in the early 1880s, and along with the 9th H.L.I. (Glasgow Highlanders) was one of the earliest outside the regular army. From the outset the band movement enjoyed close ties with the community and with other forms of popular entertainment. The first open competition for pipe bands – won by the Govan Police – was held by Rangers Football Club at Ibrox Park. A similar event, at Tynecastle in 1902, was won by the Aberfeldy Band under the pipe-maker Gavin MacDougall.[11]

Although regarded by the purist as a 'modern excrescence', exotic, unregulated and sometimes disturbingly plebeian, pipe bands sprang up in towns and villages all over Scotland. But they were expensive to equip and run, and money was always a problem. The Shotts and Dykehead Caledonia Pipe Band, founded in 1906, met in a cart-shed at the back of a local hotel, and experienced typical early difficulties. It was 1914 before it could afford uniforms.[12] The Edinburgh City Police Pipe Band, founded in 1901, held a series of concerts to raise money for material to be made up into bonnets, plaids and kilts by the force's own clothing department (which was run by the band's Pipe-Major Graham, who made all the brooches and buckles himself).[13] The Dalzell Highland Pipe Band from Motherwell, formed in 1910, shows the frequently close links with local business, financial support being given by the Colville family in return for adopting the name of the Dalzell Steel and Iron Works. The band remained essentially self-supporting, however, with a weekly levy of 5/- a head on its members, and a ladies' committee in charge of fund-raising.[14] The pipe-band movement was an autonomous and self-regulatory response by the performer community to the opportunities of an urban environment. Although financial support was essential to such activity, it tended to be communally-based: individual patronage, where available, tended to come from commercial or professional rather than landed sources, and was not accompanied by attempts to gain control of the music.[15]

A distinctively 'pipe band' style of playing emerged at an early date. It was seen in some quarters as founded in rapid and incorrect learning of a few simple tunes, and as posing a threat therefore to the long and exacting training traditionally considered essential to the making of a piper. In the winter of 1890 a correspondent signing himself 'Morna' wrote to the *Oban Times*:

11 'The City of Glasgow Police Pipe Band', *Piping and Dancing*, no.3, October 1935, p.13; 'Looking Backward By Highlander', *Piping and Dancing*, no.4, November 1935, p.19.

12 'The Shotts and Dykehead Caledonia Pipe Band', *Piping and Dancing*, no.4, November 1935, p.13.

13 'The Edinburgh City Police Pipe Band', *Piping and Dancing*, no.7, February 1936, p.13.

14 'Dalzell Highland Prize Pipe Band', *Piping and Dancing*, no.11, June 1936, pp.14–15.

15 An interesting echo of the involvement of the Glasgow business community in the early Falkirk competitions.

. . . the present day exponents of bagpipe music differ vastly from the old master hands. Certain it is that every person is not capable of mastering all the difficult movements which characterise pipe music, but the inferiority of our present day pipers is not owing to incapability in every sense of the term, but to proper and careful and persevering tuition. In the olden times it took years and years to acquire a perfect knowledge of pipe-music and pipe-playing, more particularly pipe-playing. When a person designed one of his boys for the profession of a piper, which was once held in high esteem, he was placed under an experienced tutor at ten or twelve years of age, and in many cases far earlier, and he was a bearded young man before he could return to his father's roof, branded as a piper. But . . . modern performers – most of them, not all I am happy to say – are bearded young men before they ever think of trying to learn, and you can turn out a thoroughly equipped piper, 'kilt and feather and a' in six months, in far less time than some of the old masters could acquire a single difficult movement on the chanter . . . There is what is called the 'army style' of pipe-playing, which most of our young pipers adopt, because it is easy to acquire. In army and volunteer, in fact in all pipe bands, the tunes are set in such a plain and easy style that the greatest dupe can play them in the shortest possible time . . . This is how most of our fine old marches and quicksteps are strangled, and set down in torn and bleeding bars to suit the untutored piper of our day. If you ask one of those modern pipers to play a certain tune you merely get the skeleton of it. There are none of the difficult grips and movements and siubhals which characterized the old original, and in executing which the exquisite performers of past days felt so much pride . . .[16]

But the band movement covered a wide range of technical skill, and as the 20th century dawned a competition circuit similar to that of the solo pipe began to develop.[17] The premier contest was held at the end of August each year at the Cowal Highland Gathering in Dunoon. By 1907 up to twenty senior bands competed for the Argyll Shield and eight juvenile bands for the 'Glasgow News' Shield, numbering over 400 pipers and drummers in all.[18] In the years before the Great War the senior events were dominated by the bands of Volunteer

16 'Modern Bagpipe Playing', from 'Morna', *OT*, 22/11/1890 p.3.
17 'A Pipe Band for Oban'. from 'Highlander', *OT*, 1/6/1895 p.3; 'The Inverary Pipe Band Annual Tour', giving the history of the band, its formation by Lord Archibald Campbell, details of its uniform, etc., 19/9/1896 p.5; see also 'The Scale of the Highland Bagpipe Chanter', from Charles Bannatyne, 19/1/1907, p.3. For a brief note of championship bands in the later 1890s, including the Govan Police, the Wallacetown Band and the Aberfeldy Pipe Band, see 'Cowal Highland Gathering', from 'Calum Mor', 21/8/1926, p.3.
18 'Cowal Highland Gathering', from H. S. Strafford, *OT*, 17/8/1907, p.3. See also Allan Chatto, 'The Cowal Highland Games', Parts 1–2, *The Voice*, vol.27, no.3–4, Fall-Winter, 1998–9, pp.34–5, 37–9.

Battalions, such as the 5th H.L.I., whose pipe-major was John MacDougall Gillies, one of the first professional pipers of the foremost rank to become actively involved in the pipe band movement. They disputed the crown with the 4th Royal Scots, the 7th Scottish Rifles, the Govan Police and the 7th. H.L.I. (the so-called 'Brigton Slashers') under Pipe-Major William Fergusson – later of the 52nd Lowland Division, the City of Glasgow and Clan Macrae pipe bands – an outstanding composer and one of the founding fathers of the modern movement. Competition was intense and there were claims after the Govan Police were runners-up three years in succession (1906–08) that the judges were systematically favouring the Volunteer bands. It was suggested that they should be placed under cover, and that the word of command be given by a soldier, so that they could not hear the Pipe-Major's voice.[19] Even so, judging in the pipe band world seems to have been much more systematic, open and accountable than in solo piping. The Secretary of the Cowal Gathering, H. S. Strafford, published the piping scores of the top bands in the 1908 contest, adding

> I think it will be admitted that the system of marking covers all the attributes of a high-class performance, and if the pipe-majors singly or collectively can suggest a better I will be glad to know of it:

Name of Band.	Start.	Break-off	Piping.	Total.
5th H.L.I.	10	10	29	49

(Judges' remarks – A fine performance, steady and accurate in time, tone and finish).

Govan Police	9	10	27	46

(Judges' remarks – Did not get away well. March 'squeaky.' Performance in other respects perfect. Tone exceptionally good. A little luck would have gained this band 1st).

4th R. Scots, Edinburgh,	10	9	28	47

(Judges' remarks – A good band with a fine steady tone; bad break-off march to strathspey and reel, and an error or two in strathspey).

7th Scot. Rifles, Glasgow,	9	9	27	45

19 'The Judging of Bagpipe Playing', from A.[lexander] Hutcheon, *OT*, 25/5/1907, p.3. Inspector Hutcheon, who hailed from Ellon, Aberdeenshire, was Pipe-Major of the Govan Police. For his obituary with pictures and details of his activities as a reed-maker and teacher and powerfully formative influence on young pipers in Glasgow during the first third of the 20th century, see 10/8/1929.

(Judges' remarks – Tone of this band not up to mark, but a good all round performance).

7th H.L.I., Glasgow.   8   10   29   47

(Judges' remarks – A fine band. Players did not all get away together, and this cost the band two marks. They played well all over, and their reel was the finest of the day).

Piping	Start	Break-off	Drumming	Marching	Total	Band
29	10	10	9	9	67	5th H.L.I.
27	9	10	9	12	67	Govan Police
28	10	9	9	10	66	4th R. Scots
27	9	9	9	12	66	7th Scot. Rifles
29	8	10	7	11	65	7th H.L.I.[20]

As in solo piping the technical gap between the top bands and the rest was huge, and the same few ensembles, largely from the west central Lowlands, continued to dominate Cowal in the years before the Great War.

But despite the demonstrable excellence of the élite, the conviction that pipe bands were, generally speaking, bad for technique refused to be laid to rest. George MacKay writing from Edinburgh gave voice to a widespread anxiety when he complained that

Pipers nowadays are 'made' as if by machinery wholesale at shortest notice so to speak, and pipe bands spring up like mushrooms in the night. This cannot be conducive to good playing . . .

Let us take just one note, the 'Taorluadh', by way of illustration . . . The prevailing idea in regard to this important note seems to be, that a 'dab', so to speak, is all that is necessary in the making of it. There could be no greater fallacy . . . The deficiency is not by any means confined to beginners; among very good players the notes are seldom made distinct enough, the detail not being sufficiently emphasised to give them any meaning or to indicate their character.

The old 'champions' were most particular as to this, and it was considered a serious defect to be 'too light fingered', as they termed it.

The minor music, marches and reels, is generally played too fast.[21]

But how fast was 'fast'? Solo performers used a wide range of tempi in march playing, and there were various opinions about what speeds were best for playing

---

20 'Cowal Pipe Band Contest', from H. S. Strafford, *OT*, 19/9/1908, p.3.
21 'The Cult of Ceol Mor Or the Story of "the Pibroch"', from George Mackay, *OT*, 9/9/1922, p.3.

for dancing. The fiddle maestro James Scott Skinner preferred 20 seconds for a 32–bar strathspey, and 16 seconds for a reel, but some felt that dancers were more comfortable at 23/4 seconds for a strathspey and about 18 seconds for a reel.[22] For pipe bands, of course, the problem was still more acute. A relatively moderate speed might confer technical advantage on a band in competition by permitting cleaner ensemble play, and to prevent this the organisers of the Cowal Gathering set an official tempo for march playing, penalising those who departed significantly from it. But what the optimum tempo should be was subject to considerable debate.

A correspondent of the *Oban Times* signing himself 'J. C.' suggested as a simple standard the infantry regulation drill pace of 120 to the minute.[23] He had been playing since the 1880s and claimed that march playing had become a good deal faster during the last two decades of the 19th century as the pipe changed its role to become a regimental marching instrument.[24] Of course this was in theory. In reality Highland regiments usually clocked in at about 118, the Guards at about 112. Troops in full marching order used the standard Quick Time pace of 108 to the minute.[25] The Cowal committee set its metronome at 112.[26]

This was absurdly fast for competition marches, claimed Glasgow piper Archie McNeill: no pipe corps in Scotland could play such material cleanly at above 104 – he had tested it with his own metronome.[27] (Even 104 was very quick; most late twentieth century bands play in the 80 to 90 range.) But the Cowal tempo had not been arrived at by chance. It all depended on what one thought pipe bands were *for*. A correspondent signing himself 'C', agreed that

> 112 is much too fast to make anything but a 'guddle' of a tune like 'Donald Cameron'. Though why any alteration . . . should be made, I fail to see. The fundamental idea of having a Pipe Band is surely to provide music to march to . . .
>
> If . . . the bands which compete at the Cowal Gathering find it necessary to make a bid for the prizes by putting in such 'big' flashy tunes, there is surely something wrong somewhere. Practically all the best known competition marches sound perfectly horrible if taken at too fast a pace, say 112 or over, and drums do not as a rule, improve them. Simpler tunes, properly accentuated by the drums, are much more attractive . . . if by setting a higher

22 'The Judging of Piping and Dancing', from J. A. Mackay, *OT*, 13/6/1925, p.3.
23 See Murray, *Music of the Scottish Regiments*, pp.12–13 for the various regulation paces. The light infantry pace was 140. It was sometimes possible to spot pipers who had served in the old H.L.I., because of the electrifying speeds at which they liked to play: it seemed to affect their internal clock.
24 'Bagpipe Marching Time', from 'J. C.', *OT*, 20/6/1925, p.3.
25 'Marching Times for Pipe Bands' from 'C', *OT*, 29/8/1925, p.3.
26 'Bagpipe Marching Time', by H. R. Strafford, Hon. Secy, Cowal Gathering, *OT*, 27/6/1925, p.3
27 'Pipe Band Contests at Cowal Games', from A. McNeill, *OT*, 15/8/1925, p.3.

pace and crowding out tunes which were written to exhibit the execution of
soloists, and not for performance by bands at all, [the judges at the Cowal
Gathering] become unpopular with certain bands who rely on such tunes,
they would still deserve the thanks of the nation.

The standard of playing, could, I am sure, be much improved by enforcing
melodious renderings of simpler music, and I am quite certain the judges
themselves would be relieved from the appalling prospect of having to listen
to 'Donald Cameron' some 20 times in one day.[28]

It emerged that McNeill had taken his metronome to Cowal and actually timed
the senior bands. He claimed that they were mostly playing at about 104–8 and
some actually slower.[29] Strafford retorted that the Cowal metronome was well
and truly set; indeed he set it himself, and one judge was solely occupied timing
the bands with its aid. Nearly all played up to this tempo and some were even
quicker, a few playing at over 120.[30] McNeill had to agree to differ, although he
did concede that it was tricky getting a dependable result from a metronome
balanced on top of a pipe case in the middle of a field.[31]

The Cowal tempo, as the correspondent 'C' had guessed, was a deliberate
attempt to increase the technical demand of simple tunes for the purposes of
competition, whilst at the same time inducing the top bands to drop what was
deemed unsuitable solo material by making it virtually impossible to play.
Ultimately it was an attempt to establish the relatively low technical standards of
the army bands as a norm, which of course was exactly what the élite were trying
to break free from. It is important to remember that Volunteer formations like
the 5th and 7th H.L.I., were not only streets ahead of the regular battalions in
terms of technique and musical ambition, but they were for all practical purposes
civilian outfits, since the military did not consider their personnel to be soldiers.
John MacDonald, whilst actually serving Pipe-Major of the 4th (Volunteer)
Battalion Cameron Highlanders, was regarded by the War Office as a less than
ideal instructor of the Army Class because they deemed him to be a civilian.

The career of William Fergusson is a reminder of how vital and diverse the
pipe band movement was to become in the inter-war period. Here after all was a
new pathway to eminence, as pipe-major of the new-style technically virtuosic
civilian band – the exact equivalent in ensemble terms of the top flight solo
performer, at its best a walking marvel of problem solving – operating in a
dynamically expanding competitive environment. It was a demanding role,

28 'Marching Times for Pipe Bands', from 'C', *OT*, 29/8/1925, p.3.
29 'Contest at Cowal Games', from A. McNeill, *OT*, 19/9/1925, p.3. It is a tribute to
   their technical skill that they could manage even this, although from a musical point
   of view the resulting Gadarene rush can hardly have been pleasing.
30 'Judging Piping at Highland Games', from H. S. Strafford, *OT*, 26/9/1925, p.3; 'Pipe
   Band Judging', from same, 10/10/1925, p.3.
31 'Pipe Band Judging', from A. McNeill, *OT*, 10/10/1925, p.3.

combining great technical expertise with high-level managerial, interpersonal and training skills, and many fine players were attracted by its challenges preferring its highly charged and gregarious atmosphere to the disciplined isolation of a solo career. Fergusson had learned to play in the 102nd Boys Brigade and then studied under Farquhar MacRae, a pupil of Sandy Cameron. Most of his compositions, which include 'Kintara to El Arish' and the superb 'Australian Ladies':

'The Australian Ladies', pt. 1, by William Fergusson

were apparently written during the Great War years. Thereafter he succeeded Farquhar MacRae as Pipe-Major of the City of Glasgow Pipe Band (later the Clan MacRae), and fashioned it into the leading ensemble of the early '20s. This was a tribute not only to Fergusson's ability but to the rapidly growing number of pipe-band competitions there to be won, including the World's Championship in 1921, 1922, 1923, 1925; the Sir Harry Lauder Shield, 1921, 1922, 1923, 1924 and 1925; the Glasgow Championship, 1922, 1923, 1925; the Polmaise Challenge Cup, 1921, 1922; Alloa 1923, 1924; Greenock, 1922, 1924; Lanark, 1922, 1925; Grangemouth, 1925; Inverkeithing, 1925, 1928; Aberdeen, 1925; Birnam, 1924, 1925, 1926; Comrie, 1922, 1924; Bathgate, 1925, 1926; Edinburgh, 1925; Isle of Man, 1928; and Morpeth, 1928. In 1929 and 1931 he undertook personal tours of Canada to great acclaim.[32]

Cowal remained the premier band event for many years, but the Cowal committee was not even remotely in a position to enforce the kind of control over playing styles exercised by the Piobaireachd Society in the field of ceòl mór. So that while there was a clear urge in certain quarters to impose a check on the forces of change, to stop the clock, to preserve the repertoire at the level of development it had achieved in Uilleam Ross's day, it proved impossible to enforce. The world of ceòl beag was too diverse to be regulated in this way. The

32 'Fergusson's Bagpipe Melodies', a brief notice of the publication of William
    Fergusson's collection, *Fergusson's Bagpipe Melodies. Compositions and Settings by Pipe
    Major Wm. Fergusson late of 7th. H.L.I., 52nd (Lowland) Division & Clan MacRae Pipe
    Bands* (Lond., 1939), praising 'the almost world famous "Kintara to El Arish"'. The
    cost was 2/6, *OT*, 7/10/1939, p.3. See Cannon, *Bibliography*, p.246. See 'Noted Piper
    for Canada', *OT*, 27/4/1929, p.2, which gives an account of his career and lists his
    many competition successes during the '20s. For obituaries see 'The Late Pipe-Major
    William Fergusson', an appreciation by Robert Reid, 16/7/1949, p.3, and 'Glasgow
    Letter. Death of Pipe-Major W. Fergusson', *same*.

performer community did not lose control of this music and how it should be played, and the flood-tide of creativity continued unchecked.

G. S. McLennan was probably the most gifted light-music composer of the period. He was born in 1883, son of Lt. John McLennan and Elizabeth Stewart, and was a child prodigy, playing before Queen Victoria by royal command at the age of ten (she described him as 'this marvellous boy') and winning numerous amateur competitions while barely into his teens. His ambition was to be a sailor, but his father, who was also his teacher, was anxious to prevent this loss to piping and enlisted him in the Gordons, of whose 1st Battalion he quickly became Pipe-Major. A glittering competitive career followed, leading to more than 2,000 awards. He had a superb technique and used it to pioneer the new faster and more heavily decorated style which was developing during the opening decades of the twentieth century. Contemporaries thought him easily the best light music player of his generation. He also won great fame as a composer, publishing a selection of his tunes as an appendix to his father's book *The Piobaireachd as Performed in the Highlands for Ages till about the Year* 1808 (Edinr., 1924) and in his own collection, *Highland Bagpipe Music compiled by George S. McLennan* (Aberd., 1929), issued in the year of his tragically early death.[33] The Gordons gave him a funeral fit for a head of state. His remains were born through the city of Aberdeen on a gun-carriage drawn by six horses and preceded by forty pipers. An estimated 20,000 people lined the route of the procession, and traffic in the city centre was brought to a standstill.[34]

The most obvious feature of McLennan's style as a composer was his bounteous melodic gift, the sparkling variety, wit and invention of his tunes. He had the ability to exploit to the maximum the expressive potential of the inherited musical vocabulary in a highly lucid and systematic manner, coupled with the ability to do the startlingly unexpected with results that, far from seeming eccentric or odd (as was sometimes the case with the only one of his immediate contemporaries to rival him in terms of sheer originality, namely Peter MacLeod), usually turned out to be supremely idiomatic – indeed he significantly extended the idiom of the light music of the pipes. In 'King George V's Army', for example, he establishes one ending phrase:

33 He even won a composing competition posthumously, when his unpublished tune 'The Braemar Gathering' so impressed judges R. U. Brown and R. B. Nicol, that they awarded it first prize after it had been submitted anonymously by G. S.'s half brother D. R. McLennan. See 'The Braemar Gathering. New Pipe Tune Chosen', *OT*, 2/9/1950, p.5.

34 For a life of G. S. McLennan, see Graham and MacRae, 2, viii-xvi. See also Mackenzie, *Piping Traditions*, pp.30, 47–51. See also 'Notices of Pipers, McLennan, George S. (1884–1929) in *PT*, vol.25, no.7, April 1973, p.28; for obituaries and details of his funeral, see 'Famous Pipe-Major's Last Lament Played on His Death-bed. Passing of a World-famous Piper', in *Evening Express*, 1/6/1929, p.1; 'Lochaber No More. Pipe-Major McLennan. Impressive Scenes at Military Funeral' *same*, 5/6/1929, p.3; 'The Land o' The Leal' and 'The Last Lament. Passing of a Famous Piper', *Bon Accord*, 8/6/1929, pp.1, 7.

which is normally one of the most stable things in a pipe tune, and suddenly transforms it:

having first mutated the figure:

as a way of getting from C to F and back again, into this:

so that it could form a pleasing sequence with his new ending:

The characteristic symmetry of McLennan's work is emphasised by the way bars 1 and 2 reappear in 3 and 4 transposed up a tone, yet the effect remains light and graceful, without the slightest feeling of effort or contrivance.[35]

He could do remarkable things with apparently the simplest of materials. For example, there seems little more to the 6/8 march 'Major John McLennan' at first sight than a sequence of balanced rising and descending figures, a common enough procedure in tunes of this type:

35 McLennan, *Piobaireachd As Performed in the Highlands,* p. 11. Apparently McLennan got the basic idea for the tune while listening to a corps of drums working up a beating for 'The East Neuk of Fife': Graham and MacRae, i, 11; for the tune see above Chapter 10, p.217.

But the pattern is rather exceptional: dotted crotchet/quaver triplet followed by quaver triplet/dotted crotchet which is sustained right through the tune giving it a unique rhythmical thumbprint. If one were to tap it out with a drumstick, an experienced piper would readily identify the tune. The unexpected change of key at the beginning of the second part:

comes from McLennan's use of a piobaireachd technique in which bars two and three of the first line are reversed and occupy the beginning of the second line, just as they would in certain kinds of ceòl mór. One has the feeling that there is no way that this outrageous stunt ought to work. But it does.[36]

In the reel 'Alick Cameron the Champion Piper':

he typically focuses on a pair of contrasting figures, a rising arched and a descending stepwise one:

which are extended to move up:

36 McLennan, *Piobaireachd as Performed in the Highlands*, p.12.

and then down the chanter:

Finally the arched figure is inverted and becomes the basis of the last part:[37]

One of his most famous tunes, the reel 'Mrs MacPherson of Inveran':

written for the wife of his colleague Angus Macpherson, shows a similar taste for extended ascending and descending sequences, sometimes tonally provocative, such as EGDFCE below – hitherto unheard in pipe music – but accepted by the listener as somehow inevitable and right:[38]

Figures which might have been left by other composers as standard recurring blocks were frequently and subtly varied,[39] while aspects of teaching finger technique that in other hands would have resulted simply as exercises were shaped by G. S. McLennan into superbly original tunes like the 'The Jig of Slurs'. (The slur being one of the 'artful cuttings', a means of separating two notes at the same pitch by a gracenote at a lower pitch somewhat thus):

The Jig of Slurs

37 McLennan, *Piobaireachd as Performed in the Highlands*, p.13.
38 McLennan, *Highland Bagpipe Music*, p.40.
39 See, for example 'Kilworth Hills', *Highland Bagpipe Music*, p.23.

That dramatic plunge into the subdominant harmony at the beginning of part three is a typical McLennan touch, but a stroke that could have been pulled off by few of his contemporaries – and few also perhaps of his successors.[40]

G. S. McLennan's ability to handle large scale highly integrated subjects is probably seen at its best in 'The Little Cascade' which enjoys an almost cult status and is regarded by some as one of the wonders of modern Scotland. It is based on a pentatonic scale in the fifth mode, BDEFG, arranged in an asymmetrical double-tonic sequence with a contrasting scale, ADEFG, giving it a tonality probably unique in Scottish bagpipe music. Its scurrying stepwise figures and jazzy syncopated rhythms, the exotic slightly decadent quality of its tonality, the atmosphere at once frenetic and troubled, seem in many respects the very epitome of 'modernism' – reminding us that the forces which produced Weill and Bartók were by no means confined to the concert hall:[41]

40 McLennan, *Highland Bagpipe Music*, p.33. For the composer's assessment of this tune, see Graham and MacRae, ii, 30.

41 McLennan, *Highland Bagpipe Music*, p.39; for the origins of the tune, see Graham and MacRae, ii, 25.

McLennan's skill as an arranger of other people's material was also a by-word among pipers and can be seen to advantage in tunes like 'The Braes of Castle Grant' and 'Biddy from Sligo'.[42]

And so the light music of the Highland pipe, still little more in 1869 than a twinkle in Uilleam Ross's eye, had become by the 1920s a mature and sophisticated form, rivalling piobaireachd in technical difficulty and by far outstripping it in creative vigour. And another Ross, the brilliant Willie of the Castle, was about to enshrine a major part of this achievement in one of the classic editions – *Pipe-Major W. Ross's Collection of Highland Bagpipe Music* published in five volumes, 1923–1950 and including more than two hundred tunes set by Ross himself in the very latest style. The inside cover bore a photograph of the compiler: an imposing looking man in the full vigour of middle life, immaculately turned out in Highland evening dress, pipes carried lightly under the left arm, and beaming piratically – he was a man of legendary charm – half turning as he ascended a flight of stately neo-classical steps, as if he were just popping in to see the King. By contrast with its author, the book was modest in appearance – oblong-shaped and practical, paper jacketed, portable and cheap. It did not at all look like Angus MacKay.

In the summer of 1923 Willie Ross was in South Uist, holding classes under the auspices of the local Piobaireachd Society:

> On June 8th a smoking concert was held in Daliburgh School, and Pipe-Major Ross was the guest of the evening . . .
>
> Looking back, the Chairman said, to a period of about forty years ago, it appeared that piping would soon be a lost art. About that time there were three or four first-class pipers appearing at all the Highland Gatherings, but no young pipers were coming forward. Then . . . a Piobaireachd Society was formed in South Uist. For a time they had been successful in securing the services of that king of pipers and instructors, Pipe-Major John MacDonald, for a few months every year, and the young pipers of Uist had just begun to make a name for themselves when the War broke out and the local Piobaireachd Society had to cease activities. The Society has been revived, and owing to the kindness of the Scottish Piobaireachd Society they had been able to recommence their classes. Pipe-Major Ross had shown himself a worthy successor of Pipe-Major MacDonald as instructor in piping . . .
>
> Pipe-Major Ross replied that he felt it easy to work in such a piping 'atmosphere' and with the conviction that he was among friends.
>
> The evening passed with selections on the bagpipes and reminiscences of old pipers and bygone contests with many a hint to young pipers interspersed. Too soon they had to say good-bye for Pipe-Major Ross was leaving

---

42 McLennan, *Highland Bagpipe Music*, p.3, Donald MacLeod, ed., *Pipe Major Donald MacLeod's Collection of Music for the Highland Bagpipe* (5 vols., Glasg., n.d., but 1954 ff.), iii, 31.

Lochboisdale by steamer at midnight. The pleasure of having met Pipe-Major Ross is one which none of those present will ever forget.[43]

Volume one of the new collection must already have been in the press. It was advertised in September 1923 and was almost immediately the subject of a long and appreciative review in the *Oban Times*, which showed a keen awareness of its significance, remarking on major changes of style during the previous 25 years, and how Willie Ross's notation indicated, with a precision hitherto unattained, exactly how the tunes should be expressed:[44]

> This book, which is certain to be welcomed warmly, is probably unique in at least two respects. No previous collection of Marches, Strathspeys and Reels has appeared in print at a moment when the author's fame as a successful winner of prizes was at its zenith, and no such previous Collection has exhibited the same signs of careful preparation.
>
> The title page states the contents to be as played by Pipe-Major Ross himself, and those who have the good fortune to be familiar with his playing will find this to be an accurate description not only of the settings, but also of the manner of rendering them. The elaborate system of pointing adopted is a more serious attempt to demonstrate the exact method of playing than any which we can recollect in other publications, and is particularly noticeable in the reels, which previously were often represented by a long row of quavers of equal length.
>
> To the student of Highland music in general and of pipe music in particular the most interesting arrangements are those of familiar competition marches such as 'The Abercairney Highlanders', 'Angus Campbell's Farewell to Stirling', 'Bonny Ann', 'The Glengarry Gathering', and 'The Highland Wedding'. In the seventies of the last century prizes for marches at the Northern Meeting were won with simple tunes in 6/8 time. The more intricate four and six parted march in 2/4 time was brought into prominence . . . by the late William McLennan . . . and was developed still further by his famous successors, Angus MacRae and John MacColl. Throughout the last twenty-five years the tendency has been to embellish this class of music with more and more grace notes, largely, we believe, as the result of the uncanny facility for such ornamentation displayed by an illustrious contemporary of our present author [a reference to G. S. McLennan] . . . the difference between any one of the tunes mentioned above as played on a platform in the early nineties and as played to-day is considerable . . .

There was no appeal here to authority, or fixed texts, or a concept of tradition founded upon antiquity and invariance. It was assumed that pipers would choose, or not, to play these settings and that on their exercise of that choice

---

43 'Piobaireachd Classes in South Uist', *OT*, 16/6/1923, p.3.
44 Advertisement for Willliam Ross's book 1, *OT*, 15/9/1923, p.2.

would depend the popularity of the collection. Its status derived from the compiler's standing in the performer community, and he accepted individual responsibility for the settings as a fellow interpreter of the common art. Above all, perhaps, was the sense that change was a natural and expected feature of a living form and might as easily bring gain as loss:

> The popularity of the competition march, strathspey and reel music of to-day, whether or not it will endure, is at the present moment established firmly. If it is a mere phase, it is a phase in the history of Highland music which no conscientious historian can ignore, and Pipe-Major Ross's book . . . is, in the first place, a valuable historical record of what is considered in the year of grace 1923 to be competition music in its highest form . . .
>
> Secondly, there are doubtless many pipers in the Dominions who have never heard a competition in Scotland and who now have an opportunity of seeing exactly how prizes are gained there . . .
>
> Thirdly, and principally, nine out of ten pipers all the world over cherish an ambition to excel in difficult marches, strathspeys and reels, and they will find here precisely what they have long hoped to obtain, instruction for which one of the most famous performers of the time has assumed responsibility . . . In some of these the elaboration of grace noting is almost startling, but it is in faithful accordance with modern practice.
>
> The book contains a few recent compositions of merit, and of them 'Mrs J. MacColl', march by John MacColl; 'Kantara to El Arish', march by Pipe-Major W. Ferguson of the famous City of Glasgow Pipe Band, and 'Mrs Hugh Calder', march by Roderick Campbell, are worthy of special attention.
>
> It is hoped that the useful series of which this book is the beginning will be a long one. There is no question of the value of the first part, and the appearance of the second will be awaited eagerly.[45]

In the light music of the Highland pipe there was a continuous ferment of activity stirred by an insatiable hunger for the new. Here we see the performer community extending the repertoire, redesigning the genres, pushing out the frontiers of idiom, devising fresh approaches to ensemble, seeking out new and subtle refinements in pitch and timbre. A reasonable conclusion would seem to be that – left to its own devices – change was the normal condition of a traditional art form. Continuity, not fixity, was its essence. Stability did not mean invariance – it sprang from a deeper level than the text and worked in more subtle ways than the 'educated' sponsors of fixed scores could begin to comprehend.

Meanwhile in the troubled world of ceòl mór the Piobaireachd Society was preparing to re-launch its *Collection* in a new second series, and relations with the performer community were about to enter their main twentieth-century phase.

---

45 'A New Collection of Highland Bagpipe Music', *OT*, 29/9/1923 p.3.

18

'So far from the original':
The Piobaireachd Society's Second Series

The first volume of the Piobaireachd Society's second series was published in November 1925 and contained twelve tunes. The *Oban Times* received it with qualified enthusiasm. Its reviewer wrote:

> This book marks a new era in the editing of Piobaireachd. It is the first book of its kind to be furnished with a critical apparatus. Fifteen unpublished MSS are enumerated and described. The edition is founded on these unpublished MSS. Editors of former collections have generally fixed on settings that happened to appeal to themselves . . . The critical and explanatory notes reveal a balanced judgement. They suggest to the reader how the most popular tunes, just because of their popularity, are the very pieces that are most liable to undergo change throughout the generations.[1]

The volume represented the collective conclusions of its editor J. P. Grant and his colleague Archibald Campbell of Kilberry, formed over more than a decade since they had gained control of the Society's Music Committee in 1912. It established a characteristic 'house style' which was to be repeated with minor modifications in most of the later volumes – fifteen in all, the last being published in 1990. Altogether the collection was to contain some 244 tunes, and it rapidly became the standard 20th century edition and the basis for most public performance of ceòl mór. Since the Society published the volumes at below cost, effectively eliminating commercial competition, it was for some years the only available source.[2] Volumes appeared at roughly two-yearly intervals and by 1939 eight books had appeared, covering the classic heart of the repertoire.[3] Following volume one, J. P. Grant was succeeded as editor by Archibald Campbell. Although the Music Committee bore a nominally collective responsibility and the Society always referred to its 'Editors', volumes 2 to 9 were edited solely by Campbell.

---

1 'Piobaireachd. A New Publication Issued by the Piobaireachd Society', *OT*, 6/2/1926 p.3.
2 Piobaireachd Society Papers, NLS, Acc.9103/9 Correspondence, 1929–1950, Archibald Campbell to George Campbell: 'not only are we the only piping society to publish pipe music, but we take the risk of doing so at a loss deliberately, for the sake of propagating knowledge', 2/6/1946.
3 Cannon, *Bibliography*, pp. 232–7.

A system of standard abbreviations with a key was used, an adaptation of Thomason's practice in *Ceol Mor,* meaning that all but the longest tunes could be reproduced on a single folio page:

A' Ghlas Mheur (The Finger Lock), P.S. vol. 1, 8

Abbreviations used.

Thomason had replaced Angus MacKay's clear and logical manner of dividing up the tune: 'Variation 1, 2, 3, Crun-luath, Doubling of Crun-luath' and so on, with an abbreviated code in which the variations were numbered and identified by type. Grant and Campbell adopted a more elaborate system involving contractions, brackets and upper-case Roman numerals: 'I. Urlar. II. Var. I. III. Var. I. Doubling. IV. Var. II. (V) & V. Doubling (V')'. Each line was numbered in the left-hand margin and there was an extensive assortment of signs and symbols above the stave: bracketed arabic numerals referring to various points in the editorial commentary, square brackets enclosing instructions regarding variants and repeated parts, and frequent fermata and mordent signs.

The music was written in a simplified style, extending the process begun by Angus MacKay in 1838. All conventional movements were reduced to a single form, representing a further narrowing of expressive register. General Thomason had eight different gairms and eallachs. The Society had one, which Grant rendered like this:

and Campbell like this:

Each represented a departure from earlier practice.[4]

A complete text for each tune was given in staff notation, often stated to represent the playing of Alexander Cameron (the younger) and John MacDougall Gillies. A canntaireachd version for each main text also appeared in Nether Lorn vocables. There were editorial notes identifying certain alternative printed and manuscript settings, specifying some of their differences from the preferred text and offering an apparently detailed account of the editorial procedures which had been applied to the main text. For the first time multiple versions of tunes were described in a single source carrying the stamp of institutional authority, so that – in theory – performers could choose between different settings. But this appears seldom to have happened in practice. In 1954, J. P. Grant was to write of the *Piobaireachd Society Collection* (first series) that:

> the Society published books with single settings and without explanatory notes, and laid down that no competitor who did not play those exact settings, would be eligible for a prize at their competitions. In many cases the settings were without proper authority, and in some they were fantastically conjectural.
>
> Nevertheless, competing pipers, assuming that the Society possessed or must possess a store of ancient manuscript authorities, believed that the settings were conclusively authentic, and accepted them as such.
>
> There have been two results, both of them to be deplored. Firstly, some survivors of those competitors or of their pupils still adhere to those settings as genuine bequests by old masters. Secondly, a belief if not a conviction, still persists that if at a Piobairachd Society's competition a competitor does not play a tune exactly as set out in the music part of the Society's present series of publications he might as well keep his pipes in the box.[5]

But it was scarcely surprising that the majority of performers should continue to treat the Society's main texts as prescriptive and attempt to play them as written,

4 See above pp.112, 222, 237, 330, 352.
5 NLS, Acc.9103/10 Correspondence 1951–54, J. P. Grant to College of Piping, 18/3/1954.

since the Society's judges had been systematically enforcing this practice for more than a generation.[6] It meant, in turn, that what was heard in public from the later 1920s onwards was increasingly determined by how Archibald Campbell set the tunes.

Archibald was the youngest of the Kilberry brothers who had founded the Piobaireachd Society in 1903. He was born in 1877 and educated at Harrow and Pembroke College, Cambridge. Entering the Indian Civil Service in 1900, he rose to become a junior High Court Judge on the Lahore Circuit. Retiring in 1928, he became lecturer in Indian Law to the Board of Indian Civil Service Studies at the University of Cambridge between 1929 and 1941. According to his own published account, he had begun to learn the pipes in 1894 but did not start seriously until 1897, in his twentieth year, when he had some lessons from Angus MacRae and John MacColl. He went to MacDougall Gillies about 1900 and remained in contact with him until the latter died in 1925. His studies were interrupted by long tours of duty in India – amounting to some twenty-seven years in all – but he had three weeks instruction from John MacDonald of Inverness when home on furlough in 1905, and another three weeks from Sandy Cameron in 1911. Although the latter had by then stopped playing the pipes as the result of a hand injury, Campbell considered him by far the best of his teachers and compiled an extensive set of notes on what he considered to be Cameron's distinctive style.[7] He prided himself on his fidelity to his main instructors and the accuracy with which he thought he had depicted their style, and he frequently criticised other editors for exercising their own judgement, noting that 'What I have put down in the score and in the notes . . . is what I have been taught, not what I have evolved as my own ideas'.[8]

6 In 1927, when Seton Gordon was acting Secretary to the Society, he felt obliged to write to the *Oban Times* stressing that any 'recognised' setting could be played: 'It cannot be emphasised too strongly that the Piobaireachd Society does not lay down the condition, or even desire, that pipers in their competitions should play its own settings. Any setting is accepted, provided it be a recognised one. It merely publishes the tunes; pipers may adopt its settings or not as they please. I think this point should be made clear because there is a widespread belief among pipers that there is a moral obligation to play the Piobaireachd Society's setting', 'Piobaireachd Music', 9/7/1927, p.3. But see also 'Piobaireachd Music', from Angus Macpherson, 23/7/1927, p.3, contradicting Seton Gordon and declaring that the Piobaireachd Society was in fact ruthless in excluding people who did not play from the stipulated printed settings. For details of the Society's judges continuing to enforce its style as written, of competitors being penalised for accenting the first note of the a mach group, now regarded as 'unorthodox', but in accordance with older practice, and also for playing the 'redundant' low A see 'Piobaireachd: the Mach Beats', from 'Mach', 8/10/1932, p.3.

7 Extracts of these were published by James Campbell in *Sidelights* and *Further Sidelights*. See *Sidelights* , pp. 6–7 for details of Archibald Campbell's periods of instruction. See also 'The Highland Bagpipe. Pt. IV', by Archibald Campbell, *PT*, vol.15, no.1, October 1962, pp.6–8.

8 *Sidelights*, p.6.

In the volumes of the *Piobaireachd Society Collection* (second series), edited by Archibald Campbell, some 35 tunes are stated to reflect the teaching of Alexander Cameron and John MacDougall Gillies, both of whom were by now dead, Cameron in 1923 and Gillies in 1925. These include most of the classic competition repertoire – 'The Blue Ribbon', 'Glengarry's March', 'Craigellachie', 'The Desperate Battle', 'Black Donald's March', 'The Lament for Donald of Laggan', 'The Lament for the Earl of Antrim', 'John Garbh MacLeod of Raasay's Lament', 'The King's Taxes', 'The Lament for the Children', 'The Lament for the Only Son', 'The Old Men of the Shells', 'MacCrimmon's Sweetheart', 'MacDonald of Kinlochmoidart', 'Macfarlane's Gathering', 'McIntosh's Lament', 'The Lament for Mary MacLeod', 'My King has landed in Moidart', 'The Lament for Patrick Og MacCrimmon', 'The Rout of Glenfruin', 'Scarce of Fishing', 'Seaforth's Salute', 'The Sound of the Waves against the Castle of Duntroon', 'A Flame of Wrath for Squinting Peter', 'Mary's Praise' and 'The Battle of Waternish'.

However, there are frequent differences between what Campbell wrote down as the style he had learned from Alexander Cameron and John MacDougall Gillies, and what appears in Colin Cameron's and MacDougall Gillies's manuscript books. Alexander Cameron's own manuscript book, which was apparently still in existence in the early 1920s, has disappeared, although Campbell confirmed in a note dated 16 June 1949 and attached to Colin Cameron's manuscript that '. . . the tunes . . . correspond, many if not most of them with what was taught to me by Donald's son Alexander, and by the latter's pupil, John MacDougall Gillies'.[9] In the volumes of the Piobaireachd Society's second series edited by Campbell there was frequent – and silent – addition of a mach variations not present in the original sources, while instructions to repeat the ground at various stages within the tune, which were present in the original sources, were silently removed.[10] A fosgailte a mach

9 *Sidelights*, p.45. See also the *Oban Times* review, 'Piobaireachd. A Second Book of 12 Tunes', 21/7/1928, p.3: 'The book is worth getting if for no other reasons than that it contains opinions of pipers of such repute as J. Macdonald of Inverness, the late Alexander Cameron, and the late J. MacDougall Gillies'.

10 Archibald Campbell wrote to Seton Gordon: 'Sandy Cameron did not tell me that a Crunluath a mach should always be played. He did tell me that the proper way to play a piobd was to repeat the ground after the Taorluath doubling and again to finish up with. He was not, however, teaching me as a competitor . . .' Seton Gordon Papers, General Correspondence 1927–9, NLS, Acc.7451, 4/4/28. He had earlier remarked to Gordon, 'we nowadays play piobaireachd in flat contradiction of what was considered proper for a long line of pipers up to and including Donald Cameron. These always played the ground 3 times (1) at the start (2) after the Taorluath Doubling, (3) to finish up with. I myself remember . . . that it required an effort to prevent competitors at Oban doing this'. General Correspondence 1913–1926, 25/3/ 1925. For a comment on this latter point see 'Glen's Collection of Piobaireachd', from 'Piob', *OT*, 4/1/1930, p.3, enquiring why David Glen's settings, which always included instructions to repeat the ground within the tune differed so greatly from those ascribed to MacDougall Gillies by the Piobaireachd Society.

was introduced, and although criticised by Angus Macpherson and others as spurious and previously unknown, was applied to all appropriate tunes of this type.[11] Campbell's notes of his teaching from Alexander Cameron compiled in 1916–17 contained an instruction to: 'Play the Crunluath a mach . . . after the doubling wherever possible. I was actually instructed to do so in the following tunes – 'Too Long in this Condition', 'The Groat', 'Maol Donn', 'Cill Chriosd', 'Lament for Clavers' and (I think) 'The King's Taxes'.[12] In the published notes to 'The Lament for Clavers' [usually known as The Lament for Viscount Dundee'], the first tune to receive this addition in the second series of the Society's *Collection*, it was stated:

> The open Crunluath fosgailte . . . is . . . on the authority of Alexander
> Cameron, who said that a third Crunluath movement in this form was played
> by his father, here and in certain other tunes of similar character. The Editors
> understand that some pipers are doubtful of the correctness of such a practice.
> They themselves regard the matter as one of minor importance, dependent
> upon individual taste. They consider it their duty to record the Cameron
> view, and the fact that it is dissented from, and to suggest that pipers should
> make their own choice.[13]

Traditional sanction was thus invoked for the fosgailte a mach as a distinctive practice of the Cameron school. Yet in the main published source of Cameron settings, General C. S. Thomason's *Ceol Mor*, this feature was absent. Nor did it appear in Colin Cameron's MS. And while a number of letters supporting Angus Macpherson's objections to the variation were received by the *Oban Times*, not a word was raised in its defence. John MacDonald of Inverness, who had been one of Campbell's teachers, and had himself studied with Sandy Cameron, instructed his pupils that the movement was wrong and they were not to play it. Later he explained:

> Calum Macpherson told me that an Amach should be played to every
> Crunluadh – but no Amach should be played to a Crunluadh Fosgailte. I
> once heard Sandy Cameron put an Amach on the Crunluadh Fosgailte of
> 'The Big Spree'. I asked him why he did it. He said: 'The reason I put it is
> for a finger exercise, because it is a short tune and has no singling in the
> Crunluadh,' then he added: 'It was never put in by the old pipers'. I myself
> can vouch for that. Neither Calum Macpherson nor Colin Cameron, nor the
> MacDonalds from Morar ever put in an Amach after a Fosgailte.[14]

11 See above, pp.334–6.
12 *Sidelights*, p.12.
13 Vol.i, 33.
14 *OT*, 4/4/1942, quoted in Macpherson, *Highlander Looks Back*, pp.66–68; for 'Big

General Frank Richardson, who had studied with John MacDonald as a private pupil, raised the matter with Archibald Campbell who replied:

> . . . nor can I say much about open crunluath fosgailte than that Sandy Cameron told me to play it. Personally I do not care for it but this fact weighs nothing with me, whose sole object is to play as he was taught and not as he fancies . . . I don't know what John MacDonald's recollection is of what Colin and Sandy Cameron said to him. I did not argue with or question Sandy but just accepted what he said.[15]

Since Alexander Cameron was dead, there was no obvious way of checking the source, and by virtue of his pivotal role in determining what was 'authoritative' and what was not, Campbell was in a position to enforce this practice. The Society continued to edit fosgailte tunes in a similar manner in its later publications.

Archibald Campbell's teaching notes show time values conveyed by laboriously detailed verbal instructions which do not suggest a quick or retentive ear, and he spoke of his problems in capturing correct timings even after frequent repetitions and the use of a metronome.[16] Troubled by what he thought were differences in style between Cameron and Gillies, he adhered to his written record of Cameron's teaching. Discussing the double echo beat on D, for example, he remarked:

> *Hiharara.* Gillies taught me expressly to play C and I played it for years. When I was under John MacDonald in 1905 he passed this, that is to say he made no demur to my playing it so. When I came under Sandy Cameron in 1911 he corrected me and said that the gracenote must be low G as written by Angus MacKay. I told Gillies that Sandy had said this. All that Gillies said was 'Isn't that curious?' I entered into no further discussion. If you begin arguing with these people you get nothing out of them.[17]

An example of the movement he was discussing is given below. In playing the difference would be slight, unless one were accustomed to give the C or low G gracenote a good deal more than its notated value:

---

cont'd   Spree' should probably be read 'Little Spree'. MacDonald stated that 'Colin Cameron sometimes played the closed, sometimes the open variety. BUT NEVER BOTH': Seton Gordon Papers, NLS, Acc.5640/2 (1), 'Notes of a conversation . . . with John MacDonald, May 3rd 1941'.

15 MacNeill and Richardson, pp.87–88.
16 *Sidelights*, and *Further Sidelights*, *passim*; for his use of the metronome, see *Sidelights*, p.53.
17 MacNeill and Richardson, p.84.

With C gracenote   With low G gracenote
as taught by Gillies   as taught by Cameron

His approach was not that of a normal learner. He wrote:

> I have tried to get everything I can out of Sandy Cameron and MacDougall
> Gillies and I have done my best to get all the information I can and forget
> about the playing. I must get the information and I am only sorry that I
> haven't got time to play more but if I can amass as much information as I
> can . . . then I shall be satisfied.[18]

In editing the Piobaireachd Society volumes Campbell tended to ignore precise
technical advice from Willie Ross and John MacDonald, relying instead on the
notes he had assembled in 1916–17 of his lessons with Alexander Cameron in
1911.[19]

Some who heard Archibald Campbell perform described his style as 'ponder-
ous' and declared that he was 'not a pleasing player'.[20] This would seem to be
supported by the remarks on expression contained in his notes. Although there
were occasional instructions to play briskly and not to drag, these were heavily
outweighed by directions to prolong notes beyond their expressed value, to time
low G and A melody notes 'pretty long', to play various different movements
'long and weighty'.[21] Ideas like this determined much of his editorial practice.[22]
Here, for example, is his version of 'The Unjust Incarceration', the opening tune

---

18 Letter to Alasdair Anderson quoted in Campbell, 'History of the Piobaireachd
Society', p.45.

19 See for example Piobaireachd Research Papers of Archibald Campbell, NLS, MS.
22103, letters from Willie Ross and John MacDonald suggesting that 'The Lament for
Donald Ban MacCrimmon' should be set in 6/8 time. Campbell set it in 4/4: see *PS*
ii, 66. See also NLS, MS.22112, Letter from Willie Ross re 'Mary MacLeod', 18/3/1934,
counselling against the high G quaver at the beginning of bar 3 line 3 in variation 1
doubling and in corresponding positions later in the tune. Ross played high A here,
and so did Roderick Campbell a prominent pupil of Sandy Cameron's, and so did
John MacDonald as a note from J. P. Grant indicated. Archibald Campbell favoured
the G, relying on his record of the tune made nearly twenty years previously,
indicating in the published notes merely that 'some pipers play high A plain', *PS* v,
155–6.

20 MacNeill and Richardson, pp.115, 119.

21 *Sidelights*, pp. 8–11, and *passim*. We find here, too, the novel suggestion that three
note cadences 'All are played practically alike throughout piobaireachd . . . The three
notes are all the same length . . .'

22 See, for example, NLS, MS.22102, f.22, Campbell's note on 'My king has

in the Piobaireachd Society's second volume. Settings by Colin Cameron and John MacDougall Gillies are included for comparison:

The Unjust Incarceration, line 1. Colin Cameron's MS., f.32

An Ceapadh Eucorach, line 1. John MacDougall Gillies's MS, f.6.

An Ceapadh Eucorach (The Unjust Incarceration), line 1. Archibald Campbell, P.S. Collection, ii, 42.

The published note to the tune stated 'the printed setting is the one played and taught by Alexander Cameron and J. MacDougall Gillies.'[23] Yet there are a number of differences in note values and rhythm between Colin Cameron and Gillies, who are very similar in approach, and Archibald Campbell who draws ostensibly upon the same source. The frequent substitution of crotchets for quavers and the awkward redistribution of accent which results is characteristic of a good deal of his work.

We see this in 'The Battle of Waternish', where Angus MacKay and Colin Cameron approach the ground with a lighter, more idiomatic touch. The opening A, timed as a semi-quaver by MacKay, becomes in Campbell a crotchet with a fermata:

cont'd   landed in Moidart': 'Correct as given by A Mackay. Play fairly slow. Where A & G
        occur at the end of bars as in the first & second bars they are played longer than written,
        almost as long as the note which precedes them.' MS.22101, f.143, 'MacLeod of Rasay's
        Salute': 'The first note of each bar in the ground should be dwelt upon & played practically
        as long as the crotchet following'. MS.22099, f.26, 'Too Long in this Condition': 'The last
        two notes of such bars as the 3rd & fifth of the ground are played smoothly of even length,
        & pretty slow'. Same, f.86, 'The Rout of Glenfruin': 'The tune is pretty straightforward to
        play. The A quavers in the ground preceded by low G grace note are hardly represented
        correctly [by Angus MacKay] as one third or one half of the value of the preceding note.
        They are almost the same length & where they finish a three-note cadence time E quite as
        long if not longer. This turn [darodo] is done "heavy" throughout the tune'.

23 Vol.ii, 43.

Druim Thalasgair (na) Blàr Bhaterneish, The Battle of Waternish, line 1. Angus MacKay's MS. i, f.46.

The Battle of Vaternish (Baiteal Bhaternish), line 1. Colin Cameron's MS, f.50

Blar Bhatairnis (The Battle of Waternish), line 1. Archibald Campbell, P.S. ii, 48.

MacDougall Gillies's timing of the tune was practically identical with Colin Cameron's.[24] Yet Campbell's published note stated 'The setting printed is that of Angus MacKay, with some few alterations in the pointing based on the teaching of Alexander Cameron and J. MacDougall Gillies'.[25] There would seem to be a considerable gap here between what was taught and what had been learned. Since Campbell treated his introductory notes as gracenotes, he did not allow time for them in the bar, which meant that the remaining notes had to be lengthened to make up the quantity and keep the musical arithmetic consistent. But this created a dilemma for players. While the relative time-values of what were deemed to be 'melody notes' were, generally speaking, plain enough, (except where blurred by frequent use of the fermata), exactly how much time should be allowed to introductory notes in the resulting scheme remained ambiguous. This was to lead to much uncertainty in competition playing during the next two generations as Society derived styles continued to dissolve inherited idioms.

Placed in the context of earlier work Campbell's settings often seem coarse. In 'Catherine's Lament', for example, for which there is substantial evidence from John MacGregor and Angus MacArthur onwards, we find the uniform pre-ference of the earlier tradition for a quaver/semi-quaver rhythmical pattern rejected. Campbell opened with two crotchets and placed the fermata in such a way as to indicate that phrase endings should be significantly prolonged,

24 John MacDougall Gillies MS., f.56.
25 Vol.ii, 50.

although this meant dwelling on what in the earlier scores seem to have been intended as passing notes:

Highland Society of London MS., Piobaireachd No.11 [Catherine's Lament], line 1.

Cumha Chaitrine Katherine's Salute, line 1, Angus MacKay's MS. i, f.13

Catherine's Lament, line 1, Colin Cameron's MS., f.1.

[Catherine's Lament], line 1, John MacDougall Gillies's MS., f.59.

Cumha Catriona (Catherine's Lament), line 1, Archibald Campbell, Piobaireachd Society, v, 133.

The published note to the tune cited the manuscripts of Angus and John MacKay and stated 'Except that the B marked (4) is low A in the two MacKay MSS., [this occurs in the second line of the ground which is not reproduced in the present example] the setting printed corresponds with theirs. The pointing of the Urlar is according to Alexander Cameron's and J. MacDougall Gillies's teaching'.[26]

Campbell set the tune 'Maol Donn (MacCrimmon's Sweetheart)', as follows:

26 *PS*, v, 133–4. See also *Further Sidelights*: 'I learnt this tune from Gillies and afterwards went through it with A. Cameron. Semi-quavers in the ground should not be cut and the pause marks observed. The ground is pretty slow.' p.32. Archibald Campbell's standards of accuracy were higher with tunes he had not been taught; but these tended to lie outside the classic core of the repertoire.

Maol Donn (MacCrimmon's Sweetheart), ground line 1, Archibald Campbell, Piobaireachd Society, vii, 205.

According to the published note, 'The setting printed was taught by Alexander Cameron and J. MacDougall Gillies'.[27] Campbell's 1916–17 notes state: 'I learnt this tune from Gillies and went through it with A. Cameron . . . The low A's at the beginning of bars in the ground should be played long. They are about the longest notes in those bars. Gillies played them short, but Cameron corrected me promptly'.[28] He continued 'The B's marked A should be sounded well'. [i.e. given more than their notated value].

There are two settings of the tune in MacDougall Gillies's manuscript book and one in Colin Cameron's, as follows:

MacCrummen's Sweetheart. John MacDougall Gillies's MS., version 1, f.50

MacCrummen's Sweetheart. John MacDougall Gillies's MS., version 2, f.51

MacCrummin's Sweetheart. A Mhuil Duin. Colin Cameron's MS., f.86

In none of these is it apparent that A should be considered the opening themal note and as such take the accent, which would appear in each case to fall on the first C. Angus MacKay's setting implies a similar approach, his even E/A quavers suggesting an anacrusis leading on to a dotted C quaver:

27 Vol. vii, 206.
28 *Sidelights*, pp.26–8. The [A] signs occur in the 1916–17 notes.

Cumha Mhuil Duin Suposed to be a Lament for Muil Duin Son of Conol King of Cantyre, Angus MacKay's MS. i, 134

No A in MacKay's text receives a value greater than a quaver. The opening note in his last bar is timed as a semi-quaver. In Campbell it is a crotchet. The perceived instructions of one of his teachers seem, once again, to lead to outcomes different from most of the written record, with corresponding loss of fluency and distortion of melodic contour. The published note to the tune in the Piobaireachd Society's *Collection* states 'Angus MacKay's Urlar is the same as the text, except for slight differences in timing some of the notes'.

Campbell's treatment of MacKay's settings was often perfunctory. He stated of 'The Rout of Glenfruin' that 'The setting printed was taught by Alexander Cameron and J. MacDougall Gillies . . . Angus MacKay's version corresponds with the text . . .'[29] But this was not the case. Campbell began with four straight crotchets: Mackay with quaver/semiquaver/semiquaver/crotchet/quaver/ crotchet/quaver, giving a much more varied rhythmical pattern:

Ruaig Ghlinne Fruin. The Rout of Glenfruin 1602, ground line 1, Angus MacKay's MS., ii, 65

Ruaig Ghlinn Fraoin (The Rout of Glenfruin), ground line 1, Archibald Campbell, Piobaireachd Society, viii, 221

Likewise, the sequence of eight crotchets which ended the line in Campbell's version was not present in MacKay.

His note to 'The MacDougalls' Gathering', published in volume V of the *Piobaireachd Society Collection* (second series) stated that 'The setting printed is that of Angus MacKay's MS'. Editorial responsibility was accepted for two minor emendations in MacKay's ground, as follows:

29 *PS*, viii, 221–2.

The G marked (4) and the preceding notes appear thus in Angus MacKay's MS.:

It is assumed that this is meant to represent the grace-note turn written in the text, which, though not a common one, is nevertheless found in other tunes, e.g., Albain Bheadarach, above referred to, and the Nameless Tune on p.27 of this book. MacDougall Gillies, however, and perhaps Duncan Campbell wrote

Such grace-note groups as those on the high G's marked (3) and (4) are always written by Angus MacKay without the last E, but, if High G is fingered with the second finger down, an E must almost inevitably be sounded, and, according to Alexander Cameron, it is correct both to play and to write an E as the last note of the group.[30]

Angus MacKay set the tune as follows:

'N. 29 In the H. S. of London's MSS.' ground of [The MacDougalls' Gathering], Angus MacKay's MS., i, 27.

Campbell set it like this:

Cruinneachadh Cloinn Dughaill(The MacDougalls' Gathering), ground,
Archibald Campbell, Piobaireachd Society Collection, v, 141

In Campbell's score MacKay's even quaver echo-beats were accented, one of his
E cadences cut (in bar 7), one not present in his score inserted (at bar 15);
MacKay's idiomatic quaver/semi-quaver rhythms were replaced by strings of
crotchets – fourteen in a row in line 5 above. Altogether more than fifty changes
were silently made to the original score. Not a single bar of the Campbell version
was the same as it had been in MacKay.

The impression of scholarship created by the editorial apparatus led to a
general assumption that Archibald Campbell had been scrupulous in handling
the traditional texts to which he had privileged, and in some cases unique,

access.[31] When Volume V of the *Piobaireachd Society Collection* was published in 1934, for example, there was no copy of Angus MacKay's manuscript in the public domain, and it is only in the last quarter of the 20th century that sufficient documents have become available to permit an informed assessment of his work.[32] Archibald Campbell's editorial papers, dealing with some three hundred tunes, were deposited in the National Library of Scotland in 1984.[33] Each tune has its own file containing a range of settings, manuscript material including photographic copies of MacDonald's and MacKay's MSS, single sheets cut from published volumes – ranging from Donald MacDonald to the Piobaireachd Society's first series, and frequently also material from MacPhee and Glen's published collections. There are editorial notes and accounts of different people's teaching, transcriptions, largely by Campbell, of oral texts, and occasional letters from J. P. Grant, Willie Ross, John MacDonald and others. In a number of cases, therefore, it is possible to trace how Campbell evolved the published scores. In 'Mary's Praise', for example, the note accompanying the tune in Volume V of the Society's *Collection* published in 1934 said that 'The setting given of this tune was taught by Alexander Cameron and J. MacDougall Gillies, and differs from the other versions printed or in the manuscripts. Alexander Cameron learnt it from his father, Donald Cameron'.[34] There were previous settings in the published

---

31 Even so, public protest continued to be made. See, for example, 'The Piobaireachd Society Publications', from 'Musician', *OT*, 29/11/1941, p.3; and 'A Criticism of Piobaireachd Tunes. (1) Clan Ranald's Gathering; (2) Lament for Queen Anne; (3) The Old Men of the Shells' 28/8/1948, p.3 and 4/9/1948, p.3: this was taken sufficiently seriously to elicit a rare signed response from Archibald Campbell, see 'A Criticism of Piobaireachd Tunes' 4/9/1948, p.3. It revealed a curiously inconsistent attitude: on the one hand he claimed that the received text was sufficiently sacred to prevent the unauthorised excision of fosgailte-type variations if they occurred in conjunction with duinte-type later variations (which the unnamed correspondent had complained about), whilst immediately conceding the correspondent's related point that he, Campbell, had freely added a mach movements to many tunes in which they had not originally been present. He made no allusion to the Society's introductory movement on low A, which had been one of the main subjects of criticism. For a comment by Campbell on this episode, see his letter to Seton Gordon, 2/9/1948, in Seton Gordon Papers NLS, Acc. 7451/2/2.

32 There were complaints about this from an early period: see 'Piobaireachd In MS. Fourteen MSS Unpublished', from A. K. Cameron, *OT*, 22/1/1927, p.3, urging that the Society should publish the original MSS as the birthright of the people and not hoard them away where nobody could see them. See also 'The Piobaireachd Society's Tunes', from 'A Lover of Piobaireachd', 30/8/1932, p.3, and 'The Music of the MacCrimmons', from Malcolm MacInnes, 6/1/1934, p.3. Copies of the MSS of Donald MacDonald, Angus MacKay, and Angus MacArthur were deposited by the Society in the National Library of Scotland in the summer of 1936, see 'Piobaireachd Manuscripts in the National Library of Scotland', from Archibald Campbell, 8/8/1936, p.3.

33 Campbell, (Archibald), Jurist & Piper. Piobaireachd Research Papers of (ca. 1903–1963, n.d.), NLS, MS22098–22117.

34 *PS*, v, 145–7.

books of Donald MacDonald, Donald MacPhee, David Glen and General
Thomason, and in the manuscript of Angus MacKay. In all of these the ground
was in triple time.[35] Campbell set it in 4/4. He had before him MacDougall
Gillies's manuscript book, an additional loose manuscript transcript in Gillies's
hand, all the published sources of consequence, the photographic copy of Angus
MacKay's MS, and two transcriptions in his own hand of how he thought
MacDougall Gillies and Alexander Cameron had timed the tune during lessons
in the early years of the century. The MacDougall Gillies manuscript book sets
the piece as follows:[36]

Mary's Praise. John MacDougall GilliesMS., f.52

The second Gillies setting in the loose manuscript is on similar lines, although
bearing alterations to time values apparently by another hand:[37]

There was also a transcription made by Campbell when he had been taught the
tune by Gillies and claiming to reflect the latter's style:

Between the first example and the third, four quavers and semi-quavers have
turned into crotchets, one crotchet has become a dotted crotchet and one
crotchet has become a minim. Presumably this represents what Archibald
Campbell thought he heard when Gillies taught him. Campbell's transcription
of what he considered to be Sandy Cameron's style shows similar qualities of
perception:

---

35 MacDonald, *Ancient Martial Music*, p.73; MacPhee, *Collection of Piobaireachd*, i, 10;
     Glen, *Collection of Ancient Piobaireachd*, p.182; Thomason, *Ceol Mor*, p.30; MacKay
     MS, i, 67.
36 MacDougall Gillies MS, f.52.
37 Piobaireachd Research Papers of Archibald Campbell, NLS, MS22100.

It appears that the subtleties of rhythmical balance and contrast exploited by the master pipers largely eluded their pupil. He turned their notes into words. And when he later tried to turn the words back into notes, much was lost.

At any rate with these settings before him, Campbell proceeded to evolve his own text, which he marked 'Probably safest way to write it out . . .':

The tune was published in the Society's fifth volume in 1934, supported by two folio pages of minutely circumstantial notes on the stylings of Alexander Cameron, John MacDougall Gillies and John Bàn Mackenzie, lists of variants in Colin Campbell's canntaireachd, Donald MacDonald's by now rare published book, and Angus MacKay's manuscript, of which there were perhaps three copies in existence. What the notes did not make clear was that the main text was reproduced, with minor alterations, from Donald MacPhee's published book, the relevant page of which – neatly cut from the original source – lay before Archibald Campbell as he worked on the tune:[38]

Mary's Praise, ground line 1, Donald MacPhee's *Collection of Piobaireachd,* i, 10.

Mary's Praise, ground line 1, Archibald Campbell, Piobaireachd Society Collection, v. 145

38 For a selection of further examples of silent changes to cited sources, increased note values, reduced rhythmical flexibility and inadequate or misleading annotation in vols. ii–v of the *Piobaireachd Society's Collection,* (second series), see 'The Battle of Auldearn (no.2), *PS,* ii, 46: cf. Cameron MS, f.62; MacDougall Gillies MS, f.104; Uilleam Ross's MS, f.92. 'Hector MacLean's Warning', *PS,* ii, 51: cf. MacArthur MS, f.19

Campbell's work suggests an innate mistrust of melody. He divided ceòl mór into two categories, 'heavy stuff' – of which he approved – and 'tuny stuff', of which he was wary. Typical 'heavy stuff' was the strong bottom-handed tune whose tonality lay in the lower range of the chanter and which depended strongly for its effect on intervallic and rhythmical tension. The 'tuny' stuff was forced to depend on melody and was therefore considered inferior. General Frank Richardson who knew Campbell personally and had judged with him on a number of occasions, quoted a letter from him written just after the Second World War:

> There seem to me to be two classes of piobaireachd. a) the 'heavy stuff' and b) the 'tuny stuff'. Rightly or wrongly a) was always the favourite with the earlier pipers of the 19th century – we can't go back much further. Examples are 'The Finger Lock' – pre-eminently a favourite – 'Cill Chriosd', 'The Groat', 'The Vaunting' 'The Bells of Perth', 'The End of the Great Bridge', etc. 'Padruig Og' is a sort of hybrid. It dabbles in b) in Var 1, otherwise it is wholly a). Examples of b) are 'Scarce of Fishing', 'MacCruimen's Sweetheart', 'Donald Duaghal MacKay', 'Captain MacDougall' and many others. I fear that in the Army at any rate (and be it whispered, with our own P.S. instructor [Willie Ross]) b) holds the field entirely.[39]

On a later occasion Richardson had to reassure the Seaforth Highlanders that their Pipe-Major Donald MacLeod's new piobaireachd 'Cabar Féidh gu Bràth'

---

cont'd   [original mispaginated]; MacKay *Ancient Piobaireachd*, p. 37. 'The End of the Great Bridge', *PS*, ii, 54: cf. MacDonald *Ancient Martial Music*, p.111; MacKay MS, i, 186; Cameron MS, f.34; MacDougall Gillies MS, f.10. 'Glengarry's March', *PS*, ii, 57: cf. MacDonald, *Ancient Martial Music*, p.30; MacKay MS, i,169; Thomason *Ceol Mor*, p.13 (citing Keith and Colin Cameron as sources). 'The Bells of Perth', *PS*, ii, 60: cf. MacDonald MS, f.46; MacArthur MS, f.15, MacKay, *Ancient Piobaireachd*, p.106; MacPhee, *Collection of Piobaireachd*, p.42. 'The Gathering of Clan Chattan', *PS*, ii, 63: cf. MacKay MS, ii, 36; Uilleam Ross MS, f.168; MacDougall Gillies MS, f.30. 'The Lament for Donald Bàn MacCrimmon', *PS*, ii, 66: cf. MacDonald MS, f.64; Reid MS, f.59; MacKay MS, i, 85; Cameron MS, f.41; Uilleam Ross MS, f.206. 'Donald Gruamach's March', *PS* ii, 71: cf. MacKay MS, i,178; MacDougall Gillies MS, f.90. 'The Lament for MacDonald's Tutor', *PS*, iii, 85: cf. MacKay MS, ii, 5; Cameron MS, f.65. 'Black Donald's March', *PS*, iii, 87: cf. MacDonald *Ancient Martial Music*, p.106; MacKay MS, i,192; MacDougall Gillies MS, f.60. 'The Red Speckled Bull', *PS*, iv, 105: cf. MacDonald MS, f.258; MacKay MS, i, 104; MacDougall Gillies MS, f.93. 'The Lament for Red Hector of the Battles', *PS*, iv, 111: cf. *Ross's Collection of Pipe Music*, p.106; *Ceol Mor*, pp.211–2. 'The Old Woman's Lullaby', *PS*, iv, 113: cf. Cameron MS, f.55; MacDougall Gillies MS. f.58. 'Duncan MacRae of Kintail's Lament', *PS*, iv, 121: cf. MacKay MS, i, 213; *Ross's Collection of Pipe Music*, p.103; *Ceol Mor*, pp.204–5. 'The Lament for Mary MacLeod', *PS*, v, 155: c.f. MacKay MS, i, 203; *Ross's Collection of Pipe Music*, p.104.

39   MacNeill and Richardson, pp.112–3.

was indeed ceòl mór despite the fact that it alarmingly resembled a tune, adding that, as such, Archibald Campbell would certainly have disapproved of it.[40] He continued:

> If one were to admit that there is something slightly less respectable, slightly less purely classical, in 'tuny stuff', of which Kilberry gave me several illustrative examples, then one must look slightly askance at some of the finest and most stirring moments in our music, and, by analogy, at some of the great classical compositions for more civilised instruments.
>
> Though I hesitate to set my own opinion against so great an academic authority I doubt whether it is really necessary for Caledonia to be as stern and wild as all that.

With Archibald Campbell mediation escaped from the preface, introduction and notes and entered the musical text. The 'educated' classes of Scotland were persuaded that piobaireachd was an artistic form whose chief characteristic was its difference from other kinds of music. Its adherence to loose 'non-classical' prosodic rhythms and its unique expressive idiom meant, they thought, that pleasing musicality was, at best, an incidental quality and a distraction from the main business at hand. Campbell in particular seems to have regarded it as a blemish to be edited out of the score as far as possible. The less this supposedly esoteric and demanding Celtic art-form sounded like music the better.[41] It was no good leaving things to the players. Their predilection for melody led them to interpret ceòl mór in an irresponsibly tuneful fashion. It was the duty of the Scottish landed élite to spring to the defence of tradition and rescue piping from the pipers. This was why the Piobaireachd Society had been founded in the first place.

In such a context, it was quite natural that Campbell's own synopses should assume primacy over the written record of leading players, and that his notes should become in effect the copy-text for the *Piobaireachd Society Collection* (second series) volumes 2–9. Much was done in the name of John MacDougall Gillies and the Cameron family. But the fact that each had compiled substantial manuscript books which might have allowed them to speak with their own voices was largely erased from the record, allowing the Piobaireachd Society's editor to appear as their privileged representative and spokesman and clothe himself in the authority of 'tradition'.

During the first half of the 20th century the important manuscripts steadily

---

40 NLS, Acc.9103/17 'Copies of various older piobaireachd', 8/7/1960. He tactfully refrained from pointing out that 'Cabar Féidh gu Bràth' was a gentle parody of one of their own regimental pipe calls, deploying phrase materials transposed into a different key of the march 'Highland Laddie', used in the Seaforth for 'Fall in for Staff Parade': see *Standard Settings of Pipe Music The Seaforth Highlanders* (Lond., n.d. but 1936), p.6.

41 MacNeill and Richardson, pp.73–4. For Archibald Campbell's view that 'piobaireachd is music for the expert few and not for the non-expert masses', see 'The Highland Bagpipe', Pt.3, *PT*, vol 14, no 12, Sept. 1962, p.11.

passed into the possession of the Piobaireachd Society, withdrawing them from circulation and making them inaccessible to the performer community. For a number of years only Archibald Campbell had access to them, giving him an eventually unchallengable authority – especially since his notes to the published volumes of the Society's *Collection* were framed in such a way that nobody in the performer community could be certain what he had got or how he had used it.

For example, the John MacDougall Gillies manuscript book was lent by its compiler to Archibald Campbell, probably in the early '20s, returning to Campbell's possession after MacDougall Gillies's death in 1925.[42] As we have seen, Campbell made frequent appeal to Gillies and to Gillies's teacher, Alexander Cameron, to support the interpretations he favoured. But the MacDougall Gillies manuscript was not included in the list of authorities given for the Piobaireachd Society's second series, although the contemporary MSS of Ewen Henderson, D. S. MacDonald, General Thomason, Donald MacKay (the younger), Duncan Campbell of Foss, and William Lamont of Deeside were. The first direct reference to the existence of a Gillies manuscript book in the *Piobaireachd Society Collection* occurred in two passing references in notes to little-played tunes in volume 9, issued in 1958. No indication was given of the manuscript's size or content.[43] Until it was deposited in the Special Collections Department of the University of Glasgow Library in 1977 by Campbell's heirs it was effectively lost to view for more than half a century. Gillies was not fortunate in his trustees. One of his major pupils, Robert Reid, gave instructions – actually carried out it would appear – that his 'priceless' collection of Gillies-derived manuscript material should be destroyed at his death.[44]

The manuscript of Colin Cameron was bought by the Piobaireachd Society in the summer of 1949, and immediately deposited in the National Library of Scotland. Although it was an important source for the playing style of the Cameron family from whom a good many modern players – including Archibald Campbell – traced their descent, there were only three passing references to it in the subsequent seven volumes of the *Piobaireachd Society Collection* and they gave no indication of its size, date, or content.[45]

42 A letter dated 19 September 1923 from John MacDougall Gillies to Archibald Campbell attached to the manuscript acknowledges its return. Presumably it was subsequently bought from or donated by Gillies's family. The flyleaf is now stamped 'A. Campbell'.

43 *PS*, ix,.263, 265. Nor was this information included in Cannon, *General Preface*, p.16, which simply states 'John MacDougall Gillies (1854–1925). Manuscript. Glasgow University Library, MS Gen. 1457' without further comment. Archibald Campbell went through Gillies's papers after he died: see NLS, MS22101, ff. 174, 179.

44 'Letters of Robert Reid', in *Piper & Drummer*, vol.15, no 1, November 1997, pp.32–3.

45 *PS*, ix.247, 269; xi,.353. It was not included amongst the manuscript sources used by the Society in Cannon, *General Preface*. An account of the manuscript by Archibald Campbell did appear, however, in 'A Checklist of Bagpipe Music Manuscripts held in the National Library of Scotland. Prepared by The Historical Committee of The Piobaireachd Society. 1986. Part 2', *PT*, vol.38. no. 8, May 1986, pp.44–7, (44).

After 1925 time had increasingly taken its toll on the representatives of the performer community who remembered how the music had been played in the days before the Society, and who were in a position to question Campbell's settings. The musical literalism promoted by the Piobaireachd Society had been entrenched for nearly a generation and had begun to sound 'normal'.[46] Since its editor alone had access to all the sources, it was impossible to mount a challenge to the scores on the basis of the written evidence. Senior players like John MacDonald and Willie Ross had contractual and other ties with the Society which made it difficult for them to oppose it directly. In any case, the livelihood of each depended ultimately on his ability to equip professional pupils to win major prizes at competitions, where the Society's scores were the set texts and the chief judges were likely to be either J. P. Grant or Archibald Campbell or both. And there seems little doubt that this affected what they taught. John MacDonald instructed pupils to play certain things one way while he himself played another, and did not explain why.[47] One source records that Willie Ross's mother had interrupted him 'shouting and banging her walking stick on the floor. "Rubbish," she yelled. "Do you tell me my son is teaching you that rubbish?"' and that Willie Ross had said '"You know, my mother is quite right. But you say you hope some day to compete and if you want to get prizes that's the way you must play that tune."'[48] G. S. McLennan 'taught others the Piobaireachd Society approach so that they would not be condemned' while maintaining his own style. But, as a result of his wartime service, he died, aged 45, in 1929 and the leading performer voice of the younger generation was lost.[49] Those who continued to protest publicly were branded as 'mavericks' and marginalised.[50]

As the 1930s progressed there was unrest in the upper echelons of the Piobaireachd

46 See, for example, 'Pipe-Major Meldrum on Champions Past and Present. A Veteran Piper's Reminiscences. Part 3', *OT*, 13/7/1940, p.3, on how timing of grounds had become more bookish and unmusical during his lifetime.

47 R. B. Nicol in conversation with the writer. See also, George Moss, 'Ceol Mor Playing – Old and New Styles', *PT*, vol 8, no.11, August 1956, pp.18–19: 'The style played by Johnnie MacDonald in his youth was very different from, and more correct than, the style played and taught by him in later life'. See also, 'Piobaireachd Playing', *PT*, vol 9, no.8, May 1957, pp.6–7, by the same writer, launching a fierce attack on MacDonald for compromising the traditional style. For a comment on the innate variety of MacDonald's interpretations with the implication that this was a characteristic of a traditionally-trained master, see Frank Richardson: 'He certainly taught his pupils differently at different times. If you went back to him some seven years later as I once or twice did he would teach you something quite different . . . in certain moods he wanted you to play it thus and then the mood had changed in five years and he had changed his mind entirely about how he wished you to play it.' quoted in Campbell, 'History of the Piobaireachd Society', p.44.

48 'James Matheson, Lairg,' by I. MacKay, *PT*, vol. 42, no. 10, July 1990, pp.21–2 (21).

49 Graham and MacRae, ii, p.xi

50 See David Murray, 'The Maverick: George Moss 1903–1990', in *The Voice*, Spring 1997, pp.31–35.

Society about the editorial methods of the second series and their departure from traditional idiom. But here, too, opposition was stifled. In February 1938, Somerled MacDonald, a founding member of the Society, senior judge, and one of the best amateur players of his generation, wrote despairingly to Seton Gordon:

> . . . I have been much distressed at the way things have gone . . . Some years ago I did get together a few notes (perhaps a little more than that) upon the subject generally, including methods of teaching by some of the old masters . . . [but] any book that I wrote would be ridiculed at once . . . the whole thing really has its origin in jealousy . . .
>
> Kilberry . . . will pocket my knowledge at least he has never acknowledged that I know anything whereas . . . the West coast piper lore that he has emanated . . . mostly from my cousin Kenneth Cameron who was my pupil . . .
>
> Of course it became known that I was writing a book upon the pipes and I think Hitler and Mussolini [Archibald Campbell and J. P. Grant] wish to discredit me as an authority.
>
> Why should a man like Campbell be allowed to constitute himself the one and only authority. Why should I have to listen to a 'running commentary' on what the piper competing is playing, when I know perfectly well that I could teach the said commentator who cannot even finger the Chanter . . .
>
> . . . all this has happened through an ignorant man – Kilberry – taking too much upon himself and not submitting the music to an expert John MacDonald for correction.
>
> The whole of the music put out by the present committee and indeed ever since Kilberry became secretary must be scrapped. It is wrong, and most flagrantly wrong . . . I met John MacDonald yesterday . . .
>
> He is justly very perturbed at their conduct and says that if he (John) were to die Kilberry could say anything he liked . . .
>
> John MacDonald . . . [states that] . . . all the music is wrong and that Sandy Cameron did not give it to him [Archibald Campbell] as he says . . .[51]

Somerled MacDonald sought with Gordon's support to lay a resolution before the Society's Annual General Meeting

> to the effect that the recent publications of the Piob. Soc. have given general dissatisfaction to the pipers as the music differs considerably from the way it has been handed down to them . . . the Piob. Soc. is not carrying out that which it was intended for viz. – the correction of the tunes and research. The whole thing is done by an ignorant man in Secret . . .
>
> Unless something is done now the Piobaireachd will be lost. John MacDonald and a few others must be made members of the Society.[52]

51 Somerled Macdonald to Seton Gordon; Seton Gordon Papers, General Correspondence 1936–8, NLS, Acc.7451 (5), 10/2/1938, 30/8/1938.
52 *Ibid.*

This depended on John MacDonald's willingness to rescue the Society from its predicament, but he doubted that his advice would be acted upon and he was well aware of what had already been done in the names of Sandy Cameron and John MacDougall Gillies. In any case, he seriously questioned the ability of conventional staff notation to represent the music and thought that merely tinkering with the time values of the Society settings was unlikely to be effective.[53] Writing to Seton Gordon he said:

I don't see why the P.S. Music Committee do so much altering of the tunes they publish. A. Campbell says in the notes that Gillies performed with the rest on the final note [of 'The Little Spree']. Gillies and I had a few words about this about 26 years ago. I asked how he played it his reply was that he didn't play the tune. They have other alterations in other tunes with which I am not too happy, and in my opinion they dont add to the beauty of the melodies, and unfortunately these go down to posterity as the correct settings . . . Piobaireachd playing will soon become like the 'Gaelic', it will go so far from the original that it wont recover . . .

I am pleased you are attending the Music Committee Meeting of the P.S. but I would not like you to bring up a motion that I should be consulted in the settings of the tunes or anything in connection with their publications. I don't know who constitutes the Music Committee, but they have already done some things I would not wish to have my name associated with . . .

To me, it seems quite evident, from results of the last 15 years that the preservation of our ancient and traditional music, with all its beautiful and melodious airs, and sentiment, has passed into the wrong hands, and it will take a long time, if ever, before it can be restored to its original standard . . .[54]

Despite his high profile within the Piobaireachd Society, Archibald Campbell had limited personal contact with piping in Scotland. On his return from India, he settled in the south of England and kept himself informed through a network of correspondents. He had seldom heard John MacDonald play since before the Great War, but he was anxious to tap his knowledge and channelled a stream of enquiries through Seton Gordon.[55] It is not clear whether MacDonald was aware of the source of these or the ultimate destination of his replies, but in a bid to counter the damage being done by the printed scores, he stepped up his teaching

53 Apparently he thought that time signatures and bar lines should be omitted: Archibald Campbell to Seton Gordon, NLS, Acc.7451, General Correspondence, 1945–50, 2/9/1948.

54 Seton Gordon Papers, NLS, Acc.5640/2 (1), 11/9/1938, ff.3–4; 13/1/1939, f.9; 30/3/1939 f.10; 8/9/1940, f.17; see also, 2/7/1941, f.25.

55 *Ibid.*, NLS, Acc.7451, General Correspondence, 1927–9, Archibald Campbell to Seton Gordon, 11/4/1929: 'Many thanks for your letter telling me what John MacDonald says. I will place it in the file of Mary Macleod as a piece of evidence to assist in confuting the anti-high G heretics . . . It will be very helpful if you can send my anything else hereafter that J.M. may say about any tune'.

activities, aiming to build a corps of master players, including R. U. Brown, R. B. Nicol, and Donald MacLeod, equipped to resist further encroachment of the bookish Society style.[56] Campbell in the meantime privately attempted to disparage MacDonald and undermine his standing as an authority.[57]

But there was another major obstacle to the supremacy of Campbell's interpretations – General Charles Simeon Thomason. His book was on the record, and, although scarce, could still be consulted. The General's personal authority was great. He had an extensive knowledge of the written record and had been the leading spokesman of the Cameron school, having had long-term personal contact with most of the Cameron family, which Archibald Campbell had not. He could not easily be dismissed as an ignoramus, or as a mere book expert devoid of practical knowledge. Yet the account he offered of the music in the pages of *Ceol Mor* was significantly different from that presented in the *Piobaireachd Society's Collection*, as the *Oban Times* reviewer had noticed at once on the publication of the first volume of the Society's new series in 1925.[58]

Campbell claimed to have been 'intimately acquainted with General Thomason, and was privileged to acquire "inside information" on every detail concerning [*Ceol Mor*]'.[59] He played at Thomason's funeral at Grantown-on-Spey in 1911 and shortly afterwards was allowed to go through the General's papers, as a result of which several documents including the Thomason and Ballindalloch MSS came into his possession.[60] In the 'Introduction' to *The Kilberry Book of Ceol Mor*, Campbell's personal anthology published by the Piobaireachd Society in 1948 (which will be considered in Chapter 20), he offered an apparently generous assessment of Thomason's work as a 'wonderful production', and commended his 'conspicuous intellectual ability, fine musical taste, and sound judgement', declaring that 'The two great names of the 19th and 20th centuries' history of piping are Angus Mackay and General Thomason'.[61] In an

56 *Ibid.*, Acc.5640/2 (1), 18/7/1940, f.14; 5/8/1940, f.15; 23/5/1941, ff.23–4.

57 *Ibid.*, Acc.7451, General Correspondence, Archibald Campbell to Seton Gordon, 23/10/1947, dismissing leading John MacDonald pupils as unimpressive performers; and 24/6/1948: 'Poor [R. U.] Brown . . . It is very disturbing that so admirable a person and so keen a devotee of Ceol Mor should drag his tunes so lamentably. But that is the way with all John MacDonald's pupils. It is very melancholy. I have never heard a pupil of John Macdonald play the least like him . . . Sandy Cameron was a more successful teacher. I have heard pupils of his in the nineties make some good jobs. Those were the days in which John MacDonald was usually among the 'also rans'. Duff said to me the other day that in those days John MacDonald habitually 'broke down'.

58 'Piobaireachd. A New Publication Issued by The Piobaireachd Society', 6/2/1926, p.3.

59 Campbell, *Kilberry Book*, 'Introduction', p.12. It is odd, therefore, that Campbell apparently did not know that Thomason had enjoyed extensive access to Angus MacKay's MSS thanks to transcripts and correspondence for many years before the publication of *Ceol Mor*: see *Kilberry Book*, 'Introduction', p.13.

60 These were deposited by Campbell's heirs in the Library of the University of Glasgow in 1977.

61 Campbell, *Kilberry Book*, 'Introduction' p.13.

adjacent section of the 'Introduction', however, he set forth the 'great name's' deficiencies at considerable length, claiming that:

(a) The author was not a good player. He was never properly taught, because he never had the opportunity of being so. His weakness on the practical side is abundantly clear from the number of non-existent note groups for which he was at pains to devise symbols.

(b) Too much reliance was placed on Donald Mackay . . . [who] was not regarded by his contemporaries as a great player or authority. MacDougall Gillies told the writer that Donald Cameron accepted him as a pupil for the sake of his father and uncle, but was never satisfied with him . . .

(c) General Thomason necessarily was out of touch with Scotland and the pipers there when the book was compiled . . . and he had actually heard played by experts a very few of the tunes which he recorded.

(d) Not knowing of the survival of Angus MacKay's MS., he commenced his work on Donald McDonald's productions which in many details are faulty, and he contracted a habit of emending on conjectural grounds . . .

(e) He was too intolerant of anomalous exceptions to rules and of apparent irregularities . . . and his piping education had not been complete enough to enable him to appreciate the presence of these where they occur in piobaireachd music . . .

(f) Instead of then devoting himself to a thorough revision of Ceol Mor, he branched off into an investigation of the pipe scale, and . . . wasted his abilities over matters which were beyond his means and his capacity . . .[62]

Brief words of extravagant praise were offset by detailed and destructive criticism, and there seems little doubt which was calculated to leave the stronger impression in the reader's mind.[63]

By the time these words were written, General Thomason had been dead for thirty years and Archibald Campbell had reached a position of apparently unassailable power in piping. Frank Richardson was to write: 'Kilberry and Rothiemurchus – Rothiemurchus and Kilberry – probably few pipers today can imagine the extent to which these two giants of the piping world ruled the roost in their heyday. Both men of the Law, their word was law to pipers'.[64] By the time of his death in 1963, Campbell was 'Universally regarded as the greatest living authority on the bagpipe, its history, and its music',[65] 'one of the great

---

62 Campbell, *Kilberry Book*, 'Introduction' pp.12–13.
63 There was also fairly frequent disparaging comment about Thomason in the notes to the Society's published *Collection*. See for example vol.v, 140, 142; vol. vi, 165, 173, 191; vol.vii, 198, 202.
64 MacNeill and Richardson, p.108.
65 J. Graham Campbell of Shirvan, 'Archibald Campbell of Kilberry', *PT*, vol.15, no.9, June 1963, pp.8–9 (8).

authorities on *piobaireachd*,[66] deemed to possess 'a major intellect' and commended for his 'scholarship and lucidity',[67] whose *Kilberry Book* 'could be recommended without reservation to the general musical reader'.[68]

66 Collinson, *Bagpipe*, p.146.
67 D. J. S. Murray, 'Foreword', to Campbell, *Sidelights*, p.3.
68 Cannon, *Highland Bagpipe*, p.171.

19

'Return from the Cave of Gold':
The Creation of the MacCrimmon Metaphor

The dedication of a commemorative cairn at Boreraig in August 1933 marked the climax of nearly a century of growing concentration on the MacCrimmons as the fountainhead of authenticity in piping. This was reflected in the creation of new bodies like the MacCrimmon Memorial Trust (1914) and the Clan MacCrimmon Society (1936), whose activities helped to re-shape the Highland past and give an aura of legitimacy to contemporary institutions. Both enjoyed over-lapping membership with the upper echelons of the Piobaireachd Society.[1]

The MacCrimmon family were hailed as the inventors of piobaireachd as a form and creators of the classic repertoire. The other teaching dynasties progressively faded into the background and a writer like W. L. Manson could declare in *The Highland Bagpipe, its History Literature and Music* that:

> The MacCrimmons were never excelled or even equalled as pipers and
> composers of pipe music. Their productions were all peculiarly appropriate to
> the instrument, and remain its classics to this day. They produced no second-
> rate pieces, and this was the secret of their success. But they did not compose
> off-hand, as any good piper can compose a strathspey or quickstep. They took
> a long time to a tune, sometimes several months, but they made it perfect.
> Strathspeys and quicksteps they looked on as inferior music, and all their
> attention was devoted to pibrochs. They were very studious and practised a
> great deal, rising early in the mornings to play by themselves.[2]

How he can have known most of this is unclear, since there is little direct evidence for any of it. But his remarks reflected beliefs which had become widely current since James Logan had launched the process in the letterpress portions of MacKay's *Ancient Piobaireachd.*[3] The MacCrimmons were increasingly conceived by 'edu-cated' commentators as a kind of officer class among traditional musicians, proud, highly educated descendants of the Druids whose mystical meditative techniques they had retained and practised in the creation of ceòl mór.[4]

Yet there was little agreement about what the MacCrimmons taught and how they taught it. How long, for example, did a course at the college of Boreraig last? Five to

---

1 Senior Piobaireachd Society member who were also members of these other bodies included John Bartholomew, J. Graham Campbell of Shirvan, J. P. Grant, and Seton Gordon, see 'Clan MacCrimmon Society', from G. C. B. Poulter, *OT,* 14/11/1936, p.3.
2 Manson, p.268.
3 See above, pp.156–8.
4 Seton Gordon, *The Charm of Skye the Winged Isle* (Lond., 1929), pp. 107–16. For bardic

eight years said some; seven, said others, but often much less; a few held out for twelve years with a certificate at the end.[5] There was similar dispute about when the MacCrimmon college had been founded, and for how long it had continued in existence. Archibald Campbell suggested in 1948 that its founder may have been Patrick Òg MacCrimmon some time after the year 1670, giving it a lifespan of rather less than a hundred years.[6] Seumas MacNeill, writing in 1987, was sure that the college must have been 'a mature and vigorous institution by the middle of the seventeenth century'.[7] Both estimates seem modest in the light of the declaration of the MacCrimmon Memorial Trust in 1933 that the school went back to 1500 at least.[8]

A wide-ranging search for information by individuals and organisations like the Clan MacCrimmon Society turned up nineteenth and twentieth century MacCrimmons in considerable numbers all over the world. It appeared, too, that the name had once been quite common in Glendale in Skye, and in Glenelg on the adjacent mainland, with outposts in Speyside and Aberdeenshire.[9] But it proved difficult to trace the all-important Boreraig family with any degree of certainty beyond the later years of the seventeenth century. The

cont'd   compositional techniques, see Thomson, *Gaelic Scotland,* pp.258–9. For the MacCrimmons as technically superior and their compositions as possessing a distinctive majesty and grandeur, see 'Dr. K. N. MacDonald and Bagpipe playing', from John Johnston of Coll, *OT,* 12/9/1896, p.3. For the MacCrimmons as fiddle players, and also harpers, see 'The Glenelg MacCrimmons', from Donald MacCrimmon, 6/8/1910, p.3, and 'The Great Highland Bagpipe and its Music', from Charles Bannatyne, 10/6/1911, p.3.

5 Leader, 'Bagpipe Music', *OT,* 15/2/1896, p.4; MacNeill and Richardson, pp.23–4; Charles Bannatyne, 'Pipes, Pipers, and Piobaireachd. Part III', *OT,* 16/5/1903, p.6; see also Collinson, *Bagpipe,* p.155. For details of the supposed certificate, see Gordon, *Charm of Skye,* p.117.

6 Campbell, *Kilberry Book,* 'Introduction', p.9.

7 MacNeill and Richardson, p.22.

8 See MacLeod, *MacCrimmons of Skye,* p.142. Fred MacLeod was one of the originators of the Trust, and was largely responsible for the celebrations on Skye to mark the unveiling of the monument. For further details of the Trust, its membership and activities, see *OT,* 'The MacCrimmon Memorial', 17/5/1913, p.3; 6/12/1913, p.3; 7/3/1914, p.3; 21/6/1930, p.3; 16/8/1930, p.3; 5/9/1931, p.3; 6/4/1932, p.3; 23/4/1932, p.3; 29/7/1933, p.5; 5/8/1933, p.5; 19/8/1933, pp.3,5.

9 See 'The MacCrimmon Ancestry', and 'The Glenelg MacCrimmons,' from Donald McCrimmon, *OT,* 9/7/1910, p.3, 6/8/1910, p.3; 'The MacCrimmons', from T. D. M., 11/12/1915, p.3, which gives the story of the rout of the MacCrimmons at Glaisbheinn in Glenelg in considerable detail; 'The MacCrimmons', from W. A. Tod, 19/6/1920, p.3, gives details of the Speyside and Aberdeenshire MacCrimmons; see also, 'The MacCrimmon Genealogy', from G. C. B. Poulter, 17/11/1934, p.3. 'The Glenelg MacCrimmons' from G. C. B. Poulter, and 'The MacCrimmon Genealogy Evidence from Dates and Times', from G. F. Ross, 1/12/1934, p.3, with details of how tunes dedicated to MacLeods or MacLeod relatives were automatically being assigned to MacCrimmon composers; 'The MacCrimmon Genealogy', from G. C. B. Poulter, 29/12/34, p.3, and from G. F. Ross, 12/1/1935, p.3; 'Clan MacCrimmon Society', from G. C. B. Poulter, 14/11/1936, p.3.

search was hampered by gaps in the family papers of the MacLeods and the records of the parish of Duirinish, which stretched from Waternish to Idrigill and included both Dunvegan and Glendale. In 1845, the minister, Archibald Clerk, stated that there were none in existence for a period further back than about thirty years.[10]

The MacCrimmon succession seems first to have been committed to paper by James Logan in 1838, setting out the lineage accepted by most later accounts, and stretching from the early 17th to the early 19th century as follows:

Donald Mòr
|
Patrick Mòr,
|
Patrick Og,
|
Malcolm
|
Iain Dubh.

The sources of this information appear to have been entirely traditional, as were most of those used by Fred.T. MacLeod of the MacCrimmon Memorial Trust almost a century later.[11] In his book, The *MacCrimmons of Skye*, he stated:

I am inclined to place the commencement of the MacCrimmon era, so far as their relationship with the MacLeods of Dunvegan is concerned, approximately as 1500, and the termination thereof as 1822. One of my reasons for doing so is that we find that in 1651 one of the family was publicly acknowledged as the Prince of Pipers. In the old chronicle detailing this incident the name of the piper upon whom this honour was bestowed is given as John Macgurmen (MacCrimmon), which I believe to be a mistake for Patrick MacCrimmon, he who composed the well-known port, 'I gave a kiss to the hand of the King'. If the old adage is true that it took seven years of a

10 'Parish of Duirinish', *The New Statistical Account of Scotland,* vol.14, Inverness – Ross and Cromarty, (Edinburgh, 1845), p.341.
11 MacLeod cited Norman MacLeod's, *Caraid nan Gaidheal*; MacLeod of Gesto's *Collection of Pibaireachd or Pipe Tunes*; C. S. Thomason's *Ceol Mor*, W. L. Manson's *The Highland Bagpipe*, Archibald Clerk in the *New Statistical Account*, 'Fionn' (Henry Whyte)'s *Martial Music of the Clans*, and Dr. Neil Ross's articles 'Ceol-mor agus Clann MhicCruimein', in the *Celtic Monthly*, which MacLeod pronounced 'the most valuable and reliable' of these sources. Ross extended the MacCrimmon line back to Finlay a' Bhreacain and made many attributions of specific tunes to named MacCrimmon composers (which were widely accepted subsequently) on the authority of oral testimony collected from unnamed sources in Skye.

man's life and seven generations of pipers before him to make a perfect piper,
the date 1500 is by no means too remote. While not dogmatising upon the
point, I offer the following list as comprising the members of the family who
held office between the years 1500 and 1800: –

Finlay a' Bhreacain.
Ian Odhar
Donald Mór
Patrick Mór
Patrick Og
Malcolm
Donald Bàn
Angus Og
Ian Dubh
Donald Ruadh.[12]

The 'old chronicle' abruptly amended by MacLeod is in fact one of the rare
contemporary written sources, recording a contest of musicians at the royal camp
near Stirling in 1651 in the presence of the youthful Charles II:

> Never was Prince more taken up with an army as our King was, especially
> with the Scotch Highlanders, whom he tearmed the flour of his forces . . .
> There was great competition betuixt the trumpets in the army: one Axell, the
> Earl of Hoomes trumpeter, carried it by the King's own decision! The next
> was anent the pipers; but the Earle of Sutherlands domestick carried it of all
> the camp, for non contended with him. All the pipers in the army gave John
> Macgurmen [MacCrimmon] the van, and acknowledged him for their patron
> in chiefe. It was pretty in a morning [the King] in parad viewing the
> regiments and bragads. He saw no less then 80 pipers in a crould bareheaded,
> and John M'gyurmen in the middle, covered. He asked What society that
> was? It was told his Majesty: Sir, yow are our King, and yonder old man in
> the midle is the Prince of Pipers. He cald him by name, and comeing to the
> King, kneeling, his Majesty reacht him his hand to kiss; and instantly played
> an extemporanian port, Fuoris Pòòge i spoge i Rhì', I got a kiss of the Kings
> hand; of which he and they all were vain.[13]

If John MacCrimmon was indeed the leading representative of his family in the
middle of the seventeenth century then something was wrong somewhere. There
was no mention of such a person in Logan's account which had Patrick, not
John, playing before King Charles.[14] So that when a real MacCrimmon appeared

12 MacLeod, *MacCrimmons of Skye*, pp.30–31.
13 James Fraser, *Chronicles of the Frasers*, ed., William MacKay (Edinr., 1905), pp.379–80.
14 MacKay, *Ancient Piobaireachd*, p.14, 'Historical and Traditional Notes', p.4.

in the historical record, he was promptly edited out again to preserve the accepted pattern.[15]

A substantial list of tunes became attached to the MacCrimmon name during the later 19th and 20th centuries, largely by appropriating anything relating to the MacLeods, their relatives and dependants, and notable events in the history of Skye. But the earlier sources show little unanimity about who composed what. Joseph MacDonald had spoken merely of the 'first Masters & Composers in the Islands of Sky & Mull'.[16] Donald MacDonald offered a precise attribution for just one piece, 'Too Long in this Condition', which he, or his mediator, claimed to have been composed by 'Great Peter McCruimen Piper to McLeod of Dunvegan Isle of Skye, After being Stripped of all his Clothes by the English at the Battle of Sheriff-Muir in 1715'.[17] But this was two generations after Patrick Mór was supposed to have flourished according to Logan.[18] And there were other stories attached to the tune suggesting at least one alternative composer and date.[19] Other attributions by Donald MacDonald were rather vague and general. Altogether five tunes out of the seventy one in MacDonald's published book and MSS. – less than 10% of the total – were identified in any way as being MacCrimmon compositions.[20]

In MacKay's *Ancient Piobaireachd* (1838), James Logan attributed twelve tunes to five MacCrimmon composers as follows:

15 There is at least one other story about the tune, which makes no mention of Patrick or John or indeed of any MacCrimmon, assigning it to quite a different period and composer: 'Fuair mi pòg o lamh mo Rìgh, was composed at Holyrood in 1745 by "Ewen MacDomnhuill Bhuidhe", a Macmillan from Glendessary and piper to Lochiel, on seeing his chief kiss Charles Edward's hand at a levee held in the palace of his ancestors by that Prince a day or two after the victory at Gladsmuir'. Quoted in 'An Old Pipe Tune', from 'Fionn' (Henry Whyte), *OT*, 23/5/1908, p.3. For an attribution of the tune to Donald Mór MacCrimmon see 'An Old Pipe Tune', from 'Fionn', 20/6/1908, p.3.

16 Cannon, *Joseph MacDonald*, p.25.

17 MacDonald, *Ancient Martial Music*, pp.34–37.

18 C.1640–1670 are the dates usually accepted by later commentators. See MacNeill, *Piobaireachd*, p.37.

19 See, for example, 'Celtic Scraps', by 'Fionn' in *OT*, 7/6/1890, p.3, for a tale linking the tune with Donald Mór MacCrimmon in the early seventeenth century and featuring the traditional verse: "'S fhada mar so, 's fhada mar so, / 'S fhada mar so tha mi; / 'S fhada mar so gun bhiadh gun deoch, / An tigh mo charaid Mhic Aoidh tha mi . . . Too long am I thus, too long am I thus, too long in this condition; I am too long wanting food and drink in the house of my friend MacKay'.

20 'An Groatha The Groat' was 'Composed by McCruimen Piper to McLeod of Dunvegan on the Christening of Rory More the Chief's Son'; 'The Lament for the Union' was 'composed by Macriumen'; 'MacLeod's Rowing Piobaireachd' is given as 'Composed by his piper, (Macriumen) the greatest of all pipers in the known world'. MacDonald attributes 'The Lament for Donald Ban', an historically recent tune, as follows: 'This long and grand piece, was composed by his brother, in the Isle of Skye, when he heard that Donald was killed, at the battle of Culloden in 1746." Donald MacDonald MS, NLS. MS, 1680, f.2; see also ff.4, 5.

Donald Dughal Mackay	
MacLeod's Rowing Tune	
MacDonald's Salute	Donald Mór
MacLeod's Controversy	
The Earl of Ross's March	
I got a Kiss from the King's Hand (dated 1651)	
Lament for John Garve M'Leod (dated c.1648)	Patrick Mór
The Lament for the Children	
The Pretty Dirk	Patrick Òg
The Half Finished Piobaireachd	Patrick Òg and John Dall Mackay
MacCrimmon will Never Return (dated 1745)	Donald Bàn
The Glen is Mine	John MacCrimmon.

But only one of Logan's list, namely 'MacLeod's Rowing Tune', coincided with Donald MacDonald's. A number of MacDonald attributions were queried in Angus MacKay's MS, and there are many tunes nowadays included in the MacCrimmon canon, such as 'A Flame of Wrath for Squinting Peter' which are not ascribed to them either by MacDonald or MacKay.[21] Niel MacLeod of Gesto did attribute the 'Flame of Wrath' to a MacCrimmon source, but not to Donald Mór MacCrimmon as later writers did, and in any case Gesto's tune is now known as 'Macdonald's or 'Duntroon's Salute', and is quite different from the one which later bore the 'Flame of Wrath' title.[22] Only three of Gesto's twenty tunes taken from the dictation of Iain Dubh MacCrimmon are directly attributed to MacCrimmon composers. Of the two hundred and forty two tunes in Angus MacKay's published book and manuscript collection, the percentage assigned to MacCrimmon composers is in low single figures. In addition, many of what later generations have come to consider the greatest tunes in the tradition are not ascribed to MacCrimmon sources by either MacDonald or MacKay.

The theory that antiquity was the defining characteristic of Highland institutions, had been applied to the MacCrimmon family from the days of James Logan onwards, and was visible in a tendency to push the line of succession ever further back into the mists of time. The line of argument used

---

21 NLS, MS 3753/4, i, 75, 85,153.
22 'Remarks by Captain MacLeod', *Celtic Magazine*, pp.434–5; *Pibaireachd or Pipe Tunes*, pp.25–6, MacKay MS, ii, 119.

to show that there must have been a college at Boreraig a century and a half before 1650, could be used to extend the MacCrimmon genealogy even further back if the writer were so minded. Clearly, if the institution existed in 1500, the MacCrimmons must already have achieved a degree of eminence, implying several previous generations of master players and teachers and permitting a further backward somersault into a past constructed almost wholly in terms of conjecture.

During the rest of the 19th century, there had been only one further significant addition to the MacCrimmon story claiming the status of fact. The source for this was the Rev. Dr. Norman MacLeod 'Caraid nan Gaidheal' [Friend of the Gael] (1783–1862), father of Norman of the Barony, whose contributions to Highland periodicals such as *Teachdaire Gaelach* (The Gaelic Messenger) *Cuairtear nan Gleann* (The Traveller of the Glens) and *The Mountain Visitor*, had marked a new era in popular Gaelic journalism. In a piece entitled 'Clann 'ic-Cruimein, Pìobairean Dhun-bheagain' later reprinted in his selected writings, he had stated

> Cha robh Pìobairean ann an Albainn cho ainmeil ri Cloinn 'ic Cruimein an Dùin. Fad iomadh linn bha iad 'n am pìobairean aig cinn-fheadhna nan Leòdach. Tha iad ag ràdh gun' d'thàinig a' cheud fhear de a'n ainm so maille ri Mac Leòid o bhaile anns an Eadailt d' am b' ainm *Cremona*. Bu chruitear a bha 's an duine so. Bha e 'n a fhear-ciùil ainmeil 'n a latha 'us 'n a linn féin. Gabh e ainm an àite anns an d'rugadh e; agus na thàinig uaithe, dh' ainmicheadh iad, Clann 'ic-Cruimein.

> [i.e., There were no pipers in Scotland so renowned as the MacCrimmons of the castle. For long ages they were pipers to the lairds of MacLeod. It is said that the first of the name came along with MacLeod from a town in Italy called *Cremona*. This man was a harper. He was a famous man of music in his day and generation. He took the name of the place of his birth and those that came after him took for their name Clann 'ic-Cruimein.][23]

'Caraid nan Gaidheal' had been to Skye and met a MacCrimmon when, as a child, he had accompanied the chief, General Norman MacLeod, homeward bound from military service in America and India. He recorded that:

> On reaching the old Castle of Dunvegan we were met by many of the gentlemen, tacksmen of the MacLeod estates, and MacLeod was welcomed to the home of his fathers by Captain Donald MacCrimmon (the representative

---

23 *Caraid nan Gaidheal (The Friend of the Gael.) A Choice Selection of the Gaelic Writings of Norman MacLeod, DD.* Selected, & Edited by Rev. A. Clerk LL.D. Minister of Kilmallie. With a memoir of the Author by his Son, Norman MacLeod, D.D. of the Barony Parish, Glasgow. (Edinr., 1899), pp.378–382.

of the celebrated MacCrimmon pipers who had for ages been connected with
the family), who had gained his commission and no small share of renown
with his Chief during the American war.

I can never forget the impression which the whole scene made on my
youthful mind, as MacCrimmon struck up 'Fàilte Ruairidh Mhóir', the
famous tune of the Clan.[24]

He spent three months at Dunvegan, and may have heard the Cremona story
there. We know that it was later accepted as true by MacCrimmon descendants
and seems to have been widely current in the Isle of Skye, although how much
this may be due to 'Caraid nan Gaidheal's' own influential published account is
now impossible to say.[25]

In 1910 the tale was given new focus by the startling news from Australia that a
mysterious written history of the MacCrimmons had been discovered and that a
certain Simon Fraser, a whip-plaiter of Warnambool, Victoria, had mastered its
secrets. Fraser claimed that Captain Niel MacLeod of Gesto, editor of *Pibereach
or pipe tunes, as taught verbally by the McCrimmen pipers in Skye to their apprentices*
(Edinr., 1828), had written an earlier and much deeper work entitled 'The
History of the MacCrimmons and the Great Pipe' giving a complete account of
the family and its two canntaireachd systems: the imperfect 'old' system which
Gesto had used in the 1828 collection and a 'new' improved notation introduced
about the middle of the seventeenth century by Patrick Mór MacCrimmon
following a period of study in Italy. The claim was that Gesto's book had reached
proof stage in 1826 but been 'suppressed'. Only two copies survived. And Fraser
possessed one of them. The story unfolded in stages in the correspondence
columns of the *Oban Times* between the spring of 1910 and the eve of the Great
War. The first letter said:

There are very few persons alive now who know that Neil Macleod, Gesto,
printed a book called 'The History of the Maccrimmons and the Great Pipe',
in the year 1826. Unfortunately this book contained opinions offensive to a
good many people of that time, and Macleod's friends would not let him
publish it. There was a complete history of the Maccrimmon pipers in this
book, and it contained 50 of their best pibrochs. It also contained their old
system of sheantaireachd, and also a new system perfected by Patrick Mhor
Maccrimmon on his return from Italy in or about the middle of the
seventeenth century. Had this book been published, I have no doubt that the
ordinary system would never have been adopted. The book contained
complete scales and time marks, and was very easy to read and understand. I

24 *Ibid.*, pp.133–4.
25 See 'The MacCrimmon Ancestry' from Fred T. MacLeod, *OT*, 23/4/1910, p.3, which
   while withholding support from the Cremona story, reports its widespread diffusion in
   Skye, and gives an interesting example from St. Kilda.

have only seen two copies of it, and they are both now out of existence.

Macleod, being offended, published another book about 1828, a copy of which I have, and I have another of the same book printed in the year 1880 by J.& R. Glen of Edinburgh. The tunes in this book are in the old system, and all kinds of devices are used to mislead, so that only an expert can translate the tunes. Different beats, which mean the same thing, occur; lines are left out; some tunes of 16 lines have only 12; beats are misplaced; some lines are not complete, and so on. As he said on more than one occasion: 'I have given them something to puzzle them'.[26]

Fraser claimed to have been taught by Peter Bruce, son of Sandy Bruce, who had migrated to Australia in the middle years of the nineteenth century. The suggestion was that the line of teaching had become corrupted in Scotland and preserved in purity only in Australia in the family of Simon Fraser.

Further tantalising details quickly emerged: the MacCrimmons, said Fraser, had left Italy during the fifteenth century, and settled in Ireland. There they had invented piobaireachd and the original canntaireachd system used by Gesto. The later 'new' MacCrimmon system, hitherto lost to the world, would shortly be published in Fraser's forthcoming book.[27]

But the book did not appear. According to Fraser, there were 'jealousies' on the part of other pipers and the expense of printing the special notation proved unexpectedly high. However he continued to elaborate his theories in the *Oban Times* making ever more detailed and ambitious claims to reinforce his personal authority. He was claiming by the late summer of 1911, for example, that his father had acted as amanuensis to Gesto when Iain Dubh MacCrimmon was dictating tunes to him and had passed on all his knowledge to his son Simon, so that the latter had a double line of descent from the MacCrimmons, through the Bruces and through the Frasers. And this was not all. He claimed that his mother was a grand-daughter of Charles MacArthur and had possessed the secrets of the MacArthur canntaireachd which she had duly passed on to her son, so that he was heir of the second most prestigious teaching dynasty as well.[28]

Next it emerged why the Gesto volume of 1826 had been suppressed. This, claimed Fraser, was because of religious heresy: 'Gesto did not agree with the clergy as to the numerous creeds that have done a lot of harm to pure Christianity. Like myself, he believed in primitive Christianity, free from theological puzzles and all the different creeds'.[29]

No evidence for any of this was ever produced.

26 'Piobaireachd Society's Music', from Simon Fraser, *OT*, 28/5/1910, p.3. For a collection of piobaireachd settings by Simon Fraser, see Orme, *The Piobaireachd of Simon Fraser*, pp.63 ff.

27 'The Piobairachd', from Simon Fraser, *OT*, 3/9/1910, p.3.

28 'Canntaireachd', from Simon Fraser, *OT*, 23/9/1911, p.3.

29 'Sheantaireachd', from Simon Fraser, *OT*, 23/11/1912, p.3.

Yet Fraser corresponded privately with a number of quite important figures in the piping world who were attracted by his ideas, and did what they could to publicise them. Thus it was the distinguished Highland music editor and authority on puirt-a-beul, Dr. K. N. MacDonald – Gesto's own grandson – who signalled the next development in this increasingly heady cocktail of conspiracy theory and cryptographic fantasy. In a piece in the *Oban Times* published in the spring of 1913, and entitled 'The Early History of the MacCrimmons. Related by Themselves to Captain MacLeod of Gesto' K. N. MacDonald gave further precise and colourful details of the MacCrimmons' supposed Italian descent, supplied by Simon Fraser from the alleged volume of 1826 which, it should be recollected, nobody, least of all K. N. MacDonald, ever actually saw:

> Giordano Bruno, an Italian philosopher and Pantheist, one of the boldest and most original thinkers of the age, was born at Nola about 1550 . . . He embraced the doctrines of Calvin at Geneva, but free discussion not being in favour there, he went to Paris, where he gave lectures on philosophy, when he made many bitter enemies . . . he returned to Padua in 1592, and went afterwards to Venice, where he was arrested in 1598 by the Inquisition, and sent to Rome . . . and on the 17th of February, 1600, he was burned at the stake as a heretic . . .
>
> A relation of his, Petrus Bruno, about or before this time, left Cremona, in Italy, and went over to Ireland and settled there. He had to leave on account of his religious opinions. He . . . believed strongly in primitive Christianity, and he got access to some original documents which, to his mind, proved that the Bible had been tampered with about the beginning of the second century, and he held, therefore, that creeds have nothing to do with the true teachings of Christ.
>
> Gesto was disappointed that his book of 1826 was interfered with by friends, and determined to leave a nut behind him . . . that would be difficult to crack. 'The Lament for the Laird of Annapole', No. 18 in his book of 1828, is in reality a lament for Bruno the philosopher. It will be noticed how much the letters r u n o are used in this particular tune, [the letters do not appear in this combination anywhere in the tune] which is pretty stiff to translate and play; also 'trun' and 'drun' in the finish and the 'hi die dru' beats, which have puzzled so many. Well, to shorten the story of Petrus Bruno, he took the name of 'Cremmon', and added 'Mac' to it. Whether this is true or not, Gesto did not invent it, and it was for mentioning it that some of his friends prevailed upon him not to publish the work, which was a great loss to lovers of piobaireachd . . . Petrus, it is said, was the original inventor of the 'Sheantaireachd', or pipers' language, which was used by the MacCrimmons not only as music, but to conceal their religious opinions as well . . .
>
> About the middle of the seventeenth century Patrick Mór went to Italy to study, and to see if he could prove the truth of Petrus Bruno's contentions regarding tampering with the Scriptures. He found out what led him to

believe that all that Petrus said was correct . . . It was for having mentioned this in his first book that brought Gesto into conflict with some people of his time, and he deferred to their wishes.[30]

The final version of the story was given by G. C. B. Poulter, the founder of the Clan MacCrimmon Society, in his book *The MacCrimmon Family*. Poulter stated that:

> Petrus is credited with having invented sheantaireachd or the 'piper's language,' which he derived from the Bible; and it is further stated that it was a code by which original copies of the Scriptures were preserved from interference and alteration, the key being in Genesis III. 24: 'So he drove out the man; and he placed at the east of the garden of Eden Cherubims, and a flaming sword which turned every way, to keep the way of the tree of life'. One of the important vocables is 'tre' in various forms. It is said that one method of interpretation of the MacCrimmon music has been handed down by chance through the illness of Mr. Simon Fraser, who became gravely ill as a baby in July, 1853 and at the crisis his mother 'threw up her hands and wailed the Lament for the Children in the vocables'. From that moment he began to recover, and Mrs. Fraser afterwards explained the strange singing to him on condition that he would not divulge it for fifty years . . .
>
> Petrus Bruno is said to have had three sons (1) Pàdruig, who stayed in Ireland, (2) Angus, and (3) Findlay of the Plaid or Finlay a' Bhreacain, otherwise Fionnlagh na Plaide Bàine, who was the father of Iain Odhar MacCrimmon.[31]

Simon Fraser and his disciples were the source of a good deal of the gradual appropriation of the repertoire to supposed MacCrimmon composers. For example, the tune 'Corrienessan's Salute' had been compiled by Dr Charles Bannatyne from a fragment he found amongst Angus MacKay's papers when they came into his possession in 1904, and was published by him in vol.2 of the Piobaireachd Society's first series.[32] By the time it had passed through Fraser's hands, the tune had acquired a new title, 'Cumha na Ceol More – Lament for the Great Music –' and an attribution to Patrick Òg MacCrimmon. It had also picked up a supporting tale to the effect that it was a parody or companion tune to 'The Lament for the Harp Tree' which, although anonymous in all earlier

30 'The Early History of the McCrimmons. Related by Themselves to Captain MacLeod of Gesto. By Dr. K. N. MacDonald', *OT*, 5/4/1913, p.3; see also 'The History of the MacCrimmons', from K. N. MacDonald, 17/5/1913, p.3.

31 George C. B. Poulter and Charles P. Fisher, *The MacCrimmon Family Origin; Music; Iain Odhar; Padruig Mor; Padruig Og; The descendants of Donald Donn from 1740 to 1936*, (Camberley, 1936), pp.7–8.

32 *PS.* (second series), viii, 223–4.

sources – including the MSS of Donald MacDonald and Peter Reid, and Angus MacKay's published book – was attributed by Fraser to Patrick Mór Mac-Crimmon, noting that 'Patrick Og said to his father, "I will compose a tune as near as I can to yours but I will call it 'Lament for the Great Music' – Cumha na Céol Mòr."'[33] 'The Lament for Samuel', anonymous in Donald MacDonald's published book which was the single earlier source for the tune, was attributed to Patrick Òg MacCrimmon by Simon Fraser. 'The Sound of the Waves against the Castle of Duntroon' which appeared anonymously in Peter Reid, Angus MacKay and Colin Cameron's MS, was called by Simon Fraser 'Hector MacLean of Duntroon's Lament – by Patrick Mor MacCrimmon', with the note that 'it is not a warning tune'. This would seen to indicate that Fraser was using Thomason's Ceol Mor as his copy text here where the tune is called 'Duntroon's Warning', the title it also bears in MacKay's MS.[34]

The internal inconsistencies and shifting chronology of the various Fraser-inspired narratives were commented upon at the time by critics like Malcolm MacInnes who declared 'the whole thing is bunkum'.[35] Little evidence was offered for any of it. Fraser's genealogies rested upon mere assertion. He referred frequently to the 'new' improved notation invented by Patrick Mór, but it did not differ very significantly from the 'older' one which he said it had replaced. He claimed to have inherited the large manuscript collection of piobaireachds in canntaireachd notation said by Alexander MacGregor to have been in the possession of Niel MacLeod of Gesto, and to have later sold it to a MacCrimmon descendant in Canada; but no trace of this has subsequently been found.[36] A

33 Orme, pp.129–131. See also MacDonald MS.ff.207–15, Reid MS. ff.3–4, MacKay, *Ancient Piobaireachd*, pp. 85–88. For the first publication of 'Corrienessan' see 'The Piobaireachd Society's Collection. The Notes on the Tunes', from 'Fionn', *OT*, 30/6/ 1906, p.3; and 'The Piobaireachd Society's Publications', from John McLennan, 14/7/ 1906, p.3.

34 Orme, p.161, 173, 182–3. *Ceol Mor*, p.26; MacKay MS, i, 97–100. Fraser's attempts to 'regularise' his texts would seem to indicate a considerable debt to C. S. Thomason. He seems also to have been influenced by Lieut. John McLennan's recent arguments in favour of the minim rather than the crotchet as the basis of piobaireachd metre.

35 'Piobaireachd Canntaireachd and Tosh', from Malcolm MacInnes, *OT*, 26/2/1921, p.3; see also 'The MacCrimmon Genealogy Evidence from Dates and Times', from G. F. Ross, 1/12/1934, p.3. See also Ross's *Some Piobaireachd Studies*, pp.8–19, which accepted and publicised some of Fraser's claims. See 'Letters to and concerning G. F. Ross', Piobaireachd Society Papers, NLS. Acc. 9103/25, A. K. Cameron to William Gray, 21/ 11/1932: 'The notes in G. F. Ross's "Some Piob., Studies" are from the 1826 book. He payed pretty sweet for that!'

36 Orme, p.35. The papers which passed after Fraser's death in 1934 into the possession of A. K. Cameron of Montana (now in the National Library of Scotland, Acc. nos 9613–24), seem to contain nothing resembling this. For a fruitless later search in the United States, see Pearson, 'North American "Piping Fanatic"', pp.183–90. For MacGregor's account of a large canntaireachd collection in Gesto's possession, see pp.139–40.

comparable document, Colin Campbell's Nether Lorn canntaireachd, even in its incomplete form, contained more than sixty tunes not recorded elsewhere. The hundred and seventeen surviving Fraser settings contain virtually nothing which had not appeared previously in written or printed sources. Above all, Fraser was unable to produce an actual copy of the alleged 1826 Gesto volume, claiming that his had been destroyed by children playing in his workshop.[37]

People writing privately to Simon Fraser quickly discovered that the 'secrets' were for sale.[38] Some saw at once what this must mean, but he had a curious ability to tap into deep rooted cultural anxieties amongst his clients and his claims were accepted by a number of otherwise sensible people who had been conditioned to accept the possibility of a lost realm of Celtic lore, a part of whose appeal lay in its magical exemption from the constraints of logic or proof. The mystical conception of canntaireachd as an esoteric language of power, widely current in a diffuse kind of way in the piping world, took on a highly charged and specific form amongst the followers of Simon Fraser, who considered it as a hermetic code, a system of ciphers by means of which religious truths had been darkly bodied forth. Here, for example, is A. K. Cameron of Montana writing to William Gray in November 1931:

> First of all – *and this is private*, mind that – Piob., is not Highland music, but Italian music. See? Now. You are mad, – I suppose. Oh! rest a while till a few things sink in . . . The MacCrimmons were Christians who believed in the Simple teaching of Christ. – free from priestcraft – & Theological Dogma.

---

37 *Poulter*, p.7. For an attempt to make sense of the chronology and to trace Fraser's genealogy of learning from an alternative branch of the MacCrimmon family, namely that of Donald Donn MacCrimmon, see 'The MacCrimmons of Boreraig', from G. C. B. Poulter, *OT*, 23/7/1938, p.3, and for Poulter's eventual rejection of the Cremona story, 5/11/1938, p.3.

38 See, for example, Papers of the Piobaireachd Society, NLS, Acc.9103/8, 'Correspondence, 1895–1928', Robert MacGregor to J. P. Grant of Rothiemurchus, 22/12/1919: 'I have been making a study of the articulate pipe music for several years and wrote Simon Fraser, Australia regarding the Subject, he replied and said that he was the only person alive that knew the System, and that he was afraid the art would be lost, he therefore offered to write all the beats and scales in Canntaireachd for a round little Sum of money Something equal to what would buy two or three of the best piobaireachd books, However I took no heed of him and went on in my own way'. After Fraser's death, A. K. Cameron had to threaten his heirs with legal proceedings in order to recover certain MSS and other papers which he had paid Simon Fraser to annotate or compile: see A. K. Cameron of Montana Papers, N.L.S.MS. 9618 'Miscellaneous scraps of piobaireachds in various hands, inc. Simon Fraser, A. K. Cameron, and Dr. J. D. Ross Watt, c., 1920–1930; letters from John L. MacArthur, and letters to A. K. Cameron in connection with the recovery of his papers from the heirs of Simon Fraser, 1935–8', 79ff. See 9614–5 'J. F. Campbell's pamphlet, inscribed A. K. Cameron, Powderville Montana U.S.A., August 24th 1927', for certain of the sums involved.

They were always at loggerheads with the clergy of their day. Patrick Mor wrote a Treatise of the failings of religion as then taught, – but was afraid to publish it, as it might bring hardship on his family – It was buried with him. – Fraser claims.

Sheanntaireachd means: Sing to Christ. See? And every letter in His name is in this word. Canntaireachd is another mutilation! It is a secret form of singing & playing by which the MacCrimmons were able to worship God in their own manner. – & no one was the wiser. Sheann., is based on Genesis, Chapter 3 verse 24 as a Key in which are the principal vocables of the System and also all the letters used in the system. The time marks are taken from verse 24.

The system is English.

. . . Now, the figure 3 had a deep Theological meaning. It was considered the Perfect nonmutable System because the figure 3 could not be divided.

Now, The Taorluath or '*Tri*' – luadh is a Symbol of the Holy Trinity and its three notes – like the three leaves of the Shamrock are symbolic of the Three figures in the Trinity. *It is Three A notes on the fundamental note of the Chanter.* [this is the theological vindication for the 'redundant' low A] . . . Siubhal means Bochim. – the place of weeping, or the Vail of Tears. See: Judges: – Chapter 2 v.,1.4.5. *Bibles are not all the same.*

See Jeremiah Chapter 48, v 31 & 36.

It is the Weeping Wall of the Jews till this day. Do you begin now to see what Piob., really is? I didn't dare use this information in O[ban]. T[imes]. although I hinted at it. G. F. Ross advised me to keep religion out of the matter entirely, but I cannot see why, because the *truth* & *Secret* of it must be imposed before they begin to understand it.

. . . S. Fraser: – '664 has a deep meaning in MacCrimmon music. – meaning 3 or Trinity, as they knew the meaning of this Theological puzzle'. The meaning was given in the book of 1826. – *one reason for Suppression.* – See. Now, I tried to get this meaning from Fraser for years. But he won't come through!! The Pope of Rome has 6 6 6 figures on his cap. – Another Mystery. – See.'[39]

To appreciate why these ideas might be entertained with such passion it is necessary to consider the wider context. As we have seen, the MacCrimmons were assigned an increasingly important symbolic role as standard bearers of Highland culture. The changing circumstances of that culture in the period from about 1870 onwards were reflected in a continuous reshaping of the

---

39 A. K. Cameron to Pipe-Major William Gray, in Papers of the Piobaireachd Society, NLS Acc. 9103/25, 'Letters to and concerning G. F. Ross', 22/11/1931. Gray was later to allege MacCrimmon involvement in freemasonry, see NLS, Acc.9103/10 Correspondence 1951–54, William Gray to J. P. Grant, 26/7/1954 ; J.P.G .to W.G., 31/7/1954; W.G. to J.P.G., 2/8/1954.

MacCrimmon metaphor. This brought a number of motifs together: an urge, at once assertive and defensive, to include the Highlands within the general context of high European culture, on a basis of equality, so that a person might reasonably turn his back on Renaissance Italy to go and be a piper in the isle of Skye. It invoked for the pipe itself the protective aura of high antiquity, linking it with similar qualities claimed for the Gaelic language and hence, by extension, with the vaunted primacy of Celtic civilisation in the West. It sought to dignify canntaireachd by investing it with esoteric religious meaning, asserting its kinship with the Scriptures and with the immense power of the word. It forged a link between the classical music of the Highlands and that of Italy, the cradle of cultivated western music, implying claims of similar authority and permanence (an interesting parallel to the situation in the Lowlands during the first half of the 18th century, when many of the classic Scottish songs were attributed to Mary Queen of Scots' Italian secretary David Rizzio).[40]

But the symbol was ambiguous. The cluster of meanings centring on the college at Boreraig could be read in ways that were anything but comforting. In the sense that it might be refounded, it could be read as a sign of vitality and renewal and of the ultimate sustainability of Celtic institutions.[41] On the other hand, it patently had not been renewed. At any given moment of contemplation, it was a pile of useless rubble on the isle of Skye, giving eloquent expression to the fearful underside of the 'Celtic Revival' that the culture was in truth bankrupt and could not sustain itself without creative intervention from outside. The MacCrimmon genealogy contained a recurring exotic strain, with suggestions that the family were originally Italian, Irish, or Norse. It did not matter what version one preferred because it ultimately had the same effect: namely to devalue the creative potential of the native Gaelic community.[42]

---

40 See Fiske, pp. 17–22. For a later account of the Cremona motif, see T. Pearston, 'In Search of the Italian Bagpipe', *PT*, vol. 4, no.10, July 1952, pp.6–8; and 'A Piper's Diary' p.9. See also Collinson, *Bagpipe*, pp.143–6.

41 *OT*, Leader, 'Bagpipe Music', 15/2/1896, p.4; 'Origin of the Highland Bagpipe', from 'Piob Mor', 30/3/1912, p.3; 'Piobaireachd', from W. G. Burn Murdoch, 12/4/1919, p.3.

42 For Irish attempts to appropriate the MacCrimmons and their music see *OT*, Leader, 'The Story of the Bagpipe' reviewing William H. Grattan Flood's *Story of the Bagpipe* (Lond., 1911), 6/1/1912, p.4. Flood held that the pipes were introduced into Scotland from Ireland, that the MacCrimmons had learned their art there, and that Scottish music was a relatively recent and derivative strain of an Irish parent stock: Flood, pp.42, 130–131. See also 'The MacCrimmon Pipers. Part 1', by Lieut. John McLennan, *OT*, 3/5/1919, p.3, which traced the MacCrimmons into the fabulous reaches of Irish mythical history, deducing their descent from the *Crimthainn* – a priestly class to which St. Columba had belonged. For the Norse connection, see 'The Sutherland MacCrimmons', from G. C. B. Poulter, 25/9/1937, p.3, citing the tradition that before their service with the Macleods of Dunvegan, the MacCrimmons had long been hereditary pipers to the Earls of Sutherland at Dunrobin. It would have to be added that there was much stout assertion of the native origins of the family.

The association of the MacCrimmons with doom and tragedy was particularly relevant here, and frequently echoed in contemporary sources. The literate superstructure was founded in a strain of folk tradition which was increasingly available in published form, and included such tales as 'MacDonald of the Isles's Big Ploughman and the Black Chanter', collected by Hector MacLean, J. F. Campbell's chief assistant, and published in Lord Archibald Campbell's, *Records of Argyll Legends, Traditions, and Recollections of Argyllshire Highlanders Collected Chiefly from the Gaelic* (Edinr., 1885) and 'The Black Lad MacCrimmon and the Banshee', in James MacDougall's, *Folk Tales and Fairy Lore in Gaelic and English Collected from Oral Tradition*, ed., George Calder, (Edinr., 1910). In Highland folklore the family's pre-eminence was attributed to supernatural assistance, the possession of a magical chanter, either black or silver, and to a technical expertise likewise rooted in the paranormal, a perilous and ultimately fatal gift.[43] In two of the best-known groups of tales, 'The MacCrimmon Tragedy' and 'MacCrimmon's Lament', these features were strongly marked.

For the fairies' gift, a price had to be paid and MacCrimmon was fated to enter the Cave of Gold, never to return.[44] It is a deep and folkish motif, involving the capture of mortals, a magical object, a descent into the underworld, with parallels in tales of many different places and periods, not least the ancient myth of Orpheus – although the Highland version is darker: it is the musician himself who is the sacrifice. In one of the tales, the MacCrimmon pipe is called 'the Black Gate'; it permits entry to the Otherworld, but not, unlike the Golden Bough, return. There are numerous versions of the Cave of Gold story, and the song which accompanies it, with its refrain:

Mo dhìth, mo dhìth gun trì làmhan.
Mo dhìth, mo dhìth gun trì làmhan,
Dà làimh 'sa phìob, dà làimh 'sa phìob,
Dà làimh 'sa phìob, 's làmh 'sa chlaideamh.

43 See Campbell, *Records of Argyll*, pp.337–8; the Big Ploughman's violation of the taboo against fairy food leads to the gift of the magic chanter, and MacCrimmon's subsequent theft of it placed the latter also under fairy jurisdiction, for the rules governing which see Lowry C. Wimberly, *Folklore in the English and Scottish Ballads* (New York, 1959, first published 1928), pp.275–98. For 'The Black Lad MacCrimmon', see MacDougall, *Folk Tales*, pp. 174–179, reprinted in Neil Philip, ed., *The Penguin Book of Scottish Folktales* (Lond., 1995), pp.466–7; this latter involves at least three distinct layers of fairy entrapment – MacCrimmon speaks to the fairy, he allows her to tie her hair round his reed, and he lets her touch him; any one of these actions would have been enough to place him in her power. For the fairies assisting Macpherson pipers, see W. Y. Evans Wentz, *Fairy Faith in Celtic Countries* (Oxford, 1911), pp.103–4.

44 For an early version of the story, see Martin, pp.204–5, which locates it in Trotternish in the vicinity of Hungladder; Martin also mentions a Golden Cave in Sleat.

(My loss, my loss that I lack three hands!
Two hands to the bagpipe and one to the sword).[45]

The perils encountered by the piper differ, but they were plainly once supernatural: some texts refer to 'the green bitch' (green being the characteristic fairy colour) or 'the great grey she-one'.[46] Indeed the whole point of the three hands motif is that the piper dare not stop playing; only his music can hold the supernatural at bay – as soon as he resorts to earthly means of defence he is doomed.[47]

A version of this tale was used to announce the fundraising concert to launch the MacCrimmon Memorial Trust on 13th of March 1914, attended by senior Piobaireachd Society members, including John Bartholomew, who occupied the chair, and J. P. Grant. There were Gaelic songs from Marjorie Kennedy Fraser and pipe music by John MacDonald of Inverness:

> The MacCrimmon Tragedy, or the 'Cave of Gold', is remembered for the sad cadences of its story. Not far from Kilmuir . . . is Uamha an Oir, the Cave of Gold. It is at Rudh Bhaile na Skillog, and is supposed to extend for several miles underground, and at one time was believed to be inhabited by wild beasts, who devoured and destroyed all intruders. It was believed that they could be charmed by music and rendered harmless, and in order to test this point one of the MacCrimmons of Borreraig, at the head of a band of bold adventurers, entered the cave, MacCrimmon marching at their head playing the bagpipes. The people above ground heard him and followed the course of the music for upwards of a mile inland, and to indicate his dangerous situation they heard MacCrimmon strike up the following: –
>
> > Mo dhi, mo dhi, gun tri lamhan,
> > Dha laimh 's a phiob, 's na chlaidheamh.
>
> And again, on giving up hope of returning alive, they heard him play
>
> > Bithidh na laoigh bheaga 'n an crodh bainne
> > Mu'n till mise a uaimh an oir,
> > Bithidh na minn bheaga 'nan gaibhreachrocach,
> > Mu'n till mise a uaimh an oir.[48]

---

45 Quoted in Tolmie, pp.157–60. For a full text see Matheson, 'Three Fairy Songs', pp.280–284. I am indebted to Prof. Colm O'Boyle for drawing these sources to my attention. See also in Manson, the chapter entitled 'Pipers in Enchanted Caves', pp.247–256.
46 *Tocher*, p.281, Tolmie, p.158.
47 For an interesting Lowland parallel, the ballad of the 'Wee Wee Man' (Child 38) with fairy revels and pipers playing for dancing in a hall of gold, see Wimberly, p.191; and for the power of music over supernatural beings more generally, 161, 293–4, 332–5.
48 'The MacCrimmon Memorial', *OT*, 7/3/1914, p.3. This means roughly, 'the little calves will be milk cows, little kids full grown goats before I return from the Cave of Gold'. For a full translation of these and related images, see *Tocher, op.cit.*

As the belief in fairy lore declined, the essential point of the Cave of Gold stories began to be lost, and MacCrimmon's presence in the cave was often, as above, attributed to mere adventurousness; but some twentieth century sources preserve the motif of fairy entrapment, which would seem to have been the original implication. Neil Ross published a Gaelic version in a series of articles in the *Celtic Monthly* in 1910 entitled 'Ceol-mor agus Clann MhicCruimein' which goes roughly as follows:

Once a brown-haired youth of this worthy race of musicians, was playing on the great pipe of the drones in the pipers' hollow, when his eyes were struck with wonder and his blood leapt as he saw a wonderful creature more beautiful than any living maid. No match for her was to be found in all the four quarters of the world. She had a silver chanter in her hand, and she offered it to MacCrimmon. She told him it would give him victory over all the world's musicians; but that in a year and a day he would have to enter the Cave of Gold. The young man seized the silver chanter and so he fell under her spell. He would not part with it for all the riches in the world. When he played upon the instrument of beautiful notes, then could be heard music without equal. The skylark and the thrush came and listened raptly. The deer of the bens and the mist came and attended to that sweet incitement; the brown otter came to the river bank and the seal of the waves hearkened to his tune. The sick became whole, and the sorrowing were comforted; the age of joy had come. Delight endured for a year and a day. But came the hour and came the minute. One fine summer morning the young man had to go on his journey. He turned his back to his friends and left the world of the living. He made his way to the Cave of Gold and sang a song of which the words are but these: 'Cha tig mise, cha ruig mise,/Cha tig mis' a Uamh an Oir,/ Bidh na minn beaga/Nan gabhair chreagach,/'S a chlann laga nam fir-àir;/ Bidh na mic uchda/Nam fir aca,/Mun tig mis' a Uamh an Oir.'[49]

The second group of tales is more historically rooted, and centres on Donald Bàn MacCrimmon, who was killed at the Rout of Moy in February 1746. These

49 *Celtic Monthly*, vol.18, nos. 2–4, February-April, 1910, pp.26–8, 45–7, 65–7 (45–6). See also 'MacCrimmon's Silver Chanter', in MacDougall, pp. 180–81. For further Cave of Gold material in the *Oban Times*, see 'The Legend of a Highland Piper' from 'Morag', 31/7/1915, p.3; 'The Legend of the Highland Pipes', from John MacGregor, giving a version of the story from Lewis, 7/8/1915, p.5; 'Legend of the Highland Piper', from 'A[netta]. C. W[hyte].' 1/8/1925, p.3, with a version from Mull, including a tune in sol-fa notation; 'Scottish Folklore. New society to be formed' containing proposals for a Scottish Gaelic Folklore Society or Institute, and pointing to the wide diffusion of the legend, including an Edinburgh version linked with the Castle and Holyrood, 19/7/1947, p.3. A piobaireachd entitled 'The Cave of Gold' is published in G. F. Ross, *Collection*, pp.22–3. For discussion of the motif from a folkloristic point of view, see V. S. Blankenhorn, 'Traditional and Bogus Elements in "MacCrimmon's Lament"', in *Scottish Studies*, vol.22, 1978, pp.45–67, and Alan Bruford, 'Legends Long Since Localised or Tales Still Travelling?', in *same*, vol.24, 1980, pp.43–62.

interweave the doom of Donald Bàn with the end of the MacCrimmon pipers, and of the wider Gaelic culture they had come to represent. The MacLeods had supported the Hanoverian side in the '45, and Donald Bàn was with an advance party of Lord Loudon's northern army which tried to surprise and capture Prince Charles Edward Stuart in a night attack on Moy House, not far from Inverness. The Jacobites were warned, there was some desultory shooting and, seemingly alone of the attacking force, Donald Bàn was killed.[50] Within a relatively short period of time he began to figure in a complex of related tales. As early as 1763, for example, we find him linked with the weird and supernatural in a collection of stories of the second sight compiled by William MacLeod of Hamer in Skye under the pseudonym 'Theophilus Insulanus':

> Patrick MacCaskill . . . declared to me That, in the evening before the Earl of Loudon attempted to surprise the young Pretender, at the Castle of Moy, Donald MacCrummen, piper to the independent company, (commanded by the young Laird of MacLeod), talked with him on the street of Inverness, where they were then under arms, to march, they did not know whither, as their expedition was kept a secret: And that, after the said Donald, a goodly person, six feet high, parted with him about a pistol-shot, he saw him all at once contracted to the bigness of a boy of five or six years old, and immediately, with the next look, resume his former size. The same night MacCrummen was accidentally shot dead on their long march, which concluded the operation of that night's enterprize.[51]

James Logan recorded a new motif suggesting Donald Bàn's presentiment of his fate, and quoted from the song attributed to his sweetheart, with its now famous refrain, 'Cha till, cha till, cha till MacCriomain':

> Dh'iadh ceò nan stùchd ma aodann Chulain;
> Gun sheinn a bhean shì a torgan mulaid:
> Tha sùilean gorm, cùin, san Dùn ri sileadh;
> On thriall thu bh'uain's nach till thu tuille.
> Cha till, cha till, cha till MacCruimin,
> An cogadh, na sìth, cha till e tuille:
> Le airgiod, na nì, cha till MacCruimin;
> Cha till gu bràth, gu là na cruinne.[52]

50 For a full account of these events, see Ruairidh H. MacLeod, 'Everyone who has an intrigue hopes it should not be known: Lord Loudoun and Anne Mackintosh – An Intrigue of the '45', in *Transactions of the Gaelic Society of Inverness*, vol. 55, 1986–8, pp.256–323.
51 Quoted in MacLeod, *MacCrimmons of Skye.*, pp.44–5.
52 MacKay, *Ancient Piobaireachd*, 'Historical and Traditional Notes', p.4. For a suggestion that the song was composed by Norman MacLeod ('Caraid nan Gaidheal'), see Cameron, *History of Skye*, pp. 106–7.

Professor John Stuart Blackie (1809–95) created an English version of the song, still widely sung:

> Round Cullen's peak the mist is sailing,
> The banshee croons her note of wailing;
> Mild blue eyne with sorrow are streaming
> For him that shall never return, Maccrimmon!
> No more, no more, no more, for ever,
> In war or peace, shall return Maccrimmon;
> No more, no more, no more for ever
> Shall love or gold bring back Maccrimmon![53]

The aptness of the doomed piper as a symbol of Gaelic culture, was recognised at an early date, as we can see in Sir Walter Scott's re-working of the song to accommodate the theme of the Highland Clearances. Scott had visited Dunvegan in the summer of 1814, spent a night in its haunted chamber, and actually heard Donald Roy MacCrimmon play. He dressed up the '45 in typical pseudo-mediaeval panoply, but there was an edge of implied social criticism mingling with the sense of loss:

> Macleod's wizard flag from the grey Castle sallies.
> The rowers are seated, unmoored are the galleys;
> Gleam war axe and broadsword, clang targe and quiver
> As MacCrimmon plays 'Farewell to Dunvegan for ever.'
>
> Farewell to each cliff on which breakers are foaming,
> Farewell each dark glen in which red deer are roaming;
> Farewell lonely Skye, to lake mountain and river;
> Macleod may return, but MacCrimmon shall never . . .
>
> Too oft shall the note of MacCrimmon's bewailing
> Be heard when the Gael on their exile are sailing;
> Dear Land! to the shores when unwilling we sever;
> Return, return, return, we shall never.[54]

One literary variant of the tale presented Donald Bàn as a fervent Jacobite, and as having composed a wonderful salute for Prince Charlie, given its first – and final – performance as he lay dying on the moor.[55]

---

53 Quoted in Magnus MacLean, *The Literature of the Highlands*, (London, 1925, first published 1903), pp. 260–1. For a particularly fine rendition, see 'MacCrimmon's lament' in *Jeannie Robertson The Great Scots Traditional Ballad Singer*, Topic Records, 12 T96.

54 Quoted in MacLeod, *MacCrimmons of Skye*, pp.43–4.

55 *Ibid.*, pp.82–4. See also *OT*, 7/8/1880, p.3, 8/3/1919, p.3, 15/3/1919, p.3, 22/3/1919, p.3, 5/4/1919, p.3.

On 2nd August 1933 on a rugged knoll looking down on Loch Dunvegan this complex of ideas was formally commemorated in the unveiling of the Mac-Crimmon cairn. There were glowing reports in the *Oban Times* and a large photograph depicting 'The Gallant Chief of the Clan MacLeod Landing from his Galley [actually a small motor launch] at Boreraig, Isle of Skye'.[56] A group of top pipers were present playing well known MacCrimmon compositions: John MacDonald played 'I got a Kiss of the King's Hand', Robert Reid, 'The Lament for the Children', Angus Macpherson, 'MacCrimmon's Sweetheart', and his brother John, 'MacCrimmon will never Return'. At the end of the ceremony, they played 'The Lament for Donald Bàn' ensemble.

That afternoon a memorial plaque in Kilmuir Kirkyard at Dunvegan, where ten generations of MacCrimmons were thought to be interred, was unveiled with heady oratory by the Very Rev. Dr. Norman MacLean. He began by quoting 'The March of the Cameron Men' (not perhaps the happiest allusion in the circumstances) and although it was evident that he had little idea of what a piobaireachd actually was, he painted an inspiring picture of the men of the Isles charging at Bannockburn to the sound of the pipes. There was no evidence that this had actually happened, to be sure, but 'Tradition says that it was so; and tradition is more reliable than the historian'.[57] He recollected how at Waterloo the sound of the pibroch rose loud and shrill where the fire was hottest; how when Sir Colin Campbell had cried out 'Forward, Forty-Second' at the Alma, the notes of the pipes had made the blood surge in their veins; how at the relief of Lucknow the strains of the pipes sounded as heralds of miraculous deliverance; how at Dargai the pibroch of a wounded piper sent the Gordons storming up the heights; how at the funeral of Earl Haig,

> It was only when the piper came down the nave, below the tattered flags that saw many a battlefield on which the seed of Empire was sown in blood, pouring forth the strains of that Lament which enshrines the woes of Flodden and all the dead of all the Floddens of history, only then did the eyes grow dim with tears, and the sob rise in the throat . . . The world can change beyond recognition. But the heart of men changes not. To-day is the product of all the yesterdays. If to-day the bagpipes commit to the winds of heaven the deepest emotion of the Scotsman's heart in joy and sorrow, in war and peace, so was it yesterday, and so will it continue so long as the waves wash the feet of MacLeod's Maidens standing sentinel in the Minch'.[58]

He depicted how the famous college had sprung up at Boreraig at the behest of Alasdair Crotach, chief of the MacLeods from 1480–1540, how the name of MacCrimmon had cast a spell over the Highlands and been intertwined with the

56 *OT*, 19/8/1933, p.5.
57 MacLeod, *MacCrimmons of Skye*, pp.147–8.
58 MacLeod, *MacCrimmons of Skye*, pp.148–9.

romance of Scottish history. He described how sorrow and wistful sadness was the keynote of their music, evoking for the Gael as nothing else could the themes of exile and death, and concluded:

> No man can judge the bagpipes or set a value on the MacCrimmons unless he has been familiar with the sound of the piobaireachd in its native element . . . As naturally as the curlew to the shore, or grouse to the moor, or the seal to the sea, so naturally belong the bagpipes to the open air. The MacCrimmons are the musicmakers of the great bens, of the deep valleys, and of the sea breaking round rock-bound promontories. When you hear a piobaireachd over still waters at eventide under the shadow of the everlasting hills, you realise the meaning of deep crying to deep – the depth of the human heart crying to the depth of the encompassing mystery . . . 'The world,' says an ancient Gaelic proverb, 'will come to an end, but love and music will last for ever'.[59]

The MacCrimmon metaphor continued to develop during the later 20th century, with the suggestion that they were not only the greatest players and composers of piobaireachd, but had actually invented the form. This idea seems to have been first advanced by Simon Fraser and was extended during the 1920s and '30s as people like John Grant and A. K. Cameron struggled to enlist the authority of the MacCrimmons in support of their views.[60] But it was in the pages of the *Kilberry Book of Ceol Mor* in 1948, that the idea received its first considered expression, its author, Archibald Campbell, declaring that:

> It is difficult to resist the conclusion that the MacCrimmons were responsible for the form of piobaireachd which has come down to us, and that they evolved it as that particular combination of sounds most effective in bringing out the best of which the Highland pipe of their day was capable.[61]

This claim was intended to counteract the suggestion contained in the essay 'Of the Influence of Poetry and Music on the Highlanders' prefixed to Patrick MacDonald's *Highland Vocal Airs* (1784) – which Campbell assumed had been written by MacDonald – that the music was of Norse origin.[62] Twenty years later, in Francis Collinson's *The Bagpipe the History of a Musical Instrument*, Campbell's fairly cautious formulation had evolved into this:

---

59 MacLeod, *MacCrimmons of Skye*, pp.149–154.
60 See, for example, 'Piobaireachd', from A. K. Cameron, *OT*, 6/1/1934, p.3.
61 Campbell, *Kilberry Book* (2nd edn., Glasgow 1953), 'Introduction', p.16.
62 Archibald Campbell, 'The Highland Bagpipe', *PT*, vol.14, no. 10, July 1962, pp.6–10. See above, pp.56–7. This idea first appears in his correspondence in the early '30s: 'most of the good piobaireachds were made either by the MacCrimmons or under their direct influence . . . piobaireachd is a peculiar MacCrimmon form of music.' Archibald Campbell to Seton Gordon, NLS, Acc.7451, General Correspondence, 1930–1935, 23/10/1931.

The chief interest of the MacCrimmons as far as the story of the pipes is concerned lies not so much in their origin as in the fact that they are generally thought to have been the inventors of *piobaireachd,* or *ceòl mór,* the 'great music' of the pipes.[63]

This position rested – like most of the rest of the structure – almost entirely upon conjecture. Collinson had access in 1975 to little more accurate information about the MacCrimmons than James Logan had in 1838. Yet in the intervening period the interpretation of the family's role in Highland culture and the significance imputed to them had been transformed.

It would be easy to dismiss this simply as bad history and worse folklore – of which, indeed, there is little shortage in the literature of the pipe.[64] But the MacCrimmon metaphor sprang directly from developing power-relations within the institutions of piping during the later 19th and 20th centuries and it was this which ultimately gave it coherence. The construction of a past out of which a hierarchical and authoritarian present could plausibly have emerged required the elevation of one of the teaching families into an officer-class (reducing the rest to the ranks in the process) in order to validate their 'successors' as self-appointed custodians of tradition. This was the historical equivalent of the search for fixity, the quest for the authoritative original text which would banish the phantom of variance and break the hold of the performer community on the music. By confining the concept of authenticity within narrow channels to which only cultural privilege could give access, the MacCrimmon metaphor directly re-inforced the supremacy of institutions like the Piobaireachd Society (by virtue of its monopoly of the written sources) and asserted the value of an ordered, historic legitimacy against a dangerously creative and uncontrolled present.

63 Francis Collinson, *Bagpipe,* p.146. For further sentiments to this effect see MacNeill, *Piobaireachd,* p.16: 'This almost legendary family was largely responsible for the development of piobaireachd, and was certainly responsible for the dissemination of it throughout the Highlands'.

64 One could find as late as 1987, an ostensibly responsible historical account referring to Pietro and Giordano Bruno, and treating the phantom 1826 Gesto edition as an established fact: see MacNeill and Richardson, p.19. See also the entry 'MacCrimmons' in Thomson, *Companion to Gaelic Scotland,* pp.162–3.

20

'A Matter of National Importance': Broadcasting, Recording and the Passing of John MacDonald

The new technologies of broadcasting and electrical recording began to affect the piping world from the early 1920s onwards. In December 1921 the Music Committee of the Piobaireachd Society reported that it had explored the possibility of 'recording the correct method of playing piobaireachd tunes by means of gramophone records', but concluded that at £21 per disc, the cost would be prohibitive.[1]

The first piobaireachd broadcast took place from the Edinburgh Station of the British Broadcasting Company in the last week of March 1927 and comprised a talk on ceòl mór by writer and naturalist Seton Gordon, a senior member of the Piobaireachd Society who was to become the usual provider of spoken commentary in such programmes, at the end of which Willie Ross played 'The Lament for Sir James MacDonald of the Isles'. The script conveyed the basically pessimistic view of piobaireachd set forth at greater length in Gordon's influential book *The Charm of Skye the Winged Isle*, published in 1929, whose thinking descended in a clear line through James Logan and Donald MacDonald's mediator from the Prefatory Essay by John Ramsay in Patrick MacDonald's *Highland Vocal Airs*. Gordon stated that in creative terms the form had 'entirely died out' – which was not the case – and that 'many beautiful compositions of piobaireachd had been destroyed and lost' which, if it had ever been true, had long since disappeared over the horizon of demonstration or proof.[2]

On the radio, then, the classical music of the pipe was presented to the wider world in the distinctive tones of the Anglo-Scottish establishment, and this was to be the case for many years to come.[3] Gordon and people like him were not just spokesmen. They were often involved a good deal more actively than the programme notes might suggest. In November 1933, for example, the Piobaireachd Society's editor, Archibald Campbell, wrote,

---

1 Piobaireachd Society Papers, NLS, Acc.9103/2 'Loose Minutes, 1905–6, 1910, 1913–1924, 1919–21, 1955–63', Report of the Music Committee to the Annual General Meeting, 6/12/1921.

2 'Mr Seton Gordon Broadcasting. Pipers of the Past', in *OT*, 3/4/1926, p.3.

3 It was regarded as rather a daring departure when, in the early sixties, R. U. Brown was allowed to introduce his own broadcast recitals, in a voice bearing audible traces of Aberdeenshire rather than a staff announcer speaking flawless R.P.

I wonder whether you heard John Macdonald on the wireless last month. I was responsible for the choice of tunes. I thought that tunes avoiding the high notes might be tried, as the Lament for the Children previously tried was not much of a success, I thought. I hadn't a very good machine to listen on, but I thought that these two were a distinct improvement. I took a lot of trouble in a way. I got John Macdonald to play both tunes at Inverness in his house, timed them carefully, told Seton exactly how long he would have to talk, even told him what to say (but of course he didn't say it). S. has got about 50 letters of appreciation from all sorts of weird people which he has sent me & which are very interesting to read.

Ranging from one of the few denizens of Soay to the lady at Pulborough, Sussex, who, when she heard the piobaireachd, got up and put a peat on the fire . . .[4]

The Piobaireachd Society was able to extend its control of what was heard and how it was interpreted into the broadcasting media at an early period, therefore, a control which was later given institutional form in the B.B.C.'s advisory Piping Panel, whose leading member was J. P. Grant.

The ability of the pipes to communicate over the radio seems to have been remarkably effective, however, even in the early days. In October 1934, for example, the Empire Department of the B.B.C. broadcast two piping recitals by John MacDonald and Willie Ross and received enthusiastic letters from all over the world:

One listener . . . writing from Bermuda . . . said 'I did not think I should ever have the honour of hearing Pipe-Major John MacDonald play and I thank him for that glorious Piobaireachd he played. When is Edinburgh going to get a broadcasting station so that we can hear more of our beloved Scottish music?'

From Kenya Colony an enthusiast wrote – 'I had an urgent message from a friend to come to his house as Pipe-Major Ross was to give a piping recital that evening. The road to his house is appalling; but I would have tackled the Pentland Skerries rather than miss Pipe-Major Ross. The reception was perfect; the tone and harmony of the pipes were magnificent and his fingering was faultless.'

A Skyeman exiled in Bengal wrote that the pipes came through with great strength and clarity despite lightning flashing all round the horizon and a cyclone in the offing. From Chile, from Siam, from the West Indies, and from Brazil came letters of congratulation.

Among the last to be received was one from Western Australia, where a listener was so thrilled by John Macdonald's piobaireachd he sat up half the

4 NLS, Acc.9103/9 Correspondence, 1929–1950, Archibald Campbell to J. Graham Campbell, 10/11/1933.

following night to hear a re-transmission from an electrical record of the broadcast.[5]

Listeners nearer home, while they may equally have relished the piping, tended to find the B.B.C.'s provision woefully deficient with regard to Scottish music and culture more generally. One wrote from Ballachulish in 1926 that 'Many listeners find the Glasgow programmes disappointing in the paucity of Scottish national music presented . . . In the South of England, Scottish items are frequently included, while in Glasgow at times nothing national is given for a week at a time'.[6] Another wrote condemning 'the substitution of meaningless garbage from the backwoods of America [presumably jazz] for our beautiful old Celtic and Scottish music and songs'.[7] In response E. L. Marshall, Director of the Glasgow Station, pointed out that the B.B.C. transmitted on average nearly one programme a week containing 'characteristically Scottish matter'.[8] But by 1928 people were already making adverse comparisons between the niggardly approach of Glasgow as opposed to Dublin to the broadcasting of Celtic music.[9] And by the early thirties there were further complaints about quality of service and cultural bias. One long-suffering listener was forced to complain of a broadcast céilidh from the Inverness Mòd in 1936 that it 'was a complete washout as far as reception was concerned. It sounded more like machine gun fire than a musical entertainment'. This was married at the same time with a keen sense that London was using this powerful new medium to seize control of the cultural agenda and reduce Scotland to the status of a province.[10]

The complaints went on in a steady stream throughout the 'thirties. The B.B.C. did not seem to have noticed that Scotland was full of mountains, which cut much of the country off from its services. On the other hand those who could receive the signals fretted about cultural disruption, seeing radio as a direct threat to the céilidh as a social institution and to the ultimate well-being of Gaelic culture.[11] The content of such programmes as were devoted to Scottish life and culture also attracted criticism. In the rare broadcasts of Gaelic songs, for example, only Mòd Gold Medallists were ever heard and a whole wealth of traditional singing was unrepresented. In

5 'Piping to the Empire. John MacDonald M.B.E. and William Ross', *OT*, 15/12/1934, p.5. For the script of Gordon's talk, see Seton Gordon Papers, NLS, Acc.5640/2 (1), 12/10/1934, 25/10/1934.

6 'Glasgow Broadcasting Programmes. Lack of Scottish and Highland Music', from Lachlan Grant, *OT*, 12/6/1926, p.3.

7 'Glasgow Broadcasting Programmes', from R. Munro, *OT*, 26/6/1926, p.3. For a view that interest in piping was declining in the north owing to the impact of jazz, see 'Piping in the Northern Highlands', from 'Pipe-Major', 30/3/1935, p.3.

8 'Glasgow Broadcasting Programmes', *OT*, 3/7/1926, p.3.

9 'The B.B.C. & Gaelic', *OT*, 18/2/1928, p.3.

10 'Broadcasting Neglect of Scotland', from 'Manu Forti', *OT*, 23/5/1931, p.3.

11 'Wireless Ousting the Ceilidh?', *OT*, 13/11/1937, p.3.

instrumental music, only the pipes featured; there was nothing of other instruments such as the fiddle, harp, melodeon or trump.[12] Within the piping world itself, there were complaints about solo playing being preferred to bands. When regular band broadcasts began in the early 'forties they were billed as 'experimental'.[13]

Broadcasting and recording had a considerable impact, therefore, but should not be overestimated. The heavy re-chargeable batteries used limited the spread of radios, especially in country districts, and the extension of the mains power grid was patchy: Skye, for example, did not get mains electricity until after the Second World War. A portable wind-up gramophone could be bought for just over £3.00 in the '20s, which was less than half the price of even a basic stand of pipes, and records could be bought by post. But the choice was rather limited for Scottish music enthusiasts. High initial production costs might mean that profitability could only be achieved on runs greater than the Scottish domestic market could sustain. In the early '20s it cost £120.00 to make six double-sided ten inch records, excluding performance fees, and one needed to sell 250 of each simply to cover production costs.[14]

One might also bear in mind the culture of positive resistance to canned entertainment in certain contexts, a point which emerges strongly in David G. Adams's study of farm-life in Angus at this period, *Bothy Nichts and Days* (Edinr., 1991):

> Radios, or wirelesses as they were ca'd, were very rare afore the war. Apairt fae the expense o buyin een ye needed tae tak the weet batteries tae a shop tae get them rechairged every sae offen. Even wee wind-up gramaphones were seldom seen in the bothy but there wis near aye some lad that could play the trump or the moothie or aiven a melodian, or the fiddle or pipes, or cud sing cornkisters. It wis a' Scottish music of coorse . . . some lads were able to play a tune o some sort, ithers were real guid musicians and micht tak lessons fae somebody like Jim Cameron fae Kirrie[muir]. He wis eence a bothy lad himsel, and wis a plooin champion as weel's a champion fiddler afore he had a dance band. A great mony dance band musicians started oot in the bothy, in fact maybe the maist o them did . . .[15]

---

12 'Gaelic Wireless Programmes', from 'Ethereal', *OT*, 3/10/1936, p.3. See also 'Lack of Pipe Band Music on the Wireless', from J. Mackerral-Brown, 6/3/1937, p.3; 'Broadcasting Pipe Music', from 'Tibicen', 1/1/1938, p.3.

13 'Pipe Band Music for Broadcasting simpler or competitive Tunes', from 'Fiosrachadh', *OT*, 26/4/1941, p.3.

14 'Gaelic Gramophone Records', *OT*, 28/1/1922, p.3. The evidence here is difficult to interpret. The Piobaireachd Society was quoted startlingly different break-even figures by various companies for proposed recordings of John MacDonald in the early 1930s. See below, pp.428–30.

15 Adams, pp.42–3 .

The first commercial recording of piobaireachd was made by John MacDonald of Inverness on the Columbia label in 1927. Amongst the crowd of well-wishers and onlookers who gathered at the Company's studios in Petty France in London were a number of senior Piobaireachd Society members including Sir Douglas Ramsay of Bamff and Seton Gordon, who was probably responsible for the unsigned article which appeared in the *Oban Times* shortly afterwards describing the event:

> It was an interesting and memorable experience to be present at the making of the records, which was done by the new electrical process. Pipe-Major MacDonald played in a large room, and the records were made in an adjoining smaller room. Within a minute of the playing of the urlar or ground . . . it was played over on the gramophone, and the notes were so clear and true that it might have been John MacDonald himself playing at a little distance. It was found that a single record would hold only the ground of a Piobaireachd, and so one record was devoted to the ground and another to the first variation . . .
>
> It was interesting to notice that even the officials who were taking the records soon came under the influence of the Piobaireachd spell, though as Englishmen with no knowledge or experience of the pipes, they had little interest at first in the making of the records.
>
> It is to be hoped that these records will be the means of attracting and educating public opinion to the beauty of Ceol Mor . . . and it is satisfactory that a project, which was discussed more than once before the war has been successfully carried through.[16]

The tunes concerned were the grounds and opening variations of 'The Lament for the Children', 'MacCrimmon's Sweetheart', 'The Little Spree' and 'The Lament for Patrick Òg MacCrimmon'. From a piping point of view, they were reckoned a great success, with MacDonald playing outstandingly well.

By the early 'thirties recording costs had dropped significantly and some senior members of the Piobaireachd Society including J. P. Grant, Seton Gordon and Frank Richardson, felt that it might be an appropriate time to secure additional recordings of John MacDonald, as an enduring record of his style and for private study and teaching purposes. They approached B.B.C. London with this in mind in the autumn of 1933 and were quoted £8–£12 for a dozen 'pressings' of a forthcoming MacDonald broadcast. They were informed that the Corporation intended to record the transmission for its own archives and that this could be copied by the Society for its own use via a commercial recording company.[17] But

16 '"Record" Performance. Piobaireachd and Gramophone. Pipe-Major John MacDonald', *OT*, 26/3/1927, p.5.

17 NLS, Acc.9103/9 Correspondence, 1929–1950, C. G. Graves (on behalf of the BBC, London) to Seton Gordon, 27/9/1933; George I. Campbell to C. G. Graves, 7/10/1933; [C. G. Graves to George I. Campbell?], 13/10/1933.

the companies showed little interest in the project. H.M.V. did not think it was commercially attractive. They were willing to do the job privately, i.e. not as a commercial venture forming part of their catalogue, but their quotation ran to hundreds of pounds. Columbia were equally unenthusiastic. Sales of MacDonald's previous recordings had been 'disappointing', and they understood that the same had been true of Willie Ross's light music recordings with Parlophone. Times were hard, and they did not feel inclined to lay out money 'excepting for certainties'. It was doubtful, they thought, that the B.B.C.'s equipment was compatible with their own and Columbia were quite unimpressed by the Piobaireachd Society's assurances about foreign sales. A few hundred expressions of interest was scarcely adequate in view of the fact, so the Company claimed, that they had to sell 2,000 units to cover the initial cost of production.[18]

Meanwhile Archibald Campbell, who regarded MacDonald – quite mistakenly – as 'the beautiful player of a very few tunes' and questioned his historic significance in comparison with MacDougall Gillies and Sandy Cameron, was expressing serious reservations about cost. This was important because as Secretary of the Music Committee and editor of its published *Collection*, he was the most powerful man in the Society. Without his ultimate approval nothing could happen. But Grant and Richardson persevered, approaching Parlophone and a number of smaller 'pirate' companies 'outside the ring' looking for a manageable quotation.[19] Negotiations dragged on through the spring and summer of 1935, until Andrew Stewart, the B.B.C.'s Scottish Programme Director, suggested that the northern end of the Corporation might make an archive recording, copies of which could then be made available to the Society. George Campbell of Succoth, the Society's Secretary, thereupon wrote formally, in December 1935, requesting a series of broadcasts: 'My Society are convinced that the recording of Pipe Major Macdonald's playing is a matter of national importance and it is on this score particularly that they appeal to the B.B.C. for their help and collaboration in the matter'.[20]

But in January 1936 the project hit the rocks. The General Committee of the Society finally balked at the expense. It remitted the matter to the Music Committee, effectively handing the decision to Archibald Campbell, and the Music Committee duly decided to stop exploring commercial outlets and await developments at the B.B.C., on the principle that it would be foolish of the Society to pay for what it might eventually get for nothing.[21] But the question had already been overtaken by events. John MacDonald – now in his seventieth

18 NLS, Acc.9103/9 Correspondence, 1929–1950, A.W.L. Parkhouse to George. I. Campbell, 9/11/1933.

19 NLS, Acc.9103/9 Correspondence, 1929–1950 Archibald Campbell to J. Graham Campbell, 10/11/1933; J.P.Grant to Frank Richardson, n.d. and 3/10/1935.

20 NLS, Acc.9103/9 Correspondence, 1929–1950, Andrew Stewart, BBC, to Frank Richardson , 8/10/1935; George I. Campbell to Andrew Stewart, 11/12/1935.

21 NLS, Acc.9103/9 Correspondence, 1929–1950, George I. Campbell to J. P. Grant, 25/1/1936.

year – suffered a slight stroke, which ended his career as a top-flight player. And so the opportunity was lost.

During the '30s the focus of piping shifted further towards light music and the pipe band, and this was reflected in the columns of the *Oban Times*. The volume of correspondence devoted to piobaireachd began to decline, its place being taken by letters on piping, drumming, and judging in band contexts. Advertisements for band uniforms and equipment became a regular feature. Drumming scores and pipe-settings in staff notation suitable for ensemble play began to be published, amongst them original compositions by John MacLellan of Dunoon, including 'Bonnie Dunoon', 'Men of Argyll' and 'My Dream Valley on the Road to Glendaruel', the latter with song-lyrics by the composer.[22] During the 1920s and '30s the competing pipe band came of age. Amongst the leading formations were the Clan MacRae Society Pipe Band, founded by Farquhar MacRae as the City of Glasgow Pipe Band, based on a core of players from the old 7th H.L.I., later affiliating to the Clan MacRae Society and taking its name. Under William Fergusson it had enormous influence on ensemble playing during the inter-war years. A contemporary remarked:

> It is beyond doubt that the present high standard of Pipe Band playing generally is due in no small measure to the pace set by the MacRaes whose standard has been the ambition of all other Bands. They have been the pioneers so far as band work is concerned of many outstanding tunes and it is remarkably true to say that what the MacRaes are playing to-day the bulk of the bands will be playing tomorrow.[23]

An able pipe-major was the essential catalyst in raising a local group to national prominence, as we see in the case of Tom McAllister who joined Shotts and Dykehead Caledonia in the '20s and laid the foundations for three generations of competition success, beginning with a tie for first with the temperance outfit, the Rutherglen Rechabites, at Alloway, and gaining the Lauder Shield at Cowal in 1935.[24]

22 'New bagpipe march and drum setting of "Bonnie Dunoon" by Pipe-Major John MacLellan of Dunoon', *OT*, 21/11/1936, p.2; 'A New Pipe March. Men of Argyll. By John MacLellan of Dunoon', 5/3/1941, p.5; 'My Dream Valley on the Road to Glendaruel. Melody and Lyric by Pipe-Major John MacLellan, Dunoon'. This reveals that MacLellan was in the habit of writing the lyrics first, and then working out a tune to fit them, as was the case in three of his best known compositions, 'Heroes of Vittoria', 'Lochanside' and 'The Highland Brigade at Magersfontein', 30/5/1942, p.5. For examples of drum settings see 13/2/1932, p.3; 19/3/1932, p.5; 16/4/1932, p.5; 11/6/1932, p.2; 18/6/1932, p.2; 13/8/1932, p. 2; 5/11/1932, p.5; 7/1/1933, p. 3; 18/11/1933, p.3. In the west of Scotland there were a hundred pipe bands attached to the Boys' Brigade alone during the 1930s: see Maurice Forsyth, 'The Liberton Pipe Band – A Well Abused Melody', *PT*, vol.51, no.1, October 1998, pp.34–6.
23 'The Clan MacRae Society Pipe Band', in *Piping and Dancing*, no.12, July 1936.
24 'The Shotts and Dykehead Caledonia Pipe Band', *Piping and Dancing*, no.4, November 1935, p.13. See also 'End of Era for McAllister', by Tommy Millar in *The Piper Press*, no.5, March 1998, pp.30–1.

The MacLean Pipe Band, three times world champions during the twenties and thirties, was formed in 1920 and had its roots in the old Glasgow Y.M.C.A. Band. Its progress during the next several years shows a typical pattern of meeting and overcoming difficulties with regard to accommodation and equipment:

> In June, 1921, a uniform was borrowed from a welfare club in Rutherglen. With this the band took part in a contest held at Scotstoun, winning 3rd prize, £10 . . . In April 1924, the Caledonian Gardens Association granted the use of their hall . . . This proved to be the turning point in their affairs. Within three months of taking up their new abode, the band was able to buy a uniform through the generosity of members, friends, and well-wishers. True, it was ex-army stuff, and probably more useful than ornamental; still it was a Seaforth kilt and a khaki tunic dyed blue, and it enabled the band to appear at Cowal and get a fourth prize in the civilian championship, and first for bands that had not won at Cowal before.
>
> From this point the band moved on, winning one contest after the other, till they had won the supreme award at Cowal in 1927 . . . in the meantime, they bought and paid for a uniform costing £400 . . .[25]

It was from the MacLean Band that the initiative came in October 1930 to found the [Royal] Scottish Pipe Band Association, the regulatory body which later became responsible for all serious competitive playing in this field, overseeing the administration of competitions, the consistency of judging, and the grading of bands. The support of the competing bands was canvassed and an initial meeting held at the MacLeans' practice hall. Its Pipe-Major Sloan was elected the first President. The creation of the R.S.P.B.A. was an autonomous response of the performer community to the growing importance of competitive ensemble play, and formed, as such, an instructive contrast to at least one other institution which took upon itself to legislate for the art. There were many bands, of course, which did not win – or even aim at – competition success, but were none the less the focus of important networks of social ties and relations, relying on contributions from and contributing much in turn to their various communities. The Michael Colliery Prize Pipe Band, for example, seems to have been in some ways a typical pit band, going through the usual round of bazaars and concerts to raise funds, but it had strong trade-union links and appears to have been supported by a voluntary levy paid by the workforce. It cost about £250 a year to run. Such was the scale of its fund-raising for good causes that it was called 'The Charity Band'. A march to St. Andrews during the General Strike of 1926 raised £20 for the local soup kitchen.[26]

25 'The MacLean Pipe Band, Champions of the World, 1927–30–35', *Piping and Dancing*, no.2, Sept. 1935 p.18.
26 'Michael Colliery Prize Pipe Band', *Piping and Dancing*, no.6, January 1936, p.17. Apparently colliery bands were regularly supported by workers' levies, a modern urban example of an old-established rural practice: for the pipers of Urqhuart and Glenmoriston being supported by a kind of local tax, see pp.184–5.

The advent of the Second World War brought a hiatus in civilian piping like that of 1914–18. But this time the Piobaireachd Society continued its activities, devoting its efforts to the training of pipers for military service.[27] The Society's instructor, Willie Ross, was placed at the disposal of the War Office for the duration of hostilities and the Army Class which he had taught since 1919 was re-organised to deliver a greatly accelerated programme. Hitherto aspirants for appointment as Pipe-Major had undergone a course of higher instruction lasting for several months, following a syllabus heavily weighted towards musical literacy skills:

First Month Theory of music, reading and writing elementary.
Second Month Learning and memorising Piobaireachd and writing from memory into books – about four tunes each pupil.
Third Month Theory, reading and writing advanced.
Fourth, Fifth and Sixth Months Learning, memorising and writing from memory more Piobaireachd, and also difficult marches, strathspeys and reels, with the result that at the end of the course each pupil must know and must have written out at least twelve of each of the four classes of music.[28]

From 1923 to 1939, 99 students passed through this programme.[29]

It was now replaced with crash courses in basic piping lasting a month and designed to keep pace with what the military called 'wastage'. At the estimated rate of 80% per annum this meant replacing 200 pipers a year, effectively double what Willie Ross could turn out.[30] Notwithstanding this, by the end of the war he had taught some 700 personnel. But the relentless pressure had begun to take its toll, and he was in any case approaching his seventieth year. He received an M.B.E. for his services, and the Society began to cast about for a successor. But there were difficulties. They could afford to pay him a pension, or engage another instructor, but not both. And in any case Archibald Campbell did not think that any of the younger generation of master players such as R. U. Brown, R. B. Nicol or Donald MacLeod was up to the job.[31] At the same time, he was keen to maintain the Society's influence in this area:

27 'Piping News. Piobaireachd Society carries on', *OT*, 23/12/1939, p.5.
28 NLS, Acc. 9103/8, Correspondence 1895–1928, 'Note of the work done during the six months course of instruction for Army pipers at Edinburgh Castle'; see also the exam papers for the course ending in March 1927: 'Examination of Army Piping Class. Edinburgh Castle. 18th March. 1927'.
29 NLS, Acc.9103/9 Correspondence, 1929–1950, George I. Campbell, to Lord Nathan, Under Secretary of State for War, 14/9/1946.
30 NLS, Acc.9103/9 Correspondence, 1929–1950, '*Supply of Pipers for Scottish Regiments*', 11/2/1945.
31 NLS, Acc.9103/9, Archibald Campbell to George I. Campbell, 30/6/1945; 16/3/1946; 2/6/1946; 21/9/1946; 2/10/1946; 23/3/1947; NLS. Acc.9103/10 Correspondence 1951–54, J. P. Grant to George I. Campbell, 14/4/1953; 1/1/1954, 22/3/1954; Archibald Campbell to George I. Campbell, 6/10/1954.

'the Piping world' . . . is inclined to say that the Piobd. Society is wasting its time using the Army as a means for improving piping. Before the P.S. instruction of Pipe Majors started the contrast between (1) the regimental pipe band, and (2) the civilian or City Territorial band was deplorably to the disadvantage of the first named. The gap is still considerable, but has been greatly narrowed since our classes started. Because Ross has been a noted prize winner, the prestige of our teaching is high in the piping world. Take away Ross, and Army piping once more becomes the subject of mockery to the 'piping world'. The Army could start its own school of instruction for pipe majors, but this would only be jeered at . . .

In short, if the Piobd. Society support were withdrawn, Army piping would go down flat, both in efficiency and prestige.[32]

The situation continued unresolved for nearly a decade. The Army was restive but Campbell was adamant that there was no plausible replacement for Willie Ross. He wrote:

If we sever our connection with the Army, we may lose prestige in the bar of the New Club. But we should gain prestige in the general piping world, which thinks, on the whole, that that connection has been a mistake all through.

Certainly we have not got much out of the Army, beyond the satisfaction of having been of great benefit to it. I daresay that nowadays I am one of the very few who can testify to the appalling state of regimental piping previous to 1910.[33]

The post-war period brought continuing difficulties with the B.B.C. and with the new Edinburgh International Festival. In 1947 a number of distinguished visitors had commented adversely on the absence of Scottish music at the latter. One, Dr. Eric Simón of the Instituto Cultural Anglo-Uruguayo, had proposed that 'performances by the best pipers available in the country should be given daily in one of the smaller halls'. At least he had intended to propose this. Unfortunately when he arrived at the B.B.C. to give the broadcast talk of which this was to form part, he discovered that all reference to it had been cut from his script.[34] George Campbell of Succoth, the Society's secretary, duly wrote to the London-based Glyndebourne Society which organised the Festival, making a formal proposal along the lines suggested by Simón. He received the following rather discouraging reply:

32 NLS, Acc.9103/9 Correspondence, 1929–1950, Archibald Campbell to George I. Campbell, 15/8/1946.
33 NLS, Acc.9103/10 Correspondence, 1951–54, Archibald Campbell to George Campbell, 31/7/1953.
34 NLS, Acc.9103/9, Correspondence, 1929–1950, George I. Campbell to the British Council, 7/2/1948.

Dear Sir,

   I refer to your recent suggestion that Piobaireachd Music, the classical
music of the pipes, be represented at the Festival.

   This matter was duly considered at a recent meeting of my Committee and
I regret to inform you that as Programme arrangements are now completed it
is not possible to meet your request.

   I am instructed to suggest to you, however, that you might approach the
Saltire Society, which might be interested in this type of music.[35]

But there was one wholly unexpected outcome of the 1947 Edinburgh Festival.
The city's great libraries had unearthed an assortment of interesting old items for
display and one of them, from the University of Edinburgh, turned out to be the
original manuscript of Joseph MacDonald's *Compleat Theory of the Scots Highland Bagpipe*. Mairi A. MacDonald hurried to Edinburgh to examine the find.
Here was proof of the integrity of a text she had struggled to defend for twenty
years and, better still, perhaps, proof of her father Alexander MacDonald's good
faith. But this long and complicated story had another complication still in store.
When J. P. Grant examined the manuscript he said it was not the one he had
previously seen. In his student days before the Great War, he was almost certain
that he had handled another copy in the Signet or Advocates' Libraries in
Edinburgh and this was not it. Both he and Mairi MacDonald instituted
searches, but no trace of the document was to be found.[36] Nearly fifty years
later, it was the Edinburgh University manuscript which formed the basis of
Roderick Cannon's edition of 1994, the first reliable published version in the
text's long and chequered history.

   Piping broadcasts were also to prove a bone of contention during the
immediate post-war years. In the winter of 1947/8, for example, the B.B.C.
commissioned a programme of original piobaireachds written and played by the
Scottish composer Donald Main, overruling the objections of its advisory piping
panel led by J. P. Grant which stated that the tunes were worthless and that Main
played the pipes so badly that he was likely to bring the instrument into
disrepute.[37] The B.B.C.'s view – that this was proper music and therefore none
of the piping panel's business – was not a conciliatory one. In any case, J. P.
Grant's relations with what he called the 'Morningside-Gorbals combine' which
ran the B.B.C. in Scotland had not been good. He had criticised them in the past
over piping and Scottish dance music, especially their enthusiasm for 'frightful
bands', by which, presumably, he meant people like Jim Cameron and Jimmy

35 NLS, Acc.9103/9, Wm. Grahame, asst. Secretary, Edinburgh Festival Society Ltd. to
    George I. Campbell, 6/3/1948.
36 NLS, Acc.9103/9 , W. Park, Keeper of the National Library of Scotland to J. P.
    Grant, 29/3/1949; Cannon, *Compleat Theory*, pp.111–2, *n* 47.
37 The programme was broadcast in the B.B.C. Home Service 'Modern Scottish
    Composers' series, 19/3/1948.

Shand.[38] Now he wrote to the *Oban Times* appealing for support.[39] And he received a great deal. More, perhaps, than he had bargained for. High words passed: 'outrage', 'travesty', 'insult to Scotland'. Even people who had not heard the broadcast condemned it most bitterly.[40] Main mounted a vigorous defence accusing the Piobaireachd Society of being the chief culprit in the modern decline of the art. He claimed to have spent twelve years analysing piobaireachd as a result of which:

> The findings of my research show the music to be a well-developed art form which can only properly be practised by the educated musician.
>
> This is contrary to the belief of the sentimentalists, a traditionalist school, of whom Sheriff Grant is head dictator. Hence the propaganda war.
>
> The issue is quite clear: Either the MacCrimmons, and their fellow composers, were rude, half-savages making a crude uncivilised unrhythmic din such as we hear from the military school of piobaireachd to-day – and I am therefore in the wrong; or those ancient composers were educated musicians with a highly intellectualised technique working in the medium of a highly stylised sonata form – which I can prove to anyone who cares to enquire.[41]

He dismissed the Piobaireachd Society as 'blindly emotional devotees of the MacCrimmon cult' whose *Collection* was a 'morass of sentimental hyperbole and illegitimate staff notation'.[42] He condemned Grant and those like him who insisted that piobaireachd was a special kind of music with its own rules which only 'experts' like himself were qualified to interpret, and scornfully rejected 'that final, shameful absurdity, "Piobd. is a *different kind of music*" – a sort of "navvy's music", a tinker-dialect divorced altogether from every orthodoxy, outside all law of music structure . . . as one "expert" told me, "Piobd. isn't MEANT to be music". The whole attitude is shameful and repugnant'.[43]

38 NLS, Acc.9103/9 Correspondence, 1929–1950, J. P. Grant to George I. Campbell, 6/1/1946.

39 'Piobaireachd Music', from J. P. Grant, *OT*, 3/4/1948, p.5. See also 'The BBC Piping Broadcast', from Herbert Wiseman, Head of Scottish Music, 10/4/1948, p.5.

40 'Ancient Piobaireachd', from John Grant, *OT*, 10/4/1948, p.5; same, from Malcolm MacInnes, 10/4/1948, p.5; 'The BBC Piping Broadcast' from Archibald Campbell of Kilberry, 17/4/1948, p.5; from George Bain, defending Main, 17/4/1948, p.5; from 'Loch Boisdale', 24/4/1948, p.5; from J. A. MacLellan, 24/4/1948, p.5; 'The BBC Piping Broadcast. Piobaireachd Music', from Archibald MacNab, 1/5/1948, p.5; 'Discussion on Piobaireachd', from Seumas MacNeill, 20/5/1948, p.5; and 'The B.B.C. Piping Broadcast. Piobaireachd Music', from P. Porteous, 1/5/1948, p.5 supporting Main.

41 'Piobaireachd Music', from Donald Main, *OT*, 10/4/1948, p.5.

42 'Celtic Piobaireachd', from Donald Main, *OT*, 24/4/1948, p.3.

43 NLS, Acc.9103/25, 'Letters to and about G. F. Ross; 1925, 1961, 1946, n.d. with notebooks and typescripts of his work on piobaireachd analysis'. Notes and corrections to G. F. Ross's *Piobaireachd Studies*, by Donald [Main].

The piping people huffed and puffed, but perhaps the most damaging retort came from novelist and critic James Barke, in his radio programme, 'Arts Review', of 31 March 1948, which contemptuously dismissed

> . . . Mr. Main and his so-called pibrochs . . . All Scottish musicians, known to me, outside the circle of pibroch players, are so abysmally musically ignorant of pibroch playing that they cannot distinguish the most wretched piping from good piping; and, in terms of pipe music, cannot distinguish 'Pop goes the Weasel' from the 'Leonora Overture' numbers 1, 2 or 3 – to say nothing of 'Sodger lie doon on your wee pickle strae'.
>
> This is a sweeping indictment of non-piping Scottish musicians; but if it errs, it errs in not being sweeping enough.

Barke declared that Main's compositions were 'pathetically derivative' and 'completely devoid of feeling or inspiration'. And that in terms of execution, 'Never in some forty years of listening to piping have I heard playing so downrightly wicked'.[44]

These were interesting times. In the summer of 1947 the pipe-band world was also engulfed in controversy. The Scottish Pipe Band Association wanted to move the World Championship competition from Dunoon to Edinburgh to get a bigger audience and there was a blazing row with the Cowal Committee which refused to comply with the move. In the resulting schism there were effectively two World Championships, one in Dunoon and one in Edinburgh. The Association laid an embargo on Cowal, threatening any of its members who competed there with immediate suspension. The current World Champions, the City of Glasgow Police, defied the ban and were stripped of their title.[45]

Moves had been under way in Glasgow for some time to rationalise the teaching of piping in the city which had major implications for piping institutions throughout the country. There was a tremendous post-war boom in demand for instruction – one pipe-maker in the city had a waiting list of 900 for practice chanters – and it was felt that the traditional agencies were inadequate for the purpose. A series of meetings of interested organisations was held in the Highlanders' Institute under the chairmanship of Dr. Kenneth

---

44 NLS, Acc 9103/28, Memoranda concerning Piobaireachd Society publications [BBC radio script} 'Arts Review' – Wednesday, 31st March 1948, 7.30–8.00 p.m. Modern Scottish Composers – Donald Main, reviewed by James Barke.

45 The sequence on the World's dispute begins in the *OT,* 14/6/1947; see also 'Edinburgh Letter', 21/6/1947, p.3; 'Pipe Band Dispute. Cowal banned by the Association', 23/8/1947, p.5; 'World's Pipe Band Championship. Notable Success at Edinburgh', 13/9/1947, p.3; 'Pipe Band Contest Dispute. Move to reach a Settlement', 25/10/1947, p.3; 'Pipe Band Championship', revealing that the SPBA made more than a £1,000 profit on the Edinburgh event, 21/2/1948, p.3; 'Pipe Bands Dispute', showing the SPBA still refusing to acquiesce to Cowal's demands 20/5/1948, p.3.

MacKay, representing the Scottish Pipers' Association. Much of the impetus behind this came from Seumas MacNeill representing The League of Young Scots (Comunn na h-Alba), the parent organisation of The College of Piping. The goal was to set up an overall controlling body which would introduce a system of grading and certification for teachers, players and judges. Anybody could set up as a teacher of piping, since there was no formal qualification, and there were fears that, as a result, a good deal of technically dubious instruction was going on. If a recognised certificate for teachers could be achieved, this might clear the way for higher status and remuneration and for standardised courses of instruction as well. A central governing body would be required to administer the board of examination. This would take the form of a co-ordinating committee of participating societies which would be empowered to devise courses of instruction, administer examinations for teachers and players, and grant certificates in various grades. It would also hold a register of approved teachers.

Two grades of instructors were contemplated: one, holding a Junior Teacher's Diploma, the other a Senior Teacher's Diploma, the main difference lying in knowledge of piobaireachd, the Senior Teachers having to be able to play, read, and write ceòl mór, and demonstrate knowledge of its construction and history. There were to be four grades of players: Elementary (practice chanter only); Junior (Tuning and care of pipes. Theory of music as applicable to piping. March, strathspey and reel of competition type. Piobaireachd notes and exercises); Senior (involving all of the above 'with simpler piobaireachd which may be sat as desired'); and finally holders of the Diploma of Piping (covering 'the whole of piobaireachd as may be selected'). There was a suggested scale of fees as follows:

Elementary test 5/-
Junior Certificate 10/-
Senior certificate 21/-
Diploma of Piping 42/-

Teachers, Junior Certificate, 21/-; Senior certificate 42/-[46]

Some within the Piobaireachd Society felt that it should support the scheme, and that the Society might find itself isolated if it held aloof. Archibald Campbell took a different view. The Society's delegates had been instructed to oppose certification for players, but the other societies were determined to have it in.

46 NLS, Acc.9103/9, Correspondence, 1929–1950 'Minute of Representative Meeting in the Highlanders' Institute Glasgow. Thursday, 5th December, 1946'; 'Proficiency Tests in Piping Second Representative Meeting in The Highlanders' Institute . . . Glasgow, 27th March, 1947'; 'Proposed Scheme for Certification of Teachers and Pipers', 26/6/1947.

Without the Piobaireachd Society's blessing, however, Campbell knew it could not go ahead, and in any case the scheme was flawed. The proposed fees were substantial, and it seemed unlikely that many teachers would pay them or submit themselves for examination, at least voluntarily, when there was little apparent practical advantage to be gained by so doing. He indicated that the Piobaireachd Society should decline to participate.[47]

Many of the aims and objects of the Glasgow Representative Committee were to take institutional shape in The League of Young Scots College of Piping, an attempt to re-create Boreraig in a modern urban setting, which was to enjoy a considerable influence in the piping world during the following fifty years. Under its Honorary President Flora MacLeod of MacLeod, and Joint Principals Thomas Pearston and Seumas MacNeill it was dedicated

1. To raise the prestige of Piping and the status of the Piper.
2. To improve the general standard of Piping, particularly by systematic instruction, and by the training of qualified Instructors.
3. To provide facilities for all boys, especially those of limited means, to learn the Art of Piping.
4. To encourage the study and playing of Piobaireachd.
5. To stimulate research in the methods of the manufacture of Bagpipes and Accessories with a view to their general improvement.
6. To improve the running of Solo Piping Competitions and methods of adjudication at present employed.

Such aims might be thought to have commanded wide support in the piping world. But a request by the new institution for financial assistance preserved amongst the Piobaireachd Society's papers is docketed 'no' in Archibald Campbell's hand.[48]

In April 1948 The Professional Pipers' Union was formed with Seumas MacNeill as honorary secretary and a programme designed to raise prize money, and tackle poor standards on the bench by supplying games committees with lists of accredited judges.[49] Archibald Campbell wrote 'The Glasgow professional pipers now have a Trade Union, the policy of which is to put a pistol to the heads of Games Committees about the amounts of prize money. I believe last year a threat of boycott was levied at Dunoon and only withdrawn after a last minute settlement . . . Does the

47 NLS, Acc.9103/9, Archibald Campbell to George Campbell of Succoth, 31/7/1947, 2/10/1947; memo 'To all Members of the General Committee – The Piobaireachd Society, 13th October, 1947. Proposed Scheme for Certification of Teachers and Pipers emanating from the Scottish Pipers' Association, Glasgow'.

48 NLS, Acc.9103/9 The League of Young Scots (Comunn na h-Alba) 181 Pitt Street, Glasgow, C.2, attached to a letter from College of Piping Hon. Sec. Ada Pearston requesting financial support.

49 'Piping and Judging', from Seumas MacNeill, OT, 12/3/1949, p.5.

Dunoon Committee want PS "cooperation" as a weapon with which to fight a threatened strike?'[50]

In some ways these were difficult years for Archibald Campbell. While he was very busy with his editorial work, there were a number of developments in the piping world of which he intensely disapproved. For example, the General Committee of the Piobaireachd Society, without referring to him, had agreed to take into its keeping the research papers of G. F. Ross, author of *Some Piobaireachd Studies* (1926) and *A Collection of MacCrimmon and Other Piobaireachd* (1929) which had been strongly critical of the Society's editorial methods. Campbell wrote:

> I suppose that I must go and examine the stuff some time. There is not likely to be anything among it, which will be of any value to the Piobaireachd Society. The rough idea which Rothiemurchus and I had was that any printed books worth preserving should be handed over to the Scottish Pipers Society of London, of which Mr. Ross was the President, and that most of Mr. Ross's M.S. work should be destroyed. The difficulty is how to effect this latter, for Mrs. Hepworth, the sister, regards such work as of great value. But on the other hand, [I] think that it may mislead future generations into thinking that the Society gave it its approval by accepting it as a gift, and keeping it.

He added in a note to J. P. Grant: 'What do you think? Has the PS been let in for the expense of packing and storing this stuff for an indefinite period? Or do you think that it can go to Rothiemurchus and have decent though surreptitious cremation there?'[51] There was a further unpleasant surprise in the autumn of 1950, when he discovered that the General Committee had acceded to a request by the War Office that Gurkha pipers be considered for the Army Class at Edinburgh Castle. He had to threaten to resign before he could ensure that this remained a dead letter.[52]

Meantime he had not been idle. Volume 8 of the Piobaireachd Society's *Collection* had appeared in September 1939, and he devoted the war years to an ambitious new project, an anthology eventually numbering 118 tunes entitled *The*

---

50 NLS, Acc.9103/9 Correspondence, 1929–1950, Archibald Campbell to George Campbell of Succoth, 22/1/1951. Writing to Seton Gordon, he declared 'The Glasgow Pipers Union seems to be rather an unfortunate bit of work. The Socialist schoolmaster element is at the bottom of it', Seton Gordon Papers, NLS, Acc.7451, General Correspondence, 27/8/1949.

51 NLS, Acc.9103/25, Letters to and about G. F. Ross, Archibald Campbell to 'Mr. Aiken', 21/6/1951, and to J. P. Grant, n.d. Campbell's approach to the sources was highly selective: for example he advised against purchase of an early edition of Angus MacKay's *Ancient Piobaireachd* with the errors corrected in MacKay's own hand, Piobaireachd Research Papers of Archibald Campbell NLS MS. 22102, 24/12/33.

52 NLS, Acc.9103/9 Correspondence, 1929–1950, memorandum from Archibald Campbell, 13/10/1950.

Kilberry Book of Ceol Mor (Glasg., 1948, 2nd edn., 1953 and later reprints) containing nearly all of the central competition repertoire in piobaireachd, the tunes appearing without accompanying notes, but prefixed by a substantial historical and textual essay.[53] *The Kilberry Book* was quickly adopted as an approved text for competition, and for most practical purposes became the book of books. Possessing this, the ordinary piper attracted to, or obliged to play, piobaireachd need look no further. As one commentator remarked some fifty years later 'the vast majority of aspiring piobaireachd players today begin their study via the famous Kilberry Book of Ceol Mor'.[54]

The 'Introduction' was generally accepted as a definitive scholarly statement and became the dominant source of conventional wisdom about piobaireachd throughout the second half of the 20th century. Yet it flowed from a past substantially misunderstood. Believing, as he did, that the introductory 'Essay' to Patrick MacDonald's *Highland Vocal Airs* had been written by Patrick MacDonald, and that the letterpress portions of Angus MacKay's book had been written by Angus MacKay, Campbell gave ready credence to the idea that the tradition had been in peril until rescued and preserved by the Highland Societies of London and Scotland, concluding that 'it is not unreasonable to say that the piobaireachd has survived largely through the Army, and by means of the competition system.'[55] But little evidence was offered to support these conclusions. Nor is it easy to reconcile them with the author's opinion – stated above – that standards in the Army had been historically low and continued to be so relative to the world of civilian piping. His brief account of the Piobaireachd Society alluded to early 'disagreements about . . . policy' but made no mention of the secession of the founders, the overthrow of General Thomason, or the hostile reception which had greeted both series of the Society's *Collection*. In his sketch of the important piping families, the MacCrimmons were presented as the inventors or at least perfecters of piobaireachd and as the ultimate source of authenticity in piping. Much was also made of the authority of Angus MacKay, Campbell stating that:

> Other MSS. have been recorded since the publication of Angus Mackay's book. In none of those written by pipers of repute has the writer seen any of the tunes contained in Angus Mackay's printed book, which are not exact copies . . . This is cogent evidence of what has been described already as the reverence paid to Angus Mackay by all pipers of any note since Angus Mackay's book was published' . . . [adding that] 'up to the publication of *Ceol Mor* in 1900, most printed books of piobaireachd

53 Cannon, *Bibliography*, pp.247–8.
54 'Highland bagpipe music's finest authority', *Piper Press*, no.5, March 1998, pp.20–23 (20).
55 Campbell, *Kilberry Book*, 'Introduction', p.8. See also Archibald Campbell, 'Highland Bagpipe', *PT*, July 1962, pp.6–10, (8–10).

music consisted largely, and sometimes wholly, of facsimile copies from Angus Mackay's book.[56]

But these statements were not correct. The main Victorian manuscripts, with the exception of Thomason's and David Glen's, avoided recording tunes already in MacKay's book, while Thomason and Glen used notational procedures very different from those of Angus MacKay. Indeed MacKay's notation never succeeded in fully establishing itself, except perhaps for a brief period in the *Piobaireachd Society Collection* (first series), to whose existence Campbell did not allude. Far from being copied from MacKay, none of the piobaireachds in Uilleam Ross's *Collection* (1869) had been published before, and we have seen differences between the settings of MacKay and Donald MacPhee provoke heated discussion in later Victorian Scotland. With regard to composition, also, – a crucial point marking the boundary line between a tradition which, however attenuated, could still be regarded as living, and one which had become largely of historical interest – an equally misleading impression was created. Campbell poured scorn upon C. S. Thomason's compositions, claiming that it was futile of him even to have attempted such a thing given the innate conservatism of pipers, and declaring that 'It has often been said that the art of composing piobaireachd is dead. Certainly no good player since John Ban MacKenzie is known to have attempted anything serious in that line'.[57] While he must have known the published compositions

56 Campbell, *Kilberry Book*, 'Introduction', p.12. Yet as noted above, Campbell blocked attempts to purchase a first edition of *Ancient Piobaireachd* discovered during the 1930s with the errors corrected in MacKay's own hand: Piobaireachd Research Papers NLS. MS. 22102, 24/12/33.

57 *Ibid.*, pp.13, 16. Campbell wrote 'Both [Willie] Ross and John MacDonald (I gather) consider Donald MacLeod to be the outstanding piper of the day . . . I rather wonder at a man like that bothering, or being permitted by John MacDonald to bother, with a thing like 'Hail to my Country'. I know a lot about that tune . . . It is not Ceol Mor at all, but very inferior third rate Ceol Beag . . . the General told me about 'Hail to my Country'. After many years absence in India he came on leave and woke up in the train on a fine summer morning at Dalwhinnie to see the beginnings of the Spey as he got towards Kingussie. He was so uplifted that the first line of the ground come into his head . . . The second line was taken from the General's interpretation of the second part of ['Ossian's Lament for his Father'] . . . It was very unfortunate that the General included tunes of his own composition in Ceol Mor. If I could have got at him sooner I should have protested . . . The General's own explanation to me was that he had put in his own compositions, not because he was proud of them, but in the hope that he would [?]incite others to compose piobd. – which showed a lack of appreciation of the situation.

I fear neither this tune nor any more of the General's compositions is worth anything. People now regard him as having been a great piper. He was never this. He was a man of great ability, but he was never through the mill properly with a teacher'. Archibald Campbell to Seton Gordon, Seton Gordon Papers, General Correspondence 1940–5, 19/9/1942.

of Uilleam Ross and Donald MacPhee, it is curious that a man whose name 'could be said to be synonymous with piping in the twentieth century',[58] should apparently be unaware of the work in this field of John MacColl, Calum Piobaire, William Laurie, William MacLean, G. S. McLennan, and Angus Macpherson.[59] Indeed he had composed at least one piobaireachd himself, 'A Lament for Angus Campbell', his elder brother who had died in 1908 at the age of 35. It is a potentially attractive tune with a melodic quality quite absent from his normal editorial work, suggesting perhaps just how seriously the latter was affected by the Paradigm and the cultural expectations that flowed from it.[60]

The 'Introduction' re-iterated the now familiar injunction that this was slow music to be played slowly: 'The groundwork is often very slow, and the general effect of the whole piece is slow . . . Slowness is a characteristic of Highland music, as anyone will agree who has heard the untutored Gaelic singer, or the precentor at a Highland church service.'[61] And the settings seem to have been constructed with this characteristic specifically in mind – to a markedly greater extent than in corresponding arrangements of the same tunes in the *Piobaireachd Society Collection* (second series). Low themal notes were drawn out and cadence phrase endings lengthened to give the music the kind of weight that Campbell now considered appropriate:

58 John A. MacLellan, in *Comunn na Piobaireachd: The Piobaireachd Society Present a Collection of Ceòl Mór Composed during the Twentieth Century* 1930–1980 (Glasg., 1980), 'The Composers'.

59 For John MacColl's piobaireachd compositions, see MacNeill, 'John MacColl', Part 4, p.19. For William Laurie see above, p.273. For Calum Piobaire's 'Lament for Cluny Macpherson', see *A Highlander Looks Back*, pp.15–16. For Angus MacPherson's 'The Cairn at Boreraig', 1933, see *ibid.* For his 'Salute to Seton Gordon', 1929, see Eagle, p.129 and his 'Salute in Praise of William Ross, M.B.E.', Mackenzie, *Piping Traditions*, p.114. For the circumstances of William MacLean's powerful 'Lament for the Earl of Seafield' (who was killed at Loos Sept 27, 1915, commanding A. Coy. 5th Camerons), see Piobaireachd Research Papers of Archibald Campbell, NLS, MS.22117, ff.157–60. For G. S. McLennan's 'Lament for Lieut. John McLennan' see his published *Highland Bagpipe Music* (1929); and for an unpublished composition, 'Piobaireachd', see the A. E. Milne MS, AUL, MS.2904, ff.306–7. There are a number of interesting original compositions in the Glen MS. including 'Failte Iain 'ic Aonghais', 'Miss Emma Haldane's Lament', by Angus Cameron, 'J. S. Macdonald of Monachyle's Salute', by William Sutherland of Airdrie, 'The Vale of Keppoch is become desolate', by James Mauchline, and 'The Royal Salute' by Charles Bannatyne: NLS, MS.22120, ff.408–11, 422–4, 390–91, 419–21, 163–4.

60 *Ceòl Mór Composed during the Twentieth Century*, pp.2–3.

61 Campbell, *Kilberry Book*, 'Introduction', p.6.

Lament for Captain MacDougall, Ground line 1, Piobaireachd Society , vi, 164. 1936

Lament for Captain MacDougall, *Kilberry Book of Ceol Mor*, p.5. 1948.

Lament for MacSwan of Roaig, Var.1. line 1, Piobaireachd Society, i, 39. 1925.

Lament for MacSwan of Roaig, Var.1. line 1, *Kilberry Book of Ceol Mor*, p.6. 1948.

Tulach Ard, Var.11. line 1, Piobaireachd Society, vi, 172. 1936

Tulloch Ard, *Kilberry Book of Ceol Mor*, p.7. 1948

My King has landed in Moidart, Ground line 1, Piobaireachd Society, v, 157. 1934.

My King has landed in Moidart, Ground line 1, *Kilberry Book of Ceol Mor*, p.61. 1948.

The Kilberry Book followed the general style of the Piobaireachd Society volumes, but there were certain interesting departures from the conventions of the latter text. For example Crunluath Breabach movements were now pointed 'down' as opposed to the even quavers hitherto favoured, and there was a curious new a mach movement which departed from previous notational practice by eliminating the internal semi-quaver, presumably to make the movement consistent with the McLennan style used elsewhere in the later variations. In the past the movement had been rendered as in the first three examples below:

Donald MacDonald   Angus MacKay   Piobaireachd Society   Kilberry Book

However varied the implied timing, the first three contained eleven notes. The version in *The Kilberry Book* had only ten.[62]

Campbell concluded his 'Introduction' with a number of statements about the stylistic preferences of the people who had taught him, ending, 'The majority of the tunes in the book were taught carefully to the writer by one, or by two, or by all of his three teachers, Alexander Cameron son of Donald Cameron, J. MacDougall Gillies, and John MacDonald'.[63] In the *Piobaireachd Society Collection* (second series) he had done much in the name of Cameron and Gillies, both recently dead. But the third of the authorities now identified in the *Kilberry Book of Ceol Mor* for the first time publicly as one of his major teachers – John MacDonald of Inverness – was still alive, and most unhappy about what Campbell was doing, so much so that in 1940 he had described David Glen's *Collection of Ancient Piobaireachd* as 'the most reliable we have today.'[64]

The published reviews ranged from the dutifully respectful to the gushingly positive. The *Piping Times* spoke of Campbell and the Piobaireachd Society sieving tradition to establish the true styles in the face of differing authorities, adding that 'During the past few years the Piobaireachd Society's books have become increasingly difficult to obtain, and with the advent of the Kilberry Book of Ceol Mor the reason for the scarcity of the older collections became clear, as in the one collection the piper obtained the accepted styles of the Piobaireachd Society and the reference book of the future for the piobaireachd competitions at Oban and Inverness and other gatherings'.[65] Angus Macpherson hailed the *Kilberry Book* as

---

62 For a discussion of this point see Dugald B. MacNeill, 'Crunluath a mach', in *PT*, vol.50, no.4, January 1998, p.27; with correspondence from James Hamilton, vol.50, no.6, March 1998, pp.9–11; and 'Crunluath a Mach', by Neville T. MacKay, vol.50, no.8, May 1998, pp.16–17.

63 *Kilberry Book*, 'Introduction', p.17.

64 John MacDonald to Dr. W. M. MacPhail, 9/7/1940, in Shone, p.58.

65 Vol.2, no.11, August 1950, p.10.

containing 'most of the best compositions of Ceol Mor, suitable for the highest nobleman's library, and the daily use of the enthusiast', declaring that Campbell had left 'a legacy of inestimable value'.[66] Malcolm MacInnes described the book as 'a monument to the study and devotion of an enthusiast's life'.[67] John MacDonald of Inverness took a different view. His pupil R. B. Nicol visited him at this time and was examining the new collection as it lay on a table. John MacDonald came in. R. B. Nicol said he had never seen him so angry. Gesturing at the volume, he said 'Piobaireachd is dead, Nicol, and *that* is its epitaph!'[68]

MacDonald wrote to Seton Gordon:

> Yes, I have a copy of 'Kilberry's Book', and my opinion of it is that it is the beginning of the end, of our traditional Piobaireachd playing as handed down to us, I certainly dont agree with any of his comments on the Camerons or Gillies, and I have had so much to do with him before he went to India and since his return that I am almost justified in saying he is untruthful . . . I am not continuing teaching the tunes for this year's competitions as written by the P. S. I am too old now to adopt the modern ideas of Piob. – and am quite happy to keep what I got from the old Pipers . . . I will say no more until I have an opportunity of a personal talk with you.[69]

His dismay at Campbell's settings and the institutional power that enabled them to be enforced was well known during the 'thirties and 'forties. He had long ago severed his formal connection with the Society, but he refused to engage in public controversy, concentrating instead on building a new generation of master players equipped with a detailed appreciation of the limitations of the official scores. During the war years he kept anxious track of Brown, Nicol and MacLeod, by now serving Pipe-Majors in the Gordons and Seaforth, and tried to get them released for further instruction at a revived army class at Inverness taught by himself. While the Piobaireachd Society threw its weight behind the mass production of basically-trained pipers for the Scottish Regiments, Mac-Donald was anxious, as ever, for the higher branches of the art. He wrote:

> Nicol is somewhere in England, and I heard Brown is missing, although this is not confirmed . . . I am only too anxious to impart all I can in the right

66 'The Kilberry Book of Ceol Mor', from Angus Macpherson, *OT*, 26/2/1949, p.5. A curious change of mind in view of his expressed opinion in 1942 that 'Ceol Mor has many irresponsible onslaughts made upon it', and alluding to 'the various books and scores in circulation, some of them being more of a curiosity than anything else, and would be serving a better purpose at this time in the hands of the waste-paper collector . . .', 'Piping Reminiscences of John MacDonald MBE', *OT*, 18/4/1942, p.5.
67 'Mr Archibald Campbell's "Kilberry Book of Ceol Mor"', by Malcolm MacInnes, *OT*, 19/3/1949, p.3.
68 R. B. Nicol, in conversation with the writer, Ballater, 30/7/1975.
69 Seton Gordon Papers, NLS, Acc.5640/2 (1), 28/1/1949, f.38.

direction. At the same time it would be a pity to waste time and money on *purely military* piping . . . I would very much like to have . . . *McLeod of the Seaforths* . . . who, in my opinion is likely to be one of the best Piob. players. He has got a natural aptitude and has got a mind of his own to stick to what he gets instead of copying anyone he may hear play . . . It would be realy a tragedy to allow all the good results of the labours of recent years to go to waste, and this opportunity [of restarting the army class at Inverness] would help to keep up the enthusiasm and standard of our national music, until better times return . . . they are the only ones who are likely to carry on when the older men have faded out.[70]

But by 1949 Archibald Campbell seemed unassailable, and *The Kilberry Book of Ceol Mor* went on, as he had feared it might, to become the basic text-book used in piobaireachd playing throughout the second half of the 20th century and to exercise a major influence on the way that the music was perceived and performed.

John MacDonald did not have much longer to live. Although he had given up competitive playing on medical advice following a slight stroke in 1935, he continued in high demand as a teacher and his pupils were amongst the finest performers of the following generation. His superb technique and expressive style were the admiration of his contemporaries and he dominated competitive piobaireachd playing in Scotland for nearly forty years. A legend in his own lifetime, his death on the 6th of June 1953 at the age of 87 marked the passing of an age. He was buried in Cluny Hill Cemetery, Forres, in the grave of Helen Gibb, his second wife, on 8th June 1953.

R. U. Brown, R. B. Nicol and Donald MacLeod went on to become the leading teachers of the second half of the 20th century. But the role for which he had prepared them was swiftly overtaken by technical change. The diffusion of cheap portable tape recorders from the mid 1960s onwards was to create a new audio democracy, transforming the mechanisms of transmission by giving instant permanence to hitherto fleeting oral forms. The Piobaireachd Society, hampered by its ideological stance which prevented it from endorsing the work of living players, was unable to deploy the medium, and J. P. Grant's enthusiastic recognition of its potential was frustrated by the opposition of Archibald Campbell. But John MacDonald's pupils were unaffected by such considerations, and eagerly exploited the new technology. Indeed Brown and Nicol were already experimenting with it in the year of MacDonald's death.[71] Tape-recording represented not just a rival to staff notation, but a potentially superior method of storage and transmission, which reflected the nuances of the music far

70 John MacDonald to Seton Gordon, 5th Aug 1940 f.15; J.M. to S.G., 18 July 1940, f.14; J.M. to S.G, 23 May 1941, f.23–4; see also J.M. to S.G., 13/11/1944, f.34

71 NLS, Acc.9103/10 Correspondence 1951–4, J.P Grant to George Campbell of Succoth, 23/11/1953, 30/12/1953, 1/1/1954.

more precisely than the older system, and was much superior to it as an instructional aid. Brown and Nicol saw at once that tape was the nearest approximation possible to the old method, undermining the primacy of the fixed score, acknowledging the essential diversity of the tradition, preserving the freedom of the player to interpret, and deplored that it had not been available a generation previously.[72] As they were also aware, the new technology altered the balance of power between the institution wielding print media and traditional face-to-face teaching by creating a new kind of 'text', and therefore a new kind of 'authority' which did not at all lend itself to centralisation or control. Tape-recorded lessons once made, could be reproduced indefinitely, greatly increasing the circle of potential pupils, and much extending the master teachers' range. Thus, as the 20th century entered its second half, the relationship of the oral dimension with the fixed institutionally-sponsored score was to enter a significantly new phase.

72 R. B. Nicol in conversation with the writer, Ballater 10/6/1975, 8/7/1975.

Appendix: Canntaireachd and the Oral Mode

John MacDonald and his pupils were not alone in their dissatisfaction with the Piobaireachd Society's methods, and during the 1950s attention began to focus on other possible methods of representing the tradition. In 1959, Dr. Roderick Ross, son of Neil Ross, and pupil of Angus and John Macpherson, published the first volume of his piobaireachd collection, *Binneas is Boreraig*, which eventually extended to five volumes and included much of the core competition repertoire. This used staff notation, but in a radically altered form, on a three line stave without time signatures or bar lines, designed to reflect phrase patterns more clearly, and encourage a more fluent and idiomatic approach to the music. Ross returned to the notational principles of Thomason and the McLennans, although with a new freedom which allowed the melodic contour of the tunes to influence rhythmical values on the page, and assigned to the cuttings a purely conventional value to reduce visual clutter and assist ease of reading. The settings were based on the work of a living performer, Malcolm Macpherson (the younger), son of Angus Macpherson and pupil of John MacDonald, and the printed scores were accompanied by tape recordings of Macpherson playing the tunes.[1] Here is the first line of 'MacLeod of Colbecks' in the new notation:[2]

Although seeming to reflect an idiomatic style, however, Dr. Ross began by writing down the Piobaireachd Society's settings of the tunes concerned, and then altering this score to reflect Macpherson's note values, although he did not do this fully. Macpherson held some notes more than *Binneas is Boreraig*

1 Cannon, *Bibliography*, pp.257–9.

2 *Binneas is Boreraig*, (5 vols., Edinr., 1959–1967), i, 6–7. Dr Ross has preserved what appears to be a misprint in the version published in MacKay, *Ancient Piobaireachd*, namely the D semi-quaver at the beginning of bar 10 in the ground, p.149. Since the tune is built on a scale gapped at D, this is corrected in the above transcript.

indicates and cut some more likewise, but Ross believed that if he were to render them accurately the scores would not be 'accepted'. The end results were sent to J. P. Grant and Archibald Campbell for approval.

There was renewed interest also in canntaireachd. Its frequent citation in volumes 1–9 of the Society's Collection (second series) in the written system developed by Colin Campbell, had by now made a considerable portion of it available for study. There were claims that the Society had systematically misrepresented the source, silently omitting things that were in it and inserting things that were not.[3] There were also calls that staff notation as the vehicle of the 'mutilated authorised versions' should be abandoned altogether, and that there should be a return, in Dr. Calum MacCrimmon's words, to 'the true medium of teaching – [the] canntaireachd or oral system.'[4] What this would entail, of course, was an immediate resumption of control by the performer community of the mechanisms of transmission and an end of the institutionally-sponsored texts, an acknowledgement, in short, that ultimately this argument was about power, and the ownership of tradition.

In its written form, canntaireachd provided the basis of the indigenous notational system and it was brought to its most developed state by Colin Mór Campbell of Nether Lorn, in Argyll, at the end of the 18th and beginning of the 19th century. Although Campbell's work was almost immediately superseded by a form of staff notation adapted specifically for the pipe, and remained unpublished and unrecognised until well into the 20th century, it remains an important achievement and gives valuable insight into the musical organisation of ceòl mór.

Canntaireachd is a form of solmisation developed for teaching and learning in an oral setting. It is not known how or when it originated, although it has certain features in common with other systems in western Europe arising from about the 11th century onwards. For example, the use of the fingers of the hand to inculcate musical principles, known to have been in use amongst the master pipers, has an interesting parallel in the so-called 'Guidonian Hand', in which different solmisation syllables were assigned to different joints and segments of the fingers and thumb, apparently to help teachers inculcate modes and scales and the means of modulating accurately between them.[5] Canntaireachd has the additional feature of being a 'relative' system in its sung form, but an 'absolute' one in its written form: i.e. in the former the vocables have value relative to one another

---

3 Moss, 'Canntaireachd', pp.16–21. The Society's handling of the Campbell canntaireachd had been attracting adverse comment for some time: see, for example, 'Piobaireachd Society Publications', from Malcolm MacInnes, *OT*, 7/12/35, p.3, and 'The Glencoe Pibroch', 4/11/1939, p.3.

4 A. Macaulay, 'The Passing of Dr. Calum MacCrimmon', *PT*, vol. 14, no.10, July 1962, p.11. Both John MacDonald and Angus Macpherson had urged that canntaireachd should remain central to the transmission of the repertoire during the '40s: see, 'The Piping Reminiscences of John MacDonald M.B.E.' *OT*, 4/4/1942, p.5, and 'same' from Angus Macpherson, 18/4/1942, p.5.

5 Cannon, *Compleat Theory*, pp.64–5; for the Guidonian Hand, see Rastall, pp.129–30.

and can be assigned to any starting pitch the singer cares; in the latter, the vocables indicate specific notes on the chanter.

The basic principle of canntaireachd is beautifully simple: melody notes are represented by vowels and diphthongs, and gracenotes are represented by consonants with the addition of various 'releasing' and 'arresting' particles at the beginnings and ends of the resulting vocables.[6] In Colin Campbell's system, low A is represented by

'en'

low A with a high G gracenote by

'hin'

a siubhal movement at this pitch by

'hinen'

As the movements become longer and more complex, so do the vocables. The taorluath on low A is:

'hindarid'

and the crunluath:

'hinbandre'

6 See Christine Knox Chambers, 'Non-Lexical Vocables in Scottish Traditional Music', Ph.D. Dissertation, Edinburgh University, 1980, p.35. This is the widest-ranging account of the various branches of canntaireachd. In a specifically piping context, the best modern guide is the series of articles published by Frans Buisman in the *Piping Times*, although these assume a high level of prior knowledge: 'From Chant to Script', vol. 39, no.7, April 1987, pp.44–49; 'More Evidence on Colin Campbell and the Development of the Campbell Notation: MS. SRO 112/1/803', vol. 47, no. 11–12, August-September 1995, pp.21–27, 28–34; 'Canntaireachd and Colin Campbell's Verbal Notation – An Outline', vol.50, no.3–4, December 1997–January 1998, pp.24–30, 28–33. see also, Roderick D. Cannon, 'Angus MacKay's "Specimens of Canntaireachd"' Parts 1, 3–4, *same*, vol.41, no.5–7, pp.17–25, 20–38, 41–47; and A. G. Kenneth, 'The Campbell Canntaireachd', vol.17, nos.8–9, May-June 1965, pp. 18–20, 6–9.

Every aspect of the piper's finger technique is allotted a conventional syllabic equivalent, so that a 'grip' movement on B, say, would be 'hiotro':

or a 'throw' on E, 'dre' or 'edre' (depending on whether it was played from a note below or above it in pitch):

A piper who knew the system and had a clear idea of what the music ought to sound like (considerations applying also to staff notation) could take a sequence of written vocables such as 'hindorodin hiendo, hiotroa hioemto' and realise them like this:

The standard Western syllabic system, *ut re mi fa sol la*, developed by the musical doctors of the Mediaeval church, was based on a fixed equivalence between note and verbal token. Each syllable conveyed a single piece of information: namely the position of the designated note relative to others on a fixed scale. But written canntaireachd was more subtle. The vocable had to contain several pieces of information, indicating not only which note was to be played, but also how it was to be ornamented, and even sometimes how it was to be approached, whether from a higher or a lower pitch. It had therefore to be capable of modulation, and be responsive to the exact musical context.

Sung canntaireachd used in face-to-face instruction does not require the internal consistency of written forms and exhibits a correspondingly wide range of personal styles. For example, a pupil of the leading Victorian master, Malcolm Macpherson (Calum Pìobaire), recalled his rendering of the opening phrase of 'MacLeod of Raasay's Salute' in a lesson which must have taken place in the closing years of the nineteenth century. He recorded it like this:

7 'Canntaireachd System of Notation', from Malcolm MacInnes, *OT*, 14/6/1924, p.3.

Humbayo hahbrabun
Tahayabo brobhun[7]

On the staff this would be:

humbayo hahbrabun   tahaya----bo brobhun

We can compare this with a sample from R. U. Brown of Balmoral dating from the mid 1950s. Brown was a leading pupil of John MacDonald of Inverness who was, in turn, a leading pupil of Calum Pìobair. This is the first line of 'The Lament for the Union', Deeside style:[8]

'Lament for the Union between Scotland and England', ground, line one, David Glen's MS, f.3

eeyo travree endee lechyo eeyo landee edreh yayechyo bwdreeodray andee raychyo

chyinda chyoodra yeeundun

There have been a variety of approaches to canntaireachd down the years. Some commentators have regarded the system as essentially descriptive, for example, attempting to show that the terms for the movements derive from the names of the fingers that act in their production, and that the canntaireachd scale is based on the vowel sounds deriving from the ordinal numbers of the fingers involved in each note. It has been further suggested that rhythmic patterns may be determined by prosodic relations between the syllables, to meet the objection that the written system gives pitch values only and does not indicate accent and duration.[9]

'Colin Campbell's Instrumental Book' was compiled over a period of about thirty years. Although only two of his original three volumes appear to have survived, these contain 169 tunes. When complete, the Campbell collection must have been by a considerable margin the largest assembled during the

8 Transcribed from the writer's tape recording collection.
9 See the series of papers in six parts entitled 'Highland Music and Canntaireachd' by
   Charles Bannatyne, *OT*, 30/1/1904 – 5/3/1904, p.3, apparently representing the joint
   conclusions of Bannatyne himself, 'Fionn' (Henry Whyte), Lieut. John McLennan,
   and the music publisher David Glen; see also 'Gesto's M'Crimmon Pibroch Vocables',
   from J. Cameron, 24/9/1927, p.3.

period. Equally impressive is the lucid and systematic arrangement of the contents. Tunes are grouped according to their opening formulae, in a sequence gradually ascending in pitch, suggesting that the collection was conceived as a whole on an explicit plan. It begins with a sequence of forty four tunes starting with the classic opening motif on A, 'hiririn', (called by Campbell 'hiharin'), like this:

'2nd.Called Porst na Striane
Hiharintro hiharintra Twice Over, hihhambambao hiotrotra . . .'

This is followed by a section of tunes opening on B and descending, such as

'47 Called Robt. Sinclairs Wife Lament
Hioendaen hioem hiririechi hedariIe hihararaha'

Then come tunes starting on the arched 'hindorodin' A – C – A opening formula played up to an expressed C, like:

'50th Called Bhan bhi dh'lan n'a bhi pos'a [The Old Woman's Lullaby]
Hindorodin hodindro hiodrorodin hiodintro hindili hieheho cherede chevedili'

Then twenty tunes opening 'hindre', 'hiodre' or 'hodre', which is A, B or C played up to an expressed E with a 'throw':

Then follow ten tunes opening with the rising figure 'hindro', i.e. from A to an expressed C with a 'grip':

Then eight tunes opening with a double echo-beat on E, called in Campbell's system 'cherede':

and so on.

Despite its literate form, then, and its clever translation of acoustic terms into visual analogues, Colin Campbell's taxonomy remains a fundamentally oral/aural one. Compared with the typically quite haphazard arrangement of material in twentieth century collections, it has a high degree of organisation. It serves as a reminder that this music emerged and reached artistic maturity in a substantially oral setting. We can see something of what this might mean by considering the opening sequences of the following pieces:

Vol.1, '1st Called Kepper Eaggarich [The Unjust Incarceration]
Hiharin hioen, hodrooen, himen hoen, hiotroenem . . .'

Vol.1, '6th Called Spaddarich Bharoch [The Pride of Barra]
Hiharinodin hiharindo, hiodrorodin hiham bantro . . .'

Vol.1, '7th Called McNab's Gathering
Hiharinodin hiharindro, hihorodohodin hihorododro . . .'

Vol.1, '9th Called Bhratich Bhan' [MacKay's White Banner]
Hiharinodin hihodaro,do, hiharinodin hihodaro,do, himhinhodin hiodrodin
tro . . .'

Nameless (based on Angus Mackay's MSS)[10]
'Hiharinodin hiharindro, hiharinodin hiharindro, hiemdanodin hiharindro . . .'

The musical organisation is strongly formulaic, with melodies closely related in tonal range and rhythm, in phrase sequence, mode and melodic line, so that however the pieces might diverge in their variations we could consider that, as regards their grounds at least, they are basically five slightly different ways of looking at the same pair of related motifs.[11]

The conventions governing the composition and transmission of music and song in non-literate communities have received a good deal of study during the 20th century. In the absence of a written text, or other form of recording, the music exists solely in performance. But performance may be a much more subtle and creative process than in a 'modern' setting where a written or printed score (generated by another musician called the 'composer', whom the performer need never have met) has overriding authority and delimits the performance in all

10 NLS, MS. 3753–4, i, 237–9 where it appears in staff notation – introductory movement standardised with other examples, and tune re-set from 3/4 to 6/8 for the sake of comparison. The Campbell canntaireachd vocables are supplied by the writer.
11 For an interesting study of 'tune families' in Anglo-American folk-song, see Bayard, p.105, 108, 110–11, 135–8.

kinds of ways. In some oral communities the distinction between composer and performer is much harder to define. What is transmitted is not a fixed body of knowledge, but a process. The music is creatively re-enacted in performance, the musician clothing related clusters of ideas from appropriate suites of melodic formulae. No two performances need be the same. Each performance may be a separate 'text'. There may be no essential distinction between composition and transmission.[12]

But it would be wrong to regard the resulting process as in any way artless or casual. We can see something of what it may have been like from work in related fields, like that of Milman Parry and Albert Lord during the 1930s on the heroic song traditions of the Balkans. Parry was a Homeric scholar who, starting from the observation that the *Iliad* and *Odyssey* were built from metrically standard conventional units frequently repeated with minor variations, argued that this must be a sign of oral composition. It was a familiar enough proposition: the eighteenth century Scottish classicist, Thomas Blackwell, had long before suggested that Homer was essentially an oral artist, a master improviser whose songs had been committed to writing long after his death.[13] The originality of Parry and his assistant and successor Albert Lord was that they were able to devise a research programme which tested this hypothesis in the field by examining the still living heroic song traditions of the former Yugoslavia. There they found oral compositional principles similar to those posited for Homer still in use after the passage of almost three thousand years. Typically the singer would perform in a bar or coffee house accompanying himself on a single-stringed fiddle called a *gusle*, and unfold for his audience one of the old heroic tales from the wars of the Christians and the Turks. The performance might last a few hours. It might go on for considerably longer. Much depended on the virtuosic skill of the singer of tales and the critical acuity of the audience. Lays of several thousand lines might be performed in the process. Clearly this was too long for simple memorisation. There must be some other principle involved. As they studied their recordings, preserved on hundreds of aluminium discs, it began to dawn on Parry and Lord that the performer was actually creating the song as he sang it to his audience. He was not improvising, quite; at least not freely. Detailed comparison of texts revealed that he was drawing upon an inherited stock of metrically interchangeable verbal formulae and a repertoire of standard narrative-shapes that enabled him to tailor his song to the audience in front of him, to conduct his story rapidly with broad descriptive strokes on one occasion, or develop it at epic length and with sumptuous descriptive detail on another, and to achieve either with an effortless professionalism, maintaining throughout a smooth and unbroken narrative flow. Composition-in-performance was a sophisticated and rule-bound mode. Although the ingredients were traditional, the singer of tales used his materials in a way that was ultimately personal; he might never do it exactly the

12 Albert Lord, *The Singer of Tales*, (Cambridge, Mass., 1960), pp.99–102.
13 Blackwell, *Enquiry*, pp.104–5, 119ff.

same way twice. So that, from a certain point of view, these old tales were as new as the day of their last performance. Lord summed up the position as follows:

> In a sense each performance is 'an' original, if not 'the' original. The truth of the matter is that our concept of 'the original', of 'the song', simply makes no sense in oral tradition. To us it seems so basic, so logical, since we are brought up in a society in which writing has fixed the norm of a stable first creation in art, that we feel there must be an 'original' for everything. The first singing in oral tradition does not coincide with this concept of the 'original'. We might as well be prepared to face the fact that we are in a different world of thought, the patterns of which do not always fit our cherished terms. In oral tradition the idea of an original is illogical. It follows, then, that we cannot correctly speak of a 'variant', since there is no 'original' to be varied . . . 'oral transmission', 'oral composition', 'oral creation', and 'oral performance' are all one and the same thing.[14]

The 'oral-formulaic' is by no means the only compositional method used in non-literate societies and Parry and Lord's work, while extremely influential, has not gone unchallenged. Not all oral communities would seem to work in the way they describe. There are objections that the theory can account for variety but not creativity, and that 'texts' performed by oral artists in other cultures have frequently revealed a remarkable stability over quite lengthy periods of time. This latter was exactly the point of James Macpherson (who along with Thomas Blackwell anticipated so much of this argument) regarding the transmission of *Ossian*, even down to specifying in detail how such stability could be achieved.[15] But the 'oral formulaic' theory does seem to offer suggestive parallels with the compositional/performance procedures of Highland pipers when the art of ceòl mór was at its height, building tunes from ready-made expressive units fitting into a pre-existing constructional matrix. The piper, too, had his formulae, and

---

14 Lord, p.101. For the broad outline of the development of the theory and its major implications, see pp. 13–17, 22, 24, 36, 79, 99, 100–101, 124–5, 130, 136–38. Lord suggested that the introduction to reading and writing of once non-literate poets was not fatal to their art, what did the damage was their subsequent acceptance of the fixed published text as the authoritative version: see also Albert B. Lord, 'The Nature of Oral Poetry', in John Miles Foley, ed., *Comparative Research on Oral Traditions: a Memorial for Milman Parry* (Columbus, 1987) pp. 313–349.

15 See Ruth Finnegan, *Oral Poetry its Nature, Significance and Social Context* (Camb., 1977), pp.69–84; G. S. Kirk, 'Homer and Modern Oral Poetry: Some Confusions', in *Homer and the Oral Tradition* (Camb., 1976), pp. 113–128; Douglas Young, 'Never Blotted a Line? Formula and Premeditation in Homer and Hesiod', in *Arion*, vol.6, no.3, Autumn 1967, pp. 279–324, but esp.295–9. For the idea that change is not incompatible with the concept of 'tradition', see Jack Goody, *The Domestication of the Savage Mind* (Camb., 1977), pp.112–128. For Blackwell and Macpherson, see above Chapter One.

his 'narrative' shapes. In his laments, salutes, marches and gatherings, he, too, had his set themes. He, too, could be expansive or curt as the occasion required. Above all, like the singer of tales, he may not have been performing a memorised set text, but with similar virtuosity and creative freedom manipulating the elements of his inherited musical vocabulary using a knowledge based on long study, practice and training of how such elements could best be combined.

The absence of written scores until a remarkably late date, which is a distinctive feature of pipe music, may also have parallels in non-, or partially, literate societies elsewhere. In many such instances the oral mode has been deliberately preferred for the transmission of culturally important material in the belief that it was inherently superior, that writing things down distorted and debased them. In classical Greece, Plato defended face-to-face oral instruction as against the written text on precisely these grounds; and in the same way the sacred Indian texts, the Rig Vedas, were, for many centuries, deliberately not committed to writing. Orality continued to prevail in certain cultural strata even within civilisations where writing technology had long been available. The south Slavs had possessed a written literature for a thousand years before this began to affect the singers of tales.[16]

An apparently similar complex of values and assumptions was current amongst the master teachers of the Highland pipe in Scotland, generations after the introduction of compulsory mass literacy in the 1870s. This was reflected in a number of ways, such as the preference for teaching by singing in a face-to-face situation; by the maintenance down the generations of the valued 'genealogies of learning' by which pipers trace their musical descent through the various schools; or even in the guru-type status of the charismatic master teachers mediating their esoteric knowledge with despotic authority.[17] Also striking was the culture of active resistance to the medium of print, and the growing importance of staff notation.

As we have seen, such views can be encountered well into the 20th century. Here, for example, is the correspondent signing himself 'Lochgorm' writing in the *Oban Times* in 1929:

> Piobaireachd is slipping further away from us every day . . . because no piper who has not had instruction can play it from scale. Why? because it is not played as written, and again, it is impossible to do so. If there is any doubt here, let anyone take into consideration the thousands of pipers who can read the scale of nine notes for ordinary March, Strathspey and Reel, and yet throw aside Piobaireachd as hopeless. There is something wrong! . . . The fault with Piobaireachd lies in changing over to Staff notation. It surely stands to reason that the old pipers could not read it, far less speak English, and would not have heard of a crochet or quaver cadence time signatures and such

16 Lord, *Singer of Tales*, pp.134–5. See also Jack Goody and Ian Watt, 'The Consequences of Literacy', in *Comparative Studies in Society and History*, vol.5, 1962–3. pp.304–45, esp. p.327–8.

17 See Jack Goody, ed., *Literacy in Traditional Societies*, (Cambridge, 1968), pp.1–24.

like. They measured their phrases, which the modern piper does not attempt, from a different angle altogether. They did not measure as John MacDougall Gillies used to say, by twelve inches to the foot, but in a manner which let itself into their art . . .[18]

John MacDonald of Inverness, in 1942, defended the value of an explicitly oral regime, declaring that 'piobaireachd must be transmitted by song from one piper to another in order to get the soul of it; the lights and shades. Most of the piobaireachd players of the present day rely on the score, but you cannot express in musical notation what you would like to. It is really impossible'.[19]

R. U. Brown, a leading pupil of MacDonald, trained during the later 1920s and '30s, stated that:

Staff notation for me was just a very good reference for the initial memorising. Then, when I had the tune memorised, shut the book, go to him, and learn it by singing, as this is the only way one can get the proper lights and shades, or scansion of the bars and phrases with which one can make a tune live. The composers of these fine tunes were trained in a certain way, passed it on by canntaireachd, and only by the continuance of this method can it be kept pure.[20]

R. B. Nicol, another pupil of John MacDonald and himself one of the most influential teachers of the third quarter of the 20th century, shared this mistrust of staff notation: 'I think the worst thing that ever happened to piobaireachd was the day it was put into staff notation . . . the timing of tunes been altered, didn't do it any good . . . you see, something's lost. They drew lines, and so many notes have got to go in there, and so many in here . . . something's drifted'.[21] But Nicol did not disapprove of printed scores as such, valuing the work of Ross and Glen, MacPhee and (above all) Thomason. Indeed, there seems little doubt that amongst 20th century masters, some at least of this attitude was a historically specific response to the shortcomings of the Piobaireachd Society settings. Underlying their apparently genuine belief that the medium could not adequately convey the message, was a conviction that the official scores had been incompetently done, and resentment at the way the sponsoring institutions had imposed them on the performer community. When Nicol exclaimed 'The book, the book, the bloody book, I can't do with it at all', he had specific books in mind: namely the *Piobaireachd Society Collection* (second series) and the *Kilberry Book of Ceol Mor*.[22] Of the editor,

18 *OT*, 31/8/1929, p.3.
19 "The Piping Reminiscences of John MacDonald M.B.E. Honorary Piper to His Majesty The King", *OT*, 4/4/1942, p.5. See also pp.213–4.
20 From a tape recording in the writer's possession.
21 School of Scottish Studies Archive, Edinburgh University, SA 1972/246.
22 School of Scottish Studies Archive, Edinburgh University, SA1977/164.

Archibald Campbell, he declared 'this is one work that he should have left alone. You could be a very clever man, yet no musician'.[23] These remarks should be seen in the context of more than a century of gathering doubts about transmission. By the 1970s Nicol even contemplated the possibility of publishing scores in canntaireachd notation only, which might compel the learner to seek the assistance of a good teacher in order to master the idiom properly. This, he thought, would begin to temper the crude and bookish approach – straight off the staff – so frequently heard, which in his view was ruining modern piobaireachd playing.[24]

Relations between the oral and written mode in the music of the Highland pipe are a good deal more complicated than a simple literacy vs. orality model might imply. Indeed in the light of the Scottish evidence it is doubtful if the equation of orality with 'tradition' can be sustained. As suggested in Chapters 10 and 17, the explosion of creativity in the light music of the pipe during the past hundred and fifty years, seems to have been closely connected with the spread of musical literacy. But any suggestion that the music had thereby ceased to be 'traditional' would immediately be rejected by the performer community. The written and oral modes have interacted over long periods of time, and it is not obvious – as has sometimes been assumed – that they represent irreconcilably antagonistic modes of thought. In canntaireachd written and oral systems co-existed for centuries. In piobaireachd the printed scores worked within the context of a performance tradition orally transmitted. In the light music of the pipe there was a similar dialogue: only the outcomes in the form of finished tunes were written down or printed (and not always invariably so even at the end of the 20th century); the anterior stages – the rules, procedures and conventions which enabled these outcomes to be achieved – were not committed to paper.

The argument about the concept of tradition is complicated by the fact that many of the theoretical assumptions have been drawn from the verbal arts, which are affected by literacy in significantly different ways from music. In music, teaching and learning are substantially oral/aural processes; performance tradition inhabits a similar dimension, as also does composition, even at the most sophisticated level: Stravinsky 'heard' *The Rite of Spring* in 1912, for example, but it took him nearly two years to work out how to write it down. Nor was there any attempt historically to achieve mass compulsory literacy in music. Models derived from literary sources might seem to be of limited usefulness, therefore, but they have been routinely applied to the indigenous music of Scotland since the days of *Ossian* onwards, leading to the application of concepts of authority and fixity fundamentally at odds with the variety and interpretational freedom characteristic not only of the oral mode, but also much of the written record in the period surveyed by this book.

23 *Ibid.*
24 R. B. Nicol in conversation with the writer, Ballater, 10/6/1975.

Conclusion

This book has described the construction of the concept of 'tradition' in relation to the Highland pipe and its music and examined how people came to the conclusions they did about tradition, and how it worked. The basic model was created by James Macpherson in the essays and notes attached to the poems of Ossian in the early 1760s. In various crude and simplified ways this was applied to all Highland art-forms for two centuries thereafter. The Macpherson paradigm encouraged people to think of the great period of creativity as lying in the distant past, and of contemporary tradition as moribund, although this was not the case. It encouraged a view of the traditional performing arts as requiring 'rescue' and 'preservation', although they appear to have stood in need of neither. It promoted a view of the performer community as an ineffective steward of tradition, which seems likewise to have been wrong. It fostered a view of piobaireachd as a wild and irregular form – which it was not – whose chief characteristic was its dissimilarity to 'normal' music, which was also in error. It sanctioned the programme of the Highland Societies of London and Scotland, continued in the 20th century by the Piobaireachd Society, which led to their assuming control of the competition circuit, introducing standardised settings, and attempting to reduce the classical music of the pipe to conformity with a set of cultural expectations which were largely mistaken.

The knowledge of the 'rescuers' was usually inadequate. Sir John Graham Dalyell, who was mainly responsible for turning the 19th century national competitions at Edinburgh into a theatrical spectacle, regarded piobaireachd as a primitive affair and having spent almost thirty years superintending these events, continued to hold the instrument and its music in contempt. His fellow judges, who manned the benches by virtue of title or landed possession, tended to have little personal knowledge or skill and standards in this area remained low throughout. The institutional 'guardians' were often careless with the written sources. Sir John MacGregor Murray bought and then lost a volume of the most important early manuscript, Colin Campbell's 'Nether Lorn' canntaireachd. No serious attempt was made to preserve the manuscripts awarded premiums at the Highland Societies' competitions. Those which were kept by the Highland Society of Scotland were subsequently lost by the Highland Society of London. While many of the latter's papers were destroyed, the important MacArthur/ MacGregor manuscript survived because the performer community had previously removed it from the Society's possession and ensured it was looked after. The Highland Society of Scotland, when offered the piobaireachd manuscripts of

Angus MacKay which contained nearly the whole of the tradition as it was then known, refused them on the grounds – quite mistaken – that all the best tunes were probably already in MacKay's published book. Several important publications later assumed to have been called into being at the Societies' instigation were done without, or even despite them. Joseph MacDonald's *Compleat Theory of the Scots Highland Bagpipe* was published by his brother Patrick after they had sat on the project for twenty years. Donald MacDonald's *Ancient Martial Music of Caledonia* was published by MacDonald himself, to his severe financial loss, when the support he had reasonably expected was withheld. The Highland Society of London subscribed to Uilleam Ross's *Collection* in 1869, but the Highland Society of Scotland did not. Neither supported the collections of Donald MacPhee, C. S. Thomason or David Glen. In a century rich in surviving manuscript sources, only one was called into being at the Societies' behest. Their expenditure on publications was modest and largely recoverable. Their competitions, when not in profit, were at least self-financing. The commonly made claim that without their intervention the music would have died is not supported by the evidence. The Highland Societies' role as cultural sponsors has been greatly overstated. It was the performer community which ensured the survival of piobaireachd into the 20th century.

As soon as cheapening print and rising working-class incomes made published pipe music affordable, collections made by pipers for other pipers began to appear, including those of Donald MacPhee, David Glen and John McLennan. In 1903 when the founders of the Piobaireachd Society were proclaiming that 'Men are dying, tunes are perishing, knowledge is waning', virtually the whole of the repertoire was currently in print and presumably, therefore, being bought and played – a situation which was not achieved again until the 1970s when reprints from the E.P. Publishing company of Wakefield in Yorkshire made five of the older collections briefly available. Growing musical literacy and access to print made it possible for the Piobaireachd Society to use its social power more effectively than the Highland Societies to promote fixed texts and gain control of tradition. In many respects, however, its activities followed a familiar pattern. There was the assumption that the traditional arts were simple and could be quickly mastered so that 'educated' outsiders could successfully mediate them; the cult of the amateur which ensured that gentility remained incompatible with serious musical ambition and skill; the pseudo-militaristic and secretive atmosphere in which its activities were conducted; the culture of social exclusion which denied membership to professional pipers; the characteristic combination of little knowledge with much power.

The Piobaireachd Society *Collection*, edited by various members and issued in two series, provided the set texts for the important competitions throughout the 20th century. As these were normally played as written, their standardised and simplified style affected idiom as well as the content of the repertoire. Neither series can be regarded as successful. The first (published in five volumes 1905–1912) fell so far short of the Society's stated goals, that it was received with open derision. The second series (fifteen volumes, 1925–1990) was also seriously flawed, Archibald Campbell representing the central core of the competition repertoire in such a way as to make the volumes he edited virtually worthless as an accurate account of the tradition, a process carried still further by *The Kilberry Book of Ceol Mor*. The Society failed to pursue a number of important objects specified in its original constitution, including the publication of the numerous manuscript sources and the collection of piping folklore. In the mid-20th century it blocked initiatives designed to widen the institutional base of piping, raise standards on the bench, and make good-quality teaching more widely available. In 1972, its editor stated that the location of a number of manuscripts once in the Society's possession was currently unknown.

The development of a concept of 'authority' which justified the appropriation of tradition was central to the Highland and Piobaireachd Societies' activities from the early 19th century onwards. The traditionally-trained master players and teachers were gradually displaced by gentlemen enthusiasts wielding institutional power, but the means by which this was achieved were more ambiguous than the simple replacement of one hierarchy by another. The names of leading experts in the performer community were appropriated by third parties of doubtful standing who assumed their authority and spoke on their behalf. Who would have listened to John Ramsay if he had not been thought to be Patrick MacDonald, or to James Logan if he had not been thought to be Angus MacKay, or to Archibald Campbell if he had not been thought to be Sandy Cameron (and John MacDougall Gillies and John MacDonald of Inverness)? Yet it may have been inevitable that something like this should happen. The idea of 'tradition' need not imply reverence for the past. It is an important part of the ideological process of modernisation. It is the means in a progressive, scientifically-minded ethos by which the past is erased, and links with earlier social and cultural phases cut. There may be no conscious intention to do this; indeed it is to preserve and rescue 'tradition' that bodies like the Highland and Piobaireachd Societies ostensibly exist. Their very formation may be a fatal sign, however, because of their fundamental assumption of discontinuity between past and present, their conclusion that the past is over and done with and incapable any longer of nourishing the present, that the past is fixed, and its heritage perishing, its ways of doing obsolete, its conclusions wrong, so that it must be abolished and replaced by something more in keeping with modern notions. The new order was carefully presented as springing legitimately from the old. But the world of piping had long been partitioned into carefully segregated communities of producers and consumers, differing widely in income, status, education, outlook, and for much of our period also, in language. The commentators who shaped the official view came from a highly but conventionally educated professional élite so deeply conditioned by 'modern' society that they assumed its cultural conventions to be axiomatic. They knew little of oral transmission or what it might imply, and failed to appreciate that the simultaneous co-existence of multiple variants might be a normal and healthy condition. They interpreted it as a sign of disintegration and decay, and concluded – quite wrongly – that the tradition was at risk and that they must intervene to preserve it. They were also led into fundamental error about the role of the performer community. Regarding the creative phase of tradition as a separate episode, long ago concluded, they viewed contemporary tradition-bearers as mere transmitters of an already fully-developed heritage. Tradition, in its modern phase, was considered as a degenerative process in which change took place as a result of faulty memorisation. The evidence of change and variety in the written record was therefore taken as proof that the performer community had failed in its stewardship. In consequence, 'authority' must be transferred from performance to score, and from the players to the sponsoring institutions. The Piobaireachd Society scores, supported by an arbitrary selection of written and printed sources (to which the Society's editors alone had access) arbitrarily interpreted, became the sole legitimate sources of 'authenticity'.

The cultural assumptions of the regulatory institutions with regard to ceòl mór resulted in serious impairment of expressive idiom and creative vitality. Even in the wider context, there is little positive achievement to record. Generations of wealthy and powerful people attempted to 'rescue' and 'preserve' the classical music of the pipe. But as the 20th century drew to its close, the Scottish universities had scarcely begun to consider it as an object of serious study. In the libraries of Scotland piping material accumulated on a largely haphazard basis, chiefly as a result of loans and gifts, and no single archive had a full spread of sources. There was little informed interest by the media, and public ignorance remained great. When one adds that a comprehensive and reliable edition of this music had yet to be published, that the important manuscripts – with the exception of Joseph MacDonald's – had been permitted to remain in manuscript, and that piping folklore was still largely uncollected, a disinterested observer might be forgiven for thinking that this was little to show after 200 years.

Meanwhile the part of the repertoire where there was no attempt at 'rescue' or control, namely ceòl beag (the light music of the pipe), presented a very different picture. Here the period was one of remarkable achievement, with a ferment of creative activity lasting for nearly a century and a half. There was vigorous growth in the popular market for published pipe music. Divorced from institutional control, print constituted little threat to the performer community or its musical autonomy, so long as there also prevailed a view of tradition which did not exclude the concept of change. By the time the 20th century reached its mid point, however, there had come to be two different and fundamentally opposed concepts of tradition applied to the music of the Highland pipe: one descending from the performance-centred view articulated by Joseph MacDonald which strongly stressed vitality and on-going cultural enterprise and had come to be focused on ceòl beag; and one deriving from the Macpherson paradigm which regarded tradition as fixed and unchanging and was focused on ceòl mór. Only in the latter view could the present be considered as creatively irrelevant, and the performer community as a threat to the music of the pipe.

The second half of the 20th century was to witness a further deepening of regulatory structures and the Macpherson paradigm continuing to influence cultural expectations.[1] Several further volumes of the *Piobaireachd Society Collection* (second series) were issued, and, along with the *Kilberry Book of Ceol Mor*, continued to provide the set texts. The Society's list of tunes for 1999 nominated 24 pieces for competition at various levels, giving details of their locations in the above two sources, adding:

> Competitors are not restricted to these settings and any other setting may be played. The Judges, however, may take into consideration the merits of such settings, their authenticity and authority for such settings. Competitors are advised to give advance notice should they intend to include any settings NOT contained in either Staff or Editorial notes in the Society's Collections.[2]

What might be considered 'authentic' or 'authoritative' was made no more explicit than it had been in 1920. As a result pipers continued 'to treat the published score as holy writ, and to play every tune doggedly through exactly as published'.[3] Serious doubts about the coherence of these scores were voiced by leading Piobaireachd Society members such as Peter Cooke and David Murray; but benches of judges continued to treat the Society's main texts as prescriptive, and could penalise players for offering alternative settings even when derived from the Society's own editorial notes.[4] The resulting narrowness of interpretation in public performance continued to be blamed – as it had been for nearly a hundred years – on the rigidity of the players. But since virtually the whole of the competition repertoire had been edited by Archibald Campbell of Kilberry, it was his reading of tradition which continued to determine the way the music was played. At the end of the 20th century the only interpretation of real value in a

---

1 In the 'Introduction' to the first volume of his technically innovative collection, *Binneas is Boreraig*, published in 1959, Dr Roderick Ross spoke of mystical Celtic affinities, of witchcraft and curses and the invocation of ancestral spirits, of gory battlefields and ancient heroic virtues, declaring: 'The piobaireachd man is ominous and tragic, and the heavy stare of his large and motionless eyes conveys the impression of dreary contempt and smouldering passion; and the far-off look of tragedy in his set and melancholy gaze is so often veiled in impenetrable concentration.'

2 *PT*, vol.51, no.1, October 1998, p.12.

3 D. J. S. Murray, reviewing 'Piobaireachd Society's Collection Book 13', *International Piper*, vol.2, no.12, April 1980, p.6; for continuing adherence to the time values of the book as the century neared its end, see Hugh MacCallum, 'Northern Meeting the Gold Medal', *The Piper Press*, no.9, November 1998, pp.11–15 (15).

4 Duncan Watson, 'A Day at a Games: Scarce of Good Judging', in *The Piper Press*, no.12, May 1999, pp.37–9. See also, David J. S. Murray, 'More on "The Way it Was"', *The Voice*, vol.27, no.1, Spring 1998, pp.35–8. See also Jack Taylor, 'Piobaireachd: Has it Changed? Should it Change?', *Piper and Drummer*, vol.12, no.1, 1994, pp.14–16.

living tradition – namely the way the performer himself or herself thought the tune should go – was the one interpretation certain to be unacceptable in a piobaireachd competition in Scotland.[5]

In light music, the second half of the 20th century was a period of great vitality, especially in the pipe band world which was increasingly part of an international culture, with much creativity and innovation in ensemble play, great openness to outside influence, and a compositional scene so active that towards the century's end, new collections of tunes were appearing at the rate of about one a month.[6] The players who struggled with the prescriptive competitive regime in piobaireachd were the same as those who, left in charge of the music, transformed and enriched ceòl beag. Indeed it was the ability and tenacity of the performer community which ultimately enabled ceòl mór to survive nearly two centuries of insensitive intervention in its expressive idiom, its structural organisation and its compositional-transmissional mode. The reflection that at no time did ceòl mór ever cease to be composed, and played and freely taught, may leave one with a sense of remarkable underlying resilience.

5 For an exploration of Gaelic song as an alternative pool of stylistic 'authenticity', see Allan MacDonald, 'The Relationship between pibroch and Gaelic song: its implications on the performance style of the pibroch urlar' Edinburgh University, M.Litt. thesis, 1996.

6 Iain Duncan, 'A Fund of Music for All to Share', *Piper Press*, no.12, May 1999, pp.23–5 (25); for a stimulating overview of technical innovation and change in the band world, see 'On Top of the World's: an Interview with P/M Robert Mathieson by Peter Kent and Charlie Glendinning', in *The Voice*, vol.26, no.3, Fall 1997, pp.18–29.

Readers' Guide:
Piobaireachd and the Great Highland Pipe

Understanding Piobaireachd

Piobaireachd is a secular, monodic art music, performed upon the Highland bagpipe by a class of highly-trained professional or semi-professional musicians originally under the patronage of the great Highland families. The repertoire contains about four hundred pieces. Piobaireachd takes the form of a theme and variations, the ground or theme being developed through a number of relatively fixed variation types with periodic returns of the theme.

Its emotional range is often considered to be intense but narrow, to be confined, indeed, to the evocation of bloodshed and grief. But piobaireachd covers a wide range of musical subject-matter: there are tunes of welcoming and gathering, pastoral and descriptive pieces, bacchanalian tunes and satires, as well as battle pieces and laments. Piobaireachds can be long or short, with few variations or many and last from four or five minutes to about half an hour, depending on the mood and scale of the piece. While very much a ceremonial and public form, the range of musical expression is wide, ranging from the abstract and architectural at one end of the spectrum, to a striking melodic richness and lyricism at the other.

Here are the opening sequences of one or two famous tunes to give an idea of their flavour. Pipe notation is used, but they are given also in plain staff notation to help the reader who may need this support to develop a feel for the flow of melody. Key signatures are not required on the pipe and are usually dispensed with. Sometimes time signatures are omitted as well in the notation of piobaireachd:

'Lament for the Children', ground, line 1, John MacDougall GilliesMS, f.88

'Lord Anapole's Lament', ground line 1, Highland Society of London's MS, f.93

'The Fishers of Geogh Brodinn' [more commonly known as 'Scarce of Fishing'], *Ross's Collection of Pipe Music*, p.22

Sometimes the *ùrlar*, (the technical name for the ground or theme) may not contain the most important melodic strand, but prepare the way for internal parts of still greater expressiveness, as, for example, the first variation of the 'Lament for Donald Bàn MacCrimmon':

'Donald Bain MacCrummen's Lament', variation 1 doubling, line one, Colin Cameron's MS. f.42

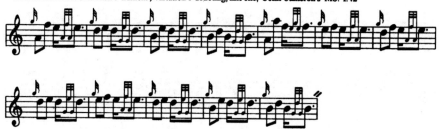

or the powerful first variation of 'In Praise of Morag'

Variation 1 doubling, line one, Colin Cameron's MS ff.90-1

or the first variation of the graceful 'Red Alexander MacDonell of Glengary's Lament'

Variation 1 doubling, Angus MacKay's MS, i, f.168

Once the ùrlar has been stated, it is usually then compressed: stripped down to its underlying tonal core. The resulting musical outline then becomes the basis for further development, the important themal notes being 'framed' in a number of possible ways.

This can best be illustrated by a melodically bold and simple tune, with a typical organisation, such as 'The Lament for MacDonald's Tutor' whose musical tension arises from the interplay of two adjacent gapped scales, ACDE/GBDE. Here is the ùrlar:

'Lament for the MacDonald's Tutor', ground, Angus MacKay's MS, ii, 5

The tonal framework of the tune is defined by the variation which follows, called the *siubhal,* (pron. 'shoowell' a word implying traversing), in which the key notes are 'shown' with varying degrees of emphasis. Since the flow of sound from the chanter or melody pipe is continuous and dynamic levels cannot be varied, then various devices involving duration and harmony must be used in order to achieve this. The important notes are accented, by making them longer than the others, and pairing them with a short low A. Since the drones of the pipe also sound at this pitch, this tends to make the paired note 'disappear' because of its consonance with the drone and the frequency of its repetition while at the same time emphasising the themal note because it alone changes in pitch, establishing keenly felt symmetrical patterns of proximity or distance from the tonic or tonics:

'Lament for the MacDonald's Tutor', siubhal, Angus MacKay's MS, ii, 5

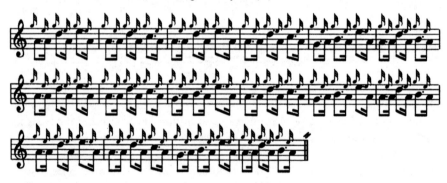

Next comes a *siubhal sleamhainn* (pron. 'shoowell slewin/slevin' implying something smooth or sliding) which uses repetition in a different way, with the themal notes being 'doubled' at the same pitch in characteristic dotted quaver/semi-quaver figures:

'Lament for the MacDonald's Tutor', siubhal doubling, line one, Angus MacKay's MS, ii, 5-6

The siubhal of 'MacDonald's Tutor' shows the basic pattern for piobaireachd variations, appearing once, *singilte*, (pron. 'sheengltche') as a 'singling', possessing various fixed properties, and once again *dùbailte*, (pron. 'doobaltche') as a 'doubling', in which some of these properties undergo, usually conventional, further modification as above.

When we turn to the technically more complex *taorluath* (pron. 'toorla') and *crunluath* (pron. 'croonla') variations which bring the tune to its climax, as they do in most piobaireachds, we can see some of the typical strategies involved. Here is the taorluath singling of 'MacDonald's Tutor'.[1] Since it exactly follows the tone row of the siubhal, a few bars should make the point clear:

'Lament for the MacDonald's Tutor', taorluath singling, line one, Angus MacKay's MS, ii, 6

This looks like a more elaborate version of the siubhal singilte, with a taorluath movement following each of the themal notes. Although it looks similar on the page, however, there is significant difference in performance because of the dramatically percussive effect of the taorluath movement. This is owing to its execution and the clever way it exploits the tonality and timbre of the chanter. It is done as follows: all the holes on the chanter are covered briefly sounding low G – the boldest note, given additional emphasis by the fact that it may lie at some considerable intervallic distance from the preceding melody note – this is followed by a tonally related D gracenote, executed on low G which automatically sounds that note again, then there is a smart return to low A, reinforced by a tonally related E gracenote – so that in effect the two contrasting tonics, A and G, are fiercely compressed and achieve momentary fusion, with great release of energy.

As in most singling movements there is much use of rubato to emphasise the

---

1 The taorluath and crunluath movements are given here in conventional modern form: they occur in a slightly different style in MacKay's MS. For further details see Chapter 16, 'Pipers' Challenge'.

phrasing, further heightened, as here, by the inclusion of conventional figures known as 'cadence notes' to mark the phrase endings. Examples may be seen at the end of bars four and six above. Cadencing is a form of musical punctuation, a way of signalling the end of the phrase. The piper has to work in this way because he does not have other signalling devices, such as dynamic change, or silence, at his disposal. So cadences are important in helping the listener to organise the music.

In the doublings the cadence notes are replaced by taorluath figures at the appropriate pitch, the tempo is raised, and the variation played through with a more flowing approach to line:

'Lament for the Macdonald's Tutor', taorluath doubling, line one, Angus MacKay's MS, ii, 6

At this point in a traditional performance the ground would be repeated.[2]

The crunluath then brings the tune to its climax. This arrangement of gracenotes is the largest and most complex nowadays played. It resembles an arpeggiated chord, and its characteristically swinging movement framed within the space defined by the principle tonic and dominant builds a high charge of musical tension and energy.

Here is a little of the crunluath doubling of 'MacDonald's Tutor':

'Lament for the Macdonald's Tutor, crunluath doubling, line one, Angus MacKay's MS, ii, 7

Not all tunes are as simple as this. Some are developed a good deal more subtly; but 'MacDonald's Tutor' shows a common basic pattern.

---

2 For repetition of the ground within the tune, see above pp.41, 127, 183, 378, *n*.10.

A particular point to note is that musical development proceeds at more than one level. The original structure is expanded, in that the ùrlar is followed by successive variations in which the ornamentation becomes progressively more elaborate. But there is movement also in the other direction, as we see when the tone row is reduced to its ultimate economy in the doubling of the siubhal, stabilising thereafter. Some tunes take this process of concentration a good deal further, showing a gradual contraction of metre and tonal range until in the final variations a plethora of ostinato ornamental figures effectively reduces them to a handful of artfully tensioned notes.

These are some of the basic principles governing the links between the different parts of a tune. We must now consider how musical ideas are organised *within* these parts.

The basic structural unit in piobaireachd is the phrase. This is, typically, of two bars in length, and distributed according to certain fixed patterns of which the simplest is nowadays called 'Primary Piobaireachd'. In a Primary Piobaireachd, only two phrases are used. For the sake of convenience we can call them 'phrase A' and 'phrase B', and they are arranged asymmetrically in three lines as follows:

> Line one – A, A, B,
> Line two – A, B, B,
> Line three – A, B.

as if to say,

> Line one – 'S seo, 's seo, '*s sin,*
> (And this, and this, *and that,*)
> Line two – 'S seo, '*s sin,* '*s sin,*
> (And this, *and that, and that,*)
> Line three – 'S seo, '*s sin.*
> (And this, *and that.*)

So that the direct juxtaposition of phrase A with phrase B, which ultimately balances the structure, is artfully delayed until the final line, giving the musical sentence its powerful onward pull.

To illustrate this point, here is a typical Primary Piobaireachd, a rowing tune, called 'The Laird of Coll's Galley', also known as 'The Battle of the Pass of Crieff'. First the ùrlar:

'The Battle of the Pass of Crieff', *Ross's Collection of Pipe Music*, p.75

Following the ùrlar comes a succession of siubhal, taorluath and crunluath movements, but although the variations change in character, the phrase pattern is strictly maintained throughout. Here, for example, are the first lines of the siubhal, taorluath and crunluath singling:

'The Battle of the Pass of Crieff', siubhal singling, line one, *Ross's Collection of Pipe Music*, p.75

'The Battle of the Pass of Crieff', taorluath doubling, line one, *Ross's Collection of Pipe Music*, p.76

'The Battle of the Pass of Crieff', crunluath doubling, line one, *Ross's Collection of Pipe Music*, p.76

The pursuit of concentration and energy is carried sometimes to very considerable lengths, as we see in tunes which share musical material between the A and B phrase, so that every alternate bar within a part is identical, creating a surging, antiphonal effect, as we see in 'Weighing from Land', for example:

'Weighing from Land', ground, John MacDougall Gillies MS, f.66

Although the musical content changes as the piobaireachd moves through its successive variations, this relationship remains constant. Here are the first lines of the siubhal, taorluath and crunluath fosgailte:[3]

'Weighing from Land', siubhal singling, line one, John MacDongall Gillies's MS, f.66

'Weighing from Land', taorluath fosgailte singling, line one, John MacDougall Gillies's MS, f.66

'Weighing from Land', crunluath fosgailte singling, line one, John MacDougall Gillies's MS, f.66

3 Gracenotes have been added to the siubhal and taorluath, left unornamented in the score.

The last two lines show a common variant of the basic taorluath and crunluath pattern of gracenotes, called the *fosgailte* (pron. 'foskiltche') or 'opened' form. As the term implies, the chanter is not 'closed' during the execution of this movement, i.e. at no point is low G sounded, unless as an initial melody note. In the taorluath fosgailte, the basic motif – namely the impression of three notes occurring in quick succession – is maintained, but they are 'shown' differently, being ornamented by gracenotes predominantly at a higher rather than a lower pitch. The crunluath fosgailte occurs in two forms. It is played from a low G, low A or B quaver with the internal B, C or D semi-quaver held in the open position whilst a throw on E is executed above it. Alternatively the chanter may be closed to low A immediately before the throw, giving a more brittle and percussive effect, like so:

Crunluath fosgailte movements in two styles

The fact that there are at least four different kinds of taorluath and crunluath is a reminder of the richness and variety of piobaireachd which is one of its attractions as a musical form.

Although the phrase is the basic structural component, the various 'movements' which together make up each phrase are the fundamental building blocks out of which piobaireachd is made. These are extremely conventional, although frequently used with a high degree of resourcefulness and invention. Since the chanter or melody pipe produces a continuous flow of sound, then mastery of the extensive gracenote system is necessary to produce most of the available musical effects, from the simple illusion of two separate notes at the same pitch (which done like this):

to the more elaborate structures shown in earlier examples.

Here, for example, is the movement 'hiririn', described in the 'Introduction' to this book, in two of its basic forms:

It is used typically as an opening or closing gesture. But it is not an isolated phenomenon. It is a member of a whole suite of similarly timed figures called *buillean* or *crahinin* (pron. 'boolyin'/'crahinin' with the implication of a flourish, stroke or blow), the chanter being struck by the appropriate finger to produce a gracenotes at a pitch below that of the affected melody note. Their English name is 'echo beats', and they occur at a variety of pitches. One of the early guides to the subject, Angus MacKay's *Ancient Piobaireachd* (1838), represents them as follows:

Whole musical sequences can be built from these echo-beats, and some powerful moments in piobaireachd involve their use:

'Ronald MacDonald of Morar's Lament', ground, Angus MacKay's MS, i, 110

Of course the melodic qualities of piobaireachd as a genre are ultimately determined by the tonal possibilities of the chanter or melody-pipe, and its related drones. In order to appreciate this, it is now necessary to consider the instrument itself.

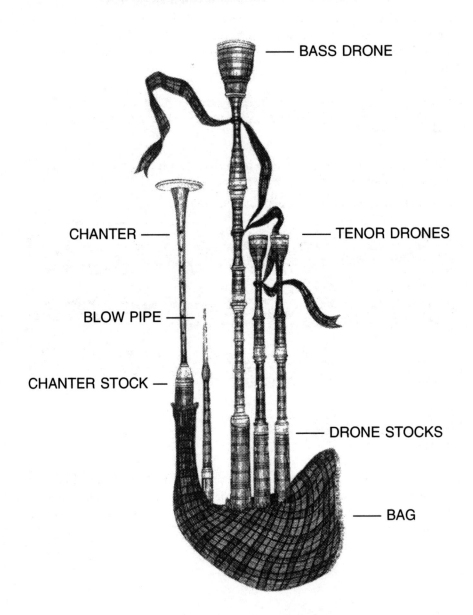

BASS DRONE

CHANTER

TENOR DRONES

BLOW PIPE

CHANTER STOCK

DRONE STOCKS

BAG

The Great Highland Pipe

The *pìob mhór*, or great pipe, (pron. 'peep vore') looms largely in the popular imagination, if rather vaguely as to its precise geometry and functioning. The basic idea is that a reservoir of air is sustained in a leather bag (*am màla* or *am balg*), deep-bellied towards the rear, and tapering to a narrow mouth at the front end where the chanter or melody pipe (*am feadan* or *an sionnsair*) is located.[4] Bags can be bought in various sizes to fit the proportions of the player. Sheepskin has traditionally been thought best for Scottish conditions although climatic variations may dictate different choices elsewhere, and the skin is seasoned with various concoctions to render it supple and airtight. These have ranged from the traditional treacle (*dràbhag siùcair*) or honey, to the commercial preparations used nowadays the secret of whose composition is jealously guarded, but which are thought to consist largely of glycerine and size.[5]

Into the bag are tied five short wooden tubes called 'stocks' (*na stuic*) – three in a row just forward of the mid-point of the bag, to support the drones (*na trì chruinn*). The drones themselves are three in number, one large and two small (*aon chrann mòr, agus a dhà bheaga*), and they sound a fixed fundamental note: the small or tenor drones one octave below low A which is the main tonic of the chanter, and the great or bass drone at two octaves below. A well-regulated pipe also produces a rich series of harmonics above the fundamental, adding greatly to the tonal colour and general aesthetic appeal. Each drone comprises a series of jointed sections, two in the case of the tenor drones, three for the bass. The pitch is adjusted by altering the length of the column of air vibrating inside the drones. This is done by changing the length of the drones themselves by manipulating the moveable upper joints. The drones are tied near their tops by loops of cord made of braided wool or silk or lengths of ribbon.

The blowpipe stock is located several inches in front of the drones in a line along the top of the bag. Into this is inserted a tube called the blowpipe (*an gaothaire*) which carries air into the bag. In the neck of the bag is the chanter stock, into which the chanter fits. The sites of the drone and blowpipe stocks are first marked on the skin of the bag, which is then cut, and the stocks are inserted and tied firmly in using waxed cord, so that an airtight joint is produced. This is a job requiring some craft and strength of hand, and pipers nowadays tend to have it done for them by professional firms.

Like many modern instruments, the pitch of the bagpipe has tended to rise during the past two centuries, perhaps as a result of the growing importance of the light music – or *ceòl beag* (pron. 'kyol bek' comprising marches, strathspeys,

---

4 The Gaelic terms used here for the various parts of the pipe are taken from "The Poetry of Piobaireachd. Part 1", by 'Gleannach' [Alexander MacDonald], *OT*, 18/4/1925 p.3. See also Edward Dwelly, *Illustrated Gaelic-English Dictionary* (Lyminge and Herne Bay, 1902–11 and numerous later editions) under 'pìob'.

5 See John J. van Ommen Kloeke, 'Seasoning: Brew Your Own?', in *PT*, vol.42, no.11, August 1990, pp.34–6.

jigs and reels) – and the consequent search for an ever brighter and more brilliant tone. As a result, the low A of late 20th century chanters is often closer to B flat (467 cycles per second). Whether the result can be viewed entirely in terms of gain is subject to debate. Traditionalists would probably support the view of Pipe-Major Donald MacLeod, one of the leading composers and competitors of the later 20th century, that modern competition pitch was 'an eldritch screech' to which many of the subtler effects of the instrument had been sacrificed.[6]

Four reeds (*na ribheidean*) are used, three drone reeds and one chanter reed. The drone reeds are tubular, sealed at one end, with a single up-cut blade, and inserted into reed-seats in the lower sections of the drones, enclosed by the stocks. The chanter reed is double bladed, the blades being bound to a metal staple, and positioned in the reed seat of the chanter, so that it is enclosed within the chanter stock. Once the pipes are set going, a continuous stream of sound is produced. There is no way of making the instrument itself play louder or softer (although there are various ways of producing the illusion of dynamic change).

Since the reeds are of different types, and they are exposed to a continuous flow of warm moist air, they alter in pitch at unequal rates and require frequent re-tuning until a stable plateau is reached. How long this takes depends upon how well or badly made and maintained the instrument is, and how knowledgeably it has been reeded-up, the latter requiring a good deal of experience, time and attention, and access to a good reedmaker. The writer knew a famous piper once who, asked why he had never married, replied 'ach, I have enough trouble with my reeds'.

Good intonation depends on a variety of factors. The same bagpipe can sound very different when played by different people. Much of the beginner's attention is devoted merely to winding the instrument steadily. Really poor piping (of which there is a good deal to be heard) will certainly include unsteady blowing – and hence involuntary pitch fluctuations – amongst its shortcomings. Good teaching and hard work can overcome many technical problems, but the ills of the flesh must also be taken into account. The moisture content of people's breath varies. There are 'dry blowers' and 'wet blowers' – regardless of the level of proficiency – and the latter have problems, because excess moisture in the system is one of the main causes of instability in pitch and tone. Technology comes to the rescue at least to some extent. There are various different sorts of water-trap, for example, ranging from a simple collar fitted into the blowpipe stock to retain moisture running down the inside of the bore, to more elaborate contraptions involving various kinds of plumbing inside the bag. Since the pipe is frequently played out-of-doors, climate also enters the equation. Cold weather increases condensation because of the temperature difference between warm moist human breath and the chilly outer instrument wall. It has implications for fingering as well. Execution gets increasingly difficult as the temperature goes down and here again some people are more adversely affected than others.

6 Alluding to the passage in Burns's poem 'Tam o' Shanter', in which the warlocks and witches pursue the hero from Alloway's auld haunted kirk 'wi' mony an eldritch [unearthly] screech and hollow'.

Reeds have been made from a variety of substances. There is a bush called 'the piper's tree', or *craobh nam piobairean*, (probably bourtree, or elder) from the tubular branches of which reeds were once made.[7] Vulcanite and whalebone, and various kinds of plastic have also been tried, but by far the most common material is *arundo donax*, or Spanish cane. This has been used for instrument and reed-making since classical antiquity, and it is not known when it was introduced into Scotland. Since bundles of cane were used as packing between barrels of imported wine, the presence of this material probably represents long standing contacts with the Mediterranean basin as we might guess from the frequent references in Gaelic poetry of the 17th century and later to 'the red wine of Spain'.[8] The quality of cane varies with the growing season. Pipers look for a good hard close-grained cane promising pitch stability and long playing life. Much of the piper's existence revolves around reeds and the endless search for perfection in terms of tonal accuracy, richness of timbre, freedom of response, and general reliability. And yet, perhaps curiously, reedmaking remains an arcane business, difficult even for pipers, unless they are themselves reedmakers, to penetrate. James Robertson the bagpipe-maker summed it up rather neatly in his pamphlet, *The Highland Bagpipe Some Interesting Information on the Materials used in the Manufacture of the Highland Bagpipe* when he said: 'Reed-making is a most particular industry, and its secrets are jealously guarded. The less the writer says on this subject, the better his chance of living to a good old age'.[9]

The great pipe itself appears to have been in use in the Highlands for at least five centuries, although there has been much dispute about its antiquity. Following its adoption as a national symbol during the later eighteenth century, there was a corresponding need, as we see elsewhere in this book, to emphasise its pre-eminence in point of age, martial vigour and indigenous development free from external influence.[10] The debate was hampered by the relative scarcity of early specimens of the instrument. There had been some attempts at preservation, such as the Great Speckled Pipe at Dunvegan, but bagpipes are fragile

---

7 'The Pipe and its Music. By Mr J. P. Grant, [of Rothiemurchus] Jun.', *OT*, 13/12/ 1913, p.3.

8 See 'Importation of Bagpipe Reeds', *OT*, 18/7/1942, p.3.

9 (Edinburgh, n.d. but ?*c.* 1930), p.15. For further particulars on reeds and reed-making see the appendix on 'Materials', in Collinson, *Bagpipe*, pp.204–10.

10 For typical positions in the dispute on the antiquity of the pipes, see, 'Pipes, Pipers, and Piobaireachd', 'The Bagpipes. Their Antiquity in Scotland', 'The Great Highland Bagpipe and its music', by Dr. Charles Bannatyne, *OT*, 2/5/1903, p.2, 27/2/1904, p.3, 13/5/1911, p.3; 'The Age of the Bagpipes', from 'J. W. M.', 16/3/1907, p.3; 'The Great Highland Bagpipe and its Music', from 'Morag', 6/5/1911, p.3; 'Deirdre, The Children of Usnach and the Bag-pipe', from K. N. MacDonald, 12/8/1911, p.3. For a modern overview of this subject, see Keith Sanger, 'The Origins of Highland Piping', *PT*, vol.41, no.11, August 1989, pp.46–52.

For discussion of the relative merits and antiquity of the two drone as opposed to the three drone configuration, see 'Puirt-a-Beul Concluding Remarks', by K. N. MacDonald, *OT*, 23/ 3/1901, p.3; 'The Great Highland Bagpipe and its Music', from Lieut. John McLennan, 3/6/ 1911, p.3; same, from 'Sassenach', 27/5/1911, p.3; 'The Highland Bagpipe', from G. Mackay, 25/4/1925, p.3, same, from 'Gleannach' [Alexander MacDonald], 16/5/1925, p.3.

things, made of several yards of delicately turned wood, and subject to a thousand mortal shocks.[11] Many instruments must have been literally played to pieces down the generations, and many fine stands of pipes have been buried with their possessors – a practice not unknown even in the present day.

Piping has become increasingly specialised during the last two centuries. Modern master players are usually content to teach and perform, to interpret and compose. But at one time, there seems to have been a wider range of skills involved. J. F. Campbell's informant, Duncan Ross, spoke of the stories he had learned as he worked the treadle for his teacher John Bàn MacKenzie (d.1864) as the latter turned pipes on his lathe.[12] A number of leading nineteenth-century players, such as Donald MacDonald, Donald MacKay, Malcolm Macpherson, Duncan and Gavin MacDougall of Aberfeldy, were also pipe-makers.[13] But it is said of John Bàn that he was the last of the old school, who with his own hands could kill the sheep, and fashion the bag, and turn the pipe, and cut the reeds, and compose the tune, and play it – with equal facility.

Many of the older instruments were probably made locally in this fashion, using native hardwoods such as holly and laburnum, and decorated with readily-available substances like horn and bone. But there is reference from a fairly early period to the making of pipes, presumably by specialist instrument makers, outside the Highlands.[14] During the 18th century the native woods were progressively laid aside in favour of tropical hardwoods such as cocus wood from the Caribbean, and ebony and blackwood from Africa which would appear to have produced significantly greater resonance and brightness of tone. Imported materials were increasingly used for decoration as well, and silver and ivory become commonplace adornments on the better sort of pipe. From the later 18th century onwards, bagpipe makers appear in the records with increasing frequency, with firms tending to concentrate in Edinburgh and Glasgow, and also in towns around the Highland fringe with good communications, like Aberfeldy, Greenock and Tain. The first of the named pipe makers, some of them still famous, and whose instruments are still sought after, begin to enter the record: people like Hugh Robertson, Donald MacDonald and the Glen family in Edinburgh, Peter Henderson in Glasgow, the MacDougalls of Aberfeldy, and a host of lesser names whose instruments can still be met with like Thow of Dundee, Center of

---

11 For further details on the Speckled Pipe (in its present form largely a 19th century reconstruction) and the Black Chanter of the Macphersons, see Collinson, *Bagpipe*, plate 20(a)/(b), and pp.136–7.

12 J. F. Campbell, *Canntaireachd*, p.33; for John Bàn MacKenzie as a pipe maker, see Jeannie Campbell, 'Notices of Bagpipe Makers' Part 7, in *PT*, vol.50, no.12, September 1998, pp.45–7.

13 In a recorded interview for the School of Scottish Studies, Angus Macpherson recollected his father, Calum Pìobaire, who died in 1898, turning bagpipes out of laburnum wood, see Collinson, *Bagpipe*, p.210.

14 Hugh Cheape, 'The Making of Bagpipes in Scotland', in Anne O'Connor and D. V. Clarke, eds., *From the Stone Age to the 'Forty-Five* (Edinr., 1983), pp. 596–615.

Edinburgh, or MacLeod of Tain.[15] Each had his individual style, affecting the external appearance of the pipe: characteristic ways of combing the wood, the shape and size of projecting mounts, and the 'bells' (*na duis*) at the tops of drones, and instruments from different makers had – and have – their own characteristic tone and feel, based upon subtle differences in internal dimensions and finish.

The most important part of the pipe is the chanter, which is conical in section and produces nine melody notes, sustaining two adjacent scales, a^1-a^{11} and g^1-g^{11}, from which a number of modal scales can be constructed.[16] One of the most thoughtful writers on this subject, J. P. MacLeod of Tain, identified several such scales, the three most important being a pentatonic (or five note) scale from G, thus:

– G (low), A, B, D, E.

the neighbouring pentatonic scale with A as its tonic:

– A (low), B, C, E, F sharp.

the overlap of these two scales giving a third as follows:

– A, B, D, E, F sharp.

MacLeod's survey of 238 piobaireachds in General C. S. Thomason's *Ceol Mor* – the largest collection in existence – revealed about forty pentatonic tunes belonging to the first of these scales, a further forty in the second, and some sixteen in the third. There were a further ten tunes in the key of G, strictly pentatonic in character, in which F occurred as a passing note, giving a total of 106 purely five note tunes out of those he had examined. In the key of A, he found 87 tunes based on scales which were gapped in various ways as opposed to a mere handful which contained all nine notes of the chanter; in the key of G this feature was even more pronounced. MacLeod deduced five scales altogether as follows:

1. Doh, ray, me, soh, lah.
2. Ray, me, soh, lah, doh'.
3. Me, soh, lah, doh', ray'.
4. Soh, lah, doh', ray' me'.
5. Lah, doh', ray', me', soh'.

. . . the complete Scottish pentatonic scale . . . consists of five notes and five modes. The first and second scales generally appear together, the second as a

15 For details of Hugh Robertson, Donald MacDonald, Donald MacKay, the Glens, the Mac-Dougalls of Aberfeldy, and David Thow and James Center, see Jeannie Campbell, 'Notices of Bagpipe Makers. Parts 1–3/5/7/9', in *PT*, vol. 50, nos.6–8/10/12, March-September 1998, pp.19–23, 34–6, 42–5, 17–22, 43, vol.51, no.2/4, November 1998/January 1999, pp.43–6, 26–9.

16 See Seumas MacNeill, *Piobaireachd*, pp. 25–29. See also Francis Collinson, 'A Possible Vocal Origin of the Bagpipe Scale', in *PT*, vol.16, no. 8, May 1964, pp.6–8. Statements about the allegedly unique bagpipe scale and its peculiar intervals should be treated with caution. There is no standard pitch. Historically it has been difficult to get two chanters from different makers to sound in unison: in the early twentieth century there were perceptible differences between those made in Edinburgh and those made in Glasgow. Reeds from different makers produce different intervals from the same chanter.

modulating scale. The fourth and fifth also appear together ('Donald Ban MacCrimmon's Lament'). But by old authorities the first and fourth were thought to be the original scales. The third scale, or part of it, was used by the old composers of pibrochs as a modulating scale.[17]

Each of these scales was thought to possess a distinctive emotional flavour making it more suitable for some kinds of composition than others. Joseph MacDonald's *Compleat Theory of the Scots Highland Bagpipe* (c. 1760), the earliest theoretical account of the music of the pipe, discusses this topic in some detail, giving examples of which scales lent themselves to marches and battle tunes, and which were better for laments and 'rural' pieces.[18] It is clear from his analysis that whilst a tune may use all the available notes in a particular scale, all notes do not have the same importance: there is a hierarchy of pitch relationships. The tonic is, obviously, the chief note; thereafter, depending on the 'taste' of the composition, may come other intervals of the scale, such as the third, fourth or fifth. We may see some of these points illustrated in the 'Lament for Patrick Òg MacCrimmon', one of the greatest tunes in the tradition, whose use of MacLeod's first pentatonic scale on G: G, A, B, D, E, seems deliberately designed to exploit the expressive possibilities of that mode. Here is the doubling of the first variation:

'Patrick óg MacCrummen's Lament', variation 1 doubling. Angus MacKay's *Ancient Piobaireachd* p.82

As Joseph MacDonald remarked of a similar use of this scale, 'The Disposition of the Notes . . . is Lamentable; & obvious to a Competent Judgement'.[19]

This is an intriguing and complex subject but enough has been said, hopefully, to convey some idea of the intimate connection between the tonality of the pipe and its musical repertoire, as well as a sense of being in the presence of a sophisticated and precise aesthetic.

17 'The Bagpipe Scale', from J. P. M.[acLeod of Tain], *OT*, 9/10/1915, p.3. For a brief recent discussion of this topic see Cannon, *Highland Bagpipe*, pp.36–8.

18 Cannon, *Compleat Theory*, pp. 67–73. See above, Chapter 2.

19 Cannon, *Compleat Theory*, p.69.

Bibliography

The literature of the Highland Pipe is extensive, and touches on a number of different disciplines. Much of the material exists only in periodical and other ephemeral sources, and a comprehensive bibliography would itself make up a substantial work. In the selected list of sources which follows only works have been included which have been helpful in the preparation of the present book. The *Oban Times* has been a major source: since much of the material is pseudonymous, however, individual contributions appear in the footnotes and index and are not listed separately here.

Unpublished works

Aberdeen University Library:
A. E. Milne, MS. 2904.
'Colin Campbell's Instrumental Book, 1797', MS. 3586 – MF copy of NLS MS. 3714.
Angus MacArthur, Collection of Piobaireachd, MS. 3587 – MF copy of NLS MS. 1679.
Donald MacDonald's Manuscript, MS. 3588 – MF copy of NLS MS. 1680.
The Peter Reid Manuscript, MS. 3589 – MF copy of NLS Acc. 22118.
Angus MacKay's Manuscript, MS. 3590, MF copy of NLS MS. 3753–4.
Colin Cameron, Piobaireachd Manuscript, MS. 3591 – MF copy of NLS MS. 3745.
William Ross, Collection of Pipe Music, MS. 3592 – MF copy of NLS MS. 3040.
C S Thomason, 'Ceol Mor Legends', MS. 3593 – MF copy of NLS MS. 3749.
David Glen's Manuscript, MS. 3594 – MF copy of NLS MS. 22120.

Edinburgh University Library:
Alexander Campbell, 'A Slight Sketch of a Journey made through parts of The Highlands & Hebrides; undertaken to collect materials for Albyn's Anthology by the Editor: in the Autumn, 1815', La III: 577.
———— 'The Cameron Gathering in Syllables', La.II. 51.
Christine Knox Chambers, 'Non-Lexical Vocables in Scottish Traditional Music', Ph.D Dissertation, 1980.
Sir John Graham Dalyell, MSS, Gen 353D, 425D.
Allan MacDonald, 'The Relationship between pibroch and Gaelic song: its implications on the performance style of the pibroch urlar' M.Litt. Thesis, 1996.
Iain MacInnes, 'The Highland Bagpipe: the Impact of the Highland Societies of London and Scotland', M.Litt. Thesis, Edinburgh University, 1989.
School of Scottish Studies Archive, SA 1972/246, SA1977/164.

Glasgow University Library:
Ewen Henderson MS, MS Gen. 1458.

Donald MacKay MS, MS Gen. 1455.
John MacDougall Gillies MS, MS Gen. 1457.

Ingliston House Library:
Highland Society of Scotland Papers.

Mitchell Library:
Glasgow Gaelic Club Minutes, Glasgow City Archives.

National Library of Scotland:
A. K. Cameron papers, MS. 9613–24
Colin Cameron Piobaireachd Manuscript, MS. 3745.
David Glen Manuscript, MS. 22120.
Seton Gordon Papers, Acc. 5640/7451.
Hannay-MacAuslan Piobaireachd Manuscript, Dep.201.
Highland Society of London Papers, Dep. 268.
Highland Society of London's MS, MS. 1679.
Donald MacDonald, 'A Select Collection of the Ancient Music of Caledonia, called
    Piobaireachd', MS MS. 1680.
Angus MacKay's Manuscripts, MS. 3753–6.
John V. Pearson, 'A North American "Piping Fanatic": Alexander K. Cameron (1882 – 1956)
    Montana's Bagpipe Essayist'. M.A. Thesis, University of Montana, 1981, Acc. 8424.
Piobaireachd Research Papers of Archibald Campbell (ca. 1903–1963, n.d.), MS. 22098–
    22117
Piobaireachd Society Papers, Acc.9103.
Peter Reid Manuscript, Acc. 22118.
Willliam Ross, Collection of pipe music, MS. 3040.
C. S. Thomason, 'Ceol Mor Legends', MS. 3749.

Open University Library:
G[eorge]. K[irk]. McGilvary, 'East India Patronage and the Political Management of
    Scotland 1720–1774', PhD Thesis, Open University, 1989

Newspapers and Magazines

Bon Accord	*Northern Chronicle*
Celtic Magazine	*Oban Times*
Celtic Monthly	*People's Friend*
Edinburgh Advertiser	*Piper and Drummer*
Edinburgh Evening Courant	*Piper Press*
Evening Express	*Piping and Dancing*
Falkirk Herald	*Piping Times*
Highland News	*Scottish Highlander*
Inverness Courier	*The Voice*
Kelso Chronicle	

Published works:

Adams, David G., *Bothy Nichts and Days: Farm Bothy Life in Angus and the Mearns* (Edinr., 1991).

Alburger, Mary Anne, *Scottish Fiddlers and their Music* (Lond., 1983).

Anderson, William, *The Scottish Nation; or the Surnames, Families, Literature, Honours, and Biographical History of the People of Scotland* (3 vols., Edinr., 1866).

[Anon.] *Crieff: Its Traditions and Characters with Anecdotes of Strathearn* (Edinr., 1881).

Anton, James, *Retrospect of a Military Life, during the most Eventful Periods of the Last War* (Edinr., 1841).

Arnold, Matthew, *On the Study of Celtic Literature and other Essays* (Lond., Everyman, n.d.; originally published 1867).

Baines, Anthony, *Woodwind Instruments and their History* (Lond., 1957).

Baptie, David, *Musical Scotland Past and Present* (Lond., 1894).

Bayard, Samuel P., 'Prolegomena to a Study of the Principal Melodic Families of Folk Song' in MacEdward Leach and Tristram P. Coffin, *The Critics & the Ballad* (Carbondale, 1961).

Best, Geoffrey, *Mid-Victorian Britain 1851–75* (Lond., 1979).

Blackwell, Thomas, *An Enquiry into the Life and Writings of Homer* (Lond., 1735).

Blair, Hugh, *A Critical Dissertation on the Poems of Ossian, the Son of Fingal* (2nd edn., Lond., 1765).

Blankenhorn, V. S., 'Traditional and Bogus Elements in "MacCrimmon's Lament"', *Scottish Studies*, vol.22, 1978, pp.45–67.

Böker, Uwe, 'The Marketing of Macpherson: The International Book Trade and the first Phase of German Ossian Reception', in Howard Gaskill, ed., *Ossian Revisited* (Edinr., 1991), pp.73–93.

Bourgault-Ducoudray, Louis Albert, *Melodies populaires de Basse-Bretagne* (Paris, 1885).

Bremner, Robert, *Scots Reels or Country Dances* (Edinr., *c.* 1757).

Broadwood, Lucy, 'Introduction' to Frances Tolmie's 'Songs of Occupation from the Western Isles of Scotland', *Journal of the Folk-Song Society*, no.16, vol. IV, (Lond., 1911).

Bromwich, Rachel, *Matthew Arnold and Celtic Literature A Retrospect 1865–1965* (Oxford, 1965).

[Browne, James], *A Critical Examination of Dr. Macculloch's Work on the Highlands and Western Isles of Scotland* (Edinr., 1825).

Bruford, Alan, 'Legends Long Since Localised or Tales Still Travelling?', *Scottish Studies*, vol.24, 1980, pp.43–62.

Buisman, Frans, 'An Anonymous Manuscript and its position in the History of Piobaireachd Playing', Part 1, *PT*, vol. 38, no.3, December 1985, pp.23–7 (23–4).

———— 'Gleanings from pre-Mackay Piobaireachd: Clialudh', in *PT*, vol. 39, nos 3–5, December-February, 1986–87, pp.34–8, 33–6, 36–41.

———— 'From Chant to Script', *PT*, vol. 39, no.7, April 1987, pp.44–49.

———— 'A Stock Tune in Older Piobaireachd Teaching and a device of Practising and Instruction,' *PT*, vol. 40, no. 7, April 1988, pp.44–9.

———— 'The Reflexive Shake: An Ancient Piobaireachd Ornament', Parts 1–3, *PT*, vol.41, no. 8–9/11, May-June, August 1989, pp.21–31, 47–53, 38–40.

———— 'A Note on the MacKenzie Manuscripts', *PT*, vol. 43, no.5, February 1991, pp. 47–53.

———— 'The Early History of Leumludh', Parts 1–2, *PT*, vol.43, no.9–10, June-July 1991, pp.27–38, 36–51.

———— 'Dungallon's Lament/Salute Playing Styles and the Exchange of Tunes in Ceol Mor', Part 1, *PT*, vol 45, no.6, March 1993, pp.25–9.

———— 'More Evidence on Colin Campbell and the Development of the Campbell Notation: MS. SRO 112/1/803', *PT*, vol. 47, no. 11–12, August-September 1995, pp.21–27, 28–34.

———— 'The Earliest Editions of Donald MacDonald's Collection of the Ancient Martial Music of Caledonia, called Piobaireachd' Parts 1–2, in *PT*, vol.50, no.1–2, October-November 1997, pp. 51–5, 32–4.

———— 'Canntaireachd and Colin Campbell's Verbal Notation – An Outline', *PT*, vol.50, no.3–4, December 1997–January 1998, pp.24–30, 28–33.

Buisman, Frans and Wright, Andrew, eds., *The MacArthur-MacGregor Manuscript of Piobaireachd (1820)* (Glasg., 2001).

[Burns, Robert, and James Johnston, eds.], *The Scots Musical Museum* (Edinr., 1787–1803).

Calhoon, Robert McCluer, *The Loyalists in Revolutionary America 1760 1781* (New York, 1965).

Cameron, Alexander, *History and Traditions of Skye* (Inverness, 1871).

Campbell, Alexander, *Albyn's Anthology Or a Select Collection of the Melodies & Vocal Poetry Peculiar to Scotland and the Isles* (2 vols., Edinr., 1816–18).

Campbell, Lord Archibald, ed., *Records of Argyll Legends, Traditions, and Recollections of Argyllshire Highlanders Collected Chiefly from the Gaelic* (Edinr., 1885).

———— *Waifs and Strays of Celtic Tradition* 1. Argyllshire Series (Lond., 1889).

Campbell, Archibald, (of Kilberry) and others, eds., *Piobaireachd . . . edited by Comunn na Piobaireachd (The Piobaireachd Society)* (15 vols., Glasg., 1925–1990).

Campbell, Archibald, ed., *The Kilberry Book of Ceol Mor* (Glasg., 1948, 2nd edn., 1953).

———— 'The History and Art of Angus MacKay', *PT*, vol 2. no.5, February 1950, pp.8–9

———— 'The Playing of 'The Prince's Salute' by Donald Ruadh MacCrimmon in 1815', *PT*, vol.3, no.7, April 1951, pp.6–7.

———— 'The Highland Bagpipe, *PT*, vol.14, no.10–12, July-September 1962, pp.6–10; 6–9; 10–14; vol.15 no.1, October 1962, pp.6–8.

———— *Sidelights on the Kilberry Book of Ceol Mor Notes on instruction received by Archibald Campbell of Kilberry*, James Campbell, ed., (Glasg., 1984).

———— *Further Sidelights on the Kilberry Book of Ceol Mor*, James Campbell, ed., (Glasg., 1986).

[Campbell, Archibald], 'Highland bagpipe music's finest authority', obituary, first published in *Oban Times*, reprinted in *Piper Press*, no.5, March 1998, pp.20–22.

Campbell, Donald, *A Treatise on Language, Poetry and Music of the Highland Clans: with Illustrative Traditions and Anecdotes, and Numerous Ancient Highland Airs* (Edinr., 1862).

Campbell, George Douglas, 8th Duke of Argyll, *Scotland as it Was and as it Is* (2 vols., Edinr., 1887).

Campbell, James, 'History of the Piobaireachd Society', *Proceedings of the Piobaireachd Society Conference*, 1977, pp.30–48.

———— 'The Elusive Appoggiatura', *PT*, vol.40, no.9, June 1988, pp.22–5.

Campbell, Jeannie, 'The Argyllshire Gathering – The Early Years', *PT*, vol.42–3, no.9–11/2, June-August/November 1990, pp. 30–4, 15–19, 40–5, 32–6.

———— 'J. F. Farquharson', *PT*, vol. 50, no.11, August 1998, pp.52–5.

———— 'Notices of Bagpipe Makers' Parts 1–13, *PT*, vol. 50–51, March 1998 – February 1999.

Campbell, J. F., ed., *Popular Tales of the West Highlands* (Edinr., 1860, 2nd. edn., 4 vols., Paisley, 1890).

—— *Canntaireachd: Articulate Music*, (Glasg., 1880).

Campbell, John Lorne, ed., *Highland Songs of the Forty-Five* (Edinr., 1984, first published 1933).

Cannon, Roderick D., *A Bibliography of Bagpipe Music* (Edinr., 1980).

—— *The Highland Bagpipe and its Music* (Edinr., 1988).

—— 'Angus MacKay's "Specimens of Canntaireachd"' Parts 1, 3–4, *PT*, vol.41, 1989, no.5–7, pp.17–25, 20–38, 41–47.

—— *General Preface to the Piobaireachd Society Collection* (Glasg., 1997).

Cannon, Roderick D., ed., *Joseph MacDonald's Compleat Theory of the Scots Highland Bagpipe* (Glasg., 1994).

Cannon, Roderick D. and Sanger, Keith, eds., *Donald MacDonald's Collection of Piobaireachd vols. 1–2* (Piobaireachd Society, 2006, 2011).

Carmichael, Alexander, ed., *Carmina Gadelica Charms of the Gaels Hymns and Incantations With Illustrative Notes on Words, Rites and Customs, Dying and Obsolete; orally Collected in the Highlands and Islands of Scotland* (6 vols., Edinr., 1900–71).

Chambers, Robert, ed., *Biographical Dictionary of Eminent Scotsmen* (9 vols., Glasg., 1853–55).

Chapman, Malcolm, *The Gaelic Vision in Scottish Culture* (Lond., 1978).

Chapman, R. W., ed., *Johnson's Journey to the Western Islands of Scotland and Boswell's Journal of a Tour to the Hebrides with Samuel Johnson, LL.D.* (Oxford, 1930).

Chatto, Allan, 'The Cowal Highland Games', Parts 1–2, *The Voice*, vol.27, no.3–4, Fall-Winter, 1998–9, pp.34–5, 37–9.

Cheape, Hugh, 'The Making of Bagpipes in Scotland', in Anne O'Connor and D. V. Clarke, eds., *From the Stone Age to the 'Forty-Five* (Edinr., 1983), pp. 596–615.

Cockburn, Henry, *Circuit Journeys* (Edinr., 1888).

Collinson, Francis, 'A Possible Vocal Origin of the Bagpipe Scale', *PT*, vol.16, no. 8, May 1964, pp.6–8.

—— *The Traditional and National Music of Scotland* (Lond., 1966).

—— *The Bagpipe: the History of a Musical Instrument* (Lond., 1975).

Colquhoun, Iain, and Hugh Machell, *Highland Gatherings: being accounts of the Braemar, Northern and Luss Meetings* (Lond., 1927).

Cooke, Deryck, *The Language of Music*, (Lond., 1964).

Cooke, Peter, 'Changing Styles in Pibroch Playing Cadence E's and Beats on A'. Pts. 1–2, *International Piper.*, vol. 1 nos. 2–3, June-July, 1978, pp.12–14, 11–13.

—— 'Letter from Peter Cooke', *International Piper*, vol.2, no.7, November 1979, pp.20–1.

—— 'Elizabeth Ross and the Piping of John MacKay of Raasay', *Proceedings of the Piobaireachd Society Conference* (Glasg., 1985).

—— 'The Pibroch Tradition and Staff Notation', in Tokumaru Yosihiko and Yamaguti Osamu, eds., *The Oral and the Literate in Music* (Tokyo, 1986), pp. 400–13.

Crawford, Thomas, *Walter Scott* (Edinr., 1982).

—— 'Lowland Song and Popular Tradition in the Eighteenth Century', in Andrew Hook, ed., *History of Scottish Literature: Volume 2 1660–1800* (Aberd., 1987), pp.123–139.

Curtis, L, P, jr., *Anglo-Saxons and Celts A Study of Anti-Irish Prejudice in Victorian England* (Bridgeport: Conn., 1968).

Dalyell, John Graham, *Musical Memoirs of Scotland* (Edinr., 1849).

Davidson, James D. G., *The Royal Highland and Agricultural Society of Scotland A Short History* 1784–1984 (Edinr., privately printed, 1984).

DeMond, Robert O., *The Loyalists in North Carolina during the Revolution* (Hamden, Conn., 1964).

Dixon, George A., 'From the Past', *PT*, vol.36, no.5, February 1984, pp.35–6.

Dolmetsch, Arnold, *The Interpretation of the Music of the XVII and XVIII Centuries* (Lond., new edn., 1946).

Donaldson, William 'The Glencairn Connection: Robert Burns and Scottish Politics 1786–1796', *Studies in Scottish Literature*, XVI, 1981, pp. 61–79.

———— *Popular Literature in Victorian Scotland* (Aberd., 1986).

———— *The Jacobite Song: Political Myth and National Identity* (Aberd., 1988).

———— 'Change and Invariance in the Traditional Performing Arts', *Northern Scotland*, vol.17, (1997), pp.33–54.

Donington, Robert, *The Interpretation of Early Music*, (Lond., new revised edn., 1989, first publ. 1963).

Dorson, Richard M., *The British Folklorists: a History* (Lond., 1968).

Dunbar, John Telfer, *History of Highland Dress* (2nd. edn., Lond., 1979).

———— *The Costume of Scotland* (Lond., 1981).

Duncan, Iain, 'A Fund of Music for All to Share', *Piper Press*, no.12, May 1999, pp.23–5.

Durkacz, Victor Edward, *The Decline of the Celtic Languages* (Edinr., 1983).

Eagle, Raymond, *Seton Gordon The Life and Times of a Highland Gentleman* (Moffat, 1991).

Edmonds, J. E., *History of the Great War: Military Operations France and Belgium*, 1914 (2 vols., Lond., 1922).

Ellis, Alexander J., trans., *On the Sensations of Tone as a physiological basis for the Theory of Music* (Lond., 1875).

Fairrie, Angus, *The Northern Meeting* 1788–1988 (Edinr., 1988).

Farmer, Henry George, *A History of Music in Scotland* (Lond., 1947).

Faujas, B., de Saint Fond, *A Journey through England and Scotland to the Hebrides in* 1784, ed., Archibald Geikie, (2 vols., Glasg., 1907).

Ferguson, J. De Lancey, and G. Ross Roy, eds., *The Letters of Robert Burns* (2 vols., Oxford, 1985).

Ferguson, William, *The Identity of the Scottish Nation: An Historic Quest* (Edinr., 1998).

Fergusson, William, *Fergusson's Bagpipe Melodies. Compositions and Settings by Pipe Major Wm. Fergusson late of* 7th. *H.L.I.,* 52nd *(Lowland) Division & Clan MacRae Pipe Bands* (Lond., 1939).

Finnegan, Ruth, *Oral Poetry: its nature, significance and social context* (Camb., 1977).

———— 'Tradition, But What Tradition and For Whom?', *Oral Tradition*, vol.6, no.1, 1991, pp.104–24.

———— *Oral Traditions and the Verbal Arts A Guide to Research Practices* (Lond., 1992).

'Fionn' [Henry Whyte], *The Martial Music of the Clans* (Glasg., 1904).

———— 'Clann an Sgeulachie, A Famous Family of Pipers', *Celtic Monthly*, vol.20, 1912, pp.207–8.

Fiske, Roger, *Scotland in Music A European Enthusiasm* (Camb., 1983).

Flood, William H. Grattan, *The Story of the Bagpipe* (Lond., 1911).

Forbes, Norman Hay, 'The Highland Bagpipe: Its History, Music and Romance', *Celtic Monthly*, vol. 5–6, 1897, pp.216–218, 237–40.

Forsyth, Maurice, 'The Liberton Pipe Band – A Well Abused Melody', *PT*, vol.51, no.1, October 1998, pp.34–6.

Fraser, A.[lexander] Duncan, *Some Reminiscences and the Bagpipe* (Edinr., n.d. but 1907).

Fraser, James, *Chronicles of the Frasers: The Wardlaw Manuscript*, ed., William MacKay, (Edinr., Scottish History Society, 1905).

Fraser, Simon, ed., *Airs and Melodies peculiar to the Highlands of Scotland and the Isles* (Edinr., 1816).

Furber, Holden, *John Company at Work A Study of European Expansion in India in the Late Eighteenth Century* (New York, 1970; first published Cambridge Mass, 1948).

Gaskill, Howard, ed., *Ossian Revisited* (Edinr., 1991).

────── *The Poems of Ossian and Related Works* (Edinr., 1996).

Gibson, John G., *Traditional Gaelic Bagpiping 1745–1945* (Edinr., 1998).

Gilchrist, Annie G., 'Note on the Modal System of Gaelic Tunes', prefixed to Frances Tolmie's collection of 'Songs of Occupation from the Western Isles of Scotland', *Journal of the Folk-Song Society*, no.16, vol. IV, (Lond., 1911).

Gillies, William A., *In Famed Breadalbane* (Perth, 1938).

Glen, David, ed., *David Glen's Collection of Highland Bagpipe Music* (Edinr., 1876 – 1900).

────── *A Collection of Ancient Piobaireachd or Highland Bagpipe Music.* (Edinr., 1880–1907).

────── *Music of the Clan MacLean* (Edinr., 1900).

────── *The Edinburgh Collection of Highland Bagpipe Music Pibrochs, marches, quick-steps, strathspeys, reels & jigs, compiled & arranged by David Glen* (Edinr., 1903–8).

Glen, John, ed., *The Glen Collection of Scottish Dance Music Strathspeys, Reels, and Jigs, Selected from the Earliest Printed Sources or from the Composer's Works* (Edinr., 1891).

Goody, Jack, ed., *Literacy in Traditional Societies* (Camb., 1968).

────── *The Domestication of the Savage Mind* (Camb., 1977).

Goody, Jack, and Ian Watt, 'The Consequences of Literacy', in *Comparative Studies in Society and History*, vol.5, 1962–3. pp.304–45.

Gordon, Seton, *The Charm of Skye the Winged Isle* (Lond., 1929).

────── 'John MacDonald of Inverness M.B.E.', *PT*, vol.14, no.5, February 1962, pp.6–7

Gow, Niel, *Collection of Strathspey Reels* (4 vols., Edinr., 1784–1800).

Graham, E. Maxtone, (E. Blair Oliphant), *The Oliphants of Gask: Records of a Jacobite Family* (Lond., 1910).

Graham, Henry Grey, *Scottish Men of Letters in the Eighteenth. Century* (Lond., 1901).

Graham, Peter and Brian MacRae, eds., *The Gordon Highlanders Pipe Music Collection* (2 vols., Lond., 1983, 1985).

Grant, Ann, *Letters from the Mountains; being the real Correspondence of a Lady, between the years 1773 and 1803* (3 vols., Lond., 1806).

Grant, I. F., *The MacLeods The History of a Clan 1200–1956* (Lond., 1959).

Grant, John, *The Royal Collection of Piobaireachd* (Edinr., privately printed n.d. but 1908).

────── *Piobaireachd its Origin and Construction* (Edinr., privately printed, 1915).

Grant, J.P., 'The Late Pipe-Major John MacDonald M.B.E. of Inverness An Apprecia-tion', *PT*, vol. 5, no. 10, July 1953, pp.4–6.

Gray, William and John Seton, *Bagpipe and Drum Tutor* (Glasg., 1922).

Greetham, D. C., *Textual Scholarship An Introduction* (New York, 1994, first published 1992).

Grimble, Ian, *The World of Rob Donn* (Edinr., 1979).

Haddow, Alexander John, *The History and Structure of Ceol Mor: a Collection of Critical and Historical Essays* (n.p., privately printed, 1982).

Haldane, A. R. B., *The Drove Roads of Scotland* (Lond., 1952).

Halford-MacLeod, Ruairidh, 'Early MacCrimmon Records', *PT*, vol.29, no.5, Feb. 1977, pp.11–13.

———— 'The MacCrimmons and the '45', *PT*, vol.29, no.6, March 1977, pp. 11–13.

———— 'The End of the MacCrimmon College', *PT*, vol.29, no.8, May 1977, pp.15–18.

———— 'The Highland Society of London and the publishing of Piobaireachd' Pts.1–2, *PT*, vol.34, nos.9/11, June/Aug. 1982, pp.25–31, 28–32.

———— 'Everyone who has an intrigue hopes it should not be known: Lord Loudoun and Anne Mackintosh – An Intrigue of the '45', in *Transactions of the Gaelic Society of Inverness*, vol. 55, 1986–8, pp.256–323.

———— 'James Logan, Part 3', *PT*, vol. 42, no. 5, February 1990, pp. 24–27.

———— 'The Top Twenty Piobaireachds 1824 to 1844 – and the influence of Donald MacDonald and Angus MacKay', *PT*, vol.47, no.8, May 1995, pp.50–4, Part 3, *PT*, vol. 47, no. 10, July 1995 pp.23–6.

———— 'Donald Ruadh MacCrimmon in North Carolina', pts. 1–2, *PT*, vol.49, nos.2/4, November/January 1996/7, pp.33–8, 46–7.

Hamilton, James, 'Crunluath a mach', *PT*, vol.50, no.6, March 1998, pp.9–11.

Havelock, Eric A., *The Literate Revolution in Greece and its Cultural Consequences* (Princeton, 1982).

Henderson, Diana M., *Highland Soldier: A Social Study of the Highland Regiments*, 1820–1920 ((Edinr., 1989).

Herd, David, ed., *Ancient and Modern Scots Songs* (Edinr., 1769).

Hogg, James, *The Jacobite Relics of Scotland; being The Songs, Airs, and Legends, of the Adherents to the House of Stuart* (Edinr., 1819–21).

Home, John *The History of the Rebellion in the year 1745* (Lond., 1802).

Honko, Lauri, ed., *Tradition and Cultural Identity* (Turku, 1988).

Hook, Andrew, 'Scotland and Romanticism: The International Scene' in Andrew Hook, ed., *The History of Scottish Literature Volume 2 1660–1800* (Aberd., 1987), pp.307–322.

Hunter, James, *A Dance Called America: The Scottish Highlands the United States and Canada* (Edinr., 1994).

Johnson, David, *Music and Society in Lowland Scotland in the Eighteenth Century* (Lond., 1972).

———— 'Musical Traditions in the Forbes Family of Disblair, Aberdeenshire', in *Scottish Studies*, vol.22, 1978, pp.91–93.

———— *Scottish Fiddle Music in the 18th Century a music collection and historical study* (Edinr., 1984; 2nd edn., Edinr., 1997).

Johnson, Edgar, *Sir Walter Scott: The Great Unknown* (2 vols., Lond., 1970).

Kennedy-Fraser, Marjorie, *A Life of Song* (Lond., 1929).

Kenneth, A. G., 'The Campbell Canntaireachd', *PT*, vol.17, no.8–9, May-June 1965, pp. 18–20, 6–9.

———— 'Re-Publishing Piobaireachd', *PT*, vol.24, no.10, July 1972, pp.8–11.

———— 'Some mistakes in Angus MacKay's settings, and where they came from', *PT*, vol. 36, no.6, March 1984, pp.13–14.

Kirk, G. S., 'Homer and Modern Oral Poetry: Some Confusions', in *Homer and the Oral Tradition* (Camb., 1976), pp. 113–128.

Kloeke, John J. van Ommen, 'Seasoning: Brew Your Own?', *PT*, vol.42, no.11, August 1990, pp.34–6.

Lang, Andrew, *Pickle the Spy: or The Incognito of Prince Charles* (Lond., 1897).

Lawson, Philip, *The East India Company: A History* (Lond., 1993).

Lehmann, William C., *Henry Home, Lord Kames, and the Scottish Enlightenment: a Study in National Character and in the History of Ideas* (The Hague, 1971).

Lenman, Bruce, *The Jacobite Risings in Britain 1689–1746* (Lond., 1980).

Leyden, John, *Journal of a Tour in the Highlands and Western Islands of Scotland in 1800* (Edinr., 1903).

Logan, James, *The Scottish Gael; or, Celtic Manners, as Preserved among the Highlanders: being an Historical and Descriptive Account of the Inhabitants, Antiquities, and National Peculiarities of Scotland; more particularly of the northern, or Gaelic parts of the country, where the singular habits of the aboriginal Celts are most tenaciously retained* (2 vols., Lond., 1831; 2nd edn., Rev. Alex Stewart, ed., Inverness, 1876).

———— *The Clans of the Scottish Highlands, Illustrated by Appropriate Figures, Displaying their Dress, Arms, Tartans, Armorial Insignia, and Social Occupations. From original sketches by R. R. McIan, Esq. With Accompanying Description and Historical Memoranda of Character, Mode of Life, &c. &c. By James Logan, Esq.* (2 vols., Lond., 1845-7).

———— *Logan's Collections*, James Cruickshank, ed., (Aberd., 3rd Spalding Club, 1941).

Lord, Albert B., *The Singer of Tales*, (Cambridge, Mass., 1960).

———— 'The Nature of Oral Poetry', in John Miles Foley, ed., *Comparative Research on Oral Traditions: a Memorial for Milman Parry* (Columbus, 1987), pp. 313–349.

Love, James, ed., *Antiquarian Notes and Queries reprinted from the Falkirk Herald* (Falkirk, 1908–1928).

MacAulay, Alexander, 'The Passing of Dr. Calum MacCrimmon', *PT*, vol. 14, no.10, July 1962 p.11.

———— 'The Art and History of the MacDougalls of Aberfeldy', *PT*, vol.16, no.4–5, January-February, 1964, pp.7–10, 9–14.

MacCallum, Hugh, 'Northern Meeting the Gold Medal', *The Piper Press*, no.9, November 1998, pp.11–15.

[MacDonald, Alexander, aka Alasdair MacMhaighstir Alasdair], 'Journall and Memoirs of P . . . C . . . Expedition into Scotland Etc. 1745–6. By a Highland Officer in his Army', in George Lockhart of Carnwath, ed., *The Lockhart Papers: containing Memoirs and Commentaries upon the Affairs of Scotland from 1702 to 1715* (2 vols., Lond., 1817), ii, 479–510.

MacDonald, Alexander, *Story and Song from Loch Ness-Side being principally Sketches of Olden-Time Life in the Valley of the Great Glen of Scotland with particular reference to Glenmoriston and Vicinity* (Inverness, 1914).

MacDonald, Alexander, ed., *A Compleat Theory of the Scots Highland Bagpipe. By Joseph MacDonald* (Glasg., 1927).

MacDonald, Donald, ed., *A Collection of the Ancient Martial Music of Caledonia, called Piobaireachd* (Wakefield 1974, facsimile reprint of 3rd edn., Edinr., 1822).

———— *A Collection of Quicksteps, Strathspeys, Reels, & Jigs. Arranged for the Highland Bagpipe* (Edinr., 1828).

MacDonald, Joseph, *A Compleat Theory of the Scots Highland Bagpipe containing all the shakes, introductions, graces, and cuttings, which are peculiar to this instrument, reduced to order and method; fully explained & noted at large in 58 tables and examples – with all the terms of art in which this instrument was originally taught by its first masters and composers in the Islands of Sky & Mull.* (Edinr., 1803; reprinted Glasgow 1927, Wakefield, 1971; see also R. Cannon, ed., 1994).

MacDonald, K. N., ed., *The Gesto Collection of Highland Music* (Leipzig, 1895).

———— 'Rev. Patrick MacDonald of Kilmore. The First Collector of Gaelic Music', *Celtic Monthly*, vol. 6, 1898, pp.135–6

———— *Puirt-a-Beul* (Glasg., 1901).

McDonald, Patrick, *Proposals for Publishing, by Subscription, a Collection of Highland Vocal Airs, never hitherto published. To which will be added a few of the most lively country Dances, or Reels of the North Highlands and Western Isles.*

―――― *A Collection of Highland Vocal Airs, never hitherto published. To which are added as few of the most lively country dances or reels, of the North Highlands, & Western Isles: and some specimens of bagpipe music* (Edinr., n.d., but 1784).

MacDougall, James, *Folk Tales and Fairy Lore in Gaelic and English Collected from Oral Tradition*, ed., George Calder, (Edinr., 1910).

MacDougall, Stewart, 'Thig Crioch air an T'saoghal/ Ach mairidh gaol is ceol', *Galley of Lorn*, March 1911, pp.43–4.

McGibbon, William, *Collection of Scots Tunes* (Edinr., 1742, 1746, 1755).

MacGregor, Alex., 'Piobaireachd agus Ceol nan Gaidheal', *Transactions of the Gaelic Society of Inverness*, vol.2, 1872–3, pp. 6–25.

―――― 'John MacDonald – an Adherent of Prince Charles', *Celtic Magazine*, vol.3, 1878, pp.462–6

―――― 'The Aged Piper and his Bagpipe', in *Celtic Magazine*, vol.5, 1879, pp.404–405.

―――― *Life of Flora MacDonald and her Adventures with Prince Charles* (Inverness, 1882).

McIan, R. R., *Gaelic Gatherings; or The Highlanders at Home, on the Heath, the River, and the Loch With Descriptive Letter-Press by James Logan, Esq, FSA, &c.* (Lond., 1848; reduced facsimile, Glasg., 1900).

MacKay, Angus, *A Collection of Ancient Piobaireachd or Highland Pipe Music* (Wakefield 1972, reprinted from 3rd edn., Aberd., 1899; first published Edinr., 1838).

MacKay, Angus, M.A., *The Book of Mackay* (Edinr., privately printed, 1906).

MacKay, I., 'James Matheson, Lairg,' *PT*, vol. 42, no. 10, July 1990, pp.21–2.

MacKay, John, *The Music of MacKay* (n.p. 1984).

McKay, N. T., 'Crunluath a Mach', *PT*, vol.50, no.8, May 1998, pp.16–17.

―――― 'Andrew Robertson (1777–1845) and his Role in Recording Ceol Mor in Written Form', *PT*, vol.51, no.4, January 1999, pp.19–24.

MacKay, William, *Urquhart and Glenmoriston: Olden Times in a Highland Parish* (Inverness, 1893).

'A.M'. [Alexander Mackenzie] 'Canntaireachd, or Articulate Music', review of J. F. Campbell's pamphlet, *Celtic Magazine*, vol 5, 1880, pp.483–89.

Mackenzie, Alexander, *History of the MacDonalds and Lords of the Isles* (Inverness, 1881).

―――― *History of the MacLeods with Genealogies of the Principal Families of the Name* (Inverness, 1889).

MacKenzie, B.D., 'General Thomason and Ceol Mor', *Transactions of the Gaelic Society of Inverness*, vol. 57, 1993, pp.58–72.

―――― 'The Life and Work of General Thomason', *PT*, vol.49, no.5–6, February-March 1997, pp.37–44, 33–41.

Mackenzie, Bridget, *Piping Traditions of the North of Scotland*, (Edinr., 1998).

Mackenzie, Henry, *Report of the Committee of the Highland Society of Scotland, appointed to inquire into the nature and authenticity of the poems of Ossian* (Edinr., 1805).

Mackenzie, Osgood Hanbury, *A Hundred Years in the Highlands*, (new edn., London, 1949).

MacKinnon, Donald, and Alick Morrison, eds., *The MacLeods – the Genealogy of a Clan. Section Three. MacLeod Cadet Families* (Edinr., 1970).

McLachlan, John, ed., *The Piper's Assistant* (Edinr., 1854).

MacLean, Magnus, *The Literature of the Highlands*, (London, 1925, first published 1903).

MacLellan, Angus J., 'From the Past', *PT*, vol.50, no.4, January 1998, pp.17–20.

MacLellan, John A., 'Angus MacKay of Raasay', *PT*, vol.18, no.6, March 1966, 10–14.

―――― 'The Literature of the Highland Bagpipe The Highland Society of London's Manuscript', in *International Piper*, vol.1, no.12, 1979, pp.8–11.

—— 'The Literature of the Highland Bagpipe Peter Reid's Manuscript', *International Piper*, vol. 3 no. 8, December 1980, pp.14–15.

MacLellan, John A., ed., *Comunn na Piobaireachd: The Piobaireachd Society Present a Collection of Ceòl Mòr Composed during the Twentieth Century 1930–1980* (Glasg., 1980).

McLennan, George S., *Highland Bagpipe Music* (Aberd., 1929).

[McLennan, George S.], 'Notices of Pipers, McLennan, George S. (1884–1929), *PT*, vol.25, no.7, April 1973, p.28.

McLennan, John, *The Piobaireachd as MacCrimmon played it: with instructions how to read and understand music* (Edinr., privately printed n.d. but 1907).

—— *The Piobaireachd as performed in the Highlands for Ages, till about the Year* 1808 (Edinr., privately printed, n.d., but 1924).

MacLeod, Donald, ed., *Pipe Major Donald MacLeod's Collection of Music for the Highland Bagpipe* (5 vols., Glasg., n.d., but 1954 ff.).

—— 'Some Memories of John MacDonald', *PT*, vol.14, no.6, March 1962, pp.6–7.

—— 'More Memories of John MacDonald', *PT*, vol.14, no.8, May 1962, pp.14–15.

MacLeod, Donald, *Memoir of Norman MacLeod, D.D* (Toronto, 1876).

MacLeod, Fred. T., *The MacCrimmons of Skye Hereditary Pipers to the Macleods of Dunvegan* (Edinr., 1933).

MacLeod, Niel, *Pibereach or pipe tunes, as taught verbally by the McCrimmen pipers in Skye to their apprentices* (Edinr., 1828; reprinted Edinr., 1880).

—— 'Remarks by Captain MacLeod, as far as he has been informed by the late John Maccrimmon, piper, Dunvegan, Isle of Skye', *Celtic Magazine*, vol. 8, 1883, pp. 434–5.

MacLeod, Norman, *Caraid nan Gaidheal (The Friend of the Gael.) A Choice Selection of the Gaelic Writings of Norman MacLeod, D.D. . . . With a memoir of the Author by his Son, Norman MacLeod, D.D. of the Barony Parish, Glasgow*, A. Clerk, ed., (Edinr., 1899).

MacLeod, Norman, 'Reminiscences of a Highland Parish', in *Works by Norman MacLeod. D.D.* (Lond., 1891).

MacLeod, R. C., ed., *The Book of Dunvegan: being Documents from the Muniment Room of the MacLeods of MacLeod at Dunvegan Castle, Isle of Skye* (2 vols., Aberd., 1938–9).

McLynn, Frank, *The Jacobites* (Lond., 1985).

MacNeill, Archie, 'Early Piping Days', *PT*, vol.12, no.6, March 1960, pp.16–22.

MacNeill, Dugald B., 'Crunluath a mach', *PT*, vol.50, no.4, January 1998, p.27.

MacNeill, Seumas, *Piobaireachd: Classical Music of the Highland Bagpipe* (Edinr., 1968)

—— 'John MacFadyen Remembered', *PT*, vol.42, no.10–11, July-August, 1990, pp.26–38, 24–8.

—— 'The Life and Times of John MacColl', *PT*, vol.50, nos.5–8, February-May, 1998, pp.18–22, 46–9, 22–5, 19–23.

[MacNeill, Seumas], 'Ardvasar Seminar', *PT*, vol.41, no.2, November 1988, pp.32–40.

MacNeill Seumas, and Frank Richardson, *Piobaireachd and its Interpretation: Classical Music of the Highland Bagpipe* (Edinr., 1987).

McNicol, Donald, *Remarks on Dr. Samuel Johnson's Journey to the Hebrides: in which are contained observations on the antiquities, language, genius, and manners of the High-landers of Scotland* (Lond., 1779).

MacPhee, Donald, *The Bagpipe Works of Donald MacPhee* (Wakefield, 1978).

Macpherson, Angus, *A Highlander Looks Back* (Oban 1970; first edn., 1953).

Macpherson, James, ed., *Fragments of Ancient Poetry, collected in the Highlands of Scotland, and translated from the Galic or Erse Language* (Edinr., 1760).

—— *Fingal, An Ancient Epic Poem. In Six Books: together with Several Other Poems composed by Ossian, the Son of Fingal* (Lond., 1761).

—— *Temora, an Ancient Epic Poem in Eight Books: together with Several Other Poems composed by Ossian, the Son of Fingal* (Lond., 1763).

—— *An Introduction to the History of Great Britain and Ireland* (Lond., 1771).

Malcolm, C. A., *The Piper in Peace and War* (Lond., 1927).

Manson, W. L., '"Callum Piobair" The World's Greatest Pibroch Player', *People's Friend*, September 26, 1898, pp.709–710.

—— *The Highland Bagpipe Its History, Literature, and Music with some account of the Traditions, Superstitions, and Anecdotes Relating to The Instrument and Its Tunes* (Paisley, 1901).

Marshall, P. J., *East India Fortunes – The British in Bengal in the Eighteenth Century* (Oxford, 1976).

Marshall, William, *Historic Scenes of Perthshire* (Edinr., 1880).

Martin, Martin, *A Description of the Western Islands of Scotland* (Edinr., 1994: facsimile reprint of the 1934 Stirling edition; first published Lond., 1703).

Matheson, William, ed., *The Songs of John MacCodrum: Bard to Sir James MacDonald of Sleat* (Edinr., 1938).

—— *The Blind Harper: the Songs of Roderick Morison and his Music* (Edinr., 1970).

Matheson, William, (recorded from) 'Three Fairy Songs', *Tocher*, no.47, 1994, pp.280–284.

Mathieson, Robert, 'On Top of the World's: an Interview with P/M Robert Mathieson by Peter Kent and Charlie Glendinning', in *The Voice*, vol.26, no.3, Fall 1997, pp.18–29.

Maurice, F., *The History of the Scots Guards from the Creation of the Regiment to the Eve of the Great War* (2 vols., Lond., 1932).

[Menzies, Daniel], *The Bagpipe Preceptor; or, the art of playing the great Highland bagpipe rendered perfectly to every capacity; by which any one who has a taste for music may soon acquire a knowledge of that grand and warlike instrument, without the aid of a master* (Edinr., 1818).

Merriam, Alan P., *The Anthropology of Music*, (Northwestern University Press, 1964).

Millar, Tommy, 'End of Era for McAllister', *Piper Press*, no.5, March 1998, pp.30–1.

Mitchell, Arthur, 'A List of Travels, Tours, Journeys, Voyages, Cruises, Excursions, Wanderings, Rambles, Visits, etc., Relating to Scotland' in *Proceedings of the Society of Antiquaries of Scotland*, 3rd. Ser., vol. 35, 1900–1, pp.431–638; vol. 36, 1905, pp.500–27; vol. 44, 1910, pp.390–405.

Mitchison, Rosalind, *Agricultural Sir John The Life of Sir John Sinclair of Ulbster 1754–1835* (Lond., 1962).

Moss, George, 'Ceol Mor Playing – Old and New Styles', *PT*, vol 8, no.11, August 1956, pp.18–19.

—— Piobaireachd Playing', *PT*, vol 9, no.8, May 1957, pp.6–7.

—— 'Canntaireachd', *PT*, vol.12, no.1, October 1959, pp.16–21.

Mossner, Ernest Campbell, *The Life of David Hume* (Edinr., 1954).

Murchison, T. M., 'Glenelg, Inverness-shire: Notes for a Parish History', *Transactions of the Gaelic Society of Inverness*, vol. 39–40, 1942–1950, pp.204–333.

Murray, David, 'Piobaireachd Society's Collection Book 13', *International Piper*, vol.2, no.12, April 1980, p.6.

—— *The Piper's Day Regimental Duty Tunes of the Queen's Own Highlanders*, (Inverness, 1991).

—— *Music of the Scottish Regiments* (Edinr., 1994).

—— 'The Maverick: George Moss 1903–1990', in *The Voice*, Spring 1997, pp.31–35.

—— 'More on "The Way it Was"', *The Voice*, vol.27, no.1, Spring 1998, pp.35–8.

Nicolaisen, W. F. H., *Scottish Place-Names their Study and Significance* (Lond., 1986; first published 1976).

North, C. N. McIntyre, *Leabhar Comunn nam Fior Ghaél The Book of the Club of True Highlanders. A record of the Dress, arms, customs, arts and science of the Highlanders. Compiled from printed and manuscript records and traditions and illustrated with etchings of Highland Relics, and the Keltic Vestiges of Great Britain and Ireland* (2 vols., privately printed, Lond., 1881).

O'Boyle, Colm, 'Some Irish Harpers in Scotland', in *Transactions of the Gaelic Society of Inverness*, vol.47, 1971–2, pp.143–71.

———— *Eachann Bacach and other MacLean Poets* (Edinr., 1979).

O'Brien, D. P., *The Classical Economists* (Oxford, 1975).

Oliphant, T. L. Kington, *The Jacobite Lairds of Gask* (Lond., 1870).

Orme, B. J. Maclachlan, ed., *The Piobaireachd of Simon Fraser with Canntaireachd* (n.p. 1979).

Pearston, T., 'In Search of the Italian Bagpipe', *PT*, vol. 4, no.10, July 1952, pp.6–8.

Pennant, Thomas, *A Tour in Scotland and Voyage to the Hebrides, MDCCLXXII* (Chester, 1774).

Philip, Neil, ed., *The Penguin Book of Scottish Folktales* (Lond., 1995).

Piobaireachd Society Collection (series one/two), see under 'Stewart, William' and 'Campbell, Archibald'.

Piping and Dancing:
  'The MacLean Pipe Band, Champions of the World, 1927–30–35', no.2, Sept. 1935, p.18.
  'The City of Glasgow Police Pipe Band', no.3, October 1935, p.13.
  'The Shotts and Dykehead Caledonia Pipe Band', no.4, November 1935, p.13.
  'Looking Backward By Highlander', no.4, November 1935, p.19.
  'Michael Colliery Prize Pipe Band', no.6, January 1936, p.17.
  'The Edinburgh City Police Pipe Band', no.7, February 1936, p.13.
  'Dalzell Highland Prize Pipe Band', no.11, June 1936, pp.14–15.
  'The Clan MacRae Society Pipe Band', no.12, July 1936.

Poulter, George C. B., and Charles P. Fisher, *The MacCrimmon Family Origin; Music; Iain Odhar; Padruig Mor; Padruig Og; The descendants of Donald Donn from 1740 to 1936*, (Camberley, 1936).

Prebble, John, *The King's Jaunt: George IV in Scotland, August 1822 'One and twenty daft days'* (Lond., 1988).

Purser, John, *Scotland's Music: a History of the Traditional and Classical Music of Scotland from Earliest Times to the Present Day* (Edinr., 1992).

Quantz, Johann Joachim, *On Playing the Flute*, ed., Edward R. Reilly, (Lond., 1966).

Ramsay, Alexander, *History of the Highland and Agricultural Society of Scotland with notices of Anterior Societies for the Promotion of Agriculture in Scotland* (Edinr., 1879).

Ramsay, Donald Shaw, ed., *The Edcath Collection of Highland Bagpipe Music and Drum Settings* (3 vols., Edinr., 1953–1968).

Ramsay, John, 'Of the Influence of Poetry and Music upon the Highlanders', in Patrick MacDonald, ed., *Highland Vocal Airs* (Edinr., n.d. but 1784), pp.9–15.

———— *Scotland and Scotsmen in the Eighteenth Century*, ed., Alexander Allardyce, (2 vols., Edinr., 1888).

———— *Letters of John Ramsay of Ochtertyre 1799–1812*, ed., Barbara L. H. Horn, (Edinr., 1966).

Rastall, Richard, *The Notation of Western Music An Introduction*, (Lond., 1983).

Reid, Robert, 'Letters of Robert Reid', in *Piper & Drummer*, vol.15, no 1, November 1997, pp.32–3.

Richardson, Frank M., 'Memories of John MacDonald, M.B.E.,', in *Proceedings of the Proboireachd Society conference*, 1985, pp.1–15.

Robertson, James, *The Highland Bagpipe: Some interesting Information on the Materials used in the Manufacture of the Highland Bagpipe* (Edinr., n.d., but *c.* 1930).

Robertson, James Irvine, *The First Highlander: Major-General David Stewart of Garth* CB. 1768–1829 (East Linton, 1998).

Robertson, Jas., and Donald Shaw Ramsay, eds., *Master Method for Highland Bagpipe With a Selection of Modern and Traditional Marches, Strathspeys, Reels and Jigs* (Lond., n.d., but 1953).

Rose, Hew, and Lachlan Shaw, *A Genealogical Deduction of the Family of Rose of Kilravock*, Cosmo Innes, ed. (Edinr., 1848).

Ross, David, 'Some of the old pipers I have met', *PT*, vol. 26. no. 4, January 1974, pp. 9–17.

Ross, G. F., ed., *Some Piobaireachd Studies* (Glasg., privately printed, 1926).

———— *A Collection of MacCrimmon and other Piobaireachd* (Glasg., privately printed, 1929).

Ross, Neil, 'Ceol-mor agus Clann MhicCruimein', *Celtic Monthly*, vol.18, nos.2–4, February-April 1910, pp.26–28, 45–7, 65–7.

Ross, Roderick, ed., *Binneas is Boreraig* (5 vols., Edinr., 1959–1967).

Ross, William (1823–1891), *Ross's Collection Pipe Music* (Lond., 1869; rev. edn., 1885; reprinted Wakefield, 1976).

Ross, William (1878–1966), *Pipe-Major W. Ross's Collection of Highland Bagpipe Music* (5 vols., Lond., 1923–1950).

Sachs, Curt, *Rhythm and Tempo a Study in Music History* (Lond., 1953).

Sanger, Keith, 'The MacArthurs Evidence from the MacDonald Papers', *PT*, vol.35, no.8, 1983, pp.13–17.

———— 'The Origins of Highland Piping', *PT*, vol.41, no.11, August 1987, pp.46–52.

———— 'Mull and the Maclean Pipers', *PT*, vol.42, no.9, June 1990, pp. 38–43.

———— 'Donald MacDonald', *PT*, Vol. 49, no. 1, October 1996, pp.24–31.

Saunders, Laurence J., *Scottish Democracy 1815–1840* (Edinr., 1950).

Scobie, I. H. MacKay, *Pipers and Pipe Music in a Highland Regiment* (Dingwall, 1924).

Scott, Hew, ed., *Fasti Ecclesiae Scoticanae: The Succession of Ministers in the Parish Churches of Scotland from the Reformation, A.D. 1560, to the Present Time* (3 vols., Edinr., 1866–71).

Scott, Sir Walter, *Minstrelsy of the Scottish Border*, ed., T. F. Henderson, (4 vols., Edinr., 1902).

Seton, Sir Bruce, and John Grant, *The Pipes of War A Record of the Achievements of Pipers of Scottish and Overseas Regiments during the War 1914–1918* (Glasg., 1920).

Shils, Edward, *Tradition* (Lond., 1981).

Shone, J. H., ed., *Some Letters of Archibald Campbell of Kilberry 1935–1949* (Cockenzie, 1980).

Simonsuuri, Kirsti, *Homer's Original Genius: Eighteenth-century Notions of the Early Greek Epic (1688–1798)* (Cambridge, 1979).

Sinclair, Rev. John, *Memoirs of the Life and Works of the Late Right Honourable Sir John Sinclair, Bart* (2 vols., Edinr., 1837).

Skinner, Andrew S., *Adam Smith and the Role of the State*, (Glasg., 1974).

Slaven, Anthony, *The Development of the West of Scotland: 1750–1960* (Lond., 1975).

Smith, N. A. Malcolm, ed., *The First One Hundred Years A History of the Royal Scottish Pipers' Society* (Dunfermline, n.d.).

Smith, Robert, 'Poem *on the Building of the Schoolhouse of* Glenshee', in *Poems of Controversy Betwixt Episcopacy and Presbytery*, (Edinr, 1869, first published 1714).

Smout, T. C., *A History of the Scottish People* 1560–1830, (Lond., 1969).

Stafford, Fiona J., *The Sublime Savage: A Study of James Macpherson and the Poems of Ossian* (Edinr., 1988).

——— 'Introduction: The Ossianic Poems of James Macpherson', in Howard Gaskill, ed., *The Poems of Ossian and Related Works* (Edinr., 1996).

Standard Settings of Pipe Music The Seaforth Highlanders (Lond., n.d. but 1936).

Statistical Account of Scotland (21 vols., 1791–99).

New Statistical Account of Scotland (15 vols., 1845).

Third Statistical Account of Scotland (1951–).

Stewart, Neil, *Collection of the best Reels or Country Dances* (Edinr., 1761–4).

[Stewart, William of Ensay], *et.al.*, eds., *A Collection of Piobaireachd. Selected and edited by the Piobaireachd Society* (5 vols., Inverness, Glasgow, 1905–1912).

Stocking, George W., Jr., 'Scotland as the Model of Mankind: Lord Kames' Philosophical View of Civilisation', in Timothy H. H. Thoresen, ed., *Towards a Science of Man: Essays in the History of Anthropology* (The Hague, 1975), pp.65–89.

Strang, John, *Glasgow and its Clubs* (Glasg., 1856).

Taylor, Jack, 'Piobaireachd: Has it Changed? Should it Change?', *Piper and Drummer*, vol.12, no.1, 1994, pp.14–16.

Thomason, C. S., ed., *A Collection of Piobaireachd, as played on the Great Highland Bagpipe. Ceol Mor* (privately printed, Lond., 1900, reprinted as *Ceol Mor: A New and Abbreviated System of Musical Notation for the Piobaireachd as Played on the Highland Bagpipe*, Wakefield, 1975).

Thompson, Frank G., 'John Francis Campbell', *Transactions of the Gaelic Society of Inverness*, vol 54, 1984–1986, pp. 1–57.

Thomson, Derick S., *The Gaelic Sources of Macpherson's 'Ossian'* (Edinr., 1951).

——— *Companion to Gaelic Scotland* (Oxford, 1983).

Thomson, George, ed., *Select Collection of Original Scottish Airs* (Edinr., 1793–1841).

Tolmie, Frances, 'Songs of Occupation from the Western Isles of Scotland', published as *Journal of the Folk-Song Society. No.16. Being the Third part of Vol.IV*, (Lond., 1911).

Vining, Elizabeth Gray, *Flora MacDonald Her Life in the Highlands and America* (Lond., 1967).

Watson, Duncan , 'A Day at a Games: Scarce of Good Judging', *Piper Press*, no.12, May 1999, pp. 37–9.

Webster, David, *Scottish Highland Games* (Edinr., 1973).

Wentz, W. Y. Evans, *Fairy Faith in Celtic Countries* (Oxford, 1911).

Williams, Morag, *History of the Crichton Royal Hospital* 1839–1989 (Dumfries: privately printed, n.d., but 1989).

Wimberly, Lowry C., *Folklore in the English and Scottish Ballads* (New York, 1959, first published 1928).

Woodward, C. H., 'An Analysis of "A Compleat Theory of the Scots Highland Bagpipe" by Joseph MacDonald. Compiled 1760–63. First published 1803', *PT*, vol.27, nos.6–10, March-July 1975, pp.21–4, 14–17, 15–17, 14–17, 25–27; vol.28, nos.4–5, 7–8, January-May 1976, pp.28–32, 28–33, 16–19, 29–32.

Young, Douglas , 'Never Blotted a Line? Formula and Premeditation in Homer and Hesiod', *Arion*, vol.VI, no.3, Autumn 1967, pp. 279–324.

Youngson, A.J., *After the Forty-Five The Economic Impact on the Scottish Highlands* (Edinr, 1973).edit

Index

See also listings of Pipers and Pipe Tunes. Musical quotations appear in bold type.

Pipe Tunes

Piobaireachd